THE BENGAL
BORDERLAND

Anthem South Asian Studies
Series editor: Crispin Bates

THE BENGAL BORDERLAND

BEYOND STATE AND NATION IN SOUTH ASIA

Willem van Schendel

Anthem Press

This edition published by Anthem Press 2005

Anthem Press is an imprint of
Wimbledon Publishing Company
75-76 Blackfriars Road
London SE1 8HA

or

PO Box 9779, London, SW19 7QA

British Library Cataloguing in Publication Data
Data available

Library of Congress in Publication Data
A catalogue record has been applied for

1 3 5 7 9 10 8 6 4 2

ISBN 1 84331 144 5 (Hbk)
ISBN 1 84331 145 3 (Pbk)

Typeset by Footprint Labs Ltd, London
www.footprintlabs.com

Printed in India

CONTENTS

FIGURES

PLATES

TABLES

ABBREVIATIONS

BDR   Bangladesh Rifles; the border guards of Bangladesh
BJP   Bharatiya Janata Party
BOP   Border outpost, usually manned by 20 to 25 border guards
BSF   Border Security Force, the border guards of India
CHT   Chittagong Hill Tracts
CID   Central Intelligence Department
CPI(M)   Communist Party of India (Marxist)
EB   East Bengal
EBR   East Bengal Regiment
EP   East Pakistan
EPR   East Pakistan Rifles, the border guards of East Pakistan
IMDT   Illegal Migrants (Determination by Tribunals) Act of 1983
ISI   Inter-Services Intelligence, Pakistan's foreign intelligence agency
Nasaka   Border Administration Force of Burma/Myanmar (also spelled Na Sa Ka)
PIF   Prevention of Infiltration Force
Re., Rs.   Rupee, Rupees (the currencies of India and Pakistan)
SAARC   South Asian Association for Regional Cooperation
Tk.   Taka (the currency of Bangladesh)
VHP   Vishwa Hindu Parishad
WB   West Bengal
WP   West Pakistan

NOTE

The modern history of the region explored in this book has been turbulent. The region has been named and renamed, and as a result there is a confusing multiplicity of geographical and political designations. The following explanation may help some readers.

East Bengal, East Pakistan and **Bangladesh** refer to the same territory, now the independent state of Bangladesh. In 1947 the region of Bengal was divided and its eastern part joined the new state of Pakistan. In 1971 it broke away from Pakistan and formed the independent state of Bangladesh.

India, Hindustan and Bharat refer to the same state, India.

Burma and Myanmar refer to the same state, currently known as Myanmar in official parlance.

Assam, a state (province) of India, gradually broke into several smaller states: Arunachal Pradesh, Assam, Manipur, Meghalaya, Mizoram and Nagaland (See *Appendix Figure 2*).

The official spelling of many towns and districts has varied during the period under review, for example **Dacca/Dhaka, Calcutta/Kolkata, Gauhati/Guwahati**. For current spellings of district names, see *Appendix Figure 1*.

ACKNOWLEDGEMENTS

This book has wound its way through many relationships and chance meetings. I could not have written it without the help of four groups of people. First, the many interlocutors in various parts of the borderland who offered insights, hospitality, documents and bittersweet stories. Second, my travel companions in the borderland, in particular Md. Mahbubar Rahman (North Bengal, Assam, Meghalaya, Teknaf, Chittagong Hill Tracts, Sylhet), Gautam Chakma (Tripura, Assam, Mizoram), Md. Ahsan Habib (Panchagarh), Mitu Chakma (Chittagong Hill Tracts), Shahriar Kabir (Darjeeling), Suborno Chisim (Mymensingh) and Ellen Bal (Mymensingh, Meghalaya). Not only did they make my travels much more enjoyable, but they were also invaluable for their interviewing skills and practical help. Third, without the very generous help of the staff of the National Archives of Bangladesh in Dhaka (especially its director, Dr. Sharif Uddin Ahmed, and its senior archivist, Md. Hashanuzzaman Hydary), I would not have been able to access the rich historical documentation contained in their collections. Finally, I am very grateful to Manpreet Kaur Janeja and Mrs Manjit Kaur Janeja (Calcutta), and Kubra (Rajshahi), for assistance in searching old newspapers.

Many others helped me with material, suggestions, comments, criticism, opportunities to present my findings, and other support, especially Itty Abraham, Aftab Ahmad, Imtiaz Ahmed, Reaz Ahmed, Shahidul Alam, Jenneke Arens, Champak Barbora, Sanjib Baruah, Avtar Singh Bhasin, Sugata Bose, Jan Breman, Shib Shankar Chatterjee, Partha Chatterjee, Joya Chatterji, Sanjay Chaturvedi, Binay Bhusan Chaudhuri, Lucy Chester, Suranjan Das, Abhijit Dasgupta, Anindita Dasgupta, Satyajit Das Gupta, Subhoranjan Dasgupta, Anjan Datta, Leo Douw, Nienke Klompmaker, David Ludden, Erik de Maaker, Muntassir Mamoon, Nilufar Matin, Hans Meier, Tanvir Murad, Nipa, Silvia Rivera Cusicanqui, Jan Reynders, Mario Rutten, Ahmad Saleem, Henk Schulte Nordholt, Kathinka Sinha-Kerkhoff, Laura van Schendel, Tobias van Schendel, Jacqueline Vel, Brendan Whyte, Thurein Yazar, Shaduz Zaman and Vazira Zamindar. Michiel Baud deserves special thanks for his detailed criticism of the entire text.

Most of the photographs reproduced in this book are mine, and therefore they appear without acknowledgement. All others are duly attributed to those who made them, and I thank the photographers for their permission to reproduce them. In the few cases in which my attempts at identifying or locating the copyright holders have not been successful, copyright holders are invited to contact the publisher.

Some of the material presented in this book has also been used in articles published in the *International Review of Social History*, *South Asian Refugee Watch*, *The Journal of Asian Studies* and *Modern Asian Studies*. The University of Amsterdam, the International Institute of Social History (IISH), and the Indo-Dutch Programme on Alternatives in Development (IDPAD) provided important financial and logistic support. Among the many archives and libraries consulted in the course of this study, the Oriental and India Office Collections at the British Library (London) and Ain-O-Shalish Kendro (Dhaka) deserve special mention.

I thank them all.

Willem van Schendel
September 2003.

1

STUDYING BORDERLANDS

On a border road in India, a truckload of border guards encounter a rickshaw. They quarrel over who has the right of way. The guards give the rickshaw-puller a beating and then open fire, killing five bystanders and wounding two. In protest, local political parties declare a general strike. Later, in Delhi, borderland Members of Parliament accuse the guards of habitually humiliating and assaulting the border population, but the Deputy Speaker concludes a fierce parliamentary debate with the words:

> We are proud of our [Border Guards] and other Forces. The Members cannot irresponsibly utter anything and everything on the Forces ... I will not allow you to say anything more ... Nothing will go on record.[1]

This is an everyday story from one of the world's many borderlands. It points to the complicated relationship between borderlanders and their rulers. This book explores that relationship. It looks at what happens when a border is imposed on an unsuspecting population, how a new borderland takes shape, and what relationships develop between borderlanders and their states.

Borders come about in many ways. Some are like earthquakes. When the earth's tectonic plates move, the ground heaves and roars. Houses crumble, trees snap and people run around in panic. A deep fissure suddenly separates one half of the landscape from the other. And then it is all over. An eerie silence hangs over a land that is forever scarred, broken, double. A little later, aid teams rush to the site; they comfort the victims and help them pick up their lives. In the media, seismologists explain that earthquakes are both inevitable and unpredictable. And then the world moves on. When the world's political tectonic plates move, they create fissures known as international borders. Many of these come about in ways that, for those who experience them, are just as overpowering, devastating and unpredictable as earthquakes. But there are no political seismologists and no border aid teams, and what happens during and after such upheavals is little known. The study of borders is a curiously neglected no man's land.

The Bengal borderland

This book deals with the territorial and human consequences of a border whose birth, had it been an earthquake, would have registered way up on the Richter scale. We look at the fissure itself – a huge territorial gash of over 4,000 kilometres – and at how it became part of the everyday lives of millions of people living near it. This border separating India, East Pakistan (Bangladesh from 1971) and Burma became the backbone of a new borderland to which I refer as the 'Bengal borderland' because it bisects and encircles a region historically known as Bengal (see Appendix, Figure 2). The story of the Bengal borderland is important for those who wish to understand social change in South Asia, but this book also aims at linking it to broader concerns in social theory, particularly to the study of borders and border communities, and to how we conceptualize social space.

In August 1947, the tectonic plates of South Asian politics shifted abruptly. British colonial rule in India came to an end, the colony was split and the Bengal borderland was born with such suddenness that nobody actually knew its exact location till several days later.[2] Nothing had foreshadowed its geographical position, and its creation took the people who now found themselves to be living in a borderland by surprise. As one of them recalled, it was a time of great confusion:

"You should realize that the separation happened all of a sudden and people were not well informed. Many people thought that it was only temporary and that the two countries would one day be one again."[3] Only gradually did it dawn on most of them what it meant to be living near an international border. "They turned our world upside down ... Nobody asked us, we did not know what was happening till much later ... Our lives were amputated."[4]

This book explains how these borderlanders and their states coped with a new, previously unimagined reality. We will see that the border remained a highly emotive issue: even today, its very location is contested in many places and there are groups who refuse to accept its legitimacy. The new border created a volatile region, linking India, Bangladesh and Burma, that has experienced wars, border conflicts, regional revolts and many forms of everyday resistance.[5]

The story of this region does not support the idea that the world is becoming borderless as it globalizes. On the contrary, the Bengal borderland is increasingly being policed, patrolled, fenced and land-mined. And yet, throughout its existence, it has been the scene of large transnational flows of labour migrants and refugees, of trade in many goods, and of exchanges of ideas and information.

Most of these flows were unauthorized by the states concerned, indicating continual struggles between the powers of territorial control and those of cross-border networking.

The changing social geographies of the borderland were bound up not only with these struggles, but also with a multiplicity of identities, old and new, that borderlanders juggled in their efforts to make sense of their new situation and shape a future for themselves. These in turn deeply influenced borderland culture, the policies of the new states, and the transnational networks facilitating cross-border flows. All these reasons make the Bengal borderland an important example of a modern borderland: thoroughly modern in the sense that it was created less than 60 years ago, it reverberates with the tensions noticeable in contemporary borderlands all over the globe.

Why study borderlands?

For a long time social scientists showed no more than a limited interest in the study of borderlands. In recent years, however, a concern with the processes of global restructuring has led to a perceptible increase in research on borderlands all over the world. Today, the study of borderlands is providing new insights into the relationship between modern states and transnational linkages.[6]

Borderland studies can tell us much about states because borders form a clear link between geography and politics.[7] The state's pursuit of territoriality – its strategy to exert complete authority and control over social life in its territory – *produces* borders and makes them into crucial markers of the success and limitations of that strategy. The ubiquity of international borders in today's world is a testimony to the importance of state territoriality: a recent survey calculated that there are 226,000 kilometres of land border worldwide, more than five times the earth's circumference.[8] Territoriality is inherently conflictual and tends to generate rival territorialities. Hence, borders need to be constantly maintained and socially reproduced through particular practices and discourses that emphasize the 'other.' Territoriality actively encourages the 'zero-sum games' that characterize geopolitical, national and border conflicts.[9]

But borders are also reproduced by transnational reconfiguration. They play a central role in regulating transnational flows and are in turn deeply influenced by them. As social scientists turn their attention from the 'virtual' world of global investment and speculation to the 'real' world of cross-border linkages and inter-territorial economies, borderlands emerge as core objects of transnational research.[10]

Increasingly, this new interest in borders merges with work on identity, ethnicity, citizenship and culture. The study of border cultures (or cultural landscapes that transcend political borders) is necessary in order to shift the focus from state strategies and global economic change to the people living in the borderland. Borderlanders' perceptions, practices, identities and discourses are central to the social reproduction, maintenance or subversion of borders. How do people in borderlands negotiate cultural elements to symbolize their membership in local, regional, national and international communities?[11] How do they juggle multiple identities in the midst of great change? How do these identities impinge on the formation of states, nations and transnational networks? Cross-border cultural landscapes cannot be 'inferred or deduced from a knowledge of the political and economic structures of the states at their borders', but are a matter of empirical research.[12]

Finally, studying the transformation of international borderlands in a period of global reterritorialization requires a historical approach. The historicity of borderland space is obvious. Whether borderlands are created with earthquake-like suddenness or not, their formal beginnings are usually well documented, and so is their formal demise. As spatialized social relations, borderlands may be long-lived; indeed, they may have an afterlife well beyond the states that created them.[13] During their existence, they are changing geographies, shaped and reconfigured by social struggles and negotiations whose outcome is not predetermined.[14] Mapping and comparing these transformations requires historical research.

At another level, the historicity of borderlands lies in their symbolic uses. They are often portrayed as the material embodiment of a state's (or nation's) history as encapsulating its struggle for sovereignty and self-determination.[15] As such, dominant historical narratives may sacralize borderlands and make them pawns in the 'performance' of sovereignty.[16] Borderlanders may develop counter-narratives (e.g. irredentist ones) in which the historical significance of the border that separates them is minimized. In other words, borderlands are often battlefields of historiography, of the politics of selective remembering and forgetting.

Shaking off the 'iron grip' of the nation-state

The study of borderlands can play an important role in rethinking wider social theory, especially with regard to how we conceptualize social space. In the social sciences, it has long been customary to imagine the world as divided into distinct 'societies', 'cultures' and 'economies', and to think of these as fixed to specific territories. This is not surprising given the fact that the social sciences developed during the period in which the modern interstate system came into being. This is a system based on the territorialization of state power 'through which each state strives to exercise exclusive sovereignty over a delineated, self-enclosed geographical space.'[17] Consequently, the modern state employs a strategy of *territoriality*, a spatial strategy to 'affect, influence, or control resources and people, by controlling area.' It is a form of enforcement that involves the active use of geographic space to classify social phenomena.[18]

This strategy of territorializing state power and sovereignty has proved to be very successful: during the nineteenth and twentieth centuries a web of contiguous state territories spread to cover the entire globe.[19] Social scientists were so deeply influenced by this development that their work came to reflect a *territorialist epistemology* that entailed a

> transposition of the historically unique territorial structure of the modern interstate system into a generalized model of sociospatial organization, whether with reference to political, societal, economic, or cultural processes.[20]

Adopting this model had far-reaching consequences for how social scientists studied the world. Most of them took state territories as a 'preconstituted, naturalized, or unchanging scale of analysis', and their work tended towards a methodological territorialism that analysed all spatial forms and scales as being self-enclosed geographical units.[21] In this way, their social imagination was stifled by the 'iron grip of the nation state'; they fell into a 'territorial trap.'[22]

In recent years, a rebellion has been gathering against this state-centred epistemology and its commitment to 'received' units.[23] It opposes the idea that the modern state's territorial form can be a general model for societies, cultures and economies. Certainly, each state claims to produce a 'space wherein something is accomplished, a space, even, where something is brought to perfection: namely, a unified and hence homogeneous society.'[24] But this claim should not be confused with its realization. This is what social scientists do when they treat states as the conceptual starting point for their investigations, when they accept states as the rules of the game.[25] The inherited model of state-defined societies, cultures and economies has become highly problematic and social theorists are devising new models.[26] Studying borderlands – zones within which international borders lie– can be one way of challenging the inherited model, because the only way to study borderlands adequately is to understand them as much more than merely the margins of state territories. Borderland practices challenge the inherited model because they are based on ways of imagining power and space that differ from the 'heartland' practices that underlie much social science theorizing. Social scientists have tended to marginalize borderland practices, making them appear far more peripheral than they really are. As we shall see, borderland dynamics have a direct and fundamental impact on the shape of states, heartland practices and transnational linkages.

A borderless world?

In recent years it has become popular to herald the demise of the state and the emergence of a borderless, globalized world. The idea is that the geography of territorial states is being 'deterritorialized'. The forces of globalization – transnational flows of capital, people, goods and information – are progressively undermining the strategy of territoriality, the attempt to classify and control by means of geographical fixity, borders and enclosure. As a result, it is argued, new post-territorial geographies of networks and flows are supplanting the inherited geography of state territories.[27]

This deterritorialization thesis does not take sufficient account of the historical complexities of territoriality, nor of the fact that global flows cannot occur unless they are 'premised upon various forms of spatial fixity, localization and (re)territorialization.'[28] In other words, it is not a matter of pitching territorialization against deterritorialization or globalization, but rather one of understanding changing patterns of historical territorialization.[29]

In world history, the bundling together of territoriality and state sovereignty is a relatively new phenomenon. It received arguably its strongest impetus from the emergence of industrial capitalism in the eighteenth and nineteenth centuries, and has been described as the geographical solution to a dilemma facing the emerging capitalist class: how to balance competition and mutual cooperation. Nation-states provided arenas in which this balance could be struck: they protected the interests of a national capitalist class and maintained control over the working class. Nation-states emerged as the 'basic building blocks of the advanced capitalist system,' and, in Neil Smith's powerful image, dramatically reconstructed the world as a giant 'jigsaw puzzle of national pieces.'[30] But this dispensation was not permanent. After the Second World War, the internationalization of markets and production processes rendered the national scale of economic organization 'increasingly obsolete'. The state found it more and more difficult to function as a gatekeeper state that provided both extraterritorial opportunities for national capital and security against the perceived social costs of internationalization, especially immigration.[31] It was only by means of a 'Ramboesque reaffirmation of national boundaries' (trade and immigration restrictions, currency controls, militaristic display, the United Nations) that states were able to extend the association of territoriality to state sovereignty up to the early 1970s. Then the pieces of Smith's jigsaw puzzle were thrown into the air, and new relations between economies, territorial polities and cultures came into being.[32]

The point being stressed by a number of theorists is that this did not imply a deterritorialisation of the world, but rather a new phase of territorialisation in which the link between territory and sovereignty became partially 'unbundled.'

Increasingly this process is being referred to as *re-scaling*, after the core concept of a new approach, geographical *scale*.[33]

The construction of scale

The concept of scale is of particular significance in the study of borderlands. Theorists of scale criticize the social sciences for generally treating space as self-evident, unproblematic, and unrequiring of theory, and for viewing 'history as the independent variable, the actor, and geography as the dependent – the ground on which events "take place," the field within which history unfolds.'[34] They deplore that social scientists have foregrounded time and society in their studies but have marginalised space. Rather than treating space as an equal partner to time and society, most social scientists have relegated it to a neutral backdrop of socio-historical relations, assuming space to be a fixed material essence waiting for humans to figure out how best to use it to economic or social advantage.[35] These theorists argue that occluding the spatial from social analysis is a serious mistake because space is not merely a material essence – on the contrary, its importance lies in its being socially constructed. Human life is unthinkable without spatial connotations and much of human life revolves around struggles over space. This social dimension of space is highlighted in studies of scales, the levels of spatial representation that we use constantly in our social analyses. For example, the local, national, or global scales that we are all familiar with are in no way natural or pre-given but are socially constructed. They are the result of human activities and are best understood as 'temporary stand-offs in a perpetual transformative ... socio-spatial power struggle,' or as provisional geographical resolutions of power struggles that are historically produced, stabilised and transformed.[36] These stand-offs (scalar configurations, or scalar fixes[37]) can be quite long-lived. They can become so stabilised as 'scaffoldings' of certain forms of power and control that we experience them as natural and permanent.[38] But they are always finite.

Theorists of scale recognize that geographical scales are produced, contested, and transformed through an 'immense range of sociopolitical and discursive processes, strategies, and struggles that cannot be derived from any single encompassing dynamic.'[39] Conversely, the study of these processes, strategies and struggles must pay more serious attention to their spatial aspects, including the historical variability of scales.[40] In this view, current changes in the world are linked to the emergence of a new scalar fix to replace the one that was dominant till the early 1970s. What is going on, then, is *not* the demise of the territorial but a *reterritorialisation* such as has not happened since the creation of the nation-state.

In this process, it is most unlikely that the national scale, and international borders, will simply evaporate. The strategy of territoriality is alive and kicking, but it is no longer clustered primarily around the level of the nation-state. Transnational capital has largely replaced national capital and this is a root cause why the national level has lost its pivotal position as the pre-eminent geographical unit. The bundling of territory and sovereignty at the state level, which was the cornerstone of the previous scalar fix, is weakening. This has led states to develop 'concerted strategies to create new scales of state regulation to facilitate and coordinate the globalization process: at both sub- and supra-national levels.'[41] In other words, they are active agents in the regulation of transnational flows that always need to be grounded in spatial fixity and localization. State strategies of territoriality have proved adaptable; they are now employed more than before at levels other than the national, particularly at that of the sub-national (export zones, growth regions, metropolises) and at that of the supra-national (free trade zones, growth triangles, unions of states, international organizations and alliances). In other words, territoriality is being re-scaled by states that should be seen as active partners in global restructuring, and not as passive victims of deterritorialization.

At the same time, countervailing strategies by groups – corporations, advocacy networks, criminal organisations, international labour migrants – that are out to circumvent the power of territorial organisation, or to dismantle entrenched scalar morphologies, are also being re-scaled.[42] They too now manifest themselves at scales that are at once more global and more local than before. Since the early 1970s, the 'politics of scale' have been increasingly characterized by this 'jumping of scales,' thereby contributing powerfully to a reterritorialization of the world.[43] We can comprehend these developments only if we become more aware of how social processes work across scales. This requires that we are neither state-obsessed nor globe-entranced.[44]

Re-imagining the study of borderlands

These reflections on the need to escape the iron grip of the nation-state are, of course, extremely relevant for the study of borderlands. A 'borderland' is a zone, or region, within which lies an international border, and a 'borderland society' is a social and cultural system straddling that border.[45] Borderland studies have been deeply marked by the territorialist epistemology of the social sciences (the tendency to study the world as a patchwork of state-defined societies, economies and cultures) and its corollary, methodological territorialism (the tendency to analyse spatial forms as self-enclosed geographical units). This approach predisposes students of international borderlands to treat these not as units in their own right, but primarily as the margins of states, societies, economies and cultures. The state territory is the implicit centre of gravity, the point of reference, and borderlands are seen in their relationship to that territory. For this reason, we know much more about how states deal with borderlands than how borderlands deal with states.[46] A reconfigured study of borderlands which takes both sides of an international border as its unit of analysis provides a powerful corrective to the current territorialization and state-centricity of the social imagination. Research on borderlands undermines 'lazy assumptions' that state and society, state and nation, or state and governance are synonymous or territorially coterminous.[47] It is important to realize that borders not only join what is different but also divide what is similar.[48] They create what Oscar Martínez has termed a borderlands milieu.[49]

Insisting on the historicity of social space is essential for the study of borderland societies. Borders are too often seen as spatial fixtures, lines in the landscape, separators of societies – the passive and pre-given ground on which events take place. But if we think of spatiality as an aspect of social relations that is continually being reconfigured, borders become much more significant. It is here that the strategy of state territoriality is dramatized and state sovereignty is flaunted. It is also here that many countervailing strategies contesting state territoriality are clustered. The struggle between these strategies continually reproduces, reconstructs, or undermines border regions. In other words, there is nothing passive about borders; in borderlands, the spatiality of social relations is forever taking on new shapes, and we need conceptual tools to analyse these transformations.

But this is only part of the story. Now that the global politics of scale themselves are undergoing major change, international borders have become crucial localities for studying how global restructuring affects territoriality, how global reterritorialization takes place. When people, goods, capital and ideas flow across borders, what happens to them and to those borders? The contributions of borderland actors (including states) to the present round of global restructuring, and the resultant reconfiguration of social relations in borderlands, are little understood. The rhetoric of 'globalization' suggests prime movers being located in centres of production and consumption, with flows moving between them. But these flows do not move in thin air and are not disembodied. We need to incorporate the social relations of transport and distribution, and their spatiality, in analyses of global re-scaling. And although borders *may* be localities of importance when it comes to production and consumption, they are *always* localities of importance when it comes to transport and distribution – another reason to take them seriously in studies of global restructuring.

The study of borderlands and 'scale'

Borderland studies benefit from the endeavour to escape from the iron grip of the nation state not only because this endeavour provides a corrective to the current state-centricity of the social imagination, or because it highlights a dynamic site of transnational reconfiguration. Borderland studies can also refine the concept of scale. As we have seen, scales are ways in which we frame conceptions of spatial reality, and the outcomes of these framings have material consequences.[50] In an international borderland, geographical scales of various levels cut across each other. Borderlands obviously mark the national scale because two national units meet here, providing 'an already partitioned geography within which social activity takes place.' For example, citizenship based on a territorial definition of the nation separates people living on either side of the border, and provides them with an identity around which control is exerted and contested.[51] But an international border may also mark the border of other scales. The border between Greece and Bulgaria doubles as a border between the European Union and the outside world, just as, before 1989, it formed the border between the Socialist Bloc and the Capitalist Bloc. The border between Burma and Bangladesh separates two states but also two world regions, Southeast Asia and South Asia.[52] And the border between Mexico and the United States is often held up as marking the border between the North and the South (or the developed and developing world).[53] By contrast, a borderland may *not* be a partitioned geography when we consider other scales, e.g. a linguistic community (the Arab world), a production system (the *maquiladora* system on the U.S.-Mexican border), or an international military alliance (NATO).

For these reasons contemporary borderlands provide privileged sites for research on how particular scales become constituted. In borderlands, the struggle over scale redefinitions is always intense and highly visible, and the current worldwide re-scaling of the state makes borderlands even more salient research sites. Studying the politics of scale in borderlands forces us to be more precise about the concept of scale itself. Richard Howitt argues that we need to explore more carefully the genealogies and contents of the many spatial metaphors that have become prominent in the social sciences. Criticizing an overemphasis on the usual metaphors for scale – scale as size (as in map scale) and scale as level (as in a pyramid or hierarchy of scales) – he suggests that we think of scale primarily as a web of relations.[54] While some people have access to webs at different levels, or webs with a wider geographical span, others do not.[55]

Two sets of questions present themselves here. On the one hand there is the issue of how we imagine such webs to be bordered. What are the spatial limits of scales? How do they come about, how are they maintained, and how are they overcome? The second set of questions has to do with how different groups imagine scale. Social scientists' geographical imaginations are important because they have an impact on their understanding of social, cultural and material realities, and, to varying degrees, ultimately on those realities themselves. But it is the geographical imaginations of groups involved in particular social struggles – *their* analysis of webs of relations of different levels and sizes in which they are involved, or from which they are excluded – that determine their strategies in a politics of scale. Research on scale has begun to engage with this issue, and this is essential because scale-literacy and theorizing about scale require an understanding of various alternative styles of 'scaling the world.'[56] Unfortunately, both the question of the bordering of scales and that of styles of scaling still tend to be looked at within national frameworks. Therefore, a focus on borderlands may provide powerful new insights into dynamics and complexities of scale that have not yet been explored.

The case of the Bengal borderland

The Bengal borderland provides a perfect case for developing a new style of borderland studies. First, to most people this is one of the world's most marginal places, the periphery of the periphery. Located in a poor, powerless and largely ignored part of the world, it forms the perimeter of societies that are themselves seen as of little consequence in world affairs. As a result, it has hardly been studied. Ignorance may not breed contempt but it certainly breeds prejudice. In this book, I demonstrate that the Bengal borderland is far from the sleepy backwater in a lost corner of the world that many imagine it to be. It is a dynamic site of transnational reconfiguration, a hotbed of re-scaling, and an excellent place to help us shake off a state-centric social imagination. It provides a strong case for re-imagining social space.

Second, the case of the Bengal borderland underlines the need for borderland studies to be historical. It provides us with an unusually crisp, laboratory-like situation. Here a largely unprepared population had to cope with a very sudden, and well-documented, imposition of an international border. Their society was brusquely partitioned and the resultant permutations show clearly the myriad individual and group strategies that go into the invention of borderlands, and thus they drive home the historicity of all social space.

Finally, the Bengal borderland demonstrates how borderland studies have to struggle with state simplifications, the tendency inherent in statecraft (and a fair bit of social science) to represent only that slice of social reality that interests the official observer.[57] The Bengal borderland figures very prominently in the fiery political rhetoric and historical imaginations of the adjoining states, but these states have never felt the need to commission comprehensive empirical studies. As a state simplification, the borderland is considered to be 'known.'

It is therefore no surprise that public debates on the Bengal borderland in South Asia are replete with stereotypes that need to be challenged. For example, it is commonly assumed that the creation of the borderland, at the midnight hour of 14 to 15 August 1947, was essentially a question of drawing a North-South border through Bengal, that Bengal was cut in two, that East Pakistan was carved out of India, and that population dislocation was overwhelmingly the flight of Hindus from Pakistan to India. All of these are wrong, as the following chapters will explain. The unchallenged persistence of such basic misconceptions is a comment on the near-absence of critical academic research in this field.

This state of affairs is a result of the dominance of state simplifications, but also of the methodological territorialism and state-centred bias that are as strong among social scientists active in this region as anywhere else. In addition, the state elites of the region have displayed a pervasive concern with sovereignty, security and territorial control. They have kept the borderland fairly inaccessible and this also has dissuaded academics from studying it.

Accessing the Bengal borderland

The lack of academic research on the Bengal borderland cannot be blamed on a dearth of material. As two recent contributions, by Joya Chatterji and Ranabir Samaddar, have demonstrated, there is sufficient source material to develop a rich field of borderland studies in this region – to invent the borderland as a unit of research.[58] But there are no ready-made methodologies and we have to feel our way towards the best methods of accessing and interpreting the available material. Paul Nugent has suggested for another borderland that it is in the nature of the subject matter that the spotlight pans across a wide field.[59] I have based myself largely on archival records and on interviews in different parts of the borderland. In addition, I have used material in the public domain, especially newspaper articles, memoirs and books. It is also true, however, that much historical and contemporary information that would be freely available to students of borderlands elsewhere in the world, is treated as highly confidential and restricted by India, Bangladesh and Burma.

The strategies of territoriality employed by these states are remarkable for relying on measures of blocking information that are becoming rare in today's world. For example, in an age in which satellite tracking and remote sensing provide extremely detailed geographical information to states and armies around the world, inhabitants of this borderland (and other citizens of these states, including researchers) are still barred from getting even moderately accurate maps of the border regions. Ranabir Samaddar described his experiences when he was doing research on transborder migration in West Bengal (India) in the 1990s:

> I was shown a number of maps which underscored the point being made by the [Indian security] officers that the Indo-Bangladesh border is no border at all given the terrain, ponds, rivers, small canals and rice fields which remain connected and interlocked. But the moment I asked, in all innocence, why should these maps not be published so that the people can see for themselves how difficult the job of border policing was, the officers shrank back. In fact, raising any questions about the maps or asking for a copy of a map raises suspicion. They wanted to know why exactly did I need it? Then followed the hedging advices, such as, oh, you can get that from Calcutta's X office or Y bureau ... I was advised to leave the maps out. Maps are a barred subject.[60]

In South Asia, such bureaucratic panic reflects an unbroken tradition of secrecy about maps going back to the establishment of the Survey of India in 1767. Even today the Indian Ministry of Defence sees itself as the 'owner of Indian geographic data' and enforces severe restrictions on their public use.[61] South Asian geographers have long denounced this policy as irrational, ludicrous and anachronistic, but to no avail.[62] Secrecy is particularly intense regarding border and coastal areas and it is not restricted to recent maps showing the location of the border.[63] Even pre-1947 survey maps of what is now the borderland are off-limits because this information is considered to be too strategically sensitive to share with the public. Of course, many of these maps are freely available abroad. The same reasons of state are invoked to block access to decades-old records and statistical data, and the national press is cautioned to 'exercise restraint' in reporting on border matters.[64] In addition, all three states have declared large parts of the borderland physically out of bounds for anyone but borderland residents and state personnel, plus a lucky few who are given a special permit. Since 1947, the public in South Asia has had no access to accurate maps showing a band of some 80 kilometres either way of the land borders. The borders that play such an important role in South Asian politics are, quite literally, left to the imagination.

These restrictions, which account partly for the undeveloped state of borderland studies in this part of the world, point to an official politics of forgetting, an elaborate attempt to obliterate the contested origins and nature of the border.[65] This politics of forgetting is clearly part of what Sankaran Krishna describes as 'postcolonial anxiety': a fear of national disunity and fragmentation that produces actions and policies that may in fact hasten precisely that very outcome.[66] Attempts to keep South Asia's borderlands under wraps – to retain them as geographies of ignorance[67] – are being confronted with demands to democratize geographical knowledge. Predictably, it has been quite impossible to forget the Bengal border: it has remained a live – and at times violently explosive – issue surrounded by a whirlwind of disinformation, confusion and misrepresentation.[68]

Such restrictions and emotions make a study like this difficult but not impossible. Most of the archival material that I have used is accessible in the National Archives of Bangladesh. Here the confidential records of the Home Ministry of East Bengal proved to be an especially rich source for the period between 1947 and the mid-1960s. These records present not only the viewpoints of the Government of East Bengal (= East Pakistan, today: Bangladesh) but also those of its counterparts across the border: they contain many government documents, reports, letters and telegrammes from India (especially Assam, Tripura, West Bengal, Bihar) and Burma. In addition, it is possible to hear the voices of many non-state actors in the petitions, verbatim reports of interviews, letters, newspaper clippings, pamphlets and censored material that are included in these government records. Unfortunately, the quality and quantity of the archival records tapers off sharply in the late 1950s and few records are available for the period after 1965.

Borderlanders themselves provided the second major source of information for this book. In the course of many discussions and interviews over a period of fifteen years, they opened my eyes to many aspects of borderland life. My interest in the borderland theme began during fieldwork in West Bengal (India) and Bangladesh in 1988.[69] It developed further when I was doing research on the Chittagong Hill Tracts (Bangladesh).[70] Over the years, I visited dozens of localities on both sides of the border and I had numerous further discussions with borderlanders that took place in non-borderland localities. Md. Mahbubar Rahman and myself jointly took many of the interviews quoted in the text; others were conducted by just one of us.[71]

In the public domain, newspapers provided a crucial body of information. A large number of newspapers were published in all three countries during the entire period under review. Metropolitan newspapers (from cities such as Dhaka, Calcutta, Karachi, Delhi and Rangoon) provided rather uneven coverage of events in the borderland. Local newspapers from the borderland might have filled the gaps but it proved impossible to locate more than occasional copies because libraries rarely collected them systematically. Nevertheless, newspapers were an essential source of information, particularly for the period since 1965, and their coverage of borderland affairs improved over time.

These three bodies of information (archival records, interviews and newspapers), together with photographs and the published material listed at the end of this book, made it possible to write this study of the Bengal borderland.

But at the same time these sources were often fragmented and episodic; they put definite limits on what I could see and forced me to make clear choices.[72] For example, the first chapters of this book are more archive-based and focus on the earlier decades (1940s to 1960s) whereas later chapters draw more heavily on newspapers and interviews and tend to focus on the more recent past. Despite this overall chronological approach, the fragmented material lent itself more easily to a thematic account when it came to presenting detail. As a result, the book consists of thematic chapters that show chronological sequences to the extent that the available material allowed.

My decision to emphasize borderland perspectives also led me not to delve too deeply into several matters that come up with great regularity in the archival material, e.g. internal discussions between officials stationed in the borderland and their superiors in provincial and national capitals, or the evolving structure of state bureaucracies in the borderland. Some readers may be surprised that certain historical events that receive much attention in mainstream historiography are treated in rather a cursory manner in this book. Sometimes this is because there is still a lack of detailed information on how these events unfolded in the borderland (e.g. the Bangladesh war of independence in 1971) and sometimes because the available information suggests that their effects on the borderland were not particularly significant (e.g. many changes in government).

Despite its limitations, the material at hand allows me to present a fairly complex image of the Bengal borderland – a modern border landscape created less than 60 years ago – and its transformation during the current period of world reterritorialization. My intention is not just to show how this region evolved. In addition, I explore the ways in which borderlands may help us understand processes of territoriality and global restructuring, because 'some things can only occur at borders.'[73]

How the book is organized

The book consists of a number of chapters presenting substantive evidence on selected aspects of borderland society. These are prefaced by Chapters 2 and 3, which provide brief comments on the historiographical context. The story of the Bengal borderland has always been incorporated into the story of the break-up of British India and the creation of independent India and Pakistan, known as 'Partition.' Chapter 2 ('Partition studies') examines some conventions of this historiographical tradition: an emphasis on Partition as a unique event, a tendency to extrapolate from the historical experience of one particular province (Punjab), a periodization that takes 1947 as the end point of Partition, a strong emphasis on high politics, and a tendency to invoke the border as a representation of Partition without actually studying the border as a lived reality. I argue that these conventions are problematic and should be reconsidered, and that the study of Partition needs to be advanced and enriched by bringing the border back in. Chapter 3 ('Radcliffe's fateful line') gives a brief introduction to the genesis of the border and the remarkable role of a single colonial official in deciding its location. The chapter goes on to examine three widespread misconceptions about the making of this border – that it bisected Bengal, that it provided a border to Muslim-majority areas, and that it separated Hindus (in India) from Muslims (in Pakistan).

The following chapters form two groups. Chapters 4 and 5 focus on state actions in the borderland, mainly in the early years of its existence. Chapter 4 ('A patchwork border') details the new states' efforts to inscribe the border in the landscape, and the insurmountable problems they faced regarding moving rivers, unsurveyed land and mapping errors. Their inability to agree on, demarcate and normalize many parts of the border ensured a subsequent history of border conflict, borderland volatility and diplomatic unease that continues to the present day. Chapter 5 ('Securing the territory') looks at how the new states took control of the borderland. It presents their main tools: an expanding bureaucracy, the use of paramilitary forces, and mechanisms for homogenizing the borderland population and for resolving interstate border conflict.

From Chapter 6, attention shifts more to the activities of non-state actors in the borderland. In Chapter 6 ('Defiance and accommodation') we explore how borderlanders dealt with the new reality of having an international border in their backyard. We look especially at what happened to local social, economic and cultural relations that had suddenly become 'international,' e.g. people who lived on one side of the border but who had a job, or owned land or a business, on the other. How did they cope? And how did agents of the new states react to borderlanders who chose to ignore or defy the border?

Chapter 7 ('The flow of goods') plots the ways in which borderland trade flows adapted to the imposition of the border and to subsequent state attempts to manipulate them. The chapter details the failure of these attempts and the emergence of a subversive borderland economy based on various forms of unauthorized trade. Instead of regulating cross-border trade, the states ended up being themselves increasingly re-scaled by unauthorised forms of trade flowing through the hands of borderlanders.

Chapters 8 and 9 consider the movement of people passing through the borderland. Chapter 8 ('Narratives of border crossing') presents three powerful state-centred narratives regarding cross-border migration – homecoming, infiltration and denial – and their ominous consequences for transborder migrants. Chapter 9 ('Migrants, fences and deportations') shows how state attempts to stop unauthorized cross-border migration failed. The tools employed

– fencing the border, identification cards and deportation – proved to be no match for the forces that were driving people to go abroad to make a living. Analysing cross-border migration requires us to acknowledge the immense Bangladeshi diaspora and to focus on the strategies of individual migrants, the networks supporting their international migration, and the roles of borderlanders and state personnel in these networks.

Chapter 10 ('Rebels and bandits') presents the considerable political and military challenges to state power in the borderland, and considers how the many borderland rebellions of the past 60 years have had a contradictory effect. One the one hand they have challenged the state strategy of territoriality but on the other, they have reinforced the border as a lived reality.

Chapter 11 ('"Rifle Raj" and the killer border') is concerned with border violence. Based on recent newspaper coverage, it examines the levels of violence, the factors involved, the perpetrators and the patterns of border violence that can be distinguished. This analysis of the 'violence of territoriality' has a narrow scope: for reasons of measurement, only acts of violence that occurred on, or very near, the actual borderline have been included.

Chapter 12 ('Nation and borderland') sketches ideological and symbolic struggles in the borderland. It looks at the imprint of the nation on borderland culture and at symbols of state territoriality. At the same time it explains to what extent symbols of borderland cultural unity have been used to resist the hegemony of the nation in the borderland. The chapter concludes with a brief exploration of how the borderland is imagined in nationalist discourse.

Finally, in Chapter 13 ('Conclusion: Beyond state and nation') we return to the themes outlined in this introduction, especially to the issue of how borderland studies can contribute to sociospatial theory. The links between borderland and time, borderland and politics and borderland and scale are briefly touched upon, as are those between the everyday transnationality of borderlanders' life routines and the larger issues of global re-territorialization.

Notes

1 This incident took place in West Bengal, India. For details, more references, and similar cases in Bangladesh, see chapter 11. 'BSF road-rage shooting kills 5 in Cooch Behar,' *The Statesman* (4 December 1999); 'XIII *Lok Sabha Debates, Session II (Winter Session), Monday, November 29, 1999/Agrahayana 2, 1921 (Saka)* (available from: http://alfa.nic.in/lsdeb/ls13/ses2/17291199.htm); XIII *Lok Sabha Debates, Session II (Winter Session), Thursday, December 9, 1999/Agrahayana 18, 1921 (Saka)* (available from: http://alfa.nic.in/lsdeb/ls13/ses2/31091299.htm).

2 For details, see chapters 2 to 4. Some 1,500 km to the west a second borderland (now separating India and Pakistan) was created at the same time.

3 Abdul Alim (born c. 1935), interviewed by Md. Mahbubar Rahman in the border town of Rajshahi in January 1999. My translation (as in the case of all other interviews in

Bengali quoted in this book).

4 Anonymous inhabitant of the border town of Tlabung (Demagiri), interviewed by Willem van Schendel, December 2000.

5 In official parlance, Burma is currently known as Myanmar. Because of the longer-term view we take here, and because the term Myanmar is fiercely contested by the democratically elected government-in-exile, I refer to the country as Burma throughout this book.

6 In their excellent overview of border studies, Donnan and Wilson speak of a 'burgeoning literature on borders.' Hastings Donnan and Thomas M. Wilson, *Borders: Frontiers of Identity, Nation and State* (Oxford and New York: Berg, 1999), xiii. Cf. Michael Rösler and Tobias Wendl (eds.), *Frontiers and Borderlands: Anthropological Perspectives* (Frankfurt am Main, etc.: Peter Lang, 1999).

7 D. Rumley and J.V. Minghi (eds.), *The Geography of Border Landscapes* (London: Routledge, 1991), 2.

8 If this figure, calculated by Foucher, is correct, and if we take the depth of the borderland to be an arbitrary 10 km on either side, the world's borderlands cover an area of 4,500,000 km^2. Foucher measured the length of the world's borders at the scale of 1/250,000. He also counted 264 'dyads,' or stretches of border shared by two contiguous states. Michel Foucher, *Fronts et frontières: Un tour du monde géopolitique* (Paris: Fayard, 1991), 15.

9 James Anderson and Liam O'Dowd, 'Borders, Border Regions and Territoriality: Contradictory Meanings, Changing Significance,' *Regional Studies*, 33:7 (1999), 598.

10 Anderson and O'Dowd, 'Borders, Border Regions,' 600.

11 In a non-exhaustive list, Alvarez distinguishes 16 different identities among people living on the U.S.-Mexico border; he speaks of the lives of border people as 'a life-long trajectory of accommodation and negotiation' and 'constantly shifting and renegotiating identities.' Robert R. Alvarez Jr., 'Toward an Anthropology of Borderlands: The Mexican-U.S. border and the Crossing of the 21st Century,' in: Rösler and Wendl (eds.), *Frontiers and Borderlands*, 228-229.

12 Donnan and Wilson, *Borders*, 10-12.

13 For examples, see John W. Cole and Eric R. Wolf, *The Hidden Frontier: Ecology and Ethnicity in an Alpine Valley* (New York: Academic Press, 1974); and Daphne Berdahl, *Where the World Ended: Re-Unification and Identity in the German Borderland* (Berkeley etc.: University of California Press, 1999).

14 Anssi Paasi, *Territories, Boundaries and Consciousness: The Changing Geographies of the Finnish-Russian Border* (Chichester, etc.: John Wiley & Sons, 1996).

15 'A claim to sovereignty on the part of an institution is a special type of claim to authority: a claim to being the highest authority for some defined group or area. Like all claims to authority it is rarely established and uncontested.' Joe Painter, *Politics, Geography and 'Political Geography': A Critical Perspective* (London, etc.: Arnold, 1995), 17, cf. 40-42.

16 For a case study, see A. Kemp and U. Ben-Eliezer, 'Dramatizing Sovereignty: The Construction of Territorial Dispute in the Israeli-Egyptian Border at Taba,' *Political Geography*, 19 (2000), 315-344.

17 Neil Brenner, 'Beyond State-Centrism? Space, Territoriality, and Geographical Scale in Globalization Studies,' *Theory and Society*, 28 (1999), 47. For an institutional approach to the emergence of a system based on territorial states in post-feudal Europe, see Hendrik Spruyt, *The Sovereign State and its Competitors: An Analysis of Systems Change* (Princeton, N.J.: Princeton University Press, 1994).

18 Anderson and O'Dowd, 'Borders, Border Regions,' 598, quoting Robert David Sack,

Human Territoriality: Its Theory and History (Cambridge: Cambridge University Press, 1986), 21-34. See also John Torpey, *The Invention of the Passport: Surveillance, Citizenship and the State* (Cambridge: Cambridge University Press, 2000).

19 The Treaty of Westphalia (1648) recognized 'the existence of an interstate system composed of contiguous, bounded territories ruled by sovereign states committed to the principle of noninterference in each other's internal affairs ... This bundling of territoriality to state sovereignty is the essential characteristic of the modern interstate system' (Brenner, 'Beyond State-Centrism?' 47). The system was, however, far from perfectly constituted. For a case highlighting the limitations of the strategy of territoriality in two modern states, see Willem van Schendel, 'Stateless in South Asia: The Making of the India-Bangladesh Enclaves,' *The Journal of Asian Studies*, 61:1 (2002), 115-147.

20 Brenner, 'Beyond State-Centrism?' 48.

21 Brenner, 'Beyond State-Centrism?' 45-46.

22 John Agnew, 'The Territorial Trap: The Geographical Assumptions of International Relations Theory,' *Review of International Political Economy*, 1:1 (1994), 53-80; John Agnew and Stuart Corbridge, *Mastering Space: Hegemony, Territory and International Political Economy* (London and New York: Routledge, 1995), 78-100; Peter Taylor, 'Embedded Statism and the Social Sciences: Opening Up to New Spaces,' *Environment and Planning A*, 28:11 (1996), 1917-1928; cf. Brenner, 'Beyond State-Centrism? 40.

23 Pandey speaks of 'received unities.' Gyanendra Pandey, 'Voices from the Edge: The Struggle to Write Subaltern Histories,' in: Vinayak Chaturvedi (ed.), *Mapping Subaltern Studies and the Postcolonial* (London and New York: Verso, 2000), 281.

24 Henri Lefebvre, *The Production of Space* (Oxford: Blackwell, 1991), 281.

25 Josiah Heyman describes states as 'aggregations of rules for social and economic action and the bureaucratic organizations required to implement these rules; for short, states are the rules of the game.' Josiah McC. Heyman, 'The Mexico-United States Border in Anthropology: A Critique and Reformulation,' *Journal of Political Ecology*, 1(1994), 51.

26 Brenner, 'Beyond State-Centrism?' 40.

27 Brenner, 'Beyond State-Centrism?' 60.

28 Brenner, 'Beyond State-Centrism?' 62.

29 For two critiques of globalization and deterritorialization, see Frederick Cooper, 'What is the Concept of Globalization Good For? An African Historian's Perspective,' *African Affairs*, 100, 399 (2001), 189-213; Gearóid Ó Tuathail, 'Borderless Worlds? Problematising Discourses of Deterritorialisation,' in: Nurit Kliot and David Newman (eds.), *Geopolitics at the End of the Twentieth Century: The Changing Political Map* (London: Frank Cass, 2000), 139-154.

30 Neil Smith and Ward Dennis, 'The Restructuring of Geographical Scale: Coalescence and Fragmentation of the Northern Core Region,' *Economic Geography*, 63 (1987), 160-182.

31 'The "gatekeeper state," the task of which is to provide extraterritorial opportunities for national territory-based capital (thus intensifying the process of globalization) while, somewhat paradoxically, providing security against the perceived social costs unleashed by globalization – especially immigration.' Joseph Nevins, *Operation Gatekeeper: The Rise of the "Illegal Alien" and the Making of the U.S.-Mexico Boundary* (New York and London: Routledge, 2002), 178.

32 Cf. Anderson and O'Dowd, 'Borders, Border Regions,' 600-601.

33 An important source of inspiration for this approach is the work of Henri Lefebvre, especially his *De l'État* (Paris: Union Générale d'Éditions, 1976-78, 4 volumes) and *The*

Production of Space. For an overview, see Sallie A. Marston, 'The Social Construction of Scale,' *Progress in Human Geography*, 24:2 (2000), 219-242.

34 Neil Smith, 'Contours of a Spatialized Politics: Homeless Vehicles and the Production of Geographical Scale,' *Social Text*, 33 (1992), 61, 63.

35 Allen presents this criticism vigorously in this sentence in an overview article: 'The normative discourse of social science has violently relegated those things spatial to its semiotic refuse heap where dead and vacuous signifiers lay wasting as victims of being fully and essentially "understood".' Ricky Lee Allen, 'The Socio-Spatial Making and Marking of "Us": Toward a Critical Postmodern Spatial Theory of Difference and Community,' *Social Identities*, 5:3 (1999), 250, 252, 253.

36 Erik Swyngedouw, 'Excluding the Other: The Production of Scale and Scaled Politics,' in: Roger Lee and Jane Wills (eds.), *Geographies of Economies* (London: Arnold, 1997), 169.

37 Neil Smith, 'Remaking Scale: Competition and Cooperation in Prenational and Postnational Europe,' in: Heikki Eskelinen and Folke Snickars (ed.), *Competitive European Peripheries* (Berlin: Springer, 1995), 59-74.

38 For a schematic history of scalar fixes since the late 19th century, see Neil Brenner, 'Between Fixity and Motion: Accumulation, Territorial Organization and the Historical Geography of Spatial Scales,' *Environment and Planning D: Society and Space*, 16 (1998), 459-481.

39 Brenner, 'Between Fixity,' 461.

40 'Starting any geographical analysis from a given geographical scale (local, regional, national) is deeply antagonistic to apprehending the world in a dynamic, process-based manner ... The theoretical and political priority, therefore, never resides in a particular geographical scale, but rather in the process through which particular scales become (re)constituted' (Swyngedouw, 'Excluding the Other,' 169).

41 Brenner, 'Beyond State-Centrism?' 66.

42 See e.g. Margaret E. Keck and Kathryn Sikkink, *Activists Beyond Borders: Advocacy Networks in International Politics* (Ithaca, N.Y.: Cornell University Press, 1998); David Kyle and Rey Koslowski (eds.), *Global Human Smuggling: Comparative Perspectives* (Baltimore and London: The Johns Hopkins University Press, 2001). For other examples, see Kevin Cox, 'Spaces of Dependence, Spaces of Engagement and the Politics of Scale, or: Looking for Local Politics,' *Political Geography*, 17:1 (1998), 1-23.

43 According to Neil Smith's original formulation of this concept, to jump scales is 'to organize the production and reproduction of daily life and to resist oppression and exploitation at a higher scale.' (Smith, 'Contours,' 60). Crucially, such struggles not only use scales but also influence them: 'These struggles change the importance and role of certain geographical scales, reassert the importance of others, and sometimes create entirely new significant scales, but – most importantly – these scale redefinitions alter and express changes in the geometry of social power by strengthening power and control of some while disempowering others' (Swyngedouw, 'Excluding the Other,' 169).

44 'Until recently political geographers remained intellectual prisoners of the first stage of geopolitics in the 1890s, but now seem to have begun to see the past in terms of the workings of processes across scales. In my view this seems likely to become an important feature of a non-state obsessed but equally non-globe entranced political geography.' John Agnew, *Making Political Geography* (London: Arnold, 2002), 139.

45 Cf. J.R.V. Prescott, *Political Frontiers and Boundaries* (London: Unwin Hyman, 1987), 13-14. Prescott distinguishes the boundary (the line that demarcates state territory),

the border (areas fringing the boundary) and the borderland (the transition zone within which lies the boundary). Since it is not clear when the 'border' merges into the 'borderland', I use the latter term as defined here, and reserve the term 'border' (and occasionally 'boundary') to refer to the line demarcating state territory. Cf. Donnan and Wilson, *Borders*, 45.

46 For a fuller treatment, see Michiel Baud and Willem van Schendel, 'Toward a Comparative History of Borderlands,' *Journal of World History*, 8:2 (1997), 211-242.

47 'The discourse of transnationalism is based on a productive critique of the inherent imperfections of traditional representations of nations, states and cultures as geographically discrete and politically pacific. It suggests a radically different definition of space and occupancy in which entities other than those defined by, contained within, or tantamount to states and nations become significant elements of human experience ... Studying communities which live across borders, survive despite them, routinely cross them and constantly network around them has become an indispensable aspect of the discourse.' Dan Rabinowitz, 'National identity on the frontier: Palestinians in the Israeli education system,' in: Thomas M. Wilson and Hastings Donnan (eds.), *Border Identities: Nation and State at International Frontiers* (Cambridge: Cambridge University Press, 1998), 142; cf Anderson and O'Dowd, 'Borders, Border Regions,' 602-603.

48 Tobias Wendl and Michael Rösler, 'Introduction: Frontiers and Borderlands: The Rise and Relevance of an Anthropological Research Genre,' in: Rösler and Wendl (eds.), *Frontiers and Borderlands*, 2.

49 He suggested that the borderlands milieu is shaped by transnationalism, social separateness, otherness, ethnic conflict and accommodation, and international conflict and accommodation. Oscar Martínez, 'The Dynamics of Border Interaction,' in: Clive H. Schofield (ed.), *Global Boundaries: World Boundaries, Volume I* (London: Routledge, 1994), 8-14.

50 'The construction of scale is not simply a spatial solidification or materialization of contested social forces and processes; the corollary also holds. Scale is an active progenitor of specific social processes. In a literal as much as metaphorical way, scale both *contains* social activity, and at the same time provides an already partitioned geography within which social activity *takes place*.' (Smith, 'Contours,' 66). Cf. Katherine T. Jones, 'Scale as Epistemology,' *Political Geography*, 17:1 (1998), 27; Marston, 'The Social Construction,' 221.

51 Smith, 'Contours,' 66, 75.

52 Willem van Schendel, 'Geographies of Knowing, Geographies of Ignorance: Jumping scale in Southeast Asia,' *Environment and Planning D: Society and Space*, 20 (2002): 647-68.

53 Cf. Peter Andreas, *Border Games: Policing the U.S.-Mexico Divide* (Ithaca and London: Cornell University Press, 2000).

54 He emphasizes the need to recognize 'scale as a Relation – a factor in the *construction and dynamics* of geographical totalities – rather than simply as a *product* of geographical relations (a handmaiden to 'real' causal factors) or simply as a matter of size and level.' Richard Howitt, 'Scale as Relation: Musical Metaphors of Geographical Space,' *Area*, 30:1 (1998), 56.

55 'While the rich and powerful revel in their freedom and ability to overcome space by commanding scale, the poor and powerless are trapped in place.' Swyngedouw, 'Excluding the Other,' 175.

56 See e.g. John Agnew, 'The Dramaturgy of Horizons: Geographical Scale in the

"Reconstruction of Italy" by the New Italian Political Parties, 1992-95,' *Political Geography*, 16 (1997), 99-122; Philip F. Kelly, 'Globalization, Power and the Politics of Scale in the Philippines,' *Geoforum*, 28:2 (1997), 151-171.

57 James C. Scott, *Seeing Like a State: How Certain Schemes to Improve the Human Condition Have Failed* (New Haven and London: Yale University Press, 1998), 3.

58 These two contributions can be considered as the first building blocks towards a field of border studies in the region. Both deal with one particular section of the border, the West Bengal-Bangladesh stretch. Joya Chatterji, 'The Fashioning of a Frontier: The Radcliffe Line and Bengal's Border Landscape, 1947-52,' *Modern Asian Studies*, 33:1 (1999), 185-242; and Ranabir Samaddar, *The Marginal Nation: Transborder Migration from Bangladesh to West Bengal* (New Delhi, etc.: Sage Publications, 1999).

59 Paul Nugent, *Smugglers, Secessionists & Loyal Citizens on the Ghana-Togo Frontier: The Lie of the Borderlands Since 1914* (Oxford: James Curry / Athens: Ohio University Press / Legon: Sub-Saharan Publishers, 2002), 115.

60 Samaddar, *The Marginal Nation*, 109.

61 In 2003 the Survey of India protested against the Ministry of Defence's ruling that no fewer than 43 types of detail had to be deleted from maps that the Survey was preparing for civilian use. These included such basic and seemingly innocuous items as contour lines and the intersections of latitudes and longitudes. Officials of the Ministry of Defence were not fazed by the argument that knowledge of contours was essential ecological information in preparing realistic development and infrastructural projects. They countered: 'Allowing contour lines on maps will endanger the country's security ... If the matter is of military consequence, it has to be controlled.' 'Civilian maps to get "flatter",' *The Times of India* (18 February 2003).

62 See e.g. Ravi Gupta and Sanjay Kumar, 'Rules on Mapping Technologies in India Heading Nowhere!' *GISDevelopment* (November-December 1998); S.V. Shrikantia, 'Restriction on Maps in India: An Anachronism That Needs Removal,' *GISDevelopment* (March-April 1999); S.M. Mathur, 'Restrictions on Survey of India Maps: Logic and Rationale,' *GISDevelopment* (July-August 1999); and many other articles in the same magazine. See also: http://www.gisdevelopment.net/policy/india/technology/index.htm. Cf. Mark Monmonier, *Spying with Maps: Surveillance Technologies and the Future of Privacy* (Chicago: University of Chicago Press, 2002).

63 'All topographical and geographical maps of the Survey of India (and maps derived from them) on the scale of one-million or larger of areas roughly 80 km wide inland along the coast and along the international borders ... are not available to the general public.' Mathur, 'Restrictions'; cf. Shrikantia, 'Restriction.'

64 E.g. the Ground Rules on border management state that 'much harm is caused by alarming reports which are occasionally published in the press. We recommend that the press on both sides be persuaded to exercise restraint and not to publish material which is likely to inflame the feelings of the population on both sides.' *Ground Rules Formulated by the Military Sub-Committee of the Indian and Pakistan Delegations* (20 October 1959), reprinted in Avtar Singh Bhasin (ed.), *India-Bangladesh Relations: Documents – 1971-2002* (New Delhi: Geetika Publishers, 2003), V, 2741-2742. A historian from North Bengal University, presenting a research paper on the merger of Cooch Behar with West Bengal (1950) and challenged because of a lack of references, replied that 'the Government of India is still not allowing any access to these sources.' 'Cooch Behar's merger,' *The Assam Tribune* (2 July 2003).

65 Anderson and O'Dowd, 'Borders, Border Regions,' 596.

66 Sankaran Krishna, *Postcolonial Insecurities: India, Sri Lanka and the Question of Nationhood* (Minneapolis: University of Minnesota Press, 1999), 240-241. The break-up of East Pakistan (Bangladesh) and West Pakistan is a case in point. Discussing India, Abraham and Pandian argue: 'What is most troubling is the all-too-easy recourse to invoking the sacred cow of national security when in trouble and the even greater ease with which so many intellectuals and commentators swallow this line ... What we mean in practice by national security are usually the activities of one or another Government Ministry or agency which is keen not to have its activities scrutinised by the public.' And: 'What one must question is the colonial mentality that suggests that an airing of one's shortfalls leads to a decline in the nation's well being. It could rather be the opposite. It is only a confident nation that allows free expression on all matters, with the assurance that the outcome will lead to a stronger public and greater legitimacy for the state.' Itty Abraham and M.S.S. Pandian, 'Autonomy of Scholarship and the State,' *The Hindu* (15 August 2001).

67 Cf. Willem van Schendel, 'Geographies of Knowing, Geographies of Ignorance: Jumping Scale in Southeast Asia,' *Environment and Planning D: Society and Space*, 20 (2002), 647-68.

68 For example, several national newspapers in India, reporting on a border incident with Bangladesh in April 2001 in which 19 border guards got killed, published maps showing the place of the incident several hundreds of kilometres from its actual place of occurrence.

69 See Willem van Schendel, 'Easy Come, Easy Go: Smugglers on the Ganges,' *Journal of Contemporary Asia*, 23:2 (1993), 189-213; Willem van Schendel, *Reviving a Rural Industry: Silk Producers and Officials in India and Bangladesh, 1880s to 1980s* (Dhaka / Delhi: University Press Ltd. / Manohar Publications, 1995); Baud and Van Schendel, 'Toward a Comparative History of Borderlands.'

70 See Willem van Schendel, 'The Invention of the "Jummas": State Formation and Ethnicity in Southeastern Bangladesh,' *Modern Asian Studies*, 26:1 (1992), 95-128; Willem van Schendel, Wolfgang Mey, and Aditya Kumar Dewan, *The Chittagong Hill Tracts: Living in a Borderland* (Bangkok: White Lotus, 2000).

71 Some of this material has been used in previous publications, e.g. Willem van Schendel, 'Stateless in South Asia: The Making of the India-Bangladesh Enclaves,' *The Journal of Asian Studies*, 61:1 (February 2002), 115-47; and Md. Mahbubar Rahman and Willem van Schendel, '"I Am *Not* a Refugee": Rethinking Partition Migration,' *Modern Asian Studies*, 37:3 (2003), 551-584. Shahriar Kabir and Willem van Schendel jointly conducted one interview cited in this book.

72 For an introduction to discussions regarding the *necessarily* fragmented nature of evidence pertaining to histories of 'subaltern' groups, see Pandey, 'Voices from the Edge.'

73 Donnan and Wilson, *Borders*, 4.

2

PARTITION STUDIES

The demise of colonial India, followed by the phoenix-like emergence from its ashes of the new states of India and Pakistan, is commonly known as the Partition. There are two reasons why any study of the Bengal borderland must start from this event. First, the border was created at that moment, so Partition coincides with the birth of the Bengal borderland. And second, the border has always been looked at through the lens of Partition (for a map of the borderland, see Appendix Figure 1).

In the Indian subcontinent, the word 'Partition' conjures up a particular landscape of knowledge and emotion. The break-up of colonial India in 1947 has been presented from vantage points that privilege certain vistas of the postcolonial landscape. The high politics of the break-up itself, the violence and major population movements it caused, and the long shadows it cast over the relationship between India and Pakistan (and from 1971 Bangladesh) have been the topic of much myth-making, intense polemics and considerable serious historical research. As three rival nationalisms were being built on conflicting interpretations of Partition, most analysts and historians were drawn towards the study of Partition as a macro-political event. A second trend in the literature has focused on Partition as a cultural and personal disaster, the fissure of two major regional cultures (Punjab and Bengal) that were divided between the successor states, and the suffering of millions of uprooted refugees and their descendants.

These viewpoints hardly exhaust the possibilities of coming to terms with the complexity of Partition. It is necessary to develop alternative perspectives to do justice to the plethora of experiences that together form Partition. Studying the Partition borderlands and their inhabitants provides a particularly important additional perspective because, as David Ludden has pointed out:

> The pain of partition was very unevenly distributed and afflicted a small proportion of the total population [of South Asia]. For most people, partition was a national trauma that affected people far away in other regions. Non-border regions had little disruption ... Almost all the pain fell on three historical regions that partition divided between India and Pakistan: Punjab, Bengal and Kashmir. In each region the new international borders were unprecedented; their local details were also quite arbitrary.[1]

The pain of Partition fell disproportionately on the new borderlands. Here disruption was overwhelming and almost all people were directly and personally affected. The borderland experience of Partition was immediate and acute and therefore differed from the experience of Partition in other parts of South Asia. This makes a borderland perspective indispensable as a component of any rounded view of Partition. This chapter, far from being an overview of the huge literature on Partition, merely comments on a few conventions in the historiography that I have found problematic when looking at Partition from a borderland angle.

One of a kind?

One convention in the study of Partition has been to analyse it against a rather restricted, regional backdrop. The voluminous literature is strikingly unanimous in presenting Partition as a unique event, a monument to political processes that took place in late-colonial India.[2] But how unique was it? What was unique about it? These questions have rarely been addressed until quite recently. Radha Kumar, Rada Iveković and Gurharpal Singh are among the first to develop a comparative perspective, bringing in wider questions of social theory – especially regarding the causes and long-term effects of state fragmentation.[3]

Comparing partitions. Obviously, the collapse of older polities and the redistribution of political spoils is an unavoidable phase in the age-old process of state formation. If we follow Aaron Klieman, who defines partition simply as the act of dividing into two or more units an area previously forming a single administrative entity, the Partition of India takes its place among numerous other moments of state reconstitution, and many of its apparently unique features have their historical counterparts.[4]

But most observers think of partition as a more restricted category. For Robert Schaeffer it is not only a division but also a devolution of power. He excludes the disintegration of dynastic states or the redistribution of territories between imperial powers (e.g. the absorption by the British and French Empires of territories formerly belonging to the Ottoman Empire). Instead, he reserves the term partition for situations in which 'political power was not merely redistributed between great powers but transferred to and divided between indigenous successors.'[5] Twentieth-century partitions that fit this description occurred as by-products of three developments: decolonization, democratization and the Cold War. These developments should not be understood separately because each of them was associated with the emergence of the new interstate system in the world.[6] The Partition of India bore the imprint of the intertwining of these three processes of decolonization, democratization and the Cold War.[7] In their intense concern with territoriality and sovereignty, Pakistan and India reflected the moment of their birth. As the British handed over power to their former subjects and installed two new state elites in territories henceforth known as Pakistan and India, the inhabitants of these territories demanded to be treated as citizens and to be given the rights that had been promised to them during the anticolonial struggle. At the same time, the Cold War descended upon the world, providing the state elites of India and Pakistan with a completely novel structure of political and military opportunities, resources and limitations.

A third way of studying the Partition of India is by placing it in a more restricted comparative framework. Edward Said has drawn attention to partition as a 'parting gift of Empire,' a legacy of imperialism, 'as the unhappy cases of Pakistan and India, Ireland, Cyprus, and the Balkans amply testify, and as the disasters of 20th century Africa attest in the most tragic way.'[8] Within this more restricted category of imperial partitions, it is easy to recognize similarities. For example, Said's point about Israel and Palestine is of direct relevance to South Asia today:

> So let us see these new partitions as the desperate and last-ditch efforts of a dying ideology of separation, which has afflicted Zionism and Palestinian nationalism, both of whom have not surmounted the philosophical problem of the other, of learning how to live with, as opposed to despite, the other. When it comes to corruption, to racial or religious discrimination, to poverty and unemployment, to torture and censorship, the other is always one of us, not a remote alien.[9]

Linking the literature on the partition of the subcontinent with work on other major twentieth-century partitions appears to be a major challenge confronting us. A moot question will be to what extent such partitions are best understood as parting gifts that European empires bestowed around the globe or as regional processes propelled primarily by local forces.[10]

Above all, comparative partition studies will break the habit of viewing the fragmentation of colonial India as *sui generis*, a peerless event, too horrendous to be bracketed with other events in world history. Essentializing Partition (with a capital P) presents the same pitfalls as, for example, essentializing the Holocaust (with a capital H): they are somehow placed outside history and it becomes unthinkable, even sacrilegious, to juxtapose them with other partitions and holocausts. This precludes the historical inquiry and understanding that is indispensable if we are to find ways of preventing such events from recurring in the future.

One into four. A comparative approach to Partition should also be applied within South Asia itself, for even if we look only at the subcontinent, the Partition of 1947 is not one of a kind, a peerless, unique event. The dismantling of the enormous colony of British India, stretching from Iran to Thailand, involved three separate moments of partition (*Figure 2.1*). The Partition of 1947 stands between the creation of a separate colonial state of British Burma in 1937 and the collapse of the state of Pakistan (and emergence of Bangladesh) in 1971. Over a period of 34 years, the colonial state was carved up and its four pieces appropriated by four different state elites. In their eagerness to present the Partition of 1947 as a unique event, however, writers have tended to ignore its embeddedness in this longer-term process, thereby marginalizing the relevance of the first (Burma) and third (Bangladesh) partitions. A proper

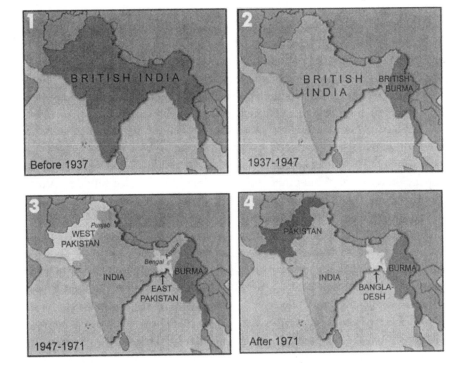

Map 1: Till 1937, British India stretched from Iran to Thailand.
Map 2: In 1937, it split into two colonies: British India and British Burma.
Map 3: In 1947, British India split into India and Pakistan (the divided regions of Punjab, Assam and Bengal are in italics).
Map 4: In 1971, Pakistan split into Bangladesh (formerly East Pakistan) and Pakistan (formerly West Pakistan).

Figure 2.1: **One into Four – State fragmentation in Southern Asia.**

understanding of major themes in the Partition of 1947 – for example the concept of homeland, the process of territorial division, the dislocation of populations, and the political use of violence – requires us to recontextualize it by comparing it with both its precursor and its successor.[11]

Moreover, Partition threw up a number of territorial issues that have not yet been settled. The best known of these is the status of Kashmir, but the following pages reveal a host of smaller and less well known, but no less inflammable, territorial disputes between India and Bangladesh, and between Bangladesh and Burma. It may be argued that the process of Partition, in its narrowest political and geographical sense, will not be complete until these outstanding issues have been resolved by the post-Partition states.

Beyond Punjab

Another peculiarity of most major studies of the Partition of 1947 is that they highlight events in one particular region, Punjab, and as a result we know more about what Partition meant there than in other provinces.[12] In the absence of similarly detailed knowledge of Partition elsewhere, Punjab has come to figure as a model of sorts, as shorthand for what Partition entailed, as the prime case from which to draw general conclusions.[13] It is helpful for students of Partition to take a more serious look at what was happening in other parts of the subcontinent and to reconsider the case of Punjab.[14] This is already happening, with new scholarship becoming available on Bengal,[15] an area with twice the population of Punjab,[16] but other provinces directly involved, e.g. Bihar, Assam, Sindh, or Rajasthan, have so far received little scholarly attention and remain marginalized in accounts of Partition.[17]

Research on these regions is bound to lead to a reappraisal of standard assumptions about Partition. For example, there were two partitions creating two huge borderlands – one between India and West Pakistan ('Partition-in-the-west') and another some 1,500 km to the east between India and East Pakistan/Bangladesh and Burma ('Partition-in-the-east'). Some of the best-known stereotypes on Partition-in-the-east are that it was essentially a question of establishing a North-South border through Bengal (ignoring the much longer border in the North and East, and the fact that Assam was also partitioned), that Bengal was cut in two halves (in reality it broke into 4 large parts and 197 small ones), that East Pakistan was carved out of India (ignoring the simultaneous surgery creating a novel and isolated 'Northeast India'[18]), that population dislocation in the east was primarily the flight of Hindus from East Pakistan to West Bengal (ignoring both the large flows of Muslim refugees coming into East Pakistan from West Bengal, Bihar and Assam, and the movement of refugees from East Pakistan to Tripura and Assam), and that population dislocation in the east was much smaller than in Punjab. The unchallenged persistence of such basic misconceptions reveals the lack of balance in Partition studies and points to the need for comparative work within the subcontinent.

Closing a disciplinary divide

In the postcolonial division of academic labour, Partition has been treated as a disciplinary divide. Historians have taken it as the final chord in the symphony of colonialism, the denouement of the nationalist movement, the end of an era. For many, it also marks the boundary of the historian's domain. Countless books have taken August 1947 as a 'natural' closing date and have presented the formal transfer of state power as the clear-cut end of a period and, in a sense, of history. In similar vein, other social scientists have treated Partition as the beginning of their domain, the jumping-off point for economic, political, social and cultural analyses of contemporary South Asia. This division of labour was not a serious problem in the early postcolonial years but gradually a worrying chasm has opened up. As most social scientists kept on focusing on the present and many historians looked no further than the 1940s, the study of social change in the intervening decades came to be increasingly neglected. Today, the third quarter of the twentieth century is perhaps the least studied in the modern history of South Asia, a state of affairs that obstructs our understanding of long-term social change in the subcontinent.

This is particularly clear in the study of Partition. Here sophisticated analyses of processes leading up to the crisis of August 1947 continue to provide fuel for lively and important debates among historians. But we do not have equally careful recent studies analysing what happened *after* that date. For example, if we want to understand how government institutions were reconstituted in partitioned Bengal, or how a new political culture developed, we have little more to go on than the fragmentary evidence contained in the memoirs of administrators – the rich unpublished records of the 1940s, 1950s and 1960s lie largely forgotten and unexplored.[19]

Reassembling a partitioned academy

In addition to the disciplinary gap, however, a second academic gap has hampered the development of new insights. This is the partitioning (or 're-scaling') of academic communities between the study of India, Pakistan and Bangladesh. Scholars in the subcontinent found themselves in one of these states and took part in the various discussions that developed in the reconstituted scholarly communities of which they were members.[20] These communities were both influenced by and very active in new discourses regarding nation, citizenship, state, history, memory and development that differed considerably between India, Pakistan and (later) Bangladesh.[21] Strained relations between these countries have seriously hampered free academic exchange and dialogue ever since.[22] The 'academic partition' also extended to foreign scholars studying the post-Partition subcontinent. As any international conference of South Asian studies will demonstrate, most opted for the study of just one successor society, and very few indeed maintained or developed a research interest across Partition boundaries.

The study of Partition itself has been one of the principal victims. Over the past half-century, three rival nationalisms have fashioned and refined their own interpretations of Partition, and these are not compatible.[23] On the contrary, they have powered the confrontational politics that continue to dominate interstate relations in South Asia despite many attempts at reconciliation. Few historians or social scientists have been able to stay aloof from the dominant interpretation in their own country and they have, often unwittingly because of limited contact with their colleagues across the border, contributed to a veritable epistemological and historiographical minefield. It will take much intellectual effort to close this gap: it requires sustained dialogue, revisiting the most emotionally charged events, the unlearning of national reflexes, and the joint reworking of by now longstanding academic traditions. Such a 'counter memorial reading' of the events surrounding Partition is both urgent and important. Without it, the conceptual and political minefield that Partition represents in South Asian public and academic discourses will only become more convoluted.[24]

A social history of Partition

As already mentioned, the primary concerns that have given direction to Partition studies so far are the high politics leading up to the split, the violence and major population movements it caused, the long shadows it cast over the relationship between India and Pakistan (and from 1971 Bangladesh), and the price that regional cultures had to pay. Surprisingly little is known about the effects of Partition on the social life of tens of millions who were neither top politicians nor cross-border refugees. In this sense, Gyanendra Pandey's remarks on India are equally applicable to Pakistan and Bangladesh:

> the historians' history of Partition has, in India, been a history of crisis for the Indian nation and the nationalist leadership. It has been a history of the machinations that lay behind this event, and the lessons to be drawn by the nation for the future. This is not a history of the lives and experiences of the people who lived through that time, of the way in which the events

of the 1940s were constructed in their minds, of the identities or uncertainties that Partition created or reinforced. Even as a history of crisis for the Indian nation, therefore, this history is inadequate.[25]

If we are to make sense of how 'the people who lived through that time' have shaped post-Partition societies, we need to pay much more attention to the *social* history of Partition. This requires a reconsideration of the historical sources that have informed Partition studies so far. Students of Partition have been like miners returning time and again to a few particularly rich seams: high-level official records (most famously the ones published in *The Transfer of Power*[26]) and the private papers, correspondence and memoirs of prominent politicians and bureaucrats. The possibilities offered by other source material have been much less diligently explored. As a result, the voices speaking from low-level and local records, newspapers, and oral and written testimony by ordinary people are rarely highlighted.[27] Convincing social histories of Partition cannot be constructed without foregrounding these voices.

Conclusion: Bringing the border back in

A crucial way of enriching the study of Partition is to look at its foremost territorial representation: the newly created international border.[28] Obviously, that border divides the three countries as much as it connects them. So many of the political problems between these countries have originated in the borderland, that one Pakistani observer in the 1960s was moved to comment ruefully: 'Our relations with India will improve only if by some miracle of modern science we could physically get away from its border.'[29]

Understanding and unravelling the post-1947 realities of Partition requires an intimate knowledge of the borderlands that were created and the permutations they experienced. The role of borderlanders in the shaping of post-Partition societies, economies and states remains almost completely unexplored.

First, it is essential to stress the fact that *Partition happened here*. There is no doubt that the break-up of colonial India was felt all over the subcontinent, ripping apart communities, bringing trauma to many individuals, and leading to a 'division of hearts.'[30] It inscribed itself in innumerable lives and this process was at least as calamitous in the borderlands as anywhere else. But in the borderlands Partition also inscribed itself indelibly in the landscape. It was here that South Asians learned first-hand what it meant to be allocated to different modern states and to be separated by international borders. It was here that the earthquake occurred, fissuring the land and making permanent scars that can never be ignored. The physical signs of Partition continue to exert an overwhelming influence over everyday life in the borderlands, and this makes them crucial sites for students of Partition.

And yet, border studies in South Asia is a weak field in terms of the quantity of work done as well as in terms of the methods applied and the conceptual range covered. There is much scope for developing a comparative perspective by linking work on the Partition borders with the general field of border studies.[31] The peculiarities of the Partition borders can best be explored by comparing them with borders and borderlands elsewhere, not least those resulting from other late-imperial partitions such as in Ireland or Palestine/Israel.

Second, systematic comparisons between different *parts* of the Partition borderlands hold much promise. Not only were two huge borderlands created – one between India and West Pakistan and another some 1,500 km to the east between India and East Pakistan/Bangladesh and Burma – but we will also see that these borderlands consisted of sectors that differed enormously from each other. If we wish to make general statements about the borderland, we can do so fruitfully only if we know much more about these differences.

Third, in the case of the Partition border, the gap between the academic disciplines has led to a startling contrast. Historians have provided us with detailed accounts of the bureaucratic and political processes leading up to the decisions of the Boundary Commissions (for Punjab and for Bengal/Sylhet) but they have been almost completely silent about what happened after those decisions were made public. Social scientists who take up the story from 1947, on the other hand, have treated the border as an unproblematic given, a *fait accompli*, the outer skin of new nations, the margin of new states. Hardly anybody has bothered to study how the decisions of the boundary commissions were implemented on the ground, explore the long period of uncertainty and confusion, or look at the border as a social reality that was shaped by borderlanders themselves over the decades following 1947.[32] It is possible to narrow down this gap by using information that is available and by employing the research techniques of both historians and other social scientists.

Fourth, writers on the Partition border have usually been unable to free themselves from partisan positions when it comes to interpreting disputes, incidents and the cross-border movement of people and goods. Understanding the borderland as a social reality requires, however, that we move beyond such positions. National discourses and received wisdoms do not travel well across the border, and creating the preconditions for reassessing such discourses and wisdoms is an urgent task. A first step is to consider them in the light of the historical evidence that is available on the Partition borderlands.

Fifth, a study of borderland society – rather than merely a study of the border – allows us to begin constructing the social history of those in whose backyard an international border suddenly appeared in 1947. Being a borderlander was as important a way of 'living the Partition' as was being a cross-border refugee: henceforth there was no way you could imagine your life without direct reference to the trauma of 1947. Taking this as a critical event that shaped both the identities and the actions of borderlanders, we can explore how Partition led them to initiate new social arrangements. These arrangements could point towards undermining the border and maintaining cross-border connections but also towards strengthening the border as a social, economic and cultural divide. The social uses made of the border varied enormously according to location along the border, the age of the border, and the social, economic, ethnic, religious or gender group to which borderlanders belonged.

Finally, it is necessary to consider carefully how and why scholars on Partition and its aftermath have come to imagine the borderland as a denigrated, residual and distant space.[33] We have routinely marginalized the borderland and privileged political, economic and cultural processes emanating from centres of state power. The following pages will demonstrate that the Partition border strongly influenced how such 'central' processes actually unfolded and, even more signficantly, that political, economic and cultural processes emanating from the borderland deeply affected the centres of state power.[34] Since its sudden birth in 1947, the 4,000 km long borderland between India, East Pakistan/Bangladesh and Burma has left a deep imprint on each of these states and on their uneasy coexistence. Border disputes, the movement of unauthorized migrants across the border, smuggling, border rebellions, and interstate war are just a few of the problems that have persistently dogged the rulers of these states and forced them continually to engage with the borderland in both material and symbolic ways. In borderland studies, such engagements have been described as the 'border effect' on state formation.[35] By studying this interaction in the case of Partition borderlanders and state power holders we can enrich not only borderland studies but also analyses of economic policy, security, nation building, law enforcement and diplomacy in South Asia.

Bringing the border back in requires a consideration of how it was created. The next two chapters take up this task. Chapter 3 looks briefly at how the border was conceived and at the necessity of qualifying some common assumptions about its birth. Chapter 4 details how the border was actually established on the ground.

Notes

1 David Ludden, *India and South Asia: A Short History* (Oxford: Oneworld Publications, 2002), 226.

2 For an analysis of the construction and collapse of such 'sites of memory,' see Pierre Nora (ed.), *Les Lieux de Mémoire* (Paris: Éditions Gallimard, 1997).

3 Radha Kumar, 'The Troubled History of Partition,' *Foreign Affairs*, 76:1 (1997), 22–34;

Radha Kumar, 'Settling Partition Hostilities: Lessons Learnt, the Options Ahead,' *Transeuropéennes*, no. 19/20 (2000–2001), 9–28; Rada Iveković, 'From the Nation to Partition, Through Partition to the Nation: Readings', *Transeuropéennes*, no. 19/20 (2000–2001), 201–25; Gurharpal Singh, 'The Partition of India in a Comparative Perspective: A Long-term View,' in: Ian Talbot and Gurharpal Singh (eds.), *Region and Partition: Bengal, Punjab and the Partition of the Subcontinent* (Karachi: Oxford University Press, 1999), 95–115. See also Thomas G Fraser, *Partition in Ireland, India and Palestine: Theory and Practice* (London: Macmillan, 1984) and Gilles Bertrand (ed.), 'La partition en question: Bosnie-Herzégovine, Caucase, Chypre,' *Cahiers d'études sur la Méditerranée Orientale et le Monde Turco-Iranien*, 34 (2002), 137–233. For a discussion of a different strand of 'partition theory,' see Nicholas Sambanis, *Ethnic Partition as a Solution to Ethnic War: An Empirical Critique of the Theoretical Literature* (Washington, DC: The World Bank, 1999).

4 Aaron S Klieman, 'The Resolution of Conflicts Through Territorial Partition: The Palestine Experience', *Comparative Studies in Society and History*, 22:2 (1980), 281. For example, if we consider Partition as 'the unintended outcome of an unsuccessful effort by a minority to secure a more federal political dispensation and the unwillingness of the party of the majority ... to countenance [it],' we discern tensions between centralization and decentralization that have undone many other states. And if we consider Partition as 'a consciously developed and deliberately deployed spatial strategy of eliminating real or imagined differences', we recognize a classic trend among politicians to seek a territorial solution to intense ideological conflict. Quotations are from Sankaran Krishna, *Postcolonial Insecurities: India, Sri Lanka and the Question of Nationhood* (Minneapolis: University of Minnesota Press, 1999), 239; and Sanjay Chaturvedi, 'The Excess of Geopolitics: Partition of "British India"', in: Stefano Bianchini, Rada Iveković, Ranabir Samaddar and Sanjay Chaturvedi, *Partitions: Reshaping States and Minds* (forthcoming), 119–53. Cf. Stanley Waterman, 'Partitioned States,' *Political Geography Quarterly*, 6:2 (1987), 151–70.

5 Robert K Schaeffer, *Severed States: Dilemmas of Democracy in a Divided World* (Lanham, MD: Rowman and Littlefield, 1999), 6.

6 Schaeffer, *Severed States*, 2.

7 Schaeffer (*Severed States*) treats these processes as following each other and dominating successive phases – decolonization partitions being followed by Cold War ones and democratization ones in the second half of the twentieth century – but it is also possible to observe them interacting in different mixes in individual partitions.

8 Edward Said, 'Partition as a Parting Gift of Empire,' *Dawn* (22 November 1999). See Fraser, *Partition in Ireland*.

9 Said, 'Partition.'

10 The last Viceroy of India was clearly concerned about this question when he manoeuvred to 'divert odium from the British' and 'avoid turning a day of rejoicing over Indian and Pakistani freedom into one of mourning over disappointed territorial hopes.' The same dilemma is expressed in WH Auden's poem 'Partition'. In the following fragment, 'you' is Sir Cyril Radcliffe, the chairman of the Boundary Commissions:

> The only solution now lies in separation.
> The Viceroy thinks, as you will see from his letter,
> That the less you are seen in his company the better,
> So we've arranged to provide you with other accommodation.

We can give you four judges, two Moslem and two Hindu,
To consult with, but the final decision must rest with you.

See HV Hodson, *The Great Divide: Britain - India - Pakistan* (New York: Atheneum, 1971) and WH Auden, *City without Walls and Other Poems* (London: Faber and Faber, 1969).

11 Each of these three moments could be teased apart in the way suggested by Pandey for the 1947 event. He speaks of three partitions taking place simultaneously: the achievement of Pakistan as a homeland for South Asian Muslims, the splitting up of the Muslim-majority provinces of Bengal and Punjab, and the mass migrations and mass violence that occurred. Gyanendra Pandey, *Remembering Partition: Violence, Nationalism and History in India* (Cambridge: Cambridge University Press, 2001), 21–44.

12 Among the reasons for this orientation on Punjab are the swift, bloody and almost complete expulsion of minority populations from both its parts immediately following Partition, the fact that the seats of government of both India and Pakistan came to be located in this region, the comparatively large state effort at supporting and rehabilitating refugees here, and the high proportion of educated and vocal refugees who were able to represent the plight of Punjab refugees in the media, literature, government policies and academic research. Cf. Md. Mahbubar Rahman and Willem van Schendel, '"I Am Not A Refugee": Rethinking Partition Migration', *Modern Asian Studies*, 37:3 (2003), 551–84.

13 For many writers on Partition, the Punjab bias needs no justification. It is quite rare for authors even to recognize it as a serious problem. In three recent publications, however, the authors do struggle with it. Menon and Bhasin highlight the ambiguity in their groundbreaking study of women's experiences during Partition: 'The choice of Punjab was obvious for personal and historical reasons both, and because it had been the site of maximum relocation and rehabilitation.' In a footnote they add that they had originally wished to include West and East Bengal but after initial interviewing and discussion they realized that 'the Bengal experience was so different that it merited a separate study.' For this reason their book covers only Punjab. Similarly, and equally problematically, Mushirul Hasan excludes Bengal on the basis of its 'difference' from Punjab. His influential article on rewriting the histories of partition 'does not cover the historical writings on the Bengal province, especially Bangladesh, where the histories of partition are being written differently since 1971.' Finally, in his book *Remembering Partition*, Gyanendra Pandey points to the extent of his linguistic abilities, and the very vastness of his subject, as the main reasons for focusing his study on the Punjab, Delhi and Uttar Pradesh, and for excluding Bengal. Ritu Menon and Kamla Bhasin, *Borders & Boundaries: Women in India's Partition* (Delhi: Kali for Women, 1998), 12, 26n. Mushirul Hasan, 'Memories of a Fragmented Nation: Rewriting the Histories of India's Partition', *Economic and Political Weekly* (10 October 1998), 2662; Pandey, *Remembering Partition*, 18.

14 For an overview of Partition historiography, see Tai Yong Tan and Gyanesh Kudaisya, *The Aftermath of Partition in South Asia* (London: and New York: Routledge, 2000), 1–28. For a comparison of the differential way in which the Indian authorities treated refugees entering the country from West Pakistan and those entering from East Pakistan, and the claim that the latter were discriminated against, see Joya Chatterji, 'Right or Charity? The Debate over Relief and Rehabilitation in West Bengal, 1947–50', in Suvir Kaul (ed.), *The Partitions of Memory: The Afterlife of the Division of India* (Delhi: Permanent

Black, 2001), 74–110; cf. 'East is east, west is west,' in 'Porous Borders, Divided Selves: A Symposium on Partitions in the East,' *Seminar*, no. 510 (February 2002), 47–53.

15 On Bengal, see Joya Chatterji, *Bengal Divided: Hindu Communalism and Partition, 1932–1947* (Cambridge: Cambridge University Press, 1995) and her 'The Fashioning of a Frontier: The Radcliffe Line and Bengal's Border Landscape, 1947–52', *Modern Asian Studies*, 33:1 (1999), 185–242; Ranabir Samaddar (ed.), *Reflections on Partition in the East* (Delhi: Vikas Publishing House, 1997); Prafulla K Chakrabarti, *The Marginal Men: The Refugees and the Left Political Syndrome in West Bengal* (Calcutta: Naya Udyog, 1999); Niaz Zaman, *A Divided Legacy: The Partition in Selected Novels of India, Pakistan, and Bangladesh* (Dhaka: University Press Limited, 1999); Willem van Schendel, 'Working Through Partition: Making a Living in the Bengal Borderlands,' *International Review of Social History*, 46 (2001), 393–421; and 'Porous Borders, Divided Selves'.
There are few studies of the economic impact of Partition on the borderland; for a lone case study of post-1947 technological and agrarian change in the adjacent border districts of Nadia (India) and Kushtia (Bangladesh), see Abhijit Dasgupta, *Growth with Equity: The New Technology and Agrarian Change in Bengal* (Delhi: Manohar, 1998). For a more general study of the economic impact of Partition, see CN Vakil, *Economic Consequences of Divided India: A Study of the Economy of India and Pakistan* (Bombay: Vora & Co., 1950).

16 In 1947 the Bengal Presidency had a population of 60 million, Bihar 36 million, Punjab 28 million, Assam 10 million and Sindh 4 million. Cf. Ludden, *India and South Asia*, 217–18.

17 On Bihar, see Papiya Ghosh, 'Partition's Biharis,' *Comparative Studies of South Asia, Africa and the Middle East*, 17:2 (1997), 21–34. On Assam, see Sanjib Baruah, *India Against Itself: Assam and the Politics of Nationality* (New Delhi: Oxford University Press, 1999); Anindita Dasgupta, 'Denial and Resistance: Sylheti Partition "Refugees" in Assam', *Contemporary South Asia*, 10:3 (2001), 343–60. On Sindh, see Sarah Ansari, 'The Movement of Indian Muslims to West Pakistan after 1947: Partition-Related Migration and its Consequences for the Pakistani Province of Sind,' in: Judith M Brown and Rosemary Foot (eds.), *Migration: The Asian Experience* (Oxford: St. Martin's Press, 1994), 149–68; Vazira Zamindar, 'Divided Families and the Making of Nationhood in India and Pakistan 1947-65' (PhD thesis, Columbia University, 2002). On Rajasthan, see Ian Copland, 'The Further Shores of Partition: Ethnic Cleansing in Rajasthan, 1947,' *Past and Present*, 160 (1998), 203–39.

18 Subsequently, the term 'Northeast India' came to be resented by many groups in the region because they felt it was a category, applied by 'mainland' Indians, that betrayed ignorance and arrogance. Most groups argued against the unity of the region, emphasizing the completely different problems facing people living in different parts. To them, the term 'Northeast India' implied a refusal to accept the existence of these very real differences. Others in the region simply refused to accept that their territory belonged to the new state of India. In this book, I use the term advisedly to refer to the geographical region created by Partition and not to lump together the distinct populations inhabiting it.

19 For East Pakistan, see e.g. Khan and for West Bengal Chakrabarty. The problem certainly was exacerbated by the way in which the postcolonial states have restricted scholars' access to post-1947 state records; but even the available material, including press reports, has been severely underused. Mohammed Ayub Khan, *Friends Not Masters* (London: Oxford University Press, 1967); Saroj Chakrabarty, *With Dr. B.C. Roy and Other Chief Ministers (A Record up to 1962)* (Calcutta: Benson's, 1974).

20 Of course there were early hopes of retaining a unity of vision regarding South Asia's past and future but these were soon dashed. The desire to preserve what Shahid Amin calls 'the Grand National' was expressed clearly in Mohammad Habib's address at the Indian History Congress in December 1947: 'It is absolutely unnecessary to state that, so far as the historian of India is concerned, the country has always been one and indivisible, and will always continue to be so. The unity of India is one of the fundamental postulates of Indian moral consciousness, and the longing for centralised administration has been one of the most visible and persistent demands of the political spirits of the Indians throughout the ages.' Quoted in Shahid Amin, *Alternative Histories: A View from India* (Calcutta: Centre for Studies in Social Sciences/South-South Exchange Programme for Research on the History of Development (SEPHIS), 2002), 5–6.

21 'Within India, there is a stable and disambiguated history of Partition and Independence in 1947. According to this story, Indian nationalism was cleft along two contending principles: the Congress Party's secular, inclusive, and progressive version of history versus various retrogressive, communal interpretations of nationalism represented by Jinnah and the Muslim League, the Hindu Mahasabha, and other parochial parties based on religion, language, caste, class, or other inferior rubrics. Despite their best efforts, the story goes, secular and pluralist Congress leaders could not carry with them the insecure minority leader, Muhammad Ali Jinnah, who squandered the inheritance by leaving the family with his moth-eaten share. To many Indians, the post-1947 survival of a plural, secular India and the breakup of a Pakistan founded on the basis of religious nationalism demonstrate the historical veracity of the secular Congress position and the bankruptcy of religious nationalism ... This particular narration of the origins of India and Pakistan is crucial in the Indian claim to a hegemonic status in the region.' Krishna, *Postcolonial Insecurities*, 233.

22 Cf. Vazira Zamindar's comments on the 'enormous difficulties for Pakistani citizens to do research in Indian archives as well as for Indian citizens to do research in Pakistan,' a situation that 'enforces some national limits on local scholarship and constrains the writing of shared histories.' Zamindar, 'Divided Families', 28.

23 To give but a single example of this continual fashioning and refinement: over several years a prominent weekly in Bangladesh, *Holiday*, has been running a series of articles entitled 'Mountbatten's India Bias' that by early 2002 had run into over 220 weekly instalments.

24 Cf. Krishna, *Postcolonial Insecurities*, 241. Attempts at bridging the divide have been under way, especially since the commemoration of the 50th anniversary of Partition in 1997. So far, such attempts tend to focus on bringing together historians from India, Pakistan and Bangladesh with a view to reworking perspectives on the politics of Partition. A good example is Amrik Singh (ed.), *The Partition in Retrospect* (Delhi: Anamika Publishers, 2000).

25 Gyanendra Pandey, 'The Prose of Otherness,' in: David Arnold and David Hardiman (eds.), *Subaltern Studies VIII: Essays in Honour of Ranajit Guha* (Delhi: Oxford University Press, 1994), 194.

26 Published in 12 volumes by Her Majesty's Stationery Office, London, between 1970 and 1983, and edited by Nicholas Mansergh, Penderel Moon, EWR Lumby and others.

27 Recent analyses on the basis of such material demonstrate how rich it is. See Menon and Bhasin, *Borders & Boundaries*; Chatterji, 'The Fashioning'; Dipesh Chakrabarty, 'Remembered Villages: Representation of Hindu-Bengali Memories in the Aftermath of the Partition', *Economic and Political Weekly* (10 August 1996), 2143–51; Urvashi Butalia, *The Other Side of Violence: Voices from the Partition of India* (New Delhi: Penguin Books,

1998); Gautam Ghosh, '"God is a Refugee": Nationality, Morality and History in the 1947 Partition of India', *Social Analysis*, 42:1 (1998), 33–62; Urvashi Butalia, 'An Archive with a Difference: Partition Letters', in Kaul (ed.), *The Partitions of Memory*, 208–41; and Pandey, *Remembering Partition*.

28 For a map of the borderland, see Appendix, Figure 1.

29 Mian Ziauddin, 'Pakistan's Foreign Policy,' *Pakistan Times* (23 March 1964).

30 Butalia, *The Other Side of Violence*, 8.

31 For an overview, see Hastings Donnan and Thomas M. Wilson, *Borders: Frontiers of Identity, Nation and State* (Oxford and New York: Berg, 1999).

32 For a pioneering study in this field, however, see Chatterji, 'The Fashioning'.

33 Ricky Lee Allen, 'The Socio-Spatial Making and Marking of "Us": Toward a Critical Postmodern Spatial Theory of Difference and Community,' *Social Identities*, 5:3 (1999), 250.

34 Cf. Michiel Baud and Willem van Schendel, 'Toward a Comparative History of Borderlands,' *Journal of World History*, 8:2 (September 1997), 211–42.

35 Thomas W Gallant, 'Brigandage, Piracy, Capitalism, and State-Formation: Transnational Crime from a Historical World-Systems Perspective,' in: Josiah McC Heyman (ed.), *States and Illegal Practices* (Oxford and New York: Berg, 1999), 25–61.

3

RADCLIFFE'S FATEFUL LINE

'I was so rushed that I had not time to go into the details,' said Cyril Radcliffe, the draughtsman of Partition, '... What could I do in one and a half months?'[1]

The decision to split British India came at the very tail end of the colonial period. In June 1947, a mere six weeks before British rule ended, the Viceroy of India formed the Bengal Boundary Commission. This Commission had to decide where the new border between India and Pakistan was to be located.[2] Its members had an impossible task. They had accepted an unclear brief and a six-week deadline. They were besieged by lobbyists and pressure groups that sought to influence them as they were about to take a decision that would affect millions. Not surprisingly, the Commission could not come to a unanimous decision and ultimately had to resort to an artful ruse.

There is an extensive literature on these hectic final days of colonial rule in the summer of 1947. Rather than summarizing this literature, this chapter seeks to dispel three widespread misconceptions: that the new border bisected Bengal; that it provided a border to Muslim-majority areas; and that it led to a Hindu–Muslim divide.

The brief

When the Viceroy constituted the Boundary Commission on 30 June 1947, he instructed it to:

> demarcate the boundaries of the two parts of Bengal on the basis of ascertaining the contiguous areas of Muslims and non-Muslims. In doing so, it will also take into account other factors.[3]

The chairman, Sir Cyril Radcliffe, was to submit the report by mid-August, when British rule would cease and the colony was to be divided.[4] The political leaders of the independence movement in British India had failed to reach agreement over a united postcolonial future; instead, there was to be a territorial partition. Two states were going to be created: Pakistan, a homeland for Muslims, and India, for all others. The instruction to the Bengal Boundary Commission was therefore phrased in terms of 'Muslims' and 'non-Muslims': the idea was to separate areas where Muslims formed a majority of the population from those where they did not.

The Boundary Commission's instruction contained two terms that were particularly vague. First, what was the Commission to make of the term *areas*? How should it define an area? It could be a province or a lower administrative unit, or it could be any other slice of territory. All of these definition had been toyed with in the intense public discussions that had preceded the constitution of the Boundary Commission. The choice would have far-reaching consequences. For example, Bengal was a Muslim-majority province containing many non-Muslim majority districts. Each district was a mosaic of *thanas* (smaller units sometimes referred to as police stations) that could be Muslim or non-Muslim majority areas. And below the *thana* level there were even smaller units that could be taken to be an 'area'.[5] The Viceroy's instruction left the Boundary Commission free to make its own choice, and after fierce internal debate its decisions were based largely on *thanas*.[6] Figure 3.1 shows what the pattern of Muslim majority and non-Muslim majority *thanas* looked like, based on what were then the latest population figures, collected during the Census of India of 1941.

If the instruction had been simply to separate Muslim and non-Muslim majority areas, the Boundary Commission could have demarcated the new border by drawing a line between contiguous grey and white areas, no doubt giving rise to questions about what actually constitutes a 'contiguous' area.[7]

But here the second vague term in the Viceroy's instruction came into play. The Boundary Commission had been told to take into account *other factors*. What were to be considered other factors? And how important should they be? These concerns became the topic of correspondence and discussion among worried politicians and bureaucrats in July 1947. But even after the Commission itself had asked the Viceroy for clarification, the term was kept deliberately vague: 'it is entirely for the Commission itself to decide what these other factors are and how much importance should be attached to all or any of them.'[8] In other words, the Commission was on its own.

It is not easy to deduce the full range of other factors that played a role in the Commission's decisions.[9] From the final report, it is clear that an important consideration was the 'claim' of great port cities to be in control of their hinterlands, especially their river systems. This argument was used twice: the southeastern port city of Chittagong pulled a non-Muslim majority district (the

Chittagong Hill Tracts[10]) into Pakistan, and Calcutta was assigned to India, together with one district (Murshidabad) and parts of two other districts (Nadia and Jessore) with Muslim majorities (see Appendix Figure 1). The river-system argument also played a role in assigning Khulna, a non-Muslim majority district, to Pakistan.

But in the end, the Commission could not agree about the best way to divide Bengal.[11] The way out was to leave the decision to chairman Radcliffe alone

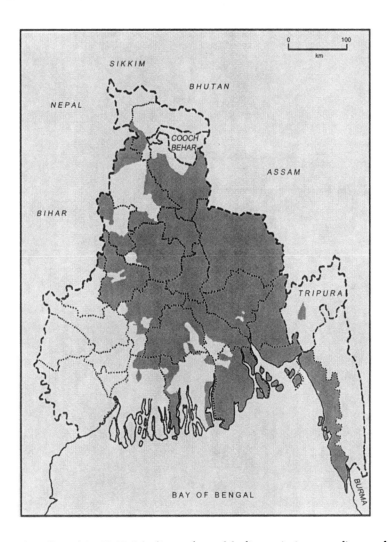

Figure 3.1: Bengal in 1947: Muslim and non-Muslim majority according to thana population figures (Muslim-majority thanas are in grey).

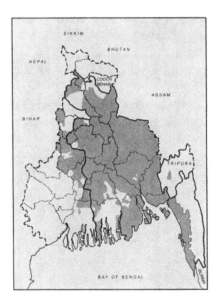

Figure 3.2: The Radcliffe line through Bengal

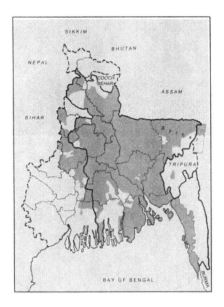

Figure 3.3: The Partition border. The Radcliffe line through Bengal and through Sylhet. The only difference between Figures 3.2 and 3.3 is the addition of the northeastern district of Sylhet.[12]

and it was he who wrote the report and took responsibility for it. Therefore the Bengal border, more than any other twentieth-century border in the world, can be seen as the creation of a single individual (see Figures 3.2 and 3.3).

Three misconceptions

The decisions of the Boundary Commission have been subject to endless debates ever since. There have been speculations of undue pressure on the Commission as well as accusations of various biases and incompetence. As in any messy divorce, the separation of the two political elites (Pakistan's Muslim League and India's National Congress) has produced interpretations of history that are antagonistic. These interpretations share a view of Cyril Radcliffe as the major bogeyman of the endgame of British rule. Whether this reputation is deserved is an issue that need not concern us here. But whereas the dominant interpretations have paid much attention to the politics of border-making, they have largely neglected the border itself. As a result, several misconceptions and simplifications crop up regularly in contemporary discussions.

Bengal bisected?   In discussions about the Partition of Bengal, it is usually assumed that the Bengal Boundary Commission bisected the province. The image is that of a north–south line dividing West Bengal from East Bengal, with the former joining India and the latter Pakistan. The reality is far more complex. The Radcliffe line did not carve two halves out of the province of Bengal; it made the province fall into *four* large pieces (see Figure 3.4). The largest of these was a group of sixteen districts at the centre. These joined Pakistan under the name of East Bengal, later East Pakistan (which ultimately seceded from Pakistan as Bangladesh).[13] East Bengal was surrounded by three territories (shaded in Figure 3.4) that joined India. To the east was Tripura, a Princely State that would formally merge with the Indian Union in 1949. To the north was a territory consisting of two regular districts and the Princely State of Cooch Behar. And to the west was a group of twelve districts. The northern and western territories did not touch, but despite this non-contiguity they were administered as one state, named West Bengal. Cooch Behar became a district of West Bengal when it merged with India in 1950.[14] In addition to these four large parts, however, Partition created no less than 197 minuscule territories, or enclaves, in northern Bengal. 74 Pakistani enclaves were located within the territory of India, and 123 Indian ones within that of Pakistan.[15] In brief, the Boundary Commission's territorial surgery of Bengal resulted not in the simple bisection that is usually imagined but in the creation of no less than 201 territorial units.

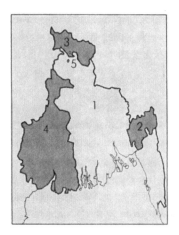

1 = East Bengal (sixteen districts of Bengal that joined Pakistan in 1947).
2 = The Princely State of Tripura that joined India in 1949.
3 = North Bengal (two districts that joined India in 1947, and the Princely State of Cooch
Behar that joined India in 1950).
4 = West Bengal (twelve districts that joined India in 1947).
5 = 197 enclaves.

Figure 3.4: The 201 parts of partitioned Bengal

A border to Muslim areas?   According to the instructions given to him, the
chairman of the Bengal Boundary Commission decided where the Bengal border
was to be. It encircled most of the Muslim-majority areas of Bengal (and most
of Sylhet district of Assam) and consequently it has usually been treated as a
border between Muslim and non-Muslim populations, or even as a border
between Muslim and Hindu populations. But if we look at the borderland that
the border created, things are much less straightforward and the communal
simplicity breaks down.

For almost three-fifths of its length, the border was *not* a Muslim/non-Muslim
divide. Only 26 per cent of the border separated a Muslim-majority area in
East Pakistan from a Hindu-majority one in India, and an additional 15 per
cent separated a Muslim-majority area in East Pakistan from a Christian- or
Buddhist-majority area in India ('Other' in Table 3.1).

In other words, there was no sharp discontinuity between Muslim territory
in Pakistan and non-Muslim territory in India. Table 3.1 reveals that, for half of
its length, the border cut through areas where the same religious majority
(Muslim, Hindu or other) dominated on both sides. On the Pakistan side, there
were non-Muslim majority areas for two-fifths of its length; on the Indian side,
Muslim-majority areas made up one-fifth of its length. Fifteen per cent of the
border did not cut through either Muslim- or Hindu-majority areas; here other

religions dominated on both sides of the border. Finally, there were even stretches of the border where the Pakistan side was Hindu-dominated and the Indian side Muslim-dominated.

Table 3.1: Hindu, Muslim and other populations on the Bengal border (percentages of total length of border)[16]

	Majority population							Total
Pakistan	Muslim			Hindu			Other	
India/Burma	Hindu	Muslim	Other	Hindu	Muslim	Other	Other	
Total	26%	20%	15%	16%	3%	5%	15%	100%

Figure 3.5 illustrates how fragmented the borderland was in this respect. It also shows the peculiar way in which the Bengal Boundary Commission interpreted its terms of reference: 'to demarcate the boundaries of the two parts of Bengal on the basis of ascertaining the contiguous areas of Muslims and non-Muslims [and] also take into account other factors.' In the borderland it was obvious that contiguity had been taken very loosely and that the vague 'other factors' argument had been used to cut a borderline that in most places actually *failed* to demarcate the contiguous areas of Muslims and non-Muslims.

This was true for the entire border as well as for separate segments. Less than half the West Bengal/ East Pakistan segment (slightly over one-third of the entire Partition border[17]) showed the expected pattern of a Muslim/ non-Muslim divide, and that only intermittently – broken up into seven short stretches. And the Assam/ East Pakistan segment (almost one-third of the entire border) showed the pattern for only 15 per cent of its length. The widespread idea that the Bengal border was a Muslim/non-Muslim border is only true in the sense that it encircled Muslim-majority areas; in most of the borderland itself it made no sense.

A Hindu–Muslim divide?   Throughout the literature on the Partition of Bengal there is an almost unchallenged assumption that the border separated Muslims from Hindus. It is crucially important, however, to acknowledge that 'non-Muslim' cannot be equated with 'Hindu'. Whereas the non-Muslim stretches of the West Bengal border were all Hindu-dominated, in Assam there were no Hindu-dominated areas *at all* facing Muslim-dominated areas in East Pakistan. The 15 per cent section mentioned above as being a Muslim/ non-Muslim divide was located along the Garo Hills/ Khasi and Jaintia Hills (now Meghalaya)

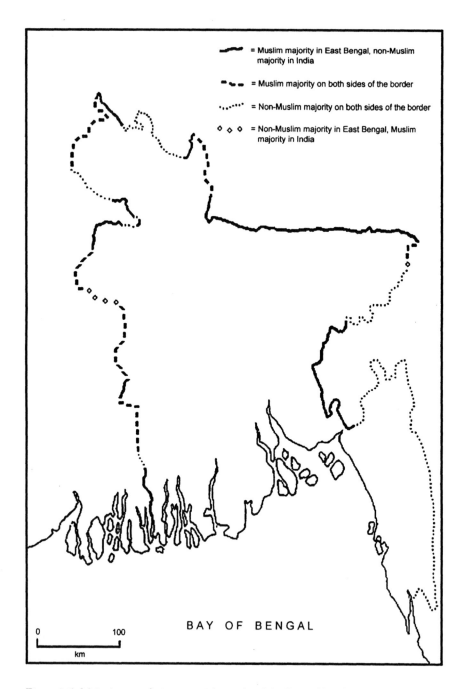

Figure 3.5: Majority populations on either side of the Bengal border

stretch that was Christian-dominated on the Indian side (see Appendix, Figures 1 and 2). In all, the non-Muslim majority areas on the Indian side of the border were three-fifths Hindu and two-fifths Christian or Buddhist.

The false assumption that there was a Muslim–Hindu divide reflects two persistent biases in thinking about the Bengal border. The first is the idea that the border that actually *matters* is the segment dividing East Pakistan and West Bengal (where 'non-Muslim' was overwhelmingly, but not exclusively, Hindu). The historiography thereby reproduces a dominant view among the political and intellectual elites of the region that narrows down the history of the region to that of the Bengalis and marginalizes all others.[18] The East Pakistan/ West Bengal segment of the border ran right through the Bengali heartland, separating tens of millions of Bengalis on one side from tens of millions of Bengalis on the other. The trauma of this separation has dominated the historiography, creating an ethnic bias and ignoring the fact that for most of its length the border did *not* separate Bengalis. Not only did similarly separated ethnic communities occur along the Assam, Tripura and Burma segments of the border, but in many places the border also marked a rather clear discontinuity between Bengalis and non-Bengalis. Here the Muslim/ Hindu dichotomy broke down. For example, among the other communities that the border separated were the Garo (whose majority religion is Christianity), the Tripura (Hindu) and the Rakhaing (Buddhist).[19] Long stretches of the border were not inhabited by Bengalis at all, for example the Chittagong Hill Tracts/ Assam (now Mizoram[20]) border where neither Islam nor Hinduism were important religions. Finally, where the border separated Bengali-majority areas from non-Bengali-majority areas (as in Tripura and Assam), it was often a case of Bengalis (both Muslims and Hindus) on one side and non-Bengali Christians or Buddhists on the other. The Partition borderland was much more than its West Bengal/ East Pakistan segment, and its dynamics cannot be reduced to those of that segment.

The view of the border as a Muslim/ Hindu divide also reveals another bias: the dominance of nationalist perspectives. From the mid-twentieth century to the present, much of the historiography of the region has been unable to escape from the pressure of antagonistic nation-building. In view of the categories that informed the decisions of the Boundary Commission, the post-Partition nations had little option but to legitimate themselves in terms of the Muslim/ non-Muslim dichotomy. Dominant political interpretations, however, narrowed this down to the categories of Muslims and Hindus and these were treated as overarching, unproblematic and antagonistic. As a result, history writing shaded easily into patterns of thought that were dualistic and left little room for other players in the historical drama of the region.[21] This in turn reinforced the tendency to view the East Pakistan/ West Bengal segment of the border as a *pars pro toto* for the entire border because it was here that the simple polarity of Muslim vs. Hindu worked best.

Conclusion: From notional border to national border

In August 1947, the reality of the Radcliffe line descended upon a population that had been neither asked for their opinion nor informed properly.[22] This lack of information was to cast long shadows over subsequent events. In the final days of colonial rule the administration invented the concept of the 'notional boundary'.[23] This had to do with preparations for a division of the spoils that commenced well before the actual partition. Administrators and politicians needed to agree on a rough (notional) idea of where the Boundary Commission was likely to fix the border, and proceed on that assumption. But the concept took on a new significance when it became clear that the decisions of the Boundary Commission would not be made public till after India and Pakistan became independent states on 14–15 August 1947.[24] Therefore, the governments of East and West Bengal were instructed to 'take charge up to the *notional* repeat *notional* boundary pending publication and implementation of the Award [Boundary Commission's decision].'[25]

This is exactly what happened. For example, Murshidabad, a district with a Muslim majority, gained independence as a district of East Pakistan. Its inhabitants raised the flag of Pakistan and Pakistani administrators took charge. After a few days, however, the district had to be transferred to India: the Radcliffe line turned out unexpectedly to separate Mushidabad from contiguous Muslim-majority districts to the east, and Murshidabad became a district of India.[26] In the same way the non-Muslim-majority Chittagong Hill Tracts gained independence as a district of India only to be transferred to Pakistani administration a few days later.[27] Similar scenes occurred all along the border wherever the Radcliffe line chopped off *thanas* and smaller units from their parent districts and joined them with the neighbouring country. Such confusion and initial identification with the 'wrong' nation cast doubt upon the allegiance of the inhabitants of these areas to the nation to which they were ultimately assigned. In some cases the events of 15 to 17 August 1947 came to be 'critical events' in the subsequent construction of community identities vis-à-vis the new nation.

This happened most destructively in the case of the Chittagong Hill Tracts. On 15 August 1947, people in this district with a 98 per cent non-Muslim population raised the Indian flag, believing that their district had joined that country. A few days later Pakistani forces removed these flags. In the Pakistani nationalist discourse these events were construed as the core symbol of the district's treason to the state of Pakistan, literally *avant la lettre*. It was the beginning of a historical development that would lead the Chittagong Hill Tracts down the road to marginalization, repression, armed rebellion and protracted war.[28]

The case of the Chittagong Hill Tracts demonstrates clearly the need to dispel the popular simplifications – regarding the bisection of Bengal, the bordering of Muslim-majority areas, and the equating of 'non-Muslim' with 'Hindu' – that continue to dog studies of Partition-in-the-east. Radcliffe's line turned out to be so fateful for so many people in so many different localities precisely because the unforeseen realities that it created were much more complex than these simplifications suggest. In the late-monsoon weeks following 16 August 1947, information about the Boundary Commission's decisions ('awards'[29]) percolated through the societies of Assam, Bengal and Burma. The news set off a concatenation of events and activities on the part of millions of people, both in the Partition borderland and beyond, which turned Radcliffe's ominous red line from a mere cartographic embellishment into an undeniable political and social reality. During more than half a century it was local residents, refugees, district administrators, traders, and a host of other local agents whose actions created, transformed and reinforced the border, arguably often in much more direct and significant ways than the national politicians who continue to dominate accounts of Partition and postcolonial state formation. In the next chapter, we will look at this process from the vantage point of the states attempting to establish exactly where the border was and how to maintain a measure of control over it.

Notes

1 Cyril Radcliffe, interviewed in the 1960s. Kuldip Nayar, *Distant Neighbours: A Tale of the Subcontinent* (Delhi: Vikas, 1972), 35.

2 There were two Boundary Commissions, one for Bengal/Assam and one for Punjab. Sir Cyril Radcliffe chaired both. For a detailed account of boundary making in Punjab, see Lucy Payne Chester, 'Drawing the Indo-Pakistani Boundary During the 1947 Partition of South Asia' (PhD thesis, Yale University, 2002). Cf. Kuldip Nayar, *Distant Neighbours: A Tale of the Subcontinent* (New Delhi: Vikas, 1972), 45–7; Tai Yong Tan and Gyanesh Kudaisya, *The Aftermath of Partition in South Asia* (London: and New York: Routledge, 2000), 78–100.

3 Cyril Radcliffe, *Report of the Bengal Boundary Commission* (New Delhi, 12 August 1947), 1 (Government of East Bengal, Home (Political) Department, 3R-12 (B. Proceedings, December 1948) (hereafter Plt. 3R-12 (12–48)).

4 The Commission consisted of four judges (two each nominated by the Indian Congress Party and the Muslim League) and the chairman, Sir Cyril Radcliffe, nominated by the Governor-General of India. Strangely, the terms of reference mentioned 'areas of Muslims and non-Muslims' rather than areas with Muslim and non-Muslim majorities.

5 Administrative units in Bengal formed a hierarchy from province via division, district, sub-division, *thana*, union, and ward, to *mouza* (or revenue village).

6 The non-Muslim members of the commission wanted *thanas* to be the basic unit of Partition and the Muslim members advocated the *union*. For arguments and counter-arguments, see *Partition Proceedings, Volume VI: Reports of the Members and Awards of the Chairman of the Boundary Commissions* (New Delhi: Government of India, Partition Secretariat, 1950).

7 The contiguity argument was a concern especially with regard to the largely non-Muslim northern Bengal districts of Jalpaiguri and Darjeeling that were not contiguous with other non-Muslim districts in Bengal but did link up with non-Muslim districts in Assam. Radcliffe, *Report*, 2.

8 Nicholas Mansergh (editor-in-chief), *The Transfer of Power, 1942–7: Constitutional Relations between Britain and India* (London: Her Majesty's Stationery Office, 1983), Vol. XII, 329. See also letter from the Governor-General to Sir A Hydari (Assam), 'It is for Boundary Commission to interpret their terms of reference. I have been asked more than once to define them but I have had to refuse.' (321; cf. 64–5, 304). And yet, later he did interpret those terms of reference when he suggested to Radcliffe that the Bengal Boundary Commission should understand the term 'adjoining districts' in the case of Assam to be 'districts of Assam that adjoin Sylhet, not any districts of Assam that adjoin Bengal' (484).

9 The most thorough account of the political environment and the work of the Bengal Boundary Commission is Joya Chatterji, 'The Fashioning of a Frontier: The Radcliffe Line and Bengal's Border Landscape, 1947–52', *Modern Asian Studies*, 33:1 (1999), 185–242. For the role of 'other factors,' especially in the division of Punjab, see Chester, 'Drawing the Indo-Pakistani Boundary', 175–208. See also OHK Spate, 'The Partition of the Punjab and of Bengal', *The Geographical Journal*, 110 (1948), 201–22; HV Hodson, *The Great Divide: Britain – India – Pakistan* (New York: Atheneum, 1971), 346–55; SA Akanda, 'Referendum in Sylhet and the Radcliffe Award, 1947', *Journal of the Institute of Bangladesh Studies*, 14 (1991), 21–47; M Kar, *Muslims in Assam Politics* (New Delhi: Vikas Publishing House); and Tan and Kudaisya, *The Aftermath*, 78–100.

10 Cf. the confidential report of the meeting at Government House, New Delhi, 16 August 1947, reprinted in Avtar Singh Bhasin (ed.), *India-Bangladesh Relations: Documents – 1971–2002* (New Delhi: Geetika Publishers, 2003), Vol. V, 2682–3. For a picture of Indian Prime Minister Jawaharlal Nehru in 1960, still fuming over the awarding of the Chittagong Hill Tracts to Pakistan, see Bhasin (ed.), *India-Bangladesh Relations*, V, 2761.

11 The two Muslim members agreed with each other and wrote a joint report, as did the two Hindu members. The two reports were incompatible. See *Partition Proceedings, Volume VI: Reports of the Members and Awards of the Chairman of the Boundary Commissions* (New Delhi: Government of India, Partition Secretariat, 1950).

12 Sylhet did not belong to the province of Bengal (but to Assam) and therefore was not included in the Partition of Bengal. The Bengal Boundary Commission wrote a separate report on the partitioning of Sylhet. Its western part was incorporated in Pakistan and joined the eastern Bengal districts to form East Pakistan. Sylhet's eastern *thanas*, together with the Tripura part of the province of Bengal and the rest of the province of Assam, joined India. For details on the partition of Sylhet, see Kar, *Muslims in Assam Politics*, 31–85.

13 Officially, the territory has been known as East Bengal from 1947 to 1956, as East Pakistan from 1956 to 1971, and as Bangladesh since 1971. In order to reduce this confusing multiplicity, I have used 'East Pakistan' even for the period up to 1956, whenever it seemed suitable.

14 The Maharani-Regent of Tripura signed the Agreement of Merger on 9 September 1949, and Tripura became a Union Territory of the Indian Union on 15 October 1949; in 1972, it became a State. The merger of Tripura remained contested. Half a century later, rebel groups in Tripura denounced it as a 'trick' and organized a day of protest on 15 October. The Maharaja of Cooch Behar signed the Agreement of Accession on 28 August 1949, after which Cooch Behar became a centrally administered area; on 1 January 1950 it was made a district of West Bengal. The Khasi states in Assam refused to sign an Instrument of Merger with India; their leaders found in 1950 that their territories had simply been turned into a district of Assam. *Tripura District Gazetteers: Tripura* (Agartala: Government of Tripura, 1975), 118; *West Bengal District Gazetteers: Koch Bihar* (Calcutta: West Bengal District Gazetteers, 1977), 138–9; cf. *Keesing's Contemporary Archives*, VII (1948–50), 10456; 'Mixed response to "black day",' *The Telegraph* (17 October 2002).

15 The 74 Pakistani enclaves were all located in Cooch Behar (India) and the 123 Indian ones in Dinajpur and Rangpur (Pakistan). For details, see Brendan R Whyte, *Waiting for the Esquimo: An Historical and Documentary Study of the Cooch Behar Enclaves of India and Bangladesh* (Melbourne: Research Paper 8, School of Anthropology, Geography and Environmental Studies, University of Melbourne, 2002); Willem van Schendel, 'Stateless in South Asia: The Making of the India-Bangladesh Enclaves,' *The Journal of Asian Studies*, 61:1 (2002), 115–47.

16 Majority areas at thana level according to Census of India 1931.

17 Including the Cooch Behar and Bihar sections, i.e. the West Bengal border as it was created in 1956.

18 Cf. Willem van Schendel and Ellen Bal (eds.), *Banglar Bohujati: Bangalir Chhara Banglar Ononyo Jatir Prosongo* (Calcutta: International Centre for Bengal Studies, 1998); Willem van Schendel, Wolfgang Mey and Aditya Kumar Dewan. *The Chittagong Hill Tracts: Living in a Borderland* (Bangkok: White Lotus, 2000), 3–4, 297–302.

19 The term 'partitioned culture areas,' which Asiwaju introduced in the study of African borderlands, may be of relevance in developing a comparative perspective on the cultural effects of partition, both in South Asia and generally. AI Asiwaju, 'Partitioned Culture Areas: A Checklist,' in: AI Asiwaju (ed.), *Partitioned Africans: Ethnic Relations Across Africa's International Boundaries 1884–1984* (London and Lagos: Christopher Hurst and University of Lagos Press, 1985), 252–9.

20 For the post-1947 administrative fragmentation of the Indian state of Assam, see Appendix, Figure 2.

21 Willem van Schendel, 'Bengalis, Bangladeshis and Others: Chakma Visions of a Pluralist Bangladesh,' in: Rounaq Jahan (ed.), *Bangladesh: Promise and Performance* (Dhaka: University Press Limited/London & New Jersey: Zed Press, 2000), 65–105.

22 Only Sylhet district of Assam went through a referendum to establish the will of the people. See Akanda, 'Referendum in Sylhet.'

23 The Indian Independence Act of 18 July 1947 listed the Bengal districts that were 'provisionally included in the new province of East Bengal,' i.e. were expected to go to Pakistan. The following did not in fact end up in Pakistan: Jessore (partitioned), Murshidabad, Nadia (partitioned), Malda (partitioned), Dinajpur (partitioned). The Act did not foresee that the districts of Khulna and Chittagong Hill Tracts would go to Pakistan and that Jalpaiguri would be partitioned. Kanti B Pakrasi, *The Uprooted: A Sociological Study of the Refugees of West Bengal, India* (Calcutta: Editions Indian, 1971), 165.

24 For the tactics employed by the Viceroy not to have to receive the boundary awards

before that date in order to 'divert odium from the British' and 'avoid turning a day of rejoicing over Indian and Pakistani freedom into one of mourning over disappointed territorial hopes', see Hodson, *The Great Divide*, 351.

25 Telegram from Rear-Admiral Viscount Mountbatten to Sir F Burrows (Bengal), 13 August 1947. A similar telegram was sent to the government of Punjab but not, apparently, to that of Assam. Mansergh (editor-in-chief), *Transfer of Power*, XII, 693. The decisions of the Boundary Commission came to be referred to as (non-negotiable) territorial 'awards'.

26 Birendra Kumar Bhattacharya, *Murshidabad: West Bengal District Gazetteers* (Alipore: West Bengal Government Press, 1979), 7. Saroj Chakrabarty, *With Dr. B.C. Roy and Other Chief Ministers (A Record upto 1962)* (Calcutta: Benson's, 1974), 64. For eyewitness accounts of how government officials who had opted for Pakistan and were posted to Murshidabad had to be swapped with their counterparts who had opted for India and were given jobs in Khulna (a district that was given to Pakistan), see Md. Mahbubar Rahman and Willem van Schendel, 'I Am Not A Refugee: Partition Migration Reconsidered,' *Modern Asian Studies*, 37:3 (2003), 551–84.

27 S Mahmud Ali, *The Fearful State: Power, People and Internal War in South Asia* (London & New Jersey: Zed Books, 1993), 176. The Pakistan flag was also hoisted atop the town hall of Darjeeling from 14 to 18 August 1947. BG Verghese, *India's Northeast Resurgent: Ethnicity, Insurgency, Governance, Development* (Delhi: Konark, 1996), 270.

28 See Van Schendel, 'Bengalis, Bangladeshis'. On critical events, see Veena Das, *Critical Events: An Anthropological Perspective on Contemporary India* (Delhi: Oxford University Press, 1995).

29 The decisions of the Boundary Commission were referred to as territorial *awards* because this made them non-negotiable decisions.

4

A PATCHWORK BORDER

When the leaders of India and Pakistan first learned about the location of the new border, they were appalled. The decisions ('awards') of the Boundary Commissions pleased no one. The last British Viceroy, who presided over the meeting, observed:

> If it had not been so serious and rather tragic their mutual indignation would have been amusing. Neither the Congress, the [Muslim] League, nor the Sikhs were in any way satisfied or grateful for any advantages they may have got out of the awards; they could only think of the disadvantages and complain bitterly. It was only after they had been complaining loudly for some time that they appeared to realise that there must be some advantages for them if the other parties were equally dissatisfied; and so after some two hours very delicate handling, we arrived at the conclusion that the awards must be announced and implemented loyally forthwith.[1]

As borders go, the Bengal border was an amazing innovation. With a length of over 4,000 kilometres, it was huge.[2] And moreover, no part of it had ever been an international border before.[3] In fact, the inhabitants of this region had no previous experience with modern international boundaries at all; other territories under British control had long surrounded their territory.[4] Remarkably, the Bengal border was the longest new international boundary to come into existence during the worldwide decolonization process of the second half of the twentieth century. It also turned out to be the longest border that India shares with any country.

In this chapter, we consider how the states of Pakistan and India established the border on the ground, a process in which they had to cooperate with each other. Despite much tension and antagonistic rhetoric, they managed to devise ways of dealing with most legal and political disputes. But today this process is still far from complete. Several border issues remain unresolved between India and what has now become Bangladesh. These lead to regular cross-border confrontations, and are potentially explosive because political forces in either country can exploit them. By comparison, the almost 200-kilometre border between East Pakistan/ Bangladesh and Burma is relatively unproblematic.

The initial patchwork

Unlike many borders created under the aegis of colonial rule, the border between East Pakistan/ Bangladesh and India owed little to modern concepts of spatial rationality. The new border was anything but a straight line; it snaked through the countryside in a wacky zigzag pattern (see Appendix, Figure 1). It showed no respect for history and cut through numerous ancient geographical entities, for example the ancient capital of Gaur, one of Bengal's most important archaeological sites. Some of Gaur's famous mosques and forts ended up in India, others fell to Pakistan (later Bangladesh) (Plate 4.1). A poet of the region, Jasimuddin, has likened the Bengal countryside to the intricate embroidery that rural women make on patchwork quilts. The handiwork of the Boundary Commission could also be likened to an embroidered quilt but one made by someone with an excessively baroque mind.[5]

Plate 4.1: After the political earthquake. Standing at the edge of no man's land, Bangladeshi day-trippers observe ancient fortifications of the city of Gaur that now fly the Indian flag. The border crossing is named Shona Masjid (Golden Mosque) after two fifteenth-century mosques, one now in Bangladesh, the other in India.[6]

A close look at the border reveals that it was a patchwork of seventeen segments. Figure 4.1 shows that fourteen of these had been boundaries between colonial administrative units before, involving *thanas* or police stations (5 segments), districts (3), provinces (3), Princely States (2) and colonies (1). Three segments had not been administrative borders; here the international border followed a railway or a river.

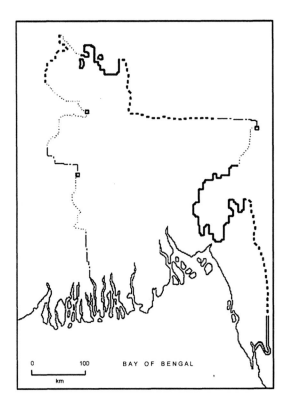

▬▬ = border with another colony (Burma)
▬▬ = border with a Princely State (Cooch Behar, Tripura)
▬ ▬ ▬ = border with another province of British India (Assam, Bihar)
—·— = district border
········ = *thana* border
▫ = not previously an administrative border

Figure 4.1: **Component parts of the Bengal border**

It was a situation fraught with possibilities for conflict. There had never been any need to inscribe the boundaries between subordinate colonial administrative units in the landscape. The clear lines that appeared on the maps used by colonial officials, including the Bengal Boundary (or Radcliffe) Committee, did not correspond with anything visible 'out there'. There was no way unequivocally to recognize the new border on the ground.

It was a colonial legacy, the system of taxation, which saved the day. It proved to be a godsend for those who had to identify the new border. In most of Bengal, an intricate land-based system of tax collection had been in place for over one and a half centuries. Under this system, landlords/ tax collectors known as *zamindars* had collected land tax (or land revenue) from cultivators and handed part of it over to the colonial state. Over the years the state had refined this system by gathering extremely detailed information on landholding. Successive surveys had established the exact size, location and productivity of individual fields all over Bengal, and this information was available locally.[7] There were detailed survey maps showing the location of the tiniest individual plots. These maps – tools of colonial control and order – now turned out to be of immense value for postcolonial officials in the Bengal borderland, providing them with a non-partisan, neutral tool for determining the exact location of the new border. The maps allowed them to agree on most of the borderline, but there were three problems that the maps could not resolve for them: rivers, unsurveyed land and mapping errors.[8]

Rivers. Borders are usually visualized as lines on the ground. This image is completely inadequate when we consider the Bengal border. For about 1,000 km, it runs through water. In many places it follows the course of a river, and it crosscuts dozens of rivers flowing from the surrounding mountains into the great Bengal delta.[9]

Generally speaking, rivers make problematic borders. There is a whole legal literature on how to demarcate borderlines in rivers. The border can be held to run through the middle of a river or to follow its deepest channel. It also can be fixed along one of the riverbanks or follow an arbitrary line through the river.[10] The Bengal Boundary Committee had omitted to specify their definition of a river border, and this created uncertainty in the minds of state officials having to establish the border.[11] Since none of the rivers had been demarcated before, it was no surprise that many border disputes between India and Pakistan focused on rivers. Even the most 'border-like' and stable of rivers, the Naf, which separated the colonies of British India and British Burma, turned out to be of no help at all:

When some previously uninhabited islands in the Naf river were occupied by people from Burma shortly after Partition, the Pakistan authorities went on a wild goose chase in offices in Dhaka, Chittagong and Cox's Bazar for documents and maps which could establish their right over these islands.

Eventually they had to concede that 'the boundary between Chittagong and Arakan districts along with the Naf river do not seem to have been formally demarcated after the separation of Burma. The latest Record in this point is the Revenue Settlement map, prepared in 1929.'[12] (see Figure 4.2)

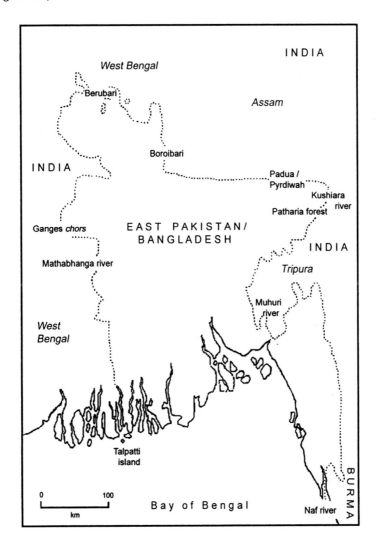

Figure 4.2: Border disputes mentioned in this chapter

Although border officials were aware of different options in fixing a river border, in practice they opted for the assumption that the border ran through the middle of a river. But rivers posed border problems for different reasons as well: they tended to move.

Wandering streams.   Much of the Bengal border ran through a landscape known as an active delta. In active deltas rivers tend to be mobile. Only in some parts of the borderland – in hilly terrains in the east and south – rivers formed a relatively stable border because they flowed through 'fixed' hill valleys (Plate 4.2).

But in the north and west, the borderland was flat and here rivers frequently shifted their course. They could move their main channel unpredictably from year to year, eating away one bank and throwing up land on the other. The inhabitants of Bengal were accustomed to entire villages being destroyed in this way and agricultural land disappearing under water. This natural process had always been the cause of much population movement within Bengal, and from the mid-nineteenth century it had fuelled settler emigration to Assam and other areas. It had also given rise to special regulations regarding land rights along riverbanks and even 'under water.'[13] When such wandering rivers came to mark an international border, they were bound to create mayhem.

The Bengal Boundary Committee based its decisions regarding the border upon scrutiny of the maps that had been produced during the land taxation surveys outlined above. It had no time to examine the situation on the ground, nor was it provided with aerial or hydrographic surveys. In other words, the

Plate 4.2: An Indian motorboat on the Karnaphuli, a 'stable' border river between Mizoram (India) and the Chittagong Hill Tracts (Bangladesh), 2000.

Boundary Commission worked on the basis of maps that were often several decades out of date.[14] It is unclear to what extent the Commission was aware of the fact that many segments of the newly designated border were in fact rivers, or of the wandering nature of these rivers.[15] In the report, the border segments are described in terms of administrative units but river courses that marked a district or *thana* boundary in, say, 1920 could well have moved hundreds of metres since then. A district border that ran through the middle of a waterway in 1920 might now cut off little bits and pieces of both banks, creating isolated pockets of India on the Pakistan side of the river, and vice versa.

The inhabitants of the Indian village of Malopara near the busy border crossing of Bongaon-Benapol in West Bengal found themselves in that position. Separated from the rest of India by a large body of water and surrounded by Pakistan (later Bangladesh) territory, the village became moribund after 1947. Although India claimed the territory and posted border guards at Malopara, it did not include the village in its development programmes. Fifty years after Partition, there was no school in the village, no electricity, no health facility, no shop and, most importantly, no bridge. During the rainy season, the village was effectively cut off from the rest of India and had to depend on Bangladeshis. By the early 1990s, only 13 families remained out of 100-odd in 1947, and in 1997 their number had dwindled to seven. 'For all practical purposes,' said the commandant of the Bangladesh border guards, 'the residents of the village depend on us. We look after their needs.'[16]

All along the border, such cross-river pockets sprang up, the unintended and bizarre outcomes of the decisions of the Bengal Boundary Commission.[17] It should be recognized, however, that with the passing of time even the most careful delineation of mid-river borders in 1947 would have thrown up similar pockets. The wandering rivers of the Bengal delta simply do not fit rigid state borders.[18]

Troubled waters. The Bengal Boundary Commission Report made explicit comments on three border rivers, and in all three cases the Commission got into trouble. The wording of the passages in the report was so ambiguous that it led to intense disputes between Pakistan and India. The two countries were unable to resolve these disputes; eventually they had to create an international tribunal (known as the Bagge Tribunal) to mediate.[19]

In two of these cases the Boundary Commission had deviated from its usual practice of drawing the border along an administrative border (which might be a river), opting instead for drawing the border along a river course that had not previously been an administrative border. Let us take a brief look at two cases:

the Mathabhanga river in the west and the Kushiara river in the east (see Figure 4.2).

According to the report of the Bengal Boundary Commission, the Mathabhanga, a small river flowing through the district of Nadia, was to mark the border between East Pakistan and West Bengal (India).

> From the point on the river Ganges where the channel of the river Mathabanga takes off, the line shall run along that channel to the northernmost point where it meets the boundary between the thanas of Daulatpur and Karimpur. The middle line of the main channel shall constitute the actual boundary.[20]

Both countries accepted that the border was to run along the channel of the river but Pakistan contended that the Boundary Commission had not shown it correctly on its map.[21] India agreed that, although the map showed the river, 'there is no river at that place.' Nevertheless, 'Sir Cyril ... finds the Mathabhanga channel and draws it on the map [and] ... river or no river – there is a rigid line as indicated on the map.' In other words, India argued that the map might be faulty but it still constituted the Boundary Commission's decision: the evidence of the map should prevail over the written description.[22] Pakistan wanted a flexible border between two fixed points, where the border would be the channel of the river even if it shifted. India claimed a reaffirmation of the Commission's line, irrespective of possible shifts by the river. In 1950 the mediation tribunal (the Bagge Tribunal) established 'that the aerial map of 1948 and Pakistan's documents proved that the Mathabhanga as drawn by Sir Cyril Radcliffe did not exist in reality.'[23]

Now the problem was how to establish a mutually acceptable border. Should it run along the Mathabhanga channel as it existed in August 1947? But who could reconstruct that authoritatively? Finally, the tribunal decided to take neither the situation in 1947 (which it could not reconstruct) nor that of the date of the aerial survey (1948) or of the tribunal's decision (1950), but to defer it to the date on which a joint survey would demarcate the border: the border should be ascertained 'as on the date of the [Radcliffe] award, or if this was not possible, as on the date of the demarcation of the boundary.'[24]

Here, a combination of a faulty map and the likelihood of a river shifting its course created uncertainty about the location of a segment of the border. The tribunal could not remove this uncertainty; it entrusted the resolution of the problem to joint demarcation at some later date. As we will see, the process of fixing the border often got stalled at the stage of demarcation, creating a new patchwork of demarcated and non-demarcated border segments.[25]

The other case, that of the Kushiara (Kusiyara) river in Sylhet, also resulted from the Bengal Boundary Commission's lack of detailed knowledge of local circumstances. The border river that they identified as Kushiara does not actually bear that name. Like many rivers in Bengal, this is a river that often bifurcates, and various sections also bear different names. The question was which branch of the Barak-Boglia-Kushiara river should be accepted as the border. On the basis of eighteenth- and nineteenth-century maps produced in evidence, the tribunal decided in favour of Pakistan's claim but India could not accept this adjudication.[26] As a result, this part of the border is one of several that remain disputed today.

Islands on the move. Establishing the border in the rivers of Bengal held more surprises. Many of the silt-laden larger rivers are dotted with silt banks and islands that are inherently unstable. These are known as *chors*. One day a small *chor* may appear in the middle of a river and grow rapidly. Next year it may be gone but, if not, it will be colonized by plants, animals and people. Cultivation will start and if the *chor* continues to exist, cultivators will settle on it.[27] Historically, states in Bengal have considered *chors* and their inhabitants as troublesome. *Chor* people are hard to tax because they are always on the move, and they are hard to control because during the rainy season most *chors* are beyond the reach of law enforcement. *Chors* have attracted the independent-minded and *chor* communities have long had a reputation for self-reliance, religious sectarianism and defiance of outside authority. Their loyalty to successive states has always been doubtful.[28]

Suddenly, an international border ran through such rivers and indeed across their poorly administered *chors*.[29] This turned what had been an internal state frontier into an exposed and vulnerable part of the national territory. Both India and Pakistan were now faced with a double dilemma: how to establish and control the border on undemarcated *chors* and how to win the allegiance of their inhabitants. Immediately after Partition, it became clear that the Radcliffe line was highly debatable when it came to *chor*-filled rivers. What is the main channel of such a river? Is it in fact still a single river or should the two streams flowing on either side of large *chors* be considered as two separate rivers? Depending on the answers to such questions, a *chor* could be claimed by either party, or it could be divided between them.

The most violent and long-term dispute involving *chors* occurred in the river Ganges (here also known as Padma).[30] In the months following Partition, tension increased rapidly and several clashes occurred. The head of the District Intelligence Branch of Rajshahi (Pakistan) reported to his superior a string of clashes during 1948. For example,

On 6.10.48 on big launch of W.B. [West Bengal, India] accompanied by another small launch carrying about 100 personnel, military and police and equipped with Bren guns, machine guns, rifles and steel helmets trespassed into our area at the point of Panka, P.S. [police station, or *thana*] Shibganj and Narayanpur, P.S. Nawabganj. 50 of the personnel landed at the char and proceeded towards Narayanpur camp [a Pakistani border outpost] in order to attack our force ... Our men took position and local people rushed out to help our force. The W.B. force retreated ... On 18.10.48 armed forces of Indian dominion came in launches ... and acquired forcible possession of the Char Ghughumari. They hoisted Indian flag, dug trenches and retained their forces there ... On 19.10.48 three launches and several boats full of 200 armed personnel of Murshidabad district [in India] came to our jurisdiction at Diar Manikchak and Illismari and they landed at the chars and took forcible possession of them ... On 22.10.48, the Indian Force stationed at Illismari approached Sahibnagar from two directions and opened fire at our men. The fire was replied by our men.[31]

The number of border posts was increased, patrols by launch were introduced and 'people in the Char areas were organised to help the police parties when required. It was impressed upon them that it was their duty to defend their homeland ... Some seized shot guns were distributed to local people in strategic areas and the local people trained to use them.'[32]

The *chor* disputes were fought with threats, intimidation, feints and occasional skirmishes resulting in arrests, casualties and deaths. But they were also fought with arguments. In December 1947 a Pakistani patrol officer posted on *chor* Ghughumari was visited by a boatful of policemen from India whose leader

showed me his maps and advanced that Ghughumari was supposed to be under the jurisdiction of ... Murshidabad district [India], and as such cajoled me to vacate the place, but I also showed him Survey Maps and explained that my camp is in [Pakistan] proper and so he had no occasion to ask me to leave the place. Then I politely asked him to take the matter at higher level and made him agreeable when he departed.[33]

Adjudicating the dispute over the Ganges *chors* was another major task of the Bagge Tribunal. Once again, Pakistan wanted a flexible border (a line through the middle of the river, which might shift over time) and India a rigid one (a fixed line irrespective of where the river was).[34] In early 1950, the tribunal decided on a fixed line 'following the course of the midstream of the main channel of the River Ganges as it was at the time of the award given by Sir

Cyril Radcliffe', and added that demarcation should be completed within one year from the date of the publication of its decision.[35] In reality, demarcation was to take much longer, and an area of 114 km² remained disputed.[36] And the longer the demarcation was delayed, the more difficult it became. A case in point was *chor* Nowshera, on which a temporary boundary had been fixed in 1950. Three-and-a-half years later, officials from Murshidabad (India) and Rajshahi (Pakistan) visited the disputed *chor*, apparently for the first time since 1950, with a view to finalizing the demarcation. They could not locate the border at all, left thoroughly confused and disoriented, and ordered another survey.[37] It would take till 1964 before Pakistan and India could decide on a joint demarcation of their Ganges border. Even so, conflicts over shifting *chors* in the Ganges have continued.[38]

Meanwhile, the local population was at a loss. Take the case of Intaz Ali. Intaz was born in 1947 and grew up in Chor Madhobpur, a village on the southern bank of the Ganges that was part of East Pakistan. He was a Pakistani. When he was in primary school, however, he and his fellow-villagers learned that the Bagge Tribunal had awarded their village to India. What to do? Were they Indians or Pakistanis? Should he go to high school in the nearest town in Pakistan, or in India? It turned out that the decision by the tribunal was not implemented, and in 1959 Intaz's father decided to send his son to a high school on the Indian side and to change his citizenship to Indian. But three years later anti-Muslim disturbances broke out in Intaz's village, and his father sent him across to Pakistan for safety. It was there that Intaz completed his high school and eventually became a Pakistani citizen again. A few years later, Bangladesh was born and Intaz made the fourth 'nation-switch' of his 24-year-old life.[39]

Unsurveyed land. As we have seen, the maps produced during the land-tax surveys of the late-colonial period made it relatively easy to establish the location of the new border on the ground. But not all land had been surveyed. In these areas anything resembling a clear guideline was absent, and trouble was bound to develop.

The most intense dispute occurred in a forest in Sylhet, the district of Assam that had been cut in two by the Boundary Commission. Western Sylhet joined Pakistan and eastern Sylhet joined India. The new border ran straight through the Patharia forest in central Sylhet, and this would be a bone of contention for years to come (see Figure 4.2). The forest had been under the administration of the Assam Forest Department. It formed the border between two *thanas* but had never been surveyed. Whether the border ran along the eastern boundary of the forest (as Pakistan claimed), or zigzagged through the forest (as India claimed) had never been of much concern to anyone. Now it became an important international issue, not least because the area was thought to contain natural gas and oil.[40] Clashes began to occur, forest guards were abducted, and territorial claims were emphasized by constructing and destroying forestry outposts. For example, in August 1948, eight Pakistani Forest staff 'while asleep in their camp at Patharia Reserve Forest were kidnapped by Home Guards of Assam and Patharkandi Police (Indian Union) ... Forest guards reported to have been assaulted by the Assam force. They were, however, released on bail.'[41]

The small Patharia dispute sent tremors up to the highest levels of the state bureaucracies of Pakistan and India. In 1948 it was put on the agenda of the Inter-Dominion Conference at New Delhi; the resulting Delhi Agreement proposed 'interim agreements' to defuse the tension and decided to put it forward as one of the four border disputes to be adjudicated by the Bagge Tribunal.[42] The interim agreements quickly percolated down both state bureaucracies, leading to detailed instructions to local forest staff, and the Bagge Tribunal began its work in December 1949.[43] In early 1950, the tribunal decided that the Boundary Commission's zigzag line through the forest was the correct border.[44]

Although both India and Pakistan had said that they would abide by the adjudication of the tribunal in this case, neither of them did and incidents continued to occur. In January 1951 a group of Indian Forest Guards and tea garden labourers crossed the border and abducted a Pakistani Forest Guard and some labourers.[45] There were further conflicts in 1951 over the building of sheds and the posting of Assamese armed police in the disputed area. In 1952 the Assamese authorities protested that 'a Pak Divisional Forest Officer accompanied by one Forester ... removed the forest reserve signboard fixed by Pakistan authority ... and tried to refix it further inside Indian territory but was prevented.'[46] The dispute dragged on and occasionally led to cross-border shootings.[47] Further high-level meetings proved fruitless until a compromise was reached in 1959; since then the Patharia forest has been enshrined in the ninth amendment to the Constitution of India.[48]

Mapping errors. Although detailed maps were available for almost the entire border area, some contained errors, and these became a third cause of border disputes. At the time, many of these were not perceived as major conflicts, but it would be wrong to suppose that border disputes were restricted to the four that India and Pakistan agreed to put before the Bagge mediation tribunal. Quite the contrary: countless disputes occupied the minds of border district officials and acted as irritants in relations between the two administrations. In one highly publicized case the name of the district written on the margins of a colonial-era *mouza* map was incorrect, and this caused considerable correspondence.[49] In another there was a dispute over a border road: did the border run on this side of it or that?[50]

The Boundary Commission itself also made more mapping mistakes than the ones already mentioned (for example in the case of the Mathabhanga river). In what seems to have been a simple drawing error on their map, a section of the border between the northern districts of Dinajpur (Pakistan) and Jalpaiguri (India) follows a straight line rather than the wavy *thana* border, as intended. As a result, 'a territory about the size of an entire union' was administered by India but claimed by Pakistan.[51] This case became known as the Berubari dispute. At first perceived as only a local issue, it led to cross-border shootings in 1952 and was discussed at high-level meetings till an agreement was reached in 1958.[52] This was not the end of the story, however. The agreed transfer was blocked by considerable popular resistance in India against giving any territory to Pakistan, leading to a case in the Supreme Court.[53] Berubari was later linked with a proposed exchange of the many enclaves in this region (another territorial conundrum that has remained unresolved till today) and continues to be a potentially explosive issue.[54]

Demarcating the border

India and Pakistan were lucky to have such detailed maps on which to base border-making decisions. Still, the ways in which these maps represented realities on the ground sometimes created problems, making it impossible for the two states to agree on the exact location of the border between their territories. Some of these cases turned into persistent trouble spots but in many others the states were able to sort out their differences. In the long run, most of the border came to be fixed by mutual consent. But this was only the first step. Next came the task of demarcating the border for all to see, by means of boundary pillars and other physical markers of sovereignty.

How was this done, especially in view of the unfriendly relationship that developed between these states? Despite the political rhetoric of enmity and mistrust, both state bureaucracies realized their shared interest in defining their territorial sovereignty, and they cooperated with each other. Immediately after Partition, India and Pakistan agreed on a working definition of the borderline. In December 1947, officials in border districts in both countries were told by their superiors to stick to the 'status quo in all branches of administration viz. Civil, Revenue and Criminal ... until the final determination of the boundary is made by a Joint Boundary Commission.' As we have seen, such instructions were insufficient to bring peace to the borderland, and top-level bureaucrats blamed this largely on their subordinates.[55]

Then, in a remarkable act of cooperation, the Home Ministries of East Bengal

(Pakistan) and West Bengal (India) issued *joint* instructions to their border officials, who received identical letters in May 1948 ordering them to meet their colleagues across the border '*as early as possible* with a view to determine *what the status quo is* regarding all chars and border villages, the jurisdictions of which are in dispute or are likely to be so.' With the help of officials in charge of land records, they were to write a joint report 'on the *factual position* as it stood on the 15th August, 1947.' They were also told in no uncertain terms that recommendations regarding the demarcation of the border were not welcome. It was not *their* task to demarcate the border, but that of a future joint boundary commission; 'once this point is clearly grasped by you and officers subordinate to you', there should be no difficulty in drafting the report.[56]

Soon after this, in December 1948, the Prime Ministers of Pakistan and India gave the formal go-ahead for demarcation.[57] It would be an operation at the provincial level and, for the purpose of demarcation, the border was divided into 'provincial segments' for which the procedures and arrangements differed.[58] India and Pakistan had already completed an aerial survey of their East Pakistan/ West Bengal border and would prepare a map on that basis.

East and West Bengal would now 'attempt to come to an agreement as regards the correct boundary line between the two Provinces after examining all relevant maps and records and the line so agreed upon will be shown on the map. [It] will be demarcated on the ground by the Survey staff of the two Provinces and will be marked by permanent pillars jointly by them.'[59]

Similar procedures were worked out between East Pakistan and Assam, and East Pakistan and Tripura. But in each case demarcation ran into serious trouble that would delay it for many years. First, there was a lack of information. For example, even the officials most directly concerned did not know the length of the border. Remarkably, as late as 1953 the East Pakistan authorities thought that the total length of the border line with India was 2,126 km – not even close to its real length of 4,095 km.[60] Second, as the demarcation process dragged on, it was overtaken by administrative reforms in India that brought new parties into it.[61] Third, political questions complicated the administrative procedure. As a result, six years after Partition only one-fifth of the border had been demarcated, and 18 years after Partition not more than two-thirds (Table 4.1).[62]

In 1974, the Prime Ministers of India and newly independent Bangladesh signed an agreement to complete the demarcation of the land border between their countries (the maritime border remained undefined[65]). They listed 15 sectors of the border that remained to be demarcated and decided how they should be dealt with. This 'Indira-Mujib agreement' was ratified by the Bangladesh government but not by the government of India, and as a result the 15 sectors are still not authoritatively demarcated today.[66]

Table 4.1: Demarcation of the Bengal border, 1947–2003[64]

Year	Demarcated	Which segments
1953	827 km (19%)	West Bengal (827 km = 37%) Assam (none) Tripura (none) Burma (none)
1965	2,713 km (66%)	West Bengal (1,736 km = 78%) Assam (681 km = 67%) Tripura (296 km = 35%) Burma (none)
2003	4,088 km (95%)	West Bengal (almost all)[A] Assam (almost all)[A] Tripura (almost all)[A] Burma (none)

[A] According to various press reports, between 6 and 125 km of the Indo-Bangladesh border remained undemarcated (and disputed) in 2003.[63]

Surveying and demarcating. Demarcating the border was a difficult and delicate job that was entrusted to survey teams made up of surveyors from both countries. To begin with, they were exposed to the contradictory territorial expectations of their superiors. Not surprisingly, quarrels often broke out between members of joint survey teams. For example, during demarcation operations on the Assam border in 1951, 'the representatives of Assam Survey Staff while leaving Sunamganj sector after a joint survey with the Pak Survey Party obliterated 14 boundary marks and demolished 5 out of 14 pillars in the northern border of Sunamganj.'[67]

A few months later another joint party surveying this segment of the border disagreed sharply over the demarcation of a disputed village and the proper surveying methods, prompting both states to send in troops and suspend all demarcation work along the Assam/East Pakistan border.[68] It took over a year to defuse the tension sufficiently to take up demarcation again, but the work halted almost immediately because Assamese members of the joint survey party were arrested by Pakistani officials on the charge of smuggling pulses from Pakistan to India.[69] Such harassment by officials was a common hazard for surveyors, especially because, in the course of their work, they had to cross the borderline all the time.[70]

Surveyors also had to contend with opposition from borderlanders. Wherever they went, they felt the full weight of local public opinion and they could not do their work without the protection of armed guards. Even so, sometimes they were attacked. When a group of West Bengal surveyors, escorted by East Pakistan police, were proceeding along the Rajshahi border, villagers assaulted them and refused to let them take the goods they were carrying back to India. In the words of one of the team's porters, Ram Sumer,

> 'We had travelled for about 15 minutes from the place of our rest when I heard Khalasi Muneswar shouting for help. I ran to the front cart and saw him, red in the face, surrounded by three armed men shouting … in Bengali which I could not understand. But I soon saw about 40 armed men running towards us from the adjoining village. We were afraid and we ran behind shouting for help from the Police.' Another member of the survey party added: 'The constables used the Butt-end of their rifles to disperse the gang. The men grew afraid and started running away … The S.I. [Sub-Inspector] left us at the Border about half a mile further up from the camp and we heaved a sigh of relief on reaching back safe in the Home Land.'[71]

In view of such tensions, it was not surprising that the demarcation of the border was a slow and uneven process. Among the four main segments, West Bengal was the most successful: by the mid-1960s four-fifths of it had been demarcated. Assam had a later start but here two-thirds had been demarcated by that date. The situation in the Tripura segment was different. On the one hand, a border had been demarcated here between British Bengal and the Princely State of Tripura in the 1850s and 1860s, and boundary pillars had been erected to mark it.[72] On the other hand, there was a conflict over the acceptability of this border, and this stalled effective demarcation; by the mid-1960s only one-third had been covered.[73]

Finally, the almost 200-km-long Bangladesh-Burma border remains completely undemarcated despite demarcation agreements in 1966, 1980 and 1998.[74] In 1993 the armed forces of Burma (Myanmar) began laying anti-personnel mines in the borderland.

> The mines do not discriminate when it comes to taking lives. Among the victims were BDR Jawans [Bangladesh border guards], Myanmar's Nasaka security forces personnel, Myanmar regular army troopers, Rohingya infiltrators and Bangladeshi woodcutters. A total of 35 Bangladeshis have been killed and 22 wild elephants perished due to landmine blasts at the border areas during the six-year period.[75]

A meeting between the survey departments of the two countries was held in Rangoon (Yangon) in September 1998, and a land boundary treaty was signed in November 1998.[76] Demarcation began right away but when it was in progress a powerful anti-personnel mine exploded at the border near Lemochhari. As a result, demarcation was immediately suspended. The lack of demarcation could easily lead to disagreements, as in 2001, when Bangladesh and Burma came to blows over the construction of a dam in the Naf river.[77]

Patchy normalization

By the early 21st century, more than 50 years after the sudden birth of the Bengal border, the initial patchwork of 17 component parts had disappeared. The states concerned had accepted the international stature of the border and had actively worked to normalize it. They had succeeded to the extent that, both nationally and internationally, the Bengal border had come to be seen as a single unit, the outer skin of the state of Bangladesh that it shares with India and Burma.

But normalization is incomplete because not all border disputes have been settled and therefore conclusive demarcation of the border is impossible. A new patchwork of demarcated and non-demarcated segments has sprung up. There are long stretches of border that are (or, at least, seem to be) routinized, but there are also 'flash points' that remain in dispute and volatile.[78] India and Bangladesh have been unable to 'transform their border into a border of eternal peace and friendship,' as they pledged in 1972.[79] Despite high-minded agreements, they have found that border disputes involving perhaps a few hectares or square kilometres of territory have baffled their powers of resolution. The new patchwork is dynamic because new areas of dispute appear quite regularly, on the land border as well as on the maritime border.[80] These spots are political time bombs that may throw a spanner in the works whenever the two countries seek to normalize their relations.

This is illustrated by an incident in 1999, a year in which the governments of India and Bangladesh were striving hard to improve the political climate. With much fanfare they had established a direct bus link between Dhaka and Calcutta and worked out an agreement to allow Indian goods to travel across Bangladesh territory to another part of India. But then, quite unexpectedly, they found themselves face to face with an almost forgotten border dispute.

The Muhuri is a small river that flows through Tripura before it enters the eastern Bangladesh district of Noakhali (see Figure 4.2). Since 1947, India and Bangladesh have a disagreement over a small area along the Muhuri, including a *chor* that surfaced around 1960. India has occupied this *chor* – unlawfully, according to Bangladesh – since the India–Pakistan war of 1965. On 22 August 1999, reacting to a conflict between *chor* cultivators, the border guards set up a meeting to mediate. When this failed, both sides resorted to cross-border machine gunning that continued for several days. There were casualties, villagers fled from their homes, troops at the border were reinforced and the press began to report on the incident. The image of two friendly nations co-operating harmoniously received a blow. It was by no means the first time that this tiny dispute flared up; in the previous two decades no less than 59 inconclusive gunfights had been fought over it between Indian and Bangladeshi border guards.[81]

Relations between modern states depend heavily on the illusion that they are sovereign political entities in complete control of well-defined territories. In the contemporary Bengal borderland territorial confusion – which detracts from this illusion – results largely from unresolved *Radcliffian* (as opposed to *McMahonian* and *Kashmirian*[82]) issues. But the prolonged patchiness of border normalization has also given an opportunity for new disputes to emerge. The *chor* that surfaced in the Muhuri river well after Partition is an example.[83] Another, which hit the headlines worldwide in April 2001, was the case of a tiny plot of Bangladeshi territory that India had occupied in 1971.

In 1971, the Bangladesh Liberation War turned the province of East Pakistan into an independent country. During this war, Bangladeshi freedom fighters were given active support and training by Indian border guards. One of their training camps was in the East Pakistani border hamlet of Padua (Pyrdiwah) on the Sylhet/ Meghalaya border (see Figure 4.2). After the war was won, the freedom fighters left and the Indian border guards who had given them training stayed and turned the training camp into an Indian border outpost. In this way, 95 hectares of Bangladeshi territory came to be held 'in adverse possession' by India. This fact, virtually unknown except to locals for almost 30 years, led to sudden diplomatic crisis between India and Bangladesh in 2001, when a group of Bangladeshi border guards, apparently without the backing of their government, entered the hamlet and encircled the Indian border outpost. The incident, widely reported as an 'invasion' in the Indian press, led Indian border guards to enter Bangladesh-held disputed territory in retaliation. As their entry point the Indians chose Boroibari (a few hundred kilometres to the west of Padua), which had been disputed and undemarcated since 1947.[84] In this disastrously miscalculated confrontation, 16 Indian and 3 Bangladeshi border guards were killed, at least 22 people were injured, and thousands fled their homes (Plate 4.3). The worst border incident to occur between these two 'friendly' countries, it caused enormous political and diplomatic damage.[85]

Nobody knows how many other undiscovered 'flash points' may yet lie hidden along the Bengal border but in view of the patchy pattern of border normalization it is likely that there are many.[87] As long as the Bengal border remains a patchwork of disputed and undisputed sectors, demarcated and undemarcated

Plate 4.3: A guard of honour stands next to the flag-covered coffins of Indian border guards killed at the India-Bangladesh border, April 2001.[86]

parts, and various areas 'in adverse possession', it cannot be normalized (Plate 4.4). It will continue to act as an effective obstacle to any attempts at routinizing territorial relations between these states.[88] Disputed territory is not just a political

Plate 4.4: Bangladeshi border guards training their gun at India after the border incident at Boroibari on the Roumari/ Mankachar border, April 2001.[89]

irritant between neighbouring states and, as we will see, a tragedy for the local population. It is also a tool that political parties, governments, bureaucrats, border guards and many others can use to destabilize polities and torpedo unwanted (national) policies and political arrangements. In this way, a patchwork border serves many purposes and its survival is a comment on the peculiarities and interests of the states that maintain it.

Conclusion: Normalizing the border

An unequivocal definition of national borders is essential for any modern state because the global state system is based on the territorialization of state power and on each state's striving to exercise exclusive sovereignty over a delineated, self-enclosed geographical space.[90] This is why both Pakistan and India were eager to spend much money and manpower on fixing and demarcating their borders. And this is why the unfinished nature of border demarcation today is an embarrassment to the state elites of India, Bangladesh and Burma.[91] It highlights the fact that their strategies of territoriality have not resulted in a self-enclosed national territory, and that they are incapable of exercising sovereignty over parts of the territory that they claim to be theirs.

As a historical process of bureaucratic classification and control, however, the establishment of the Bengal border has been rather successful. For the bureaucracies involved, the process of gaining a clear understanding of the location of the border was a lengthy one. At the local level, it required studying survey maps and colonial notifications, visual inspection of border sites, joint enquiries, rapid responses to border incidents and endless reporting to one's superiors. These superiors in turn sought legal advice, devised instruments (conferences, committees, agreements) to deal with border issues, applied diplomatic pressure, built up military presences at the border, and tried to sway public opinion. Gradually these highly complex activities normalized the border in most places. Here the states developed ways of dealing with each other, the border became a routine issue, and disputes over the border became a thing of the past. Incidents might still occur – a cow straying across, or smugglers being caught – but these could no longer upset the regular pattern of administration. Half a century after the painful separation, despite the danger of half-forgotten 'flash points' erupting, the borderland had not quite acquired the natural feel of an 'adult' borderland, but in many places it was on its way.[92] In the next chapter we will look more closely at how this transformation was achieved, focusing especially on the tools of territorial control that the states employed to establish sovereignty and legitimacy, not just over the border itself but over the new borderland and its inhabitants.

Notes

1 Viceroy's Personal Report No. 17 (16 August 1947), in: Nicholas Mansergh and Penderel Moon (eds), *The Transfer of Power, 1942–7: Constitutional Relations between Britain and India*, Vol. XII: The Mountbatten Viceroyalty, Princes, Partition and Independence, 8 July–15 August 1947 (London: Her Majesty's Stationery Office, 1983), 774.

2 Figures on the length of the India/ Bangladesh/ Burma border are inconsistent. According to the Home Minister of Bangladesh, the border that his country shares with India and Burma (Myanmar) is 4,427 km. The CIA thinks it is 4,246 km (4,053 km with India and 193 with Burma). The Embassy of India reports, however, that the border with Bangladesh is 4,095 km. If we add 193 km for the Bangladesh/ Burma border, the total comes to 4,288. But according to Burmese figures the land border with Bangladesh is 208 km and the river border 64 km. The Indian Embassy gives the following figures for the length of the border of various Indian states with Bangladesh: West Bengal 2,216 km, Assam 262 km, Meghalaya 443 km, Tripura 856 km and Mizoram 318 km. Since no authoritative statement on the exact length of the border is available, I use the following approximation in this study:

Total length:	4,288 km;
West Bengal segment:	2,216 km (including Cooch Behar 422 km and Bihar 214 km);
Assam segment:	1,023 km (later disaggregated into Assam 262 km, Meghalaya 443 km and Mizoram 318 km);
Tripura segment;	856 km;
Burma segment:	193 km.

See 'Resist smuggling Nasim tells BDR personnel', *The Daily Star* (22 March 1999); *The World Factbook 2000* (Central Intelligence Agency; http://www.cia.gov/cia/publications/factbook/); 'Union Home Secretary Chairs a High Level Empowered Committee' (Washington, DC: Embassy of India, 10 December 1998). Cf. SK Ghosh, *Unquiet Border* (New Delhi: Ashish Publishing House, 1993), 710; *Basic Facts on the Union of Myanmar* (Yangon: Public Relations and Information Division, Ministry of Foreign Affairs, Government of the Union of Myanmar, 1996).

3 Strictly speaking, a short stretch in the far Southeast had functioned for ten years previously as an 'inter-colony' border between two British possessions: India and Burma. Burma had been an integral part of the British colony of India till the British Parliament passed the Government of Burma Act of 1935, which created a separately administered colony of Burma. The reforms came into operation in 1937.

4 This is also why it makes little sense to compare the 1947 Partition-in-the-East with the provincial reshuffle of 1905 that is sometimes referred to as the 'first partition of Bengal.' In 1905 the British rearranged the administration of colonial Bengal by separating the eastern half from the western half and joining it with Assam to form the new province of Eastern Bengal and Assam. This provincial rearrangement, which was undone six years later, merely led to the creation of new provincial boundaries within the colonial context. These boundaries did not coincide with the later Radcliffe line.

5 Jasimuddin, *Nokshi kāthar math* [The Field of the Embroidered Quilt] (1928).

6 The Chhota ('Small') Shona Masjid is in Bangladesh and the Bara ('Big') Shona Masjid in India. On the Bangladesh side the checkpoint is known as Shona Masjid, on the Indian side as Mohodipur. Photograph taken in 2001.

7 Following the collapse of the precolonial *kanungo* system of maintaining land records in the mid-eighteenth century, the colonial state built up an impressive system of land registers. Starting with the Quinquennial Registers (from 1789 onwards), the mapping of land in Bengal developed into a finely tuned operation. The most important instruments were the six major land surveys, of which the best known are the Thakbast Survey (1845–77), the Revenue Survey (1846–78) and the Cadastral Survey (1888–1945). Copies of the printed land records and maps produced during the Cadastral Surveys were kept by the cultivators, their landlords, and in state offices (local *tohsil* offices as well as the District Record Rooms). For details, see Sirajul Islam, *Rural History of Bangladesh: A Source Study* (Dacca: Tito Islam, 1977); Willem van Schendel, *Peasant Mobility: The Odds of Life in Rural Bangladesh* (Assen: Van Gorcum, 1981 / New Delhi: Manohar, 1982).

8 In a rare interview in the 1960s, Cyril Radcliffe would blame the inadequacies of the Bengal Boundary Commission's decisions partly on the quality of the district maps. 'I was so rushed that I had not time to go into the details. Even accurate district maps were not there and what material there was was also inadequate. What could I do in one and a half months?' The British poet WH Auden echoed this view when he portrayed Radcliffe in this fragment of his poem 'Partition' of 1967:

> He got down to work, to the task of settling the fate
> Of millions. The maps at his disposal were out of date
> And the Census Returns almost certainly incorrect,
> But there was no time to check them, no time to inspect
> Contested areas. The weather was frightfully hot,
> And a bout of dysentery kept him constantly on the trot,
> But in seven weeks it was done, the frontiers decided,
> A continent for better or worse divided.'

Although there were certainly errors in the district maps (see below), what is much more striking is how accurate they turned out to be over most of the length of the border. From Radcliffe's comment it is also clear that the Boundary Commission restricted itself to the use of district maps and ignored the much more detailed *mouza* (revenue village) maps on which these were based. Kuldip Nayar, *Distant Neighbours: A Tale of the Subcontinent* (Delhi: Vikas, 1972), 35; WH Auden, *City Without Walls and Other Poems* (London: Faber and Faber, 1969).

9 According to Nazem, there are at least 54 rivers that flow into Bangladesh from India and Burma. A smaller number flow from Bangladesh territory to India, and a few weave in and out of the two territories. Nurul Islam Nazem, 'The Impact of River Control on an International Boundary: The case of the Bangladesh-India Border,' in: Carl Grundy-Warr (ed.), *Eurasia: World Boundaries, Volume 3* (London and New York: Routledge, 1994), 101–10. Many irritations between India and Bangladesh revolve round these rivers, particularly because of interventions by the upper-riparian partner, in most cases India. The most vexed disputes are those concerning the waters of the Ganges (Farakka barrage), the Tista (Tista barrage) and the Meghna (Tipaimukh dam). Cf. Ben Crow with Alan Lindquist and David Wilson, *Sharing the Ganges: The Politics and Technology of River Development* (Delhi: Sage Publications, 1995); 'Go ahead for dam in Assam: Meghna faces Padma's fate,' *The New Nation* (15 July 2003).

10 Nafis Ahmad, 'The Indo-Pakistan Boundary Disputes Tribunal, 1949–1950', *The Geographical Review* (New York), 43:3 (1953), 329–37; Nazem, 1994.

11 Cyril Radcliffe, *Report of the Bengal Boundary Commission* (New Delhi, 12 August 1947) and Cyril Radcliffe, *Report of the Bengal Boundary Commission (Sylhet District)* (New Delhi, 13 August 1947).

12 Plt. 20M-60/50 (3-53). On the disputed island of Totadia in the middle of the Naf river, see S Mahmud Ali, *The Fearful State: Power, People and Internal War in South Asia* (London: Zed Press, 1993), 187. On continuing difficulties in deciding the river border, see 'Developments along Myanmar border being monitored,' *The Independent* (25 March 2002),

13 Villagers often retained claims on lands that had been 'eaten up' by a river but sometimes reappeared after a generation or more. There was a special type of land surveys in Bengal (*diara* surveys) that dealt exclusively with the settlement of land rights along rivers.

14 The cadastral survey had started in Chittagong District in 1888 and had gradually worked its way from district to district till it was completed with a revisional survey of Bakarganj district in 1945.

15 River changes could be rapid. The Ganges (Padma) 'is so erratic that its bed has been changing frequently, and the boundary laid down in the last Survey Settlement Operation has considerably changed in course of last 20 years; even the boundary existing in 1940 is not the same as the present. The whole area has to be resurveyed before final demarcation. At this state it is not possible to say what is the exact district boundary' (letter from the Commissioner of Rajshahi, 13 May 1948 (Government of East Bengal, Home (Political) Department, Confidential Records Branch, 1B2-4/49 (B. Proceedings, July 1952) (hereafter CR 1B2-4/49 (7-52)). Cf. Alamgir Hossain, 'Padma gobbles panchayat', *The Telegraph* (10 April 2003).

16 Tapash Ganguly, 'The Forgotten Village,' *The Week* (Kottayam), 13 April 1997. On a similarly located village in Assam, see Faruque Ahmed, 'They are Indian but earn their livelihood in Bangladesh: With no health care centre, no post office, no grocery shop, 900 Bhogdanga villagers deprived of basic necessities', *The Northeast Daily* (14 November 1999). On a border village in Tripura dependent on Bangladesh for marketing, health care and even drinking water, see 'Tripura villagers abducted by ultras in Bangla territory', *The Assam Tribune* (14 May 2003).

17 For example, Pakistan claimed land west of the Nagar river (on the Bihar/Pakistan border) and north of the Pyain river (on the Assam/Pakistan border) as late as 1953. (CR 3A-6/52 (8-53b); CR 3A-1/53 (4-54a)). In November 1965, Indian and Pakistani armed forces fought for several days for the possession of the hamlet of Lakshmipur, 'separated from the Indian mainland by two canals forking out from the Kapotakshe river and by a small stretch of marshland'; 16 of its houses were located in 24-Parganas (India) and 4 in Jessore (East Pakistan). '10 Pakistanis killed at Lakshmipur', *The Statesman* (10 November 1965).

18 In the 1990s, the Tumburu watercourse moved from Burmese territory to Bangladeshi territory, causing great friction between Burmese border guards (Nasaka), who continued to use it, and their counterparts in Bangladesh. In April 2000, Burma finally agreed that the watercourse had moved out of reach. 'Nasaka won't use Tumburu canal', *The New Nation* (29 April 2000). Similar tensions occasionally flared up over the disputed Dabfari canal on Totarbari Island in the river Naf. In their border agreement of 1966, Pakistan and Burma undertook not to construct dams on the border river; and this agreement was renewed in 1980. When the Nasaka started constructing a 'frontier dam' in early 2001, this led to a rapidly escalating conflict. 'BDR, Nasaka trade gunfire over dam construction', *The Independent* (9 January 2001); 'Ceasefire follows flag meeting: BDR,

Nasaka trade fire over embankment on river Naf', *The Daily Star* (10 September 2001);
'Mutual inspection of the creeks of the Naaf river between Bangladesh and Burma',
Narinjara News (20 March 2002). For similar attempts by Indian authorities to construct
groynes in the border river Mahananda to prevent it moving further towards the
Bangladesh side, see 'Indians' bid to construct groynes: BDR, BSF gunfight near
Banglabandh', *The New Nation* (25 February 2001); 'India agrees to demolish 2
controversial groynes', *The New Nation* (10 February 2002). A similar conflict over a
jetty in the border river Kalindi led to extensive cross-border shooting. 'BSF jettisons
jetty over Kalindi: Situation tense despite flag meeting', *The Daily Star* (18 November
2002); 'BSF snubs BDR, firm on jetty at Shamshernagar', *The Times of India* (18 November
2000); Jayanta Gupta, 'Fresh trouble erupts at Bangla border', *The Times of India* (24
November 2002). Conversely, Indian authorities objected to Bangladeshi protective
constructions, e.g. along the border river Chhoto Jamuna (Panchbibi, North Bengal) in
2003. 'BSF halt construction of river revetment', *The Independent* (10 May 2003).

19 The official name was the Indo-Pakistan Boundary Disputes Tribunal, but it became
better known as the Bagge Tribunal, after its chairperson, Algot Bagge, a former member
of the Swedish Supreme Court. This tribunal was recommended as early as December
1948 by the India-Pakistan 'Committee for Boundary Disputes and Border Incidents
between East Bengal–West Bengal, between East Bengal–Assam, and between East
Punjab–West Punjab' (CR 2C-41/49 (9-60a)). For its terms of reference, see CR 2C-41/
49 (9-60b). For the tribunal's decisions, see *Partition Proceedings, Volume VI: Reports of
the Members and Awards of the Chairman of the Boundary Commissions* (New Delhi:
Government of India, Partition Secretariat, 1950), 315–22, or Avtar Singh Bhasin (ed.),
India-Bangladesh Relations: Documents – 1971-2002 (New Delhi: Geetika Publishers,
2003), Vol. V, 2689–712. On the tribunal, see Ahmad, 'The Indo-Pakistan Boundary
Disputes Tribunal'; cf. A. Tayyeb, *Pakistan: A Political Geography* (London: Oxford
University Press, 1966), 91–5.

20 Radcliffe, *Report of the Bengal Boundary Commission*, 4.

21 For the Pakistan case, see 'Boundary Disputes between the Dominion of India and the
Dominion of Pakistan…' (CR 2C-41/49 (9-60a)).

22 Bhasin (ed.), *India-Bangladesh Relations*, V, 2705–6.

23 *Gazette of Pakistan Extraordinary*, 10 February 1950, 85; quoted in Ahmad, 1953, 333.

24 *Gazette of Pakistan Extraordinary*, 10 February 1950, 85; quoted in Ahmad, 1953, 333; cf.
Bhasin (ed.), *India-Bangladesh Relations*, V, 2708; Birendra Kumar Bhattacharya,
Murshidabad: West Bengal District Gazetteers (Calcutta: West Bengal Government Press,
1979), 7.

25 And even where demarcation was finalized, further movements of the river created new
disputes. For continuing friction along the Mathabhanga border, see '233 bighas of land
under Indian possession,' *The Independent* (28 June 2003).

26 The Barak River flows west through Cachar (Assam, India) till it bifurcates into the
Surma and the Boglia. The Radcliffe line follows the Surma from the north and then
runs west along the Boglia. The Boglia flows west for another 10 km and then divides
into a northern and a southern branch which both meet the Radcliffe line running
south some kilometres to the west. The dispute was about which of these branches was
actually named Kushiara. The northern branch is known as the Boglia until much further
west (inside Pakistan) it becomes the Kushiara. The southern branch is known as the
Sonai or Puran Kushiara. India wanted the border to be fixed along the northern branch,
and Pakistan tried to prove that it should be fixed along the southern branch and follow

the line on the Boundary Commission's map. See Bhasin (ed.), *India-Bangladesh Relations*, V, 2711–12; Ahmad, 334–5.

27 Mobarak Hossain, *Chorer Manush Chorer Jibon* (Dhaka: Mass Line Media Centre, 1999).

28 For example, 56 years after the establishment of the border Indian authorities were still complaining about their lack of control over the inhabitants of border *chors* in the Brahmaputra river ('people living in the Chars normally do not cooperate with the Indian forces in identifying the foreigners') and inhabitants of border *chors* reported on the absence of state administration in their area. 'State police, BSF to work in tandem against Bangla influx', *The Assam Tribune* (11 February 2003); R Dutta Chowdhury, 'Char Indians, Bangladeshis bury border barrier', *The Assam Tribune* (1 September 2003).

29 For an example of the complexities of *chor* borders, see Anindita Dasgupta's map of the India-Bangladesh border across the Brahmaputra between pillars 1045 and 1067 near Dhubri (Assam). Here a mosaic of *chors* fills the enormous river, and the border runs across eight of them as well as across the nine channels that they create. The map can be found in Sanjoy Hazarika, *Rites of Passage: Border Crossings, Imagined Homelands, India's East and Bangladesh* (New Delhi: Penguin Books, 2000), 127.

30 The main disputed *chors* were on the border of the districts of Murshidabad and Rajshahi: Alatali, Ashiaradaha Khash Mahal, Bagdanga, Bansgara, Boarmari, Diar Manikchak, Durlabhpur, Ghughumari, Ilishmari, Khidirpur, Majherdiar, Moktarpur/Rajshahi Khash Mahal, Nowshera, Panka, Thutapara and Tiklir Char. Murshidabad also had *chor* disputes with the district of Kushtia (Pakistan), notably over Char Bhadra (see CR 1B2-3/49 (7-52)). *Chor* conflicts occurred in other rivers, too. See for example the case of Daikhawar Char in the Brahmaputra river where it enters Rangpur district (Pakistan) from Goalpara (Assam) (CR 1B4-13/51 (9-53); CR 1A2-3/53 (3-54)); 'Brohmoputrer duiti dip dokhol shongkranto mitha shongbad,' *Azad* (11 August 1951); 'Brohmoputrer chor birodh', *Azad* (30 August 1951).

31 CR 3A-1/49 (11-50). KS Roy, a Minister in the West Bengal government, visited Ilishmari and Sahebnagar that were burned down by Indian police. 'He had to cross the whole space of the Ganges to reach Elishmari', commented an outraged District Magistrate of Rajshahi (Pakistan), 'How then could he agree with his Dt. officials that Elishmari was theirs?' (CR 1I-108/49 (3-51)). For an Indian view of Pakistanis trespassing on Ganges *chors* in this period, see 'Pakistan Constables Arrested: Murshidabad Border Incident', *Hindusthan Standard* (12 August 1948) (also in: Government of East Bengal, Home (Police) Department, Branch Police, P3D-4/48 (B. Proceedings, March 1949); hereafter Pol. P3D-4/48 (3-49)).

32 CR 3A-1/49 (11-50). The seizure of firearms is discussed in chapter 5.

33 CR 1W-1/49 (1-53). Incidents were exploited by both governments to present their case to the press (e.g. Pakistan's 'Press Note' on the Char Rajshahi Khas Mahal shooting, 19 April 1948; 'Rajshahir Chore Guliborshon,' *Ittehad* (11 May 1948); CR 1B2-4/49 (7-52)). But at the same time measures were taken to control them. These took the form of meetings of officials from both sides. District Magistrates would jointly report on *chor* incidents (e.g. 'Joint enquiry into the shooting incident at Majherdiar ...' 1950; CR 1B2-11./50 (3-51); cf. CR 3A-1/53 (4-54a)), and they were put on the agenda of the Chief Secretaries' Conferences (e.g. the one of 10 May 1948; CR 1I-16/48 (11-50)) but the incidents did not cease.

34 Pakistan argued that the text of the Bengal Boundary Commission Report ('the district boundaries and not the actual course of the River Ganges shall constitute the boundary between East and West Bengal') should be read together with the latest notification of

those district boundaries (of 11 November 1941) which defined them as 'the mid stream of the river Ganges all along except over a small area where the boundary line passes over the island in the river Ganges between Boalia P.S. of Rajshahi and Raninagar P.S. of Murshidabad district' ('Boundary Disputes between the Dominion of India and the Dominion of Pakistan ...'; CR 2C-41/49 (9-60a)).

35 Bhasin (ed.), *India-Bangladesh Relations*, V, 2703; *Gazette of Pakistan Extraordinary*, 10 February 1950, 76. The Tribunal later extended the time limit in this dispute up to February 1953; see correspondence by the Tribunal in CR 1B2-13/53 (9-54).

36 In reply to an Assembly Question, the Home Ministry, East Bengal, divulged that a total of 396 km^2 of East Pakistan territory was 'in wrongful possession of India since or after Partition.' Of these, 114 km^2 were in the Ganges *chor* area. It conceded that 'some territories (much smaller in area than the area in wrongful possession of India), which will fall in West Bengal after final demarcation of the boundary, are still in our possession', adding that 'it will not be to the interest of our cause to furnish data regarding possession of the territories concerned in reply to any question in the Assembly' ('Draft reply to the Central Assembly Question by Mr. Ahmed Jaffar admitted for 3rd October ,1953'; CR 3A-1/53 (4-54a)).

37 They reported: 'Since 1950 [the] topography of the locality seems to have undergone a considerable change. The middle point of a Nullah [= small channel] was made Adhoc boundary and it was agreed upon that two chains [40 metres] on either side were to be kept uncultivated by the tenants. It seemed that the condition could not be enforced. The Nullah itself has now become the subject matter for dispute. On the spot the Indian nationals urged that the Nullah existed to the north and they sought to point out the alleged course of the Nullah but no sure trace of the Nullah could be found in the locality in that direction. To the further south of the aforesaid Nullah the Pakistani nationals pointed out a track to which the Nullah was said to have passed taking bends at places. The traces of a Nullah were more vivid on that direction though with breaks at certain points. From the conflicting and confusing version it was not possible to take any agreed decision about the Adhoc boundary of 1950. It seemed that the Khash Mahal department of both [India and Pakistan] settled Khash [government] lands after the fixation of the Adhoc boundary of 1950 to their respective tenants' ('Proceedings of the Conference held between the District Magistrate, Rajshahi, and the District Magistrate, Murshidabad, on 6.6.53 and 7.6.53 at the Rajshahi Circuit House,' CR 1B1-4/53 (6-54); cf. CR 3A-10/53 (8-54)).

38 Ben Crow with Alan Lindquist and David Wilson, *Sharing the Ganges: The Politics and Technology of River Development* (Delhi: Sage Publications, 1995), 86. By 2000, the river had moved more than 8 km to the southwest on the Nadia/Kushtia border, throwing up new *chors* and creating conflicts that official meetings could not resolve. After a joint survey of one area was suspended, an Indian newspaper reported that 'Bangladeshis have built huts and begun farming parts of the Padma's char that are snarled in a border dispute. They have pulled down structures built on these 400 acres by Indians, who pay rent for the land. Santosh Biswas, 'Foreigners grab disputed Padma char,' *The Statesman* (26 March 2000).

39 Intaz Ali (interview by Md. Mahbubar Rahman, Rajshahi, Bangladesh, 1999).

40 In 1923–33, the Burmah Oil Company had drilled two wells at the Patharia forest, one of which reportedly flowed oil. After Partition prospecting for oil and gas would continue on both sides of the Patharia border. Cf. J Coggin Brown and AK Dey, *India's Mineral Wealth: A Guide to the Occurrences and Economics of the Useful Minerals of India, Pakistan*

and Burma (London: Oxford University Press, 1955), 102; *Five Years of Pakistan (August 1947–August 1952)* (Karachi: Pakistan Publications, 1952), 39; *Keesing's Contemporary Archives*, VII (1948-50), 10693; http://shakti.hypermart.net/petroleum.html; http://www.gasmin.com/energy/ex.html.

41 Report of the District Magistrate, Sylhet, to Assistant Secretary, Govt of East Bengal (Home Political) Department, 19/3/49 (CR 3A-1/49 (11-50)).

42 According to this agreement, armed forces were to be stationed no closer than five miles from the forest, the Radcliffe line was to be treated as the ad hoc border, a joint committee was to be in charge of inspections of the forest and decisions on the strength of forest staff, and no new buildings were to be built by either side (CR 1I-31/49 (3-49); CR 2C-41/49 (9-60b)).

43 The Chief Secretaries of East Bengal, West Bengal and Assam, meeting in January 1949 (a month after the Delhi Agreement), ordered a meeting of the District and Forest officials concerned. This meeting was held in Sylhet ten days later. The officials drew up a detailed list of all existing paths, roads and buildings in the forest, undertaking not to change these till the Bagge Tribunal would take a decision. Unlike the higher authorities, they were not merely concerned with territorial clarity. They were also worried that the unsettled nature of the dispute would lead to a loss of state income from forest produce, especially bamboo, honey and beeswax. Patrols were to be held to 'prevent illegal extraction of forest produce' and 'strict instructions shall be issued to the patrolling staff not to insist upon a rigid observance of the patrolling zone ... and there should be no attempt at violence or arrest' (CR 1I-31/49 (3-49); cf. CR 3C-6/49 (11-50)).

44 Bhasin (ed.), *India-Bangladesh Relations*, V, 2708–10; *Gazette of Pakistan Extraordinary*, 10 February 1950, 85, cited in Ahmad, 1953, 333–4.

45 CR 3A-6/52 (8-53a).

46 CR 1B1-2/52 (7-54).

47 E.g. in 1958 when Indian woodcutters tried to work in a part of the forest claimed by Pakistan and the border troops started firing at each other. 'Indian forces open fire again – Strong protest lodged with Assam Government,' *The Pakistan Observer* (12 May 1958); 'Indian police opens fire in Patharia sector,' *The Pakistan Observer* (2 November 1958).

48 The Nehru-Noon agreement of 1958, resulting from a meeting on border issues between the Prime Ministers of India and Pakistan, did not even mention the case. It was finally settled at a ministerial conference in 1959. For the text of these two agreements, and a detailed description of the agreed 'rational boundary in the Patharia Forest Reserve region,' see the ninth amendment to the Constitution of India (*Constitution (Ninth Amendment) Act, 1960*); also A Appadorai, *Select Documents on India's Foreign Policy and Relations, 1947–1972* (Delhi: Oxford University Press, 1982), Volume I, 96–8, 99–103; and Bhasin (ed.), *India-Bangladesh Relations*, V, 2712–807. For armed clashes on this border, see 'Indian forces withdraw from Pak territory: Heavy firing on border patrol continues,' *The Pakistan Observer* (27 March 1959). In this sector, however, the border remained highly sensitive, particularly the stretch known as Lathitilla-Dumabari. Here major firing occurred during the India-Pakistan war of 1965 and till today it remains undemarcated and disputed. On this disputed stretch, where Bangladesh occupies four villages claimed by India, see R Dutta Choudhury, 'Fences broken, river unguarded: Indo-Bangla border still porous, aiding influx,', *The Assam Tribune* (30 November 2002); '"Bangla occupying over 750 *bighas* of Assam land",' *The Assam Tribune* (11 March 2003).

49 This was the conflict over the enclave of Dohogram-Angorpota and the Tin Bigha corridor (see CR 1B2-28/52 (7-55); cf. Van Schendel, 'Stateless in South Asia.' The map in

question was a *mouza* map. A *mouza* (or 'revenue village') is the smallest administrative unit in Bengal. *Mouza* maps show details of separate plots, village roads, rivers, ponds, etc.

50 E.g. CR 3A-6/52 (8-53a); CR 1B2-28/52 (7-55).

51 Pakistan's case was based on the passage in the report of the Bengal Boundary Commission that states: 'In the event of any divergence between the line as delineated on the map and as described ... the written description is to prevail.' *Report of the Bengal Boundary Commission* (1947), 7; cf. CR 1B-39/51 (1-53).

52 The Nehru-Noon agreement of 1958, see Appadorai, *Select Documents*, Volume I, 96--8. On this and other outstanding border disputes in 1958, see also Shreedhar and John Kaniyalil, *Indo-Pak Relations: A Documentary Study* (New Delhi: ABC Publishing House, 1993), 149.

53 For a report on the 'All-India Berubari Convention' (held in New Delhi, Dec 10, 1960), see 'Protest by All-India Convention,' *The Statesman* (December 11, 1960). On official talks regarding Berubari, see 'Talks on Border Demarcation', *The Statesman* (April 27, 1961) and on the Supreme Court's dismissal of the appeal to restrain the Indian government from transferring half of Berubari Union and 512 acres of nearby Chilahati village to East Pakistan, see 'Appeal dismissed in Berubari case,', *The Statesman* (August 12, 1965). In 1965 Berubari became the scene of continual cross-border firing between Pakistan and India; see e.g. '12 killed in Dahagram firing ...', *The Morning News* (17 March 1965); 'Fresh Pakistan firing in Berubari: West Bengal sends protest note,' *The Statesman* (3 April 1965); 'East Pakistan demands Berubari transfer,' *The Statesman* (25 April 1965). By September 1965, the West Bengal government was ready to 'undertake the Berubari demarcation on the basis of the Nehru-Noon agreement' ('Accord at eastern border talks: Demarcation to start next month,' *The Statesman*, 1 September 1965). Cf. Saroj Chakrabarty, *With Dr. B.C. Roy and Other Chief Ministers (A Record upto 1962)* (Calcutta: Benson's, 1974), 402–4, 470–3. For Indian parliamentary debates on this issue, see Bhasin (ed.), *India-Bangladesh Relations*, V, 2712–807.

54 For the fate of the 197 enclaves (74 Bangladeshi ones in India and 123 Indian ones in Bangladesh), see Brendan R Whyte, *Waiting for the Esquimo: An Historical and Documentary Study of the Cooch Behar Enclaves of India and Bangladesh* (Melbourne: Research Paper 8, School of Anthropology, Geography and Environmental Studies, University of Melbourne, 2002); and Van Schendel, 'Stateless in South Asia'.

55 'At the recent meeting of the Chief Secretaries of East and West Bengal it was felt that many of the disturbances near the border appear to be the result of a failure to appreciate and carry out these instructions on the part of subordinate officers on either side' (CR 1B2-4/49 (7-52)).

56 Letters to the District Magistrates of Murshidabad (India) and Rajshahi (Pakistan), 29 May 1948 (CR 1B2-4/49 (7-52), emphasis in the original). The Directors of Land Records and Surveys in East and West Bengal were to assist them. The report was to be based on administrative records such as boundary notifications, revenue jurisdiction lists, *union board* village lists and registers, *thana* records and maps, and *khash mahal* demand and collection registers. It was not to include site visits.

57 The Directors of Land Records and Surveys of the Provinces (Assam and West Bengal in India, East Bengal in Pakistan) and States (Cooch Behar and Tripura, both in India) were to demarcate the border without further delay. They were given the freedom to do so 'assisted by such staff and in such manner as they might mutually agree upon, areas where disputes have arisen or may arise being taken up first.' Only the four cases put up

for mediation by the Bagge Tribunal were to be left out at this stage. Curiously, no mention was made in this document of the demarcation of the Bihar (India)-East Pakistan border. *Inter-Dominion Conference at New Delhi (December 6-14, 1948), Appendix V: Boundary Disputes* (New Delhi, 1948).

58 Initially there were seven segments but by the mid-1950s administrative changes in India had reduced the number to four: the West Bengal/East Pakistan border; the Assam/ East Pakistan (Rangpur to Sylhet) border; the Tripura/East Pakistan border; and the Assam/East Pakistan (Chittagong Hill Tracts) border. Of course, the East Pakistan/Burma border was not part of this agreement, and it remained undemarcated.

59 CR 2C-41/49 (9-60a). In January 1948, India and Pakistan had decided on an aerial survey of the East Pakistan/West Bengal border. The cost of the aerial photography that was carried out in 1948 (Rs. 153,714/6/-) was shared equally by them (CR 1B1-6/54 (7-54)). For the 1954 agreement on the maintenance of border pillars, see CR 1B2-36/51 (10-54).

60 Memorandum of the Director of Land Records & Surveys, East Bengal, 10 March 1953; CR 3A-1/53 (4-54a). In later sources, the figure tends to rise. The exact length of the border will remain guesswork until it has been completely demarcated. For the 'real length' given here, see footnote 2 above.

61 These reforms made the Cooch Behar and Bihar segments of the border disappear as West Bengal took over administration of these parts of the borderland (in 1950 and 1956, respectively), but they created new jurisdictions in Assam, where Meghalaya (1972) and Mizoram (1987) were created. The demarcation of the Cooch Behar/East Pakistan border was taken up in 1953–4 and that of the Bihar/East Pakistan border in 1954–5 (CR 1B2-3/53 (1-55); CR 1B2-28/52 (7-55); CR 1B2-13/55 (12-55); CR 1B5-3/50 (12-55)).

62 By contrast, India and Pakistan were able to resolve their four border disputes in Punjab and complete the demarcation of that Partition border by April 1960. Lucy Payne Chester, 'Drawing the Indo-Pakistani Boundary During the 1947 Partition of South Asia' (PhD thesis, Yale University, 2002), 271–81.

63 In 1997 Bedi reported that 78 km of the West Bengal border, 3 km of the Assam-Bangladesh border, 36 km of the Tripura-Bangladesh border, and 8 km of the Mizoram-Bangladesh remained undemarcated. In addition, the entire Bangladesh-Burma border (193 km) remains undemarcated. In recent years, however, officials of Bangladesh and India have spoken only of 6.5 km of undemarcated boundary line. These 6.5 km refer to only three of the most vexed *disputed* parts of the undemarcated total: Lathitilla-Dumabari (Sylhet/Karimganj border), Muhuri (Feni/Tripura border) and Daikhata (Jalpaiguri border). Once again, in 2002, the Indian Minister of External Affairs had to report to his parliament that the latest attempt by a joint India-Bangladesh survey team to come to a consensus regarding these 6.5 km had come to naught. The Joint Boundary Working Group, meeting shortly afterwards, could do little more than reiterate the two states' irreconcilable positions regarding these three disputes. For details, see Rahul Bedi, 'Not-so-friendly neighbourhood,' *Indian Express* (15 May 1997); cf. Kazim Reza, 'Kashmir syndrome in Indo-Bangla border!' *The New Nation* (6 April 2000); 'Joint Record of Discussion of the Second Meeting of the India-Bangladesh Joint Boundary Working Group (JBWG) I & II, New Delhi, March 26–27, 2002', in: Bhasin (ed.), *India-Bangladesh Relations*, IV, 2204–18; 'Influx posing threat to security: Jaswant,' *The Assam Tribune* (15 March 2002).

64 Since no authoritative statement on the exact length of the border is available (see footnote 2), I use the following approximation in this study:

Total length: 4,288 km;
West Bengal segment: 2,216 km (including Cooch Behar 422 km and Bihar 214 km);
Assam segment: 1,023 km (later disaggregated into Assam 262 km, Meghalaya 443 km and Mizoram 318 km);
Tripura segment;   856 km;
Burma segment: 193 km.

Sources for this table: *1953* (CR 3A-1/53 (4-54b)); *1965* (Statements by Indian Minister of External Affairs, reported in 'Pakistan Forces Stop Shooting on Border Cooch Behar, March 23', *The Statesman* (24 March 1965), and in Dinesh Chandra Jha, *Indo-Pakistan Relations (1960–5)* (Patna: Bharati Bhawan, 1972), 182); *1998* ('BSF denies push-in attempts: Border chiefs chart crime control agenda,' *The Daily Star* (29 October 1998)). For figures on border demarcation presented to the Indian Parliament in 1960, 1965 and 1968, see also Bhasin (ed.), *India-Bangladesh Relations*, V, 2754, 2793, 2805–7.

65 On the maritime border, see Bhasin (ed.), *India-Bangladesh Relations*, IV, 1908–10, 1917–19, 1926, 1930–1, 2065.

66 The 15 sectors listed are: Mizoram-Bangladesh sector, Tripura-Sylhet sector, Bhagalpur Railway Line, Sibpur-Gaurangala sector, Muhuri River (Belonia) sector, Tripura-Noakhali/ Comilla sector (remaining portion), Fenny River, rest of Tripura-Chittagong Hill Tracts sector, Beanibazar-Karimganj sector, Hakar Khal, Baikari Khal, Enclaves, Hilli, Berubari, and Lathitilla-Dumabari. *Agreement between the Government of the Republic of India and Government of the People's Republic of Bangladesh concerning the Demarcation of the Land Boundary between India and Bangladesh and Related Matters*, (New Delhi, 16 May 1974). This text was published by the Bangladesh Government as *Act No.LXXIV of 1974* (Dacca, 1974); it was also reprinted in *The Daily Star* and *The Independent* (25 April 2001). For the text, the debate in the Indian parliament, the Bangladeshi constitutional amendment, and further correspondence, see Bhasin (ed.), *India-Bangladesh Relations*, IV, 1889–1901.

67 CR 3A-6/52 (8-53a).

68 CR 1B4-13/51 (9-53); cf. 'Purbobongo-Asham shimana shorip: bondho hoar karon shomporke Asham shorkarer biggopti,' *Azad* (18 April 1952). For similar quarrels in North Bengal, see CR 1B-39/51 (1-53).

69 CR 1A2-3/53 (3-54); cf. CR 3C1-1/53 (3-54), CR 3C2-2/52 (4-54). Today, this segment of the border remains undemarcated and disputed. In April 2001, in a violent clash near the village of Boroibari, claimed by both sides, 19 border guards (16 Indians and 3 Bangladeshis) were killed.

70 For cases on the 24-Parganas/Jessore border and the Tripura/Comilla border, see CR 1J1-1/51 (10-53); CR 11C1-4/53 (2-54). The 'Ground Rules' agreed by both states in 1959 sought to protect survey parties during their work. *Ground Rules Formulated by the Military Sub-Committee of the Indian and Pakistan Delegations* (20 October 1959), reprinted in Bhasin (ed.), *India-Bangladesh Relations*, V, 2735–742.

71 CR 1J1-1/51 (10-53).

72 See 'Tripura State Northern Boundary Report of Messrs Yule and Campbell of 1851', and various other border reports in: Sahadev Bikram-Kisor and Jagadis Gan-Chaudhuri (comp.), *Tripura: Historical Documents* (Calcutta: Firma KLM Private Limited, 1994), 41–85, passim. The Cooch Behar border (another Princely State/British Bengal segment) had been similarly demarcated with boundary pillars and ditches in 1934 (CR 1B2-3/53 (1-55); CR 1B2-28/52 (7-55)).

73 In 1950 the Chief Secretaries told the Directors of Land Records and Surveys of Tripura and East Bengal to go ahead with the demarcation but no progress was made. In 1953 a circular went out to district collectors to start on 'preliminary work to the demarcation' of the border between East Pakistan and Tripura State 'during this field season [= winter 1953–4].' The two main conflicts were over the Kar/Creed border between Sylhet and Tripura and over a piece of land along the railway tracks near Akhaura. In 1954 the Tripura authorities became nervous over district survey and settlement operation undertaken in Sylhet but were assured that these would not prejudice the demarcation of the border (CR 1I-3/51 (11-53); CR 11C1-4/53 (2-54); CR 31-146/51 (2-54); CR 3I-182/54 (1-55); CR 1B3-4/54 Pt 1 (1-55)). Cf. 'Talks on border demarcation,' *The Statesman* (27 April 1961).

74 In 1966 a maritime boundary demarcation agreement, including the Naf river border segment, was signed. In 1980 a land boundary demarcation agreement followed, and this incorporated the 1966 agreement. In 1998 a third treaty was signed. None of these was implemented. In 2001, Bangladeshi officials estimated that there were about 2,500 Nasaka (Burmese border guards) stationed along the border with Bangladesh. Azizul Haque, 'Bangladesh 1979: Cry for a Sovereign Parliament', *Asian Survey*, 20:2 (February, 1980), 228; 'Border tense as Myanmar continues to mass troops: Nasaka refuses to sign joint statement', *The Daily Star* (22 January 2001).

75 According to press reports, by late 2000, 56 Bangladeshi citizens had been killed by Burmese land mines. Mohammad Nurul Islam, 'Where landmines take a heavy toll', *The Independent* (28 May 1999); cf. Arshad Mahmud, 'Conference set to expose Burma's landmine menace', *South China Morning Post* (16 March 1999); 'Work on removal of land mines yet to start in Bandarban border', *The Independent* (20 January 2001).

76 'Bangladesh, Myanmar agree to remove trade barriers', *The Daily Star* (19 July 1999).

77 Despite 'negotiating a package of proposals for the last 10 years', the two states failed to make any progress. After the border clashes of 2001, they tried once more to set up a Joint Survey Commission. Meanwhile, Bangladeshi fishermen and woodcutters would cross the undemarcated border into Burma in considerable numbers. In 1999, Burma border guards captured at least 71 of them. 'Rohingya, border issues to dominate talks with Yangon: Myanmar PM arrives May 29', *The Independent* (21 May 2000); '71 Bangladeshis return from Myanmar,' *The New Nation* (20 May 2000); 'Flag meet held: Dhaka, Yangon agree to begin joint survey', *The New Nation* (21 January 2001); 'Border tense' (2001).

78 Even the most routinized and well-demarcated stretches may suddenly become the focus of conflict. For example, in 2001, in a remarkable divergence of interest between two levels of the Indian state, the government of the state of Meghalaya suddenly disagreed with the central government in Delhi about the validity of the 50-year-old demarcation of its international border with Bangladesh. The Meghalaya government informed the State Assembly that it considered the demarcation of the boundary with Bangladesh 'as "arbitrary", "unnatural" and "unrealistic" as it was drawn erroneously in 1950 during the time of the Assam Government.' This assertion occurred in the wake of a clash between border guards of India and Bangladesh at the border village of Pyrdiwah/Padua in April 2001. Both Delhi and Dhaka considered this village to be Bangladeshi territory that had been held in 'adverse possession' by India since 1971, but Meghalaya pronounced: 'Pyrdiwah is Indian territory and there will be no compromise on this stand.' 'No compromise on Pyrdiwah: Meghalaya', *The Assam Tribune* (27 June 2001).

79 *Treaty of Friendship, Cooperation and Peace between the Republic of India and the People's*

Republic of Bangladesh, Dacca, March 19, 1972. See Appadorai, *Selected Documents*, 434, or Bhasin (ed.), *India-Bangladesh Relations*, I, 29–32.

80 For example, when a river changes course, a flood washes away a border pillar, or local authorities declare a bit of land to be unlawfully occupied by the other country. At times the maritime border has been the most fiercely disputed one. In 1981 a territorial dispute erupted over the ownership of a newly emerged island in the oil- and gas-rich Bay of Bengal, on the West Bengal/ Bangladesh border. This island, variously named (South) Talpatti/ Talpatty/ New Moore/ Purbasha and thought to have surfaced in 1970, is situated in the estuary of the Haribhanga and Raimongol rivers, which forms the border. India discovered it in 1971 and claimed it; Bangladesh followed suit in 1978. In 1981, the presence of Indian surveyors on the island led to Bangladeshi gunboats entering the area. Soon the island became a focus of protest demonstrations and meetings in Bangladesh. India withdrew its presence and the two countries decided to resolve the dispute through exchange of data and, if necessary, a joint survey. No progress was made, however, and the issue continues to block any maritime boundary agreement between India and Bangladesh. On the land border see: 'India unilaterally puts up border pillar inside Bangladesh territory', *The Daily Star* (7 January 2002); 'BSF evicts Bangladeshis, occupies char: BDR denies occupation,' *The Independent* (9 January 2002); 'Bangladesh gets back 2,000 acres of land from India,' *The Independent* (23 November 2002); 'Assam land occupied by B'desh', *The Sentinel* (16 March 2002); 'Minister sore over Bangla territory claim', *The Telegraph* (3 October 2001); 'BDR-BSF exchange fire in Tetulia: Villagers flee', *The New Nation* (30 April 2003). On the maritime conflict, see Bhasin (ed.), *India-Bangladesh Relations*, IV, 2233–72; Golam Hossain, *General Zia and the BNP: Political Transformation of a Military Regime* (Dhaka: University Press Limited, 1988), 64, 98–9; *Border and Territorial Disputes* (Harlow: Longman Group, 1992 [3rd Ed.]), 426–7; Rahul Roy-Chaudhury, 'Trends in the Delimitation of India's Maritime Boundaries' (Delhi: Institute of Defense Studies and Analysis, 1998); S Kamaluddin, 'Slap in the middle of a row: Negotiations over the ownership of a tiny island strain relations between New Delhi and Dacca', *Far Eastern Economic Review*, 108:19 (2–8 May 1980), 38; Shakhawat Liton, 'Ensure South Talpatty's sovereignty: JS body asks navy', *The Daily Star* (22 September 2003).

81 A solution for the Muhuri conflict has been on the drawing board ever since 1974, when the two Prime Ministers signed an agreement that stated:

> Muhuri River (Belonia) Sector: The boundary in this area should be demarcated along the mid-stream of the course of the Muhuri River at the time of demarcation. This boundary will be a fixed boundary. The two Governments should raise embankments on their respective sides with a view to stabilising the river in its present course. (*Agreement* (1974) Article 1)

'Firing continues at Indo-Bangla border,' *Assam Tribune* (24 August 1999); 'BDR, BSF continue trading gunfire', *The New Nation* (24 August 1999); Sadeq Khan, 'Indian BSF Go Berserk', *Holiday* (27 Augustus 1999); Shaikh Nazrul Islam, 'Muhurirchar dispute: Border officials agree to draw line', *The Daily Star* (29 December 1999). For background, see also 'Unprovoked firing by Indian troops in Muhuri river area: Protest lodged with Tripura', *The Morning News* (30 June 1965); Jha, *Indo-Pakistan Relations*, 180–1; Surya P Sharma, *India's Boundary and Territorial Disputes* (Delhi: Vikas Publications, 1971), 121; Haque, 1980, 228; 'Dhaka objects to Delhi's embankment plan on Muhuri river: Erosion feared', *The Daily Star* (9 June 2003); Bhasin (ed.), *India-Bangladesh Relations*, I, 472.

82 *Radcliffian* issues are only one variant of postcolonial border issues in South Asia. There are at least two other major ones. The first have emerged from border-making exercises in the colonial period, well before Partition, the second from postcolonial warfare between India and Pakistan. These variants could be described as *McMahonian* and *Kashmirian*, respectively. The border between China and India in Arunachal Pradesh is really a 'Line of Actual Control' (LAC). Here a border (the McMahon Line) was established by the British in colonial times but not accepted by the Chinese. The 1,030 km line remains contested, undemarcated and 'imaginary' today. By contrast, the Kashmirian 'Line of Control' separating Indian-held and Pakistan-held Kashmir did not come into existence till well after Partition. Cf. 'Open Sino-Indian border worries Arunachal CM', *The Sentinel* (11 October 2002); 'Govt aware of LAC violations by Chinese army,' *The Assam Tribune* (25 July 2003); Manoj Joshi, 'Map interpretation leads to confusion', *The Times of India* (28 July 2003).

83 Other minor irritations that could easily develop into confrontations had to do with joint maintenance surveys of border pillars. These surveys were discontinued whenever Indian and Bangladeshi members of the team quarrelled over the location of these pillars. This was the case regarding a border pillar (No. 798) that was swept away by the Tista river in the late 1980s, leading to a new dispute between India and Bangladesh over who owned what part of Jharsingheswar *char* in that river. When India decided to impose its view, an international incident was hard to avoid. In 2002, however, India and Bangladesh were able to come to an agreement over this disputed land and Bangladesh gained possession. 'India unilaterally puts up border pillar inside Bangladesh territory', *The Daily Star* (7 January 2002); 'BSF evicts Bangladeshis, occupies char: BDR denies occupation', *The Independent* (9 January 2002); 'Bangladesh gets back 2,000 acres of land from India,' *The Independent* (23 November 2002).

84 CR 1B4-13/51 (9-53).

85 Cf. numerous reports in Indian and Bangladeshi newspapers in the weeks following 15 April 2001.

86 Photograph from *The Tribune* (22 April 2001).

87 For example, in October 2001, West Bengal Minister Kamal Guha discovered a 'sinister plot by Bangladesh' to take over four border villages (Chilahat, Nautari-Debottar, Borosari and Kajaldighi) in North Bengal and called on the Delhi authorities to 'thwart the evil designs of anti-India forces.' 'Minister sore over Bangla territory claim', *The Telegraph* (3 October 2001). In April 2003 the Directors of BSF and BDR met for a high-level Indo-Bangladesh border conference in Dhaka; they were taken by surprise when three border guards were injured in a gunfight over disputed land on the Tetulia/Phansidewa river border in North Bengal. In a remarkable development, the local commanders of BDR and BSF not only set out to resolve this dispute but, a few months later, could also report complete success. They agreed that the land belonged to Bangladesh and 'the BSF authority ... handed over the documents of land to the BDR authority in a simple function.' 'BDR-BSF exchange fire in Tetulia: Villagers flee', *The New Nation* (30 April 2003); 'Bangladesh regains 150 acres of land from India', *The Independent* (19 July 2003). In June 2003, a Bangladesh newspaper reported on three previously unknown cases of disputed territory along the Mathabhanga (Nadia/Kushtia) border. '233 bighas of land under Indian possession,' *The Independent* (28 June 2003).

88 'BSF intelligence inputs show that a good portion of the 2,200-km Indo-Bangla border in West Bengal is alive with disputes of "immense international ramifications", which in turn could have serious implications for diplomatic relations between the two states.'

Anupam Dasgupta, 'BSF top gun on recce for home truths', *The Telegraph* (10 March 2003).

89 Photograph by Zia Islam, 20 April 2001.

90 Brenner, 'Beyond State-Centrism?', 47.

91 International border disputes are not the only type of border dispute in the region. The aftermath of Partition also brought many, sometimes violent disputes over the internal borders of Northeast India. For background, see Bhubaneswar Bhattacharyya, *The Troubled Border: Some Facts About Boundary Disputes Between Assam-Nagaland, Assam-Arunachal Pradesh, Assam-Meghalaya and Assam-Mizoram* (Guwahati: Lawyer's Book Stall, 1995).

92 For the difference between an 'adolescent' and an 'adult' borderland, see Michiel Baud and Willem van Schendel, 'Toward a Comparative History of Borderlands', *Journal of World History*, 8:2 (1997), 224. See also chapter 13.

5

SECURING THE TERRITORY

The men who took charge of the new states dreaded invasion and subversion from across the border. How could they secure their national territory and control a border that was only vaguely known, partly disputed and largely unguarded? They simply lacked the tools to do the job. The top army man in East Pakistan complained that 'we had virtually nothing at all; not even any maps of East Pakistan', and the Premier of West Bengal decided that he needed to enlist village youths to guard the border.[1]

In this chapter I consider how men like these proceeded to overcome early fears of disintegration and annexation, and how they developed instruments to control and dominate the inhabitants of their borderland. Among these tools, I foreground bureaucratic control, paramilitary forces, homogenizing the borderland population and techniques for resolving interstate conflict.

I should make a note here about two main sources of information on which this chapter is based: government records and press reports. The political climate of the early post-Partition period was fiercely nationalist. The press in both Pakistan and India was crucial in setting the tone. It tended to present rumours as facts, analyse events in terms of communal (religious) categories, and nurture an image of the neighbouring country as untrustworthy and out to destroy one's own nation. The Indian Prime Minister's remarks about the Calcutta press could have applied just as easily to the East Pakistani press across the border: 'I find that the Calcutta press, or most of it, is functioning in a completely communal way and they have lost all sense of balance and proportion. Their objective is communal and so inevitably, their ways and methods tend to become communal.'[2]

The extensive correspondence between the governments of East Bengal and Assam, West Bengal and Tripura reveals that many officials shared the views aired in the press, and they were inclined to give credence to information that fitted these views. Still, it is often possible to distinguish factual information from propaganda because these files present multiple sources, contain much detail, and attest to the fact that the governments often agreed that the events covered in their correspondence actually had taken place. Nevertheless, the source material for this period has to be treated with considerable circumspection. In the following pages I first outline the volatile character of borderland society, with particular regard to worries over territorial sovereignty, and then turn to an account of the political instruments developed to secure the borderland.

One border, many nations

The Radcliffe line gave territorial shape to a national ambition: Pakistan. The movement for Pakistan had claimed that there were two nations in British India, Muslims and non-Muslims, and that each should have its share of power. This became known as the 'two-nations theory'. Pakistan was conceptualized in territorial terms, as a homeland, but the movement had never been consistent in what it imagined the territory of Pakistan to be, nor what its constitutional relation with the rest of ex-British India should be.[3] Consequently, when the Radcliffe decisions ('awards') were made public, the adherents of Pakistan viewed them as both a triumph and a bitter disappointment. The nation of Pakistan found territorial expression and sovereignty, but its territory was smaller than the 'viable' Pakistan for which they had hoped.[4] Thus, despite achieving his dream – the creation of a homeland for the Muslims of British India – MA Jinnah commented in a radio broadcast: 'It is an unjust, incomprehensible and even perverse award. It may be wrong, unjust and perverse; and it may not be a judicial but a political award, but we have agreed to abide by it and it is binding upon us.'[5]

In hindsight it may seem preordained that a two-nations theory would result in two states, India and Pakistan, but this was certainly not the only possible outcome of the struggle for Pakistan. Many people thought that a single federated state comprising both Pakistan and India was a distinct possibility while others dreamed of a combination of several independent Muslim states in addition to one independent India.[6] These visions turned out to be a *fata morgana*, and they evaporated rapidly in the face of the Radcliffe awards. The Pakistan that came into existence was strange enough. It was not territorially contiguous but consisted of two separate territories administered by a single state. Obviously Pakistan's strategies of territoriality were going to be highly complicated.

By giving territorial shape to one national ambition, the Radcliffe line defeated all other national ambitions. Most historians of decolonizing India have highlighted only one of these: the ambition to keep the former colony united under one state. Proponents of the 'one-nation theory' saw India as a single nation and they experienced a sense of acute loss when the territory was divided and they had to reconcile themselves to an India that fell short of their nationalist dreams. This is how the historian Mohammad Habib expressed the sentiment in his address to the Indian History Congress in December 1947:

> It is absolutely unnecessary to state that, so far as the historian of India is concerned, the country has always been one and indivisible, and will always continue to be so. The unity of India is one of the fundamental postulates of Indian moral consciousness, and the longing for centralised administration has been one of the most visible and persistent demands of the political spirits of the Indians throughout the ages.[7]

Initially many in India and Pakistan felt that Partition was so absurd that it could not possibly be sustainable. India's Prime Minister, Jawaharlal Nehru, gave voice to this feeling when he opined that 'Pakistan was bound to come back to us.'[8] This proved to be a serious miscalculation but the sense of loss was, and continues to be, real. It is felt by many inhabitants of the post-Partition states of South Asia, and is expressed well in the poem 'Denial' by Bangladeshi poet Taslima Nasrin:

> I want to wash away the ink stain of 47
> With water and soap.
> 47 – the word pricks like a thorn in my throat
> I do not want to swallow it.
> I want to vomit it out
> I want to regain the undivided soil of my forefathers…[9]

Although India's leaders had agreed to respect Pakistan's sovereignty, this was not the case for other Indian politicians. A notable voice was that of the All-India Hindu Mahasabha whose viewpoint was explained as follows by its president during a big conference in Calcutta in 1949:

> the Mahasabha's [Great Council's] mission [is] to protect Hindudom and its honour, and to restore Akhand Bharat [undivided India] … As a solution to the sufferings of Hindus in East Bengal, in view of the common factors between West Bengal and East Bengal, it is clearly in the interest of East Bengal to align with India. Failing this, India should demand cession of two or three border districts from East Bengal to rehabilitate their refugees there.[10]

By the early 1950s this remarkable plan to create a homeland for Hindus from East Bengal/ Pakistan in the southwestern corner of East Pakistan seemed to have died a natural death, so many were taken by surprise when it made a political comeback in the 1990s.[11]

Beside these two visions, however, there were many other territorial claims and visions. The two states that resulted from Partition had to contend not only with each other's frustrated territorial ambitions, but also with those of various groups that subscribed neither to the one-nation theory nor to the two-nation theory. For them, the 'day of rejoicing over Indian and Pakistani freedom' was one of 'mourning over disappointed territorial hopes.'[12] These groups started from a 'many-nations theory', the assumption that colonial India had contained more than two nations, and that each (or at least their own) was entitled to its own sovereign territory. They envisaged a South Asia of many smaller states. For India and Pakistan, securing their newly won territories and borders implied the necessity to destroy these competing territorial designs.

In the Bengal borderland, the state elites of India and Pakistan had to confront many such dreams. Most never developed beyond the level of a 'nation-of-intent' and withered away soon after the Radcliffe line was published, but some were to haunt politicians of the region for decades.[13] One of these was the dream of a separate state covering the mountainous areas of Northeast India, East Pakistan and Burma. This idea gained a boost from within the British colonial establishment in 1942 when the Governor of Assam launched a plan for a separate 'tribal' area in northeast India that could be retained as a British crown colony after the rest of India gained independence. This 'Reid Plan' was never a serious option in the subsequent Partition discussions but it continues to live on in debates about separate statehood in Northeast India.[14] Other territorial aspirations that cut across the new border were Adibashistan (which would unite Garo people across the Mymensingh-Garo Hills border), Rajasthan (which would do the same for Rajbongshi people living in Cooch Behar, Jalpaiguri and Rangpur), Swadhin Asom (an independent Assam), Greater Mizoram (uniting Mizos living in India, Burma and the Chittagong Hill Tracts of East Pakistan), and United Bengal.[15]

Over the years, some of these cross-border territorial schemes would fade away, only to be replaced by a host of other autonomy movements whose appeal to people in the borderland would wax and wane. Most of these were based on community identities: Rohingyas in Burma fought for a separate homeland;[16] Jummas in Bangladesh struggled for regional autonomy;[17] Mizos in India dreamed of a Greater Mizoram;[18] Garos and Khasis in Meghalaya took up arms;[19] and Koch and Rajbongshis in Northern Bengal claimed a state of their own called Kamtapur (Plate 5.1).[20]

Plate 5.1: Cross-border nationalism: 'We Want Kamata Land...! No Kamata No Rest...!'
At a rally in 2002, activists protest against the division of their 'Kam(a)tapur homeland'
between Bangladesh and three Indian states.[21]

Such insurgencies posed problems for the states concerned that went beyond
the mere maintenance of law and order and the crushing of competing local
nationalisms. They raised immediate fears concerning the territorial integrity
of the state and loss of control over the borderland, exposing it to possible
interference by the neighbouring state or sympathetic citizens from across the
border. Securing the territory required dealing effectively with such insurgencies
by way of either repression or cooptation. In this respect, all three states would
have quite a mixed track record: despite considerable militarization they each
lost control of parts of their borderland for years on end.[22]

Rumours of annexation

In the period after Partition the territorial boundaries of East Pakistan and
India seemed anything but inviolate. True, the top leaders had bound themselves
loyally to accept the territories awarded to them by the Boundary Commission
but there was much talk of invasion and annexation. To cite a few of many
examples, in 1948 strong rumours circulated in the eastern districts of East
Pakistan that Tripura was about to invade East Pakistan and occupy the huge
landed estate that the Maharaja of Tripura still owned there.[23] In September
1948, police arrested a man for spreading 'propaganda' in Sylhet town in East
Pakistan:

Benay Kumar Das (C.I.D. Const. of Assam) s/o Basanta Kumar Das of Jatarpur, Sylhet town, was found to circulate at Mirabazar in Sylhet town on 19.9.48 in presence of a gathering that Hyderabad had been occupied by the Dominion of India after having fought for only 3 days and that East Bengal would also be taken within 5 or 6 days by the Military stationed at Dawki (Assam). His propaganda caused panic and alarm amongst the public.[24]

In 1951 a Calcutta newspaper disclosed that 'the Pakistani Govt. is formulating a plan of conducting a Jehad [holy war] on Arakan, a Burmese territory, and wants to annexe this territory through its Mujahids by following the example of Kashmir Jehad.'[25] And in the same year, the District Magistrate of Dinajpur (Pakistan) wrote to his superiors in Dhaka:

Some [Hindus] are on the tiptoe of expectation that Dinajpur is going to be soon occupied by Bharati [Indian] Forces. One Muslim in the interior has been already advised to keep a pigtail by his Hindu friend so that he may escape annihilation by its help when occupation is completed in a few days' time. It appears that small Indian flags have been distributed secretly by agents from India. Two have been detected.[26]

Rumours of annexation were so widespread and persistent that the governments of India and Pakistan felt constrained to write in the Delhi Agreement of 1950 that they would: 'Not permit propaganda in either country directed against the territorial integrity of the other or purporting to incite war between them and [that they would] take prompt and effective action against any individual or organisation guilty of such propaganda.'[27]

The impact of such agreements seems to have been limited. Furious letters continued to fly back and forth between Dhaka and Calcutta denouncing press reports in the neighbouring country that were deemed 'objectionable, false and malicious', and demanding 'prompt and drastic action' against newspapers publishing such vile propaganda.[28] In October 1950, the government of West Bengal complained that 'influential people, including an Hon'ble Minister of East Bengal' were spreading propaganda that Dinajpur (West Bengal) would be incorporated into Pakistan, and that there had been 'an announcement by beat of drum' at the border that Balurghat was being included in East Dinajpur (Pakistan).[29] In its turn, East Bengal complained that West Bengal did nothing to stop speeches and pamphlets by firebrand politicians such as Shyama Prasad Mookherjee who questioned the 'territorial integrity of East Bengal' and urged the Indian government to consider war with Pakistan as a means of reunifying the subcontinent and protecting East Pakistan's Hindus.[30]

The tools of territorial control

The creation of an entirely new international border presented the new states with acute security problems. How to monitor a border of 4,000 km running through some of the most densely populated countryside in the world? And how to defend it, if necessary, at short notice and in an atmosphere of mutual hostility and suspense? The regular police force in the border districts had no experience in this work and new tools of territorial control had to be invented. These were broadly: 1) expanding the state bureaucracy; 2) creating state-supported paramilitary bodies; 3) homogenizing the borderland population; and 4) devising mechanisms of inter-state conflict resolution.

Expanding the state bureaucracy. Immediately after Partition state officials moved into the newly defined borderland to establish their hold over it. In districts that fell entirely within a single country, the local administrative structure was intact, although often some personnel had opted to emigrate.[31] However, the Radcliffe border ran right through many other districts, lopping off *thanas* and smaller territories and placing them in the neighbouring country. Here serious administrative problems cropped up since officials with experience of these areas could no longer reach them, and the new administrators had no access to the relevant office files in the district town, now in another country. A lengthy process of exchange of district and *thana* files and records was set in motion.[32]

The situation was most chaotic on the East Pakistan side of the border, where the bureaucracy was in disarray because it had been cut off from the old capital, Calcutta, and had to create a new centralized state structure from scratch. In August 1947,

the new East Pakistan government was hastily housed in a College for Girls [Eden College in Dhaka[33]], with a large number of improvised bamboo sheds added to it for greater accommodation ... On partition, East Pakistan received only one member of the former Indian Civil Service who belonged to that region. Six others were hastily promoted from the Provincial Civil Service...'[34] An official publication described the predicament in heroic terms: 'For the many directorates there was no accommodation at all and these were sent to outlying districts. One Minister sat in a boat on the Buriganga river, disposing of files and transacting official business. Hundreds of officers chummed together in ramshackle tenements. Even camps were a luxury and bamboo constructions sprang up to provide shelters for officials and staff who were used to comfortable Calcutta flats and rooms.'[35]

Clearly, for a fledgling state bureaucracy trying to spread its wings over a large territory, the administration of the borderland was a huge problem. The immediate worry was to protect the borders from invasion. The General Officer Commanding (East Bengal), who arrived in January 1948, later reminisced:

> The provincial government ... was newly formed and poorly staffed. But worse still, it was politically weak and unstable. There was no army. All we had in East Pakistan at the time of Independence were two infantry battalions [one with three and one with only two companies]. We had very poor accommodation: at Headquarters there was no table, no chair, no stationery – we had virtually nothing at all; not even any maps of East Pakistan.[36]

So the borders had to be protected by the police. The armed police force in East Pakistan was about 60,000 men strong. It was disaffected and not very effective.[37] For these men, border service was just one of many duties; they were needed to establish a semblance of state control all over East Pakistan, which at the time had a population of over 42 million. The state was acutely alive to the fact that it needed more manpower if it was to establish a monopoly of violence. In its first year, it created a new army corps, the East Bengal Regiment, and a paramilitary police force, the East Pakistan Rifles (EPR).[38] The state power holders considered the grip of the armed police on the borderland to be hardly adequate. In 1957, in a spectacular attempt to curb widespread smuggling, the Pakistan army, navy and air force were given jurisdiction over a ten-mile belt all along the East Pakistan border.[39] During this campaign the armed forces set aside civil law and ruled by terror.[40] When in 1958 the campaign came to an end, the East Pakistan Rifles took over the border duties that the police had shouldered during the first years of Pakistan. After the birth of Bangladesh, the Rifles continued as the new country's border guards, now under the new name of the Bangladesh Rifles (BDR).

Administrative dislocation was less severe on the Indian side of the border. The capitals of Bengal, Assam and Tripura all fell to India. The chief problem here was one of communication between the northeastern region and the rest of India – only a narrow strip of Indian territory, squeezed between Nepal and East Pakistan and quickly dubbed the 'chicken's neck', allowed land transport. Railway lines and river routes between Assam and West Bengal now ran through East Pakistan, creating a host of strategic and administrative problems. For example, during a trip to Assam in 1948, the Chief Minister of West Bengal drafted a plan for a volunteer militia and sent the details by mail to Calcutta. However, his personal assistant forgot to put an airmail label on the letter so it was sent by rail. The assistant suddenly recalled that a portion of the rail route ran though Pakistan territory: 'The envelope, I thought, was bound to attract the attention of [the] Pakistani censor and the secret document would be known to them.' After rummaging through the mail at the post office, the envelope was found and dispatched by air.[41]

Control of the Indian side of the border, just as on the Pakistan side, was put largely in the hands of the police, backed up by border militias run by the different states of India (e.g., the Assam Rifles, Tripura State Rifles, West Bengal Rifles).[42] It was not until 1965 that these were replaced by an all-India border force, the Border Security Force (BSF).[43]

Soon after Partition hundreds of small camps sprang up all along the border. Known as border outposts (or BOPs), these were manned by perhaps 20 armed men who would patrol a stretch of border line.[44] At first these were poorly trained policemen but gradually they were supplanted by more specialized forces. Even so, it took almost twenty years before border security was put into the hands of professional border guards on both sides of the border. Since then, the East Pakistan/Bangladesh Rifles (BDR) and the (Indian) Border Security Force (BSF) have been facing each other across the border line.[45]

Border guards were not the only state personnel in the borderland. Many other branches of the state bureaucracy were visible, each playing its role in territorial control as well as in orientating the borderland population to the state apparatus to which they had been assigned. Of these branches, the customs department was most directly concerned with border matters but customs personnel were found only in a few localities along the border where cross-border traffic was officially allowed. We will see that in these places border guards and customs officials belonging to the same state often developed an antagonistic relationship with each other.

The role of customs personnel in controlling the flow of people and goods increased significantly in 1952 when the states of India and Pakistan agreed to introduce a system of passports and visas (Plate 5.2). Although before there had been restrictions regarding goods and money that could be taken across the border, people could move freely between East Pakistan and India (unlike West Pakistan and India, where travel had been restricted from 1948[46]). The new system was a rather useful tool for securing the borderland. It allowed the states not only to monitor (some) cross-border traffic but also to remove from their part of the borderland citizens from across the border who had entered the territory without authorization.[47]

Plate 5.2: States controlling their borders. India-Pakistan conference on the introduction of the passport and visa system, Karachi, May 1952.[48]

State-supported paramilitary bodies.   Initially the states simply did not have the capability to secure their territories by means of their own personnel. Surveillance and control of the borderland in particular were a constant headache. Among their populations there were, however, many who were willing to serve the state on ideological grounds. It was not long before the states began to use this resource. In doing so, they built on earlier models of mobilizing paramilitary manpower, both by the colonial state and by the anti-colonial movements.[49] In this section, I focus on the situation on the East Pakistan side of the borderland, making shorter references to parallel developments in the neighbouring Indian states.

A few months after Partition, the East Pakistan authorities decided to set up a government-sponsored paramilitary organization named the Ansars.[50] Membership of the Ansars was 'entirely honorary and voluntary, and open to all Pakistanis between 18 and 48 years of age.'[51] In early 1948 the Prime Minister of Pakistan chaired a select meeting on national security in Karachi. The second item on the agenda was the question of raising a 'volunteer corps for assistance in the maintenance of law and order'. The Chief Secretary of East Bengal proudly announced that 'in his province it was intended to enroll 1,50,000 men in the Ansar organization, of whom 15,000 would be trained in the use of arms, so that they could be embodied, when necessary, in the Police at a later stage. He said that at the present there was a large body of men willing to serve the State.'[52] Indeed, the organization grew rapidly and by early 1949 there were 118,000 Ansars, almost half of them trained in the use of firearms. The force was financed by public subscriptions and a government grant.[53]

The Ansars were organized along military lines. The unit of organization was the platoon, consisting of a platoon commander, his assistant and thirty members. The aim was to create 100 platoons in each subdivision (two or more subdivisions made up a district in East Pakistan). Ansars were recruited especially in the borderland.[54] Here they were used to prevent the smuggling of jute and other 'controlled' commodities, act as the eyes and ears of the district authorities, check emigrants at border railway stations lest they take valuables out of the country unlawfully, make occasional cross-border raids, and construct border roads.[55] They soon earned a reputation for intimidation and hooliganism, especially with regard to the non-Muslim inhabitants of East Pakistan. Whenever the border police faced staff shortages, Ansars would be 'embodied' and would serve in the border outposts.[56] The Ansars became the largest and most active armed volunteer corps in East Pakistan.[57]

On the other side of the border the Indian states employed exactly the same strategy. In March 1948, the West Bengal state formed an armed vigilante group known as the Bangiya Jatiya Rakshi Bahini (West Bengal National Volunteer Force):

The Premier [of West Bengal] received disturbing reports particularly from Nadia and some other border districts which set him thinking seriously about the need for raising a para-military force composed of village youths for guarding the border ... The West Bengal Cabinet passed the scheme which marked the opening of the Chandmari training centre, 39 miles away from Calcutta, to train village youths in defence operations. Within a year four batches of volunteers numbering nearly 2,500 completed their training.[58]

West Bengal also had its volunteer Home Guards, as did Assam and Bihar.[59] The Tripura volunteer militia was known as the Kirit Bikram Bahini.[60] Although these groups differed from the Ansars and from each other in how they were organized, they provided the same services to the state and became just as notorious among borderland Muslims.

Homogenizing the borderland population. Both states used a third tool of borderland territorial control to great effect. Creating bodies of armed men all along the border made it possible to defend the territory but did not necessarily win the hearts and minds of borderlanders. However, such armed bodies enabled the state to plan and carry out new policies of surveillance, intimidation and homogenization of the borderland population. These took various forms, from selective disarming to 'pathological homogenization' and ethnic cleansing.[61]

So far the historical literature has largely ignored the violence of nation-building in the borderland. But it is not undocumented, nor forgotten, and can still be analysed.[62] Here I will touch briefly on two of its aspects.

Disarming the enemy within.   In spite of the lofty promises and intentions expressed by the leaders of India and Pakistan, those who were labelled as members of the 'minorities' in either country were often perceived and treated as internal enemies.[63] Thus Muslims on the Indian side of the border and non-Muslims on the Pakistan side of the border were widely assumed to be disloyal to the new state and possible agents of the neighbouring one. Life became tough for them, not only because of local majority resentment and discrimination, but also because of state policies aimed at weakening their position. For example, although the East Pakistan government denied it vehemently, it had a clear policy of disarming Hindus in the border areas. A circular letter of 1948 instructed district officials: 'All arms requisitioned from Muslims … should be restored to original licensees. 75% of the arms held by Hindus in your district should be forthwith requisitioned .. Disarm all Hindus except big landlords, commercial concerns or other reliable Zamindars [in the border subdivisions]… .12 bore guns should be retained for the training and use of the Ansars … All other guns should be re-issued to deserving Muslim licensees.'[64] On the Indian side of the border, Muslims were being treated in the same way.[65]

Removing the minorities.   Disarming was often a prelude to removal. On either side of the border, intimidation easily turned into active expulsion. Sometimes it was the local population who took the initiative but quite often the push came from refugees from across the border who were looking for land and revenge. In many cases they were able to win tacit or open state support in targeting the borderland minorities.[66] Such expulsions occurred in all sectors of the borderland over a long period of time, and they were often interlinked with events across the border.[67] The fate of Muslims in India and Hindus in Pakistan became a central theme in the propaganda campaigns of both states, and it is often difficult to distinguish clearly between facts, rumours, exaggerations and fabrications.

In West Bengal, where many felt that it was 'desirable that the frontier tracts of West Bengal should be inhabited by sturdy Hindus', expulsion of Muslims to East Pakistan occurred in waves.[68] For example, in 1948 the Indian nationalist stalwart Sardar Patel gave a thunderous speech in faraway Nagpur (Central India). He demanded that Pakistan stop driving out its minorities or else be prepared to give enough territory to settle those uprooted people.[69] The next day the District Magistrate of West Dinajpur (West Bengal, India) ordered Muslim landlords to vacate their houses to make room for Hindu refugees.[70] In other parts of the West Bengal borderland (e.g. Murshidabad, 24-Parganas, Cooch Behar[71]), Muslims were reportedly 'asked to get out of their homes and find shelter inland leaving the border free for the police and for Hindus imported from the interior.'[72] When this news crossed the border, it led to reverse expulsion of Hindus from East Pakistan to West Bengal.

Such involvement by Indian officials in the expulsion of Muslims from the borderland is a recurring theme. In April 1950, Tripura officials were instrumental in the burning of Kamalpur town and the killing and driving out of its Muslim population.[73] In 1951 the Tripura government started requisitioning land owned by Tripura Muslims in the border area in order to settle Hindus who had fled there from East Pakistan.[74] In the same year government pressure on Muslims in the border areas of Assam increased, and many were compelled to flee to East Pakistan.[75] In West Bengal (India), the Progressive Workers of Nadia published a pamphlet that stated:

In 1950 the flame of communal passion rose high, as a result of a conspiracy of communalists in the two Bengals; oppression and atrocities were let loose in both Bengals and hundreds of thousands of refugees fled away from their hearths and homes in panic ... As soon as the refugees from East Bengal reached the Nadia border, a section of influential communalists oppressed in many ways the Muslim peasants of Nadia and drove out about two hundred thousand of them. In this connection it must be admitted that after Partition a section of Congress leaders and workers became communal minded. Their attitude towards Indian Muslims is extremely inimical ... The number of communally minded Government officials in Nadia is also not negligible. There is a complaint that many Government officials of Nadia were directly or indirectly involved with various communal troubles.[76]

East Pakistan officials were just as often, if not more frequently, accused of expelling non-Muslims from *their* side of the borderland. There is considerable evidence of Pakistani efforts at building up 'natural' borders.[77] The violent expulsion of large numbers of Bengali Hindus from the East Pakistan borderland is best known because we have much evidence on the long drawn-out exodus of Hindus from East Pakistan.[78] The fate of other groups is much less well known, and I take an example from one such group. The Hajongs, non-Bengali Hindus of northern Mymensingh, had been involved in a tenants' uprising from before Partition. The Pakistan state came down heavily on this movement, pushed most Hajongs across the border, and argued that almost all who fled across the borders are of communist mentality and have been involved in anti-State activities. This explains why we cannot allow such men to be rehabilitated on the borders. Besides, their houses and properties are now in possession of the [Muslim] refugees from Assam ... We cannot throw these poor Assam refugees on the road to make room for Hajongs and Banais of communist and anti-State predilections.[79]

It was not only the partitioned states of India and Pakistan that implemented policies of removing from their borderland minorities of uncertain loyalty to the state. Burma did the same. The Rohingyas (a Muslim minority group living in the Arakan borderland) were considered of doubtful loyalty to the Burmese state, partly because some of them had sought to incorporate northern Arakan into East Pakistan.[80] In 1948, armed operations were carried out and hundreds of villages were 'put to the torch and thousands were mercilessly killed, triggering a massive refugee exodus to the then Pakistan.'[81] The East Pakistan authorities welcomed these refugees as *mohajirs* (Islamic refugees) and, according to press reports, planned to build them kolkhoz-like model villages, which never materialized.[82] This was only the first of continual attempts by the Burmese authorities to deny the Rohingyas citizenship and push them across the border, leading to repeated waves of refugees into Bangladesh.[83]

In India, Pakistan and Burma, removing minorities from the border regions was never a publicly stated policy. The fact that all three states used it to improve their hold on their borderlands shows, however, that it made perfect sense as a tool to extend state control. Ideological legitimations were perhaps less significant than reasons of state: consolidating territorial power by creating 'natural borders' and fashioning demographic homogeneity where none had existed before.[84]

There is no reason to assume that officials in the borderland were more communal (anti-minority) in their attitudes than their colleagues in the capital. They were often ordered to carry out discriminatory policies. But they also worked in an environment of ruptured communities, flows of refugees, border incidents and fears of invasion and war. Many must have seen themselves as soldiers on the state's frontline: reports from the border often evinced an intensity of purpose, pride and concern that was less noticeable in the debonair communications of top-level bureaucrats in the (provincial) capital. In the borderland, the state's shibboleths were taken more seriously: embattled officials found order, clarity, security and guidance in them.

The examples above highlight the active role taken by officials, high and low, in homogenizing border populations. More often, perhaps, they acted surreptitiously, by taking no notice of minority appeals for protection, looking the other way when minorities were being discriminated or attacked, or siding with co-religionist immigrants against local minorities. Nor were states always consistent in these policies; in 1964 the East Pakistan police even installed loudspeakers on the border to persuade Garo refugees to return from India.[85]

Inter-state conflict resolution. A fourth tool for controlling the borderland – in addition to bureaucratic expansion, state-sponsored vigilante groups, and homogenizing the population – was conflict management. Soon after Partition, the new states evolved techniques to minimize inter-state conflict in the borderland. These techniques have been generally overlooked in the historiography of Pakistan and India, which has focused more on antagonistic rhetoric, unfriendly acts, mutual obstruction and territorial discontinuities. In the borderland, things often looked different. Borderland officials probably had more regular contact with counterparts of the neighbouring state than any of their colleagues in the state bureaucracy. They had to devise ways of dealing with these counterparts across the border, and they did. At times they were at odds with their own superiors for doing so, and at times they pushed their superiors to resolve border conflicts at inter-state meetings.

There were three main forms of borderland conflict management: joint enquiries, border meetings and border ceremonies. As we will see, the border was never quiet, and officials were constantly being apprised of 'incidents'. Many of these required no more action on the part of the borderland official than to inform his superior,[86] write a strongly worded letter to his counterpart across the border, or make a site visit. But if lives were lost or the incident was deemed serious for other reasons, a joint enquiry was held at the spot by officials of the two districts sharing the border. By 1950, the procedure to be followed in joint enquiries was formalized. All persons living on the border were 'advised to lodge information regarding any border incident with the nearest thana, Circle Officer or Officer-in-Charge of the Border Police outpost' who would report it to the District Magistrate (DM). On receipt of this information the DM would depute an assistant to hold a 'preliminary local enquiry' based on witness accounts and send 'the statement of the case to his opposite number across the border, who would also have had ready in most cases a similar report from officers on his side of the border.' Then the two DMs would depute officials of equal rank to hold a local joint enquiry at the place of the incident and examine all witnesses together. On the basis of this report the two DMs would meet at the place of the incident and 'try to come to a Joint agreed finding as to the facts of the case.' If there was disagreement on one or more points, they should make recommendations including whether 'further enquiry at a higher level would be desirable. In every case, however, they should devise and put into operation measures necessary to prevent the occurrence of such incidents.'[87]

Clearly, the joint enquiry was a sophisticated bureaucratic procedure for assessing and controlling border incidents. But whereas joint enquiries dealt with individual incidents, border meetings were often concerned with a large number of issues.[88] For example, a two-day meeting of top officials of the districts of Murshidabad (India) and Kushtia and Rajshahi (Pakistan) was held at Rajshahi in 1949. They discussed the cases of a boat being fired on and the killing of a boatman on the border river, the taking away of 24 buffaloes from a disputed border *chor*, and the removal of paddy, jute and corrugated iron sheets from another island. On the second day, the company proceeded to a disputed area and decided that it 'may be left alone to be cultivated by those who possess land on the island, the latter being free to sow, reap and carry away paddy to whichever areas or districts they belong, either Murshidabad, or Kushtia or Nadia, and police on either side would neither enter nor interfere with the life of the island.'[89] In addition they decided that, if police action was needed on the island, only a *joint* Indo-Pakistan police would be allowed to act.

So what we have here is a number of district officials taking decisions regarding the territorial reach of their states that went far beyond what their states' top brass were willing to countenance: freedom for cultivators to take their produce to either state territory, a stand-off between the police forces of the two sides over a disputed area, and even the impromptu creation of a local cross-border police force.[90] The state certainly acted differently at the border.

A third instrument was the public border ceremony, intended to ease the transfer of disputed territory from one state to the other. Since such transfers were rare, this type of political theatre was performed only very occasionally. In March 1951 India and Pakistan agreed to exchange two disputed areas (Jaynagar and Bhatupara-Betai on the Kushtia/ Nadia border). Under joint supervision of the Commissioners of the Presidency Division (India) and the Rajshahi Division (Pakistan), the changeover was accompanied by the raising of flags, salutes by armed guards, prayers and nationalist speeches.[91] In this case, however, the festive ceremony failed to ease the inherent tensions. The Hindu inhabitants of Jaynagar village, which was transferred to Pakistan, left for India with all their moveable possessions and they demolished everything that they could not take with them. This was witnessed by all participants in what had been intended as a ritual of conflict resolution but instead led to new conflict and resentment.[92]

Conclusion: The borderland secured

The states that came into existence in August 1947 shared a borderland that was anything but natural to them, and that was very difficult to control and defend. In this chapter I have surveyed how the states worked to make the border a strategic, political and social reality. Burma figures less prominently in this survey than India and (East) Pakistan. There are two main reasons: the Burmese state was plunged into civil war and took much longer to gain control of its borderland, and even for the more recent period information on the Burmese state's policies regarding its relatively short border stretch with East Pakistan/Bangladesh is quite limited.

From shaky beginnings, the post-Partition states of India and Pakistan were able to establish considerable control over their shared borderland. Early worries of invasion and annexation faded into the background and a combination of instruments of control turned out to be reasonably successful. Importantly, the two states reinforced each other in the borderland. Although the exact location of the border was sometimes a bone of contention and relations between India and Pakistan were often strained, both states shared an interest in dominating the border population, controlling the cross-border movement of goods and people, and making borderlanders committed to the nation. Their very antagonism made the job easier. Every attempt at state surveillance and control on one side of the border could be used to tie inhabitants on the other side more closely to their own state. Every attempt at official nation-building implied a slur on the nation in the neighbouring state, thereby strengthening its appeal across the border (in chapter 12 we will look more closely at nation-building in the borderland). Securing the border territory became easier as the cruder forms of homogenizing the population became less noticeable and ways of resolving border conflict developed. Routines for dealing with border incidents became well established and contributed to the normalization of state rule in the borderland.

Both Pakistan and India were largely successful in their strategies to secure the borderland. They were able to do so because district officials, in their pursuit of border stability, often quietly employed practices of cooperation and conflict management that contrasted with the confrontational policies that have so far been highlighted in the historiography of relations between these two states. But states were not the only players in the borderland and at times they were not even the major ones. The following chapters take a closer look at how others played their roles in the fashioning of the borderland.

Notes

1 Mohammed Ayub Khan, who was General Officer Commanding (East Bengal) and arrived in January 1948, later emerged as President of Pakistan. Mohammed Ayub Khan, *Friends Not Masters* (London: Oxford University Press, 1967), 22; Saroj Chakrabarty, *With Dr. B.C. Roy and Other Chief Ministers (A Record upto 1962)* (Calcutta: Benson's, 1974), 118–19.

2 Jawaharlal Nehru in a letter to the Chief Minister of West Bengal, May 1950. Chakrabarty, *With Dr. B.C. Roy*, 170.

3 According to Ayesha Jalal: '[F]rom first to last, Jinnah avoided giving the demand [for "Pakistan"] a precise definition, leaving the League's followers to make of it what they wished. A host of conflicting shapes and forms, most of them vague, were given to what remained little more than a catch-all, an undefined slogan.' Jalal argues that Jinnah could do little else in view of the conflicting aspirations of Muslim Leaguers from Muslim-majority and non-Muslim-majority provinces in British India and his concern to act as spokesmen for all of them. Ayesha Jalal, *The Sole Spokesman: Jinnah, the Muslim League and the Demand for Pakistan* (Cambridge: Cambridge University Press, 1985), 4, 119.

4 Mansergh (editor-in-chief), *The Transfer of Power, 1942–7: Constitutional Relations between Britain and India*, Vol. VII, 124. For the Muslim League's claims before the Bengal Boundary Commission, see Joya Chatterji, 'The Fashioning of a Frontier: The Radcliffe Line and Bengal's Border Landscape, 1947–52,', *Modern Asian Studies*, 33:1 (1999), 197–201; cf. A. Tayyeb, *Pakistan: A Political Geography* (London: Oxford University Press, 1966), 107–10.

5 Chaudhri Muhammad Ali, *The Emergence of Pakistan* (New York & London: Columbia University Press, 1967), 221.

6 One such attempt was the plan for an independent Muslim state in northeastern Bihar, put forward by the Bihar Provincial Muslim League in a pamphlet entitled *Divide Bihar* (1947). See Papiya Ghosh, 'Partition's Biharis', *Comparative Studies of South Asia, Africa and the Middle East*, 17:2 (1997), 23. Such plans may be dormant for a long time, only to be revived by a new generation. Indian intelligence sources reported the revival of this idea in the 1990s, in the form of a 'Muslimstan' covering northeastern Bihar, Dinajpur and Rangpur. Ranabir Samaddar, *The Marginal Nation: Transborder Migration from Bangladesh to West Bengal* (New Delhi, etc.: Sage Publications, 1999), 185.

7 Quoted in Shahid Amin, *Alternative Histories: A View from India* (Calcutta: Centre for Studies in Social Sciences/South-South Exchange Programme for Research on the History of Development (SEPHIS), 2002), 5–6.

8 Quoted in Leonard Mosley, *The Last Days of the British Raj* (London: Weidenfeld and Nicolson, 1961), 77.

9 The full text of the poem is as follows:

> *India was no discarded paper that you had to tear to bits.*
> *I want to erase the word 47 with rubber*
> *I want to wash away the inkstain of 47*
> *With water and soap.*
> *47 – the word pricks like a thorn in my throat*
> *I do not want to swallow it.*
> *I want to vomit it out*
> *I want to regain the undivided soil of my forefathers.*
> *I want Brahmaputra as much as I want Subarnarekha.*
> *I want Sitakunda Hills as much as Kanchenjungha.*
> *Srimangal as much as Jalpaiguri.*
> *I want the sal forests of Bihar*
> *As well as Ajanta and Ellora*
> *If Curzon Hall is mine, Fort William belongs to me too.*
> *That man who thrashed away the two-nation theory*
> *He can never accept defeat at the hands of 47.*

From Taslima Nasreen, *Ay kosto jhēpe, jiban debo mepe* (1994), translated by Subhoranjan Dasgupta and quoted in Ranabir Samaddar (ed.), *Reflections on Partition in the East* (Delhi: Vikas Publishing House, 1997), 210.

10 Government of East Bengal, Home Department (Political), *Note on the Genesis of Communal Disturbances in West Bengal* (Dacca: East Bengal Government Press, 1950), 1, 1920 (CR 5R-1/50 (1-53b); cf CR 1I-12/50 (3-53)); cf. 'Khare Defines Mahasabha's Political Creed: Ideology of Cultural State Explained,' *The Statesman* (26 December 1949); Amalendu De, *Swadhin Bangabhumi Gathaner Parikalpana* (Calcutta: Ratna Prakashan, 1975); Chatterji, 'The Fashioning,' 204n.

11 The idea was revived when Hindutva organizations in India started campaigning for a 'Swadhin Bangabhumi' (Independent Bengal), to be carved out of Bangladesh, calling forth sharp reactions from both nationalist and Islamist politicians in Bangladesh. The 'Bangasena' (Bengal Army), an organization established in India in 1982, resumed activities in 2002. Its leader, Kalidas Baidya, summarized its aims as follows: 'We are preparing ourselves to capture six districts of Bangladesh situated on the west bank of the Padma river and create a homeland for Hindus who have fled from there to India ... We want that the six districts of the country, namely, Khulna, Faridpur, Jessore, Kushtia, Barisal and Potuakhali, be announced as an independent country.' The new country was to be named Bangabhumi and its capital Samanta Nagar. In 2003, the international general secretary of the Vishwa Hindu Parishad (VHP) put it like this: 'Capture one or two districts in Bangladesh, acquire space and send these infiltrators there.' Soon after, a group in West Bengal declared a provisional 'Hindu Republic of Bir Bangla' with a putative capital of Shaktigarh situated in the Chittagong Hill Tracts, from which the 'interim government' would launch a 'liberation struggle'. At the same time, the idea of occupying Bangladeshi territory by means of 'coercive diplomacy' was advocated by the Delhi-based society Astha Bharati. In June 2003, Gobina Bala, convenor of Bangasena in Jalpaiguri claimed another six districts from Bangladesh: Khulna, Faridpur, Jessore, Barisal, Potuakhali and Mymensingh. See 'India-Bangladesh Border: Dangerous Situation,' *Economic and Political Weekly* (30 March 1991); 'Khaleda Wants India To Hand Over "Bangabhumi Terrorists"', *The Independent* (23 March 1999); 'Editorial: Sense and Nonsense', *The Daily Star* (24 March 1999); Haroon Habib, '"Swadhin Bangabhumi" Issue Causes Concern in Dhaka', *The Hindu* (26 March 1999); Monobina Gupta, 'RSS seeks Bangla refugees' state', *The Telegraph* (18 March 2002); 'Regrouped Bangasena threatens war against jihad', *The Telegraph* (24 November 2002); Avijit Sinha, 'Bangasena sounds battle bugle', *The Telegraph* (25 November 2002); 'Send all infiltrators to a space in Bangladesh', *The Shillong Times* (20 January 2003); Aloke Banerjee, 'Hindu republic "born" in Bangladesh', *The Times of India* (12 February 2003); '"Bangasena" march towards Bangladesh: 200[0] held in W. Bengal', *The New Nation* (20 February 2003); '"Bangla land must for rehabilitation"', *The Assam Tribune* (23 February 2003); 'Bengali Hindus demand part of Bangladesh', *The Sentinel* (9 June 2003).

12 As the last Viceroy of India feared the moment of Partition might be remembered. See HV Hodson, *The Great Divide: Britain – India – Pakistan* (New York: Atheneum, 1971).

13 For the concept of 'nation-of-intent', see Mikael Gravers, 'The Karen Making of a Nation', in Stein Tønnesson and Hans Antlöv (eds.), *Asian Forms of the Nation* (London: Curzon Press, 1996), 237–69.

14 The plan, which built on ideas that JH Hutton, the deputy commissioner for the Naga Hills, had first presented to the Simon Commission that toured India in 1928–9, is variously known as the Reid Plan (after Sir Robert Reid, Governor of Assam), the

Coupland Plan (after Prof. Reginald Coupland, advisor to the Cabinet Mission), or the Crown Colony Scheme. It envisaged a territory comprising mountainous areas in present-day Bangladesh (Chittagong Hill Tracts), Burma (Chin and Kachin areas) and India (Arunachal Pradesh, Nagaland, Manipur, Mizoram, Meghalaya, Tripura and mountainous areas of Assam). Mansergh (editor-in-chief), *The Transfer of Power*, Vol. I, 649; Ashikho-Daili-Mao, *Nagas: Problems and Politics* (New Delhi: Ashish Publishing House, 1992), 31. Some British officials who chose to stay on as officials of the West Bengal administration after 1947 supported similar plans. When the government found out that two of them were 'fomenting discontent among the hill men of Darjeeling against the new state of West Bengal ... they had to be posted elsewhere.' Chakrabarty, *With Dr. B.C. Roy*, 45.

15 On Adibashistan, see Plt. 2P-23/47 (9-49); on Rajasthan, see Ranajit Das Gupta, *Economy, Society and Politics in Bengal: Jalpaiguri 1869–1947* (Delhi: Oxford University Press, 1992), 238, 253-255; on Swadhin Asom, see Udayon Misra, *The Periphery Strikes Back: Challenges to the Nation-State in Assam and Nagaland* (Shimla: Indian Institute of Advanced Studies, 2000), 80–104; on Greater Mizoram, see Malabika Das Gupta, 'Nationalities, Ethnicity and Cultural Identity: A Case Study of the Mizos of Tripura', in: B Pakem (ed.), *Nationality, Ethnicity and Cultural Identity in North-East India* (New Delhi: Omsons, 1990), 369–74. On the United Bengal plan, see Joya Chatterji, *Bengal Divided: Hindu Communalism and Partition, 1932–1947* (Cambridge: Cambridge University Press, 1995), 259–65.

16 On Rohingyas (or Bengali-speaking Muslim Rakhaing living in northern Arakan state of Burma), see for example Martin Smith, *Ethnic Groups in Burma: Development, Democracy and Human Rights* (London: Anti-Slavery Society, 1994), 54–7; Martin Smith, 'Sold down the river: Burma's Muslim Borderland,' *Inside Asia* (July–August 1986), 5–7; *Rohingya Reader* (Amsterdam: Burma Centrum Nederland, 1995), 2 volumes; Abdur Razzaq and Mahfuzul Haque, *A Tale of Refugees: Rohingyas in Bangladesh* (Dhaka: The Centre for Human Rights, 1995); and *The Newsletter Monthly, News & Views of the Rohingya Solidarity Organisation Arakan (Burma)* (published from Chittagong, Bangladesh, in the 1990s).

17 On the Jumma autonomy movement, see e.g. Siddhartho Chakma, *Proshongo: Parbotyo Chottogram* (Calcutta: Nath Brothers, 1392 BE [1985–6]); Willem van Schendel, 'The Invention of the "Jummas": State Formation and Ethnicity in Southeastern Bangladesh', *Modern Asian Studies*, 26:1 (1992); Amena Mohsin, *The Politics of Nationalism: The Case of the Chittagong Hill Tracts, Bangladesh* (Dhaka: University Press Limited, 1997).

18 On Mizo irredentism, the ambition to create a Greater Mizoram combining parts of Northeast India, Bangladesh and Burma, see Malabika Das Gupta, 'Greater Mizoram Issue and Tripura,' *Economic and Political Weekly*, 21 (13 September 1986), 1629–30; MS Prabhakar, 'Ferment in Manipur,' *Frontline*, 6:1 (1989), 32–9; Vumson, *Zo History, with an introduction to Zo culture, economy, religion and their status as an ethnic minority in India, Burma, and Bangladesh* (Aizawl: author, n.d. [c. 1992]). After the Mizo movement made its peace with Delhi, the Bru National Liberation Front would be formed to fight for autonomy for the Bru (Riang) inhabitants of Mamit district (Mizoram). See 'Bru team returns without meeting BNLF militants', *The Assam Tribune* (26 April 2000).

19 E.g. the A'chik National Volunteers' Council (ANVC; see e.g. *The Assam Tribune* (19 July 1999)) and the Hynneiwtrep National Liberation Council (HNLC; see e.g. *The Telegraph* (1 May 2000)).

20 To be known as Kamtapur or Kamatapur State. 'New militant outfit active in Cooch Behar', *The Assam Tribune* (5 July 1999); 'Kamtapur Party Leaders Held,' *The Telegraph*

(26 November 1999); 'WB Separatists Woo Assam Tribals', *The Telegraph* (27 November 1999).

21 The All Koch-Rajbanshi Students' Union (AKRSU), which organized the rally in Guwahati (Assam), stated: 'After Independence, the Rangpur district, where the [Koch-Rajbanshi] community was the largest single majority, was given to then East Pakistan; Cooch Behar and Jalpaiguri districts were included with West Bengal; Purniya district with Bihar; and Goalpara, Kamrup and Mongaldoi districts with Assam ... This fragmentation of the Kamatapur homeland has reduced the [7 million Koch-Rajbanshi] community into minority in all these areas.' The political and armed struggle for Kamtapur was, however, fought only on the Indian side of the border. Photograph from 'Kamatapur homeland stir launched, new front in Assam', *The Sentinel* (16 March 2002). Cf. Appendix Figure 1.

22 For example, the government in Delhi had to contend with an insurgency that severely restricted the government's effective power over the Mizoram border up to the 1980s, when Tripura started spinning out of control. The government in Dhaka lost its grip on the Chittagong Hill Tracts border between the mid-1970s and the late 1990s. And the government in Rangoon never really established a strong hold over its Arakan border. See also chapter 10.

23 The Chakla Roshnabad estate (CR 1B-3 (9-49); cf. CR 1B3-1/49 (3-51)). There was also the reverse rumour that East Pakistan would invade Tripura and annex it to Pakistan (CR 1B3-2/50 (7-52)); cf. PN Chopra, *The Sardar of India: Biography of Vallabhbhai Patel* (New Delhi: Allied Publishers, 1995), 173.

24 In September 1948 India invaded the Princely State of Hyderabad in the south and annexed it after a few days' struggle. CR 1A3-8/49 (11-50); cf. Pol. P4A-2/49 (4-49). CID Const. = constable of the Central Intelligence Department.

25 'Pakistani Officials Want to Fly the Crescent Flag on the Akyab Port! Plan of Making a Crusade on a Part of Burma Exposed; Pakistanis Have Been Occupying 1,500 Sq. Miles', *Rozana Hind* (9 May 1951) (cf. Plt. 2N-31/51 (4-50).

26 CR 1V-6/50 (6-54).

27 *Agreement between the Government of India and the Government of Pakistan dated the 8th April, 1950*, p. 3 (CR 1C-1/50 (11-50). The Inter-Dominion Conference (Calcutta, April 1948) had agreed: 'Any propaganda for the amalgamation of Pakistan and India or of portion thereof including East Bengal on the one side and West Bengal or Assam or Cooch Behar and Tripura on the other, shall be discouraged. The word "propaganda" shall be taken as including any organisation which may be set up for the purpose' (Plt. 1I-259/48 (2-49)).

28 The governments had developed extensive joint procedures for dealing with such press reports in the neighbouring country. The voluminous correspondence on such reports can be found in the confidential records of the Government of East Bengal at the National Archives of Bangladesh in Dhaka.

29 Letter from Dhirendra Mohan Gupta, Deputy Secretary to the Government of West Bengal to the Deputy Secretary to the Government of East Bengal, 13 October 1950 (CR 1P3-4/50 (12-52)).

30 'Chief Secretary, West Bengal, stated that ... speeches and pamphlets [by Dr Shyama Prasad Mookherjee and Sri JP Mitter of West Bengal] were ... not actionable under the existing laws of the land, although in some cases they might be contrary to the spirit of the Delhi Pact and, in a few cases, against the provisions of the Pact.' *Decisions taken at the Chief Secretaries' Conference held at Calcutta on the 20th and 21st November, 1950*

(*Eighteenth Conference*), 5 (CR 1I-3/51 (11-53b); cf. CR 5A-1/51 (3-53)). Speaking in the Indian Parliament in April 1950, SP Mookherjee suggested waging war on Pakistan in order to reunify the subcontinent and protect Hindus in East Pakistan; in August 1950 he had modified his demand to one-third of the territory of East Pakistan for the resettlement of refugees from that area. See BD Graham, 'Syama Prasad Mookerjee and the Communalist Alternative,' in DA Low (ed.), *Soundings in Modern South Asian History* (London: Weidenfeld and Nicolson, 1968), 341, 343–4. For more on the political role of SP Mookherjee, see Craig Baxter, *Jana Sangh: A Biography of an Indian Political Party* (Philadelphia: University of Pennsylvania Press, 1969). For the effect of Mookherjee's speeches in Tripura, see CR 5M-3/50 (2-53).

31 On these 'optees,' see Md. Mahbubar Rahman and Willem van Schendel, '"I Am Not A Refugee": Rethinking Partition Migration,' *Modern Asian Studies*, 37:3 (2003), 551–84.

32 Choudhuri Foyzar Rahman of Rajshahi town was involved in this transfer, as he explained in an interview with Md. Mahbubar Rahman in 1998. In 1950 Choudhuri Foyzar Rahman, then a Pakistan government employee, was sent to Malda, Balurghat and Jalpaiguri (in India) to help collect judicial records and maps and to take them to Pakistan.

33 Then a town of about 213,000 inhabitants, now about 50 times that size. For building activities in Dhaka during the first years after Partition, see *One Year of Popular Government in East Pakistan* (Dacca: Government of East Pakistan, 1957), 83–6.

34 AMK Maswani, *Subversion in East Pakistan* (Lahore: Amir Publications, 1979), 84–5.

35 *Five Years of Pakistan (August 1947–August 1952)* (Karachi: Pakistan Publications, 1952), 243.

36 Khan, *Friends Not Masters*, 22; cf. 24. For more on the development of post-1947 Dhaka, see Tai Yong Tan and Gyanesh Kudaisya, *The Aftermath of Partition in South Asia* (London and New York: Routledge, 2000), 165–72.

37 'They were not very well disciplined and even the senior officers were not all that good. The politicians [did not redress their grievances] and the result was a feeling of acute discontent and inefficiency.' In July 1948, there was a police revolt in Dhaka that was put down by the army. Mohammed Ayub Khan, *Friends Not Masters* (London: Oxford University Press, 1967), 28; cf. Jyoti Sen Gupta, *Eclipse of East Pakistan: Chronicles of Events Since Birth of East Pakistan Till October 1963* (Calcutta: Renco, 1963), 62–3.

38 In his memoirs, Ayub Khan claimed: 'The East Bengal Regiment also came into existence in my time [1948–9]. It was the first time that people from this part had been enlisted in a combatant unit. I was also able to establish the East Pakistan Rifles, a police force, and initiate a system of giving all police officers battle-training. It did the force an immense amount of good and they developed tremendous confidence in themselves.' In fact, the East Pakistan Rifles grew out of the Eastern Frontier Rifles, a force established in 1922, renamed Eastern Pakistan Rifles in 1947, and, after reorganization in 1958, East Pakistan Rifles. Up to 1958, they were responsible for 'internal security ... assisting the police in emergency'. After 1958, their new duties were 'border protection, anti-smuggling and internal security' or 'anti-smuggling activities, collection of border intelligence and limited defence.' By 1971, the East Pakistan Rifles consisted of about 13,000 men, and the East Bengal Regiment of six battalions. Khan, *Friends*, 30; *East Pakistan District Gazetteers: Dacca* (Dacca: East Pakistan Government Press, 1969), 406; Lachhman Singh, *Victory in Bangladesh* (Dehra Dun: Natraj Publishers, 1981), 52–3; Mohammed Ayoob and K Subrahmanyam, *The Liberation War* (New Delhi: S Chand & Co., 1972), 152.

39 Smuggling was seen as a serious problem at the time: 'There are smugglers of foodgrains, cloth, gold and currency on both the sides, and it is these people who give rise to many

of the border troubles while attempting to smuggle from either side. Such cases are prominent on the border between East Pakistan and India. During the year 1956–7, 231 border incidents have been reported to the Central Government.' *Ten Years of Pakistan, 1947–1957* (Karachi: Pakistan Publications, 1957), 37.

40 Later this campaign (known as Operation Closed Door) was seen as a dress rehearsal for military rule in Pakistan (established later in 1958) and a catalyst for the Nehru-Noon Accord of 1958. Hasan Zaheer, *The Separation of East Pakistan: The Rise and Realization of Bengali Muslim Nationalism* (Karachi: Oxford University Press, 1995), 65–6; Sen Gupta, *Eclipse of East Pakistan*, 370–6, 390–2, 414–15; Appadorai, *Select Documents*, Volume I, 96–8.

41 Saroj Chakrabarty, *With Dr. B.C. Roy and Other Chief Ministers (A Record upto 1962)* (Calcutta: Benson's, 1974), 118–19. India began constructing a new railway link through the chicken's neck a few months after Partition. By December 1949 it became possible for the first time to travel by train from Assam via Darjeeling to the rest of India without crossing East Pakistani territory. *Keesing's Contemporary Archives*, VII, 10426; CN Vakil, *Economic Consequences of Divided India: A Study of the Economy of India and Pakistan* (Bombay: Vora, 1950), 408. Agartala, the capital of Tripura, had depended on nearby Akhaura railway station, now just out of reach four kilometres inside East Pakistan. Half a century after Independence, Agartala still lacked a railway link with the rest of India; the same was true of Aizawl, the capital of Mizoram.

42 These forces functioned under the Indian Army but were under the administrative control of the Home Ministry and consisted of soldiers from the region ('Assam Rifles to replace Army,' *The Telegraph* (9 August 1999). In some parts of the borderland, special units played a prominent role in representing the state. In forested and thinly populated areas on the Assam/ East Pakistan and Tripura/ East Pakistan border it was the forest guards of the two countries who patrolled the borders. In the Chittagong Hill Tracts, it was a regional force, the Chittagong Hill Tracts Frontier Police. In Assam, there was the Border Police force under the Special Branch, created in 1962 and re-established as an independent force in 1972. Its task was manning the international border (until 1967, when the Border Security Force took over) and surveying border villages to detect foreign nationals. R Dutta Choudhury, 'I-cards will help in curbing influx', *The Assam Tribune* (19 January 2003).

43 At first, the BSF was run by the state governments. In 1967 it was placed under the control of the Government of India. By 1999, an inspector-general of the BSF claimed that it was 'the largest paramilitary organisation in the world.' Amiya Kumar Das, *Assam's Agony: A Socio-Economic and Political Analysis* (New Delhi: Lancers Publishers, 1982), 57; cf. 'Border force plan: Central scheme to allow for State views,' *The Statesman* (16 July 1965); SK Ghosh, *Unquiet Border* (New Delhi: Ashish Publishing House, 1993), 88–90; 'Interview of the week: Issue identity cards to people living along the borders: V.S. Sirohi', *The Northeast Daily* (19 December 1999).

44 Initially, the border police (or border militia) was organized as a special unit: a Deputy Inspector General, Border Police, was in charge of a number of border *subedars* (officers) and their constables. By 1971 there were 370 border outposts on the East Pakistan side and the number on the Indian side is likely to have been similar (Ayoob and Subrahmanyam, 155). In 1999, Bangladesh had 606 border outposts (89 on the Burma border and 517 on the India border); in 2000 the Bangladesh Home Ministry said there were 750 Indian outposts along the India-Bangladesh border (Shaikh Nazrul Islam, 'Indian border guards kill 73 in 4 years', *The Daily Star* (7 October 1999); 'BDR plea to stop

cross-border shootings: India should deploy forces having Bengali origin,' *The New Nation* (21 May 2000)).

Outposts could be a few kilometers apart, as on the West Bengal/ East Pakistan border, or bunched together, as around the tiny Bangladesh enclave of Dohogram in north Bengal, where India was reported to have 'erected a ring of eleven check posts and seventeen observation towers' (Mohammad Nurunnabi Chowdhury, 'Indian passage through Bangladesh', *The Independent* (12 August 1999)). By contrast, when the Burmese army entered Indian territory at the Mizoram/Arakan/Bangladesh border in 1999, the nearest BSF post turned out to be 36 km away ('Myanmar Army accidentally enters Indian area', *The Assam Tribune* (9 August 1999)). According to BSF chiefs, three quarters of the BSF force was employed in Kashmir and the border with Pakistan, where a battalion looked after a stretch of 27 to 32 km, whereas on the northeastern borders a battalion looked after 89 km, in Tripura after 95 km, and in Mizoram after no less 400 km. According to the Inspector-General of the BSF in the North Bengal Sector (Kishanganj, Siliguri and Cooch Behar), the 179 border outposts in his sector were about 6 km apart and should be 3.5 km apart for proper border patrolling; there were also 253 watch towers in his sector. 'Shortage of BSF personnel manning border: Mitra', *The Sentinel* (1 December 2002); 'Border fencing in Tripura sector being expedited', *The Assam Tribune* (1 December 2002); R Dutta Choudhury, 'Ethnic affinity, lack of fencing encouraging Bangla influx', *The Assam Tribune* (16 June 2003); cf. 'Porous border helping rebels in cross-border movement: Manik Sarkar', *The Sentinel* (25 August 2003).

In 2000 the Director-General of the Bangladesh Rifles (BDR) expressed concern over the fact that 559 km of the Bangladesh border were 'unprotected': in the southeast there were no BDR camps along 100 km of the border with Burma and 379 km of the border between the Chittagong Hill Tracts and India, and in the southwest along 80 km from Kaikhali to North Talpatti in the Sundarbans. He demanded an increase of the BDR to at least 70,000 to man the border, a BDR outpost on every 20 km of the Chittagong Hill Tracts border and 4 helipads in the region, and 10 gunboats to patrol the Sundarban border. According to the Bangladesh Home Ministry, the number of Indian border guards was almost twice that of Bangladeshi border guards. In September 2000, the Bangladesh government decided to recruit 18,000 men to be deployed in the 'unprotected' sections of the borderland, bringing the total number of BDR men at 56,000 ('DG of BDR concerned at unprotected borders of CHT, Satkhira', *The Daily Star* (4 July 2000); 'BDR to be deployed in CHT, Sunderbans', *The New Nation* (18 September 2000)).

45 On the East Pakistan/ Burma border the pattern was the same. The Burmese 'Border Administration Force' is known as Na Sa Ka or Nasaka.

46 For the emergence of the permit system restricting travel between India and West Pakistan in 1948, see Vazira Zamindar, 'Divided Families and the Making of Nationhood in India and Pakistan 1947–65' (PhD thesis, Columbia University, 2002), 60–83. For background information on the evolution of the passport system, see 111–43.

47 *Passport System to Regulate the Entry of Indian Nationals into Pakistan* (Dacca: East Bengal Government Press, 1952); also in Plt. 2B-17/52 (3-53).

48 Photograph from *Five Years of Pakistan*, 223. Photographer unacknowledged. The passport and visa system was introduced in October 1952.

49 They also sought to destroy paramilitary groups that had sprung up during the anti-colonial movement but were considered to be disloyal to the new state. In this way, the Muslim League National Guards were forced to disband in West Bengal, as was the

Rashtriya Swayam Seva Sangh in East Pakistan. Armed cadres of the Communist Party of India were also seen as a threat. This operation was a delicate one, as a conference of police officers in Pakistan acknowledged: 'East Bengal ... has to deal with organisations which are notorious for underground work of which large numbers belong to the minority community [= Hindus]. The banning of such organisations would probably lead to considera[ble] reactions from India on the ground of victimisation of the minorities in direct violation of promises made by the Quaid-i-Azam [= MA Jinnah] and other prominent leaders. The problem is further complicated by the lack of power to enforce any ban on such organizations due to the insufficiency of both army and police forces. Added to this is the difficulty of communications which precludes the rapid despatch of reinforcements.' *Secret Report of the Proceedings of the Conference of Police Officers held at Karachi in February 1948* (Pol. 13-1/48 (10-48)). On the use of violence (including 'goonda parties') by the West Bengal government in establishing its territorial dominance, see e.g. *West Bengal Personal Liberty League Committee's Statement* (Calcutta, 1949); *The labour to be led in fighting against disturbances;* Anti-Riot Leaflet No. 3 (Calcutta: Communist Party, 1950); CR 5R-1/50 (1-53a).

50 See Eastern Pakistan Ansars Ordinance 1948 (12 February 1948), and Ansar Act, 1948.
51 I.e. male Pakistanis. The aims of the Ansars were: '(a) To harness, for constructive purposes, the great upsurge of public enthusiasm to serve the new State; (b) To counteract influences which might threaten peace and security within the State; (c) To assist Government in promoting harmony between different sections of the people and in carrying out schemes for social and economic reconstruction; (d) To supplement the efforts of the Police in suppressing crime and other anti-social activities such as smuggling, black marketing, evasion of Customs and railway dues, etc.; (e) To act as a National Militia in case of a national emergency. At first the names 'Home Guard' and 'National Guard' were tentatively used, but the name 'Ansar' was adopted as expressing within itself, with historical and religious significance, the whole ideal of voluntary service to the community and to the nation.' *First Annual Report on the Ansars* (Dacca, 1949), 1 (Pol. P10A-76/49 (11-49)).
52 'Secret Minutes of the Joint Conference of the Hon'ble Premiers, Home Secretaries and Inspectors-General of Provinces of Pakistan, held at the Pakistan Secretariat, on the 20th and 21st February, 1948', 2 (Pol. 13-1/48 (10-48)). In his memoirs, Ayub Khan (then General Officer Commanding; President of Pakistan from 1958 to 1968) would later claim: 'Before I left the province [East Bengal, in 1949] I was able to build up an adequate *Ansar* (civil armed guards) force. In this I received great support from Aziz Ahmed who was then Chief Secretary of the provincial government. He felt that such a force would bring discipline to the masses and persuaded the provincial government to spare resources for it' (Khan, 1967, 30). The *First Annual Report* (1949, 9) shows, however, that Aziz Ahmed was actually president of the National Service Board, of which Ayub Khan was a member.
53 *First Annual Report.*
54 In September and October 1948, 'Government considered it desirable that special attention should be given to expansion of the Ansar force in Border areas.' *First Annual Report,* 5. In 1951 the West Bengal press reported that 'every union of East Pakistan border districts ha[s] been asked to raise an Ansar corps of 500 men' (a union covers a few villages). 'War Fever in East Pakistan', *Amrita Bazar Patrika* (6 September 1951) (CR 5A-1/51 (3-53)). Later, the Ansars were brought under the Deputy Commissioner (= highest district official), who supervised the Adjutant of Ansars under the heading

of 'political and border matters.' See AMA Muhith, *The Deputy Commissioner in East Pakistan* (Dacca: National Institute of Public Administration, 1968). Cf. *One Year of Popular Government in East Pakistan* (Dacca: Government of East Pakistan, 1957), 128.

55 CR 1C-2/50 (11-50); CR 1I-108/49 (3-51); CR 1A7-1/52 (4-53).

56 The first time this happened was in 1950, when jute smuggling to West Bengal was perceived as a serious threat to the national economy. The border militia was withdrawn 'as being unreliable', and Ansars were inducted to help man the increased number of border outposts (CR 1C-2/50 (11-50)); 'Purbobongo hoite beaini mal rophtani bondher chesta: Pradeshik shorkar kortrik shimanto elakay kothor bebostha', *Azad* (4 September 1950)).

57 Others were the Muslim (League) National Guards (of which there were roughly 200,000 in East Bengal/ East Pakistan in early 1948; Pol. 13-1/48 (10-48)), the Pakistan National Guards, the Mujahids and the Razakars.

58 Chakrabarty, *With Dr. B.C. Roy*, 118–19; Chatterji, 'The Fashioning,' 237–8. Other groups styled themselves Santi Sena Dal, National Cadet Corps, or Congress Volunteers. Members of the (West Bengal) National Volunteer Force were inducted into border patrols (CR 1A2-2/53 (10-54)) but also used to clear garbage during a strike in Calcutta (Chakrabarty, 119). The idea of raising a Village Volunteer Force in the border areas of West Bengal to help secure the border, curb infiltration and identify illegal immigrants was raised again 50 years later by the Border Security Force (BSF). 'BSF for more recruits,' *The Statesman* (9 March 2003).

59 For information about the subsequent history of the Assam Home Guards, see L David, 'The Civil Defence and Home Guards: Committed to keep fissiparous tendencies at bay', *The Sentinel* (5 December 2001).

60 The Kirit Bikram Bahini (= Troops of Maharaja Kirit Bikram Kishore Manikya of Tripura) were set up in Tripura State in 1948. According to East Pakistan officials, they were 'under the Command of Habul Banerji, a man of desperate character, who was externed … from Comilla [East Pakistan]. This "Bahini" is a voluntary Corps on the lines of "Azad Hind Fauj". It consists mainly of Hindu immigrants. The State has supplied this organisation with arms and ammunition. In collaboration with the State Force, this organisation is committing depredations on the border' (CR 1I-120/48 (1-51); cf. CR 1B-3 (9-49)).

61 Heather Rae uses the term 'pathological homogenisation' to bracket strategies such as the exclusion of minority groups from citizenship rights, the forced assimilation or conversion of minority groups, and their expulsion or extermination. Heather Rae, *State Identities and the Homogenisation of Peoples* (Cambridge: Cambridge University Press, 2002), 4–5.

62 Cf. Gyanendra Pandey, *Remembering Partition: Violence, Nationalism and History in India* (Cambridge: Cambridge University Press, 2001).

63 In the Delhi Pact of 1950, India and Pakistan stated: 'The Governments of India and Pakistan solemnly agree that each shall ensure, to the minorities throughout its territory, complete equality of citizenship, irrespective of religion, a full sense of security in respect of life, culture, property and personal honour, freedom of movement within each country and freedom of occupation, speech and worship, subject to law and morality' (CR 1C-1/ 50 (11-50)).

64 See the circular letter from the Chief Secretary to the Government of [East] Bengal to District Officers, dated 22 September 1948 on the subject of the Arms Act policy, Pol. P5A-138/48 (10-48). For a clever sidestepping of the issue, see the answers by the Minister

of the Interior to questions by Rajkumar Chakraverty, member of the Constituent Assembly, 16 December 1948. In the copy of the circular letter of 22 September 1948 filed with these questions, the terms 'Muslims' and 'Hindus' were changed into 'persons of proved loyalty' and 'persons of doubtful loyalty' (Pol. P3I-46/48 (2-49)). Meanwhile, the West Bengal press carried many reports, e.g. 'Seizure of Guns', *Hindusthan Standard* (26 October 1948). In 1950, a conference of Commissioners and District Magistrates of East Bengal recommended a 'liberalisation in the grant of arms licences to members of the minority community … in areas where serious crime was endemic' (CR 1C-2/50 (11-50)).

65 The Home (Civil Defence) Department of East Pakistan reported in December 1948 that 'Muslims living in border areas opposite to Maidam Border Outpost (Pakistan) are being disarmed by the authorities of Cooch Behar [India]' (CR 2A2-1/51 (3-53)). A petition by inhabitants from the Dinajpur border (April 1948) states: 'The said Santhals [on the Indian side of the border] are increasing their stock of bows and arrows and other arms, while the houses of the Muslims who, it appears, have become debarred from keeping arms for defence, are being searched for keeping anything of the kind and, if any is found, is being taken away by the police' (Plt. 1I-228/48 (7-49)). For confiscation of guns from Muslims in Assam, see CR 1I-16/48 (11-50).

66 Reconstruction of the various roles of locals, immigrants and government officials in expelling minorities has rarely been done since most observers and later writers were more interested in apportioning blame than in understanding the complexities of forced migration. For a careful reconstruction of the factors involved in the flight of Garos from Mymensingh (East Pakistan) to India in 1964, see Ellen Bal, *'They Ask If We Eat Frogs': Social Boundaries, Ethnic Categorisation, and the Garo People of Bangladesh* (Delft: Eburon, 2000), 157–206.

67 Cf. Rahman and Van Schendel, "'I Am Not A Refugee'"; Amena Mohsin, 'Partitioned Lives Partitioned Lands', in: Imtiaz Ahmed (ed.), *Memories of a Genocidal Partition: The Haunting Tales of Victims, Witnesses and Perpetrators* (Colombo: Regional Centre for Strategic Studies, 2002), 19–42.

68 'Seized Land', *Hindusthan Standard* (20 March 1951); cf. CR 3W-9/52 (3-53). The *Dainik Basumati* (Calcutta) of 10 September 1948 carried an article warning that Pakistan would create disturbances in (the Muslim majority district of) Murshidabad and force a plebiscite there. In order to protect Murshidabad, it said, 'every West Bengal Hindu and every refugee Hindu from East Bengal will have to proceed with a proper plan to make Murshidabad a Hindu majority district' (Plt. 17E-61/48 (10-50)). For a plot, by Hindu refugees in Nadia district (West Bengal), to kill a member of the West Bengal Legislative Assembly and another politician who wished to resettle Muslim refugees returning from East Pakistan on the border of Nadia district, see CR 2N1-2/51 (3-53). For Jawaharlal Nehru's objection to the policy 'to clear those areas, upto a certain depth, of Muslims,' see Chakrabarty, *With Dr. B.C. Roy*, 192–3.

69 Chopra, *The Sardar of India*, 174; cf. Sen Gupta, *Eclipse of East Pakistan*, 102. This demand was taken up more than half a century later by the Viswa Hindu Parishad (VHP; World Hindu Council) when its international general secretary, Praveen Togadia – referring explicitly to Patel – 'advised the [Indian] government to attack Bangladesh and annex three of its districts [viz. Khulna, Mymensingh and Chittagong] … for rehabilitating Hindus and Buddhists who fled Bangladesh due to persecution.' Some time later he exhorted the Indian government once again to invade Bangladesh, this time to carve out a separate place from their territory and forcibly settle the infiltrators there. In the

vocabulary of the VHP, Bangladeshi Hindus are refugees and Bangladeshi Muslims are infiltrators. 'Attack Bangladesh: Togadia', *The Times of India* (29 January 2003); "'Influx a ploy to make Assam part of Bangla'", *The Assam Tribune* (8 June 2003); 'Annex B'desh land: Togadia,' *The Sentinel* (8 June 2003).

70 CR 2C-4/49 (1-51); CR 1I-108/49 (3-51).

71 For petitions by Muslims from Cooch Behar and various accounts of how they were harassed into leaving for Pakistan, see e.g. CR 5M-4/50 (5-55).

72 CR 2C-4/49 (1-51). The Pakistani authorities were convinced that this was a longstanding policy in West Bengal. In 1951 they wrote in an internal memorandum: 'The anxiety of the Government of West Bengal to take possession of the property abandoned by Muslim refugees [after riots in early 1950 that led to an exodus of Muslims from West Bengal and of Hindus from East Pakistan] was the outcome also of a policy to expel Muslims from a five mile belt all along the East Bengal border. The policy was initiated long ago. The Chief Secretary, East Bengal, first complained about it at the Chief Secretaries' Conference on 10th/12th May, 1948 ... Muslim migrants returning to Maldah [in 1951] were definitely told by local officers that their homesteads and lands falling within that belt would not be restored to them' (CR 3I-181/51 (11-52); cf. CR 1M-6/50 (1-53); CR 1W-10/50 (1-53); CR 5M-4/50 (5-55)). See also Dhirananda Goswami, *Nodiyar Songkot*, Vol. 1 (Santipur: Nodiyar Progotisil Kormider pokkhe, 1951) and denials by the West Bengal government (e.g. CR 3I-181/51 (11-52); CR 2N1-2/51 (3-53)). There is a voluminous correspondence between the Governments of West and East Bengal, and those of Assam and East Bengal, concerning the 'non-restoration' of land and houses to West Bengal and Assamese Muslim who took refuge in East Pakistan, and East Bengal Hindus who fled to India, during the riots of 1950. Non-restoration of property in the borderland immediately led to mutual suspicion of attempting to build up 'natural boundaries.' See e.g. CR 1W-10/50 (1-53), CR 2A2-1/51 (3-53), CR 1W1-1/51 (5-53). Patel's speech apparently also triggered the setting up of the Kirit Bikram Bahini in Tripura (CR 1I-120/48 (1-51)).

73 For a detailed joint enquiry and many witness accounts of the Kamalpur massacre, see CR 1B3-2/50 (7-52); cf. CR 5M-3/50 (2-53). Already in December 1948, a worried president of a Union Board in Comilla wrote to the Prime Minister of East Bengal that the Tripura authorities were 'oppressing the local border Muslims of their own State in the shape of forcible possession of their valuables and live stocks and forcing them to migrate to Pakistan' (CR 1B3-2/49 (11-50)). See information on Tripura Muslims being used as forced labour (1950), and petition (1951) from Tripura Muslims concerning their 'miserable, helpless conditions' in CR 3T1-1/51 (5-53); cf. CR 5M-3/50 (2-53).

74 See eviction orders in the Extraordinary Issues of the *Tripura Gazette* (28 March and 1 June 1951), petitions, correspondence and newspaper reports in CR 3T4-1/51 (3-54). The proportion of Muslims in the population of Tripura fell from 21% in 1951 to 7% in 1981. SR Bhattacharjee, *Tribal Insurgency in Tripura: A Study in Exploration of Causes* (New Delhi: Inter-India Publications, 1989), 84.

75 'All-out Government drive against the Muslims in Assam: Indiscriminate arrest on false charges of espionage: Muslim officials driven out of offices and courts,' *Sangbad* (Dhaka), 10 September 1951; 'Oppression upon Muslims in Assam: Many people arrested on suspicion of being Pakistani spies,' *Azan* (Chittagong), 29 September 1951. For lists of refugees, externment order, correspondence and the controversy concerning anti-Muslim remarks by the President of the Assam Provincial Congress Committee reported in 'Regard Refugees as Brothers: A.P.C.C. President's Speech at Haliakandi', *Hindusthan*

Standard (26 June 1951), see CR 2A1-1/51 (3-54); cf. CR 2A1-1/52 (12-53).

76 Goswami, *Nodiyar Shonkot* (1951). Cf. CR 2N1-2/51 (3-53); CR 1B2-2/50 (12-52).

77 For example the letter from the District Magistrate of Rangpur that stated that it would 'be in the interest of the State that these people (i.e. immigrant Muslims) should be settled permanently in [the border *char*] area which is so close to the Cooch Behar border' (CR 5P-12/49 (4-50)).

78 Remarkably, the abundant and detailed archival material on this exodus, for example in the Bangladesh National Archives, has not so far been used at all. On the exodus, see e.g. Sen Gupta, *Eclipse of East Pakistan*; Jayanta Kumar Ray, *Democracy and Nationalism on Trial: A Study of East Pakistan* (Simla: Indian Institute of Advanced Study, 1968); Kudaisya, 'Divided Landscapes'. Recently, the fate of Hindu refugees from East Pakistan has been exploited by rightwing Hindu propagandists in India, for example in AJ Kamra's stridently communalist *The Prolonged Partition and its Pogroms: Testimonies on Violence against Hindus in East Bengal, 1946–1964* (New Delhi: Voice of India, 2000).

79 Letter by the District Magistrate of Mymensingh, 4 May 1951 (CR 6M1-1/51 (7-53); cf. Plt. 18R-4/50 (2-51); CR 4M-1/50 (3-53)). This was a response to a letter that the Indian Minister for Minority Affairs wrote to his Pakistani counterpart: 'Some of the officials in the Mymensingh district near the borders of Garo Hills [India] have even let it be known that Hajongs, Garos and other Hindus will not be allowed to live within five miles of the Indo-Pakistan border and that Muslim refugees from Assam, Bihar and West Bengal will be settled in this belt. It is reported that during the last week of January [1951], about 26,000 Muslims from Kishorganj and Tangail Refugee Camps were settled by Government on lands evacuated by non-Muslims in Haluaghat P.S.' (CR 6M1-1/51 (7-53); cf. CR 3I-97/51 (12-52)). Settlement of Muslim refugees from India in the Chittagong Hill Tracts, a Pakistan border district with a largely non-Muslim and non-Bengali population, was official policy: 'The scheme for the development of Chittagong Hill Tracts was also approved on the recommendation of the Ministry of Refugees and Rehabilitation at an expenditure of Rs. one million out of the Development Fund. This scheme will rehabilitate 50,000 refugees on land to be developed in that area.' *Five Years of Pakistan (August 1947-August 1952)* (Karachi: Pakistan Publications, 1952), 149-150. See also protest by Kamini Mohan Dewan (President, People's Association, Chittagong Hill Tracts) on 11 April 1950 (Plt. 3L-1/50 (1-51)).

80 'By 1947 the Rohingyas had formed an army and had approached President Jinnah of the newly created Pakistan to ask him to incorporate northern Arakan into East Pakistan (Bangladesh). It was undoubtedly this move more than any other that determined the present-day governmental attitude towards the Rohingyas: they had threatened Burma's territorial integrity [on] the eve of independence and could never be trusted again.' Human Rights Watch, *Burma: The Rohingya Muslims – Ending a Cycle of Exodus?* (New York, etc.: Human Rights Watch/Asia, 1996); cf. Klaus Fleischmann, *Arakan: Konfliktregion zwischen Birma und Bangladesh* (Hamburg: Institut für Asienkunde, 1981), 68–72; Martin Smith, *Burma: Insurgency and the Politics of Ethnicity* (London: Zed Press, 1994), 64, 109, 119, 194; Bertil Lintner, *Burma in Revolt: Opium and Insurgency Since 1948* (Chiang Mai: Silkworm Books, 1999), 65, 110; Sen Gupta, *Eclipse of East Pakistan*, 423–4.

81 Mohammad Yunus, *A Memorandum on the Genocide of the Rohingya Muslims of Arakan in Burma* (Arakan: Rohingya Solidarity Organization, 1995), 3.

82 '"Chottograme Arakani mohajer", Panuapathare dui hazar loker bostir byobostha,' *Azad* (14 April 1949).

83 East Pakistan (and later Bangladesh) authorities no longer welcomed these later waves. On Rohingya refugees, see e.g. Human Rights Watch, *Malaysia/Burma – Living in Limbo: Burmese Rohingyas in Malaysia* (New York, etc.: Human Rights Watch, 2000).

84 The term 'natural frontier' was used by the Calcutta paper *Hindusthan Standard* (8 May 1951) when it accused the Pakistan authorities of pursuing 'a policy intended to make "natural frontiers" between East Pakistan and Assam' by driving out non-Muslim minorities from northern Mymensingh district. The East Pakistan government dismissed this allegation as objectionable, false and malicious and demanded that the West Bengal government take 'prompt and drastic action' against the paper. (CR 3I-97/51 (12-52)).

85 Bal describes a sudden change in the official attitude after thousands of Christian Garos had fled from Mymensingh to Assam and Bengalis had occupied their lands. One Garo who stayed back reported: 'After a few months the government sent a special officer who had to receive the Mandis [Garos] who came back from India. The government also sent police to protect the Mandis who had not fled away, or who had come back already.' Bal suggests that this temporary change of heart was a result of international pressure, especially from Christian organisations. Bal, 'They Ask If We Eat Frogs', 189–90. Cf. Neville A Kirkwood, *Independent India's Troubled Northeast, 1952–69: An Australian Missionary's Story* (n.p.: Griffith University, Centre for the Study of Australia-Asia Relations, 1996), 52–65.

86 I have not come across any references to female border officials in this period.

87 CR 1A2-4/51 (3-53); CR 1C-2/53 (7-54). Such reports could be quite extensive, e.g. the 57-page 'Joint Inquiry Report into the Kamalpur Incident (Tripura)', based on 27 witness accounts (CR 1B3-2/50 (7-52)). Joint enquiries were also held when state personnel crossed the border and were arrested (CR 1A7-1/52 (4-53)). See also instructions on joint enquiries along the Tripura-East Pakistan border in CR 1C-3/49 (11-50), and extension of the agreement to the Bihar-East Pakistan border in CR 1B1-6/53 (10-54).

88 E.g. the joint conference between the Dewan of Tripura State and the District Magistrates of Noakhali and Comilla (Tippera) of 12 October 1949, which discussed twelve issues ranging from lottery tickets to grazing permits, and from the movement of motor vehicles to clearance of arrear rents (CR 1C-3/49 (11-50). Such meetings were quite common: between 1950 and 1953, at least 106 of them were held in different parts of the borderland (CR 3A-10/53 (8-54)). The practice of joint enquiries and border meetings was also enshrined in the *Ground Rules Formulated by the Military Sub-Committee of the Indian and Pakistan Delegations* (20 October 1959), reprinted in Avtar Singh Bhasin (ed.), *India-Bangladesh Relations: Documents – 1971–2002* (New Delhi: Geetika Publishers, 2003), V, 2735–42.

89 CR 1B2-3/49 (7-52). For similar arrangements concerning the Patharia forest, see the report of a meeting between district and forestry officials of Cachar and Sylhet in January 1949 (CR 1I-31/49 (3-49)).

90 Another example is that of the District Magistrate of Kushtia (Pakistan) who wrote to his counterpart in Nadia (India) in 1954, suggesting a joint raid on a group of Indian and Pakistani smugglers who could not be apprehended because they nipped across the border and the police could not. 'Whenever an attempt is made by the Police Staff of Daulatpur P.S. [Pakistan] for action against Moula Baksh, who is a surveillee, he crosses over the border in some unguarded moment and takes shelter in the house of Patit Kurmi ... I would suggest that a simultaneous raid in the houses of all the abovenamed culprits – both Indian and Pakistani – be arranged by [the police] on each side on a date

to be fixed by them so that the culprits may be apprehended and proceeded against for cur[b]ing their nefarious activities' (CR 1B2-57/54 (9-54)).

91 A Division contains a number of districts. In the event, the Commissioner of Rajshahi arrived too late, giving rise to angry correspondence in CR 1B2-2/50 (12-52); cf. CR 2N1-2/51 (3-53). Another exchange was a part of Sultanpur *mouza* to India in return for a part of Kudum Bhaja *mouza* to Pakistan. 'Duibonger shimana nirdharon karjo: Angshik shomapto boliya Dr Keshkarer bibriti', *Azad* (23 September 1951).

92 In 1959 the two countries decided to ease the possible future exchange of territories after demarcation of the border had taken place by establishing Ground Rules for border management. *Ground Rules Formulated by the Military Sub-Committee of the Indian and Pakistan Delegations* (20 October 1959), reprinted in Bhasin (ed.), *India-Bangladesh Relations*, V, 2735–42.

6

DEFIANCE AND ACCOMMODATION

It was a fine day for soccer, and the boys of Lamazuar crossed the river to play a friendly match in the next village. They had done so many times before. Only this time it was early 1948, and Partition had turned the village river into the international border between Pakistan and India. The entire soccer team was arrested and thrown in jail.[1]

In August 1947 the political elites of the nascent states of India and Pakistan had agreed to accept the Partition border. But what about the people in the new borderland? In view of the fact that there was nothing democratic about the creation of the border, or about its official acceptance, it was hardly surprising that feelings of frustration and outrage ran high. People found their social world truncated, their relatives and neighbours turned into foreigners, and their livelihoods threatened by unwelcome new arrangements. In this chapter I explore how borderlanders coped with the effects of the social, political and economic earthquake that befell them, and how they developed strategies that often brought them into conflict with state officials.

For borderlanders, there were three main aspects to the upheaval. First, the world as they had always imagined it was gone forever, their universe torn in two, and half of it lost. They were subjected to the violent rescaling that results from state formation, and that rescaling took place in their backyard. Their geographical imagination abruptly violated, they needed to reinvent themselves as people with new identities: as borderlanders, as citizens of a new state and as inhabitants of a divided landscape. The strategies they employed were complex and variable, ranging from outright defiance to acceptance, accommodation and innovation. In the following pages, I consider in particular strategies of ignoring and defying the border.

The second aspect of the upheaval was the sudden appearance of the state. Previously, the state had been a fairly distant entity for most borderlanders, but after Partition it was everywhere. The sheer number of state personnel shot up, and they began to regulate aspects of life that had never been of much concern to the state before. We will see that what irked borderlanders most were state attempts to restrict their movements, and state interference in their livelihoods. In this chapter we explore how this worked out for cross-border landholding, markets across the border and borderland commuters.

Finally, Partition led to massive population movements across the border. All over the borderland, relatives, friends, neighbours, colleagues and acquaintances simply disappeared, leaving the local social fabric in tatters. In their place arrived refugees, sometimes from nearby and relatively familiar regions, but quite often from far away. In many places, it took borderland society several generations to adjust to these newcomers; in others social upheaval became permanent: immigration still continues in these areas today. In this chapter I touch only briefly on these themes but they take centre stage in chapters 8 and 9.[2]

Rebuilding an adequate social world became a major task for everybody: locals who lost part of their social network, newcomers who had to find a social niche, and state personnel who needed to establish themselves in positions of power and authority. It is difficult to reconstruct this rebuilding process because relatively little evidence of it survives. Borderlanders themselves have not written much about it, few scholars have bothered to record their oral evidence, and no detailed studies have been done.[3] The material presented in this chapter is based largely on state records and interviews.

Ignoring the border

It took time for the importance of the border to sink in. Nowhere in the borderland did people have any previous experience with the phenomenon of an international boundary, and no effort was made to explain it to them.[4] Many new borderlanders operated with a concept of geography that had not yet adopted the idea of borders as precisely fixed lines in the landscape. They learned gradually what the new border meant, and – like the soccer players of Lamazuar – they often learned in a violent way.

Ignoring the border was one way of dealing with it. At first, long stretches of it remained undemarcated and unguarded, so initially the movement of people across it was hardly hampered. Three unrelated groups of migrants made use of this situation. Large numbers of refugees crossed the open border is search of safety and a better life, notably Hindus fleeing Pakistan and Muslims fleeing India. Apart from refugees, there were numerous cross-border settlers, for example, women who married a husband across the border, or children who went to schools or colleges across the border and then found a job in that country. A third large group were cross-border labour migrants.[5] Most of these border-crossers tried to ignore the border and the rules that came with it.

Crossing the border could also be an expression of genuine ignorance, or a feeling that somehow it did not concern you personally. For example, in 1951–2 several thousands of shifting cultivators crossed the border from Tripura (India) to the Chittagong Hill Tracts (Pakistan) and began to cultivate plots there. This was nothing exceptional because shifting cultivators had been migrating throughout these hills for many generations. But this group chose to settle in the Kassalong Reserved Forest where cultivation was not allowed. They were detected and evicted from the forest, and 'as they are Indian nationals in our reserve forests without any authority they have to go back from whence they came.' The immigrants (who belonged to the Riang group) did not agree and stood their ground:

> the Police Force … encountered some more Reang trespassers who collected in large numbers and threatened the force, and it is reported that as the situation was precarious the Police had to open fire as a result of which one person was shot dead … Even as I write, fresh reports are being received of trespass by these tribesmen from the Tripura State.[6]

These groups of immigrants clearly did not consider themselves trespassers on foreign soil; they ignored the border because they considered it irrelevant to their older claims to the land.[7] Such attitudes would persist much longer among shifting cultivators in the section of the borderland linking East Pakistan and Burma. Here the border was not demarcated, the terrain was difficult, the states were a weak presence, and many small ethnic groups straddled the border. As a result, cross-border patterns of slash-and-burn cultivation continued to be supported by strong cross-border webs of kinship and sociability.

But shifting cultivators were not the only ones ignoring the border. Many others did the same, most notably border guards who were in charge of patrolling the border but sometimes thought that they could ignore it at will when not wearing their uniform. Their cross-border socializing could lead to border incidents. A missionary observed:

> Armed Pakistan and Indian guards would sometimes cross to the other side and drink with each other; at times tea in a tea-shop, at others illicit rice beer. Sometimes an inebriated remark would set tempers aflame and [on] one occasion on the Indian side of the border such an altercation flared during a friendly drink and three Pakistanis were shot. Such situations periodically arose and the media reported "fighting between two patrols" with somewhat exaggerated claims of the number killed on the other side. A few face-saving retaliatory raids would be made to even the score.[8]

It was not uncommon for border guards to get arrested while on the other side of the border. In this way an Indian border guard was apprehended in Jessore (Pakistan) when he went to buy molasses across the border; a Pakistani border guard got himself arrested on a rape charge in the Lushai Hills (now Mizoram, India); and another got so carried away by the excitement caused by an election in the Garo Hills (now Meghalaya, India) that he joined the crowd there and was taken into custody.[9]

Defying the border

It is not always easy to distinguish between people ignoring the border and people actively defying it. Often ignoring turned to defiance when state personnel appeared on the scene and tried to prevent unauthorized border crossing. When in 1948 Bengali Hindus and Santhals, from both sides of the Dinajpur border, held a big meeting on the Indian side to take a decision about migration to India, they simply ignored its existence. But Pakistan border guards intervened when, two days later, 'at about 7 or 8 P.M. many Santhals, Hindus and armed Police of the Indian Dominion, in all about 5 to 6 hundred in number, were assisting in the shifting of movables of the said Hindus of Jagannathpur to Indian Dominion.' This turned the action into one of defiance: 'the Hindus succeeded in their work by beating them back.'[10]

There were many more occasions when large groups of people openly defied the border and challenged the local representatives of the state. Traders were quick to find out that the new border blocked important trade routes. For example, many parts of East Pakistan produced paddy that was sold in deficit areas that were now across the border in India. The East Pakistan authorities were keen to stop this: special police officers were given the task of preventing paddy leaving the country. This was not an easy task, as events after the first major post-Partition harvest in December 1947 demonstrated. One officer wrote to his superior for support. Describing himself as a 'helpless but undaunted servant of Islam and Pakistan', he explained that, after he had been stationed on the border at Rajshahi, 'I became aware of a large area in Murshidabad district [India] opposite my camp faced with an acute crisis and the smugglers on our side disastrously active. I set to work at once and was successful in stopping this huge drainage of food grains from Eastern Pakistan.' He was then threatened by smugglers, armed Indian border guards, and a Pakistani landlord, but persisted 'as a selfless Guard of my National Home.'[11]

Some of his colleagues, however, failed to stop a breakthrough. On 11 January 1948 no less than 500 boats laden with paddy were taken through Chanchkoir, on the river Atrai in Rajshahi (Pakistan), on their way to India. Police ordered them to stop, but as there were only a few policemen, they proved no match for

the many armed men accompanying the boats. The next day the police learned
that paddy boats were assembling upriver once again. This time the Cordoning
Officer detailed his men for duty. That afternoon a fleet of boats accompanied
by at least 60 armed men on the river banks came rushing towards Chanchkoir.
The boatmen and their protectors shouted 'Allahu Akbar!' (God is Great!)
and refused to listen to the officer telling them to stop and show their permits.
On the contrary, they attacked and wounded him with a pointed bamboo. He
fled to a police boat. The crowd pursued him by jumping into the water and
caught up with him in midriver. Then the officer ordered his men to open fire,
jumped into the river himself, and swam across with the crowd in hot pursuit.
The police party fired in all directions for 20 minutes, using 102 rounds of
ammunition, while the men surrounded them and pelted them with bricks.
Then the paddy boats squeezed past the police party, collecting about twenty
injured men and four dead bodies, and disappeared towards the border.[12]

It is likely that such confrontations occurred often. In April 1950, two border
guards in the district of Rangpur (Pakistan) were on patrol when they came
across 'a large number of Hindu migrants with about a thousand heads of cattle
and other restricted articles proceeding towards Cooch Behar [India] by a village
path.' When told by the senior guard to proceed to India through the prescribed
customs route, they did not pay heed to his instructions but 'adopted a defiant
attitude and tried to assault him.'[13]

Group defiance of the border also could be of a political nature. In one case
it grew out of an attempt to maintain an older pattern of sociability that was
thwarted by the border. In June 1948, articles appeared in the Calcutta press
about police in the district of Khulna (Pakistan) breaking up a Hindu festival
in the border village of Sripur.[14] Several hundreds of people from both sides of
the border had gathered there, as in previous years, to sing religious songs during
the annual Phuldol festival. This year, however, the meeting had strong political
overtones and lasted longer than usual. It turned into a display of borderland
solidarity: the gathering criticized 'the present border guard system of East
Bengal' and planned 'to form a new party for the sa[f]eguard of the border
Hindus in co-operation with borders of Taki (West Bengal).'[15] Fearing this, the
East Pakistan authorities used a colonial law (Section 144[16]) to clamp down on
the meeting.

Group defiance of the new border seems to have been a feature of the first
years after Partition but was later abandoned. One reason was no doubt that it
invited state violence that could be avoided by employing other strategies.[17]
Crossing the border in small groups or individually remained very easy in most
places, and this became the preferred strategy.[18] As we will see, such activities
often escaped the surveillance of the state, or led the state to failed attempts at
curbing them. But in three cases, the state had to come to terms with large-

scale, daily border crossings that could neither be ignored nor suppressed. These were linked to cross-border landholding, marketing and commuting.

Cross-border landholding

One of the major legal problems thrown up by Partition was that of immovable property. What was to happen to property in one territory owned by inhabitants of the other? Could Indian citizens continue to have property rights in Pakistan, and *vice versa*? Should emigrants lose their rights? Such questions occupied the minds of refugees, legislators, bureaucrats and lawyers and led to political tensions between Pakistan and India.[19] The discussion on immovables was monopolized by vocal upper- and middle-class refugees, and geared disproportionally towards the 'evacuee property' that they had left behind, especially the landed estates of *zamindars* and other tenure holders, and the urban property of professionals and businessmen.[20]

In the borderland, however, cross-border property rights took on a quite different meaning. Here the very imposition of the border created bizarre situations: cultivating 'Indians' were cut off from their fields a few yards away in Pakistan, a 'Pakistani' shopkeeper would find a border in between his home and his shop down the road in India, or a tea planter's house would be in Pakistan and his garage in India.[21] In other words, one certainly did not have to be a refugee to have one's property in two countries. Moreover, among cultivators in border villages, international migration was often extremely short-distance: tens of thousands moved only to the next village or *para* (neighbourhood) to become citizens of a new country, and continued to cultivate their fields 'back home.'[22] In many cases, this was a family strategy:

> When Partition took place, Haru Mondol, then a young boy, found that the border ran right through the family's ancestral land. Haru's father stayed put in what was now India, but Haru's uncle built a new house on the land just across the border. In this way, the two brothers and their offspring became citizens of two countries but continued to cultivate the family land jointly.[23]

Such cross-border cultivation was a feature all along the border and in many places it continued for years without much trouble. Only gradually would the border emerge as an insurmountable obstacle. At first the border was open, and cultivators moved back and forth unhindered by state interference. Then Pakistan and India began to impose restrictions on the movement of harvested crops across the border. The Inter-Dominion Agreement of 1948 stated:

Where any cultivator living in a border village of one Dominion has land in a border village in the other Dominion, he should be permitted, within a reasonable period after the harvest, to take across the border to his residence reasonable quantities of any controlled commodities produced by him for his domestic consumption with the minimum of restrictions and formalities.[24]

By 1950, the amount of paddy that could be taken across was fixed.[25] This meant that cultivators could produce crops on their fields across the border but were not allowed to take all their produce home; they had to sell everything in access of the fixed amount in the country of origin. Shortly afterwards, with the introduction of passports and visas in 1952, the movement of the cultivators themselves became restricted.[26] And finally, although the two states never agreed upon a solution to cross-border ownership, cultivators lost their hold over their lands across the border.[27] Some would exchange their plots with other borderlanders, others were forced to sell off their lands, and yet others simply lost their lands to new occupants. The India-Pakistan war of 1965 sounded the death knell for cross-border land ownership; both India and Pakistan unilaterally abolished it, and thereby dispossessed hundreds of thousands whose claims were ignored and who never received any compensation at all.[28]

The predicament of the ziratias. The most thoroughly documented case of the demise of cross-border land claims is that of the so-called *ziratia* tenants.[29] In the easternmost districts of East Pakistan, there were many thousands of people who owned land in Tripura (India, see Appendix Figure 1). These plains districts, now in Pakistan, had been part of the kingdom of Tripura till they were annexed by the Mughal Empire and later became part of British India. The hilly part of Tripura survived as a Princely State till 1949 and its Maharaja also retained huge estates in the plains.[30] The tenants in the plains had long been encouraged to reclaim lands in the Tripura hills and use hill forest resources on a permit system, thereby increasing the Maharajas' tax base. Now these arrangements suddenly unravelled as the plains fell to Pakistan and the hills to India. Tenants in the plains had a landlord who had become a foreigner, and they found their access to land in Tripura blocked by the new border. At the same time, Tripura was overrun by Hindu Bengali refugees from East Pakistan who were eager to occupy these lands.

The situation deteriorated rapidly. Those who lived in East Pakistan and held lands in Tripura became known as *ziratia* subjects or tenants. In early 1948, when it was harvest time, they formed two organizations, the *Purbo*

Shimanto Pakistani Proja Union (Union of Tenants of the Eastern Borderland of Pakistan) and the *Roshnabad Proja Shomiti* (Tenants' Organization of the Roshnabad Estate), which held protest meetings, sent out petitions to the authorities in both Tripura and East Pakistan, issued press releases, and kept in touch with each other by means of a printed bulletin (Plates 6.1 and 6.2).

They protested against a string of measures taken by the Tripura government: a ban on the export of most paddy to East Pakistan, a grazing tax on cows needed to plough the paddy fields, a tax on thatching grass, customs duties of up to 54 per cent on chillies and spices, and a quadrupling of the rates of forest permits. 'Thousands and thousands of "Ziratia" subjects are now in the margin of life and death', wrote the secretaries of these organizations, 'they are passing their days in terrible suspense ... there are people who have only the homestead in the Pakistan area and ... their entire cultivable lands are within the Tippera [Tripura] state.'[33]

They claimed 'full rights over the natural produce of Tripura State and no power on earth can deprive them of these rights' – a claim that the Tripura authorities curtly dismissed as 'absurd.'[34] Soon the armed border police of Tripura and the *ziratia* landholders were playing cat and mouse across the border. *Ziratias* smuggled their crops across the border to their houses in East Pakistan, and Tripura officials entered Pakistan to arrest *ziratias* at their homes for smuggling and non-payment of the new duties, at times shooting and killing people. By November 1948, a 'long catalogue of border incidents and bitterness' broke into violence. Offices of the Tripura government went up in flames, Tripura patrol parties were attacked by large crowds of Pakistanis, and villagers caught a Tripura forester on Pakistan soil and turned him over to the police. Widespread anger followed an incident in which a Tripura patrol party opened fire on a dozen *ziratias* who were working their land in Tripura. Two of them succumbed and their:

> dead bodies were dragged to Sonamura through the hills, and kept hanging on a branch of a mango tree in front of the Sonamura thana [police station] till the [following noon] when these dead bodies were brought down. Their curved limbs were straightened by the booted soldiers by trampling on them.'[35]

Clearly, in this part of the borderland the Inter-Dominion agreements were 'but paper transactions.'[36] The restrictions that Tripura imposed on its *ziratias* were felt to be anything but reasonable and the *ziratias*' mounting anger concerned threatened livelihoods, not communal identities, as they themselves were keen to point out.[37] After Tripura acceded to India, the Government of India responded to what they called 'border raids in the Tripura State territory

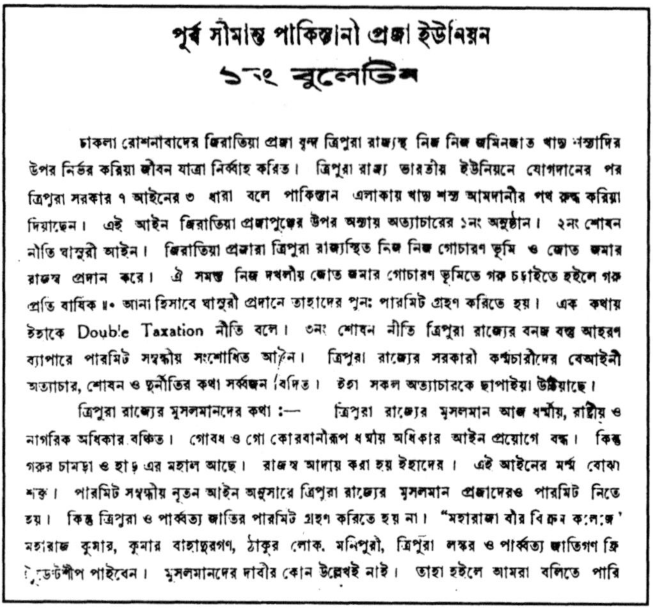

পূর্ব সীমান্ত পাকিস্তানী প্রজা ইউনিয়ন

১ম বুলেটিন

চাকলা রোশনাবাদের জিরাতিয়া প্রজা বৃন্দ ত্রিপুরা রাজ্যস্থ নিজ নিজ জমিনজাত খাদ্য সম্ভাদির উপর নির্ভর করিয়া জীবন যাত্রা নির্বাহ করিত। ত্রিপুরা রাজ্য ভারতীয় ইউনিয়নে যোগদানের পর ত্রিপুরা সরকার ৭ আইনের ৩ ধারা বলে পাকিস্তান এলাকায় খাদ্য শস্য আমদানীর পথ রুদ্ধ করিয়া দিয়াছেন। এই আইন জিরাতিয়া প্রজাপুঞ্জের উপর অন্যায় অত্যাচারের ১নং অনুষ্ঠান। ২নং শোষন নীতি খাস্‌খরী আইন। জিরাতিয়া প্রজারা ত্রিপুরা রাজ্যস্থিত নিজ নিজ গোচারণ ভূমি ও জোত জমার রাজস্ব প্রদান করে। ঐ সমস্ত নিজ দখলীয় জোত জমার গোচারণ ভূমিতে গরু চরাইতে হইলে গরু প্রতি বার্ষিক ॥০ আনা হিসাবে খাস্‌খরী প্রদানে তাহাদের পুনঃ পারমিট গ্রহণ করিতে হয়। এক কথায় ইহাকে Double Taxation নীতি বলে। ৩নং শোষন নীতি ত্রিপুরা রাজ্যের বনজ বস্তু আহরণ ব্যাপারে পারমিট সম্বন্ধীয় সংশোধিত আইন। ত্রিপুরা রাজ্যের সরকারী কর্মচারীদের বেআইনী অত্যাচার, শোষন ও দুর্নীতির কথা সর্বজন বিদিত। ইহা সকল অত্যাচারকে ছাপাইয়া উঠিয়াছে।

ত্রিপুরা রাজ্যের মুসলমানদের কথা :— ত্রিপুরা রাজ্যের মুসলমান আজ ধর্মীয়, রাষ্ট্রীয় ও নাগরিক অধিকার বঞ্চিত। গোবধ ও গো কোরবানীরূপ ধর্মীয় অধিকার আইন প্রয়োগে বন্ধ। কিন্তু গরুর চামড়া ও হাড় এর মহাল আছে। রাজস্ব আদায় করা হয় ইহাদের। এই আইনের মর্ম বোঝা শক্ত। পারমিট সম্বন্ধীয় নূতন আইন অনুসারে ত্রিপুরা রাজ্যের মুসলমান প্রজাদেরও পারমিট নিতে হয়। কিন্তু ত্রিপুরা ও পার্বত্য জাতির পারমিট গ্রহণ করিতে হয় না। "মহারাজা বীর বিক্রম কিশোর মহারাজ কুমার, কুমার বাহাদুরগণ, ঠাকুর লোক, মনিপুরী, ত্রিপুরা লস্কর ও পার্বত্য জাতিগণ ফ্রি ডুটিশীপ পাইবেন। মুসলমানদের দাবীর কোন উল্লেখই নাই। তাহা হইলে আমরা বলিতে পারি

Plate 6.1: Opening paragraphs of the first issue of the Bulletin of the *Union of Tenants of the Eastern Borderland of Pakistan*, printed in Comilla, 1948.[31]

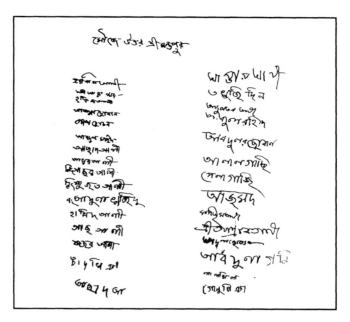

Plate 6.2: In 1951 ziratia tenants drew up a petition against the requisitioning of their land in Tripura (India) and handed it to the visiting Pakistan Revenue Minister. They attached a long list of signatures. The fragment shows those of tenants from *mouza* North Srimontopur.[32]

by Pakistan nationals' by appointing a Military Administrator and posting military pickets along the border.[38] Increasingly, *ziratias* lost control of their land in Tripura, mainly through state requisitioning, intimidation and occupation by Hindu refugees from East Pakistan.[39] Nor did their predicament get any serious attention from the Pakistan authorities. When East Pakistan abolished *zamindari* rights in the 1950s, the Maharaja of Tripura lost his huge income from the Chakla Roshnabad estate that lay in East Pakistan. By one stroke of the pen his tenants in Pakistan were freed from their landlord but they had to pay a high price: as landholders in Tripura they suffered a crushing defeat. Within a few years, they had been turned from the Maharaja's loyal subjects into Pakistani foreigners without rights. By the late 1950s, both the superior tenure holder, the Maharaja, and his lowly tenants, the *ziratias*, saw their cross-border land rights annulled.[40] The state of Pakistan now diverted the income from the Chakla Roshnabad estate to its own coffers but the *ziratias*, unlike the Maharaja,[41] were not compensated in any way.

Forcible harvesting. Uncertainties over property rights across the border also extended to standing crops. Border violence tended to intensify during the paddy harvesting seasons. It was then that borderland fields became a battleground of the unresolved issues of land ownership, citizenship and sovereignty. In these fights, the crop became the prize and elaborate plans were laid to reap and move it. This was the time for groups of borderlanders to get state forces on their side: there are many reports of border police giving protection to groups of harvesters, chasing 'foreign' cultivators across the border and thereby getting entangled in border incidents.

The disputed border between Nadia (West Bengal, India) and Kushtia (East Pakistan) was the scene of many such clashes. In November 1950, at the time of the major *amon* paddy harvest,

> about 150 Pak Muslims helped by the Pak police were harvesting paddy from the fields near the Lakshmankhali bridge [just inside India] ... and were taking away the same to Pakistan in carts. On the arrival of the West Bengal Police, the Pak Muslims began to retreat towards Pakistan while the Pak Police opened fire at the West Bengal Police. The West Bengal Police fired in return ... As a result of the firing by the Pak Police, one Pak Muslim died within West Bengal jurisdiction and he was taken to Krishnagar [India] for post-mortem examination.[42]

District officials would try to control the impact of such encounters by holding joint enquiries and threatening to bring in more armed forces. But they could do little more than react to events as these happened. Since local power relations drove these clashes, it was not surprising that local outcomes differed strikingly.

For example, during the *amon* paddy harvest of November-December 1951, the Pakistan authorities lost control of an area along the Assam-Sylhet border. Here powerful men from across the border launched a campaign to harvest paddy in Pakistan – not just paddy from land owned by Indians in Pakistan but also from land owned by Pakistanis in Pakistan – and they were successful in enlisting the help of Indian armed police. At the height of this campaign, large numbers of Indians under the protection of armed police came to Pakistan to hold meetings. At one of these, they first demanded half and then one-third of the paddy reaped by Pakistani nationals and, when this failed, the Indian police officer demanded protection money 'and they would not disturb anymore the Pakistani nationals in reaping paddy from the border area.' Here forcible harvesting became so organized as to push aside the Pakistani administration. In an enraged letter to the Deputy Commissioner of Sylhet, two prominent men from the area urged him to do something and warned: 'Our people, we men, the public are not prepared to tolerate the activities of the Bharati [Indian] men and Bharati sepoys … the public [may] be forced by circumstances to take [the] law in their own hands.'[43]

It was rare for forcible harvesting to have such a destabilizing effect on state power in the borderland. Indeed, in many other parts, the violent confrontations caused by forcible harvesting had the opposite effect: they built up the legitimacy and effectivity of both states in the borderland, and did so in roughly equal measure on either side.

The end of cross-border landholding.   The example of the *ziratias* showed how Partition could result in borderlanders being deprived of an important part of their livelihood without being able to claim any compensation. What set the *ziratias* apart from other cross-border landholders, however, was the fact that here thousands had a common purpose and a common foe, and hence could organize on a large scale. All along the India-East Pakistan border similar but largely unrecorded struggles were being fought by single individuals and small groups. The pattern was the same: the implications that the border had for landholders gradually became clear as both state personnel and local residents joined in making it more and more difficult to hang on to cross-border land.[44]

Policies regarding the rights of cross-border cultivators were inconsistent. Cultivators in the Assam-East Pakistan and Tripura-East Pakistan borderland were allowed to take some of their paddy home across the border, but on the East Pakistan-West Bengal border life was much tougher. In January 1948 the Regional Controllers of Procurement were ordered 'to allow cultivators resident in West Bengal but having lands in East Bengal to take away their produce to West Bengal, and vice versa.' But in June 1948 they were informed that 'the agreement to allow cultivators to take the produce of their land from one Dominion to the other was impracticable and should not be implemented. No movement of food grains should, therefore, be allowed between the two Provinces of East & West Bengal.'[45]

Cross-border cultivators were now supposed to sell their crops to local government officials but usually they were 'not getting reasonable facilities for selling crops like rice, paddy ... In most cases the crops are either procured by the District authorities or taken away by the local people without payment of any price.'[46] As the District Magistrate of Dinajpur (East Pakistan) observed almost two years after the letter of June 1948:

> The produce was sold by the owners to Government and the prices have not been paid yet. The residents of this district having land in India had to sell to Government their produce similarly and they have got only a small portion of the price in some cases ... If we do not pay the prices, our people in similar circumstances cannot expect to get better treatment.[47]

There were also restrictions on the export of money, so cross-border cultivators taking either their crop, or its value in money, back home were breaking the law. It was no wonder, then, that landholders took to subterfuge (e.g. moving border pillars[48]), smuggling and violence.

For years, India and Pakistan struggled with the embarrassment of large-scale cross-border landholding. As antagonistic states striving for territorial sovereignty, they found it impossible to countenance the continuation of extra-territorial landholding because it interfered with the surveillance of people and with effective control of the economy. And yet, they were unable to resolve the issue by negotiation: plans to devise a system of mutual expropriation of extra-territorial landholdings through compulsory purchase proved prohibitively expensive and came to naught. As a result, India and Pakistan could only employ methods to ensure that cross-border cultivation became less and less attractive. They forced cultivators to surrender their crops for little or no compensation, stood by – idly or protectively – as locals stole the harvest, and criminalized the cultivators' last option: to take their crop home. Some officials in East Pakistan even threatened to confiscate agricultural land owned by Indian nationals, even though this was not the official policy.[49] Borderlanders devised a host of strategies to counteract these disastrous measures but in the end most of them had to accept defeat; they gave up their land across the border through sale, exchange or abandonment. Some borderlanders were luckier than others. Those who lived along the West Bengal-East Pakistan section could benefit from an agreement to tolerate the private exchange of land between borderlanders. Here Pakistani and Indian borderlanders swapped their lands as they migrated to the neighbouring country. This was a very complex and risky practice, involving illegal border crossings, deception and bureaucratic hassles. Not surprisingly, such 'displacement by exchange' often ruined one, or both, of the exchanging parties.[50]

The end of cross-border landholding and the legal exchange of land among migrants came 18 years after Partition. In 1965 war broke out between India and Pakistan and this provided the ruling elites of these countries with an opportunity to move unilaterally on this problem that had refused to go away. Defining cultivators from across the border as enemies, both India and Pakistan simply outlawed cross-border land ownership without having to bother about compensation. In this way, they sacrificed the land rights of hundreds of thousands of borderlanders to the logic of post-Partition territoriality.

But whatever the legal position, even today some borderlanders continue to consider their land across the border as their property. As one borderlander who migrated a short distance from India to Rajshahi (Pakistan) in 1949, explained in 1999:

> I never exchanged my land. It is still all there [just across the border in West Bengal, India]. My two brothers take care of it. I go there every year ... We are still a joint family. Two good houses, about 45 *bighas* [6 ha] of land, 15 *bighas* of garden; neither I nor my younger brother took our share of the land ... And when I go there, I stay for a few weeks or a month.[51]

Such informal private arrangements showed that, even half a century after Partition, cross-border landholding had not completely disappeared.[52] But only a lucky few were in a position to retain their links with land across the border.

Markets across the border

Land was not the only reason why borderlanders continued to cross the border. Trade was another. One of the cruellest consequences of Partition was the cutting up of innumerable networks of local marketing. A prominent feature all over the densely-populated borderland was a system of interlocking village markets (*hat*) that served the rural population on alternate days. Many villages did not have shops; their inhabitants visited two or three markets in their region that assembled on different days of the week. Thus village A held its market on Sundays and Thursdays, village B on Tuesdays and Fridays, village C on Wednesdays and Saturdays, and each market had its own profile in terms of goods and services. Inhabitants from many surrounding villages visited these markets at least two or three times a week, usually on foot or by boat, to sell their produce and buy whatever they might need. The markets were crucial not only as commercial hubs but equally as centres of news gathering, social control and entertainment.

The new border had a profound effect on this web of markets because it cut through well established patterns of trade and introduced a powerful state presence into the local arena. Borderland markets continued to be frequented by people from both sides of the border but they were now observed much more closely by state personnel whose views on borderland marketing differed sharply. On the one hand, there were those who considered borderland markets as anti-national: 'Zakiganj is not a suitable place for a market or bazar due to its proximity with Karimganj (Bharat)', wrote the Deputy Commissioner of Sylhet (Pakistan) in 1951, 'It would be a good policy to close down all hats and bazars within a belt of 5 to 10 miles from the borders and it would be suicidal to have a large market within 200 yds of the borders. The market at Zakiganj has been serving and will serve only Bharat ... It may be noted that though Zakiganj is in Pakistan it is the India currency that is in frequent use there. It is [a] disgrace for Pakistan.'[53]

In the same spirit the new District Magistrate of Rangpur (Pakistan) was appalled by what went on in the border markets, which he described as 'the smugglers' Paradise.' He ordered the closure of all 44 markets that were closer than 8 km (5 miles) to the border, calling forth protests from India.[54]

Others, however, sought to establish new markets on their own side of the border with a view to drawing custom and state income from the neighbouring country. When Dawki market became Indian, the Muslim League in Tamabil, just inside Pakistan, suggested that a new market could be established there. That market, it was argued, would yield the state an annual revenue of between Rs500,000 and Rs1,500,000.[55] Sometimes, such new markets were given nationalist names, e.g. Pakistanhat or Jinnahrhat.

Views of the correct way of dealing with border markets varied not only with officials' understanding of national interest, but also with the part of the borderland in which they found themselves, and with the fluctuating level of antagonism between India and Pakistan. In the winter of 1948-9, 'the Government of Assam ... announced by beat of drums at Balu Bazar (Garo Hills) that no citizen of Pakistan would be allowed to attend that Bazar', but Indian Garos were allowed to go to market in Pakistan.[56] Meanwhile, the government of Tripura worried about the sales of its forest products and asked East Pakistan to open more customs posts because 'it had become impossible for the inhabitants of Tripura to sell their raw materials like bamboos, etc. in Pakistan markets, which they had been doing for many years past.'[57]

The official policy was clearly in favour of openness; it allowed marketing visits of up to ten miles into each other's borderland.[58] A 1957 trade agreement between India and Pakistan went into considerable detail, dividing the borderland into six sectors and spelling out which quantities of which goods could be taken across in one day. Paddy and rice products were prohibited but, for example, a person coming from the Chittagong Hill Tracts (Pakistan) could take four chickens, a head load of earthenware, or a bottle of kerosine oïl into the Lushai Hills (India), and a person going the other way was entitled to take a head load of sesame seeds, raw cotton, or bay leaves (Plates 6.3 and 6.4).[59]

But local officials had their own preoccupations. To them, those who came to market from across the border were potential smugglers, spies and victims of robbery. It was impossible to keep track of what was going on when thousands of people gathered and milled about. Some markets were actually on the borderline, causing anxiety in customs officials who were supposed to curb smuggling. For example, the eastern border crossing at Akhaura was an important transit point for Hindu emigrants from Pakistan to Tripura (India), and thorough customs checks were done there to see if emigrants took money or other 'restricted' goods with them. But twice a week a market was held at the very grounds of the customs check post. The market straddled the border and, in the words of an exasperated Pakistani customs official,

Plate 6.3: Villagers entering Rangamati (Chittagong Hill Tracts) on market day, 1940s.[60] The Karnaphuli river connects this town with Mizoram (India), making it easy for market-goers from there to visit regularly.

Plate 6.4: Market day in Bandarban, about 1962. This town served the southern
Chittagong Hill Tracts and adjacent hills in Burma.[61]

about 2 to 3 thousand people remain in movement ... frequently crossing
the border ... this market is mostly attended by people from Agartala
[India] and therefore, all people have to be checked very thoroughly ...
With the present strength of staff, it [is] very difficult to check both the
pedestrians and about 500 to 600 rickshaws passing across the border during
hat days.[62]

The two directives, to allow marketing and to curb smuggling, were often at
odds.[63] In the far north, another market in the commercial town of Sonahat
had been bisected by the border. One half lay in Rangpur (Pakistan), the other
in Goalpara (Assam, India). When a resident from the Pakistan side, who had
bought a few kilogrammes of rice from a vendor on the Indian side, was assaulted
by Indian armed police, the incident led to 'excitement and tension in the
locality,' a protest meeting and arrests. Sonahatis from both sides of the border
then formed a peace committee to 'restore public confidence,' and the district
authorities on either side decided to allow residents to buy rice across the border
up to 4½ kg, for 'bonafide domestic purposes.'[64]

Cross-border marketing and espionage were another unhappy pair. It was
not uncommon for visitors to be arrested at a border market because officials
thought they moved 'in a suspicious way', spread 'anti-state rumours', or were

too inquisitive about the strength of border defence.[65] For visitors of markets across the border, there was a further uncertainty: robbery and harassment by state personnel.[66] When people from the northernmost tip of East Pakistan visited a border market in Bihar (India), 'the border militia of Purnea District … searched Pakistan people who had gone there for marketing as they usually do and harassed, abused and assaulted them and threatened them not to come to the hat again. They also looted money of Pakistan people.'[67]

It was even more common for police to rob market-goers when they were returning home, usually late at night.[68] Occasionally, officials themselves became victims of harassment in connection with border marketing.[69] The following case reveals a difference between borderlanders and outsiders that may have been of more general significance.

Indian policemen stationed at the border outpost of Rangutia (Tripura) struck up a friendship with the station master of the nearby railway station of Mukundapur in Pakistan, and others on the Pakistan side of the border who often contacted them in the course of their joint efforts to regulate peace and order on the border. Having received Pakistani officials in their outpost on several occasions, the Indians decided to pay a return visit and also buy some fish, vegetables and eggs that were cheaper in East Pakistan. They came over and had tea with their friends. They also bought some fish and potatoes from vendors just in front of the Pakistani border outpost, and told a boy who had accompanied them to take these purchases back to their camp in India. Then the Head Constable of the Pakistani outpost (an Urdu-speaking non-Bengali) called them in, asked who they were, and arrested them for unauthorised entry into Pakistan. He suspected them of 'observing the defence measures and the camp itself' but they said they had no bad intentions. Immediately after their arrest a good number of border people assembled and pleaded for their release in order to maintain 'the existing good relationship among the border people' of both countries.[70]

Here borderland solidarity ran counter to the national interest as seen by a non-local state servant. Many borderlanders set more store by good relations and friendly contacts across the border than by statist ideas of territorial inviolability. The very sentinels of the state could get involved in these cross-border networks and it took a non-local to notice the slippage. It was no coincidence that both Pakistan and India often entrusted border duties to non-locals. On the border, it was rarely armed borderlanders who confronted each other as policemen, customs officials and army people across the Bengal border. Rather, outsiders such as Pashtuns, Punjabis and Biharis (on the Pakistan side) and Gurkhas, North Indians, Kashmiris and Lushais (on the Indian side) guarded the border on behalf of the state. Borderlanders could join the civil militias but even here immigrants seem to have outnumbered the locals.

Disruptions of smooth borderland marketing often resulted from a clash between local concepts of territorial continuity and state concepts of territorial discontinuity. What complicated the issue was that the states did not enforce complete discontinuity (i.e. closure of the border), and allowed cross-border marketing. This created a shadowy world in which the pre-Partition web of markets was not completely severed but manipulated to lessen its potential for undermining the states' territorial integrity. The states sought to monitor borderland markets by means of surveillance, permits, visas and intelligence, but could do so only haphazardly.[71] Borderlanders adapted to this new regime remarkably well, trading legally across the border when it was allowed, and resorting to 'armpit smuggling' when it was not.[72] However, they could not always escape the violence that was part of the new regime.

Borderland commuters

In addition to those who cultivated land or visited markets across the border, there were people whose work required them to cross the border regularly, sometimes on a daily basis. Some of these people were simply continuing jobs that they had done before the border was imposed.[73]

Cross-border commuters often held government jobs. Arabinda Gupta from Cachar (India) was a case in point. In 1952 he worked as an agricultural demonstrator in the East Pakistan Department of Agriculture in Sylhet. Jatindranath Ganguly from Khulna (Pakistan) was in a similar situation; he worked as a Khas Mahal peon in 24-Parganas (India) in 1948.[74] For years, many policemen served one state but continued to live in the other. Constable Nurun Nabi's home was in Murshidabad (India) but he was stationed at Tetulia (Pakistan), while Binay Kumar Das, who was a constable in the intelligence service of Assam, had his home in Sylhet (Pakistan).[75]

Other borderlanders had their own businesses or professions across the dividing line, for example a lawyer from Tripura (India) who was practising in Comilla (Pakistan), a shopkeeper from Dinajpur (Pakistan) whose shop was across the border in West Dinajpur (India), or a doctor from Rangpur (Pakistan) seeing patients in Cooch Behar (India). Day labourers were another large group of cross-border commuters.[76] When visas were introduced in 1952, detailed provisions were made for borderland artisans, pensioners and transport workers, and for people 'working with or in an established and *bona fide* business' across the border.[77]

Some borderlanders found that the border actually ran right through their workplace. About 1,000 km of the border went through water and those who worked on these rivers, lakes and marshes faced a dangerous but potentially lucrative situation. Bridges being relatively scarce, most cross-river traffic was done by boat, and there were numerous ferrymen on border rivers; these were often wage labourers employed by ferry owners. Their work was suspect because of its location: here the line between legal trade and smuggling, exploitation of domestic and foreign resources, and being a citizen or an alien was wafer-thin. And the danger was compounded when the precise location of the border was disputed. Over the years, many ferrymen – and fishermen, another large group working on border rivers – fell victim to cross-border shootings. Nobody has bothered to record systematically how many boatmen and fishermen lost their lives on the border rivers over the years but the records are full of such incidents.[78]

There were other groups of people whose work took them to both sides of the border. Some of these, such as railwaymen, telegraph linemen and people quarrying stones along border rivers, continued work that had existed before the border came into being,. Others were engaged in work that resulted from the border and the new opportunities it created, for example members of border demarcation parties (surveyors, builders of boundary pillars), coolies transshipping goods at the border, rickshaw-pullers and smugglers.

Conclusion: The half-open border

India and Pakistan had been given territories that had no previous history of separation. To turn these territories into self-contained units was a complicated task, not least because strict territorialization came at a considerable price. It was for this reason that strategies regarding territoriality hardly formed a clearly directed policy. On the contrary, as the two governments felt their way down an unknown, slippery path, they groped for *ad hoc* compromises that were often contradictory. Moreover, prime ministers and chief secretaries might make lofty statements but these could not easily be translated into feasible (and affordable) policies. Borderland officials, who were in many ways the chief protectors of the territory on a day-to-day basis, might receive *ukases* from the capital but they were largely on their own when it came to making policies out of them: they were rarely provided with the necessary wherewithal or manpower. As a result, top-level decisions were implemented differently in different parts of the borderland, and some were not implemented at all.

Among the unanticipated territorial consequences of Partition were the issues of cross-border landholding, marketing and commuting. For both India and Pakistan (much less so for Burma[79]) these issues were crucially important because they impinged on their claims to sovereignty, territorial inviolability and control of people and goods. It was because the new state elites were eminently territorial in their imagination of statehood that a peasant taking some chickens to market or tilling a plot of land across the border, or a day labourer crossing the border in search of employment, could be perceived as a threat to the integrity and defence of the national territory, and be subjected to beatings (or worse) in the name of imposing state authority. The issue of landholding was further complicated by questions of property rights and compensation (on which the states were never able to reach agreement), and the issue of marketing by considerations of benefits to the national economy. Incapable of resolving many of these unanticipated territorial consequences of Partition, the new states would authorize or prohibit the movement of crops, goods, money, cattle and people in an erratic pattern that fluctuated wildly between different sections of the borderland, between different periods after 1947, and between official policy and actual implementation.

The process of building territorial states took many casualties in the borderland: the *ziratias* whose cross-border property rights were sacrificed to the state's pursuit of revenue; cross-border cultivators who got killed or wounded in skirmishes or who ultimately lost their property; market-goers and commuters who were robbed or arrested; and many others who suffered physical, economic, social and psychological deprivation. Borderlanders employed various strategies to prevent state interference from ruining their lives. Torn between accommodation and defiance, they engaged the state in many ways. It is these struggles for control of the borderland, more than anything else, that established the Partition border as an undeniable social reality.

In this chapter I have presented the tension between borderlanders and their states in terms of defiance and accommodation. The states might define themselves in terms of exclusive dominance over a territorialized population, but many people on both sides of the international border stood to lose a great deal if such territorial dominance was enforced. For them, the main issues were to what extent (and at what risk) the border could be ignored, defied, or slipped through; how to avoid the dangers of exposure to unsympathetic state personnel on either side; and how to hang on to crucial sources of income beyond the border. As a result, the borderland witnessed an unfolding drama of territorialization and defiance. State logic won out in the case of cross-border landholding, but it took many years. It did not succeed nearly so well in the case of cross-border marketing, where strict territorialization could never be enforced and where forms of accommodation had to be found.[80]

In the following chapters we will explore how state logic was ultimately defeated in even bigger ways by cross-border networking in several arenas. We will see how labour migration expanded despite all state efforts to block it, and how it turned into one of the most contested political issues between India, Bangladesh and Burma. But first, in the next chapter, we will consider the enormous impact of legal and illegal flows of goods on the development of the borderland and on the formation of its states.

Notes

1 CR 1I-16/48 (11-50). Lamazuar is a village in Sylhet (East Pakistan). The soccer team were arrested on the plea that they had gone to India to parade. For another soccer match, in Hili (Dinajpur) in 1954, which led to border incidents, see CR 1B2-122/54 (1-55).

2 See also Md. Mahbubar Rahman and Willem van Schendel, '"I Am *Not* a Refugee": Rethinking Partition Migration,' *Modern Asian Studies*, 37:3 (2003), 551–84.

3 Except for Joya Chatterji, 'The Fashioning of a Frontier: The Radcliffe Line and Bengal's Border Landscape, 1947-52,' *Modern Asian Studies*, 33:1 (1999), 185–242; and Ranabir Samaddar, *The Marginal Nation: Transborder Migration from Bangladesh to West Bengal* (New Delhi, etc.: Sage Publications, 1999).

4 Only some parts of the Partition border had ever acted as fixed borders between states. The border between Cooch Behar (India) and Rangpur (Pakistan) reflected the territorial division between the Mughal empire and the independent state of Cooch Behar. Early British expansion had frequently halted for a generation or so before pushing on into the hills surrounding the Bengal delta. This was true of the boundary between Chittagong and the Chittagong Hill Tracts, which did not become part of the Partition border, and of the Meghalaya border, which did. The Meghalaya border had for some time, in an earlier incarnation, acted as the border between British India and independent Garo and Khasi polities but was subsequently obliterated when the British conquered the Garo and Khasi hills. On Rangpur/Cooch Behar, see Willem van Schendel, 'Stateless in South Asia: The Making of the India-Bangladesh Enclaves', *The Journal of Asian Studies*, 61:1 (February 2002), 115–47; on Meghalaya, see David Ludden, 'The First Boundary of Bangladesh on Sylhet's Northern Frontiers,' *Journal of the Asiatic Society of Bangladesh* (forthcoming).

5 Cf. Rahman and Van Schendel, '"I Am *Not* a Refugee"'.

6 Letter from the Deputy Commissioner, Chittagong Hill Tracts (9 January 1953), in CR 7C1-1/52 (1-54). The evicted (717 families, about 2,500 individuals) were Riang and Noatia (groups that are sometimes considered to be subdivisions of the Tripura/Tipra). They formed an example of non-Muslim immigration into East Pakistan but were eventually sent back to Tripura.

7 Similar attempts by people from Tripura to start cultivation in the Chittagong Hill Tracts in 1958 and 1959 were reported in 'Fresh firing by Indian troops: flagrant violation of ceasefire agreement', *The Pakistan Observer* (21 February 1959).

8 This observation was made on the Mymensingh/Assam (now Meghalaya) border. Neville A Kirkwood, *Independent India's Troubled Northeast, 1952–69: An Australian Missionary's Story* (n.p.: Griffith University, Centre for the Study of Australia-Asia Relations, 1996), 14. For cross-border drinking in the same area in 1990, see Francis Rolt, *On the Brink of Bengal* (London: John Murray, 1991), 136–40. For a more recent example in which Indian border guards 'picked a fight with some local residents while gambling near the Zero Line' in the same area, leading to a shooting that killed a man and injured a child, and another in which a drunken Indian border guard killed his colleague, see 'One hurt as BSF opens fire on mob – Police to probe incident', *The Telegraph* (6 November 2002), and 'BSF jawan guns down colleague,' *The Sentinel* (11 September 2003).

9 CR 1A2-1/51 (3-54); CR 1A4-1/52 (3-54).

10 Plt. 1I-228/48 (7-49). For West Bengal police crossing the border at Rajshahi to help Chain Mondols (a group of Hindus) migrate to India, see CR 1I-108/49 (3-51). In this case, Pakistani police prevented them taking away their moveable property.

11 Letter from Syed Ghulam Nabi Ahmadi, Patrol Officer, Ghughumari Ghat & Panka
    Ghat, to the Regional Controller of Procurement, through the Regional Cordoning
    Officer, Region I, Rajshahi, 25 February 1948 (CR 1W-1/49 (1-53)).

12 'Report of the executive enquiry on the firing resorted to by the Armed Police Party
    posted at Chanchkoir on 12.1.48' (Pol. P5E-10/48 (10-48)).

13 The confrontation ended in arrest, and confiscation (and subsequent auctioning) of
    cows. A petition, accusing the police of demanding a huge bribe, was later filed by
    Rupkanta Barman and five others of a village in PS Dimla (Pakistan), suggesting that
    these were local Rajbongshi cattle traders rather than emigrants; CR 1A3-5/50 (3-54).

14 E.g. 'Ek Sotabdir Prachin Sripurer Phuldol Utsob Pondo: Sohosradhik Noronarir Upor
    Puliser Lathi Chalona', Hindusthan (4 June 1948).

15 Pol. EBP10C-51/48 (6-49). The East Pakistan authorities were particularly worried about
    connections with various parties (Communist, Congress, Hindu Mahasabha), which
    they suspected, as well as about the fact that Sripur was the home village of Dr Bidhan
    Chandra Roy, who was then the Prime Minister of West Bengal.

16 Section 144 of the Code of Criminal Procedure, 1898, gives magistrates the power to
    issue temporary restraining orders 'in Urgent Cases of Nuisance or Apprehended Danger.'
    The section has been used frequently in the post-colonial period and is still in force. See
    The Code of Criminal Procedure, 1898 (Act V of 1898) [As Modified up to the 31st December
    1980] (Dacca: Bangladesh Forms and Publications Office, 1981), 88–9.

17 In more recent decades smugglers, rebels and bandits have become better armed, were
    less concerned about state retribution, and would once more seek confrontation. See
    chapter 10.

18 Some groups of nomadic people would continue to move back and forth across the
    border on a seasonal basis, and they were usually allowed to do so. Most notable were
    the Bede. One group of Bede, interviewed in West Bengal in February 2003, said: 'We
    have been travelling on well-laid out paths for generations ... Both [Bengals] are our
    land, we belong to wherever we can find means to earn a living. We have seasons.
    Around this time, we camp in Bangladesh to collect birds and honey. A month later,
    when the harvest is over, we sell medicinal plants and charms to villagers.' Spending
    much of the dry season in southwestern Bangladesh, they would return at the onset of
    the rainy season and 'travel the length of Bengal, from East Midnapore to North Dinajpur.'
    Alamgir Hossain, 'Nomads off beaten track', The Telegraph (7 February 2003)

19 Cf. CN Vakil, Economic Consequences of Divided India: A Study of the Economy of India
    and Pakistan (Bombay: Vora & Co., 1950), esp. 102–16; Five Years of Pakistan (August
    1947–August 1952) (Karachi: Pakistan Publications, 1952), 148–53; Ten Years of Pakistan,
    1947–1957 (Karachi: Pakistan Publications, 1957), 243–8.

20 Jyoti Bhusan Das Gupta, Indo-Pakistan Relations (1947–1955) (Amsterdam: De Brug-
    Djambatan, 1958), 188–211. India and Pakistan evolved different solutions for 'evacuee
    property' in Bengal and in the rest of the subcontinent. For background, and details on
    India/ West-Pakistan, see Vazira Zamindar, 'Divided Families and the Making of
    Nationhood in India and Pakistan 1947–65' (PhD thesis, Columbia University, 2002),
    84–111.

21 Pol. XX (3-49).

22 For example, Joy Kanta Kashya and other villagers of Golabari (Dinajpur, Pakistan)
    shifted to Baruapara (Jalpaiguri, India) during the communal disturbances of 1950. 'The
    distance of his new house from the old one in Pakistan is about 200/250 yards' (CR 1B-
    39/51 (1-53)).

23 Haru Mondol (interview by Md. Mahbubar Rahman, Lolitahar (Rajshahi district, Bangladesh), 1999). This strategy of family splitting was also recorded for other parts of the borderland, as in the case of a father living in Cachar (India), and cultivating the family's land there, while his son and wife lived nearby in Sylhet (Pakistan) and took care of the land the family owned in Pakistan. This strategy confounded the authorities because it was unclear whether such families were Indians, Pakistanis, or both (CR 1B4-10/53 (7-54)).

24 Plt. 20A-1/49 (8-49). For a separate agreement between Pakistan and the Princely State of Cooch Behar, see Plt. 1I-259/48 (2-49).

25 In 1950 the amount to be taken across the Assam-East Pakistan and Tripura-East Pakistan borders was restricted to 40 maunds (about 1,400 kg) per family. On the West Bengal-East Pakistan border even this was not allowed: cultivators could not take any paddy home across the border. By 1954, this regime was also in force on the Assam border. Tripura had imposed unilateral restrictions on ziratia subjects (see below). Just after Partition, ziratias could take their entire crop home to Pakistan but had to pay an export duty of Rs. 0/2/3 per maund (36 kg). There were also bribes to be paid to customs officers, weight takers, police and foresters. By 1949, Tripura had restricted the export of paddy to Pakistan to 28 maunds (about 1,000 kg) per family, and the export duty was raised to Rs.1/2/3. In meetings in October 1949 and November 1950, pressure from Pakistan increased the amount of paddy and lowered the duty. *Decisions taken at the Chief Secretaries' Conference held at Calcutta on the 20th and 21st November, 1950 (Eighteenth Conference)*, 8–9 (CR 1I-3/51 (11-53); cf. CR 1B-3 (9-49); CR 3I-172/49 (11-50); CR 1C-3/49 (11-50); CR 8M-1/54 (1-55)).

26 In 1948, India introduced a permit system (and in 1949 the Influx From Pakistan (Control) Act) that applied only to West Pakistan. After 1952, border traffic between India and East Pakistan was regulated officially by a passport/visa system that had a special facility for borderlanders. The Category A Visa for Pakistan was for 'Indian nationals who live in Indian territory within ten miles of the East Bengal border and who normally earn their livelihood by working in Pakistan territory within ten miles of the Indian border: (a) Cultivators who have to make frequent journeys in order to cultivate or supervise the cultivation of their own lands and their labourers and hired servants; (b) Small artisans, such as blacksmiths, wood-cutters, carpenters, petty shopkeepers and petty traders; and (c) Persons the only markets for whose agricultural produce lie in Pakistan territory within ten miles of the East Bengal border.' Persons holding such visas did not have to pass through a check post (of which there were few) but could cross the border 'at any place within the villages specified in the visa.' Government of Pakistan, Ministry of Foreign Affairs and Commonwealth Relations, *Pakistan O Bharoter Moddhe Jatayater Jonne Passport O Visa Niyomaboli / Passport System to Regulate the Entry of Indian Nationals into Pakistan* (Dacca, 1952), 1-2 (Plt. 2B-17/52 (3-53)); cf. Sen Gupta, *The Eclipse of East Pakistan*, 135–40. In 1953, Pakistan officials had the impression that there were more East Pakistani than Indian cultivators benefiting from 'A' visas (CR 8M-1/54 (1-55)).

27 In the 1950s and 1960s the superior tenures (rent-receiving interests) were abolished following the enactment of the East Bengal State Acquisition and Tenancy Act, 1950, the West Bengal Estates Acquisition Act, 1953, and the Tripura Land Revenue and Land Reforms Act, 1960. In East Pakistan, all tenures were abolished by April 1956. However, property rights in immovables were discussed many times without Pakistan and India agreeing upon a solution. By 1965, talks had stalled. Cf. Kamal Siddiqui et al.,

Land Reforms and Land Management in Bangladesh and West Bengal: A Comparative Study (Dhaka: University Press Limited, 1988); *Tripura District Gazetteers: Tripura* (Agartala: Government of Tripura, 1975), 260–1; Jha, *Indo-Pakistan Relations*, 306–12.

28 For an account based on interviews with cross-border land owners and 'exchangees,' see Rahman and Van Schendel, "'I Am *Not* A Refugee'".

29 Cf. Willem van Schendel, 'Working through Partition: Making a Living in the Bengal Borderlands', *International Review of Social History*, 46 (2001), 393–421.

30 The three parts of his Chakla Roshnabad estate in Noakhali and Comilla districts alone covered 145,000 hectares, 1,500 villages and 90,000 (under-)*raiyati* tenants. Another part of the estate was located in Sylhet district. See JG Cumming, *Survey and Settlement of the Chakla Roshnabad Estate in the Districts of Tippera and Noakhali, 1892–99* (Calcutta: Bengal Secretariat Press, 1899). After Partition, the estate yielded Rs. 1.8 million a year in rent (CR 1B-3 (9-49)).

31 Plt. 1I-77/48 (9-48).

32 The minister passed the petition on to the Home Secretary and wrote in the margin: 'I received this representation when I visited a border-area named Nayanpur. I find a statement from the High Commissioner of India here that these allegations are not true. It appears to me that the statement of the Indian High Commissioner's office is incorrect. Should facts be published by our Govt?' CR 3T4-1/51 (3-54).

33 Various petitions to the Prime Minister, East Pakistan, the District Magistrate at Comilla, and others, in CR 1B-3 (9-49); Plt. 1I-77/48 (9-48). Cf. Tripura Government Circular (CR 1I-120/48 (1-51); CR XX/50 (7-51)), and 'Bharotiyo Shoinyoder Biruddhe Obhijog', *Ittehad* (Calcutta), 23 May 1948; 'Tripurar Poristhiti,' *Zindegi* (Dhaka), 7 August 1949. The Roshnabad tenants also started a campaign to get better conditions from their landlord; one petition that has survived is entitled '*Roshnabad Zomidarir Shimantobashir O Tripura Rajyer Projagono Pokkhe Shrishrimoti Mohamanya Matamoharani Shomipe Binite O Shokorun Prarthona* [A humble and woeful petition to Her Exalted Majesty the Queen Mother on behalf of the border people of the Roshnabad Estate and the subjects/ tenants of Tripura State] 1949; Representation by Moulvi Sk. Wahidullah Chowdhary BA, Secretary, Committee of Action, Roshnabad Proja Samiti, Feni' (CR 1B-5/49 (12-49); Plt. 1I-77/48 (9-48)).

34 Letter from the Dewan (Prime Minister) of Tripura to the District Magistrate, Tippera (Comilla), 17 December 1948; in it he also describes the *ziratias* as 'the lawless elements on your side of the border' (CR 1B-5/49 (12-49)).

35 CR 1I-120/48 (1-51); cf. CR 1B3-2/49 (11-50); CR 1B3-1/50 (5-52).

36 'Pakistan-Tripura State Border Troubles: Leader's Efforts for Restoring Peace,' *Hindusthan Standard* (25 December 1948). In the Inter-Dominion Agreement of 1948, India and Pakistan agreed that: 'Where any cultivator living in a border village of one Dominion has land in a border village in the other Dominion, he should be permitted, within a reasonable period after the harvest, to take across the border to his residence reasonable quantities of any controlled commodities produced by him for his domestic consumption with the minimum of restrictions and formalities.'

37 'The background and purpose of the nonviolent, non-communal and economic Satyagraha by the subjects of Tripura Roshnabad Estate, and the resolutions carried in different public meetings,' October 1948 (CR 1B-5/49 (12-49)). In September 1948, Tripura State police arrested three Pakistani Hindus (Uday Chandra Namasudra, Lal Chand Nama and Monomohan Nama) from their home village for paddy smuggling, took them across the border and lodged them in Agartala jail (CR 1I-120/48 (1-51)).

The District Magistrate of Comilla was of opinion that the conflict had 'arisen out of discontent essentially agrarian in nature' that the Tripura State had 'always tried to give ... a political colour and make it an Inter-Dominion issue [so as] to shirk its duties and responsibilities as landlord towards the tenants who happen to be Pakistanies' (CR 3I-172/49 (11-50)). For reports on border meetings, see CR 3A-10/53 (8-54).

38 Letter by Secretary, Ministry of External Affairs, New Delhi, to High Commissioner for Pakistan in India, 15 July 1950. See also *Tripura Gazette*, 27 January 1950 (CR 5M-3/50 (2-53)).

39 CR 3T4-1/51 (3-54).

40 In 1957, *ziratia* rights were linked to railway transit facilities for Indian food grains through East Pakistan to Tripura. In exchange for these facilities, *ziratias* were allowed to take up to 40 *maunds* (about 1,400 kg) of paddy per family from Tripura to East Pakistan. When transit trade was blocked, however, *ziratia* rights lapsed. See Shreedhar and John Kaniyalil, *Indo-Pak Relations: A Documentary Study* (New Delhi: ABC Publishing House, 1993), 137–40; cf. 'Kumillay Purbo Pakistan o Tripura Rajjo shommelon: Shimanter golojog o bibhinno shomosshar mimangsha prochesta,' *Azad* (13 October 1949).

41 Who was entitled to handsome compensation under the East Pakistan State Acquisition Act. On the question of legal ownership of the estate after Tripura had acceded to India, see CR 1V-6/50 (6-54).

42 Report by Special Superintendent of Police, Intelligence Branch, East Bengal, 18/11/51 (CR 1B2-22/50 (5-52a); cf. CR 1B2-22/50 (5-52b); CR 3A-6/52 (8-53a); CR 1A1-3/51 (2-54)). Reverse cases can be found in CR 1B2-11/51 (3-53); CR 1B2-31/51 (3-53); CR 1B2-53/51 (12-52). See also 'Shimana elakay chash-abad', *Azad* (28 May 1949); 'Shimanto pulishder guli binimoy shomosha,' *Azad* (19 December 1950); 'Nodia-Kushtia shimante Bharotio shoinno o tank shomabesh', *Azad* (20 December 1950). For similar cases on the Malda/Rajshahi border, see e.g. CR 1I-108/49 (3-51); CR 1B7/50 (11-52); CR 1B2-31/51 (3-53); CR 1B2-3/51 (8-53); and on the Dinajpur/West Dinajpur border, Plt. 1I-228/48 (7-49).

43 CR 1B4-11/51 (8-53); cf. CR 1B4-3/52 (3-55).

44 For example, people from Assam who had lands in East Pakistan had to obtain a permit to till those lands (CR 1B2-42/51 (7-54)). For a case of attempted cross-border arrest of an inhabitant of the Chittagong Hill Tracts (East Pakistan) who had land in the Lushai Hills (Assam), see CR 1B2-46/51 (7-54).

45 CR 1B2-12/52 (12-52); cf. Plt. 1I-259/48 (2-49).

46 Letter from the West Bengal government to the Home Ministry, East Bengal, complaining about the treatment of cultivators living in Malda district (India) and cultivating lands in Rajshahi (East Pakistan), March 1950. Harassment of cross-border cultivators went further: 'all sorts of impediments are placed by the police as well as the local people ... against the sale or removal to West Bengal of the produce of all types like mangoes, pulses, fish, lichis, cereals, mulberry leaves, etc. obtained from lands owned by Indian nationals, the movement of which out of East Bengal is not restricted by law and that in very many cases these articles are taken away by the local people without any payment' (CR 1B2-12/52 (12-52)).

47 Letter dated 6 April 1950 (CR 1B2-12/52 (12-52)). Here, too, there were 'some people whose culturable lands wholly fall in the other dominion and vice-versa.' For cases of procurement in Kushtia and Nadia, see Pol. P10C-28/49 (6-49); CR 1B2-11/51 (3-53).

48 E.g. CR 1I-156/48 (11-50); CR 1I-120/48 (1-51).

49 For example, three Hindus who migrated from the Chittagong Hill Tracts (East Pakistan)

to India received an official note from the sub-divisional officer, Ramgarh, which read: 'It is learnt that you have migrated to Tripura Hill-Tracts leaving behind your properties here. You are asked to show cause by 29.8.53, why your properties would not be acquired.' A similar case was reported for Rajshahi (CR 1B2-12/52 (12-52).

50 For details on 'displacement by exchange,' see Rahman and Van Schendel, '"I Am Not A Refugee"'.

51 Interview of Md. Mahbubar Rahman with Abed Ali (Rajshahi, Bangladesh, 1999; my translation). A *bigha* is 0.33 acre, or 0.14 ha.

52 Cf. the case of Monwara Begum Minu, wife of Abdus Sobhan of Bijoynagar (a border village in Godagari, Rajshahi, Bangladesh). When Monwara was murdered by three men from Mushidabad, across the border in India, the motive was to get control of her paternal property in India. '3 Indians held in Rajshahi', *The New Nation* (2 November 2002).

53 Plt. 32C-1/51 (3-53).

54 CR 1B2-35/51 (1-55); 'Pakistan's new order: Hats bordering Cooch Behar closed,' *Hindustan Standard* (31 May 1951). Over half a century later, exactly the same sentiment was expressed by Indian border guards in the region who 'urged the government to ban new cattle markets within 8 km of the border and to shift all existing ones beyond the stipulated distance.' The district magistrate in West Dinajpur district was of the same opinion. He said: 'All the *haats* within [a 5-km radius of the border with Bangladesh] will be relocated once they are identified. We won't let anybody sit in these markets with their ware from now on.' When journalists suggested that this would create great inconvenience to villagers and might trigger tension in the border region, he said: 'There is nothing we can do about this. The *haats* close to the border will have to go for security reasons ... All the families [living close to the border line] are being identified. Once the identification is complete, we will relocate them to some other areas.' 'BSF on alert in Cooch Behar,' *The Statesman* (26 February 2002); Abhijit Chakroborty, 'I-D cards to check border infiltration,' *The Telegraph* (7 October 2002).

55 Plt. 5M-4/48 (7-49). Even though Tamabil market (Sylhet) was established, and flourished, Pakistanis continued to visit and own shops at Dawki market (Assam) (CR 2A/50 (1-51); CR 2A-1/50 (3-53)).

56 CR 1I-120/48 (1-51); Pol. EBP3R-56/48 (2-49).

57 *Decisions taken at the 17th Chief Secretaries' Conference held at Dacca on the 29th and 30th August, 1950* (CR 1A2-4/51 (3-53); cf. CR 3C1-1/53 (3-54); CR 3C2-2/52 (4-54)). For a plea by the Sylhet authorities, based on a petition by local businessmen, to open customs stations to allow (and tax) trade with the Khasi & Jaintia hills in Assam, see CR 3I-239/51 (8-54).

58 After 1952 with a special visa. Under the visa regulations introduced by Pakistan and India in that year, category 'A' visas were made available to 'Persons the only markets for whose agricultural produce lie in Pakistan territory within ten miles of the East Bengal border,' and vice versa (Plt. 2B-17/52 (3-53)).

59 The ten-mile belt for border trade was reaffirmed in the Trade Agreement between India and Pakistan of 22 January 1957. Once more it was only for the East Pakistan/India borderland, and it included the following stipulations: a category 'A' visa was required, persons could cross the border only once a day, goods would be free from restrictions and customs duties, and a cash amount of no more than Rs.5 could be taken across the border. For the text of the agreement and the list of items per sector, see Shreedhar and Kaniyalil, *Indo-Pak Relations* (1993), 126–37, 141–2. When a new

agreement had to be made in 1960, the 'Pakistan Delegation was of the view that border arrangement did not lead to increase in bona fide trade, but led to a number of difficulties. Nevertheless, they were prepared to consider the continuance of border trade arrangements in a modified form in respect of specially difficult areas only' (156–7). Officially sanctioned border trade ended, and the next trade agreement of 1963 did not include border trade, although it left the two governments free to make special 'arrangements relating to Border Trade' (159–81, at 161). In 1972, however, the Prime Ministers of India and Bangladesh 'approved the principles of the revival of transit trade and the agreement on border trade' (Joint Indo-Bangla Declaration, 19 March 1972, reprinted in Appadorai, *Selected Documents*, 441; 'Trade Agreement between the Government of India and the Government of Bangladesh, New Delhi, March 28, 1972', in: Avtar Singh Bhasin (ed.), *India-Bangladesh Relations: Documents – 1971–2002* (New Delhi: Geetika Publishers, 2003), III, 1283–91.

60 Photograph by Lily Smith.

61 Photograph by JF Laurence.

62 Letter from the Superintendent of Land Customs, Akhaura, 30 April 1951 (CR 2T5-2/51 (1-53)). In June 1951, Indian authorities protested because the market 'could not sit … due to the cordon made by the local Ansars preventing sellers form coming to the market' (CR 1B2-35/51 (1-55)).

63 For example, in April 1948 West Dinajpur (West Bengal) police 'seized some rice at the border in the Indian Union from a man who was taking the rice from the Indian Union to a Pakistan Hat in the neighbourhood, but the Pakistan Police and National guards obstructed the constables and chowkidars in their lawful work, arrested them and took them to Phulbari P.S. (Pakistan)' (Plt. 1I-228/48 (7-49)).

64 Pol. EBP10C-4/47 (3-48).

65 Apparently arrests for spying were quite common. The District Magistrate of Kushtia (Pakistan) wrote to his counterpart in Nadia (India) in October 1951: 'I have so far received reports of arrests of 692 Muslims in August and September last by your Police in Nadia District, 592 on the accusation that they were Pakistani spies and 100 on other charges … For our part, we don't have any spies not to speak of such a large number sprawling about in your countryside. Please permit me to add that I have a shrewd feeling that your Police are not using discretion to the extent you … would expect of them in a broader view of things' (CR 1A1-3/51 (2-54)). For cases of 'spies' arrested at markets in Jessore, Mymensingh, Sylhet and Khasi & Jaintia Hills, see Plt. 5M-4/48 (7-49); CR 1A3-8/49 (11-50); Pol. P4A-2/49 (4-49); CR 1A2-1/51 (3-54).

66 Borderlanders appear to have set great store by maintaining cross-border market links, and we have no evidence of borderlanders obstructing each other from attending markets across the border. Sometimes locals harassed non-locals visiting border markets, however, as in the case of some businessmen from Faridpur (an interior district of East Pakistan) who went by boat to Basirhat (West Bengal) in 1950 to sell about 3,600 kg of onions. They 'anchored near a "Hatkhola" by the bank of the [border] river Ichhamati. The hat is held twice a week and the men were able to dispose of their goods within 8 days (within 2 or 3 hats).' Then they were attacked by local shopkeepers (apparently over a trade deal), robbed, forced to drink alcohol, and finally ended up in the local hospital. Such attacks occurred frequently in the area (CR 1A2-12/50 (5-53); cf. CR 2A-1/50 (3-53)).

67 CR 1I-136/48 (11-50); cf. Plt. 5M-4/48 (7-49). This segment of the Indian state of Bihar was later transferred to the state West Bengal in order to link the two parts of West Bengal that Partition had created. See Appendix Figure 2.

68 E.g. some fishermen from Sylhet (East Pakistan) were returning from Mowdon (Assam) in November 1951 when three Indian constables arrested them, beat them and looted their cash and commodities (CR 1B4-11/51 (8-53)). Villagers from Malda (West Bengal) were detained at night by Pakistani border police when they were returning by boat from Rajshahi (East Pakistan) where they had bought bamboos. The policemen demanded money and released one person to go and collect it from his home in India. He did so, and then his companions and their boat were also released (CR 1B2-6/49 (7-52)). Cf. the case of two Khasis from Assam who were arrested after having bought tobacco at Borchera market in Sylhet (CR 1A2-10/49 (3-51)), and eight merchants from West Dinajpur (India) returning with groceries from Dinajpur town (Pakistan) who were detained and told that 'under no circumstances should anything go to the Indian Dominion from Pakistan' (CR 1W-1/49 (1-53), which lists several other cases).

69 E.g. the case of a Pakistani land customs inspector on the Mymensingh border, who was issuing customs permits to market vendors bringing in pineapples, betel leaves and bamboos from the Garo Hills (India) in August 1952, when he was kidnapped from Pakistani territory by an enraged Indian police officer who told him: 'You should not hold Pakistani office within our view ... Your Pakistani Police are oppressing our people and we have enough strength and we can also retaliate' (CR 1A4-1/52 (3-54); Plt. 5M-4/48 (7-49)).

70 CR 1A2-3/51 (3-53).

71 District intelligence agents routinely visited markets to pick up rumours, check information in an unobtrusive way, observe suspect individuals and learn about troop movements across the border. Their regular reports to district headquarters (of which many ended up in Home Ministry files in Dhaka) often referred to such data gathering at borderland markets.

72 To use a term used by a former Ghanaian border guard when describing small-scale cross-border trade by individual villagers. Paul Nugent, 'Power Versus Knowledge: Smugglers and the State Along Ghana's Eastern Frontier, 1920–1992', in: Michael Rösler and Tobias Wendl (eds), Frontiers and Borderlands: Anthropological Perspectives (Frankfurt am Main, etc.: Peter Lang, 1999), 93.

73 Cf. Van Schendel, 'Working through Partition'.

74 CR 3I-324/52 (9-53); CR 1A3-8/49 (11-50); cf. CR 1I-156/48 (11-50).

75 E.g. CR 1A3-8/49 (11-50); CR 1A6-1/52 (3-54); cf. CR 1A2-1/51 (3-54).

76 CR 3T3-1/51 (3-53); CR 1A7-1/52 (4-53); CR 3I-68/52 (1-54); CR 1B2-9/51 (3-54).

77 Visas were allowed for 'small artisans, such as, blacksmiths, wood-cutters, carpenters, petty shopkeepers and petty traders' (Category A), for pensioners and other recipients of periodical or monthly payments who had to make regular personal appearances (Category B), transport workers (steamer crews, railway workers) and 'Indian nationals working with or in an established and bona fide business in Pakistan' (Category E) (Plt. 2B-17/52 (3-53); cf. CR 8M-1/54 (1-55)).

78 On ferrymen being arrested, shot at, or killed by border guards, see e.g. CR 1B2-11./50 (3-51), Pol. EBP10C-23/48 (9-48), Pol. P10C-12/49 (10-49), CR 1B2-1/51 (2-54), CR 1B1-4/53 (6-54), CR 1B2-46/51 (7-54), CR 1B5-1/52 (8-54), CR 1B2-9/54 (2-55), CR 1B2-40/53 (12-55); on fishermen, CR 1B2-6/49 (7-52), CR 3I-20/53 (11-54). Others whose work took them to the border rivers were also at risk, e.g. collectors of stones in the Pyain river on the Meghalaya/ Sylhet border (see CR 1A1-6/51 (3-53)). Sometimes the categories of commuting government servant and ferryman overlapped: the district authorities of Rajshahi (Pakistan) employed ferry-men from the adjacent district of Murshidabad (India). These men got caught up in a border dispute between the two

states in 1948. They 'were severely beaten, arrested, remanded [in] custody and subsequently released on a bail of Rs.200/- each. Their relations are also being oppressed. Their fault is said to have ... originated from the fact that they are serving under an enemy and hence are traitors' (CR 1W-1/49 (1-53)).

79 In the early years after Partition, the Burmese state was only weakly present in its border regions. Civil war broke out and the powers of the government in Rangoon did not extend much beyond the central areas of the country. Even the manning of the Arakan border was thin and haphazard, and the relationship with East Pakistan was a very minor concern in Burma. As a result, the border remained much more open here than where it separated East Pakistan and India.

80 For more on cross-border marketing, see chapter 7. A brief description of cross-border marketing on the Dhubri/ Rangpur border in the 1990s can be found in 'Breaching the frontiers effortlessly', The Hindu (15 April 1998).

7

THE FLOW OF GOODS

In August 2001 the Director-General of the Bangladesh Rifles opened a glitzy shopping mall in central Dhaka. The mall, named *Bangladesh Rifles Square*, was owned by the nation's border guards. The Prime Minister had laid the foundation stone and at the grand opening the Director-General announced that the income from the shopping complex would be 'spent to serve the distressed' because 'the country's border forces have a moral obligation to serve the distressed, besides their responsibilities to safeguard territorial integrity, curb anti-state activities along the frontier and assist law-enforcing agencies in discharging their functions.' Selling pirated DVDs, smuggled Indian saris and many legal items, the multi-storied shopping complex was an interesting example of the interweaving of illegal and legal trade, mediated by state functionaries.[1]

In the previous chapters I have focused primarily on the Bengal borderland and its states. Now I turn to a powerful influence on the formation of both the borderland and the state: market forces. Partition was as much an economic process as it was an administrative one, and the commercial permutations involved in the creation of a borderland society were immensely complex. As the case of the Bangladesh Rifles Square suggests, the state played a crucial role in this economic restructuring.

All three new states laying claim to the Bengal borderland developed economic policies that sought to enclose economic relations within their national territories. To this end they categorized various cross-border flows and declared most transnational trade illegal, decisions that were to play a major role in the economy of the borderland. The opening sections of this chapter explain how the states tried to use categorization to tame trade flows. I go on to show that these attempts were largely unsuccessful, yet still had a substantial impact on borderlanders and their economic behaviour. The concluding sections discuss the emergence of a vibrant subversive economy that undermined official policies and ultimately rescaled the state.

Assassinating a regional economy

Before Partition the huge Bengal-Assam-Arakan region had been integrated in a web of complex economic ties. The region, inhabited by tens of millions of people, had a strong agricultural base and a large variety of industrial zones. For many centuries it had been linked to global commercial networks, mainly through agro-industries producing silk and cotton textiles, indigo, opium, tea, rice, sugar and jute fabrics. By the 1940s, tea and jute fabrics were its main contributions to the world market, and the region consumed large quantities of industrial and other commodities from many parts of the world.

In terms of production, trade and consumption, there was absolutely nothing that foreshadowed Partition. The events of 1947–8 precipitated what can perhaps best be described as the political assassination of this regional economy. Three states emerged and divided the region between them. All three states saw themselves as developmentalist states, in charge of promoting the development of a newly found 'national economy', defined as all economic activities taking place in the territory allocated to the new state.

What was the place of the borderland in these state-centred projects of development? It soon became clear that, in all three states, those in charge of economic policy saw the borderland as an economically suspect zone not worthy of great investment. Industrial and agricultural development initiatives tended to bypass the border areas, and the 'Development Raj' had little time for the specific economic problems of the borderland. Infrastructural improvements lagged behind – a policy bitterly regretted by the Indian state elite during its war with China in 1962[2] – and what state-sponsored development did take place in the borderland was related more to strategic worries than to concerns over the welfare of the borderland population.

Economic planners and politicians were, however, very interested in controlling the large trade flows crisscrossing the borderland. These had now become transnational flows and therefore needed state regulation. One of the first measures was to abandon the joint currency of colonial times and introduce separate currencies for the territories of India, Pakistan and Burma: the Indian rupee, the Pakistani rupee and the Burmese kyat.

In the early years after independence, Burma was in no position to develop a clear trade policy. The government in Rangoon had little authority over the regions bordering East Pakistan and only gradually established control.[3] Although India and Pakistan were in much better control of the borderland, they too were unable to develop straightforward trade policies. Both states sought to disentangle the economy of the partitioned region in order to construct an integrated national economy, yet at the same time were also keen to profit from any cross-border trade that they saw as supporting their own national economic goals by providing strategic or scarce goods, or because it could be taxed. To complicate matters, economic policy was frequently sent haywire by political considerations. A chill in the air between Delhi and Karachi/Islamabad could translate into an obstruction of trade flows in the Bengal borderland, some 1500 kilometres away. A quarrel over faraway Kashmir could easily induce patriotic state personnel to go on wildcat strikes, holding up cross-border trade. It could also lead to an official state policy of economic boycott or blockade.[4]

As a result, a high level of uncertainty surrounded cross-border trade, and borderlanders were forever picking up clues as to the newest obstructions and opportunities. Trade that was encouraged yesterday might be criminalized today, only to be tolerated unofficially tomorrow. Currencies of two or more states circulated freely in the borderland, but possession of foreign currency was officially prohibited, except for those with a special licence, and there were various restrictions regarding the export of currencies. Because of the monetary 'irregularities' that lay at the basis of cross-border trade, a threat of confiscation and punishment always hung over it.[5] The creation of the border set up a new, haphazard dynamics that nobody in the borderland could control.

Right after the establishment of the border, the flow of certain goods was interrupted or hampered, other goods continued to flow freely, and yet others began to flow in response to new opportunities opening up. Borderlanders soon learned that this pattern of flow and blockage would be subject to sudden and unpredictable change.[6] They also learned to think in terms of the main categories of cross-border trade that official discourse distinguished: transit trade and sanctioned trade, border trade and illegal trade. I will discuss these separately in the following sections.

Transit trade and sanctioned trade

One important political decision that affected the flow of goods through the borderland was an agreement between Pakistan and India to allow transit trade. This involved permission for goods originating in country A, and destined for another part of country A, to take a short route through country B. This agreement was much more important for India than for East Bengal/ East Pakistan. India faced serious transport problems between its northeast (Assam, Tripura) and the rest of the country. East Pakistan, with its more compact shape and extensive waterways, was less troubled in this respect. Not surprisingly, India was never happy with the implementation of the transit trade agreements. In a White Paper of December 1949, it stated: 'Pakistan's observation of her obligations in regard to "transit" arrangement had always been half hearted ... even goods from one part of India to another were subjected to all kinds of restrictions.'[7]

Most of the transit trade was conducted by railway, and it was in the borderland that both states did their checking.[8] Border railway stations in East Pakistan figured prominently in conflicts over goods lost in transit, confiscated, or otherwise detained. These conflicts revealed more than that India and Pakistan found it hard to cooperate smoothly. They also revealed a lack of central control over borderland officials. Transit trade was frequently caught up in tussles between customs officials, police, volunteer militias, and railway staff. Relations between these groups of state employees were proverbially bad, and it was often suggested that this was a result of fierce competition over bribes.[9] For example, Pakistan customs officials might check and pass goods on their way to India, only for Pakistan border police or Ansars to impound them.[10]

Central authorities were often unaware of what was taking place in the borderland and this gave room for all kinds of local practices that might deviate from instructions from the capital. An indication of the weakness of central control over state agents in the borderland is provided by the following case:

> In July 1948, the government of West Bengal (India) asked East Bengal (Pakistan) 'if they might post an officer of the Agriculture Deptt. at Santahar [a border railway station in East Pakistan] to help expedite the transhipment of potatoes at the station on their way from Assam to the markets of Calcutta.' The railways were consulted and 'they replied with the astonishing information that a West Bengal officer was already posted in Santahar ... This Govt. [East Pakistan] did not at any time give permission for this officer to be posted at Santahar and it is not known how exactly W.B. [West Bengal] managed to achieve this posting ... It would appear from the reminders which the West Bengal Home Deptt. have been sending us that they themselves do not know that their Agriculture Deptt. has had an officer in Santahar.[11]

The range of goods allowed to transit through East Pakistan was wide but certain items are more prominent in the sources, possibly because they were seen as being of strategic importance and therefore more likely to be obstructed. These included coal, medicines, machine parts and petrol.[12] As we will see, jute was a special case.[13]

In 1965, India and Pakistan waged war on each other and discontinued their direct rail connections. Since then, the borderland has been a zone of dead railway lines; transit goods brought in by train had to be transferred to trucks here (Plate 7.1). It was not until 2001 that the governments of India and Bangladesh, after long deliberations, cautiously began the procedure of reconnecting a single cross-border railway line (Plate 7.2).

Plate 7.1: Railway tracks coming to an end at the border in north Bengal (Burimari check post, Bangladesh), 2000. This line used to connect Darjeeling with Dhaka.[14]

Plate 7.2: After a break of 36 years, India and Bangladesh agreed to reopen one railway link. This picture of the first trial run shows the train – garlanded, bedecked with flags, and observed by borderlanders, journalists and officials – entering India at Gede (West Bengal), July 2001.[15]

Although trains carried much of the transit trade before 1965, goods were also transported in other ways, e.g. by water (Plate 7.3). In 1953 a detailed procedure was devised for transit traffic by river between Assam and Calcutta. The procedure involved steamers and barges being sealed by customs personnel as they entered East Pakistan, endorsements of lists of transit goods, clearance orders and frequent customs checks. Most of Assam's tea and bamboo destined for Calcutta took this route via East Pakistan, and cars and fertilizers went the other way.[16] Before 1965, 60 per cent of the cargo between the Brahmaputra valley and Calcutta and 80 per cent of the cargo between the Barak valley and Calcutta used this means of transport.[17]

Plate 7.3: Sanctioned trade. A Bangladeshi ship, docked at Karimganj (India) on the Kushiara River, is loading Indian coal for Bangladeshi destinations, 2002. The border between Bangladesh (Zakiganj, Sylhet) and India (Karimganj, Assam) runs midway through the riverbed.[18]

Border rivers were also used for domestic trade but this was risky. For example, when the owners of an oil-press at Barhaj (Uttar Pradesh, North India) found that it was impossible to book spare parts from Calcutta by railway, they decided to send the shipment via the Baghirathi and Ganges rivers, skirting the border with East Pakistan. Although the cargo was duly furnished with customs papers, Pakistani border police seized it when the wind blew the boat that carried it towards Char Narayanpur, a *chor* in the Ganges under Pakistani control.[19]

Road transport was also important in sanctioned trade and transit trade. As roads improved, the volume of goods crossing the border in trucks at a small

number of designated 'land ports' grew enormously. Plates 7.4 and 7.5 show
the same road in 1954 and 2000. Disputes at these border posts could lead to
gargantuan queues, with hundreds of truck drivers from all over India and
Bangladesh spending days or weeks camping out and waiting for an opportunity
to get through.

Plate 7.4: The border crossing between Tamabil (Sylhet, East Pakistan) and Dawki
(now: Meghalaya, India) in 1954. The bus from Dawki to Shillong and a goods truck
are ready for departure.[20]

Plate 7.5: Indian coal trucks waiting for clearance to enter Bangladesh, Dawki
(Meghalaya, India), 2000.[21]

In some cases, transit arrangements were made locally, and these could go against the central rules. In July 1948 there was a scarcity of rice in some parts of the Garo Hills (India). The district authorities felt that 'to feed the deficit areas ... it is necessary to send rice and paddy ... by country boats through Mymensingh district.' They asked their counterparts in Mymensingh (Pakistan) to 'allow transit and give escorts to boats till re-entry into Indian Union.' This request, which ignored the decision by the political leaders of both countries *not* to allow the transit of paddy and rice, was granted.[22]

Transit trade was supposed to flow through certain locations in the borderland only. It had to pass through one of a few designated customs posts. Such locations became centres of unprecedented economic activity, attracting traders, transport companies and labourers. They also provided employment for customs officials, police and administrators. The states invested quite heavily in infrastructure and in their bureaucratic and symbolic presence in the locations, because they needed to monitor and tax the goods flowing through them.[23] It was in these trade-ordained centres that the states first established themselves in the borderland. Here and there along the immense border, twinned 'garrison-entrepôts' faced each other across the boundary line.[24] Several of them became hyphenated entities in public discourse, e.g. Bongaon-Benapol, Agartala-Akhaura, Dawki-Tamabil, or Chengrabandha-Burimari (Plate 7.6).[25] Ensconced in these so-called 'land ports,' the states sought to control their own side of the borderland, eye the other side, and selectively squeeze or promote cross-border trade.

Plate 7.6: Travellers in no man's land. A party of Bangladeshis, followed by a coolie, are walking on the dirt road connecting the Bangladeshi checkpoint of Burimari with the Indian checkpoint of Chengrabandha, 2000. An Indian truck is coming from the opposite direction.[26]

From the borderland point of view, transit trade did not differ much from other officially sanctioned trade that was destined for domestic use rather than for re-export. In 1957 India and Pakistan came to an agreement to 'facilitate imports from and exports to each other's territories' of coal, stone boulders, wood, chemicals, machinery, cement and 55 other commodities. They agreed to trade in 109 commodities in 1960, and in 304 in 1963.[27] Such agreements concerning 'sanctioned trade' were continued after Bangladesh became independent.[28] Like goods in transit, these flows would pass through the borderland with export permits, and sometimes under the aegis of state corporations. Bangladesh also made trade agreements with Bhutan and Nepal, whose borders are close to Bangladesh but do not quite meet.[29] Trade flows between these countries have to pass through India. In the case of Bhutan, India allowed trucks to pass back and forth (Plate 7.7), but in the case of Nepal, it did not.[30] Trade agreements between Bangladesh and Burma varied over time, but official trade remained small in volume. In 2003 the crisis of foreign exchange in Burma had become so severe that the two governments decided to start a special account system under which importers would not need foreign exchange.[31]

Plate 7.7: Unloading a truck from Bhutan just inside Bangladesh, Burimari border, 2000.

Border trade

In addition to transit and sanctioned trade, the two states recognized a third category: border trade. This was the official term for the cross-border marketing that I described in the previous chapter. Officially, border trade was tightly regulated in terms of quantity per person, type of commodity and spatial extension. Because it was seen as supplying borderland markets, it was legal up to 16 km (10 miles) from the border but illegal beyond that belt. Border trade was permitted only intermittently. During periods when these flows were considered to be entirely illegal, the state saw all cross-border marketing of local produce as smuggling and as unpatriotic, anti-state behaviour.

Illegal trade

The fourth category of trade, illegal trade, existed only as a result of policies of state territoriality. It is only when states forbid – or fail to sanction – certain transnational trade flows that these come to be defined as illegal, illicit, black, underground, contraband, clandestine, smuggling, and so on. Illegal trade can be defined as all cross-border economic activity that is not authorized by the government of either the sending or the receiving country.[32] In the Bengal borderland, this category came into existence by default. India and Pakistan started from the assumption that *no* cross-border trade was legal unless it was sanctioned by both of them. And since only certain trade flows were given this double stamp of approval in the various agreements mentioned above, all others were considered illegal.

For borderlanders it was a difficult category to deal with because it changed over time. The two states were in the habit of periodically redefining which items fell under the headings of sanctioned and transit trade. And what they wrote down in their agreements, signed in offices in Calcutta, Delhi, Karachi, or Dhaka, did not necessarily percolate down correctly (or at all) to the borderland. As a result, borderland perceptions of what the states considered to be illegal trade were often considerably blurred.

By prohibiting trade in many 'illegal' commodities, India and Pakistan burdened themselves with the responsibility of actually checking these flows. They soon found out that they were incapable of doing so without desperate measures.[33] For example, trade in paddy and rice was generally prohibited even in border marketing.[34] In reality, however, trade in these goods was brisk and trade patterns were extremely complex, with paddy moving back and forth across the border depending on product qualities, seasonal variation in production, and section of the borderland. Both India and Pakistan were keen to control this trade but both soon realized that they were completely unable to do so. For example, even during the India-Pakistan war of 1965, when troops were massed along the Nadia border and shooting was going on, the government of West Bengal found to its surprise and dismay that huge quantities of rice were being moved by bicycle and rickshaw 'from the Ranaghat area [in Nadia] ... to the border and ... smuggled into East Pakistan.'[35]

Much paddy was sold across the border 'in contravention of the law and to the detriment of Government revenue', and this led to proposals for draconian measures. For example, 'in areas where extensive smuggling is proved to have taken place ... District Magistrates should come up with proposals for collective fines or quartering additional police, the cost of which would be recovered from the local inhabitants.'[36]

For a while in 1957–8, Pakistan even went so far as to militarize its entire East Pakistan borderland in an attempt to quash smuggling. This 'Operation Closed Door', in which the Army, the Navy and the Air Force collaborated,[37] brought terror to the borderland but failed completely in its aim of stamping out illegal cross-border trade.[38]

Illegal trade was easily the dominant form of cross-border trade, if only because legal (sanctioned) trade could pass the border only where customs facilities had been established. This meant that anything which passed the 4,000 km border in between the handful of designated customs posts was illegal, even if the commodity in question was on the list of sanctioned trade goods. This dominance of illegal trade was predicated on restrictive official policies, combined with insufficient state surveillance, but also on many borderlanders simply disagreeing with state-imposed categories of legality and the closure of trade across huge stretches of the border. They considered various forms of 'illegal trade' as morally justified or licit. Underlying the persistence of smuggling was their rejection of the states' authority to outlaw most borderland trade. Not only did the states fail to impose their categorization, but we will see that borderland notions of licitness also progressively subverted official notions of legality. It was a case of states overreaching – not only in terms of their powers of surveillance, but also in terms of ideological hegemony.[39]

Illegal cross-border trade not only included the bulk of transnational commercial activities in the borderland; it also covered a wide range of goods and trade relationships. For the sake of analysis it is helpful to distinguish four large flows of illegal trade. I will discuss these under separate headings: historical trade; swapping; international goods to India; and banned goods.

The disruption of historical trade.   In their pursuit of territorial control, both India and Pakistan strove to destroy many pre-existing trade networks and systems of exchange. The best-documented case of such disruption is the movement of jute fibre from the fields of East Pakistan to the jute mills around Calcutta. The case of jute demonstrates the coercion and resistance that was involved in the disruption of trade flows in the borderland.

Since the mid-nineteenth century, Bengal had been the world's leading producer of jute. The wet deltaic fields of eastern Bengal were eminently suited for the crop that factories in Scotland and Calcutta turned into jute sacks, burlap and carpet backing. Bengal jute had a truly global reach. In the form of hundreds of millions of sacks it travelled to the far corners of the world, containing anything from Brazilian coffee and Ghanaian cocoa to Thai rice and Russian oats. Twentieth-century warfare required large numbers of sandbags, and jute had a wide range of other uses, from industrial packaging to tarpaulin canvas and garden twine. Jute was a major factor linking the economy of Bengal to global commerce.

The new border imposed itself between the jute fields in the east and the jute factories and port of Calcutta in the west. Of course, there was nothing inherently ominous about this separation of raw material and processing industry. It would have made perfect economic sense to continue the production system that had existed for about a century, and that now involved trading jute fibre from fields in East Pakistan to nearby factories in India. But it did not make political sense at all.

The Pakistan government considered jute as a strategic national resource that had to be processed under state control, i.e. in the state's territory. Jute became the centrepiece of a new national development programme. The government was keen to develop a jute industry of its own, and to thwart that of its neighbour and potential competitor, India.[40] Pakistan, expecting that it would soon have the capacity to process jute in Pakistani jute factories, forbade the export of jute. The Calcutta factories, which had the capacity but not the jute they needed, were left high and dry.

It was a political decision that backfired immediately. The Pakistan state elite might well will the Indian factories out of existence, but the fact remained that a strong demand for jute emanated from these factories. Pakistan could not offer its producers the prices that jute fetched across the border, so the jute trade was driven underground. Selling jute to Calcutta had suddenly become an anti-national act, and Pakistan saw itself forced to police the trade it had declared illegal.[41]

Policing the jute trade brought the borderland into view because it was here that the state sought to intercept it. Pakistan began to establish new outposts on the border expressly to stop the smuggling of jute.[42] In 1949, the Pakistan Jute Board concluded that earlier measures to curb smuggling to India had not had the desired effect and 'smuggling is still going on on a fairly large scale.'[43] For this reason the government organized a Jute Purchase Drive in the borderland. Thirty purchase teams were formed whose task it was to 'comb through each section [of the borderland] and buy as much jute as possible.'

It was clear that they expected resistance. The mood among jute growers in the borderland was described as one of growing discontent because they were forced to hold on to large stocks of jute 'strangulated in villages', and therefore faced financial crisis.[44] For this reason, the purchase teams were accompanied by armed Ansars, and the authorities considered giving them the power to requisition jute because 'a deadlock can ensue if the growers do not sell voluntarily to our team … the power would be very useful in persuading the unwilling and stubborn type of stock holder.' In the end, requisitioning was not resorted to because it was thought that it would 'antagonize the cultivators on the border who may feel they are at a disadvantage as against cultivators in the interior.' Instead, the purchase teams relied on the power of ready cash, a price slightly higher than usual (which they could offer because they cut out the middleman), and intimidation by means of drawing up a blacklist of unwilling stock holders 'with a view to see how they dispose of their stocks eventually and prevent them smuggling it out of Pakistan.'[45]

During the 1950s the flow of jute through the borderland declined considerably, but not because of the anti-smuggling measures, which appear to have been a minor influence. There were two other factors at work. First, an East Pakistan jute industry took off and new factories in Dhaka and nearby Narayanganj were able to offer competing prices. Law also regulated the area under jute, although 'unauthorized' jute continued to be grown. Second, the cultivation of jute in India (West Bengal and Assam) increased rapidly, partly as a result of government campaigns, and this made the Calcutta factories much less dependent on East Pakistan jute.[46]

What had been one production system up to 1947 was split to form two competing jute industries, each with its own catchment area in terms of raw material and labour, and each with its own links to the world market.[47] It was a case of economic surgery in the service of state territoriality. The state elite in Pakistan saw it as a triumph of national self-reliance. Jute traders in East Pakistan were, however, less territorial in their thinking and actions: large amounts of jute continued to be smuggled to India. The state of Pakistan never succeeded in completely disrupting the illegal flow of jute through the borderland, and neither could its successor, Bangladesh. A study conducted in 1990 found that certain grades of jute were being smuggled through *all* 30 transit points on the Bangladesh-West Bengal border included in the survey, as well as through Teknaf on the Bangladesh-Burma border.[48]

The case of jute shows that state attempts at disrupting established trade patterns could make these flows more attractive. Borderlanders found themselves in a more advantageous position regarding marketing. Whereas before Partition jute sellers had had little choice but to sell to specific local traders who acted as intermediaries for the jute factories, after Partition they could sell to traders on either side of the border and, occasionally, to Jute Purchasing Teams. The border created different groups of buyers who competed with each other.

These advantages were offset, however, by new risks related to the presence of two states and their means of coercion. A good way of minimizing these risks was to involve border guards, customs officials or the police in illegal cross-border transfers of goods. Although many state employees were unwilling to become involved (for reasons of morality, allegiance to the ideal of the nation, career planning, or fear of physical danger), others were keen to be involved, or were ordered to become involved by superiors who ran protection rackets for smugglers. It is quite clear that, right from the start, state employees on both sides of the border were involved in smuggling.[49] Over the years, there have been many reports about borderland state personnel acting as core operators in highly structured networks of illegal cross-border trade.[50]

In 1992 a study revealed a well-ordered system of smuggling on the West Bengal border. Border Security Force personnel gave informal authorization to smugglers operating between Bongaon (the border checkpost) and Calcutta. Proof of this authorization were two passes, one with a 'Shiva mark' and one with a 'Ganesha mark.' Policemen also issued a pass, and for the three tokens together each smuggler had to pay Rs.3,000 a month. A similar system of tokens was reported to be operating on the Bangladesh side of the border. Here 'linemen' (engaged by police, Bangladesh Rifles and Customs officers) supervised hired smugglers locally known as *dhur*.[51]

At first, when this trade consisted overwhelmingly of disrupted trade, it was facilitated largely by a commercial alliance between law-enforcement agencies in the borderland and private entrepreneurs. But increasingly, especially when new commodities were added to these illegal cross-border flows, it became clear that high-level bureaucrats and politicians had emerged as major organizers, financiers and facilitators of illegal trade in their own right.[52] Such practices could be integrated completely into state institutions, as was the case with Burmese Military Intelligence Battalion MI 18, stationed at the border town of Maungdaw. This battalion owned a six-crew sea-going ship, the Saw Mratt Radana, used for regular smuggling to Bangladesh.[53]

Swapping. Very soon after Partition the borderland began to act as host to new trade commodities. The first to arrive on the scene were products made in the wider economies of India, Burma and Pakistan. The range of commodities that could be exchanged between these economies was enormous, and today 'informed sources claim that almost all goods, which are legally exported from and imported into Bangladesh, can safely be included as items of smuggling.'[54] Popular Indian consumer items in East Pakistani/ Bangladeshi markets were table fans, cosmetics, razor blades, medicines, exotic fruits (oranges, grapes, apples), woollen shawls from Kashmir, silk *saris* from South India, and phensidyl (a cough syrup with a high codeine content).[55] Some Bangladeshi industries, e.g. the leather industry and the brick industry, obtained their raw material or fuel from India.[56] Components of trucks and buses were smuggled in from India, to be assembled in workshops in the Bangladesh borderland.[57] Goods of Bangladeshi origin in Indian markets included ready-made clothes, medicines, biscuits, tobacco and fish.[58] Burmese goods in Bangladesh and India included soap, spices, shrimps, clothes, rice, cigarettes, whisky, beer and salt. Products from Thailand (nylon ropes, hosepipes, fish) and China (electronics, crockery) also reached these markets via Burma.[59] Among Bangladeshi and Indian goods in Burma were fertilizers, scrap metal, pulses, biscuits, kerosene and diesel, contraceptives and even rice (Plate 7.8).[60]

Plate 7.8: Burmese trader visiting the border town of Teknaf in southern Bangladesh, 2001.[61]

Closely related to this was 'unauthorized transit trade' in which Indian goods were smuggled into Bangladesh only to be smuggled back into India through another part of the borderland. Such trade, often under cover of legal consignments of transit trade, was attractive because it cut down on the high transport costs involved in the much longer route around Bangladesh.[62] For example, the route from Calcutta to Agartala (both in India) across Bangladesh is 350 km; the route from Calcutta to Agartala around Bangladesh is 1,645 km, most of it over much poorer roads. According to Indian officials quoted in a press report in the 1990s, it cost Rs.27,000 to take a truck from Agartala via Assam to Calcutta, much more than the truck fare from Calcutta to Chennai (a slightly shorter distance), which was only Rs.16,000.[63]

Increasingly, agricultural produce, as well as cattle, sugar, salt and hides, travelled from India to markets in Bangladesh (Plate 7.9):

Teenagers can be found strolling at various points on the border. They occasionally disappear from sight to emerge on the other side of the border. They go with a small packet of salt and come back with an Indian currency note ... Dinhata town in Cooch Behar district is one of the border towns in West Bengal [known] for an abnormally high consumption of salt.[64]

Plate 7.9: Swapping. Smugglers are waiting for a safe moment to run across the field that marks the border between Bangladesh (left) and India (right), 2002. Armed guards of both countries, and the check point of Tamabil/ Dawki, are 30 metres behind the photographer.[65]

Nobody knows the volume of these flows but the balance of trade seemed to be very firmly in favour of the (much larger) Indian economy. It mirrored the extremely skewed *legal* balance of trade. Available figures on legal exports from Bangladesh to India indicated that around 1990 these were only about 10 per cent of legal exports from India to Bangladesh. By the late 1990s, the figure had dropped to about 5 per cent.[66]

International goods to India.   In addition to the illegal cross-border swapping of goods produced in these countries, there was another flow of illegal trade that developed vigorously and that had a profound impact on life in the borderland. The economic policies of India and Pakistan (and later Bangladesh) differed markedly, most importantly in the much higher priority given in India to import substitution and the protection of Indian industries. This meant that foreign industrial goods were much less readily available on the Indian side of the border than on the East Pakistan side. Responding to differential demand, traders in East Pakistan began to move such goods across the border to buyers in India, and a flow of high-quality and often expensive contraband came into existence.[67] This flow expanded dramatically after the birth of Bangladesh, and especially after that country introduced import liberalization in 1980.[68]

Plate 7.10: A winter morning in an Indian border town, 2000. Before dawn a Bangladeshi trader is laying out his goods: synthetic blankets from China.

Helped by the fiscal and commercial policies adopted by the governments of Bangladesh and India, traders began to use Bangladesh as a conduit for smuggling imported goods to India. Most of these goods were imported legally into Bangladesh and then smuggled to India, which continued its protective import regime but boasted a large and expanding middle class with a strong preference for imported consumer goods (Plate 7.10). The list of items was long and varied. It included foreign calculators and watches, cameras and second-hand cars, milk powder, synthetic yarn and fabrics, foreign cigarettes and ready-made garments, but also diesel and petrol, cement, motor parts, fertilizers, insecticides, spices, edible oil, used clothes, cell phones and computer parts.[69]

The profitability of this trade was enhanced by importing raw materials or components into Bangladesh and then making products for the Indian market in garments factories, edible-oil mills, or screwdriver factories in Bangladesh. There was a clear connection between the widely noted instability of industrialization in Bangladesh and its dependence on illegal exports to India that showed dramatic booms and slumps.[70] Some of the factories were established in the border areas:

> An assembly plant for videocassette recorders was set up in Nabharon, a village in Jessore district (Bangladesh), very near the border with India. Components were shipped from East Asia to the Bangladesh seaport of Chalna, where they were imported either legally or illegally. From there they were brought to the assembly plant by road. Once the recorders were assembled, 'baggage parties' on motorcycles 'carrying two or three such items make routine trips across the borders in active connivance with the law enforcing agencies on both sides of the border.' Two aspects of such borderland industrialisation were of particular interest. First, Indian capital was involved in this factory, as is reputedly the case in many other illegal-export oriented enterprises in Bangladesh. And second, Japanese, Korean or Taiwanese brand names hid the fact that increasingly cheaper, inferior Indian components and parts were also used in these assembly factories.[71]

Much trade was in the hands of large merchants who had the capacity to organize such complex flows of components, and who rarely resided in the borderland. The border was just one element in their game, which often involved legal economic activities as well. Borderlanders were crucial in the actual transport of merchandise across the border: their local knowledge and contacts with border guards were of incalculable value.[72] But most of them were employees or agents of bigger operators in both India and Bangladesh.

Take the smuggling of stolen motorcycles from Calcutta to Bangladesh. Thieves in Calcutta got Tk.10,000–22,000 per item, depending on how new it was. Others transported the motorcycles to the border at Baghachra in Satkhira district (routes would change frequently), where 'carriers' took them across the border for a fee of Tk.2,000. At the point of crossing ('ghat'), the Indian border guards were paid Tk.3,000 and the Bangladeshi border guards Tk.5,000. The 'ghat owner' (person in charge of smuggling operations at that border location) also pocketed Tk.5,000, kept the motorcycles for a few days, and changed the brand names, chassis numbers, etc. The motorcycles were then sold by well-established motorcycle traders in Bangladeshi towns for up to Tk.50,000 apiece. In other words, borderland smugglers pocketed 14 percent (Tk.7,000) and border guards 16 percent (Tk.8,000) of the sales price while the motorcycle dealers, who were the likely operators of the business, earned between 24 and 46 percent (Tk.12,000–23,000).[73]

These operators often invested on both sides of the border. Therefore, they had a direct stake in keeping the import regimes of the two countries as different as possible and they needed personal protection. It was only natural that they tended to gravitate towards centres of political decision-making such as Dhaka, Chittagong, Calcutta, Delhi, or Agartala.

Banned goods. Finally, in addition to disrupted trade, swapping and international goods to India, there was a fourth flow of illegal trade through the borderland: banned goods such as drugs (opium, heroin and codeine, alcohol, cannabis), small arms, proscribed literature and wildlife products.[74] Unlike the goods discussed above, the possession of these goods was illegal. Gold was a borderline case, as its declared possession could also be legal but much of it was held illegally; the pattern of gold smuggling showed some similarity with the patterns described in the section on international goods to India.[75] Drugs were different, however. The borderland is roughly midway between the world's two major production areas of opium and heroin: the Golden Triangle (covering parts of Burma, Yunnan, Laos and Thailand) and the Golden Crescent (covering parts of Afghanistan, Pakistan and Central Asia). The Bengal borderland did not develop into an important channel for the trade in heroin till the 1980s, when increasing quantities of Burmese heroin began to be routed through Northeast India, Bangladesh and Nepal to South Asian ports and airports for transshipment to European and North American markets. These routes led through difficult mountainous terrain that was traversed by Chinese and Burmese mule caravans (Plate 7.11). At the same time, local consumer markets developed along these trade routes. Soon heroin addiction spread in northeast India and Bangladesh, and the borderland was no exception. Mizoram, the Arakan/ Chittagong border, the Tripura/ Comilla border and the Jessore/ 24-Parganas border became known as both transit points for heroin and locations with relatively high concentrations of users.[76] By the 1990s, the region had become well integrated into the worldwide circulation of heroin. Heroin had established itself as a routine trade item in many parts of the borderland, and some opium poppy was being grown there.[77]

Plate 7.11: Burmese mule caravan in Mizoram (India), near the border with Bangladesh, 2000.

The smuggling of small arms provided a link between illegal trading and the many insurgencies that characterized the region. The borderland saw arms crossing in many directions.[78] Some followed the sea route to an East Pakistan (later Bangladesh) port and were then smuggled to India, others came over land via India or Burma, or were flown into one of the region's airports and distributed from there. Smuggled arms varied from handguns and 'chocolate bombs' made locally in e.g. Bihar, Tripura, or Moheshkhali (an island off the coast of Chittagong), to assault rifles, submachine guns, anti-tank devices and rocket launchers produced in the United States, Russia, Israel, China or Belgium.[79] In time, Bangladesh emerged as an important small arms depot for South and Southeast Asia. According to the *Small Arms Survey 2001*:

Bangladesh is a major transit point for arms in the region. Small arms come across to Bangladesh from Afghanistan and Pakistan on the one side, and from Thailand, Singapore, Myanmar, and Cambodia on the other. From there, the weapons usually go north to rebels in India's north-east or south to the LTTE [Liberation Tigers of Tamil Eelam].[80]

One seaside town in Bangladesh, Cox's Bazar, profited especially from the small arms trade. Here customers from far afield, but also from Bangladesh itself, would come to shop for the latest merchandise, arriving largely by sea.[81] Cox's Bazar was linked with a network of local arms bazars in the borderland, for example the 'trijunction point' where India, Burma and Bangladesh meet.[82] 'You can get anything here, from the smallest handgun to a rocket launcher, from the Russian Kalashnikov to a Chinese version of the AK-47, from the American M-16 to the German HK33.'[83] Increasingly, illegal small arms were also available to local entrepreneurs and politicians, turning both cross-border trade and borderland politics into bloodier affairs than before.[84]

The significance of banned goods as items of illegal trade, like the international goods described in the previous section, was their enormous potential for involving borderlanders in transnational networks, and this in spite of vigorous state attempts at imposing territorial control. Students of the transnational tend to focus on interlinked urban areas ('global cities') but often overlook borderlands as crucial sites for studying transnational connections. At borders, appearances often deceive: what looks like insignificant local 'ant trade' (individuals crossing the border carrying only a few items) has widespread and cumulative effects. Sleepy border villages may appear to be entirely wrapped up in a small world of parochial and peripheral concerns but this may be a contrived, carefully stage-managed *mis-en-scène*, a show put on to delude suspicious outsiders. Under the cover of this innocuousness, many such border villages have come to be incorporated into transnational nexuses of illegality. It is here that, say, a Kalashnikov assault rifle is exchanged for a fistful of banknotes (derived from, say, aid donated by a foreign government, or from toll collection by an insurgent group). It is here that a consignment of heroin is swapped for a carton of Danish milk powder, or a bit of gold for some bottles of Chanel No.5. Do not be surprised to see a peasant housewife opening an earthen pot, taking out a handful of the latest Swatch watches and a box of ammunition, and ambling off to take care of her cows grazing on the boundary line.[85] And do not be surprised to find a border villager called Gokul holding half a pound of Russian uranium:

Indian authorities were astonished when they arrested Gokul Barman of Chakarman village near the border in South Dinajpur (West Bengal, India) in August 2001. He was in possession of a leather pouch containing 225 grams of uranium made in the Soviet Union in 1984 and active up to

2003. They suspected that 'the mineral had been smuggled into India from Bangladesh and was being sent to secessionist groups in Jammu and Kashmir.' They also found out that 'while one packet had been seized, another had reached the hands of terrorists.'[86]

The divide of the 1970s

When the Partition border was imposed, it cut across complex trade flows. The new states actively discouraged many of these in order to territorialize their national economies. They sanctioned only certain trade items, and these were to cross only at designated localities. After 1947, all other trade across the border was declared illegal, and therefore most trade between India, Bangladesh and Burma became smuggling.[87] Even if the states made great efforts to disrupt illegal trade, they found it impossible to put a stop to it. Official estimates of illegal trade were staggering. For example, the Indian Department of Commerce estimated in 2002 that the value of goods annually smuggled to Bangladesh from Northeast India alone was over Rs.20 billion (or about US$450 million).[88] A few months later, the Foreign Minister of Bangladesh stated that the illegal trade between Bangladesh and India was worth US$3 billion, or twice the value of legal trade.[89] Not surprisingly, officials often assumed that at least 40 to 50 per cent of the economies of both India and Bangladesh were 'black.'[90]

1947 to 1971: the states enclose the regional economy. In the early years after Partition, the cross-border flow of goods had been primarily one of regional products between different parts of the Bengal-Assam-Arakan area: crops (paddy, rice, jute, potatoes, spices, tobacco and pulses), fruits (mango, jackfruit, areca nuts, papaya), forest products (timber, firewood, bamboo, honey), cattle, fish, sugar and molasses. In many cases, these were well-established regional trade patterns, now driven underground. Smuggling was largely in the hands of regional operators and was financed locally or regionally. It targeted rural markets in the borderland as well as urban markets at short distances.

1971 to the present: global trade re-scales the state. In the years after 1970, this pattern was still recognizable but new goods, new organizational arrangements and new financial links came to dominate cross-border trade.[91] Four types of illegal goods now passed the border in different mixes at different places. These can be symbolised by *jute, saris, video recorders* and *heroin* (Figure 7.1[92]). Jute stands for 'disrupted trade' (goods that had been part of regional networks of exchange before Partition but whose trade was declared illegal by the new states); saris for 'swapping' (goods produced in the wider economies of

Bangladesh, India and Burma and traded illegally back and forth across the border); video recorders for 'international goods to India' (goods that were legally or illegally imported into Bangladesh and then smuggled to India); and

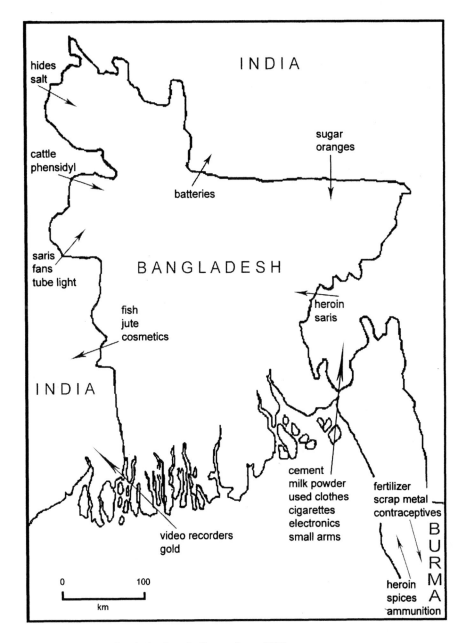

Figure 7.1: Some borderland trade flows, about 2003.

heroin for 'banned goods' (goods of foreign origin that were banned in India, Bangladesh and Burma and were traded through these countries to domestic as well as foreign markets).

The expansion of illegal cross-border trade was partly a result of sheer demographic growth. In 1941 the population of Bengal, the most populous part of the region, was 60 million. By 1971 it had doubled, and in 2001 it stood at 210 million, or a whopping 3½ times the number of inhabitants of 60 years previously.[93] But there was also another factor in the opening-up of new opportunities for profitable trade: the phenomenal growth of urban markets and middle- and upper-class consumerism in both eastern India and Bangladesh.

A larger demand for smuggled goods, as well as the introduction of new types of goods, required other organizational arrangements and financial links. The more smuggling was done in bulk, the harder it was to hide it from official eyes. In order to circumvent state tariffs, fees and duties, and in order to avoid being arrested for 'anti-national activities', privatized forms of trade protection, regulation and financing became more important.[94] Certain state employees at the border became prominent local representatives of such networks, protecting cross-border flows organized by private entrepreneurs in exchange for commissions that they might have to share with their superiors in the state bureaucracy.[95] Abdul Ghafur et al. described the arrangements between big entrepreneurs in Dhaka and Chittagong and state representatives in the southeastern coastal zone as follows:

> The liaison between the operators and the law enforcement agencies is worked out in advance. Rates of bribes are settled periodically and such bribes are distributed among the rank and file of different agencies. Any failure at any point of the chain may thwart the whole operation. Therefore, the links in the chain have to be made failure-proof. Coded messages or signs are carried by the operators and carriers as proof of proper payments … Occasional raids and confiscations are organized to show some action by the relevant agencies, but the brunt of such legal hazards is mainly borne by the petty operators at field level.[96]

In this way, illegal trade flows through the borderland came to have a phenomenal impact on state formation. These flows influenced the careers of individual state employees, attracted many people to state jobs that held the promise of tapping into illegal trade, and dampened demands for higher salaries in the state bureaucracy.[97] They shaped trade policies, undermined the judicial process and contributed to the breakdown of public safety. They supported candidates for elected office, and thereby allowed illegal traders easy access into the state structure, as the following two cases demonstrate.

On a borderland bus in Kushtia, Bangladesh border guards (BDR) found '3 sacks of heroin like powder, 20 bottles of methanol, 1 kg ganja [marijuana]' and Tk.20,000 in the possession of a woman passenger. They arrested the woman, Shahnaz Parveen, who was found to be the wife of the bus owner, a man 'known in the area as ringleader of smugglers.' The BDR handed Shahnaz over to the police but she turned out to have powerful friends. Soon Reza Ahmed, the district secretary of the ruling party (Bangladesh Nationalist Party, BNP), appeared on the scene and demanded her release because she was 'innocent.' Reza based his power on his own political office and even more so on that of his father, Ahsanul Haq Molla, a state minister of the BNP. When the BDR commander, Major Imran, refused to release Shahnaz, a brawl ensued, ending in a fist fight. Reza then mobilized local supporters who brought out an anti-BDR procession, barricaded the road, and held the BDR men hostage in the local police station till they were liberated by reinforcements.[98]

Bangladeshi customs officers at the Bhomra check post held up six truckloads of rice coming from India because these had been under-invoiced and wrongly declared as animal feed. When the customs officers proved to be insensitive to pressure from Ali Kader, a local member of parliament for the ruling party (BNP) who owned the clearing and forwarding agency involved, he sent in 40 gangsters who ransacked the customs house and smashed its furniture to smithereens. The officials were beaten up and forced to sign the clearance documents. After this revealing showdown between the bureaucratic and political faces of a state that leaned increasingly on regional fiefdoms, protection rackets and direct violence, the gangsters drove off with the trucks.[99]

As the worlds of trade, administration, politics and crime shaded almost seamlessly into each other, a new type of operator emerged. Known as *mostan*, these men mediated between the visible institutions of state and the less visible world of crime. They derived their power from illegal trade and official protection, and used it to terrorize a neighbourhood or town, and gain access to (or even control) political leaders at the local and state levels. They joined hands with political party bosses, if such an alliance was beneficial to them, but could change ideological sides at the drop of a hat.[100] Gangster rule, or *mostanocracy*, depended heavily on smuggling, the plunder of state revenues, appropriation of foreign aid, extortion and protection money.[101] Illegal cross-border trade thus emerged as a corner-stone of a new kleptocratic state.[102]

Conclusion: a subversive economy and rescaled states

The subversive economy that developed so vigorously from the 1970s was oriented much more toward the borderland than the state-centred 'Development Raj' had ever been. In the borderland, it was impossible to tell where the subversive economy ended and state power began.[103] Although the two had merged to such an extent that it was difficult to speak of an antagonistic relationship, official antagonism was still in evidence in certain state rituals and practices. Some of these were routine, such as customs checking, border patrols, the arrest of smugglers and the seizure of their goods. Others were episodic, such as the occasional visit by a top-ranking politician who would thunder against 'anti-social and anti-state crimes' and announce tighter border controls or even a sealing of the border. But borderlanders generally took these to be rituals of deception for the benefit of faraway audiences, and which impinged only intermittently on the real arrangements that had been worked out locally.[104]

The easy flow of goods across the borderland also had another impact on the worlds of trade, administration, politics and crime. In some cases the states were keen to divert to their own territory unauthorized flows of goods that were benefiting a neighbouring state. For example, competition over the expanding subversive economy prompted Bangladesh, Burma and India to invest in a long-neglected section of the borderland:

Unauthorized trade flows between Burma and northeastern India went predominantly through the river port of Teknaf on the Burma-Bangladesh border. In 2002 Burma and Bangladesh agreed to route the Asian Highway through this port, which was being upgraded to take much more (legal, and hence taxable, but mainly illegal) trade. As these plans were maturing, India sprang into action. It developed a scheme to divert this lucrative trade to its own border with Burma. Survey teams began exploring the possibility of constructing a cross-border road and a gas pipeline through the mountains linking Mizoram (India) with Chin State (Burma) at a point just east of the trijunction point where India, Bangladesh and Burma meet (see Appendix Figure 1). If Burma could be made to agree to such a scheme, India could count on a significant diversion of trade from Teknaf and so cut out Bangladesh.[105]

The borderland economy straddled the border effortlessly. For example, the presence of large contingents of border guards in the border town of Hili did nothing to prevent everyday economic arrangements that defied the very purpose of their presence:

'We come shopping to [Indian] Hili often', said [Bangladeshi] Anisur Mondal, 'We still feel we belong to the same village. There are so many friends still on both sides. The BSF usually don't stop us, for if they do, it's more of a problem for them arresting us and feeding us for 15 days!'

'I never carry any passport. I am my own passport', said trader Saukat Mondal. 'I stay in Khulna [Bangladesh], have houses on both sides of Hili border and one in Murshidabad [India]. My brother stays in Kolkata. I take saris from Delhi to Dhaka and bring back wristwatch parts to India. I started by importing bidis in 1964 and here I am today. No border has ever stopped me or will.' To demonstrate his point to an Indian journalist, Saukat and his team squat on the Indian side of the Hili border next to the [Bangladeshi] railway track running close by. As the train slows almost in front of the border check post, 'all of us walk some 50 yards into Bangladeshi territory in full view of armed BDR men. BSF personnel, too, line up on the Indian side … Shaukat shoves [two large bundles of saris] and his men into a moving compartment.'[106] (Plate 7.12)

Plate 7.12: Bangladesh border guard at Hili railway station on the border with India, 2000.

Borderlanders were well aware that it was state elites' attempts to use their political power in order to control economic activity that gave rise to illegal forms of economic enterprise. The tariffs, customs duties, consumer taxes, prohibitions and protections that formed the core of this restrictive management of the national economy created opportunities for illegal entrepreneurs. In this way, customs fraud and smuggling formed a part of foreign trade policy, just as much as protectionism did.[107] By building and maintaining cross-border trade networks, such illegal actors could be seen to reconcile arbitrary state policy with market rationality.[108]

Despite the public rhetoric, the state elite did not consider illegal entrepreneurs to be 'anti-state.' Rather, the state elite itself combined positions of power and accumulation and used these entrepreneurs as kingpins in coalitions to prop up its control of the state – which tended to be insecure either because of the unpredictable outcome of elections, or because of the threat of military coups – as well as its control of networks of accumulation. Ironically, over time, those who routinely undermined the state's territoriality emerged as its kingmakers and office bearers. In this revenge of the open border, the economic policy of enclosure and centralization found its Waterloo. The state had failed to bring the borderland economy to heel, and now the trade that it had declared illegal was rescaling the state. The rise of *mostanocracy* meant power shifting away from central state institutions, and the forging of stronger direct links between localized arenas (e.g. borderland networks) and transnational ones. State institutions were still extremely useful for various reasons – their rich pickings from tax and aid monies, their legitimizing authority, the access they provided to other states and supranational organizations, their infrastructural capacity and their military clout – but increasingly these institutions had been subverted by illegal entrepreneurs who thought globally rather than territorially.[109]

Clearly, if we want to understand the dynamics of the states in this region we must take account of their progressive failure to impose territoriality on many aspects of life, and the rescaling that resulted from this failure. In this chapter, we have looked at trade flows and we have seen how they defied enclosure by the state. But they also defy enclosure by conventional ways of looking at the economy. For example, economic planning in this region is saturated with assumptions about national space, the functioning of institutions of state, and the size and structure of national economies that demonstrate the 'iron grip of the nation-state'. Since these states have never been able to enclose trade flows and have driven many flows underground, the size of these flows is anybody's guess. Official statistics ignore perhaps half the economy. Equally important is the fact that the economic effects of these trade flows are blotted out, e.g. the ways in which they impinge on patterns of industrialization, employment, investment or consumption. The blinkers of state-centrism continue to throw up economic development plans, programmes and projects that are 'territorially challenged' and insensitive to processes of rescaling. Most development plans are blind to the politics of scale emanating from illegal trade networks, and therefore they are often wildly, even dangerously, off the mark.[110]

In the preceding pages I have explored the interaction of trade flows, territoriality and borderland society. We have seen that India, Bangladesh and Burma were not capable of channelling flows of goods according to their plans, and that they found the economy of the Bengal borderland impossible to control. In chapters 8 and 9, I will consider if they were more successful in controlling flows of people passing through the borderland.

Notes

1 'BDR has moral obligation to serve distressed people,' *The Independent* (25 August 2001).

2 When the Chinese army invaded Northeast India, it became clear to India's rulers that the road and rail links between that region and the rest of India were woefully inadequate for supply and strategic purposes.

3 Initially there were problems as the currencies of Burma and Pakistan were not convertible (cf. 'Rangoon o Pak-Borma shimante mudrar jor chorakarbar...,' *Azad* (29 May 1949)). Trade relations were much less restricted by political considerations in this section of the borderland and appear to have been less formalized.

4 For an Indian view of the difficult trade relations in the first 2½ years, see *White Paper on Indo-Pakistan Trade Relations (15th August 1947–31st December 1949)*, reprinted in Shreedhar and John Kaniyalil, *Indo-Pak Relations: A Documentary Study* (New Delhi: ABC Publishing House, 1993), 22–126. For the text of various trade agreements between India and Pakistan, see Shreedhar and Kaniyalil, *Indo-Pak Relations*, 30–181.

5 In most of the borderland, Indian *rupees* and Pakistani *rupees* (1947–1971)/Bangladeshi *takas* (since 1971) circulated freely. Bangladesh *takas* and Burmese *kyats* mingled in the southernmost section of the borderland. In the immediate post-1947 period, British currency was also a common means of payment in some borderland transactions but it was soon overtaken by the US dollar. In the northernmost part of the borderland, Bhutanese currency (*ngultrum*) was also used. On the ease of releasing counterfeit currency in borderland trade (e.g. Bangladeshi takas and US dollars in illegal deals in northern Arakan (Burma)), see 'Counterfeit banknotes flood Burma Bangladesh border', *Narinjara News* (5 September 2002). For an example, of the regular movement of large sums of Indian currency through the Bangladesh side of the borderland, see 'Huge Indian currency seized in Khulna,' *The Independent* (23 September 2003).

6 For example, in December 1950 the export of vegetables and fish through a ferry crossing on the Sylhet-Tripura border was suddenly disrupted, apparently only as a result of a new contingent of Pakistan armed forces being posted there (CR 5T-1/50 (2-53), also for similar cases).

7 Reprinted in Shreedhar and Kaniyalil, *Indo-Pak Relations*, 29. For the rules for transit trade as framed in 1948, see Shreedhar and Kaniyalil, *Indo-Pak Relations*, 50.

8 According to the East Pakistan Inland Water Transport Authority, over 1,000 million kg of goods in transit were transported by rail and 975 million kg by boat in the year ending in June 1960. *Report to the Government of Pakistan on a Survey of Labour Problems in Inland Water Transport in East Pakistan* (Geneva: International Labour Office, 1961), 5.

9 See, for example, a petition by the Muslim League of Sherpur (Mymensingh) in Pol. P10C-7/49 (9–49). This antagonism between different groups of state personnel remained a constant factor in trade across the border, occasionally bringing it to a halt when traders refused to pay multiple bribes. For example, in early 2002 over 1,000 lorries bound for markets in Bangladesh got stuck on the Indian side of the border at Hili because the Hili Exporters' and Customs Clearing Agents' Association protested against the behaviour of the Indian border guards against them and the truck drivers. Their spokesperson said: 'The BSF [Indian Border Security Force] harasses exporters and drivers even if they have the necessary clearance from Customs to move the goods across the border. Once the vehicles are cleared by Customs, the BSF has no business to stop them.' 'Trucks to Bangla held up on border', *The Telegraph* (5 January 2002).

10 'The Dewan of Tripura complained that the Police and the Ansars at Akhaura have been physically checking goods in transit to Agartala even after the Pakistan Customs had passed the same after examination of Customs papers in accordance with the Delhi Agreement' (CR 3C-6/49 (11-50)). See also complaints by Cooch Behar about obstruction and corruption in the Indian customs department and railway in the same file. Cooch Behar needed cloth from Bombay and Ahmedabad but this could not reach because of insufficient allotment of wagons and because Indian customs refused to grant a permit. The Cooch Behar authorities argued that such permits should be done away with 'if such goods are consigned to any part of the Indian Dominion, even though the goods be passing through Pakistan.' Only 17 per cent of the cloth quota for 1949 could be 'imported' from other parts of India (7 per cent had to be flown in), and only 10 per cent of salt. No cement, iron or steel was allowed to go to Cooch Behar, and there were scarcities of paper and coal as well.

11 CR 4T-15/49 (3-51).

12 On coal, see e.g. CR 4T-5/49 (3-50), CR 3C-6/49 (11-50), CR 4T-12/50 (7-52); on medicine CR 4T-5/49 (3-50), CR 6M5-1/51 (8-53); on spare parts CR 4T-5/49 (3-50), CR 2R4-19/49 (12-52); and on petrol and kerosine Plt. 6C-5/48 (9-50), Pol. EBP2M-14/48 (11-48).

13 The transit of Assamese jute through East Pakistan to Calcutta was allowed, but the East Pakistan authorities soon found out that over 75 per cent of the jute from Assam was in fact East Pakistan jute smuggled to Assam and then re-entering East Pakistan as transit goods (CR 1C-2/50 (11-50)).

14 For attempts by residents on the Indian side to re-establish a nearby railway station, see Avijit Sinha, 'Haldibari on nostalgia trip – Station loses prominence to political reality', *The Telegraph* (4 November 2002).

15 *The Daily Star* photograph (12 July 2001).

16 Standing Order No. 32/1953, Collectorate of Central Excise & Land Customs, Chittagong, Government of Pakistan (CR 11C1-2/52 (9-53)). During the India-China war of 1962, the trade was temporarily blocked because Pakistani crew went on strike. In 1965, 70 per cent of the tea sent from Assam to Calcutta was transported by this route, as were large quantities of jute, wax and bamboo. Important goods moving from Calcutta to Assam were cars, fertilizers, cement and iron. Six inland river companies

based in Calcutta daily moved over 2,000 tons of goods each way between Assam and Calcutta, using 81 steamers and 158 flats and barges. They employed over 10,000 staff, over 90 per cent of whom were Pakistanis. At the outbreak of the Indo-Pakistan war of 1965, transit trade was stopped by India, and Pakistan impounded 86 vessels (and Rs.50 million worth of goods in transit) then on its territory. The transit trade was resumed in 1972 under short-term agreements that had to be renewed every six to twelve months, and later two to three months. Cf. 'Calcutta-Assam steamer route closed', *The Statesman* (8 September 1965); 'East Pakistan impounds Indian tea flotilla: Alternative arrangements for shipment from Assam', *The Statesman* (14 September 1965); 'Pakistan strategy in eastern sector: Economic strangulation main objective', *The Statesman* (16 September 1965); Rafiq Hasan, 'Delhi seeks extension of water transit', *The Daily Star* (30 January 2003). Avtar Singh Bhasin (ed.), *India-Bangladesh Relations: Documents – 1971–2002* (New Delhi: Geetika Publishers, 2003), III, 1302, 1327, 1452–8, passim. See also Rehman Sobhan, *Transforming Eastern South Asia: Building Growth Zones for Economic Cooperation* (Dhaka: University Press Limited, 1999), 110–11.

17 'Water Transport,' *Oriental Times* (July 22–August 6, 1999).

18 The coal exported from Karimganj is high-calorie, low-ash 'Khasi coal', for which there is a great demand in brick kilns in Bangladesh during the winter season. Each vessel carries up to 600 tonnes of coal. The supply of coal to the Karimganj jetty is difficult because the road is in a bad shape. In 2001, only 11,000 tonnes were shipped to Bangladesh. 'Coal exports up', *The Telegraph* (7 September 2002); 'Ships leave Karimganj', *The Telegraph* (22 September 2002).

19 CR 2R4-19/49 (12-52); cf. CR 1B2-40/53 (12-55).

20 Photograph by Bernard Llewellyn. From Bernard Llewellyn, *From the Back Streets of Bengal* (London: George Allen & Unwin, 1955), facing 113.

21 For background on the coal trade, see Rajesh Dutta, 'Coal Export from Meghalaya to Bangladesh: A Case Study of the Barsora Trade Route', in: Gurudas Das and RK Purkayastha (eds.), *Border Trade: Northeast India and Neighbouring Countries* (New Delhi: Akansha Publishing House, 2000), 200–8.

22 Pol. EBP14M-87/48 (7-48). Similarly, in March 1948 the District Magistrate of Rangpur (Pakistan) and the Cooch Behar *durbar* made the following local arrangement: 'Goods in transit through Pakistan from one part of Cooch Behar State to another and also goods in transit through Cooch Behar from one part of Rangpur to another part of Rangpur should be exempted from payment of Export Duty and other duties, if any, subject to the condition that the movement is covered by a transit permit authenticated by appropriate authority and showing the quantity and nature of goods carried in transit.' This agreement was approved by the Chief Secretaries' Conference of May that year (Plt. 1I-259/48 (2-49)).

23 State income from sanctioned trade derived from various forms of taxation (import tax, VAT, travelling tax), pre-shipment inspection charges, fines and auction sales. 'Hilli, Burimari land ports earn Tk.115.68 cr', *The Independent* (1 August 2003).

24 Janet Roitman, who takes this term from French colonial documents on the Chad Basin, describes the garrison-entrepôt as 'a site of wealth creation, regulation, violence, accumulation, redistribution, sociability, and *political and economic subjectivity*' (emphasis in original). Janet Roitman, 'The Garrison-Entrepôt', *Cahiers d'Études africaines*, 150–152, 38:2–4 (1998), 297–329.

25 In 2003, the Bangladesh government announced it was planning to privatize the

management of 12 of its 13 'land ports': Akhaura, Banglabandh, Bhomra, Bibir Bazar, Birol, Burimari, Darsana, Haluaghat, Hili, Sona Masjid, Tamabil and Teknaf. Only the most profitable, Benapol, would be under direct state control. Government would retain regulatory authority over all land ports. '12 landports to go to private sector', *The Daily Star* (24 February 2003).

26 This land port not only channelled trade from Bangladesh to India and vice versa, but also trade between Bhutan and Bangladesh. A considerable proportion of the trucks entering Bangladesh here were Bhutanese. Like Indian trucks, they were allowed only to unload their cargo just inside Bangladesh and had to return to Indian territory immediately afterwards.

27 Over the years, the descriptions became more detailed. Several of these flows were exclusively between West Pakistan and India. In the year ending in June 1960, official figures put the traffic between East Pakistan and India by boat at 225 million kg. Shreedhar and Kaniyalil, *Indo-Pak Relations*, 127–32, 145–47, 161–71; *Report to the Government of Pakistan*, 5.

28 The 1972 trade agreement between India and Bangladesh stated that 'the two governments agree to make mutually beneficial arrangements for the use of their waterways, roadways and railways for commerce between the two countries and passage of goods between two places in one country through the territory of the other.' This agreement was renewed under different governments in 1980, 1984, 1992 and 1995. Actual transit arrangements remained restricted, however. In 1999 a proposal for a new agreement on transit trade led to much protest among opposition politicians in Bangladesh. 'Trade Agreement between the Government of India and the Government of Bangladesh, New Delhi, March 28, 1972', in: Bhasin (ed.), *India-Bangladesh Relations*, III, 1283–91, passim. 'No Anti-National Deal, Says Tofael', and 'Transit Agreed by AL in '73: Tanvir', *The New Nation* (2 August 1999); 'Transit to India: We Reviewed Agreement of 1973, Says MK Anwar', *The Independent* (2 August 1999); 'Prothom Alo-BIISS discussion on transshipment: Think regional, says Saifur – There's time to think: Tofail', *The Daily Star* (22 August 1999). For a list of officially designated (but not necessarily operative) routes from India to Bangladesh, see Trade-India.com (http:/ /www.trade-india.com/dyn/gdh/shipping_corner/bangladesh.htm).
The sanctioned trade between Burma and East Pakistan/ Bangladesh was insignificant. In 1999 it amounted to less than US$ 0.3 million. Under a trade agreement signed in 1994, Burma exported rice and paddy, wheat, shrimps and dried fish, bamboo, umbrellas and spices to Bangladesh, which exported fertilizers, cement, medicines, PVC pipes, crushed tobacco and fabrics to Burma. 'Trade with Myanmar: Jetty on Naf River Soon', *The New Nation* (4 August 1999); cf. 'Burma to lease out land to Bangladesh!' *Narinjara News* (17 March 2003).

29 For the text of various Nepal-Bangladesh agreements of the 1970s, see PK Mishra, *India, Pakistan, Nepal and Bangladesh (India as a Factor in the Intra-Regional Interaction in South Asia)* (Delhi: Sundeep Prakashan, 1979), 225–65. Cf. 'Nepal offered to use Mongla Port at less tariff,' *The New Nation* (21 September 2002); Rafiq Hasan, 'Landlocked Nepal to use Mongla port: Govt to offer 50pc discount on service charges', *The Daily Star* (13 October 2002).

30 Bhasin (ed.), *India-Bangladesh Relations*, III, 1623–6.

31 'Account trade: Dhaka sends 44-product list to Yangon', *The Daily Star* (1 August 2003).

32 Peter Andreas, *Border Games: Policing the U.S.-Mexico Divide* (Ithaca and London: Cornell University Press, 2000), 15.

33 See e.g. the rules for East Pakistan under the Pakistan Prevention of Smuggling Act, 1952 (CR 3S-11/54 (9-55)); 'Purbobongo hoite beaini mal rophtani bondher chesta: Pradeshik shorkar kortrik shimanto elakay kothor bebostha,' *Azad* (4 September 1950).

34 Some government-to-government trade was possible under the Special Rice Account, e.g. a very limited 'self-balancing' exchange involving two types of rice under the trade agreement of 1963 (Shreedhar and Kaniyalil, *Indo-Pak Relations*, 175–6). On paddy as a banned item for export in both India and Bangladesh, see Abdul Ghafur, Muinul Islam and Naushad Faiz, *Illegal International Trade in Bangladesh: Impact on the Domestic Economy (Phase II)* (Dhaka: Bangladesh Institute of Development Studies, 1991), 80, 90.

35 'Rice being smuggled into East Pakistan: P.C. Sen,' *The Statesman* (13 October 1965).

36 This plan also included 'substantial and prompt rewards' for informers (CR 1C-2/50 (11-50)). The other option was to create more customs stations in an attempt at 'canalising the trade' at places where 'people are forced to carry goods across the border' for lack of customs facilities (CR 11C1-9/52 (1-54)).

37 'The Pakistan Navy joined hands in the operation, patrolling in the rivers Jamuna, Pussur, Shipsa and in the Sunderbans area along the border with West Bengal. The Pakistan Air Force also lent its hand, especially by transporting the anti-smuggling personnel to remote places that harboured some of the worst smugglers.' *Pakistan 1957-1958* (Karachi: Pakistan Publications, 1958), 176.

38 At the time, the official assessment was much more positive: 'Smuggling of foodgrains from East Pakistan's borders to India assumed serious proportions during the later part of 1957. The Central Government, therefore, decided ... to deploy the Pakistan Army on the border of East Pakistan to check this dangerous activity. The Pakistan Army took charge from 18th December 1957. The "Operation Close[d] Door" at once received general public support and proved very successful. The Army seized and confiscated considerable quantities of foodgrains and other goods from the smugglers ... The Army's task under the *Operation Close[d] Door* was highly complex in view of the multiplicity of the smugglers' dens all along the border of the province as well as in the interior. The Army took up the challenge and within a very short time they achieved substantial results. As the security measures were tightened from day to day, smuggling along the border came almost to a dead stop. By suspending their activities abruptly the smugglers tried to lure the Army into a false sense of complacency and fulfilment. But their hopes were not realized as the Army continued their operation with ever-increasing zeal and vigilance making big hauls of men and material. Patrolling along both land routes and waterways, they combed out the entire smuggler-infested area ... It is estimated that goods worth over Rs. 400 million are annually smuggled across the borders of East Pakistan to India, and an equal amount of cash and precious metals change hands in the underground market.' *Pakistan 1957–1958*, 84, 176; cf. 181–2.

39 On the distinction between (il)legal and (il)licit, see Itty Abraham and Willem van Schendel, 'Introduction: The Making of Illicitness,' in: Willem van Schendel and Itty Abraham (eds.), *Illicit Flows: How States, Borders and Language Produce Criminality* (Bloomington: University of Indiana Press, forthcoming).

40 In this, the policy regarding jute differed from that regarding the East Pakistan cement industry, for example. Here the border also separated an industry (in Chhatak, Sylhet, Pakistan) from its source of raw materials (lime stone, coal) that were found in the nearby Khasi & Jaintia Hills (Assam, India). Despite the absence of an official border crossing in the area, Indian raw materials continued to supply the Pakistani industry. Van Schendel, 'Working through Partition', 409.

41 On the pre-Partition jute trade, see Sugata Bose, *Agrarian Bengal: Economy, Social Structure and Politics, 1919–1947* (Cambridge: Cambridge University Press, 1986); Binay Bhushan Chaudhuri, 'Commercialisation of Agriculture,' in: Sirajul Islam (ed.), *History of Bangladesh, 1704–1971* (Dhaka: Asiatic Society of Bangladesh, 1992), Vol II, 371–427. On changes in the jute trade up to the end of 1949, see Sreedhar and Kaniyalil, *Indo-Pak Relations*, 22–126.

42 Smuggling became especially attractive after India devalued its currency in 1949 and Pakistan did not. A deadlock in official trade resulted that lasted for eight months. In that year, the Indian Jute Mill Association banked on receiving at least 600,000 bales purchased by, according to Pakistan sources, their 'unscrupulous ... agents ... who could manage to evade [East Pakistan's] measures and smuggle it to Calcutta.' Pakistan government officials reasoned that 'the smuggling of jute was a question of life and death for the Bharat Jute mills and therefore all possible efforts should be made to check smuggling of jute from East Bengal to Bharat.' In North Bengal alone, the number of border outposts on the Pakistan side was raised from 85 to 162. Boats all over the country were to be checked, and within ten miles of the border 'the strictest possible measures should be adopted to check all possible modes of smuggling, including road transport.' District Magistrates were told to tour their districts and 'organise public meetings with a view to explaining the evils of smuggling of jute out of East Bengal.' Even after the signing of a trade agreement between Pakistan and India, making it possible for Indian jute mills to acquire jute from East Pakistan on a permit system, the restrictions on the movement of jute within 10 miles of the border ('specially jute moving towards the border') were retained. (CR 1C-2/50 (11-50); cf. CR 1B4-2/50 (9-54)). See Vakil, *Economic Consequences* (1950), 436–441; 'Purbobongo hoite beaini mal rophtani bondher chesta: Pradeshik shorkar kortrik shimanto elakay kothor bebostha,' *Azad* (4 September 1950); Sreedhar and Kaniyalil, *Indo-Pak Relations*, 91–110. Transport by rail was another concern. For a list of 106 border stations (most of them not for sanctioned cross-border traffic), see CR 3I-232/54 (1-55).

43 In February 1950, the East Pakistan government received 'alarming reports' that jute smuggling had 'again taken a serious shape and that the smugglers were being actively helped by certain elements in the Police, Ansars and Customs Staff' (CR 1C-2/50 (11-50); CR 1B2-35/51 (1-55)).

44 CR 1C-2/50 (11-50).

45 Plt. 5J-1/49 (1-51).

46 However, during years of shortfall, the Calcutta jute mills could get licences to import jute from East Pakistan and Thailand. In 1965 they contracted to buy half a million bales from East Pakistan but the war between India and Pakistan that broke out in that year made the contract inoperative. 'Raw jute poses new problem for industry: Steps to meet deficit and transport difficulties', *The Statesman* (15 September 1965).

47 On jute production in West Bengal, see SN Mukherjea, *A Brief Agricultural Geography of West Bengal* (Calcutta: Directorate of Agriculture, Government of West Bengal, 1956), 111, 122, 162; on East Pakistan, see James K Boyce, *Agrarian Impasse in Bengal: Institutional Constraints to Technological Change* (Oxford: Oxford University Press, 1987), 90, 92, 100–1.

48 Abdul Ghafur, Muinul Islam and Naushad Faiz, *Illegal International Trade in Bangladesh: Impact on the Domestic Economy (Phase I)* (Dhaka: Bangladesh Institute of Development Studies, 1990), 99.

49 E.g. CR 3I-20/53 (11-54), CR 1A5-1/54 (1-55).

50 CR 1C-2/50 (11-50). Ghafur et al.'s survey in different parts of the borderland in the 1980s found clear-cut evidence that 'an overwhelming proportion of illegal trade is conducted within a system of connivance and co-operation of the law-enforcement agencies with the operators in exchange of financial payments.' It also pointed to the 'widespread and increasing practice of rent-seeking among the rank and file of these agencies' and abysmally low figures for arrests and convictions of suspected smugglers. Ghafur et al., *Illegal International Trade*, I, 50; 47–8, 100. Cf. Atiur Rahman and Abdur Razzaque, 'Informal Border Trade between Bangladesh and India: An Empirical Study in Selected Areas,' in Forrest E Cookson and AKM Shamsul Alam (eds), *Towards Greater Sub-regional Economic Cooperation: Limitation, Obstacles, and Benefits* (Dhaka: University Press Limited, 2002), 129–213.

51 The study was carried out by the South Asia Research Centre in Calcutta. 'Border crime on the rise in West Bengal', *The Statesman* (15 April 1992)); cf. 'Smuggling, human trafficking go on along Meherpur borders', *The Independent* (3 October 2001)). Tokens were also in use among law enforcers and smugglers bringing contraband goods into Bangladesh through Chittagong harbour ('Outer anchorage of Ctg port "smugglers' haven"', *The Daily Star* (5 January 2002). According to Indian border officials, 'the volume of smuggling across the borders in South Bengal was large, estimated to be worth Rs.300 crore [= 3 billion] a year. With so much illegal money circulating, some border guards fell prey to temptations, sources explained. "Many of the boys in South Bengal have come in posting from Kashmir. Some may consider it an opportunity to recoup and repair"'. Nirmalya Banerjee, 'Fencing problem plagues border', *The Times of India* (16 April 2002). Cf. SK Ghosh, *Unquiet Border* (New Delhi: Ashish Publishing House, 1993), 64–8. Cf. 'Smuggling rampant along border', *The Independent* (27 June 2003).

52 Cf. Tapash Ganguly, 'Dangerous Influx', *The Week* (12 July 1998).

53 'Bangladesh returns a Burmese Military Intelligence-owned smuggling vessel at a flag meeting', *Narinjara News* (26 February 2003). Cf. 'A bizarre incident', *The Independent* (7 March 2003).

54 Ghafur et al., *Illegal International Trade*, I, 40.

55 Sometimes such items were put to unexpected use across the border. This was the case with phensidyl from India. In Bangladesh, phensidyl was prohibited as an illegal drug. In the 1990s, a large demand for phensidyl developed in Bangladesh and the syrup became a popular item in cross-border trade flows. Reportedly, phensidyl was also mixed with tea, powdered paracetamol tablets and sugar to create *phenta*, sold in cups for Tk.10. The Bangladesh government complained to India about 'the existence of unauthorized factories manufacturing spurious Phensidyl on the Indian side of the border. The Indian side assured to investigate this allegation.' See the 'Agreed Minutes of the 7th Meeting of the India-Bangladesh Joint Working Group (JWG), New Delhi, February 17, 2001,' in Bhasin (ed.), *India-Bangladesh Relations*, I, 520. Cf. Khadimul Islam, 'Drug addicts now depend on "Phenta"', *The Independent* (8 September 2002).

56 Coal from Meghalaya, which kept the brick kilns of Bangladesh burning, was exported legally but also illegally to Bangladesh. Cf. 'Coal smuggling still unabated in Khasi Hills', *The Telegraph* (1 October 2002).

57 Zahid Hossain Biplob et al., 'Vehicles being made with Indian parts, smuggling rampant before Eid', *The New Nation* (18 January 1999).

58 Trade flows would wax and wane. In the 1990s a rather bizarre trade took off: that of the skeletons of Bangladeshis who had died of lightning. Highly valued in Northeast

India for their alleged magnetic and medicinal powers, these remains, worn as amulets, were thought to remedy asthma and gout, protect their owners against accidents, and ensure them a peaceful death. 'Human skeletons being smuggled into Assam', *The Sentinel* (28 March 2000). Bangladeshi biscuits appeared in Indian markets in 2002. 'Opar biscuits bite into epar tea time', *The Times of India* (15 November 2002); Anujata D Talukdar, 'NE producers losing out to Bangla products', *The Assam Tribune* (27 December 2002).

59 Many goods from Burma were registered as goods coming from Singapore. Including these goods, the president of the Bangladesh-Myanmar Business Promotion Council estimated that official figures of Bangladesh imports from Burma (US$16.94 million) would come to US$170 million. 'Yangon's strict control creates trade imbalance', *The New Nation* (3 June 2003). Cf. Surajit Khaund, 'Myanmar market attracts buyers from India', *The Assam Tribune* (13 August 2003).

60 The complexity of trade routes passing through the Bangladesh-Burma border should not be underestimated. 'Markets along the [Bangladesh-Burma] border abound with goods smuggled across Burma – sarongs and electrical goods from Malaysia and Thailand which first have passed through customs gates belonging to the rebel Karen National Union in the south, and crockery from China channelled through territory controlled by the Kachin Independence Army or the Communist Party of Burma. Even heroin, unheard of a few years ago, is now available, though largely from offshore sources. In this impoverished backwater, however, most traders deal in basic goods – rice, fish, timber and cigars from Burma, and medicine and kerosene from Bangladesh.' Martin Smith, 'Burma's Muslim Borderland:.Sold Down the River', *Inside Asia* (July–August 1986), 5. Smugglers also used Bangladesh as a route for getting works of art (e.g. Buddha statues) out of Burma. For bulk goods, the sea route was also important. For example, the Bangladesh Navy intercepted five cargo boats with 600 metric tons of fertilizer being smuggled out of Bangladesh in 2003. 'Fertiliser worth Tk. 2 crore seized', *The Independent* (10 August 2003). Cf. '30 gold statues of Buddha recovered', *The Daily Star* (1 October 2002); 'Contraband goods from Burma seized in Bangladesh', *Narinjara News* (4 March 2003); 'Tk 30 lakh worth of smuggled Myanmarese goods seized', *The Independent* (27 August 1999); 'Smuggling rampant at Ukhiya, Teknaf borders', *The Independent* (25 April 2000); 'Three boats with Tk. One Cr Burmese salt seized in Cox's Bazar', *The Independent* (29 November 2001); Abdullah Al-Mahmud, 'Safe haven for smugglers,' *The Daily Star* (21 May 2003); 'Account trade: Dhaka sends 44-product list to Yangon', *The Daily Star* (1 August 2003).

61 For an impression of the Teknaf border area, see Francis Rolt, *On the Brink of Bengal* (London: John Murray, 1991), 71–86. For a description of illegal trade through this port and a plea to open two new 'land ports' at Naikkhyongchhari and at Kachchapia to facilitate cross-border trade by road, see Shwe Lin Yun, 'Why is the Myanmar-Bangladesh border trade ineffectual?' *Narinjara News* (28 February 2002).

62 In order to evade Indian tariffs and taxes (e.g. VAT), it was sometimes profitable to export Indian goods legally, only to smuggle them back into India. Ghafur et al., *Illegal International Trade*, I, 33.

63 BG Verghese, *India's North-East Insurgent: Ethnicity, Governance, Development* (Delhi: Konark, 1996), 192; 'Trade links with SE Asia a must for NE', *The Assam Tribune* (24 August 1999).

64 Sondip Bhattacharya, 'Kinds of kindness', *Navhind Times* (18 October 1998). For an impression of the world of 8- to 10-year-olds smuggling small amounts of sugar from

India to Bangladesh in Hili, see 'Tale of a "tiny smuggler"', *The Independent* (20 August 2001); cf. Main Uddin Chisti, 'Carrier kids in border career: Children in Cooch Behar make living ferrying smuggled goods to Bangladesh', *The Telegraph* (16 September 2002). One borderlander at Tamabil (Bangladesh) described the role of children in smuggling as follows: 'You give your order [for a bottle of Chinese gin] now ... and tomorrow morning a child will cross the border with a chicken – chickens are worth fifty *taka* on this side and seventy on the other – and will come back with your bottle. It's simple. No one bothers with the children.' Quoted in Rolt, *On the Brink of Bengal*, 135.

65 The path leads to a walled area just behind the smugglers, at the very edge of Bangladeshi territory. This is a burial ground of Bangladeshi freedom fighters who died here fighting the Pakistan armed forces in the Bangladesh War of Liberation in 1971. The Tamabil/Dawki check post is on the Sylhet (Bangladesh)/Meghalaya (India) border.

66 In 1998–9 Bangladesh's legal exports to India stood at US$60 million and its legal imports from that country at US$1,228 million. The vast bulk of these imports and exports passed through the borderland. Ghafur et al., *Illegal International Trade*, I, 29; 'Smuggling along border mounts: Trade gap with India rises to $880cr', *The New Nation* (25 August 2001). According to one observer, 1.7 million heads of cattle were smuggled from Northeast India to Bangladesh every year in the late 1990s. Another calculated that to move a truck load of smuggled cattle from the Bangladesh border to its destination required Tk.2,500 in bribes to officials to procure a 'release certificate' (thereby evading Tk.8,000 in duty and VAT) and then Tk.100 at various illegal checkpoints along the way (Tk = Taka, the currency of Bangladesh). Kaushik Ghosh, 'Cattle smuggling on the rise along Indo-Bangla border', *The Statesman* (15 August 1999); 'Trade links with SE Asia a must for NE', *The Assam Tribune* (24 August 1999); 'Cattle smuggling thru' western borders rampant', *The Independent* (4 November 2002).

67 These included Japanese electronics, French perfumes, American cosmetics, Taiwanese household appliances, Swiss watches, Korean synthetic cloth, Chinese silk yarn, Australian milk powder, and many more. Not only industrial goods were profitable items for smuggling: in the 1960s, spices from the Far East and East Africa were reported to be imported into East Pakistan and then smuggled to India where the price was at least four times higher. 'Smugglers explore new border areas', *The Statesman* (15 October 1965). For an overview of the complex mix of goods being smuggled through small riverside villages on the Rajshahi/Murshidabad border in the 1980s, see Willem van Schendel, 'Easy Come, Easy Go: Smugglers on the Ganges', *Journal of Contemporary Asia*, 23:2 (1993), 189–213. A smaller but similar flow of international goods that had duty-free access to Burma, but not Bangladesh, entered Bangladesh through Teknaf and Ukhia. Abdullah Al-Mahmud, 'Safe haven for smugglers', *The Daily Star* (21 May 2003).

68 On import liberalization in Bangladesh, see Ghafur et al., *Illegal International Trade*, II, 52–5.

69 Ghafur et al., *Illegal International Trade*, II, 1–2. For other lists of smuggled articles, see Ghosh, *Unquiet Border*, 72–4; and Srinath Baruah, 'Certain Observations on Informal Trade with Neighbouring Countries and Economic Prospects of the North Eastern Region', in Gurudas Das and RK Purkayastha (eds.), *Border Trade: Northeast India and Neighbouring Countries* (New Delhi: Akansha Publishing House, 2000), 64–86. Cf. 'Smugglers of computer parts active', *The Daily Star* (17 November 2001); Souvik Chowdhury, 'Meghalaya-Bangladesh border: The dangers of mixed loyalties', *Tehelka* (26 February 2001); Manas Paul, 'Gold smugglers in Customs net', *The Assam Tribune*

(16 December 2002). On cigarette smuggling by British American Tobacco (BAT) through Cox's Bazar and Anwara in Chittagong, see 'Int'l ring in cigarette smuggling', *The New Nation* (4 October 2002); 'Smuggling out of imported spices rampant,' *The Independent* (13 March 2003).

70 See import trends in Ghafur et al., *Illegal International Trade*, II, 4–10.

71 Ghafur et al., *Illegal International Trade*, II, 16; 'Mini TV factories in Satkhira?' *The Daily Star* (18 March 2001).

72 Certain smugglers could also occasionally appeal to border guards' leniency and pity. As an Indian border guard explained: 'We know that we should not allow any smuggling to take place but there were instances when we caught widows trying to smuggle out a few kilograms of salt and they later said that their children would starve to death if they are not allowed to [sell] the salt.' R Dutta Chowdhury, 'Char Indians, Bangladeshis bury border barrier', *The Assam Tribune* (1 September 2003).

73 Shaikh Nazrul Islam, 'Organized gangs smuggle motorbikes from India: Known as 'tana party' in Satkhira and Jessore, they also change brand, forge documents', *The Daily Star* (6 April 2002). See also Van Schendel, 'Easy Come, Easy Go'.

74 Smuggling of banned books (including novels by Salman Rushdie, pornographic writings and Islamist literature) and videos is occasionally reported. Wildlife products are increasingly being smuggling through the borderland (e.g. tiger and deer skins from Bangladesh to India, and mountain goat (cheraw) horns, pangolin skins and elephant meat from Burma to India). See for example 'Bangla fundamentalists flood Karimganj market with Laden books,' *The Sentinel* (20 October 2001); Bidhayak Das, 'Wildlife warden adds to Thanga crime dossier,' *The Telegraph* (26 May 2003).

75 Gold was imported illegally into Bangladesh (by air or sea) and then exported illegally to India across the land border. The price of gold in Bangladesh was well above the world market price but considerably lower than the gold price in India. On gold smuggling, see CR 3S-11/54 (9-55), which contains an account of a group of smugglers from Uttar Pradesh (India) who, in the early 1950s, smuggled camels into East Pakistan and brought back gold hidden in buckets with false bottoms. See also Ghafur et al., *Illegal International Trade*, I , 82–4, and II, 24–30; and e.g. 'Gold smugglers active along C'Nawabganj border', *The Daily Star* (21 August 2001). On arms smuggling (which increasingly took the form of trading Indian-made small arms to Bangladesh), see e.g. Abdul Wadood, 'Rajshahi, Chapai Nawabganj border areas: Safe routes of arms smuggling', *The Daily Star* (4 August 1999); Ghosh, *Unquiet Border*, 78–9; and (on smuggling arms to Bangladesh through the Sylhet border) 'Female arms smuggler held with revolvers', *The Independent* (12 May 2003). In the Indian Parliament, it was alleged that arms were smuggled to India from Thailand, through Burma and Bangladesh. *XI Lok Sabha Debates, Session IV (Budget)* (21 March and 12 May 1997). On arms smuggling from Burma to Bangladesh, see for example '3 Rakhain youths arrested: Bullets recovered', *The Daily Star* (27 May 2001); 'Bullet smuggling rising on Bangladesh-Burma border', *Mizzima News Group* (12 June 2001).

76 Although it is often assumed that the direction of heroin trade was from east (Burma/ Golden Triangle) to west (India), partly through Bangladesh, trade routes appear to have been much more complex and variable. Burmese heroin was also smuggled from West Bengal (India) to Bangladesh, and some heroin originating in Afghanistan travelled east through Pakistan and India to consumers in Bangladesh, and via air from Dhaka to western destinations. 'Biggest ever heroin haul', *The New Nation* (21 September 1999); 'Heroin worth Tk 10 cr seized in Meherpur', *The Independent* (12 May 2002);

'NCB detains two in Thanga case', *The Statesman* (26 May 2003).

77 Cf. Van Schendel, 'Easy Come, Easy Go'. Opium consumption was not completely new in the borderland. In 1947 a police party near Bandarban in the Chittagong Hill Tracts arrested Kong Kyaw Mogh who died shortly afterwards, apparently from eating an overdose of opium (Pol. EBP5R-9/47 (9-48)). By 1999, commercial opium cultivation had gained a foothold in the same area, and several heroin refineries were reported near the border in Chin State (Burma). A new overland route was being opened up from Paletwa (Burma) to Alikadam (Bangladesh) and from there to the port of Chittagong. 'Anti-drug operation: Army destroys poppy plants in CHT', *The Daily Star* (18 May 1999); 'Army demolish poppy fields on 144 acres in Bandarban', *The New Nation*, 28 May 1999; *The Newsletter Monthly – News and Analysis of the Arakan Rohingya National Organisation, Arakan (Burma)*, 2:2 (February 2000); 'Crackdown on poppy farmers in Bandarban', *The Daily Star* (12 May 2002).

78 According to news reports, one shipment of almost 100,000 bullets and 200kg of explosives travelled from China through Burma to Tripura (India), and was then sent through Bangladesh and West Bengal (India) to Maoist guerrillas in Nepal. It was intercepted near the Bangladesh/West Bengal border. See e.g. Anwar Ali, 'More surprises at ammo spot: 11,050 bullets, 12kg explosives found in Bogra pond', *The Daily Star* (3 July 2003); 'Cache was meant for smuggling?' *The Daily Star* (3 July 2003).

79 This crisscrossing pattern of trade across the international border can be illustrated by the following example. Fifteen arms dealers were arrested in Murshidabad district (West Bengal) 'as they were crossing over to Bangladesh with sophisticated weapons. The dealers had arrived from Munger in Bihar with the arms and were going over to find lucrative customers on the Bangladesh side.' But Bangladesh also had a sizeable home production of small arms. Police sources in Bangladesh estimated that there were more than 50 arms manufacturing workshops in Chittagong, Cox's Bazar and the Chittagong Hill Tracts, and the island of Moheshkhali alone boasted 20 illegal arms factories. Arms in the borderland were clearly linked with transnational trade networks. For example, when Indian police raided houses of the United Liberation Front of Asom (ULFA) in Chisikgre (Phulbari, West Garo Hills, Meghalaya) after mortar attacks on an oil refinery and an airport in Assam, they found '96 rocket-propelled grenades, 11 large rockets, eight rocket launchers, 15 anti-tank devices', Chinese ammunition, hand grenades, rifles, powerful wireless sets, explosives and timing and pressure release devices. According to some police sources, the neatly packed arms had come from an ULFA training camp in Gajni (Sherpur) just across the border in Bangladesh, and that they had been en route to Assam (others thought they might have been floated down rivers from camps in Bhutan). They also suspected that ULFA had procured the arms through contacts in Afghanistan, possibly through some Korean connections. Sakyasen Mitra, 'BSF on red alert at Murshidabad point', *The Daily Star* (10 May 2001). Cf. '980 handmade bombs recovered from Ctg. Village', *The New Nation* (28 March 2000); Nazimuddin Shyamol, 'Thirty criminal syndicates control arms market: Chittagong turns transit point for gun-runners', *The Independent* (12 August 2002); 'Sarbahara men's "arms factory" unearthed in Ctg,' *The Independent* (18 June 2003); '"Gunrunner" held with M16', *The Daily Star* (11 September 2003). 'Taliban, Korean link in Ulfa arms jigsaw', *The Telegraph* (13 April 2003); 'Mortar raids planned in B'desh: ULFA's rocket lady got her training in firing range outside Dhaka', *The Sentinel* (21 April 2003). Cf. Sunando Sarkar and Bappa Majumdar, 'Arms take a new route', *The Telegraph* (19 May 2003).

80 *Small Arms Survey 2001: Profiling the Problem* (Geneva/Oxford: Graduate Institute of
    International Studies/ Oxford University Press, 2001), 182. Many small arms were also
    circulating in Bangladesh itself, being used especially in the strong-arm techniques
    that national and local political entrepreneurs increasingly favoured. Cf. 'GOC: ULFA,
    NDFB buy arms from global open markets – 19 ULFA, 11 NDFB rebels surrender', *The
    Sentinel* (28 June 2003); 'The who's who of Dhaka's underworld', *Holiday* (15 November
    2002).

81 In 2001, a group of Naga insurgents from India, returning from a shopping trip to Cox's
    Bazar, were found to be in possession of the following types of arms: AK-56 assault rifle,
    Russian Dragunov sniper rifle, 303 rifle, Chinese grenade, ammunition. '4 NSCN (IM)
    ultras killed by own cadres, 5 surrender', *The Assam Tribune* (28 September 2001); cf.
    'Northeast militants go arms shopping', *The Times of India* (7 December 2002); 'Agencies
    probe origin of arms in Bandarban', *The Daily Star* (16 July 2003).

82 Other important arms bazars were in northwest Bangladesh. In 2002 the following
    prices were reported for small arms in markets in Dinajpur: Tk.2,000–5,000 (US$42–
    106) for a pipe gun, Tk.5,000–8,000 for an Indian-made Colt or Gopi pistol, Tk.9,000–
    10,000 for a shotgun, Tk.10,000–20,000 for a Smith & Wesson or Tiger revolver,
    Tk.20,000 for a cut-rifle and Tk.80,000 (US$1,700) for a Chinese rifle. Ammunition
    sold for Tk.800–1,000 per dozen. 'Dinajpur border safe haven for arms smugglers', *The
    Independent* (7 September 2002); On borderland prices of various arms, see also Amanur
    Aman, 'Racketeers active in Kushtia in smuggling firearms', *The Daily Star* (21 March
    2002).

83 Laldina, a member of the Chin Army in Chhimtuipui district of Mizoram (India), quoted
    in 'Mizoram border safe haven for gun-runners, insurgents', *The Northeast Daily* (29
    March 2000). Another important supply route ran via northern Burma and Arunachal
    Pradesh in India. For an impression, see 'One border, many insurgencies', *The Telegraph*
    (7 February 2003).

84 See for example '100 trained ultras poised to enter state', *The Sentinel* (19 March 1997);
    'NE ultras' link with Tamil Tigers exposed', *Press Trust of India* (26 March 1997); 'Assam
    NRIs funding ULFA: Govt may seek Swiss help', *The Sentinel* (18 August 1997); 'Illegal
    arms flow has changed NE security scenario: BSF', *The Assam Tribune* (29 November
    1999); 'Nasim briefs Advani on arms smuggling', *The New Nation* (27 December 1999);
    'Stop smuggling of illegal arms', *The New Nation* (28 December 1999); 'Gun-toting
    terrorists active in Chapainawabganj frontier', *The Daily Star* (4 May 2000); 'Meghalaya
    grapples with clandestine arms deal', *The Sentinel* (18 August 2002); 'People spy what
    police don't: Report of arms shipment via Bangla arriving in Sundarbans', *The Telegraph*
    (6 December 2002). Cf. chapters 10 and 11.

85 Cf. 'Arms, drugs smuggling rise in border areas: Women being used as carriers', *The
    Independent* (18 August 2002).

86 Two years later, Bangladeshi border guards seized another packet of 225g of uranium
    (estimated value Tk. 100 million, or about US$2 million) from Patnitola (Naogaon).
    This packet had a label reading 'Uranium. Produced in Kazakhstan. Quantity: 225
    grams. Date of Production: January 1998. Date of expiry: December 2008.' 'Uranium
    seized from villager in W. Bengal', *The Times of India* (27 August 2001); 'India to seek
    Bangla help in uranium case', *The Times of India* (27 August 2001); 'Seized "explosives"
    suspected to be uranium: Experts continuing tests', *The Independent* (4 June 2003). For
    an official denial, see Anujata D Talukdar, 'Reports of uranium smuggling refuted', *The
    Assam Tribune* (27 August 2003).

87 Sometimes the status of cross-border trade remained hard to define. When people in northern Arakan argued that local shortages of rice were a result of the Burmese military junta exporting huge quantities of rice and paddy to Bangladesh, it was unclear whether this allegation was true and, if so, how to establish whether this trade was legal or not. 'Price-hike of rice make people starve in Arakan,' *Kaladan News* (14 October 2002); cf. 'Yangon's strict control creates trade imbalance,' *The New Nation* (3 June 2003).

88 'Report of the Committee on Informal Cross-Border Trade' (Economic Division, Department of Commerce, Government of India). Findings and recommendations of this unreleased report can be found in Kalyan Barooah, 'Boom in unofficial exports to Bangla through NE', *The Assam Tribune* (29 August 2002). Smuggling from Northeast India to Bangladesh consisted mostly of agricultural produce (vegetables, fruits, cereals, spices), fish and textiles. In the same period, smuggling from West Bengal, omitted from the figure of Rs.20 billion, included these items as well as industrial products (bicycle parts, yarn, steel goods, batteries, imitation goods, nylon mosquito and fishing nets, carbide, dyes, cosmetics, glasses, bidis), drugs, gold bars and salt. According to Bangladeshi newspaper reports, goods to the tune of Tk.12–36 billion (US$200–600 million) were smuggled annually into just four ports (Anwara, Banshkhali, Sitakunda and Patenga) along the Chittagong coast. 'Smuggled goods worth Tk.1 crore seized in Chapainawabganj', *The Independent* (8 September 2002); Shahidul Islam, 'Smuggling rampant', *The Daily Star* (12 March 2003).

89 'Curbing smuggling will end illegal migration: Morshed Khan asks India, all political parties to unite to fight terrorism', *The Daily Star* (24 April 2003).

90 Kamaluddin puts the figure for both India and Bangladesh at 50 per cent, Kumar suggests 40 per cent for India in 1995–6, as does India's Chief Vigilance Commissioner in 2000, and the Bangladesh Chambers of Commerce and Industry suggest 50 per cent for Bangladesh in 2002. Estimates for Burma are much higher. S Kamaluddin, 'Bangladesh: The country has become a smuggler's paradise: Trade without tariff', *Far Eastern Economic Review*, 153:32 (8 August 1991), 16; Arun Kumar, *The Black Economy in India* (New Delhi, etc.: Penguin Books India, 1999), 56; Confederation of Indian Industry, *Press Release* (November 2000; http://www.ciionline.org/news/pressrel/2000/Nov/28nov2.htm)); 'Black money rules 50pc of country's economy: FBCCI', *The Daily Star* (21 May 2002).

91 There is only one detailed field survey of illegal trade flows through the borderland. It is based on investigations in 49 borderland 'smuggling centres' in the late 1980s, and paints a picture that differs markedly from that of the 1940s and 1950s. The survey selected five sectors on the Bangladesh side of the borderland: the coastal region of Chittagong, the Sylhet/ Comilla/ Noakhali sector, the Dinajpur/ Bogra/ Rajshahi sector, the Kushtia/ Jessore sector, and the Jessore/ Khulna/ coastal sector. Not covered were the Chittagong Hill Tracts sector and the Mymensingh/ Rangpur/ Dinajpur (up to Tetulia) sector. Ghafur et al., *Illegal International Trade*, I & II.

92 For a cautionary treatment of the use of arrows in the study of (illegal) trade in borderland, see Willem van Schendel, 'Spaces of Engagement: How Borderlands, Illicit Flows and Territorial States Interlock,' in: Van Schendel and Abraham (eds.), *Illicit Flows* (forthcoming).

93 Willem van Schendel, *Three Deltas: Accumulation and Poverty in Rural Burma, Bengal and South India* (Delhi, etc.: Sage Publications, 1991), 302; provisional census figures for West Bengal and Bangladesh as available for 2001.

94 Private forms of banking flourished as smuggling expanded and official banking, currency

and taxation regulations failed to liberalize. These private forms of banking, usually known as *hundi* or *hawala*, are based on trust and personal acquaintance, and are cheap because no bribery is required. They are often linked to transnational transfers involving migrants in other continents but they are also crucial in regulating cross-border smuggling between India, Bangladesh and Burma. Towns and villages on either side of the border are strongly linked by a network of financial ties that makes it unnecessary for smugglers to carry large sums of money across the border. For example, over 150 hundi agents offered their financial services to customers in the relatively small border town of Chapainawabganj in western Bangladesh in 2002. 'Hundi agents transferring local currency to India', *The Daily Star* (22 September 2002).

95 They could also link up with rebels against the state. For example, a contractor for the Border Road Construction wing of the Tripura State Public Works Department in India was kidnapped from his home by five men dressed in olive-green fatigues and taken across the border to Bangladesh. It was thought he had fallen foul of his (illegal) business associates in Bangladesh who might be (associated with) one of several rebel groups from Tripura hiding in Bangladesh. 'BSF intensifies hunt for officer', *The Telegraph* (23 May 2003).

96 Ghafur et al., *Illegal International Trade*, I, 35. Cf. Van Schendel, 'Easy Come, Easy Go'.

97 For example, the unusually high dowries that young men employed in the customs department could demand on the marriage market were a clear indication of their large income and bright prospects in the eyes of prospective in-laws.

98 'A bizarre incident,' *The Independent* (7 March 2003). Cf. 'BNP activists storm Bandarban DC office', *The Independent* (14 April 2003).

99 'Rice from Bhomra land port looted: Border trade suspended as criminals allegedly backed by local MP beat up customs officials', *The Daily Star* (14 May 2002); Quazi Amanullah, 'Bhomra land port looks deserted as MP's musclemen move freely', *The Daily Star* (21 May 2002). For another case, in which five customs officials of Bhomra were jailed by Bangladesh Rifles for smuggling eight trucks of jute seed, see 'Smuggling: 14 Indians, 4 customs officials sent to jail', *The Daily Star* (7 May 2003); 'Custom officials of land ports to observe pen down strike', *The New Nation* (6 May 2003).

100 'The who's who of Dhaka's underworld', *Holiday* (15 November 2002).

101 On mostanocracy, see Van Schendel, 'Easy Come, Easy Go', 206; Subodh Dasgupta, 'Gouribari: What Next?' *Economic and Political Weekly* (29 September 1984), 1696. For an assessment by an Indian governmental commission on the same pattern in Northeast India, where 'Ministers, MLAs, bureaucrats and the police engaged in collection of money through illegal means', see 'Illegal money collection NE's canker: Advisory Group,' *The Shillong Times* (7 May 2003). On links between 'Bihar-based criminal gangs' and leaders of some political parties in Siliguri (West Bengal), see Anupam Dasgupta, 'Bangla national's arrest puts cops on alert,' *The Telegraph* (8 May 2003).

102 Which is why Ghafur et al. argued that stepping up surveillance was useless: 'From our field investigations, we have found ample support to our theoretical premise that as long as there are economic rationales for illegal trading in various goods, no amount of tightening of the law enforcement mechanisms will effectively deter smuggling in Bangladesh, given the existing politics and the system of governance of the country.' Ghafur et al., *Illegal International Trade*, I, 49. This is one reason why government initiatives to curb smuggling inspired little confidence, e.g. the Chittagong District Anti-Smuggling Coordination Committee, consisting of representatives of 14 government bodies: the Police, the Bangladesh Rifles, the Navy, the Coast Guard, the

Taskforce for the Prevention of Smuggling, the Customs Department, the Tax Department, the Customs Intelligence Department, the Customs Excise Department, and the Drug Control Department. Nazimuddin Shyamol, 'Smuggling on rise in Chittagong', *The Independent* (28 June 2003).

103 On the 'subversive economy,' see Hastings Donnan and Thomas M Wilson, *Borders: Frontiers of Identity, Nation and State* (Oxford/New York: Berg, 1999), 87–106.

104 Andreas describes border policing as a 'ritualized spectator sport', a game whose performative and audience-directed nature often overrides its actual coercive practice. Andreas, *Border Games*, x.

105 'Dhaka, Yangon agree on road link: Two taskforces formed for feasibility study', *The Daily Star* (18 December 2002); 'Myanmar gas export to Kolkata thru' Bangladesh proposed', *The Independent* (13 January 2003); 'Indo-Burma joint survey in western Burma', *Narinjara News* (16 January 2003); Bhasin (ed.), *India-Bangladesh Relations*, III, 1776.

106 Both examples from Dhiman Chattopadhyay, 'Peaceful coexistence at Hili border', *The Times of India* (12 November 2001). Cf. 'Scores of children engaged in smuggling along Hili border', *The Daily Star* (23 August 2001). The importance of rail transport in illegal trade is highlighted in Khandker Mashiur Rahman, 'Railway carries 70% smuggled goods: 10 stations mainly used', *The New Nation* (19 August 2002).

107 As Béatrice Hibou argues for African states in Jean-François Bayart, Stephen Ellis and Béatrice Hibou, *The Criminalization of the State in Africa* (Oxford/Bloomington: Currey/Indiana University Press, 1999), 79.

108 Price differentials in new technologies helped in this effort. For example, 'in the border villages of West Bengal, in areas like South Dinajpur and Coochbehar, the [cellular phone service of Bangladesh's GrameenPhone] has come to rank just below *hilsa* [fish] in the list of things people long for from Bangladesh … [It] is cheap as the rates are low, and it is useful, as local smugglers can now warn or get in touch with counterparts across the border … A SIM card costs Bangladesh Taka 4,000 (about Rs 3,300). Postpaid connections and refills were available for denominations of Taka 300, 500 and 1,000. The big incentive is that all calls to Bangladesh are at local call rates, roughly about Rs7 per minute. A call from an Indian telecom connection entails ISD charges. Pradip, the front office manager of a money changer at the border checkpost, now carries two cellphone sets — one offering the 'Cellone' service of the Indian Government's Bharat Sanchar Nigam Ltd and the other the BGD-GP service. Those better off have a third connection — from Reliance Telecom, which holds the GSM mobile telephony licence for West Bengal. Pradip assures the BGD-GP is "really beneficial" for his trade. The trade of "export-import," or smuggling. "Most of the money changers exist on signboards … The real business is something else. And the Bangladesh Grameen Phone service keeps us wired every moment with our contacts on the other side of the border" says Pradip. "We share information about the scale of vigil by the security forces, the demand of various commodities in the market and other necessary inputs." Subrata Nagchoudhury, 'No hanging up on cross-border telephonism', *The Sunday Express* (10 August 2003). Cf. Alfred W McCoy, 'Requiem for a Drug Lord: State and Commodity in the Career of Khun Sa', in Josiah McC. Heyman (ed.), *States and Illegal Practices* (Oxford/ New York: Berg, 1999), 160.

109 One example was the cabinet minister in Bangladesh who ran a drugs line from Afghanistan via Pakistan to Bangladesh, and from there to the United Kingdom. Another example was that of a Superintendent of Customs and a Lieutenant-Colonel

in India providing bail for a Burmese dealer in heroin precursors, methamphetamine tablets, arms, rhino horn, elephant meat and other wildlife products who was caught in India. The dealer, San Niang Thanga, was thought to be in charge of operations in Northeast India of '125', a drugs organization run from China by Kim Cheung Wong. 'Biggest ever heroin haul', *The New Nation* (21 September 1999); 'Ruling party's MPs involved,' *The New Nation* (23 September 1999); 'Rhino horn trade link to Thanga,' *The Telegraph* (8 June 2003).

110 E.g. the dismal history of development planning regarding the silk industry. See Willem van Schendel, *Reviving a Rural Industry: Silk Producers and Officials in India and Bangladesh, 1880s to 1980s* (Dhaka/ Delhi: University Press Ltd./ Manohar Publications, 1995). For a general review of specious accuracy and other weaknesses of economics statistics – even without considering figures on illegal trade and its effects – see Oskar Morgenstern, *On the Accuracy of Economic Observations* (Princeton, NJ: Princeton University Press, 1963 (2nd ed.)). For consequent problems for states trying to 'read' their own societies, see James C Scott, *Seeing Like a State: How Certain Schemes to Improve the Human Condition Have Failed* (New Haven and London: Yale University Press, 1998).

8

NARRATIVES OF BORDER CROSSING

'BONAFIDE CITIZENS SHOULD NOT SHELTER FOREIGNERS' warns the signboard nailed to the gnarled tree. This Indian village, tucked away near the border with Burma and Bangladesh, is hardly a place where you would expect lots of foreigners; even most Indians need a special permit to visit it. What is going on here? Are Indians sheltering foreigners? Whatever for? And what foreigners? (Plate 8.1)

In the Bengal borderland, the categories of citizen and foreigner came into being at the time of Partition. The border assigned a state identity to people on the basis of where they lived. Previously, all borderlanders had been subjects of the British monarch, but now they were recategorized as Pakistanis, Indians and Burmese. The new states claimed authority over the movement of their citizens, both within the state territory and beyond its borders. Intense struggles ensued over that authority and over the capacity of these states to confine the

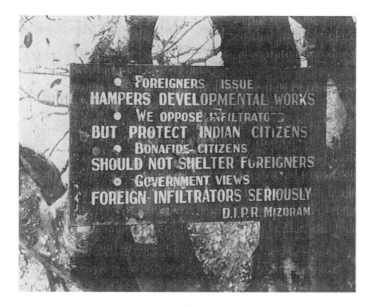

Plate 8.1: Government signboard on a tree in Chawngte/ Kamalanagar, Mizoram (India), near the 'trijunction point' where India, Bangladesh and Burma meet, 2000.

lives of borderlanders spatially. The movements of people across the border became the object of continual regulation and evasion. They also became a major irritant between these states and are likely to maintain the volatility of the relationship between India and Bangladesh well into the 21st century.

The Partition border sliced through a society that had always been highly mobile. Some of the old patterns now became cross-border movements, and new ones joined them. So far, these movements have been analysed only cursorily and our understanding has been hostage to a few dramatic narratives that conceal as much as they reveal. This chapter presents brief outlines of three dominant views that, I argue, should be abandoned because they are distorted by the 'iron grip of the nation-state.' They should be replaced by a more nuanced approach to cross-border population movements since 1947.

Narrative 1: 'Coming home'

In the master narrative of Partition, the cruelty and violence of nation-building is epitomized by the intense suffering of millions of uprooted people who had to cross the border in order to save their lives. The conceptual model has always been the Punjab, where population exchange in 1947 was swift, massive, ruthless and almost complete: it has become the touchstone of Partition migration.[1] A second case that has received considerable attention is the movement of Bengali Hindus from East Pakistan to West Bengal. As a population movement, it was less intensely dramatic because it started later, extended over a much longer time, and was less complete. As an experience for individual refugees it was, of course, just as as heart-rending and traumatic.[2]

Plate 8.2: **Muslim refugees waiting at the border railway station of Darsana (Jessore) after their arrival in East Pakistan, c.1950.**[3]

In both India and Pakistan, Partition migration has been studied and interpreted overwhelmingly within nationalist frameworks. Scholars have focused their attention on immigrants, who were seen as sons and daughters of the nation coming home, to the almost complete exclusion of emigrants, who were seen as abandoning the nation.[4] In this view, the tragedy of the immigrants was that they were members of a nation whose territory had suddenly become confined between new borders and who found themselves excluded from that territory. They were citizens by proxy and their trek across the boundary line – the spatial delimitation of the nation – was a homecoming: they joined the nation to which they belonged and in which they had full rights (Plate 8.2).[5] Their material loss, traumatic uprooting and suffering on the way were all sacrifices to the nation, and this obliged the nation to take care of them.

In the early days, both India and Pakistan welcomed immigrants and demanded that they be allowed to pass the border unmolested. A newspaper cartoon published in India in 1952 captures the mood: it expressed indignation at the humiliations to which Pakistani customs officials subjected East Pakistani Hindus migrating to India (Plate 8.3[6]). The two countries were keen to ensure that migrants from India to Pakistan and from Pakistan to India were treated in exactly the same way.[7] This led to parallel and fairly uniform arrangements in the borderland.

Passport from Pakistan

Over 2,000 refugees from E. Bengal were looted and robbed of their belongings on their way to the Pakistan border.—Report.

Plate 8.3: Cartoon from *Shankar's Weekly*, 26 October 1952.

The old spirit of welcoming immigrants into the national fold never died, and would flare up whenever refugees arrived in the wake of riots.[8] But gradually the mood changed. Later immigrants found it more difficult to establish their national credentials, and their citizens' rights were increasingly challenged.[9] This erosion of immigration rights reflected a stronger territorialization of national identities in the region. Those who had spent years on the other side of the border were seen as having acquired a measure of membership of that nation, making inclusion in their nation of immigration more problematic. This diminishing of entitlement also reflected a history of conflicts over resources, especially land, between local populations and newcomers.[10] It was not so much the spokesmen for the nation who footed the bill for the 'homecoming' as those people, often in the borderland, upon whom the immigrants physically descended.

Moreover, the communal (Muslim/ non-Muslim) basis for the creation of Pakistan and India was reinforced by experiences after 1947, as relations turned bitter and both state elites used communal symbols in their quest to establish and maintain power. Pakistan had been a communal entity from the start and non-Muslim immigration remained small. But in India, which claimed to be a homeland for all, including Muslims, Muslim immigrants were not really welcome and Hindu immigration from East Pakistan/ Bangladesh was increasingly resented.

After the mid-1960s the two-way out-migration that had been caused by Partition abated. The India-Pakistan war of 1965 made it impossible for refugees fleeing from one half of Bengal to exchange land with refugees fleeing from the other.[11] The Bangladesh Liberation war of 1971 led to the demise of the state of Pakistan and augured in a different style of dealing with communal relations in the entire region. Moreover, differential economic policies had given the Indian side of the borderland the edge over the Bangladeshi side. As a result, migration into Bangladesh tapered off but migration from Bangladesh to India continued to grow.[12]

In Bangladesh the narrative of homecoming disappeared as immigration issues dropped from the public agenda. Muslim immigration had stopped after the birth of the new state and the new nation of Bangladesh was perceived unequivocally to be rooted in the territory of the state. But in India a new discourse gained popularity as migration from Bangladesh, of both Hindus and Muslims, continued. This was the narrative of infiltration.

Narrative 2: 'Infiltration'

The view that immigration was *not* a homecoming first developed in Assam and Tripura. Here many inhabitants saw post-Partition immigrants not primarily as fellow Indians being cast out of Pakistan and in need of help but as Bengalis moving into non-Bengali areas and taking over. In Assam this discourse had begun well before Partition.[13] In Tripura, which during the colonial period had a policy of attracting Bengalis,[14] local protests against immigrants took organized form right from 1947 when Seng-krak, the first anti-refugee and anti-Bengali political union, was established.[15] It orchestrated clashes with immigrants and kidnappings when 'refugee colonies' were set up and 'tribal' land was given to Bengali newcomers.[16] The immigrants became an important vote bank and soon Bengali newcomers began to control Tripura politics, calling forth further protests by the local population. Major confrontations took place in 1953 and 1954; these focused increasingly on the ownership of land. In an attempt to defuse the tension and return some lands that immigrants had occupied unlawfully, the alienation of 'tribal' lands was made more difficult by law.[17]

The language of infiltration first surfaced in official discourse when, in 1962, the Indian government in parliamentary debates identified immigrants in Tripura and Assam as *infiltrators* and proceeded to expel them.[18] It was also used in 1964, when

about 2 lakh [200,000] people belonging to linguistic and religious minorities were physically seized by the police and left at the border without any kind of judicial process. The government had to stop the operation of the scheme after large-scale public protest and was convinced that the Foreigners' Act, 1946 was not applicable in Eastern India.[19]

In the same year, the Indian government started an international propaganda campaign on the topic of 'infiltration' from East Pakistan; from this time on, it has become commonplace in Indian political debates to talk about infiltration.[20] The term became widespread in Northeast India during the Assam movement that started in 1979, and that spoke to Assamese fears of 'being swamped by foreign nationals' as a result of 'misplaced notions of national commitment' and the failure of Indian laws to 'prevent infiltration from Bangladesh.'[21] The Assam movement criticized an Indian law of 1950 that openly encouraged free entry into Assam of Hindus who were victims of disturbances in East Pakistan. Prafulla Mahanta, the leader of the Assam movement, wrote with irony: 'In secular India, the Hindu East Pakistanis were permitted to settle as refugees and the Muslim Pakistanis were thrown out.'[22]

Since then the narrative of infiltration has been elaborated in two ways. In public debates in Northeast India there have been attempts to strengthen the insidious connotations of the term 'infiltration' by using the hyperbole of 'demographic attack'. In the words of a politician in north Bengal, the threat [of deliberate, large-scale and sustained infiltration by Bangladesh residents] is there: it is so profound that it may affect a demographic change in Indian areas around Bangladesh so much so that they may one day cease to be Indian territory. The idea of such demographic aggression against India has been there since 1958, but it has been put into practice with intensity after the emergence of Bangladesh as a nation.[23]

Such ideas gained power over time. Plate 8.4 shows how the threat was portrayed by alarming black arrows in a book published in the early 1980s. By the 1990s the idea of demographic aggression had become acceptable at the highest levels of the Indian state. In a report to the President of India in 1998, the Governor of Assam saw a sinister design behind what he called 'demographic invasion': to create a Greater Bangladesh and provide *Lebensraum* for Bangladeshis by 'severing the entire land mass of the North-East, with all its rich resources, from the rest of the country.'[24]

FOREIGN CIVILIAN INVASION
OF
ASSAM AND THE NORTHEAST REGION

Plate 8.4: Map from a book entitled *Assam's Agony* that seeks to reveal the 'unwritten conspiracy behind th[e] mass infiltration' and the dangers to national security, especially 'to "shear" the country – either along Assam-West Bengal border or West Bengal-Bihar border.'[25]

Bengali-speaking Indian citizens living in Northeast India felt threatened by such allegations. They resented being portrayed as infiltrators and as demographic front soldiers of Bangladesh. Fearing for their position, they began creating organizations to protect their interests, e.g. 'Amra Bangali' (Plate 8.5).[26]

Plate 8.5: 'If the eviction of Bengalis from Assam does not stop, all Bengal will be set afire!' Slogan of the political group **Amra Bangali** (We Bengalis) daubed on a house in a village near the border between West Bengal and Assam (India), 1981.

Although public discourse in northeast India usually equated 'infiltrators' with (Muslim) Bengalis from Bangladesh, this was not always the case. In the state of Mizoram, the warning of Plate 8.1 was directed against the immigration of (Buddhist) Chakmas from the Chittagong Hill Tracts in Bangladesh.[27]

There was a second way in which the narrative of infiltration was elaborated. This was done by state actors in other parts of India who, from the late 1970s, detected immigrants from Bangladesh and depicted them as lawbreakers and a threat to national security.[28] Many of these politicians and administrators were connected with the new political Hinduism (Hindutva, or Hindu fundamentalism), which held that Hindu India was under threat. They gave immigrants the appearance of 'destroyers of social harmony' who took away jobs from Indian citizens, committed crimes, threatened the social safety net, undermined social cohesion and subverted the Indian state.[29] Having constructed a picture of immigrants from Bangladesh as a threat to the national citizenry, they proceeded to deport them. In 1992–3, in an action code-named Operation Pushback, authorities in New Delhi and Bombay rounded up hundreds of people whom they suspected to be Bangladeshis and shipped them to the border with Bangladesh. Bangladesh refused to take them back, arguing that these were not Bangladeshi citizens, and the Indian government was forced to abandon the operation.[30] Further deportations followed in 1994, 1997, 2000 and 2003.[31] In 1998, police officers in Mumbai (Bombay) arrested 'infiltrators' and escorted them to the West Bengal-Bangladesh border to hand them over to the border guards.[32] Speaking of the deportation of 'Bangladeshi infiltrators' in the Maharashtra assembly, the Deputy Chief Minister asserted that 'This is a question of Indianness, nationalism and patriotism', and linked immigration from Bangladesh with 'a well-organised conspiracy to infiltrate ISI [Pakistani[33]] agents into the country.'[34] In 2001 the Indian Supreme Court adopted the narrative of infiltration when it declared Bangladeshi immigrants 'a threat to both the economy and the security of the country.'[35]

In short, local politicians in Northeast India developed a narrative of infiltration in the 1940s and 1950s to deny citizens' rights, and particularly land rights, to immigrants from East Pakistan. In the 1960s the narrative of infiltration surfaced in Indian government statements in connection with the first mass expulsions from Northeast India. In the 1980s, Hindu fundamentalist politicians in other parts of India took up the narrative, and by the 1990s it had become a core argument in national debates in India that sought to link immigration from Bangladesh with the planned subversion of India. According to this argument, the duty of any true Indian patriot was *not* to welcome immigrants as repatriates coming home, but to deport them as foreign agents out to destabilize, Islamize and ultimately annex entire regions of India to Bangladesh.

Narrative 3: 'Not Our Citizens'

In East Pakistan, and later Bangladesh, successive governments developed a bizarre counter-discourse: they simply denied that *any* of their citizens migrated to India at all. In 1964, Pakistani Foreign Minister ZA Bhutto stated:

It is inconceivable that hundreds of thousands of Muslims ... would surrender the safety and security of their homeland in [East] Pakistan to migrate with their women and children to the uncertainty and perils awaiting them in a hostile land beyond the border.[36]

Thirty-four years later, echoing Bhutto's incredulity, the Prime Minister of Bangladesh stated: 'We do not accept that there is any Bangladeshi national living in India. So the question of deporting any Bangladeshi by the Indian Government does not arise.' By now this line was no longer a short-term diplomatic ploy to counter an emerging Indian discourse of infiltration. It had become a mantra of negation.[37] By the early 21st century Bangladesh officials were still in denial but some had modified their position slightly: now they claimed that there were, in their opinion, no *illegal* Bangladeshis anywhere in India.[38]

The desperate tenacity with which Bangladeshi officials clung to their discourse of denial was the result of an acute sense of vulnerability vis-à-vis their huge neighbour, India. Rooted in Partition, this feeling was boosted by India's adoption of the discourse of infiltration. To the Bangladeshi state elite, acknowledging the unauthorized movement of Bangladeshi citizens across the border would reveal the inability of their state to control this movement, or worse, suggest its complicity. In their anxiety to avoid owning up to the failure of their state's strategy of territoriality – and hence its claim to full statehood – the Bangladeshi authorities chose to disown their citizens in Indian territory.

This official narrative had serious consequences for border crossers. Until 1982, 'while denying large-scale out-migration, Bangladesh at least took back infiltrators handed over by the Indian BSF. But after 1982, they refused pointblank.'[39] India's push-back policies could not count on any cooperation from the Bangladeshi authorities. As Indian border guards tried to push back what they termed 'Bangladeshi infiltrators', Bangladeshi border guards tried to foil the 'push-in' of what they considered to be 'Indian citizens'.[40] During Operation Pushback in India (which Bangladesh branded as 'Operation Push-In'[41]),

> [t]he deportation process suffered a severe setback in September 1992 when 132 deportees were sent to the border. The [Border Security Force] tonsured their heads, stripped them and burnt their belongings. The event blew up into a diplomatic row when Bangladesh accused India of trying to push out West Bengal Muslims.[42]

The Bangladesh narrative of denial clearly had terrible effects on individual migrants. Denied citizens' rights by either Bangladesh or India, they were caught in the middle. This predicament was epitomized by the fate of hundreds of hapless labour migrants who, in 2003, literally found themselves marooned for weeks in the no man's land between West Bengal and Bangladesh. Indian border guards sought to expel them but Bangladeshi border guards refused to let them in on the ground that they were 'Bengali-speaking Indian Muslims.'[43] Stuck in rice fields between two groups of menacing armed men, the frightened migrants tried to survive under the open sky (see chapter 9).

From the point of view of the Bangladesh state, a porous border was clearly a not unwelcome device to export labour.[44] Bangladesh authorities did not try to stop labour migrants from crossing into India but they vehemently opposed their forced return.[45] This position created great problems for Bangladesh as a modern territorial state. Happy to use its border to disown its mobile citizens, Bangladesh sought to protect the integrity of its border in other respects, in particular from unauthorized trade (smuggling) and unauthorized entry (Rohingya refugees from Burma, Indian border police, Jumma rebels from hideouts in India, and students from Burma being cases in point[46]). The ensuing ambiguity regarding membership of the nation and the territorial integrity of the state became one of the main problems of contemporary statecraft in Bangladesh.

By and large, opinion leaders and scholars in Bangladesh have not shown any alacrity in claiming migrants to India as expatriate Bangladeshis. In sharp contrast with the heroization of successful Bangladeshi migrants to North America and Europe, there has been a deafening silence about the ingenuity, creativity and resilience of the much larger groups of Bangladeshi migrants to India, some of whom clearly also 'made good'. There was a serious problem in acknowledging these migrants as Bangladeshis because of the older tradition of seeing them as repatriates, and therefore as traitors who opted for the rival nation of India.

By now, however, millions of Bangladeshis in India are truly transnational in three ways. First, they are not accepted as Indian citizens and live the shadow existence of 'illegal' immigrants worldwide, a floating underclass who are in India but not of it. Second, their motives for crossing the border have long stopped being related to nationalist ideologies. They have joined many migrants worldwide in pursuing the good life that is denied them back home – in terms of a decent income, freedom from oppressive social control and prospects for a better future. Research among Bangladeshis in Delhi revealed that 'for most, the dominant identity, at least for the moment, is human beings whose basic need is to fill their stomachs.'[47] And third, like their counterparts all over the world, they think transnationally when they remit money and make occasional visits back home. Unlike the early 'repatriates', they often retain regular contact with relatives in Bangladesh through transnational networks of increasing complexity.

It is not impossible that, in the future, Bangladeshi opinion-leaders will portray migrants to India as cultural heroes, people who against enormous odds were able to rely on their own wits to survive in the interstices of India's huge society, and to create new cultural and social forms of transnational Bangladeshi identity.[48] Until that time, the Bangladeshi discourse on migration to India is likely to be marked by denial, disdain and disinformation.

Conclusion: statist narratives

The three narratives that dominate contemporary thinking about cross-border migration in this region are flawed by what I have referred to as a territorial epistemology.[49] They analyse these population flows by starting from the definition of the state as a natural, self-enclosed unit. They accept the state claim that it is states, and states alone, which hold the legitimate monopoly over the movement of people across international borders. They do not challenge the right of the post-1947 states to expropriate from individuals the legitimate 'means of movement' and to deprive them of the freedom to move across certain spaces without state authorization. Nor do they place this state claim in a historical context, showing how it links up with worldwide processes whereby modern states seek to monopolize the legitimate means of movement.[50] All three narratives accept the state and its exclusionary claims as given when analysing cross-border migration.

The first of the three, the narrative of homecoming, actually consists of two parallel, state-centred arguments that mirror each other but do not touch. The Indian variant is deeply concerned with people entering Indian territory, but has nothing to say about people leaving that territory. The Pakistani/Bangladeshi variant is its exact reverse. The second narrative, that of infiltration, is equally statist in that it analyses cross-border migration only to the extent that it affects the future of the Indian state. Since this narrative presents border-crossing as an invasion of national space or a demographic attack by a neighbouring state, it is not surprising that the narrative is confined to Indian politicians, administrators and scholars – it does not exist in Bangladesh. By contrast, the third narrative, that of disowning citizens, is a purely Bangladeshi one. Its statism is obvious in the assumption that those who leave the state territory and cross over to India lose their Bangladeshi citizenship – they are no longer members of the nation. Therefore they are of no concern to Bangladeshi politicians, nor to scholars who treat their state's territory as the natural arena for social analysis.

The available narratives of cross-border migration may be dramatic but they are based on remarkably little serious investigation. They may be powerful as rhetorical devices in national politics; however, they are not powerful tools of social analysis. They tell us little about how state officials actually deal with migrants;[51] they do not even provide state officials with solid guidelines in their dealings with cross-border migrants.

This was very clear in October 2001 when Bangladeshi Hindus fled to India after repression in the wake of national elections that returned the Bangladesh Nationalist Party (BNP) to power. Officials in India were in a quandary as to how to identify these border-crossers. One law-enforcement agency thought they were 'refugees', another referred to them as 'illegal entrants' and a third considered them 'infiltrators'. District officials in Malda (West Bengal) were ready to charge them under the Foreigners' Act and push them back while their colleagues in the adjoining district of South Dinajpur wanted them to stay as refugees or 'shelter-seekers'.[52]

The three narratives do little to elucidate the causes and forms of population movement across this border, the strategies of millions of migrants, or the consequences of cross-border migration for individuals and their societies. In order to gain a better insight we need to rescale and historicize the study of cross-border migration in this region – the national scale just will not do. In the next chapter I explore how these population movements affected the Bengal borderland and how unsuccessful the states were in enclosing people bent on crossing the Partition border.

Notes

1 See e.g. *Disturbances in the Punjab, 1947* (Islamabad: National Documentation Centre, 1995); Ritu Menon and Kamla Bhasin, *Borders & Boundaries: Women in India's Partition* (New Delhi: Kali for Women, 1998); Gyanendra Pandey, *Remembering Partition: Violence, Nationalism and History in India* (Cambridge: Cambridge University Press, 2001).

2 For examples, see e.g. Kanti B Pakrasi, *The Uprooted: A Sociological Study of the Refugees of West Bengal, India* (Calcutta: Editions Indian, 1971); Prafulla K Chakrabarti, *The Marginal Men: The Refugees and the Left Political Syndrome in West Bengal* (Calcutta: Naya Udyog, 1999 (2nd ed.)); Dipesh Chakrabarty, 'Remembered Villages: Representation of Hindu-Bengali Memories in the Aftermath of the Partition', Economic and Political Weekly (10 August 1996), 2143–51; 'Porous Borders, Divided Selves: A Symposium on Partitions in the East', Seminar, no. 510 (February 2002); Chavi Sharma, 'A Division of India/A Partition of the Self', in Imtiaz Ahmed (ed.), *Memories of a Genocidal Partition: The Haunting Tales of Victims, Witnesses and Perpetrators* (Colombo: Regional Centre for Strategic Studies, 2002), 1–17; Manas Ray, 'Growing Up Refugee: On Memory and Locality', *History Workshop Journal*, no. 53 (2002), 149–79.

3 Photograph from *Five Years of Pakistan (August 1947–August 1952)* (Karachi: Pakistan Publications, 1952), 151. Photographer unacknowledged.

4 Menon and Bhasin, *Borders & Boundaries* is one of the first studies to try and overcome this bias by looking at women refugees crossing the Punjab border in both directions.

5 On the concepts of citizenship and 'proxy' citizenship in India and Pakistan, see Willem van Schendel, 'Stateless in South Asia: The Making of the India-Bangladesh Enclaves', *The Journal of Asian Studies*, 61:1 (February 2002), 115–47. On the complexities of cross-border migration and settlement in the borderland, see Md. Mahbubar Rahman and Willem van Schendel, '"I Am *Not* a Refugee": Rethinking Partition Migration', *Modern Asian Studies*, 37:3 (2003), 551–84.

6 This cartoon, from *Shankar's Weekly* (26 October 1952), led to an official protest from the Government of Pakistan (CR 3N11-1/52 (2-55)). The title refers to the introduction of a passport and visa system between East Pakistan and India in October 1952.

7 There were several agreements on the treatment of out-migrants, e.g. the Agreement between the Government of India and the Government of Pakistan dated the 8th April 1950 (Nehru-Liaquat Agreement).

8 Over the years, a veritable jungle of legal and political nomenclature would develop to refer to cross-border migrants in India and Pakistan. Here we do not concern ourselves with the niceties of distinguishing refugees, evacuees, *mohajirs*, repatriates, displaced persons, immigrants, *bastutyagi*, *bastuhara*, *asroyprarthi*, *shoronarthi*, etc. Not only were these differences of little or no concern in the border areas, but definitions also differed between India and Pakistan. For example, in the Pakistan (Protection of Evacuee Property) Ordinance, 1948, refugees from Pakistan to India were considered to be 'evacuees' and those fleeing the other way 'refugees'. What Pakistan called an evacuee, India would call a refugee.

9 Thus in India a policy was introduced in 1964 under which no direct rehabilitation was to be given to the 'new migrants' from East Pakistan in West Bengal, i.e. people who had arrived in India after 1 January 1964. *Report of the Committee of Review on Educational Facilities for New Migrants from East Pakistan to West Bengal* (Calcutta: West Bengal Ministry of Labour, Employment and Rehabilitation, 1968). The Prafulla K Chakrabarti Archive, International Institute of Social History, Amsterdam, The Netherlands.

10 On raids by West Bengal landlords on immigrant East Pakistani squatters, see Chakrabarti, *The Marginal Men*, 82–3. Similar conflicts occurred in East Pakistan; see petitions by locals against immigrants from West Bengal and Assam in the Rangpur border area, and against 'a gang of Kabulies' who squatted in Parbatipur, Dinajpur (CR 5P-12/49 (4-50), Pol. P10C-6/49 (4-49)).

11 Rahman and Van Schendel, "'I Am *Not* A Refugee'". For migration trends in two borderland villages, see Willem van Schendel, *Reviving A Rural Industry: Silk Producers and Officials in India and Bangladesh, 1880s to 1980s* (Dhaka/ Delhi: University Press Ltd./ Manohar Publications, 1995), 105–13.

12 There has been very little research on migration of Indian nationals to Bangladesh. It certainly exists and occasionally Bangladeshi police arrest 'illegal entrants' from India – see for example 'Three Indian girls arrested in Panchagarh', *The Independent* (25 January 2003).

13 M Kar, *Muslims in Assam Politics* (New Delhi: Vikas Publishing House, 1997), 86–107.

14 In 1947 the local population of Tripura consisted of many linguistic and religious groups. The majority religion was Hinduism. They are usually referred to as 'tribal', a term that has meaning only in connection with the legal category of 'scheduled tribes' in the Constitution of India. The Maharajas of Tripura had begun attracting Bengali Muslims as agricultural labourers and sharecroppers, and Bengali Hindus as professionals and clerks. In the 1870s, 36 per cent of the population had been 'non-tribal' (i.e. mostly Bengali), a figure that rose to 48 per cent in 1931, 63 per cent in 1951 and 71 per cent in 1971. Gayatri Bhattacharyya, *Refugee Rehabilitation and Its Impact on Tripura's Economy* (New Delhi/ Guwahati: Omsons Publications, 1988), 93.

15 Seng-krak was soon outlawed. It was followed by a host of successors, e.g. Paharia Union (1951), Adibasi Samiti (1952), Tripura Rajya Adibasi Sangha (1953), Adibasi Samsad (1954), East India Tribal Union (1956), Tripura Upajati Juba Samiti (TUJS; 1967), Seng-krak (revived in 1967), Tripura Sena (c. 1968), Barki Halam (1974), Tripura National Volunteer Force (TNVF; 1979), and Army of Tripura Peoples' Liberation Organization (ATPLO; 1980). After 1980, when widespread violence engulfed the state, many new organizations cropped up (e.g. All Tripura Tribal Force (ATTF, c.1985)). For details, see SR Bhattacharjee, *Tribal Insurgency in Tripura: A Study in Exploration of Causes* (New Delhi: Inter-India Publications, 1989), 127–34. Cf. Harihar Bhattacharyya, 'The Emergence of Tripuri Nationalism, 1948-1950', *South Asia Research*, 9:1 (1989), 54–71;

Panjoubam Tarapot, *Insurgency Movement in North-Eastern India* (Delhi: Vikas, 1996), 174–80.

16 In 1948, the Tripura government for the first time released almost 800 km² of tribal reserve land 'for increasing land revenue, economic growth, and particularly for refugee rehabilitation.' Bhattacharyya, *Refugee Rehabilitation*, 17–20.

17 Government of Tripura, Law Department, *The Tripura Land Revenue and Land Reforms Act, 1960*. For significant amendments in 1974 and 1975, see Bhattacharyya, *Refugee Rehabilitation*, 98-100. See also Bhattacharjee, *Tribal Insurgency in Tripura*, 114–17.

18 Parliamentary debates on the issue had been going on since May 1961. In August 1962, the Home Minister, LB Shastri, informed the Lower House that about 45,000 Muslims had 'infiltrated' into Tripura; his deputy reported 250,000 to 300,000 'infiltrators' in Assam over the preceding 10 years and similar 'infiltrations' were alleged to have taken place in Manipur and West Bengal. By late 1962, according to Indian sources, some 50,000 Muslims from Assam and some 16,000 from Tripura had been evicted. Pakistan refused to identify them as 'Pakistani infiltrators'; instead it described these deportees as 'Indian Muslims' and complained about the Indian action. It set up an enquiry committee that reported that almost all deportees were Indian citizens. It also held that over 520,000 Muslims were evicted from India up to mid-1965 (Dinesh Chandra Jha, *Indo-Pakistan Relations (1960–65)* (Patna: Bharati Bhawan, 1972), 271–86). In 1962, the Assam Pradesh Congress Committee adopted a resolution stating that it was 'of the confirmed opinion that the infiltration of Pakistani nationals without valid travel documents into Assam is likely to endanger the security of the country' (Prafulla Kumar Mahanta, *The Tussle Between the Citizens and Foreigners in Assam* (New Delhi: Vikas, 1986), 82). From mid-1962, 'India started deporting from Assam and Tripura persons whom it called *Pakistani infiltrators.'* Jha, *Indo-Pakistan Relations*, 242 (italics added). For a police officer's memories of this expulsion campaign, see Sanjoy Hazarika, *Rites of Passage: Border Crossings, Imagined Homelands, India's East and Bangladesh* (New Delhi: Penguin Books, 2000), 58–9. Cf. Kar, *Muslims in Assam Politics*, 121–48.

19 'Joint Communique by the Home Ministers of India & Pakistan, April 11, 1964', in: *Selected Indo-Pakistan Agreements* (New Delhi: Ministry of External Affairs, 1970), 30; Anindita Dasgupta, 'Thinking with the head: Foreign nationals in Assam,' *The Daily Star* (6 May 1999).

20 *Influx – infiltratie uit Oost-Pakistan* ('s-Gravenhage: Information Service of India, Ambassade van India, 1964). In 1965, the Chief Minister of Assam claimed that over one million 'illegal Pakistani infiltrators' had entered Eastern India between 1951 and 1961, and provided an uncannily precise breakdown – 220,961 in Assam, 459,494 in West Bengal, 297,852 in Bihar, and 55,403 in Tripura. 'Assam Expels More Than Half of 220,000 Infiltrators,' *The Statesman* (28 July 1965).

21 The title of a book by the leader of this movement (and later Chief Minister of Assam, Prafulla Mahanta) emphasizes the point: *The Tussle Between the Citizens and Foreigners in Assam* (1986; quotes are from 86, 89, 116). He dedicated this book 'to the law-abiding and Constitution-following citizens of India residing in Assam who have waged a relentless tussle against the invasion of illegal foreigners masquerading as minorities playing to the designs of the political tricksters and economic exploiters.' For a description of widespread anti-Bengali agitations in Assam in 1960–1 driving about 45,000 refugees into Jalpaiguri, Cooch Behar and Darjeeling districts, see Saroj Chakrabarty, *With Dr. B.C. Roy and Other Chief Ministers (A Record up to 1962)* (Calcutta: Benson's, 1974), 450–60, 488–90.

22 Mahanta, *The Tussle*, 94. The act in question is the Immigrants (Expulsion from Assam) Act, 1950. For related laws and orders, e.g. the Prevention of Infiltration from Pakistan (PIP) Act of 1964, cf. Sanjib Baruah, *India against Itself: Assam and the Politics of Nationality* (Philadelphia: University of California Press, 1999), 119; Hazarika, *Rites of Passage*, 61. For analyses of the Assam movement, see Monirul Hussain, *The Assam Movement: Class, Ideology and Identity* (Delhi: Manak Publications, 1993); Dilip Kumar Chattopadhyay, *History of the Assamese Movement Since 1947* (Calcutta: Minerva, 1990).

23 Quoted in Anil Maheshwari, 'The face behind the mask', *The Hindustan Times – Sunday Magazine* (15 August 1998).

24 SK Sinha, 'Illegal Immigration into Assam', quoted in Arun Chanda, 'Assam Governor asks Centre to seal Bangladesh border', *Rediff on the Net* (13 February 1999); cf. Samudra Gupta Kashyap, 'Diminishing Assam Border? Governor writes to President', *Indian Express* (17 December 1998); 'Bangla's "demographic attack" must be stopped: Thakre', *Assam Tribune* (20 June 1999). Such ideas were not new: the Speaker of the Lok Sabha (Indian Lower House of Parliament) expressed them as early as 1961. In 2002 Indian Home Ministry sources accused the Bangladesh intelligence community (notably the DGFI – Directorate-General of Forces Intelligence) of operating schools 'near the Indo-Bangladesh border adjoining Goalpara in the late seventies to impart training in the local dialect to wannabe migrants so that they may not get detected.' '"Bangla hand for long"', *The Telegraph* (3 November 2002). Jha, *Indo-Pakistan Relations*, 273. For similar sentiments, see also *Rajya Sabha: Supplement-I to the Synopsis of Debates; Wednesday, May 17, 2000/Vaisakha 27, 1922 (Saka)* (Available at: http://alfa.nic.in/rs/rsdebate/synopsis/189/su17052000.htm).

25 Amiya Kumar Das, *Assam's Agony: A Socio-Economic and Political Analysis* (New Delhi: Lancers Publishers, 1982), 41; cf. 31, 169.

26 Among these organizations were Amra Bangali, All Assam Citizens' Rights Protection Committee, and the Barak Valley Students' Council. In 2000 these joined hands to form the Bangali Oikko Moncho (Bengali Unity Platform) 'to protect the interests of Bengalis living in the Northeast, especially Tripura and Mizoram.' See 'Platform formed for protection of NE Bengalis', *The Northeast Daily* (1 June 2000).

27 Similarly, the All Arunachal Pradesh Students Union (AAPSU) ran a campaign to expel (Hindu) Hajongs and (Buddhist) Chakmas who had fled East Pakistan in the 1940s and 1960s, respectively, and whom the Indian government had accepted and settled in Arunachal Pradesh. Even after the Indian Supreme Court had ruled that these refugees were entitled to Indian citizenship and should have been given papers long ago, the AAPSU maintained that their stay was illegal because they did not have 'inner line permits'. In another case, the Mizoram authorities came down on unauthorized (Christian and Buddhist) migrants and refugees from Burma, leading to a stampede to the border. 'AAPSU wary of Chakmas, Hajongs', *The Sentinel* (17 May 2003). Cf. 'MZP vows to drive out Bangladeshi Chakmas', *The Sentinel* (29 June 2003); David M Thangliana, 'Myanmarese flee Aizawl: Over 1000 refugees cross Mizo border after rape sparks diktat', *The Telegraph* (31 July 2003).

28 For a slew of examples, see Ranabir Samaddar, *The Marginal Nation: Transborder Migration from Bangladesh to West Bengal* (New Delhi, etc.: Sage Publications, 1999). Cf. Avtar Singh Bhasin (ed.), *India-Bangladesh Relations: Documents – 1971–2002* (New Delhi: Geetika Publishers, 2003), Vol. V, 2390–668.

29 Cf. Sujata Ramachandran, 'Of Boundaries and Border Crossings: Undocumented Bangladeshi "Infiltrators" and the Hegemony of Hindu Nationalism in India', *Interventions*,

1:2 (1999), 235–53. The Rashtriya Swayam Sevak Sangh (RSS) accused immigrants from Bangladesh of 'indulging in criminal activities like rape and murder of innocent teenaged Hindu girls, desecration of Hindu temples and breaking up of idols thereby hurting the religious sentiments of the Hindus … abduction of Hindu citizens living in bordering areas … dacoity in the houses of even poor Hindus.' Cf. 'B'deshi militants creating chaos in Barak: RSS', *The Sentinel* (13 September 2003). For a parallel discourse on immigrants as destroyers of social harmony in North America, see Joseph Nevins, *Operation Gatekeeper: The Rise of the 'Illegal Alien' and the Making of the U.S.–Mexico Boundary* (New York and London: Routledge, 2002), 175.

30 Apparently, the Indian authorities had been able to 'push back' Bengali Muslims up to 1965, after which Pakistani (and later Bangladeshi) border guards started rejecting people whom the Indians sent across. Hazarika, *Rights of Passage*, 60.

31 Ajoy Bose, 'Nation in migration,' *Time* (11 August 1997); Anindita Ramaswamy, 'BJP's Oust Bangladeshi drive hots up,' *Indian Express* (16 September 1998); 'Delhi police not up to "find and evict" task', *The Times of India* (10 June 2000); Brajesh Upadhyay, 'Police find the going tough in drive against Bangladeshis', *The Times of India* (22 June 2000). Deportations have also been reported from Uttar Pradesh: 'UP police in N Bengal to send back 225 Bangladeshis', *The Statesman* (7 October 1999); cf. 'Haryana turns the heat on Bangladeshi migrants', *The Statesman* (3 November 2002). For an early use of the term 'physically pushing out', by the Indian Home Minister in 1963, see Jha, *Indo-Pakistan Relations*, 279.

32 The government of Maharashtra claimed that it deported over 8,000 Bangladeshi 'infiltrators' between 1982 and mid-1998. In a twist to the drama, many of the deported claimed to be Muslims from West Bengal, and sympathizers tried to free them when trains reached railway stations in West Bengal, leading to exchanges of fire between Maharashtra policemen and local policemen. The government of West Bengal opposed the move. Rajasthan and Gujarat also deported suspected Bangladeshis. 'Joshi to deport Bangladeshis from Mumbai', *The Daily Star* (13 October 1997); 'Bengal protests Maharashtra's action', *The Hindu* (25 July 1998); 'Maharashtra to fight stay on deportation of "Bangladeshis"', *Rediff on the Net* (27 July 1927); Dev Raj, 'Rights-India: Deportation of "Bangladeshis" targets Muslims', *Inter Press Service* (3 August 1998); Udayan Namboodiri, 'Illegal Immigrants: Political Pawns', *India Today* (10 August 1998); Kalyan Chaudhuri, 'Protest in West Bengal', and R Padmanabhan, 'The deportation drive', *Frontline* (15–28 August 1998); 'India acts against alleged Bangladeshi infiltrators', *BBC News* (4 February 1999).

33 ISI (Inter-Services Intelligence) is Pakistan's chief foreign intelligence agency. Indian politicians and journalists often suggest that Bangladesh, wittingly or unwittingly, is helping Pakistani agents to enter Indian territory. Much less frequently, Bangladeshi press reports mention activities of India's intelligence agency, the Research and Analysis Wing (RAW) in their country. See e.g. 'Report focus on ISI Dhaka hub', *The Telegraph* (2 December 2002); 'RAW deploys hundreds of agents to watch Bangladesh defence: Monitoring Army', *The New Nation* (1 December 2002).

34 'Deportations of illegally residing aliens will continue, says Munde', *Times of India* (10 April 1999); 'With coal comes ISI, ultras, saboteurs too to NE', *The Sentinel* (28 September 2001).

35 'Illegal Bangladeshis a threat to India: SC', *The Hindustan Times* (27 February 2001). Later that year, the state of Orissa began identifying 'Bangladeshi infiltrators' with a view to driving them out of the state. '"Bangladeshis" face purge in Orissa', *The New*

Nation (6 August 2001); Imran Khan, 'Orissa to deport 4,000 Bangladeshi migrants', *The Times of India* (26 November 2001).

36 Jha, *Indo-Pakistan Relations*, 276–7.

37 In 2000, Sheikh Hasina Wazed, then the Prime Minister of Bangladesh, was still echoing Bhutto's statement when she declared on television: 'Why should Bangladeshis go to India?' 'Hasina denies India's infiltration report', *The Assam Tribune* (11 June 2000). See also 'No Bangladeshi immigrant in India, Hasina tells CNN', *The Independent* (7 September 2000).

38 This is what Bangladesh Foreign Secretary Mobin Chowdhury said in 2003. 'No Bangladeshi in India illegally', *The New Nation* (9 January 2003). However, Foreign Minister M Morshed Khan seemed to create an opening a few months later, during a discussion at the Overseas Correspondents Association in Dhaka: 'India accused us of illegal migration. I say there is. The border is vast. But to make it an issue is ridiculous. We have found a solution to the problem – the cross-border illegal trade must be checked to control illegal migration.' 'Curbing smuggling will end illegal migration: Morshed Khan asks India, all political parties to unite to fight terrorism', *The Daily Star* (24 April 2003).

39 Partha S Ghosh, *Cooperation and Conflict in South Asia* (Delhi: Manohar, 1995), 84.

40 Ironically, in Bangladesh itself a parallel narrative of infiltration was developing at the same time. Here it was directed against the Rohingyas, cross-border migrants from Arakan (Burma) who sought refugee status. At least 100,000 of them, who were not housed in camps, were considered illegal, uncleared or residual refugees, or merely 'arrivals'. In 1999, at least 1,700 of them were in Bangladeshi jails on the charge of illegal border crossing. A Bangladeshi army officer expressed a much more general sentiment in government circles when he said: 'If caught, we are pushing the infiltrators back or sending them to jails'. *The State of the World's Refugees: A Humanitarian Agenda* (Oxford: UNHCR/Oxford University Press, 1997), 254; '25 Rohingyas languishing in Chandpur jail', *The New Nation* (27 October 1999); 'More Rohingyas infiltrating', *The New Nation* (31 May 2000); 'Situation of Rohingya refugees in Bangladesh', *The Newsletter Monthly – News and Analysis of the Arakan Rohingya National Organisation, Arakan (Burma)*, 2:2 (February 2000); Mohammad Nurul Islam, '70,000 Rohingya refugees waiting for enrolment as voters', *The Independent* (13 May 2000).

41 For documents on Bangladesh's official position on 'pushed-in' Bengali-speaking individuals from India, see Bhasin (ed.), *India-Bangladesh Relations*, V, 2546–8, 2565, 2569–70, 2646–58.

42 Partha Ghosh, 'Illegal immigration from Bangladesh – II', *The Hindu* (12 August 1998). Cf. 'Presence of illegal Bangladeshis denied', *The Hindu* (3 August 1998); 'Bangladesh terms India's claim illogical', *The Hindu* (22 August 1998); 'Push-in bid along border in Tetulia foiled', *The Daily Star* (19 August 1998); 'Envoy summoned: Delhi urged to take steps to stop push-in attempts', *The Daily Star* (26 August 1998); 'Dhaka not cooperating on deportation issue', *Hindustan Times* (18 October 1998); 'BDR foils BSF's bid to push in Indian Muslims', *The New Nation* (8 May 2002).

43 The disagreements over the identity of deportees from India were complicated by a continual mixing of national identities (citizens of India and Bangladesh) and religious identities (Muslims and non-Muslims, particularly Hindus). Bangladesh's stand that India was pushing back Indian citizens who were Muslims, rather than Bangladeshi citizens who were Muslims, ignored the fact that India was also deporting Hindus who were thought to be Bangladeshi citizens. On the other hand, Hindu nationalist politicians

in India stuck to the 'homecoming' thesis: a spokesman declared that the Vishwa Hindu Parishad (VHP) regarded 'Muslim Bangladeshis as illegal foreigners while the Hindus are refugees as they did not have any place to seek shelter except India.' See '13 Indians pushed into Meherpur', *The New Nation* (23 May 2003); 'VHP warns against Bangla influx', *The Assam Tribune* (26 May 2003).

44 Little information is available about reverse flows of Indians to Bangladesh. The discourse on 'infiltrators' in Northeast India is silent about them but they do occur. For example, about ten thousand migrants from Mizoram (India) were reported to have moved to the Chittagong Hill Tracts (Bangladesh) in 1998, and in 2002 several hundreds of Muslims fled from Gujarat (India) to Bangladesh. Occasionally, Bangladeshi police identify and expel Indians who have migrated to Bangladesh in search of jobs. Haroon Habib, 'Mizo tribals take shelter in Bangladesh hills', *The Hindu* (28 March 1998); '200 Indian Muslims flee to Bangladesh: Officials', *The Times of India* (18 May 2002); Alamgir Hossain, 'BDR pushes back Indian families', *The Telegraph* (26 February 2003).

45 Bangladesh's refusal to even consider whether persons presented by India as Bangladeshi citizens were indeed of that identity flies in the face of the *International Convention on the Protection of the Rights of All Migrant Workers and Members of Their Families.* Article 8.2 of this UN Convention, of which Bangladesh became a signatory on 7 October 1998, states: 'Migrant workers and members of their families shall have the right at any time to enter and remain in their State of origin' (United Nations General Assembly Resolution 45/158 of 18 December 1990). The ambivalent attitude of Bangladesh towards its émigré citizens was expressed by an official in Dhaka in the case of a Bangladeshi who fell seriously ill in South Korea but received no help at all from his embassy. When he returned to Bangladesh (with the support of Korean NGOs and the Korean airlines), the Dhaka official stated: 'It has always been difficult for the government to recognise any of its nationals living abroad as 'undocumented' workers and therefore difficult to render any help though official channel', Reaz Ahmad, 'Sorry tale of a migrant worker', *The Daily Star* (21 October 2001). Cf. 'Exploited Bangladeshi laborers abandoned by their embassy', *Arab News* (27 May 2002)). For a rare report of Bangladeshi border guards preventing a group of 18 men, 8 women and 4 children from districts in central Bangladesh to migrate to India, see 'BDR arrests 30 from border area', *The Daily Star* (11 August 2001).

46 Generations of Burmese Muslims in search of religious education have been enrolled in Islamic colleges (*madrasha*) in southern Bangladesh. Since the Burmese authorities did not issue passports to such students, their entry into Bangladesh was illegal but permitted informally by law-enforcing agencies in Bangladesh. In 2003, however, a group of 21 students from Burma, on their way to enrol in Islamic studies in a *madrasha* in Patiya (Chittagong), were arrested for illegal entry and put in jail in Cox's Bazar. 'Madrasah students from Burma arrested in Bangladesh', *Narinjara News* (13 March 2003).

47 Sharat G Lin and Madan C Paul, 'Bangladeshi Migrants in Delhi: Social Insecurity, State Power, and Captive Vote Banks', *Bulletin of Concerned Asian Scholars*, 27 :1 (1995), 10. For some, the dominant identity was 'Muslim' or 'cultivator', but for nearly all, their identity as Bangladeshis had 'fallen into the background'.

48 As Mexican intellectuals did with *Chicanos* (Mexicans in the USA) in the late 1970s. See e.g. Michael Kearney, 'Transnationalism in California and Mexico at the end of empire', in: Thomas M Wilson and Hastings Donnan, *Border Identities: Nation and State at International Frontiers* (Cambridge: Cambridge University Press, 1998), 117–41. In an impassioned plea to pay attention to the exodus of poor Bangladeshis, a Bangladeshi

newspaper editor recently wrote: 'Neglected by the national authorities, hounded by the police of their countries of work, they are the most despised and denigrated lot anywhere who provide the valuable foreign exchange with which we make foreign trips as VIPs.' This piece considers the condition of poor Bangladeshis in Malaysia, Pakistan, the Gulf and the West, but overlooks the much larger group of Bangladeshis in India. Afsan Chowdhury, 'Straight from the Heart: Are *miskins* people too?', *The Daily Star* (16 April 2002).

49 I.e. a tendency to study the world as a patchwork of state-defined societies, economies and cultures. See Chapter 1.

50 For an analysis of this theme for states in Europe and North America, see John Torpey, *The Invention of the Passport: Surveillance, Citizenship and the State* (Cambridge: Cambridge University Press, 2000).

51 Consider this testimony by an unauthorized Bangladesh immigrant in Delhi who was 'authorized' by Indian state officials needing to fill a family-planning quota: 'During 1975 the whole area was deluged and we sought the help of the government. The government offered help in the form of a small plot of land in New Simapuri [in Delhi] on the condition that both husband and wife undergo sterilization [vasectomy and tubectomy] operations. We accepted the proposal and were offered a tiny plot of 10 feet by 25 feet.' Possession of this plot allowed them later to erect authorized houses. Quoted in Lin and Paul, 'Bangladeshi Migrants', 9.

52 Sunando Sarkar, 'Administration torn asunder by influx,' *The Telegraph* (3 November 2001); 'Bangla immigrants to be pushed back', *The Times of India* (5 November 2001); 'Cong no to refugee status for intruders', *The Times of India* (5 November 2001); 'BJP for dual policy on Bangla influx', *The Telegraph* (6 November 2001).

9

MIGRANTS, FENCES AND DEPORTATIONS

Many considerations underpinned the drawing of the Partition border but patterns of migration were not among them. The border failed to create territories that acted as self-enclosed containers of human resources because it was imposed on a region with an expansionary population. People crisscrossed the border in their thousands, and most of these population movements were not authorized by the new states. In the previous chapter we encountered three statist narratives of cross-border migration – homecoming, infiltration and denial – and concluded that these were inadequate. In this chapter I rescale and historicize the study of cross-border migration by focusing on state measures to block it and on how these measures affected the strategies of individual migrants and the networks that supported them. The chapter concludes with an assessment of the role of borderlanders and state personnel in these networks.

Creating international migrants

The deltaic region of Bengal had long been known for its remarkably mobile inhabitants.[1] Its rich soils supported a dense agricultural population with high mortality caused by epidemic disease and natural calamities. The rivers of this delta often changed their course, forcing many inhabitants to move to new settlements. In the nineteenth century the population began to expand and economic changes contributed to more population mobility. Increasing landlessness, particularly in eastern and central parts, led to a stream of out-migrants looking for land in less densely populated areas of Bengal. Keen to expand their tax base, both the colonial authorities and landlords in adjoining regions encouraged these migrants. It was in this period that cultivators established themselves in the Sundarban wilds in the south, the Barind area in the north, and on *chors* (silt banks) in the major rivers of Bengal. Others moved into sparsely-settled non-Bengali speaking regions to the north, east and south; only in the densely-settled west there was little scope for expansion. They followed the course of the Brahmaputra river north into the Assam valley and they settled in northern Arakan and in Tripura.[2] As the population continued to grow and the economy of Bengal stagnated, would-be settlers found it harder to procure productive and safe land in Bengal. They moved onto islands in the Bay of Bengal that were dangerously exposed to hurricanes and tidal bores, and they pushed further into areas where local populations increasingly began to resist Bengali immigration. It was on this demographic scenario of increasingly desperate 'self-rescue migration' that the Partition border impinged.[3]

The creation of the border in 1947 had two effects. First, the fairly unobtrusive movement of settlers out of Bengal suddenly became *international* migration. New states came into being, claiming the right to decide who was a citizen or an alien, and to grant or withhold authorization to cross the border. When it was declared illegal to move without papers, the movement continued underground.[4] Second, the throes of state formation after 1947 led to additional out-migration, often in waves. Although the narrative of homecoming identified these newcomers as political migrants (repatriates, refugees, displaced persons) and ignored the longer-term trend of self-rescue migration, the distinction between 'economic' and 'political' settlers was often of little importance to the migrants themselves or to those on whose land they settled.

The border gave citizens who resisted migrant settlement a new argument that the state hardly could ignore, and the Indian narrative of 'infiltration' was constructed around that argument. No state could allow foreign nationals to cross the border and simply occupy land and avail themselves of the services provided by that state. This formal argument of state territoriality gained power when it could no longer be maintained that immigration from East Pakistan/ Bangladesh was overwhelmingly 'homecoming' migration by East Bengali Hindus. In the last quarter of the twentieth century, the discovery that many recent immigrants from Bangladesh were in fact Muslim coincided with the emergence of a political Hinduism (or Hindutva) in India that was based on the tenet that Hindu India was under threat.[5] It was through this political movement that Bangladeshi 'infiltration' became a national issue in India. Many immigrants refused to accept this. Rahman, a Bangladeshi living in Delhi, sought to highlight the hypocrisy of the infiltration discourse in India – officially a secular country – when he remarked in 1998: 'If we are "infiltrators" because we have come from Bangladesh, then many BJP leaders like Advani and Khurana are also "infiltrators" because they have come from Pakistan. Why doesn't the government want to deport them?'[6]

In the Indian debate on 'infiltration,' questions of citizenship dovetailed with rising communal sensibilities and paranoia, and Bengali-speaking Muslims became perfect scapegoats.[7] In Sanjoy Hazarika's words:

Too often, one meets with academics and journalists, officials and politicians in the country, especially in the North-East, who are absolutely

convinced that every Bengali-speaking Muslim is an illegal migrant who
has come over into the area in the past decade or so. Such an attitude
borders on xenophobia and skepticism is necessary if we are to look at
such emotive issues with rationality and common sense.[8]

Indian authorities took various positions in this debate, and these positions
shifted under the influence of continuing migration from Bangladesh.[9] The
Assam government switched from the homecoming thesis to the infiltration
thesis after violent anti-Bengali disturbances in the early 1980s.[10] Authorities
in Delhi and Mumbai did the same after Hinduist parties came to power there.
Only the West Bengal government stuck to the homecoming line till 1999,
when it too caved in and adopted the language of infiltration.[11]

As the experience of population exchange ('homecoming') faded into the
background and the older trend of migrants leaving eastern Bengal for less
densely populated areas continued vigorously, the narrative of infiltration gained
ground in the Indian half of the borderland.[12] Migration from Bangladesh came
to be seen as highly undesirable and measures were taken to contain it. Such
measures were taken only on the Indian side – Bangladesh never showed any
interest in keeping its citizens – but their effects were noticeable throughout
the borderland.

Three Indian measures were of particular importance in shaping borderland
society. Each was designed to enclose what had now become an international
'Bangladeshi diaspora'. Because the borderland was the territorial meeting point
of India and Bangladesh, it was here that these measures were implemented
and contested. We look at each in turn: first border fencing, then detection
and identification, and finally deportation.

A fence around the border

The idea of protecting the border with a fence was not new. Soon after Partition,
short stretches of border, especially near customs posts, had been fenced.[13]
Regional politicians in Assam first proposed erecting a fence along the entire
border so as to isolate the population of East Pakistan/ Bangladesh in the early
1960s.[14] They also advocated clearing an area 'in sufficient depth along the
border to control Pakistani infiltration', which was taken up by the government
in Delhi but not acted upon.[15] It took a violent uprising and anti-Bengali
pogroms in Assam, however, to make India's national leaders sit up. By 1985
the issue was placed on the national agenda.[16] In 1986 the Indian government
approved the Indo-Bangladesh Border Roads & Fence Project 'with a view to
preventing infiltration by Bangladesh nationals.'[17] Progress was uneven and
very slow. According to Indian press reports in 1998, 'the total border fencing

is about 190 km in West Bengal, 20 km in Assam and almost non-existent in Tripura and Mizoram', or about 5 per cent of the total length of the border (Plate 9.1).[18]

Plate 9.1: Indians (left) and Bangladeshis at Jamaldho village on the India-Bangladesh border talking to each other through the border fence, 2003.[19]

Even so, the border fence caused great offence in Bangladesh official circles 'because it humiliates and belittles us before the world.'[20] And Taslima Nasreen, a Bangladeshi poet, expressed her outrage at the fence as a symbol of the degradation of Partition when she wrote:

Two parts of the land stretch out their thirsty hands
Towards each other. And in between the hands
Stands the man-made filth of religion, barbed wire.[21]

According to the Ground Rules established between the two states, no permanent posts or defensive works of any nature can be constructed within 150 yards of the border, so where the fence came up it created a 150-yard-wide belt of no man's land on the Indian side.[22] When in 1999 the West Bengal government changed its mind about immigration and decided to contain 'infiltration' by fencing its border with Bangladesh, it found that no less than 450 villages were located within 150 yards of the border. Since these villages would lie in the fenced-off no man's land, they had to be relocated.[23] The government soon found out, however, that borderlanders were not prepared to take their relocation lying down, or to put 'national interest' before their own. A top border official explained that 'people from about 187 villages within 50 yards from the international border [in southern West Bengal] could not be relocated as yet because of court cases.'[24]

The social destruction that a border fence could bring to these villages may be deduced from a sketch of two of them:

> Every time Nazir Rahman Bhuia moves from one part of his house to another, he crosses an international boundary. For the India-Bangladesh border at marker number 2033 runs right through his home in a village set in lush green countryside in the eastern Indian state of Tripura ... the village has two names now – Motinagar on the Indian side, Dhajanagar on the Bangladeshi. The Indian village has electricity, the Bangladeshi has none. Both are inhabited by Muslims ... Life goes on as usual, even when border guards show up occasionally. The villagers meet each other, celebrate marriages and bury the dead together. "We feel strange about the border running through the village like this, but we've adjusted to it," says Bhuia.

> A group wedding [was] celebrated in a West Bengal village – three brides and two grooms were from India, three grooms and two brides were from Bangladesh. Bengalis live on both sides of the border. "The marriages were solemnized in the village council office. The people have never recognized these border pillars that were suddenly erected," adds the [Border Security Force] officer, who is responsible for policing a big part of the zanily zigzagging frontier.[25]

Sometimes the West Bengal authorities abandoned border fencing when delicate questions of sovereignty and citizenship were involved in addition to the disruption of economic and social life. This was the case in Char Meghna, an area where about 1,500 Indian citizens lived illegally on Bangladeshi territory and 'many people on both sides of the border have their places of work on the other side.'[26]

In Assam, politicians were dissatisfied not only with the very slow progress of the fencing of the India-Bangladesh border, but also with the quality of the fence.[27] An Assam Home Ministry survey covering a 100-kilometre stretch of border fencing spoke of 'a rusty, brittle structure' and a senior official admitted that 'portions of the fencing have gaping holes big enough for Patton tanks to pass.'[28] A report by the Governor of Assam argued that the fence should be 'of the same height as along Punjab's border with Pakistan', and that observation towers, speedboats and floating border outposts were necessary.[29] A description of the Punjab border fence gives an idea of what the governor had in mind:

It is a formidable barrier, erected well inside Indian territory ... at a cost of $85,000 a kilometer. It consists of two 3-m high barbed wire fences with razor sharp concertina wire running in between. It also has what border policemen call cobras: five electricity wires fixed at different heights from the ground. At night the cobras come alive, along with powerful sodium vapor lamps that illuminate the fencing ... Recently, one ... itinerant worker was electrocuted near Wagah when he tried to crawl across during a brief power shutdown – standby generators came on automatically, roasting him inside the concertina.[30]

In 1998, India was reported to be considering the erection of a 150-kilometre electrified fence on the Bangladesh border, 'charged with a low, non-fatal voltage, immigration officials said.'[31] But despite the rhetoric, the technocratic dream of sealing the India-Bangladesh border by means of fences, floodlights and motorized border patrols did not materialize.[32] The cost of construction and maintenance would have been high, the political fallout for India's relationship with Bangladesh considerable, and the efficacy of the fence doubtful. Nevertheless, Indian government officials remained committed to a further fencing of the border and to 'sanitizing' the area between the fence and the border, i.e. deporting its population.[33] Occasionally, parallels were drawn with the most high-tech forms of barricading a border in the world, at the US-Mexican border, and the ways in which Mexican migrants were able to circumvent it.[34] Clearly, as in the USA, the de facto immigration policy of the Indian government has been *not* to make the India-Bangladesh border impermeable to the passage of 'illegal' entrants, for reasons to which I will return shortly.[35]

In places where fences did come up, however, borderland society was not bisected. In densely populated areas communication across the fence often remained possible. Borderlanders who wished to cross the border simply became more dependent on the mediation of local border guards and customs officials, or they cut holes in the fence or crossed over in a fenceless section (Plate 9.2).

There were many local differences: in parts of Meghalaya where a border fence had been put up, cultivators on the Indian side complained that there was an insufficient number of gates to allow them to work their fields; as a result, their counterparts from Bangladesh had taken over the 150-yard strip of Indian territory, cultivating right up to the fence.[36] Increasingly, Meghalaya politicians voiced hesitations about the wisdom of fencing the border. In 2003 the Chief Minister of Meghalaya was:

guarded when he spoke about fencing the border and said that his government would take into account the survival needs of the people residing along the border. Most of these people depend heavily on open markets on both sides of the border and barter food and other essential commodities almost regularly. This form of exchange, called "barter trade," is their main means of sustenance and has been continuing for ages. "We will not let physical fencing affect the people's lives," Lapang said, adding that "openings and outlets will be kept" for barter trade and border hats [markets].[37]

Plate 9.2: Informal border crossing. Indian visitors entering Bangladesh near a border pillar. Tripura/ Sylhet border, 2002.

A few weeks later he was even more outspoken and roundly rejected border fencing: 'The government of India has decided to fence the border. But it does not serve any purpose as people can climb it. So we feel that instead of fencing, good roads for smooth running of vehicles are required to check infiltration.'[38]

In Assam, Indian villagers living beyond the fence were dependent on their Bangladeshi neighbours and 'the children of these villages, who have to remain cut off from their own country for half the day, cannot be expected to have any feeling for their motherland.'[39] And all along the fenced border, Indian cultivators complained of humiliating treatment by border guards every time they had to visit their fields beyond the fence (Plates 9.3 and 9.4).

Plate 9.3: Indian border villager being frisked by Indian border guards before being allowed to cross the fence and cultivate his fields, Assam.[40]

Plate 9.4: Locked-out Indian cultivators and their cow waiting at the border-fence gate to be allowed to return to their village (near Dhubri, Assam).[41]

In southern Bengal, official attempts to stop Indian border guards' involvement in smuggling to Bangladesh led to a severe obstruction of border agriculture. Here the gates were opened only for a few minutes a day, driving local cultivators to despair:

> An agitated group of villagers summoned the courage to go before the Border Security Force, near the West Bengal-Bangladesh border at Tehatta in Nadia, with their difficulties. Their bone of contention: Fencing along the border. "Our difficulties started after the new rules were implemented for opening the gate on the fence," Tehatta panchayat samity [local council] president Netai Biswas said. "Earlier, the key to the gate used to be with the gate sentry. We could easily get in to cultivate our fields across the fence. Now the company commander keeps the keys. One havildar [sergeant] manages four gates with the same key. The gate opens only for a few minutes. If a farmer is late to arrive, he can't go to his field" ... BSF sources explained that the company commander took charge of the key as a sentry manning the gate had been conniving with a few smugglers. The latter would keep their consignments handy and the sentry would open the gate briefly so that they could cross over to Bangladesh ... As a precaution [against connivance], locks were sealed when border gates were closed for the night and keys were kept in sealed boxes.[42]

But despite these examples, the general picture of the border fence was not that of a real barrier and there was certainly no evidence to show that the border fence slowed down Bangladeshi migration to India. As a local newspaper put it, crossing the fenced border remained 'as easy as slicing butter with a knife' (Plates 9.5 and 9.6).[43]

Detection and identification

A second line of defence against 'infiltrators' from Bangladesh was to identify culprits and to send them back to the Bangladesh side of the border. This was much more difficult than it seemed. First of all, migrants usually travelled without identity papers (although there was also a sizeable group of Bangladeshis who entered India on visaed passports and never returned[45]). Second, there was little to distinguish newcomers from residents. They spoke the same language, might dress in Indian-made clothes smuggled into Bangladesh, and blended in very easily. Even if they spoke an eastern Bengali regional dialect, there were many established Indian citizens in the borderland who originated from the same regions. Third, the long border was inadequately policed and crossing it was relatively easy in most places. Fourth, there was always confusion about

Plate 9.5: Triple Indian border fence 150 yards inside the Assam-Bangladesh border, 2000. To the left is the border road, used exclusively by the (Indian) Border Security Force. Bangladesh is in the background.

Plate 9.6: Posed photograph from an Indian newspaper showing Indian border guards (BSF) 'arresting' illegal immigrants from Bangladesh at a gated border fence.[44]

the cut-off point between 'homecoming' and 'infiltration' because local politicians, the government in Delhi and the Bangladesh government used different definitions. An agreement between the Prime Ministers of India and Bangladesh (the Indira-Mujib Pact) 'tacitly provided that Bangladesh would not be held responsible for persons who had illegally migrated to India before the birth of the new Republic prior to March 25, 1971.' Therefore the year

1971 was officially considered to be the beginning of 'infiltration', but earlier cut-off points (e.g. the year 1951) continued to figure in Indian political discourse.[46]

Identification of Bangladeshi immigrants was further hampered by the fact that Indian borderlanders often protected them.[47] Unauthorized migration took place within an extended community that transcended the border. Economic and political actors on either side were mutually dependent: earlier immigrants offered newcomers shelter and support, Indian employers were keen to exploit cheap labour, and Indian politicians were interested in expanding their electorate. Champak Barbora's cartoon indicates these linkages (plate 9.7).

Plate 9.7: **Cartoon by Champak Barbora, published in** *The Assam Tribune* **(7 February 2003).**

Immigrants also found it easy to make use of the imperfect registration of Indian citizens: only 30 to 40 per cent of births in India are registered (as against an even smaller 12 per cent in Bangladesh[48]). This provided ample opportunities for forgery. Many immigrants secured an 'Indian' identity by fraudulently acquiring a ration card, birth or school certificate, enrolling as voters and – ultimate proof of Indian citizenship – availing themselves of the Election

Commission's identity card.[49] And for those with money and connections it was not difficult to 'manage' a passport.[50]

The total number of post-1971 immigrants from Bangladesh to India is unknown. Guesstimates by Indian politicians and journalists have been rising steadily. In 2000, an Indian government report estimated that 300,000 illegal immigrants entered India each year, or 850 people per day.[51] In 2001, the Indian government put the number of illegal immigrants from Bangladesh 'unofficially' at 12–18 million, of whom some 5 million might have settled in West Bengal.[52] By 2003, however, following the lead of Hindutva activists, it revised this figure upward to a staggering 20 million, half of them in West Bengal and Assam.[53] If these figures are correct, the number of unauthorized Bangladeshi immigrants in the state of West Bengal alone equalled that of all unauthorized immigrants in the United States.[54]

By the late 1990s the Indian government was also improving its legal toolbox in order to detect and identify unauthorized immigrants. It was revising the Foreigners' Act of 1946 and a controversy was raging over the proposed repeal of the special anti-infiltration act for Assam, the Illegal Migrants (Determination by Tribunals) Act of 1983 (popularly known as the IMDT), because it had failed to facilitate the deportation of Bangladeshis from Assam.[55] According to press reports, since 1983 about 300,000 people had been screened under this act, but only 25,000 were tried by tribunals, and a mere 1,500 were deported as illegal immigrants.[56] In 2003, the Indian government decided to repeal the IMDT Act in order to devise a more effective way of dealing in legal terms with immigrants to Assam.[57]

Other administrative measures proved to be just as ineffectual. Border guards often found it impossible to identify persons without some form of identification:

"How can we stop infiltration?" said Mr Balbir Singh Sahal, the [BSF] Sector Commander [at the West Bengal border, Nadia district], "We do not understand Bengali. These people speak the same language, wear similar clothes and look no different. It is impossible to distinguish between a Bangladeshi and an Indian. Also, many live in houses adjacent to each other. Indians should be issued identity cards immediately."[58]

Plans to issue identity cards to Indian citizens, especially in 'sensitive' border areas, were discussed for years and floated repeatedly, in 1989, 1994, 1997, 1999, 2001 and 2003.[59] Such drives did nothing to reduce immigration. On the contrary, a report from the fenced border at Dhubri (Assam) indicated that Indian citizens encouraged immigration because they earned money by conducting Bangladeshis through the border: they rented out their passports, identity cards and residential certificates to them.[60] Any system of identity papers was vulnerable to fraud:

> An Indian reporter approaching some fresh Bangladeshi immigrants waiting
> for a train at New Cooch Behar railway station (India) found that, as soon
> as he questioned them, they whipped out certificates issued by the chief of
> a *gram panchayat* (local council), showing them to be Indians. Although
> everyone was aware that one of a 'mushrooming tribe of agents' had
> procured these for them, no Indian state official was willing, or perhaps
> able, to check the veracity of these certificates.[61]

Even in the absence of such trickery, however, identity card schemes appeared
to be doomed from the start. Not only were they very expensive and labour
intensive, but in the absence of a reliable national citizens' register it was
impossible to keep such schemes up to date.[62] For the same reason, Bangladeshis
happily voted in Indian elections (as Indian borderlanders also did in Bangladeshi
elections) because they could register as voters.[63] Before elections, there would
be enormous publicity about the cleaning up of electoral rolls in Indian border
districts, but unauthorized immigrants with political patronage and armed with
voters' identity cards could not be sent away from the polling booths.[64]

It was clearly impossible for the Indian state to handle the immigration of
Bangladeshis administratively. Its main weakness was that it could not
implement the laws and schemes that it devised because its registration of citizens
was inadequate, it employed too few border guards to monitor the schemes, it
could not trust those guards and other state personnel to put the interest of the
state before their self-interest, and it failed to check Indian citizens who
encouraged illegal immigration and registration. It was no surprise that the
state explored another means of ridding itself of unwanted Bangladeshis:
deportation.

Deportation

From their inception as separate states, both India and Pakistan practised the
removal of unwanted individuals from their territories. There were several forms
of removal. Those who were considered a threat to the state could be externed,
fugitives from the law could be extradited, and from 1952 so could those who
arrived without valid passports and visas. By far the most important form of
removal in terms of numbers was the expulsion of minorities, and we have seen
that local state representatives often played a role in this.

The deportation of people on the grounds of their being 'infiltrators' or
'foreigners' first occurred on a large scale in India in the 1960s.[65] It was not
until the 1990s, however, that deportation once more became a hot issue in

India. Public opinion was primed for these deportations by campaigns depicting Bangladeshi immigrants as a security risk, a health hazard, a law-and-order problem, and a burden on Indian society.

When parts of Mumbai were waterlogged for three days, the Shiv Sena mayor blamed the illegal Bangladeshi population for the mess. 'Their filth blocked up the gutters', he said. In Delhi, the BJP [Bharatiya Janata Party] added to its following by generating antipathy towards Bangladeshi immigrants. As civic amenities came under strain, the hapless Bangladeshi immigrant became a convenient scapegoat. The president of the Delhi BJP argued: 'Is our country a *dharamshala* [charity institution] that whoever wants to come and stay here can freely enter? It is a matter of national security ... There is too much pressure on the resources here [in Delhi]. Outsiders should be removed.' And the Chief Minister of Maharashtra linked immigrants with subversion when he said: 'we cannot tolerate this nonsense whether it is a Bangladeshi or a Pakistani national indulging in law and order problem.'[66]

Criminalization, humiliation and illegal deportation went hand in hand.[67] Police squads would check out neighbourhoods, identify Bengali-speaking Muslims (who might be Indian citizens from West Bengal, Tripura or Assam) and herd them together.

Sitting inside his dimly-lit hut in Delhi's Seemapuri, home to an estimated 50,000 Bangladeshi immigrants, 50-year-old Altaf Hussain still remembers the time his sons Milon and Haroon were caught by the authorities in the wake of an anti-Bangladeshi drive by the local BJP Government in 1994. They were paraded on donkeys, had their heads shaved, put on a train to Calcutta and, finally, forced back to Bangladesh at gunpoint. For nine days, starving and without any familiar address to call on, the two brothers wandered around, until a Good Samaritan smuggled them back to Seemapuri.[68]

Fourteen-year-old Nanu from Mumbai was rounded up but had no papers to prove that he was an Indian. With 14 other Bengali-speaking Muslims, he was taken to West Bengal by train. 'After taking us to the jungle, the police told us to keep on walking and not look back or else we would be shot.' Nanu alleged that, in the jungle, women in his group had been raped by [Maharashtra] police who were accompanying them.[69]

The rough way in which deportations were carried out led to protests and accusations of human rights abuses. Maharashtra police chained the deportees, and tied their chains to railway coach windows. A senior member of the West Bengal government commented: 'They are not cattle, to be pushed back under the cover of darkness. They should be treated like human beings.'[70]

The deportations were a disaster for the deportees because the Bangladesh border guards – true to Bangladesh's official narrative of denial[71] – refused to accept them as Bangladeshi citizens. Consequently they wandered about the borderland till they found the means to return to their places of residence. Some actually became experts at returning after having been 'pushed back'. One of them was Noori, who was deported from her Delhi home seven times, always returning triumphantly after a few weeks or months.[72] Many others were not so lucky, however: they ended up in West Bengal jails that soon ran out of capacity to accommodate them.[73] Not deterred by Bangladesh's attitude, the government in Delhi devised two new ways of identifying and isolating immigrants. In 1998 it was reportedly contemplating setting up detention camps near the India-Bangladesh border 'to ensure the success of its "push-back" scheme of illegal immigrants.' In these camps (dubbed Bangladesh Transfer Facilitation Centres) immigrants would be fingerprinted, photographed, and so on, and held till such time as Bangladesh would accept them as its nationals.[74] In 1999 the government in Delhi also sanctioned the setting up of a 3,500-strong Prevention of Infiltration Force (PIF) that it saw as 'a second line of defence against infiltration' and that would be deployed at some distance from the India-Bangladesh border.[75]

Sometimes local state bodies in India also devised policies of their own to stop immigration. For example, authorities in Assam attempted to create vigilante groups (or Village Defence Parties) on the border to help Indian border guards check illegal immigration and the possible intrusion of fundamentalist elements from Bangladesh. They did not find this easy because inhabitants of Indian border villages used their local knowledge strategically, arguing that they would be motivated to help the authorities only 'if the Government takes initiatives to develop the border areas.'[76] In Northeast India, non-state organizations also developed policies of deportation of their own. One of these was a youth organization in Nagaland that served 'quit notices' on suspected Bangladeshi immigrants and closed down shops and an Islamic school.[77]

In 2003, in a magnified replay of the deportations of 1998, the Indian government announced a 'special drive' to remove millions of unauthorized immigrants.[78] Soon police in Delhi were rounding up Bengali-speaking labour migrants and putting them on trains to the border. At the same time, 'deportation cells' were formed in police districts of Calcutta and Delhi, and West Bengal police started arresting migrants fleeing from Mumbai after heavy intimidation.[79]

Suddenly, thousands of deportees were gathered at several locations along the West Bengal/ Bangladesh border and for weeks Indian border guards tried to drive them into Bangladesh. They did so under cover of darkness, forcing the deportees out by beating them and 'terrorising them through firing blank shots.'[80] Bangladeshi border guards and villagers, for their part, blocked the way and beat the deportees back with sticks and gunfire.[81] Groups of hundreds of deportees were then trapped in the man's land where several were injured in shootings or contracted pneumonia, and at least one old man died of 'hunger and cold' (Plates 9.8 and 9.9).[82]

Plates 9.8 and 9.9: Border guards barring stranded deportees from entering either India or Bangladesh. No man's land, Satgachhi border, Cooch Behar, 2003.[83]

According to both Bangladeshi and Indian press reports, many deportees identified themselves as Bangladeshis who had been living in India for years.[84] Mamata Bibi, a deportee in the no man's land, was quoted as saying: 'I don't know why we were stopped from entering our own country.'[85] Still, the government in Dhaka stuck to the narrative of denial: it reiterated its position that there were no illegal Bangladeshi migrants in India *at all*, and denied that the deportees could be anything but 'Bengali-speaking Indian Muslims'.[86] Dismissing this as 'absurd', an Indian government spokesman pointed out that Dhaka could not continue its ostrich policy forever: 'This is not a problem which will vanish simply if you do not address it.'[87] The resulting eyeball-to-eyeball confrontation caused intense suffering to thousands of deportees, and it ended in yet another stalemate between two states unable to deal with uncontrollable population movement across their shared borderland.[88]

In short, none of the Indian state's measures were effective in disrupting the flow of Bangladeshi migrants across the border. Certainly, border fencing, identity cards, deportation drives, anti-migrant pogroms and border detention camps were crucial as rhetorical elements in the dramaturgy of Indian sovereignty. They were effective in building up in many Indian minds an image of Bangladeshi immigrants as illegal aliens, lawbreakers, health hazards and potential terrorists out to subvert India's territorial borders and disrupt the very fabric of Indian society. But in terms of actually curbing Bangladeshi immigration the impact of these measures was immaterial, and it is likely that they were not really intended to do so. They can be understood as practices of statecraft, projecting public images of territorial inviolability that mask the reality of borders that are necessarily porous to economic flows, particularly flows of cheap labour.[89]

From settler migration to the trafficking of labour

After 1971, Bangladesh society rapidly developed new global links, mainly as a result of independent statehood and a sudden increase in foreign aid. One effect was a diasporic spread of Bangladeshis all over the world. The settler migration of earlier days continued but now new flows of labour migration developed and emigration out of Bangladesh grew explosively as the country's oversaturated labour markets were completely unable to accommodate growing numbers of labourers. Many Bangladeshis left from Dhaka airport, either as short-term labour migrants to the Gulf states and Southeast Asia, or as legal or illegal migrants to highly industrialized societies in the North.[90] Some boarded ships at the ports of Chittagong and Chalna.[91] But the majority of these job-and-dignity seekers, in their quest for a better life, continued to cross the land border into India or Burma.[92]

They were not always, however, heading for Indian or Burmese destinations.

Some Bangladeshi migrants used Burma as a corridor to employment in Malaysia, Singapore, Thailand and Japan, and many Bangladeshi migrants used India as a corridor to employment in Pakistan and the Middle East. The Indian press coined the term 'exfiltration' to describe the movement of Bangladeshis from India to Pakistan.[93] In the 1990s it was estimated that there were about a million Bangladeshis in the Pakistani city of Karachi alone.[94] Much of the India-Pakistan border was difficult to cross because of heavy barbed-wire fencing, and this led Bangladeshis to opt for the most dangerous routes, often with disastrous results. One was through the hot, parched wasteland of the Thar desert and the Rann of Kutch. Here one group of nearly 40 Bangladeshi migrants, mostly women and children, died of thirst in the early 1990s.[95] Another route was through the unfenced border (or, more precisely, line of control) between Indian-held and Pakistan-held Kashmir:

'Well organised brokers charge money for accompanying them from their native places to ... West Bengal and to places near the international border in Jammu and Kashmir. Throughout their journey, they are accompanied by different brokers, who leave them near the border for crossing over to Pakistan.' If Pakistan-bound Bangladeshis were apprehended by the Kashmir police, they were not booked or produced before a court. Instead, according to senior police officers, 'the best way to get rid of them is to huddle them into a Calcutta-bound train without ticket.' Homeward bound Bangladeshis returning from Pakistan, however, were arrested under the law of the land. Some of these migrants remained lodged in Indian police lock-ups for many years, waiting for their repatriation, long after completing their jail terms.[96]

For most Bangladeshi citizens on the move, the search for a better life was now no longer oriented primarily towards finding a plot of land. Increasingly, Bangladeshi immigrants in India and beyond were looking for cash incomes. 'In Calcutta and Delhi, they appear to have carved out a niche for themselves as domestic helps, construction labourers and rag pickers. In Mumbai, they are crucial as weavers and *zari* [embroidery] workers.'[97] Even among those who stayed in the borderland, wage earners became more important. And many of them were commuters or seasonal migrants who travelled back and forth across the border.[98] Bangladeshi women from Rajshahi provided cheap labour to Indian cigarette and bangle factories just across the border in India,[99] and many rickshaw-pullers and day labourers in Indian border towns such as Agartala (Tripura), Silchar (Assam), or Siliguri (West Bengal) were Bangladeshis (Plate 9.10). According to one report, 10,000 rickshaw-pullers in Siliguri town came from Bangladesh illegally.[100]

Plate 9.10: Indian police arresting 50 'suspected Bangladeshis' hired by a contractor to work on a construction site, Guwahati (Assam, India), July 2000.[101]

The Bangladeshi diaspora took many shapes and involved many different groups. Some migrants bravely set out on their own, others took the assistance of relatives and friends, and yet others put their fate in the hands of agents.[102] And then there were those who were forced into migration. The cross-border trafficking of human beings came to be noticed from the 1980s, but had probably existed for some considerable time previously.[103]

At the border, the distinction between self-smuggling, commuting, migration-by-consent and trafficking was not always clear:[104]

> Contrary to the conventions of enforcement agencies and news reporting, which tend to identify "the bad guys" and their victims, much migrant smuggling or trafficking operates in an ambiguous area that is neither purely voluntary nor involuntary from the perspective of the migrant. Many contemporary slaves know that they will be smuggled illegally across borders to work, and they sometimes know the nature of the work – what they often do not know is the terms of the "contract".[105]

Both men and women, children and adults, were smuggled across the Bangladesh-India border but the trafficking of women has attracted most attention.[106] The prospect of employment or marriage was commonly used to entice women to cross the border.[107] For example, groups of Bangladeshi women being ferried across the Ganges to India in the 1980s thought they might get a factory job in Calcutta or a husband in Bihar.[108] Such groups were often taken by train to Calcutta, accompanied by local women who might themselves be migrants. 'A Bangladeshi woman settler who is now residing in Guma [24-Parganas, India], told the survey team that her principal vocation was trafficking in women. She accompanies a group of women every evening by train from Guma to Calcutta.'[109] In many cases it was only after the women reached their final destinations (in India, Pakistan, the Gulf states or Southeast Asia) that they realized they had been tricked: often they were sold to sweatshops or brothels.[110] Middlemen played the same trick on boys and men when they offered them jobs in faraway factories, only to sell them as bonded labourers to rural landlords or owners of workshops.[111]

In the case of many women and children, however, it was not consent or enticement but force or sale that brought them to the border.[112] Kidnapping was common, especially of young children and even babies, but some parents sold their children.[113] In this way, about 15,000 children were believed to cross the border from Bangladesh to India every year.[114] Boys aged between 2 and 12 were in high demand in the Gulf states as jockeys in camel races.[115] Young girls and boys were sought after as domestics and especially as sex workers.[116] Very young girls were said to 'command a high price as they are likely to be free from HIV/ AIDS,' and, 'in West Bengal, children used as jockeys in camel races are the most expensive, followed by those used for prostitution, while those pushed into begging or used as labourers cost the least. In Bangladesh, the prices are said to be very low, with the average ranging between Rs.1,000 and Rs.5,000.'[117]

As these migrants passed through the borderland, they might experience special exploitation. On the one hand, the border police of both countries would charge women money for crossing the border.[118] If the money was not given, sexual assault was a possibility.

Some women had their first experience of "trading" their bodies when they were raped by the police at the border for failing to pay the money they would need to buy their way into India.[119]

On the other hand, borderlanders have been known to resist trafficking in women and children.[120] In northern Bangladesh, an old woman was beaten to death by a mob charging her with having abducted children, and train passengers on routes from the border to Calcutta attacked or detained people they suspected of being traffickers and their victims.[121]

A reserve pool of labour

Human trafficking was doubtless the most exploitative and humiliating form that the Bangladeshi diaspora took. But most emigrant men and women who passed the borderland were not being trafficked against their will; they were labour migrants in search of a good and dignified life rather than human chattels.[122] The attractions of the Indian economy were considerable, as Sarat Lin and Madan Paul concluded from their study of Bangladeshi immigrants in New Delhi: 'not only are there far more job opportunities, but more jobs are full time, daily wages are higher, and prices of food and consumer goods are significantly lower ... the typical real purchasing power of an unskilled agricultural wage earner in India is at least five times that in Bangladesh.'[123]

The volume of Bangladeshi emigration shows clearly that there was a strong, sustained demand in India and beyond for the cheap labour provided by Bangladeshis. If there were indeed some 12 to 20 million unauthorized Bangladeshis in India, there were obviously millions of Indians keen to employ them. The Indian state never developed schemes either to hold these Indian citizens accountable for their illegal practice of employing 'aliens,' or to issue temporary work permits to labour migrants from Bangladesh. The following case from Ranabir Samaddar's study of the West Bengal section of the borderland shows that Indian labour contractors who recruited labourers in Bangladesh were left untouched while their labourers could be 'flushed out' of their workplaces in India.

> New contractors like Mansur Ali, Hasan Ali Molla and Shamser Gazi [of Basirhat, West Bengal, India] now operate on both sides. They employ labour-recruiting agents deep in Bangladesh who recruit labour by advancing Indian money (in the form of plastic cards). Labour supply is thus assured and production is regular. The West Bengal police and security forces had flushed out the migrants in 1993 and 1994 from big brickfields like Bharati. Labour became scarce and the price of bricks soared from Rs.1,200 per 1,000 bricks to Rs.1,500 per 1,000. Saiyad Ali Gazi, Ismail Fakir, Hafizur Sheikh, Akram Mallick, Kamrul Mandal and other Muslim migrant workers were "pushed back".[124]

When one Bangladeshi fisherman, who had been travelling back and forth to Assam for decades and was now retired in Bangladesh, was asked how cross-border migration could be stopped, he smiled and said:

> Can the river stop flowing? Can you block the rains? People who talk about such things do not know what they say. The Assamese need us, we need them.[125]

And yet, in Indian discussions about 'infiltration,' the contributions that these millions of Bangladeshi workers obviously made to the Indian economy went largely unnoticed. As nationalist Indian politicians built careers on 'infiltrator-bashing' and stressed the costs of unauthorized immigration in terms of law enforcement and state services, these politicians were supported by many who themselves employed cheap Bangladeshi domestic, agricultural or industrial labour.[126] 'Infiltrator-bashing' served not only as a vote getter, it also kept Bangladeshi labour immigrants stigmatized and vulnerable, and therefore cheap and pliable. In this way, Bangladesh served as a crucial reserve pool of labour for the economies of Assam, West Bengal, Delhi, Mumbai and other parts of India. Cross-border labour migration from Bangladesh ensured that real labour wages in these areas remained low, even where minimum-wage rates had officially been introduced, because Bangladeshi labourers were in no position to claim these rates. At the same time, the costs of the reproduction of migrant labour and the care for aged ex-labourers devolved on the Bangladesh economy.

Conclusion: emigration and the borderland

In 1947 a border was imposed on a region whose population was expansionary. For several decades the official discourse in India ignored this fact, as the official discourse in Bangladesh continues to do today. Most of the expansion took place overland, and the border turned into a whistle stop on the outward journey of millions of Bangladeshi migrants. At first, most migrants had been settlers in search of land to cultivate, and their scope had been the wider region of northeastern India and coastal Arakan (Burma). Increasingly, however, the Bangladeshis who emigrated through the borderland did so in search of wages, not land, and their geographical scope widened to include the entire world. They were now 'labour on the move' and they had become global migrants.[127]

As Indian political discourse increasingly conceived of the border as a war zone – an area where the nation was vulnerable to hostile demographic invasion – crossing the border began to require more circumspection in certain sections where surveillance had been stepped up. There is no evidence to suggest, however, that emigration was effectively hampered. On the contrary, new forms of assistance and exploitation sprung up on both sides of the border. Labour contractors, cross-border guides, providers of documents, border guards and many others could now earn better money from migrants.

In a general discussion of human smuggling, David Kyle and John Dale distinguish two ideal types.[128] A migrant-exporting industry is driven by migrant demand. It provides a packaged migration service out of a sending region, in which most of the organizational activity is at the sending side, and the contract is terminated once the migrant has arrived at the destination. A slave-importing operation, on the other hand, is set up to import weak labour for ongoing enterprises. It is usually carried out by relatively stable (criminal or semi-legitimate) organizations in the destination country, and nearly always depends on the corruption of state officials in all countries involved. In most cases, victims of such operations – who tend to come from weaker social backgrounds than the customers of migrant-exporting schemes – are duped into believing that they are embarking in a migrant-exporting scheme. In order to create this false image, seemingly well-to-do women often act as initial contact persons in slave-importing schemes.[129] The victims' own complicity is then used to facilitate making them pay off a rolling debt through coerced labour.

Although large transnational professional criminal organizations (mafias, syndicates, cartels) can be involved in such commodified migration, in many cases they are not.[130] In the Bengal borderland, human smuggling certainly was a crime that was organized, but it was not 'Organized Crime.'[131] Cross-border migration was not controlled by a few mighty Godfathers hoodwinking well-meaning but powerless states. Its social organization was far more fragmented and complex, and it involved the states in question.

The Indian state was at the receiving end of both migrant-exporting and slave-importing schemes involving Bangladeshis. Although India ostensibly sought to regulate the inflow of Bangladeshis, it was clearly unwilling to invest even remotely adequate resources into reaching that goal, and cross-border migration organizations were only slightly inconvenienced. In some sections of the borderland unassisted crossing remained as easy as ever, but where surveillance had increased, migration became more commodified as migrants had to buy the services of borderland brokers.[132] These brokers could well occupy positions in the state that they were able to turn to their own advantage. In 1993, a journalist visiting Cooch Behar [India] observed that

> I found Congress and CPI(M) politicians joining hands to bring Bangladeshis in Matador vans from the border and then putting them on to the Teesta-Torsa Express bound for the Nizamuddin railway station in Delhi.[133]

The Indian narrative of infiltration emphasized the evil of human smuggling rackets but remained completely silent about the contradictory involvement of a state that failed to target slave-importing schemes working from Indian soil, or Indian citizens who acted as slaveholders or employers of unauthorized immigrants.[134] There is much evidence that Indian state agents protected such schemes in order to benefit from them, both at the border and at places of employment (brothels, brickfields, factories, homes).

The state of Bangladesh was even more intimately involved in human smuggling. Like other 'sending states', it viewed migration as a positive benefit.[135] The export of people, authorized or unauthorized, provided a most important source of state revenue through remittances. In the last quarter of the twentieth century, Bangladesh was often described as an 'aid-dependent' society but by the turn of the 21st century the billions of dollars of international aid flowing into Bangladesh had been eclipsed by remittances sent back by 'officially exported' labour. These, together with the unrecorded funds sent back home by millions of unauthorized labour emigrants, decisively stimulated various sectors of the Bangladesh economy – including financial services, travel agencies, construction and transport – and boosted the tax income of the state. Bangladesh had become a deeply 'remittance-dependent' state. The export of labour also served important political purposes, to the extent that it curtailed 'political upheaval associated with the broken promises of failed "development" projects.'[136] Much anecdotal evidence indicates that Bangladesh state agents at various levels – in the borderland and beyond – benefited directly from both migrant-exporting and slave-importing schemes by 'taxing' them, and demanding commissions and other perks. The Bangladesh state did not interfere with the flourishing migrant-exporting industry but it did occasionally, although not very effectively, thwart slave-importing schemes destined for India. These schemes yielded much less state income and they were, moreover, a political embarrassment because domestic and foreign human rights groups made them the focus of publicity campaigns.

Borderland 'migration brokers' took advantage of two sets of circumstances that originated outside the borderland. The first was the forces that continued to compel inhabitants of Bangladesh to seek a better life abroad. The Bangladeshi diaspora will show no signs of slowing down as long as scarcity, instability and insecurity continue to dominate the Bangladesh economy, thwarting the life chances of millions.[137] Second, the narrative of infiltration that Indian politicians developed in their quest for state power had the effect of upping the stakes, thereby making the mediation of cross-border migration brokers more lucrative.[138]

While some borderlanders were doing a roaring business in assisting international migrants, the Indian narrative of infiltration began to point to an ominous future of anti-Bangladeshi pogroms.[139] Extreme proponents of this line advocated not only expulsion of Bangladeshis from India, but also territorial annexation of Bangladeshi territory. 'Capture one or two districts in Bangladesh, acquire space and send these infiltrators there', advocated an influential Indian politician in 2003.[140] At the same time, there were many in India who assumed that the state of Bangladesh itself was pursuing an evil territorial design: seeking Lebensraum for its teeming population and ultimately usurping Indian territory in order to establish a Greater Bangladesh.[141] However, it was not the Bangladesh government so much as individual migrants who were demonized and held responsible. The narrative of infiltration emphasized the supposedly free choice of individual actors, and hence the culpability of individual immigrants who were in a national space where they were not authorized to be. This perspective also exculpated the state of India of any responsibility in fostering the very immigration it claimed to want to fight, and drew attention away from the social, economic, environmental and political conditions that fuelled unauthorized international migration.[142]

The Bangladeshi counter-narrative of denial was equally ominous: never more than a short-term diplomatic device, it completely failed to address central issues of citizenship and governance in Bangladesh. It callously ignored the plight of millions of Bangladeshi citizens whose right to work and a decent life were thwarted at home and who voted with their feet, thereby exposing the multiple ways in which the economic, political and social system in Bangladesh had failed them. The Bangladeshi narrative of denial did not even blame the victims: it annihilated them. It stripped migrants to India of their Bangladeshi citizenship because they were in a national space where the Bangladesh state elite found it inconvenient to acknowledge them. By turning the Bangladeshi diaspora into a numbers game, and by variously criminalizing and disowning individual migrants, politicians in both countries gambled with the futures of millions of Bangladeshis living, by force or by choice, beyond the territory of their state.

The Bangladeshi diaspora must be one of the larger in the world, and all evidence points to its likely continuation and expansion. It may also be among the least understood diasporas in the world: little studied and, if studied at all, then from the perspectives of the states that are themselves players in cross-border migration.[143] More analysis should take place at the level of the living strategies of individual people fleeing environmental degradation, intense economic exploitation, political harassment, stifling family and gender relations, or a future that they fear holds no promise. Their simultaneous contributions to several economies, including that of Bangladesh, need to be made visible, as do the patterns of circular migration in which many of them are involved.

To this end, the scale of study must shift from the territorial state to the networks that support and sustain international migration. The borderland presents itself as an excellent scale to explore because transnational flows of people are continually reconstituting the borderland as a distinct social space, and thereby reveal the limitations and ambiguities of state territoriality. Here a partially barricaded border coexists with a borderless economy.[144] The involvement of many borderlanders in facilitating unauthorized migration constitutes a serious challenge to the state's authority and capacity to divide borderlanders into territorially defined 'citizens' and 'foreigners', and to confine their lives spatially.

The movement of people across the border is the object of continual regulation and evasion, both in terms of actual policing and in terms of identities. It is in this context that a slogan like 'Bonafide Citizens Should Not Shelter Foreigners' (Plate 8.1) makes sense. Here we hear a state addressing borderlanders in the voice of territoriality. The slogan is a weapon in a never-ending state campaign for control of the hearts and minds of borderlanders whose economic and social interests may pull them in another direction.

In the case of cross-border migration, the preferred strategy in the borderland was – and remains – the evasion of state surveillance through avoidance, concealment, collusion or dissimulation. But the borderland is also a site of open rebellion, of violent confrontations between borderlanders and agents of the state. The following chapter analyses these confrontations.

Notes

1 For an overview of these patterns in the centuries preceding British conquest, see Richard M Eaton, *The Rise of Islam and the Bengal Frontier, 1204–1760* (Berkeley: University of California Press, 1993).

2 Sajal Nag, *Roots of Ethnic Conflict: Nationality Question in North-East India* (Delhi: Manohar, 1990); M Kar, *Muslims in Assam Politics* (New Delhi: Vikas Publishing House, 1997).

3 See Willem van Schendel and Aminul Haque Faraizi, *Rural Labourers in Bengal, 1880 to 1980* (Rotterdam: Comparative Asian Studies Programme, Erasmus University Rotterdam, 1984), 48–57; Willem van Schendel, 'Self-Rescue and Survival: The Rural Poor in Bangladesh,' *South Asia*, 9:1 (1986), 41–59.

4 Passports and visas were introduced in 1952.

5 In 1991 a question was put before the West Bengal Assembly whether the Bharatiya Janata Party (BJP)'s campaign plank of a large-scale influx of Muslims had any factual basis. In his response, the Chief Minister of West Bengal presented figures to show that of the 39,000 persons caught trying to enter India in the first half of 1991, 28,000 were Muslims. 'Basu opposes ration cards for infiltrators', *The Statesman* (2 August 1991).

6 Sujata Ramachandran, 'Of Boundaries and Border Crossings: Undocumented Bangladeshi "Infiltrators" and the Hegemony of Hindu Nationalism in India', *Interventions*, 1:2 (1999), 248. BJP = Bharatiya Janata Party, the principal political party propagating Hindutva.

7 At the border, according to Indian border guards, unauthorized Bangladeshi Hindu migrants were 'apprehended with less vigour' than Bangladeshi Muslim migrants, and local-level 'apprehension figures' showed more Muslims than Hindus being caught. Ranabir Samaddar, *The Marginal Nation: Transborder Migration from Bangladesh to West Bengal* (New Delhi, etc.: Sage Publications, 1999), 101, 125–6.

8 Sanjoy Hazarika, *Rites of Passage: Border Crossings, Imagined Homelands, India's East and Bangladesh* (New Delhi: Penguin Books, 2000), 140–1.

9 Bangladeshi migrants were increasingly described as environmental and developmental refugees. See Ashok Swain, *The Environmental Trap: The Ganges River Diversion, Bangladeshi Migration and Conflicts in India* (Uppsala: Uppsala University, Department of Peace and Conflict Research, 1996). For an overview of official documents relating to unauthorized border crossing, see Avtar Singh Bhasin (ed.), *India-Bangladesh Relations: Documents – 1971–2002* (New Delhi: Geetika Publishers, 2003), Volume V, 2385–668.

10 These massacres left more than 3,000 dead and over 400,000 homeless. Mohan Ram, 'Eyeball to eyeball: The issues that triggered the massacres in Assam State in February remain unresolved, and both sides are standing firm', *Far Eastern Economic Review*, 120:20 (19 May 1983), 29. Cf. Kar, *Muslims in Assam Politics*.

11 Arup Chanda, 'Basu asks Hasina to curb infiltration,' *Rediff on the Net* (29 January 1999). By 2003, the Chief Minister of West Bengal expressed his view of migration from Bangladesh as follows: 'On the question of dealing with illegal infiltrators from Bangladesh, our state government is in agreement with the Government of India that whenever such infiltration is detected, the foreign nationals should be pushed back.' 'Buddha speaks in Delhi's voice', *The Telegraph* (9 February 2003).

12 Population densities in Bangladesh, already high at Partition, rose from about 300 per km^2 in 1951 to about 900 per km^2 in 2001. More frequently than is often realized, Indian Muslims enter Bangladesh in search of work or safety. Two families from Murshidabad (India) were found to have lived with relatives in Kushtia and earning their living from operating rickshaw-vans (carts) for over three years before police deported them. In May 2002 a group of several hundred Muslims sought refuge in Bangladesh. They said they had left Bangladesh 30 years previously and had settled in the town of Ahmedabad in the Indian state of Gujarat. Anti-Muslim rioters in Ahmedabad killed members of their families and set their houses on fire. In desperation, they saw no other option but to seek security in Bangladesh. Some of them were helped across the border by both Indian and Bangladeshi border guards. Others, however, were maltreated by Indian border guards, or sent back by Bangladeshi border guards. Alamgir Hossain, 'BDR pushes back Indian families', *The Telegraph* (26 February 2003); 'Gujarat rioters: 70 Muslims reach Satkhira for safety,' *The New Nation* (6 May 2002); 'BDR foils BSF's bid to push in Indian Muslims', *The New Nation* (8 May 2002); '300 Muslims from Gujarat cross over to Bangladesh', *The New Nation* (9 May 2002); '200 Indian Muslims flee to Bangladesh: Officials', *The Times of India* (18 May 2002).

13 For example in Hili, a border crossing in Dinajpur/West Dinajpur, a fence put up by Pakistan in 1955 'with a view to preventing the free movement of smugglers, both Indian and Pakistani' elicited a protest from India (CR 1B2-13/55 (12-55)).

14 The first suggestion of a 'complete sealing' of the border appeared in 1964. In the same year, the Government of India decided to prevent infiltration by putting up 'barbed wire fencing ... in selected areas'. Kar, *Muslims in Assam Politics*, 136, 142.

15 In the 1960s, Assamese politicians were not able to push Delhi beyond sanctioning 180 additional police watch-posts on the Assam-East Pakistan border and erecting barbed-wire fences in selected places. Another suggestion at that time was 'to clear a stretch of territory all along the border between Assam and East Pakistan so that the security forces of the State and the Centre might gain the mobility needed to prevent fresh infiltrations.' In 1964, the Government of India formulated a Four-Point Plan that included clearing a half-mile belt along the border in the Assam sector and constructing 300 miles of border road 'to facilitate movement of Security Forces.' The plan was not implemented. In the 1990s, the Indian government went so far as to float

a plan to settle 'the families of ex-servicemen and retired Indian soldiers' as a 10-km wide human belt along the borders; this plan was torpedoed by several border states. Dinesh Chandra Jha, *Indo-Pakistan Relations (1960–65)* (Patna: Bharati Bhawan, 1972), 280, 283; cf. 'Evacuation of border people, Union Plan makes little progress,' *The Statesman* (14 April 1965); Kar, *Muslims in Assam Politics*, 136, 141–2; Sanat K Chakraborty, 'Human belt to control cross-border migration,' *The Northeast Daily* (23 November 1999).

16 By means of the Assam Accord between the Indian government and the leaders of the Assam movement.

17 This project, budgeted at Rs.3.7 billion in 1986 (revised to Rs.8.3 billion in 1992 and Rs.10.5 billion in 1998), involved the construction of 900 km of border fence, 2,800 km of border roads and 24 km of bridges along the India-Bangladesh border in the states of West Bengal, Assam, Meghalaya, Tripura and Mizoram. Twelve years later, according to government sources, 800 km of fence, 2,100 km of roads and 17 km of bridges had been completed, and the project was supposed to be completed by March 2001 (Bangladeshi sources reported that only 541 km had been fenced). In mid-1999, the government gave a new date of completion, 2007. In 2001, the Director-General of the Border Road Organisation calculated that 1 km of border fence cost Rs. 2,2 million and 1 km of border road Rs. 4,5 million, and a high BSF official admitted that 'at least 80 percent of the 4,000-km land border is unfenced.' The same year the Indian External Affairs Minister told Parliament that 854 km along the India-Bangladesh border had been fenced, and the entire border would be fenced in 2006–7. There are many press reports of lack of progress and embezzlement of funds for border roads and fences. Nevertheless, in the wake of border conflicts with Bangladesh, the Indian government tripled its budget for the border in 2003. It allocated funds for border fencing and roads, and their maintenance, but also for boats and even reconnaissance aircraft for the BSF. Embassy of India (Washington DC), *Union Home Secretary chairs a high level empowered committee* (http://www.indianembassy.org/, 1998); 'Border incidents: BDR, BSF to hold meeting from Oct 24', *The Daily Star* (12 October 1999); 'Centre to complete border fencing by 2007', *The Assam Tribune* (20 August 1999); 'Fencing along Indo-Bangla border begins', *The Times of India* (10 August 2001); 'Phase I of Rs. 1,335-cr Indo-B'desh border fence to begin soon: Shenoy', *The Sentinel* (19 October 2001); 'BSF flotillas soon to patrol riverine border with Bangla', *The Sentinel* (1 December 2001); 'Indo-Bangla border: Fencing to be complete by 2007: Jaswant', *The Assam Tribune* (20 December 2001); 'Cong MLA makes mockery of border road construction in Badarpur', *The Sentinel* (19 March 2002); Pallab Bhattacharya, 'Delhi triples budget for border with Bangladesh: Rs.80 crore allocated for barbed wire fencing', *The Daily Star* (2 March 2003).

18 Udayan Namboodiri, 'Illegal Immigrants: Political Pawns', *India Today* (10 August 1998). In 1997 the Home Minister of Tripura said: 'There were repeated communications between the Centre and the State over the question of fencing the border with Bangladesh. In 1995–6, a stretch of 490 km was considered for fencing. This was duly communicated to us. But till date the budgetary provisions have not been cleared by the Centre.' Rakesh Sinha, 'Strife-worn Tripura banking on Gujral Government to come to its rescue', *The Indian Express* (19 May 1997). As for Mizoram, as late as 1999 the fencing of its border with Bangladesh was still no more than 'under active consideration by the Home Ministry', according to the Prime Minister of India. 'Plan to stop influx in NE soon: PM', *The Assam Tribune* (23 May 1999).

19 Photograph from *The Tribune*. 'Border tension eases as migrants return: Yaswant Sinha invites B'desh Foreign Minister', *The Tribune* (7 February 2003).

20 President Ershad, quoted in Partha S Ghosh, *Cooperation and Conflict in South Asia* (Delhi: Manohar, 1995), 85. Some Bangladeshi soldiers were killed and injured when they attempted to dismantle a fence that Indians were erecting along the border in Assam. Salamat Ali, 'Trouble flares up on Bangladesh border', *Far Eastern Economic Review*, 124:18 (3 May 1984), 12. Cf. Bhasin (ed.), *India-Bangladesh Relations*, IV, 1954–2028, 2071–2.

21 From Taslima Nasreen's poem 'Broken Bengal', published in the selection *Behula Eka Bhashiyechhilo Bhela* (1993), quoted in 'Porous Borders, Divided Selves: A Symposium on Partitions in the East', *Seminar*, no. 510 (February 2002), 38.

22 The Ground Rules of 1959 stipulate the following: 'After an identifiable boundary line whether real or working has been demarcated, neither side will have any permanent or temporary border security forces or any other armed personnel within 150 yards on either side of this line. Also no permanent posts will be constructed till the final demarcation has been done ... If defensive works of any nature including trenches exist in the stretch of 300 yards (150 yards on each side of the working boundary) they must be destroyed or filled up.' *Ground Rules Formulated by the Military Sub-Committee of the Indian and Pakistan Delegations* (20 October 1959), reprinted in Bhasin (ed.), *India-Bangladesh Relations*, V, 2738. The Ground Rules were confirmed in the *Joint India-Bangladesh Agreement for Border Authorities of the Two Countries, 1975*, reprinted in Bhasin (ed.), *India-Bangladesh Relations*, IV, 1902–7. It is usually Bangladesh that brings up the inviolability of the agreement (see for example 'Agreed Minutes of the 4th Meeting of the Indo-Bangladesh Joint Working Group (JWG), Dhaka, October 20, 1997,' in Bhasin (ed.), *India-Bangladesh Relations*, I, 446, or 'BDR, BSF flag meet', *The New Nation* (16 August 2003)) but India occasionally uses the argument as well, e.g. in the case of Bangladesh constructing (or repairing) an embankment on the border at Satkhira. 'BDR-BSF meet ends without decision', *The New Nation* (28 February 2002).

23 'Bengal to take up border fencing', *Rediff on the Net* (5 January 1999); cf. Nirmalya Banerjee, 'Negotiations on border fencing', *The Times of India* (4 November 2002). The harmful effects of the fence on West Bengal border villagers were also brought up in the Indian parliament in 1996. *XI Lok Sabha Debates, Session II, (Budget Session) 18 July 1996/Asadha 27, 1918 (Saka)*. On the India-Pakistan border, where 450 km were fenced, 380 fencing gates were made, of which 280 were operational in the late 1990s. To facilitate farming in the no man's land, a Border Security Force (BSF) spokesman explained, these gates would be opened one hour after sunrise and closed at 6 p.m. 'No cause for alarm over Indo-Pak border fencing gaps: BSF', *Rediff on the Net* (7 March 1998). For a similar arrangement at the fenced stretch of border at Dhubri (Assam), see 'Breaching the frontiers effortlessly', *The Hindu* (15 April 1998). Villages in 24-Parganas, West Bengal, challenged the building of the fence in the Calcutta High Court, and this 'ordered the local authorities to find a solution'. Tapash Ganguly, 'Caught in the Middle', *The Week (Kottayam)* (19 September 1999). Groups of cattle smugglers were also reported to try to disrupt the construction of the fence, attacking BSF personnel in Malda with sophisticated weapons. 'Cattle smugglers attack BSF', *The Statesman* (27 June 2000).

24 'South Bengal Frontier to strengthen border surveillance', *The Times of India* (5 December 1999); cf. 'Border farmers' woes', *The Times of India* (5 March 2002). For border villagers in Malda district protesting and demonstrating against the fence, halting

its construction, see 'India restarts fencing border with Bangladesh', *The Times of India* (10 November 2001). For residents of four border villages in Nadia (West Bengal) asking for an injunction restraining the Border Security Force from putting up a barbed wire border fence, see 'BSF asked to show cause in border fencing case', *The Statesman* (13 July 2002). In 2002 a West Bengal government circular ordered district authorities to evacuate and relocate residents living within 150 yards of the Indo-Bangladesh border 'for security reasons'. This called forth a demonstration in Jalpaiguri. Some months later, the authorities of Jalpaiguri district announced that they had surveyed the population living in the 'restricted area ... within 150 yards from the zero point' that would be outside the fence. They counted 3,543 Jalpaiguri residents (holding 2,220 acres) who would have to be removed if the circular was implemented. According to the Inspector-General of the BSF in the North Bengal Sector (Kishanganj, Siliguri and Cooch Behar), 169 villages in his sector should be relocated 'to reduce the problems of the people of these villages and also of the forces manning the border'. Avijit Sinha, 'Meet to break border blocks', *The Telegraph* (9 November 2002); 'Border survey complete', *The Telegraph* (31 January 2003); R Dutta Choudhury, 'Ethnic affinity, lack of fencing encouraging Bangla influx', *The Assam Tribune* (16 June 2003). For border villagers in Darjeeling district protesting BSF orders to clear out of a zone of 300 metres from the border without being offered any resettlement, see Probir Pramanik, 'Faulty border works failing to curb influx', *The Telegraph* (4 September 2003).

25 Maseeh Rahman, 'Separated at Birth', *Time* (11 August 1997). For an impression of the fate of villagers who refused to leave their village and were cut off from the rest of the Indian territory in North Dinajpur district when the border fence came up, and co-villagers who did move but were cheated out of their rehabilitation money, see Kousik Sen, 'Fenced-in orphans, citizens in poll time', *The Telegraph* (11 February 2003).

26 These Indian citizens, who lived in Bangladesh, were reported to vote for the Hogolberia gram panchayat (Karimpur I Block, Nadia) in India. 'BDR asks Indians to quit', *The Times of India* (23 August 2001). For earlier border trouble at Char Meghna, see CR 1B2-57/54 (9-54).

27 On the deplorable state of border fences in different parts of Assam, see for example 'AASU for anti-influx monitoring body', *The Assam Tribune* (3 March 2002); cf. 'Indo-Bangladesh border: Fencing should be at par with western border: Governors', *The Assam Tribune* (12 October 2002). On a border bridge without approach roads at Gheomari near Dhubri, see R Dutta Chowdhury, 'Faulty border works failing to curb influx', *The Assam Tribune* (4 September 2003).

28 'Dispur alarm over gaping holes in border fence', *The Telegraph* (23 August 2003).

29 Two years later, Indian border-guards were planning to start with 'five small vessels [that] would support a "mother boat" stationed in the middle of the [Brahmaputra] river with troopers equipped with hi-tech equipment.' And by 2003, Mazagaon Docks Ltd. in Mumbai had built three floating border outposts (each capable of carrying four patrol boats and 50 men) out of a planned total of 14 to be deployed in border rivers in Assam, West Bengal and Gujarat. Four of these were expected to be used in Assam. 'BSF flotillas soon to patrol riverine border with Bangla', *The Sentinel* (1 December 2001); R Dutta Choudhury, 'Floating border outposts to check influx', *The Assam Tribune* (7 February 2003); 'Floating BOPs in Assam, Gujarat, WB rivers', *The Sentinel* (8 February 2003).

30 Maseeh Rahman, 'Separated at Birth', *Time* (11 August 1997). Cf. Nirmalya Banerjee, 'Stop influx from Bangladesh, says Assam governor', *Times of India* (10 January 1999).

31 *Asiaweek* (17 July 1998).

32 Occasionally, border guards would report the arrival of new gadgets. In mid-2001, the top officer of the Indian Border Security Force in Assam told reporters that his personnel was being provided with 'new gizmos, like night vision devices, trip flares and faster motor boats', but a sustained escalation of border interdiction by technological means did not result. 'BSF reborn with vigour', *The Sentinel* (2 August 2001); cf. Nirmalya Banerjee, 'BSF to seek help of US firm to check infiltration', *The Times of India* (9 February 2002); Anantha Krishnan M, 'Scientists develop radar to check infiltration', *The Times of India* (4 July 2002); 'Governor for high-tech vigil', *The Telegraph* (13 July 2003).

33 The importance of border fencing was re-emphasized in the report by the Group of Ministers published in 2001. Although they warned that 'border fencing is not the panacaea for all the problems afflicting efficient and effective management of the border', they recommended to 'convert all single fence into double fence with concertina coils', to have parallel jeepable roads and floodlighting in all fenced border areas, and to be strict concerning people living in the fenced-off areas: 'Habitation/cultivation should not be allowed, in the area between the fence and the border, and this area should be kept sanitised. This would involve relocation of families/villages.' Government of India, *Reforming the National Security System - Recommendations of the Group of Ministers* (New Delhi: Ministry of Defence, 2001), 83–4. Apart from the ethical aspects of such draconian 'sanitizing', it is in fact very hard to achieve. For an enlightening description of the German Democratic Republic's enormous exertions to establish a 'sanitized borderland' between 1952 and 1989, see Daphne Berdahl, *Where the World Ended: Re-Unification and Identity in the German Borderland* (Berkeley, etc.: University of California Press, 1999).

34 The rapid escalation of border policing on the US-Mexico border in the 1990s resulted not in deterring undocumented immigration (of Latin Americans and Asians) but merely in making it less visible to US citizens. Migrants no longer entered via the suburbs of San Diego and El Paso but now crossed the border in sparsely populated mountainous and desert sections. Peter Andreas, *Border Games: Policing the U.S.-Mexico Divide* (Ithaca and London: Cornell University Press, 2000; Joseph Nevins, *Operation Gatekeeper: The Rise of the 'Illegal Alien' and the Making of the U.S.-Mexico Boundary* (New York and London: Routledge, 2002). For a general view of fencing as a political tool, see Olivier Razac, *Barbed Wire: A Political History* (New York: The New Press, 2002).

35 Stoddard first identified the 'implicit code' of the US border control agencies whose public task to halt unauthorized immigration was complicated by 'verbal restraints from upstairs': lobbies of agribusiness employers, in particular, made sure that unauthorized immigrants received 'adequate warning and means of concealment' whenever the border patrol launched an anti-immigration campaign. ER Stoddard, 'Illegal Mexican Labor in the Borderlands: Institutionalized Support of an Unlawful Practice', *Pacific Sociological Review*, 19:2 (1976), 175–210. Cf. Michael Kearney, 'Transnationalism in California and Mexico at the End of Empire', in: Thomas M Wilson and Hastings Donnan (eds.), *Border Identities: Nation and State at International Frontiers* (Cambridge: Cambridge University Press, 1998), 117–41; Andreas, *Border Games*. As an observer on the Bangladesh-India border at Benapol remarked: 'This business of illegal crossing has been going on forever and will continue. There is express lack of will on part of the authorities on both sides to check the phenomenon.' Syed Mehdi Momin, 'Illegal border crossing – Benapole style', *The Independent* (7 September 2003).

36 BG Verghese, *India's Northeast Resurgent: Ethnicity, Insurgency, Governance, Development* (Delhi: Konark, 1996), 203. In 1999, 16 Indian villages in Karimganj district of Assam were cut off from the rest of India by the border fence. In 2003 inhabitants of a part of the border town of Karimganj were told that the new border fence would separate them from the rest of the town (and India). In protest they presented the district Deputy Commissioner with a memorandum stating that they would have to live under the control of the Bangladesh Rifles which would be troublesome and disgusting. 'Bangladeshis cut open border fence to sneak into Assam', *The Sentinel* (21 May 2000); cf. 'Indo-Bangla border in Karimganj only in name', *Assam Tribune* (31 August 1999); 'BJP: AASU, Ministers made 10-minute border trip', *The Sentinel* (6 March 2002); R Dutta Choudhury, 'Dhubri border farmers live in India, till in Bangla', *The Assam Tribune* (17 April 2000); 'Karimganj residents fear of being outside a fence', *The Sentinel* (26 May 2003).

37 'Lapang to focus on border plan – Roads on priority list', *The Telegraph* (25 April 2003).

38 'Good border roads must to boost economy: Meghalaya CM', *The Assam Tribune* (10 May 2003).

39 R Dutta Choudhury, 'Plight of Indians who remained on the other side of border fencing', *The Assam Tribune* (2 December 2002).

40 Photograph by Shib Shankar Chatterjee (A C Dasgupta Road, Ward Number - II, Dhubri, Assam-783 301, India).

41 Photograph by Shib Shankar Chatterjee (A C Dasgupta Road, Ward Number - II, Dhubri, Assam-783 301, India).

42 Nirmalya Banerjee, 'Fencing problem plagues border', *The Times of India* (16 April 2002). Cf. Main Uddin Chisti, 'Fence bruises border villages', *The Telegraph* (3 June 2003).

43 'Indo-Bangla border in Karimganj only in name', *The Assam Tribune* (31 August 1999); 'Bangladeshis cut open border fence to sneak into Assam', *The Sentinel* (21 May 2000).

44 From Tapash Ganguly, 'Caught in the Middle', *The Week (Kottayam)* (19 September 1999).

45 See Samaddar, *The Marginal Nation*, 199–214; Bijoy Sankar Bora, 'Forest crimes in Laokhowa sanctuary: Illegal Bangladeshi nexus unearthed', *The Assam Tribune* (13 April 2002). According to figures collected by the Indian Border Security Force, the number of Bangladeshis entering India legally through six check posts in southern Bengal (Ghojadanga, Petrapole, Gede, Lalgola, Mohanpur and Hili) in 2000 was 405,000; the number leaving India that year was 375,000. Nirmalya Banerjee, 'Bangla spies killed along border', *The Times of India* (15 April 2002).

46 Verghese, *India's Northeast Resurgent*, 39. This was also the cut-off point enshrined in the Illegal Migrants (Determination by Tribunals) Act of 1983. Under this act the government of India agreed to detect and deport foreign nationals who entered Assam after that date (Prafulla Kumar Mahanta, *The Tussle between the Citizens and Foreigners in Assam* (Delhi: Vikas, 1986), 109). In 2000, however, an accord between the government in Delhi, the state government of Assam, and the major political party pushed that date back to 1951, causing a storm of protest and further confusion ('1951 to be cut-off year for indigenous peoples: AASU', *The Sentinel* (12 April 2000); 'Indigenous definition sparks row in Assam', *The Northeast Daily* (17 April 2000); 'Definition of indigenous people in '51 census report', *The Assam Tribune* (3 May 2000)). For a brief overview of immigration legislation, see 'Assam's problem of foreign infiltration', *Oriental Times*, 2:9-10 (7–21 July 1999).

47 This is well documented for West Bengal but less so for Assam. In 1965 a worried Government of India stated that 'on Assam's border, there is a large number of Muslims, many of whom give shelter to the infiltrants and regard them as old migrants.' Kar, *Muslims in Assam Politics*, 142.

48 According to UNICEF and other statistics, quoted in Georzina Moutusi Sorker, 'Registration of child birth', *The New Nation* (19 September 2002).

49 For example, Habibur Rahman, a Bangladeshi arrested for a robbery in Calcutta, produced a certificate from Abdur Razzak Mollah, West Bengal's Minister of Land and Land Reforms, attesting that Habibur Rahman was an Indian national, a permanent resident of Canning police station of South 24-Parganas district (West Bengal), and of 'good moral character'. Pronab Mondal, 'Minister "clean chit" for arrested Bangla robber', *The Telegraph* (2 September 2003).

50 For examples, see Samaddar, *The Marginal Nation*, 101–4, 119; 'Passport arrests blow lid off police-tout nexus', *The Telegraph* (2 March 2002). There was also a category of borderlanders who were genuinely unclear about their 'national' identity. In numerous villages 'the international border cuts right through the homes of villagers, putting them into a dilemma regarding their nationality.' 'Indo-Bangla border in Karimganj only in name', *The Assam Tribune* (31 August 1999).

51 Report of the Border Management Task Force, prepared by former Home Secretary Madhav Godbole, April 2000. This report was not made public but it was quoted in a speech by the former Director-General of the Border Security Force, Prakash Singh. 'Reinforcement of BSF in NE mooted', *The Sentinel* (10 October 2002).

52 In 2001, the Government of India reported on illegal immigration: 'Today, we have about 15 million Bangladeshis, 2.2 million Nepalis, 70,000 Sri Lankan Tamils and about one lakh [100,000] Tibetan migrants living in India ... There is an all-round failure in India to come to grips with the problem of illegal immigration.' India, *Reforming*, 60. In other publications, the number of Bangladeshis illegally living in India is variously estimated to be between 12 and 18 million. 'Centre, 5 states to file affidavits on immigrants', *The Assam Tribune* (13 July 1999); 'Problem of infiltration worse in Bengal: Joshi', *Hindustan Times* (2 August 1998); Udayan Namboodiri, 'Illegal Immigrants: Political Pawns,' *India Today* (10 August 1998); '1.5 crore Bangla aliens in country', *The Assam Tribune* (12 May 2000).

53 In 2001 Surendra Jain, the chief of the Bajrang Dal (a radical group who refer to themselves as the Warriors of the Hindutva Revolution), taunted the Indian Prime Minister for weakness against Bangladesh and demanded deportation of 'over 20 million' illegal Bangladeshi migrants. In January 2003 the Indian government announced its resolve to 'detect and deport [Bangladeshis illegally staying in India] as they posed a serious threat to national security'. A 'special drive' was announced, and the Indian Home Ministry estimated the number of illegal Bangladeshi immigrants in India at 20 million, 'out of which over 10 million are in Assam and Bengal alone'. The Bangladesh Foreign Ministry retorted: 'The claim regarding illegal stay of 20 million Bangladeshis in India is not only unfortunate, but also baseless and absurd.' By the time the Indian government's estimate had risen to 20 million, however, Hindu fundamentalists had already readjusted their estimates upward to 27.5 million. 'Sangh flays govt's "soft" stance on Bangladesh', *Rediff on the Net* (23 April 2001); 'States agree to identity cards – Drive to flush out illegal immigrants', *The Telegraph* (8 January 2003); http://www.hinduunity.org/bajrangdal.html; 'No illegal Bangladeshis anywhere in India', *The Independent* (9 January 2003); 'Attack Bangladesh: Togadia', *The Times of India* (29

January 2003).

54 According to calculations by the US Immigration and Naturalization Service (INS), 5 million illegal immigrants were residing in the USA in 1997, of whom 2.7 million were from Mexico. Andreas, *Border Games*, 4n.

55 'Centre may repeal Migrants Act', *Indian Express* (12 August 1997); 'Proposed amendment of Foreigners Act: Advani seeks in-depth study by Law panel', *The Hindustan Times* (7 January 1999); Utpal Bordoloi, 'Cabinet to consider repeal of Illegal Migrants Act soon', *Deccan Herald* (17 January 1999).

56 Anindita Dasgupta, 'Thinking with the head: Foreign nationals in Assam', *The Daily Star* (6 May 1999); cf. '1,501 aliens deported in last 16 years', *The Sentinel* (6 October 2002). For the chaotic style of record keeping and the process of implementation, see Hazarika, *Rites of Passage*, 131–6. According to an Assamese MP, however, between 1996 and 1999 about 250,000 Bengalis and Nepalis were singled out as foreign nationals under the Act. The Assam government sought court permission for their deportation but the courts identified only 4,000 of them as foreigners. According to the governor of Assam, 9,600 persons had been identified as foreigners since 1983. 'Move to annul IMDT Act: Fresh Plot to deport Bengalees from Assam', *The New Nation* (25 February 1999); Samudra Gupta Kashyap, 'Diminishing Assam Border? Governor Writes to President', *Indian Express* (17 December 1998); cf. R Dutta Choudhury, 'BSF, Border Police put on high alert along Assam-Bangla border', *The Assam Tribune* (5 February 2003).

57 'IM(DT) repeal Bill in next session', *The Assam Tribune* (9 May 2003).

58 Aloke Banerjee, 'Where two nations slip into each other', *The Statesman* (29 May 1993); cf. Souvik Chowdhury, 'Meghalaya-Bangladesh border: The dangers of mixed loyalties', *Tehelka* (26 February 2001).

59 As early as 1964, the Indian Home Minister proposed issuing identity cards to all inhabitants of the border areas of Assam. Jha, *Indo-Pakistan Relations*, 280; cf. Kar, *Muslims in Assam Politics*, 135–44; George Iype, 'To weed out illegal immigrants, government plans to issue I-cards for Indians and foreign nationals', *Rediff on the Net* (13 June 1997). For the failure of a similar identity card project started in 1989 on the Pakistan border, see Mihir Mistry, 'Thin dividing line raises identity issues', *Times of India* (19 June 1999). For a new plan to introduce 'multi-purpose national identity cards … initially in the border districts or may be in a 20 Kms border belt and extended to the hinterland progressively', see India, *Reforming*, 85. In early 2002, West Bengal was considering implementing this project, albeit for residents living within 30 km of the Bangladesh border; see Satrajit Moitra, 'Residential permits for Indo-Bangla border areas', *The Times of India* (10 January 2002). Another plan involved providing borderland cattle with laminated identity cards; see 'Now, I-cards for cows along the border', *The Times of India* (5 November 2001). In 2003, a 'pilot project' of multi-purpose photo-identity cards was launched in 13 states of India, including Assam, Mizoram and Tripura, and West Bengal authorities began distributing photo-identity cards to border villagers in South 24-Parganas. 'Gogoi calls for issue of photo I-cards', *The Assam Tribune* (9 February 2003); Soumen Bhattacharjee, 'I-cards for border residents roll out', *The Telegraph* (11 February 2003); 'Camp for border ID cards', *The Sentinel* (10 June 2003); 'Zoramthanga allays fear on photo I-cards', *The Telegraph* (23 July 2003); 'Indians on border to get identity cards', *The Times of India* (30 August 2003).

60 'Breaching the frontiers effortlessly', *The Hindu* (15 April 1998); cf. Anil Maheshwari, 'The face behind the mask,' *Sunday* (15 August 1998). Another technique, allegedly

practised in Karimganj district (Assam), was for Bangladeshi women to cross the border and give birth in India, thereby automatically conferring Indian citizenship on their babies. 'Citizenship by labour!', *The Sentinel* (5 April 1997).

61 Anil Maheshwari, 'The face behind the mask', *Sunday* (15 August 1998).

62 This was not helped when a new crime emerged in the West Bengal border district of Nadia in 2003: looting of birth and death certificates from municipalities and schools. 'Bangla influx: CM talks tough', *The Times of India* (11 July 2003).

63 See for example the description of Nabinnagar village, straddling the Nadia/ Kushtia border, in Aloke Banerjee, 'Where two nations slip into each other', *The Statesman* (29 May 1993).

64 Chandan Nandy, 'Voter passport for infiltrators', *The Telegraph* (30 August 1999).

65 In early 1964, 'special officers with a judicial background were appointed to scrutinize cases of Pakistani infiltrators' and later that year statutory tribunals were introduced under the Foreigners' (Tribunals) Order 1964. Employing a term from the anti-colonial movement, the Indian authorities referred to the orders they served on suspected infiltrators as *Quit India* notices. 'Assam Expels More Than Half of 220,000 Infiltrators', *The Statesman* (28 July 1965); cf. Kar, *Muslims in Assam Politics*, 135–48.

66 Udayan Namboodiri, 'Illegal Immigrants: Political Pawns', *India Today* (10 August 1998); Anindita Ramaswamy, 'BJP's Oust Bangladeshi Drive Hots Up', *Indian Express* (16 September 1998); 'Joshi to deport Bangladeshis from Mumbai', *The Daily Star* (13 October 1997). West Bengal Chief Minister Jyoti Basu stated that illegal settlers from across the border were 'a major headache for many Indian cities'. Arup Chanda, 'Basu asks Hasina to curb infiltration', *Rediff on the Net* (29 January 1999). The same discourse of crime and subversion is employed for Bangladeshi migrants in Pakistani cities. 'Syed Mohammad Kazmi – Chairman, Pakistan Small Chamber of Commerce and Industry's (PSCCI) Law & Order Committee (Karachi Division) and a member of the Human Rights Committee Pakistan – believes the illegal immigrants from Bangladesh are responsible for the decaying Karachi situation ... About the Bangladeshis crossing the border illegally through land routes Kazmi said there were reports that when these people reached the border Indian security forces, instead of arresting them, detained the men folk and let the women and children cross the border. These people were imparted training in carrying out terrorist activities and then pushed into Pakistan. Moreover, the slums of illegal Bangladeshis along the coastal areas were extended protection by the smugglers for carrying out their illegal activities, Kazmi said. According to him Ilyas Goth, Ali Akbar Shah Goth, Chashma Goth and Ali Barohi Goth in Landhi were notorious Bengali colonies ... And when these people land into Pakistan [the Bangladesh] embassy does not own them.' Rubina Jabbar, 'The Spectre of Illegal Immigration', *The News International* (Karachi) (11 September 2000).

67 On the concept of illegal deportation and detailed witness accounts, see Nivedita Rao et al., *Deportations of Bengali-Speaking Muslims from Mumbai: A Fact-Finding Report Produced by a Joint Team from CPDR, EKTA and WRAG* (Mumbai, 1998 – also available at http://www.mnet.fr/aiindex/i_csss/deport.html).

68 Udayan Namboodiri, 'Illegal Immigrants: Political Pawns', *India Today* (10 August 1998). For an overview of living conditions and migrant identities in this Delhi neighbourhood in the 1990s, see Sharat G Lin and Madan C Paul, 'Bangladeshi Migrants in Delhi: Social Insecurity, State Power, and Captive Vote Banks', *Bulletin of Concerned Asian Scholars*, 27 :1 (1995), 3–27.

69 'Bengalipura reels under fear of midnight knock', *Hindustan Times* (30 July 1998). Other

women who were deported later accused Indian border guards of repeatedly raping them. E.g. 'Two women brought for push-in "raped" by BSF members', *The Daily Star* (23 June 2003).   •

70 Deportations from Indian Punjab took the same form: chained detainees, guarded by Punjab policemen, were taken by train to the Bangladesh border without informing the West Bengal authorities. Anil Maheshwari, 'The face behind the mask', *Sunday* (15 August 1998); Avijit Nandi Majumdar and Pronab Mondal, 'Punjab in sneak Bangla pushback', *The Telegraph* (18 January 2000).

71 See chapter 8.

72 Noori was interviewed by Sujata Ramachandran in Delhi in 1998. Ramachandran, 'Of Boundaries and Border Crossings', 249.

73 According to West Bengal's Home Minister. 'Bengal to take up border fencing', *Rediff on the Net* (5 January 1999); 'Beyond the courtesies', *The New Nation* (26 November 1998).

74 'Dhaka not cooperating on deportation issue', *Hindustan Times* (18 October 1999).

75 At the same time the All-Assam Students' Union demanded that people living in the no-man's land be 'cleared' and relocated, that Indian border guards be authorized to shoot on sight anyone found in the no-man's land, and that patriotic Assamese youths be recruited into a 'second line of border forces'. In Meghalaya 'infiltration check posts' were created where policemen were stationed 'to identify infiltrators'. Three years after PIF was initiated, it had not made great strides: in 2001 only 8 posts had been established in Assam and 20 others had been 'identified'. Nevertheless, in the same year the Indian government floated a plan to rekindle the Prevention of Infiltration from Pakistan Scheme (PIF), introduced in 1962 to deal with immigration from East Pakistan, now named the Prevention of Infiltration by Foreigners Scheme (also: PIF). 'Centre to complete border fencing by 2007', *The Assam Tribune* (20 August 1999); 'Mizoram for infiltration prevention force', *The Assam Tribune* (5 July 1999); 'AASU for strict surveillance along border', *The Telegraph* (26 August 1999); 'Border fencing work not satisfactory: AASU', *The Assam Tribune* (26 August 1999); 'Centre tells State Govt: Strengthen second line of defence along border', *The Assam Tribune* (1 June 2000); 'Abducted Meghalaya cop found murdered', *The Assam Tribune* (2 September 2001); R Dutta Choudhury, 'Laden posters in Karimganj: Porous border posing threat', *The Assam Tribune* (10 October 2001); India, *Reforming*, 86–7; 'Cachar border census for identification of genuine citizens complete', *The Sentinel* (20 July 2003).

76 'Border villagers of Assam to help border guards to check Bangla influx', *The Sentinel* (15 September 2002); cf. 'Fundamentalists' intrusion feared: VDPs activated in Karimganj', *The Assam Tribune* (14 October 2001). Similarly, the North East Students' Organisation (NESO), meeting with the Prime Minister of India, demanded the creation of 'a special force with local youths to keep vigil against infiltrators along the Indo-Bangla border.' In 2003, the Assam police was contemplating to use 'people residing along the Assam-Bangladesh border' to act as informers on the movement of illegal immigrants; the police had decided 'to give preference to ex-servicemen as they are expected to function more efficiently.' 'NESO for time-bound solution to illegal influx into NE States', *The Assam Tribune* (8 August 2001). At the national level, the idea of armed 'Village Volunteer Forces' as instruments of border management and 'border area vigilance' was put forward in India, *Reforming*, 95–6; Oinam Sunil, 'Special informers to rid border of influx', *The Telegraph* (30 January 2003); R Dutta Choudhury, 'Second line of defence along border needs motivation', *The Assam Tribune* (1 December 2002);

'Assam villagers form groups to foil influx', *The Shillong Times* (7 February 2003). Cf. 'BSF for more recruits', *The Statesman* (9 March 2003).

77 The Kohima-based Lisami Youth Organisation reacted in this way to news that the Illegal Migrants (Determination by Tribunal) Act in Assam might be repealed; it wanted to prevent Bangladeshi migrants fleeing from Assam to enter Nagaland. 'Naga "Quit Notice" on Bangla migrants', *The Telegraph* (9 May 2003). Cf. 'Students in joint drive on migrants', *The Telegraph* (15 May 2003).

78 'Home ministry officials, however, don't have a clue on how to go about the drive. In the past, such exercises have yielded no returns and the problem was shoved under the carpet … A senior bureaucrat claimed that deportation of illegal aliens had proved futile. "They are taken to the border and shoved out but within days the same people are back, slipping in from another gap in the long, porous border".' 'Election heat on Bangla migrants', *The Telegraph* (31 January 2003)

79 According to Indian press reports, groups rounded up in West Bengal on 22 January 2003 had been recruited by Indian brokers to work as masons and brickfield labourers in Mumbai. They were on their way back to Bangladesh after Mumbai authorities threatened them with arrest. Bangladeshi press reports, however, spoke of 'Bangla-speaking Muslim slum dwellers who do not have ration cards' and were picked up from slums in Mumbai and Delhi. In the following days, Indian border guards tried to push thousands over the border, in at least 14 different places. Cf. 'Homeward bound Bangla infiltrators in police net', *The Statesman* (23 January 2003); 'Kolkata mission asked for more info on push-in', *The Daily Star* (24 January 2003); Shaikh Nazrul Islam, 'BDR beefs up troops as push-in bids continue: New Delhi terms claims baseless, absurd', *The Daily Star* (29 January 2003); 'Bangladeshis held in Burdwan', *The Telegraph* (30 January 2003); Chandrima S Bhattacharya, 'Flight from Mumbai and border', *The Telegraph* (7 February 2003); 'Deportation Cell set up in DP to expel illegal Bangladeshis' *Outlook* (3 January 2003); Pratyush Kanth, 'Police stop eviction of Bangladeshi migrants', *The Times of India* (1 February 2003).

80 During this deportation drive, Indian border guards cut the barbed wire border fence in order to push deportees into the no man's land, thereby demonstrating how two instruments designed to stop immigration – border fencing and deportation could be at cross-purposes. 'Foreign Minister discusses push-in issue with WB CM: Unscheduled stopover in Kolkata on way back from US', *The Independent* (1 February 2003).

81 According to the rules agreed upon by India and Bangladesh at the time, persons apprehended while attempting to cross the border should be accepted back on the basis of disclosures made by them, or within three days, if verification was needed. 'Dhaka rules out joint verification', *The Statesman* (6 February 2003).

82 Forty-eight 'push-in attempts' were reported. Among the groups stranded in the no man's land were 213 Bede, an itinerant group of snake-charmers and herb-sellers, with 150 pet snakes. They appeared to be Bangladeshi citizens who had been performing near the border when the Indian push-ins started. According to Indian press reports, they either crossed over to India at Jangipur or were handed over to Bangladesh border guards by Bangladeshi border villagers who suspected them of being cattle thieves (Bede are often seen as thieves by the settled population). The latter version included the suggestion that the Bangladesh border guards drove them into Cooch Behar (India) at gunpoint in a copy-cat 'return push-in'. The official Bangladesh position was that these were 'a floating population' and that they had been intercepted by Indian border guards while trying to cross into Indian territory at border post 867/8-c in Cooch Behar. A

stand-off of almost a week resulted. The group, among whom were many children, suffered badly in the cold winter nights, and their snakes started dying. Meanwhile troops were reinforced, local borderland residents evacuated, and the border was declared out of control. The group was also attacked by Bangladeshi borderlanders, leaving 10 of them injured – and then the entire group suddenly and mysteriously disappeared under cover of a thick night fog. 'Indo-Bangla border standoff continues', *The Assam Tribune* (3 February 2003); Main Uddin Chisti, 'Flag meet fails, Bangla border stays on the boil', *The Telegraph* (3 February 2003); Debasis Sarkar, 'No-man's land standoff continues', *The Times of India* (3 February 2003); Prakash Nanda, 'Delhi Foreign Office summons Bangladesh HC', *The Telegraph* (4 February 2003); Main Uddin Chisti, 'Mob battle on Bangla border – Delhi issues diplomatic warning', *The Telegraph* (4 February 2003); Rakhi Chakrabarty, 'Bangla border tense as impasse continues', *The Times of India* (4 February 2003); Sudipta Chanda, 'Another hard day's night on a muddy turf', *The Statesman* (5 February 2003); Main Uddin Chisti, 'Stranded snake-charmers pray as breadwinner reptiles starve', *The Telegraph* (6 February 2003); Alamgir Hossain, 'Nomads off beaten track', *The Telegraph* (7 February 2003); 'Border still tense', *The New Nation* (9 February 2003). Cf. *India/Bangladesh: "Push In - Push Out" Practices at the Border Not Acceptable* (London: Amnesty International, 2003); Jagat Mani Acharya, Manjita Gurung and Ranabir Samaddar, *Chronicles of a No-Where People on the Indo-Bangladesh Border* (Kathmandu: South Asia Forum of Human Rights, 2003).

83 Photographs by Shib Shankar Chatterjee (AC Dasgupta Road, Ward Number - II, Dhubri, Assam-783 301, India), 2 February 2003. Human rights organizations were unanimous in their criticism of the way both India and Bangladesh treated these people: 'The people at the border are not being treated as citizens of a country, but as junk,' said the general secretary of one of India's leading human rights groups, the People's Union for Civil Liberties, and an Amnesty International spokesperson said: 'People cannot be arbitrarily packed off in trucks and dumped on the border.' 'Rights groups express concern about families stranded on Indo-Bangla border', *One World* (5 February 2003).

84 This is not to say that all deportees were immigrants from Bangladesh. According to Indian press reports, razzias in Delhi slums also netted numerous Assamese migrants whose documents issued by the Assam government, and written in Assamese, were illegible to the Delhi police, who dismissed them as fraudulent anyway. In Mumbai slums, Muslim residents from West Bengal complained 'that policemen from the CID harass them continuously. "They just round us up, and, even if we have the papers, charge us Rs.500 or Rs.1,000, and then let us go. Otherwise it's *tori-paar* (deportation)".' 'Most migrants in Delhi have Assam papers', *The Assam Tribune* (6 February 2003); Chandrima S Bhattacharya, 'Paper shields to fend off Mumbai exile', *The Telegraph* (8 February 2003).

85 'Border forces push back & forth', *The Telegraph* (1 February 2003).

86 These deportations followed the Indian government's declaration that there were 20 million Bangladeshis staying illegally in India, and that they formed a threat to national security. Whereas initially senior BSF officials and the Indian deputy High Commissioner in Bangladesh flatly denied that 'push-ins' had taken place and said that Bangladesh's allegations were 'inherently false', the Inspector-General Law and Order of West Bengal, Chayan Mukherjee, said that 'such push-ins were routine ... Bangladeshis staying illegally in India are rounded up and handed over to the BSF on court orders, he said. The Petrapole border post is the most common point for such push-ins.' A government

spokesman in Delhi deftly sidestepped the issue of forcible deportation by declaring that Bangladesh's allegations regarding the push-in of Indian citizens was 'baseless' and 'absurd'. BDR foils BSF bid to push in hundreds', *The Daily Star* (25 January 2003); 'BSF kills 2 Bangladeshis – BDR foils 2 more push-in bid', *The Independent* (28 January 2003); 'India masses 4,000 for push-in: Bangla', *The Statesman* (28 January 2003); 'Dhaka hits back with push-in charge', *The Telegraph* (28 January 2003); 'Sparks fly on Bangla border', *The Telegraph* (29 January 2003); 'Stop repeated push-in bids: Dhaka expresses deep concern: BDR on high alert, asked to thwart Indian move', *The Independent* (30 January 2003); '200 push-in victims trapped in no-man's land: Flag meeting ends inconclusive', *The Daily Star* (1 February 2003); 'Border forces push back & forth', *The Telegraph* (1 February 2003); 'Panchagar shimante golaguli: BSF-er lagatar pushin chestay desher bibhinno sthane uttejona, Lalmonirhate potaka boithok bhenge gechhe', *Prothom Alo* (4 February 2003). Cf. 'Borders tense: BDR put on high alert', *The New Nation* (29 May 2003); 'No let up in push-in bid by BSF: Several attempts foiled, hundreds assembled across the border', *The Daily Star* (5 June 2003).

87 Ostrich-like though it might be, Dhaka's stance was effective in stopping the eviction drive. For example, 'a train-load of illegal migrants, who were being deported to Bangladesh, are now returning to Delhi from West Bengal ... because the Bangladesh authorities did not allow us to release them.' Pallab Bhattachariya, 'Dhaka should redress the issue, HC to Delhi told', *The Daily Star* (1 February 2003); Pratyush Kanth, 'Police stop eviction of Bangladeshi migrants', *The Times of India* (1 February 2003).

88 Deportation of illegal migrants from India also occurred regularly at other points along the border. For example, 'illegal migrants caught in the entire Barak valley and the upper Assam districts' were pushed back into Bangladesh through 'the push back point located near the last railway station near the border at Mahisashan [in Karimganj district, Assam].' R Dutta Choudhury, 'Fences Broken, River Unguarded: Indo-Bangla Border Still Porous, Aiding Influx', *The Assam Tribune* (30 November 2002).

89 'State boundaries are an extremely powerful symbol of national identity and sovereignty. Discourse around illegal immigration reflects this. Calls for "regaining control of our borders" evoke a mythic and pure past of clear and unambiguous distinctions between the inside and the outside ... Such discourse, however, only serves to mask the reality of a boundary that is *necessarily* porous to economic flows, particularly that of cheap labor. Indeed, the stability and prosperity of the "inside" depends upon such flows from the "outside". Thus, effective statecraft must maintain the image of autonomy, while implementing practices that expose the myth of national autonomy.' Nevins, *Operation Gatekeeper*, 161.

90 See for example Katy Gardner, *Global Migrants, Local Lives: Travel and Transformation in Rural Bangladesh* (Oxford: Clarendon Press, 1995); 'The Little Bangladeshes', *Indian Express* (6 August 1998); 'Bangladeshi youths struggling for a livelihood in Italy,' *Daily Star* (26 July 1999).

91 E.g. a group of 50 Bengali speakers who were detected in a suburb of Rangoon; they had arrived by schooner. '50 Bengalis held in Myanmar', *The New Nation* (1 February 2002).

92 For the term 'job-and-dignity seekers', see Mike Davis, 'Foreword,' in Nevins, *Operation Gatekeeper*, x.

93 The complex migration patterns across South Asian borders are little studied. For example, large numbers of Rohingya Muslims from Arakan (Burma) are known to have migrated through Bangladesh and India to Pakistan, and from there to the Gulf

countries, where over 200,000 were thought to reside in the 1990s. Bertil Lintner, 'Distant exile: Rohingyas seek new life in Middle East', *Far Eastern Economic Review*, 156:4 (28 January 1993), 23; Samaddar, *The Marginal Nation*, 165. On Bengali migration through India to Pakistan, see Arun Sharma, 'Bangla infiltrators go scot-free, courtesy J&K police', *Indian Express* (11 June 1998). According to the Indian government, over 3,800 Bangladeshis were apprehended at the India-Pakistan border between 1997 and 2000. 'Lok Sabha told: 3846 Bangladeshis held along Indo-Pak border', *The Daily Star* (26 April 2000). Cf. SK Ghosh, *Unquiet Border* (New Delhi: Ashish Publishing House, 1993), 100; Lin and Paul, 'Bangladeshi Migrants'.

94 As well as 200,000 Burmese, many of whom were Muslim Rohingyas from Arakan who crossed three borders to reach Karachi. 'Explaining the trafficking procedure, in case of Bangladeshis, [a member of the Human Rights Committee Pakistan (HRCP)] said some Bangladeshis in Karachi were acting as agents of traffickers. They would contact the people in Bangladesh willing to come to Karachi for jobs, etc. and ask them to send their personal details and photographs and then obtain national identity cards and passports by their name. Carrying these 20 to 25 passports the agent would go to Bangladesh and come back with the cargo of illegal immigrants. At the airport the agent would get these passports stamped by the corrupt immigration staff after which this group of new arrivals would enter into the city as a regular citizen holding the necessary legal documents to prove their status. The HRCP report said the citizenship identity card could be obtained at an under-the-counter payment of Rs.3,000 to Rs.7,000. Even passports could reportedly be had for a price: Rs.10,000 for Bengali and Rs.25,000-Rs.30,000 for an Afghan, etc. The report said there were four million unauthorized illegal immigrants in the country. Half of them were Bangladeshis, the rest Indians, Afghans, Burmese and others. The largest concentration, of 1.5 million, was in Karachi, 80 per cent of whom were Bangladeshis living in some 80 shanty towns in the city. Burmese numbered 200,000. The Afghan refugee population was close to two million. In 2000 Frederick estimated the number of Bangladeshis in Karachi at 1,5 to 2 million. Cf. Haroon Ahmed, 'Bangladeshi Immigrants in Sindh,' in: Tapan K Bose and Rita Manchanda (eds.), *States, Citizens and Outsiders: The Uprooted Peoples of South Asia* (Kathmandu: South Asia Forum for Human Rights, 1997), 345–52; John Frederick, 'The Black Route,' in: John Frederick and Thomas L Kelly (eds.), *Fallen Angels: The Sex Workers of South Asia* (New Delhi: Lustre Press/Roli Books, 2000), 68.

95 Maseeh Rahman, 'Separated at birth', *Time* (11 August 1997).

96 Arun Sharma, 'Bangla infiltrators go scot-free, courtesy J&K police', *Indian Express* (11 June 1998); cf. '48 Bangla nationals held on Indo-Pak border', *Hindustan Times* (18 February 1999); Sanghamitra Chakraborty, 'Agents take Bangladeshis for a ride – to Pakistan and detainment', *Times of India* (3 May 1998); '30 Bangladeshis held trying to cross into Pak', *The Times of India* (7 December 2002); Frederick, 'The Black Route,' 68–9; '58 Bangladeshis nabbed while entering Pakistan from Kashmir', *The Daily Star* (25 July 2003).

97 Zari (*jori*) is embroidery with gold or silver thread. Udayan Namboodiri, 'Illegal Immigrants: Political Pawns', *India Today* (10 August 1998). Cf. R Padmanabhan, 'The deportation drive', *Frontline* (15-28 August 1998). On a community of rag pickers and domestic workers in Delhi, see Lin and Paul, 'Bangladeshi Migrants'.

98 The importance of the two-way movement of people across the border and the fact that individuals often cross back and forth repeatedly, is emphasized by Samaddar, who cites borderlanders' expressions for this: 'the border means coming and going; *asha*

jawa'; '*okhane chash, ekhane lekhapara* (cultivation there, studies here)'; '*opare chash, epare bash* (land for tilling there, house for living here).' Samaddar, *The Marginal Nation*, 102, 116, passim. This book also provides a good sense of the many different roles migrants from Bangladesh play in the West Bengal economy. An example of longer-distance 'coming and going' was provided by a busload of Bangladeshis intercepted near Calcutta on their way to the Bangladesh border. None of them had passports and they were planning to cross the border with the help of brokers. 'These daily labourers were living in Delhi for the past few years', said the local superintendent of police, 'After the attack on [the Indian] Parliament [in December 2001], the Delhi police have been carrying out extensive raids. Fearing arrest, these Bangladeshi infiltrators fled the Capital.' '38 booked on bus to Bangladesh', *The Telegraph* (26 January 2002).

99 Frederick and Kelly (eds.), *Fallen Angels*, 68, 74.

100 Anil Maheshwari, 'The Face Behind the Mask,' *The Hindustan Times - Sunday Magazine* (15 August 1998); 'The Little Bangladeshes,' *Indian Express* (6 August 1998); cf. SK Ghosh, *Unquiet Border* (New Delhi: Ashish Publishing House, 1993), 36.

101 Photograph from *The Assam Times* (11 July 2000). Recruiting agents are said to come to the border *chors* of Assam to take young men to towns in Assam for work in unskilled professions. Hazarika, *Rites of Passage*, 149.

102 In the late 1990s, Bangladeshi migrants had to pay agents about US$100 to get to Pakistan and about $4,500 to get to Europe. Sanghamitra Chakraborty, 'Agents take Bangladeshis for a ride - to Pakistan and Detainment', *The Times of India* (3 May 1998); 'Bangladeshi youths struggling for a livelihood in Italy', *The Daily Star* (26 July 1999). For a description of agents (*dalal*) providing Bangladeshi migrants with a variety of services – illegal border crossings out of and into Bangladesh, help in onward travel to Delhi, Pakistan and beyond, repatriating funds in Bangladeshi currency, and help in buying land – see Lin and Paul, 'Bangladeshi Migrants,' 8–9.

103 Cases of trafficking of children within East Pakistan were not unknown. In 1949, in reply to an Assembly question, it was revealed that young boys, kidnapped from eastern districts of East Pakistan, were sold to '*ghatu* hunters' from Sylhet who turned them into *ghatus* (dancing boys) (Pol. P3I-20/49 (12–49); cf. *East Pakistan District Gazetteers: Sylhet* (Dacca: Government Press, 197)), 114).

104 For the terms self-smuggler and self-smuggling, see Andreas, *Border Games*, 20, 95.

105 David Kyle and Rey Koslowski, 'Introduction,' in David Kyle and Rey Koslowski (eds.) *Global Human Smuggling: Comparative Perspectives* (Baltimore and London: The Johns Hopkins University Press, 2001), 9.

106 Although most attention has been paid to the movement of women from Bangladesh to India, Indian women also crossed the border into Bangladesh. They could do so in search of work or to marry a Bangladeshi husband. Three Indian girls from West Bengal told a remarkable story of abandonment-by-migration. They entered Bangladesh with their fathers at the ages of 10 and 11, and went to stay with an aunt in Dhaka. After a few days their fathers left for India, assuring the girls that they would return soon. They never did. Then the aunt disappeared, and the girls were left to fend for themselves. Miraculously, they found work in a garments factory and then a light-bulb factory. After three years they decided to return to India and re-establish contact with their parents. When they got down from a long-distance bus near the border, they asked bystanders for the way to India. Puzzled, locals informed the police who took them into custody and a local human rights organization provided them with legal aid. 'Three Indian girls arrested in Panchagarh', *The Independent* (25 January 2003). Other Indian

women who migrated to Bangladesh were sex workers in Bangladeshi border towns. 'Rajshahi most vulnerable to AIDS onslaught', *The Independent* (19 June 2002). For cross-border marriages, see Md. Mahbubar Rahman and Willem van Schendel, '"I Am Not A Refugee": Rethinking Partition Migration', *Modern Asian Studies*, 37:3 (2003), 551–84.

107 Frederick and Kelly (eds.), *Fallen Angels*, 67–8, 74.

108 Field notes 1988. Cf. Kalpana's testimony in Carolyn Sleightholme and Indrani Sinha, *Guilty without Trial: Women in the Sex Trade in Calcutta* (Calcutta: Stree, 1996 / New Brunswick, NJ: Rutgers University Press, 1997), 18–19, cf. 34–51; and women's testimonies in Vorasakdi Mahatdhanobol (ed. by Pornpimon Trichot), *Chinese Women in the Thai Sex Trade* (Bangkok: Institute of Asian Studies, Chulalongkorn University, 1998); *Red Light Traffic: The Trade in Nepali Girls* (Kathmandu: ABC/ Nepal, 1996).

109 'Border crime on the rise in West Bengal', *The Statesman* (15 April 1992). Numerous newspaper reports attest to the fact that women played a prominent role as agents in the trafficking of women and children from Bangladesh. See for example 'Alleged woman child lifter held in Bogra', *The Daily Star* (21 July 2003); 'Human traffickers abducting school children', *The Independent* (22 July 2003). See also Frederick and Kelly (eds.), *Fallen Angels*, 67–70.

110 According to the Bangladesh National Women Lawyers Association, about 500 Bangladesh women were illegally transported to Pakistan every day in early 1999. A Pakistani lawyers group estimated that there were over 200,000 undocumented Bangladeshi women in Pakistan in 1998. Nadeem Qadir, 'Experts warn of rising child prostitution in Bangladesh', *Daily News* (3 February 1999); *Asian Migration News* (15 January 1998); Audity Falguni, 'Bangladeshi girls in Indian flesh market', *The Independent* (28 February 2003).

111 This fate befell ten teenage boys from the Malda borderland who were promised jobs in sugar mills, with free housing and food. After a long train and bus ride they found themselves captives in the house of a landlord in a village near Kanpur, Uttar Pradesh. Debarati Agarwala, 'Bonded boys flee heartless landlord', *The Telegraph* (10 December 2002); cf. Mehedi Hidaytullah, 'Smugglers held with 20 children', *The Telegraph* (20 September 2003). In stories of trafficking, young children are often depicted as clueless victims being bundled across the border. But things are often much more ambiguous: in the harsh world of abandoned children of the urban underclass, boys as young as six or eight years old could have well-developed migration strategies, as four of them demonstrated. When they were picked up by police as they were travelling with a man who offered them jobs and two square meals a day, they explained that they had left Dhaka to escape poverty, hunger, and abuse. In other words, there was an element of voluntariness and agency in their migration that is often disregarded. Obviously, they might still have ended up as trafficked labour slaves, but their crossing the border would have been a voluntary act. 'Trafficking: 4 boys rescued in Rupsha', *The Daily Star* (25 August 2002).

112 For a case study, see Samaddar, *The Marginal Nation*, 190–8. For a man from southern Bangladesh taking his wife and sister-in-law to Calcutta and selling them to a brothel there, see 'Man sentenced for "selling" wife at Kolkata brothel: Wife beaten to death in Satkhira', *The Daily Star* (21 September 2003).

113 E.g. Madhusudan Mondal, 'Rescued boys languishing at shelter home', *The Independent* (5 September 2003).

114 The accuracy of such figures is unclear because the methodology used to calculate

them is not explained. E.g. 'Child traffickers held with 2 babies', *The Independent* (8 July 1999); 'Trafficking in children on the rise in Nilphamari', *The Independent* (19 July 1999); PT Jyoti Datta, 'Bid to check child trafficking through Indo-Bangla border', *Business Line* (1 June 1999). Children of Muslim Rohingyas (refugees from Burma in Bangladesh), were thought to be especially targeted by child traffickers. *Asian Migration News* (15 October 1998).

115 Despite the outlawing of this notorious practice in 1993. *Bangladesh Human Rights Practices, 1995* (Washington, DC: United States Department of State, 1996); 'Court overload traps "camel boys" in home', *South China Morning Post* (14 August 1998); 'Rescued Bangladesh boys return home', *The Hindu* (20 February 1998); *Victims of Trafficking and Violence Protection Act 2000: Trafficking in Persons Report* (Washington, DC: United States of America, Department of State, 2002), 27; 'Dating death in desert: Sport of sheikhs rides roughshod over juvenile camel jockeys', *The Daily Star* (12 August 2001); Audity Falguni, 'Tale of Dubai-back camel jockey', *The New Nation* (18 July 2002).

116 '27,000 Bangladeshis trapped in Indian brothels', *Dawn* (8 April 1998). According to a United Nations report, around 300,000 Bangladeshi children were sold to Indian brothels in the mid-1990s. *The Daily Star* (15 December 1998). Many of these women ended up in Pakistani brothels. 'The flesh trade of Bengali women is still prospering shamelessly, with women lured from Bangladesh via India, more disgusting is the fact that it is patronised by the law enforcement agencies. The business is flourishing in the city as well with the immense help and support by the police and local administration who have black sheep among themselves. "At the border from Beenapur to Amritsar and then to Lahore the officers helped us in crossing the border. But they retained their privilege of keeping a lot of girls for themselves, sexually abusing them and then releasing them on the arrival of a fresh lot", revealed the wife of a pimp, Noorjehan, at the Legal Aid Centre during interrogation after the arrest. Zia says: "In Karachi, the police knows the whereabouts of all the dens run by these Bengali pimps at the Bengali paras but are a party to it, the huge commissions they extort are the price".' Farhat Anis, 'Life in the Dark', *The News International* (Karachi) (11 September 2000). The market for sex workers is a highly complex one: Bangladeshi women ended up in the sex industry in India and Pakistan, but at the same time Indian sex workers were active in Bangladeshi border towns. Boys from the borderland were also known to end up in the sex industry in India. 'Rajshahi most vulnerable to AIDS onslaught', *The Independent* (19 June 2002); 'Rescue blows lid off boy trafficking', *The Telegraph* (22 August 2003).

117 I.e. between about $25 and $125. '27,000 Bangladeshis trapped in Indian brothels', *Dawn* (8 April 1998); Sanghamitra Chakraborty, 'Repatriated Bangla children may never see their real families again', *Times of India* (19 April 1998).

118 At the Benapol-Bongaon border crossing 'local auto-rickshaw drivers, handling agents and small hotel-keepers reported that men accompanying girls and women across the border [were] a common sight, and that these men did not even bother with forged documents, they handed over the money quite openly as they came across the border.' Sleightholme and Sinha, *Guilty without Trial*, 42.

119 Shib Sankar Chakroborty, 'Special Report to Dhaka: Report to Bangladeshi High Commission on Trafficking of Women,' *Amrita Bazar Patrika* (9 April 1989), cited in Sleightholme and Sinha, *Guilty without Trial*, 42. Cf. 'BSF men face charge for rape of Bangladeshi woman', *The Daily Star* (15 January 2003); 'Migrant rape charge on border troops', *The Telegraph* (8 March 2003); 'Two women brought for push-in "raped" by

BSF members', *The Daily Star* (23 June 2003).

120 Munni Saha, 'The Protectors: Awareness in the Trafficking Borderlands: Association for Community Development', in: Frederick and Kelly (eds.), *Fallen Angels*, 74.

121 'Trafficking in children on the rise in Nilphamari' (1999); 'Bangla touts arrested', *The Telegraph* (13 May 1999); '8 Bangla guardians held for child trafficking', *The Telegraph* (27 April 1999); 'One caught while trafficking girl child', *The New Nation* (24 April 1999); '3 alleged child lifters beaten to death in Mymensingh', *The Daily Star* (1 August 2003).

122 For example, police in North 24 Parganas (West Bengal) found 88 Bangladeshi nationals and two Indian escorts in a truck making its way from the Bangladesh border to brick kilns near Calcutta. The labourers had paid Rs.500-900 each for the privilege of being trafficked. On interrogating the Indian escorts, the police found out that 'these gangs have a very good network and seem to be in business for a long time.' 'Bust nets 88 for border breach', *The Telegraph* (15 October 2001).

123 Lin and Paul, 'Bangladeshi Migrants', 5. For a contribution based on interviews among Bangladeshis in Delhi placed in the context of Hindutva, see Ramachandran, 'Of Boundaries and Border Crossings'.

124 Samaddar, *The Marginal Nation*, 120–1.

125 He also said: 'We go because we fulfil a need over there, we go also because it meets a need here. Your people need our skills and hard work, we need the money.' Hazarika, *Rites of Passage*, 194, 201.

126 Cf. the political support of Californians employing Mexican gardeners, nannies and house cleaners for politicians invoking the 'brown peril' of illegal Mexican immigrants. Nevins, *Operation Gatekeeper*. For example, when Purno A Sangma, former speaker of the Indian Parliament (Lok Sabha), created a new party in 2003, he announced that 'a campaign against illegal migration would be the political launch-pad of the Northeast People's Forum'. 'Migrants on forum agenda', *The Telegraph* (5 September 2003).

127 See Samaddar, *The Marginal Nation*, 36; Gardner, *Global Migrants, Local Lives*.

128 David Kyle and John Dale, 'Smuggling the State Back In: Agents of Human Smuggling Reconsidered', in: Kyle and Koslowski (eds.), *Global Human Smuggling*, 29–57.

129 Kyle and Dale, 'Smuggling', 34. See above for some examples of the role of women in procuring Bangladeshi workers for the Indian sex industry.

130 Cf. the examples of Ecuador and Burma in Kyle and Dale, 'Smuggling'.

131 James O Finkenauer, 'Russian Transnational Organized Crime and Human Trafficking', in: Kyle and Koslowski (eds.), *Global Human Smuggling*, 166–86. Migrant exporters could operate on a fairly large scale, e.g. the group in Dhaka smuggling women to Lebanon and other parts of the Middle East – police discovered 141 passports in their possession. 'Women rescued before emplaning: 141 passports recovered from two traffickers', *The New Nation* (16 August 2003).

132 In Benapol, a broker explained: 'It is very easy for us to arrange these illegal [crossings]. For 800 taka per person we get them across the border openly through the no-man's land. The security personnel will literally look the other way.' Those who had only 300 to 400 taka to spare were taken across the border through a different more circuitous route. Syed Mehdi Momin, 'Illegal border crossing – Benapole style', *The Independent* (7 September 2003). Cf. Faruque Ahmed, 'Dalals charge Rs 200 to 500 to facilitate illegal entry of people from Bangladesh to India: "Infiltration business" along Indo-Bangla border in Dhubri', *The Northeast Daily* (23 February 2000). On fluctuations in the rates that border-crossers have to pay to brokers, see Sandipan Chakraborty and

Soumen Bhattacharya, 'Touts make merry at the expense of the homeless', *The Times of India* (4 November 2001). Ghosh singles out Muslim organisations in India as helping 'infiltration' from Bangladesh 'rather than safeguarding national interest'. He gives no evidence to support his claim (Ghosh, *Unquiet Border*, 18, 20). On Assamese villagers' views of brokers, see Hazarika, *Rites of Passage*, 145–6.

133 'The Little Bangladeshes' *Indian Express* (6 August 1998). CPI(M) = Communist Party of India (Marxist), at the time the dominant party in the coalition ruling the State of West Bengal. Brokers were inventive in creating various covers for travelling migrants. Thus a group of Bangladeshi workers heading from the border to Delhi were travelling in a truck carrying a banner indicating that they were a religious party going to visit a shrine. Samaddar, *The Marginal Nation*, 122.

134 Samaddar, *The Marginal Nation*, 120–1.

135 See e.g. descriptions of Ecuador and Burma in Kyle and Dale, 'Smuggling'.

136 Kyle and Dale, 'Smuggling', 49; Cf. Swain, *The Environmental Trap*. Abul Barkat's study of the distribution of benefits from the US$36 billion in aid that Bangladesh received since its independence in 1971 found the following: foreign consultants took 25 per cent, Bangladeshi politicians, bureaucrats, commission agents and contractors 30 per cent, local elites 20 per cent, and 'target group' poor people 25 per cent. '75 per cent of country's foreign aid plundered,' *The Independent* (13 October 2002).

137 Cf. Lin and Paul who speak of the 'increasing necessity for the landless to seek employment outside the country [i.e. Bangladesh]'. Lin and Paul, 'Bangladeshi Migrants,' 4.

138 For example, inhabitants of Indian villages close to the Bangladesh border were reported to be earning much money from migrants hurriedly returning to Bangladesh after Mumbai police 'turned on the heat'. For a consideration, borderland touts smoothed their way past Indian and Bangladeshi border guards, and other villagers earned hundreds of rupees a day from hiring out huts where the returning migrants waited for the moment to cross the border. Pronab Mondal, 'Silent trip back to Bangla', *The Telegraph* (10 February 2003); cf. Tapash Ganguly, 'Dangerous Influx', *The Week (Kottayam)* (12 July 1998).

139 Such pogroms were strongly advocated by the Vishwa Hindu Parishad (VHP). Its international general secretary, Praveen Togadia, was quoted as demanding: 'The Gujarat incident [= killing of Muslims in Gujarat over a period of months in 2002] will have to be repeated in Assam in order to save the Hindu people living in the region from the nefarious activities of the illegal Bangladeshi Muslim infiltrators living throughout India.' Falguni Barman, 'Check Bangla influx for survival: VHP', *The Assam Tribune* (20 January 2003); cf. 'Fight evil designs of migrants: VHP', *The Assam Tribune* (19 January 2003).

140 Praveen Togadia, quoted in 'Send all infiltrators to a space in Bangladesh', *The Shillong Times* (20 January 2003).

141 Such conspiracy theories were not usually construed with regard to illicit flows of goods between India and Bangladesh. At other borders, however, power holders could easily convince themselves that smuggling was part of an underhand plot by the neighbouring state to undermine the national economy, and they would express themselves in ways very similar to the Assam Governor quoted above. For example, the head of Ghana's Border Guards stated in 1977: 'smuggling activities along the borders of Ghana, and into and from Ghana is centrally organised, planned, coordinated, directed and financed by the Togo Government against Ghana. This is a fact. It is sad and unfortunate that some Ghanaians are being used as front men.' Quoted in Paul Nugent, 'Power Versus

Knowledge: Smugglers and the State Along Ghana's Eastern Frontier, 1920–1992', in Michael Rösler and Tobias Wendl (eds.), *Frontiers and Borderlands: Anthropological Perspectives* (Frankfurt am Main, etc.: Peter Lang, 1999), 91.

142 Nevins, *Operation Gatekeeper*, 173. Cf. Swain, *The Environmental Trap.*

143 For example, the Bangladesh Economic Review 2002 simply ignored the largest group of labour emigrants when it stated that 2.6 million Bangladeshi nationals had gone abroad with jobs between 1990 and 2002. It referred merely to clients of the *state* migrant exporting schemes: labour emigrants who had been part of state-controlled manpower exporting operations and who were monitored by the Ministry of Expatriates' Welfare and Overseas Employment. Rafiqul Islam Azad, '26.4 lakh Bangladeshis went abroad with jobs since '90', *The New Nation* (10 June 2002); cf. Somini Sengupta, 'Money from kin abroad helps Bangladeshis get by', *The New York Times* (24 June 2002).

144 Cf. Andreas, *Border Games*, 141.

10

REBELS AND BANDITS

In a borderland two states meet in a display of military, administrative and symbolic power. A borderland is a showcase of state territoriality but at the same time it is often a privileged site of rebellion against the power of the state. It is here that the state finds it most difficult to classify its citizens and to make them accept its claim to sovereignty over a self-enclosed geographical space. And in addition to this paradox, there is another. A borderland may bristle with markers showing the spatial limits of two states but these markers may obscure a reality of spatially overlapping, extra-territorial state activities. As we will see, states may well have developed policies of supporting rebellions across the border.

In the preceding chapters we have come across many activities in the borderland that have challenged the authority of the states and defied their borders. These activities included smuggling, illegal migration, forcible harvesting, cattle rustling, and so on – activities that breached the territorial limits that the states sought to impose on economic and social networks. In this chapter, we focus on activities that challenged the states' military and political presence in the borderland.

In military terms, the reality of a state's claim to sovereignty is expressed in its ability to monopolize the use of violence in its territory. Law and order depend on a state's capacity to punish offenders by violent means. The legitimacy of a state in the eyes of its citizens does not necessarily depend on a show of power. On the contrary, the better state violence is hidden behind a framework of widely accepted rules and norms, the more powerful the state is likely to be. Ideally, the mere threat of violence suffices to regulate the behaviour of citizens who have internalized the authority of their state.

This ideal is particularly hard to attain in borderlands because the vicinity of another state, with different rules and norms, always provides borderlanders with an alternative. They can compare and judge their own state in ways that are usually not open to people living in the interior of a state territory. Put another way, it is more difficult for borderlanders to internalize a state unconditionally, and this makes states habitually mistrust borderlanders. In addition, a borderland provides access to the military resources of another territory and therefore becomes an excellent hunting ground for non-state 'military entrepreneurs'.[1] A state has several options to ensure that borderlanders toe the line: it can educate them to internalize the state, cajole them into state-approved behaviour, turn them into a crucial symbol of the nation, buy their loyalty, threaten them with violence, or actually unleash violence on them. If all this fails, it can expel them.

All these state strategies have been employed in the borderland where India, Bangladesh and Burma meet, with varying degrees of success. The ideal of imposing a largely internalized state on the borderlanders has remained elusive, and attempts at buying off various borderland grievances have also been fairly unsuccessful. The result has been a borderland that is remarkable for a high level of violence and lawlessness, a multitude of anti-state rebellions, and often low state legitimacy. Little known to the outside world, it has been a region of rebels and bandits, of insurgency and counter-insurgency, and of serious and sustained human rights violations.

Borderland rebels

In the late 1940s and 1950s, the new states were deeply concerned with securing control of the borderland by means of expanding their bureaucratic power, beefing up (para)military forces and homogenizing the borderland population. Even in combination, however, these tactics often proved less than successful. The states were unable or unwilling to allocate adequate resources to their borderlands, and they were unable to control their own personnel: many state officials used their positions in the borderland to pursue private aims. As a result, borderlanders soon regarded these states – each of which had started out with considerable legitimacy in the eyes of borderlanders – as part of the problem rather than as part of any solution. As protests and petitions went unheeded, borderland elites realized that they had too little influence on state affairs. It was not long before a sense of marginalization was translated into rebellions that were intended to force the states into taking notice of borderland grievances, or that had the objective of establishing a separate state.

Over time, in many parts of the borderland, the state's options for controlling the population were reduced, and the unleashing of state violence became more prominent. Increasingly, armed forces were used to retaliate and discipline. In the process, they created further grievances, and so widened the gap between state and borderlanders. These dynamics played out differently in different sections of the borderland, some sections beaten into stupefied submission, others defiantly rebellious, and yet others falling prey to chaotic internecine terror.

Since 1947, dozens of insurrectionary organizations have been (and continue to be) active in the Bengal borderland, some with a very limited range of action and others stirring up millions of people.[2] Thus far, no one has analysed these borderland insurrections jointly, and I do not attempt to do this here. Instead, I present a few case studies that illustrate ways in which the borderland was (and is) used by rebels and how rebels shaped the borderland. Figure 10.1 shows the location of these cases.

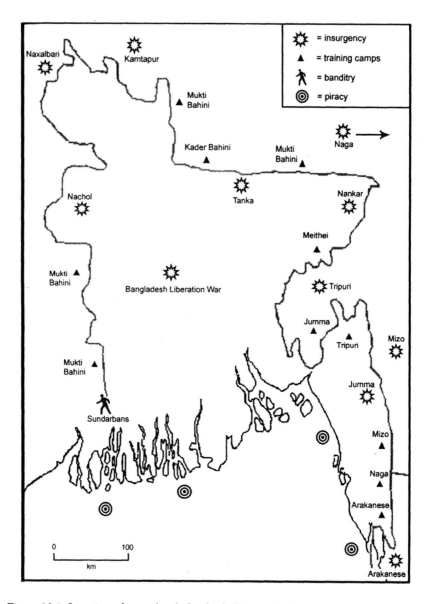

Figure 10.1: Location of some borderland rebellions , 1947–2003.

The ideological inspirations of borderland rebellions varied enormously but were underpinned by two main identities. The first was based on inequity, economic exploitation and poverty, the second on cultural identity, language and territory. These two identities, which I characterize briefly as 'class' and 'nation', were clearly not mutually exclusive, but manifested themselves in various combinations in these rebellions. In some, the dominant idiom was that of class, even though cultural identities clearly played a role as well. In others, the emphasis shifted over time, from class to nation. There was also an overall shift in the character of borderland rebellions during the period since Partition: especially after the 1970s, rebellions stressing the 'class' angle lost importance vis-à-vis rebellions in the 'nation' mode.[3] These were certainly important mixes and shifts but, for the sake of presentation, I group borderland rebellions here under the two headings of class and nation.

Rebellions in the 'class' mode. The closing years of colonial rule had been tumultuous in many parts of rural Bengal. In various places, sharecroppers had been demanding the abolition of exploitative tenancies and levies, and these demands had brought them into violent conflict with landlords and the colonial state. In East Pakistan these agrarian movements had lost much of their power by the time of Partition, mainly because tenants (who were predominantly Muslims) opted to support the movement for Pakistan as a way of ridding themselves of their landlords (who were predominantly Hindus). But this was not the case in all regional movements, especially where tenants were not Muslims. Several of these movements continued beyond the moment of Partition, and found themselves located in the new borderland.

Communists were involved in a number of these borderland movements. Both India and Pakistan feared communists and both soon outlawed the Communist party. In the borderland this fear led them to cooperate to fight communism.[4] The Pakistan authorities were especially concerned about the communist movement, which they saw as anathema to the cause of Pakistan because of its stance against Hindu-Muslim identity politics (communalism) and its experience in underground work. In East Pakistan, the problem was compounded by the fact that Hindus had dominated communist organizations. A conference of police officers in Karachi in 1948 recognized this:

East Pakistan 'has to deal with organisations which are notorious for underground work of which large numbers belong to the minority community. The banning of such organisations would probably lead to considera[ble] reactions from India on the ground of victimisation of the minorities.'[5]

Nevertheless, the government of East Pakistan played the communal card when it warned all its officers in a circular:

Since the establishment of Pakistan, the enemies of Islam 'have been busy in different garbs to undermine Muslim solidarity and to sabotage or obstruct the progress of Pakistan. One such garb is the preaching of the outwardly attractive but in fact dangerously subversive anti-Islamic doctrine of communism.' In schools and colleges, the circular added, there was a need for 'weeding out teachers as well as students who indulge in anti-Pakistan propaganda or subversive activities.'[6]

In 1949, a high official exhorted each 'administrative officer [who] is true to his job' and a 'true patriot and well wisher of the State' to contribute to 'waking up the latent energies of the people' by means of a vigorous campaign of rural reconstruction. He added that the 'campaign is also in fact a preventive or insurance against communistic and other subversive influences which gain ground when the masses suffer from social and economic grievances.' Students and teachers should be involved in the campaign so that the 'time and energies now wasted by the students in unhealthy agitations and controversies [are] canalised towards constructive nation-building activities.'[7]

In this atmosphere, borderland movements with communist connections were clearly most unwelcome.[8] Not only did they hamper state attempts at controlling the borderland, but the predominance of Hindus among communists also made Pakistani authorities fear Indian influence in these movements. It was easy to discredit Hindus involved in borderland insurgencies as fifth columnists or Indian agents, and to argue that any Pakistani ought to help destroy such enemies of the nation. In many places this proved to be an effective argument; however, several insurgencies refused to disintegrate.

One of these was in the northern belt of Mymensingh district, where thousands of Hajong tenants had turned against their landlords in what became known as the *Tanka* movement (see Figure 10.1). The Hajongs, one of several non-Bengali groups living in this area, were Hindus, as were their Bengali landlords. A third group in the conflict comprised Bengali communist workers, who had supported the Hajongs from the late 1930s and who were mostly Hindus as well. After an insurrectionary phase between 1942 and 1945, a severe crackdown followed in 1946, and the state of Pakistan inherited a disturbed border area with defiant and well-organized guerrillas.[9]

The district authorities came down on the movement with an 'anti-communist drive in the border areas.'[10] The result was that many Hajongs and communist workers fled across the new border to the Garo Hills (India). Here they were safe from attacks by the Pakistani police and they could regroup and launch attacks across the border.[11] By 1949 they were thought to be 'recruiting almost every villager now', and attacks on Pakistani police parties had become so frequent that an additional police force was quartered on almost the entire Mymensingh border area at the cost of the inhabitants.[12] The Hajong refugees were also able to mobilize the Assam authorities in their attempts to petition the Pakistan state for restitution of their land in Pakistan. Pakistan officials made it very clear, however, that Hajongs, insurgent or not, were no longer welcome on the Pakistani side of the border: 'The Hajongs as a class are communist minded and anti-Pakistanis ... They are extremely undesirable persons, notorious communists and disloyal to the state.'[13]

In other parts of the borderland the Pakistan authorities were faced with similar insurrections in which pre-Partition political alliances between tenants and communist workers persisted. In eastern Sylhet, the *Nankar* movement pitted tenants against their landlords and the police. In November 1947, a policeman described the rebellious tenants as unwitting tools in the hands of communists. Faced with police oppression, he thought, the tenants could be brought to a settlement, 'but the Hindu Communists intervened in order to keep the agitation alive and thereby to allow the disturbed condition of [a part of the] Pakistan area to continue.'[14] In 1949, intense police terror was widely reported and a police shooting that killed five led to questions in the East Bengal Legislative Assembly. The government reply laid heavy stress on the anti-state character of the movement.[15] Not long afterwards, many of the leaders crossed the border to India and the movement died down. The same happened to other movements, e.g. the *Nachol* movement in Rajshahi district, where communists had supported Shantal villagers in protests against levies. This movement collapsed after one of its leaders, Ila Mitra, was arrested in 1950. Her torture during imprisonment in East Pakistan became a *cause célèbre* in India and she left for Calcutta after being released.[16]

The main reason why these communist-supported rebellions in different parts of the borderland were able to survive the creation of Pakistan for several years was that they were not susceptible to nationalist rhetoric and communal manipulation – few Muslims were involved in them. After Partition, the emphasis of these movements changed from tenancy reform to the setting up of a separate government: they turned against the new state. Hajong rebels, in particular, were able to make extensive use of the new border as a strategic resource. In the early 1950s there were similar communist-supported agrarian movements in West Bengal (India) but these were not as closely linked with the new opportunities and problems created by the border.[17] On both sides of the border the *zamindari* system of landlordism was abolished in the 1950s, and this put a definite end to this wave of tenant rebellions.

Agrarian struggles continued in various parts of the borderland, but it was not till the late 1960s that the border region would see another communist-inspired revolt. This time it took place in the far north, where Partition had created the 'chicken's neck', a narrow strip of Indian territory squeezed in between Nepal and East Pakistan/Bangladesh. Essentially Maoist, the revolt came to be known as the *Naxalbari uprising* (see Figure 9.1).[18] It gave birth to a large number of 'Naxalite' (or Marxist-Leninist) revolutionary parties and organizations in India, Bangladesh and Nepal, many of which continue to be active today. The Naxalbari uprising has been analysed extensively, mostly as a contribution to revolutionary politics in India, or as a 'tribal' or 'subaltern' insurgency.[19] But its significance here is the fact that it was a borderland revolt of a new kind. It differed in two ways from the earlier movements that had combined rural grievances with socialist visions.

First, unlike their precursors of the late 1940s, the communist party workers who were involved in the organization of the Naxalbari uprising were themselves borderlanders who rebelled against their own party's leadership. Faced with a leadership that had recently joined the coalition government of West Bengal, some prominent members of the Communist Party of India (Marxist) – or CPI(M) – in West Bengal broke away to emulate 'China's path' of agrarian revolution.[20] The north Bengal border region seemed perfect: far from the centres of state power, with local organizations developed during tenants' and tea plantation workers' actions during the 1950s and 1960s, and providing an escape route across the border if things became too hot.[21] A group of borderland dissidents within the CPI(M), led by Charu Mazumdar (Plate 10.1), used these advantages to rebel against their party leaders, who formed part of the government, and to establish a liberated zone from which to attack the state.

Plate 10.1: A borderland rebel: Charu Mazumdar, organizer of the Naxalbari uprising (1967).[22]

The Naxalbari uprising was also notable in that it became the first rebellion in the Bengal borderland to 'jump scale' by establishing international links.[23] Although it was, on the one hand, a rebellion against local forms of agrarian oppression and exploitation, it immediately developed into an international event. Chinese media hailed it as a 'peal of spring thunder' creating 'a red area of rural revolutionary armed struggle.' They saw in it the 'front paw of the Indian Revolution' and the 'prelude to a violent revolution by hundreds of millions of people throughout India.'[24] A team from Naxalbari left for China on foot, and was given ideological and arms training there for four months before returning home.[25] In the Cold War context, Naxalbari rapidly became recognized internationally as South Asia's contribution to global revolutionary armed struggle.

Rebellions in the 'nation' mode.   I have used the shorthand 'rebellions in the "class" mode' for borderland revolts pitting themselves against inequity, economic exploitation and poverty, and expressing themselves primarily in class terms. I use the term 'rebellions in the "nation" mode' to refer to a second group of borderland revolts. These expressed themselves primarily in terms of cultural identity, language and territory.

These rebellions differed not only in their ideology but also in their relationship to the states administering the borderland. These states feared class rebellions across the border and worried that these might spill over into their own territory.[26] But borderland rebellions in the 'nation' mode were quite a different matter to them. Right from the moment of Partition, India and Pakistan had become locked into an antagonistic and competitive relationship with each other, and their antagonism was exacerbated by their drifting towards opposite Cold War powers. Most open confrontations between the two countries took place in their western borderland, especially Kashmir, but the eastern borderland also became an arena for mutual destabilization and espionage. Here both states played their smaller 'Great Games.'[27]

In contrast to rebellions in the 'class' mode, which had a very long history in the region, rebellions in the 'nation' mode were largely a product of Partition. In 1947, throughout South Asia, the idea of the nation became firmly wedded to the idea of territorial division. Post-Partition borderland nationalists of various hues were almost inevitably keen separatists. It was this 'urge to secede' that made borderland nationalisms the stuff of foreign policy. Pakistan was the first to develop a coherent policy of supporting insurgents across the border with a view to destabilizing and dismembering its neighbour. Northeastern India provided an excellent playing field. It spawned numerous insurgencies of groups that refused to accept that they belonged to the Indian nation and therefore fought against the Indian state. Leaders of these movements saw India as an occupying or colonizing power and, reasoning that the enemy of their enemy was their friend, they often sought support from Pakistan.[28]

The first such alliance sprang up in 1955 between Nagas from the far northeast of India and the Pakistan state.[29] It was followed in 1963 by an alliance between Pakistan and Mizos on the Indian side of the Lushai Hills/ Chittagong Hill Tracts borderland. In both cases the Pakistan government provided rebels from Indian territory not only with a safe haven in East Pakistan, but also with training camps in the borderland (Plates 10.2 and 10.3).[30] A third insurgent group from

Plates 10.2 and 10.3: Mizo guerrillas retreating from the Sajek hills in the Chittagong Hill Tracts (East Pakistan) in 1971.[34]

India that secured base camps in the borderland in 1967 came from Tripura.[31] In 1968, Meithei insurgents from Manipur (India) contacted the Pakistan authorities, wishing to be given shelter in Sylhet district where there were several older Manipuri villages. The timing was inconvenient for Pakistan, however, and many of these insurgents were handed over to India. But in 1970–1 some Meithei insurgents did receive arms training in Borlekha (Sylhet).[32] From the late 1940s onwards, the southern Chittagong Hill Tracts had also provided shelter to communist, nationalist and Islamic insurgents from Arakan (Burma), but these operations were on a much smaller scale than those dealing with separatists from India.[33]

This pattern of aiding and abetting, established during the Pakistan period, was interrupted after 1971 when Bangladesh emerged: its new government was on excellent terms with India. After *coups d'état* in Bangladesh in 1975, however, the honeymoon was over and Bangladesh allowed insurgent groups from Northeast India to use its territory once again (Plate 10.4). Important newcomers in this period were Assamese rebels who began using Bangladesh as a convenient conduit for contacts with Pakistan.[35]

Plate 10.4: Saluting another nation. Activists of the People's Liberation Army, fighting for the independence of Manipur state in Northeast India, at morning assembly in their camp in Chhotodamai (Sylhet) in Bangladesh, late 1980s.[36]

For a long time, India's scope for similarly exploiting insurgency in East Pakistan was limited simply because no breakaway insurgencies developed there. However, India's major chance came when a cataclysm occurred in East Pakistan. The movement for an independent Bangladesh engulfed the entire territory of East Pakistan when the Pakistan army cracked down on it, kick-starting the Bangladesh Liberation War on 26 March 1971.[37] India was deeply involved in the insurgency from the beginning and invaded the territory in November 1971, although it did not officially declare war on Pakistan till 3 December of that year. By 16 December it had occupied East Pakistan, compelled the Pakistan armed forces to surrender, and acted as midwife to a newly installed Bangladesh government. This war was no doubt the major political event in South Asia in the second half of the twentieth century; here, I examine India's overt involvement in the borderland:

> The first among those who crossed over to India were the leading cadres of the Awami League and the personnel of the EPR [East Pakistan Rifles] and EBR [East Bengal Regiment], who were fleeing from the pursuing Pakistan army. This posed to the Indian authorities a very crucial problem even in the first week following the crack down [of 26 March 1971, the beginning of the Bangladesh Liberation War], as to whether to allow these refugees to cross over and seek sanctuary in India. The Border Security Force, which was manning the Indian side of the border with Bangla Desh, permitted these refugees to cross over.

Indira Gandhi, India's Prime Minister, 'had alerted the Border Security Forces (BSF) of the Home Ministry to handle the situation on the border … It was the BSF who were the first to receive, accommodate, train and equip the force that was eventually to burgeon out into the Mukti Bahini [Freedom Fighters] of Bangla Desh.'[38] The Indian side of the borderland became populated with training camps for Indian-armed Mukti Bahini forces that carried on a guerrilla war inside East Pakistan. For several months, these forces fought a border war, operating inside East Pakistan territory, and Pakistani troops retaliated by shelling villages and towns on the Indian side of the border and making forays across the border (Plate 10.5).[39]

For nine months, the entire borderland turned into a war zone as millions of refugees poured into India to settle in makeshift camps close to the border, while East Pakistani/ Bangladeshi guerrillas used the relative safety of Indian territory to regroup and relaunch their attacks on the Pakistan army inside East Pakistan (Plate 10.6). It was symbolic for this phase of the war that the first seat of the provisional government of Bangladesh, Mujibnagar, was a border village.

Immediately after India invaded East Pakistan and established the independent state of Bangladesh in late 1971, the borderland was brought under control (Plate 10.7). The camps that had trained Naga, Mizo, Meithei and Tripuri insurgents were dismantled and their inmates fled or were taken captive.

Plate 10.5: President Yahya Khan of Pakistan is seen shooting across the East Pakistan (Bangladesh) border into Indian territory with a view to provoking Indira Gandhi into retaliation. At the time, many in Pakistan believed that Indian retaliation would prompt a renewed flow of economic and military aid to the Pakistan government. Cartoon by Ahmed, 1971.[40]

Plate 10.6: A borderlander ferries Bangladeshi freedom fighters across the Ichhamoti river that forms the border between the districts of 24-Parganas (India) and Khulna (Bangladesh) in 1971.[41]

Plate 10.7: Indian troops ensconced in the border town of Hili (Dinajpur) during the Indian invasion of East Pakistan, November 1971.[42]

Suddenly the border was completely open. Thousands of Indians took the opportunity to visit Bangladesh and vice versa. For the first time since its inception in 1947, the borderland formed a link between two friendly states rather than a divide between two bitter enemies.

The change was as remarkable as it was short-lived. Although Bangladeshis were grateful for the Indian intervention, many were also alarmed by the hegemonic behaviour of Indian troops. The inhabitants of East Pakistan wanted to establish the sovereign state of Bangladesh that they had imagined during long years of struggle; they did not want to join India. By now there was much more that separated them from India than most Indians realized. Undoing Pakistan was one thing, but undoing Partition was no option for Bangladeshis at all: the first flags of Bangladesh showed the outline of the new country, lying comfortably within the embrace of Radcliffe's line.

This mood soon made itself felt in the borderland. The Bangladesh state elite was at pains to demonstrate its newfound independence, not just of Pakistan but of India as well, and it was only to be expected that this elite would revert to the state routines that had developed during the Pakistan era. This trend became much more pronounced after 1975, when the pro-Indian government headed by Sheikh Mujibur Rahman had been replaced by a series of governments that were much less inclined towards close ties with India. Although the intense bitterness of the Pakistan era never returned, the borderland was again tense, and the warm relationship of 1971–5 was definitely over.

The change could be seen in the ways in which the two states dealt with insurgencies on each other's territories. We have seen that insurgents from India's Northeast gradually slipped back into Bangladesh. When in 1974 India was approached by Jumma insurgents from the Chittagong Hill Tracts (Bangladesh), it showed no interest in supporting their cause. But things were different a year later, when another regime had taken power in Bangladesh. For two decades India became the main patron of the Jumma guerrillas, who were fighting the Bangladesh armed forces in the increasingly militarized Chittagong Hill Tracts (Plate 10.8) and who could use the Indian side of the borderland to recuperate, regroup and get training.[43] A second Indian attempt at destabilizing the state of Bangladesh was its support for the 'Kader Bahini' that carried out regular cross-border attacks on Mymensingh district (Bangladesh) from bases in Meghalaya (India) between 1975 and 1977.[44]

Plate 10.8: Members of the Shanti Bahini, the Jumma guerrilla army active in the Chittagong Hill Tracts (Bangladesh), pose for a picture in their jungle hideout in 1986.[45]

In this way, borderland rebellions in the 'nation' mode could become tools in the mutual destabilization games of India and Pakistan, and later India and Bangladesh. The effects of these games on the borderland could vary from being small (e.g. Meitheis in Sylhet) or short-lived (e.g. the Bangladesh Liberation War) to being long-term and disruptive. During regional border wars (e.g. in the Chittagong Hill Tracts (Bangladesh) and Tripura (India) in the 1980s and 1990s), entire sections of the borderland became so chaotic and dangerous that many borderlanders had to flee their homes or were expelled (Plate 10.9).

Plate 10.9: **Inhabitants of the Chittagong Hill Tracts (Bangladesh), caught up in regional war, fleeing to safety in India after a massacre by Bangladesh armed forces, 1986.**[46]

If insurgencies had an impact on sections of the borderland, the borderland also had an impact on insurgencies. The vicinity of the border afforded borderland rebels safety and training camps as well as easy access to arms.[47] Often the policies of rebel leaders were shaped decisively by their experiences in the borderland. Some sections of the Bengal borderland became veritable meeting grounds of citizens of neighbouring countries who would never have met had it not been for their decision to revolt against their states. Here they exchanged ideas about strategy and organization, and developed cross-border networks of mutual support. At times, crucial decisions were made in hideouts across the border rather than in the heartland of the rebellion.

For example, in 1978 six borderland guerrilla groups were operating near the trijunction point where India, Burma and Bangladesh meet: the Mizo National Front (from India), the Arakanese Independence Army, the Mujahids, the Arakan National Liberation Front and the Burmese Communist Party (from Burma), and the Shanti Bahini (from Bangladesh). It was across the border in Arakan, rather than in Mizoram's capital, Aizawl, that the Mizo insurgents held conventions and took their major policy decisions.[48]

One paradox of these borderland rebellions was that they occurred in regions that state elites often saw as peripheral and far removed from their central concerns but at the same time as highly strategic and sensitive. Decisions taken by rebel leaders in border hideouts forced state rulers to sit up and take action, whether in terms of counter-insurgency, political negotiation, propaganda, or (covert) foreign policy. But it was not always a case of the tail wagging the dog. Often the tail itself was being wagged by the dog next door. Borderland rebellions could become hostage to a neighbouring state's strategies to the extent that a change in that state's priorities could lead to the collapse of a rebellion across the border. For example, withdrawal of Indian support was crucial in persuading rebel leaders in the Chittagong Hill Tracts to sign a peace agreement with the Bangladesh government in 1997. In the Bengal borderland, rebellions in the 'nation' mode often appeared to be local events, taking place on one side of the border, but their ramifications were neither local nor restricted to the territory of a single state.

Another paradox was that both rebels and state agents were keen to emphasize their mutual antagonism: the borderland bristled with markers of the territorial state and the nation against which borderlanders ostensibly revolted. But appearances could deceive: in reality there could also be a shared interest between rebels and state agents in perpetuating an unruly borderland. This was the case in Northeast India, where a government commission concluded that 'Ministers, MLAs, bureaucrats and the police ... had a vested interest in insurgency' because insurgency helped them in getting money from New Delhi.[49]

Borderland bandits

The state's control over its territory was challenged not only by insurgents but also by bandits. There is a distinction between insurgents (who fight for political ideals) and criminal gangs (who appropriate wealth by violent means) but this distinction has not always been clear in the borderlands between India, Pakistan/ Bangladesh and Burma. Here, cross-border robbery could pose as an expression of nationalist fervour, protection rackets could masquerade as donations to a revolutionary party, and cattle lifters could portray themselves as ethnic heroes. Like so much else in the borderland, definitions of what constituted criminal behaviour were contested among borderlanders, and between borderlanders and their states.[50]

Since precolonial times, weak state control had made the armed robber, or *dacoit*, a familiar figure in the social landscape of Bengal.[51] The creation of the border provided new opportunities for robbers because law enforcers could be shaken off easily. In the words of an East Pakistani official: 'This has always been a headache to us. People from across the border steal in[to] our territory & commit crimes & return to the other side. Our investigating officers cannot cross the border for enquiring into the incident due to passport regulations. This is also true of our side, i.e. our nationals act likewise.'[52]

The situation was frequently more complex than this. Borderlanders adapted to the new situation by teaming up to form what state agents would call 'Indo-Pak criminal gangs' that gathered information and weapons on either side of the border, struck wherever they wanted, and then hid on the safest side.[53]

In most of the Bengal countryside, gang robbery rarely stirred state officials.[54] But cross-border criminal alliances were another matter, especially if they challenged the state's claim to a monopoly of violence. From the 1940s to the present, the resolve to combat 'cross-border crime' runs through most reports of state officials' meetings regarding border issues; this in itself indicates how unsuccessful these states have been in curbing such activities over the years.

In the late 1940s and 1950s, violent crime in the borderland was usually a local affair, with men from one or a few villages banding together to rob and loot at night.

In February 1955, Nowab Ali, who lived in a village in Tripura (India), sold a plot of land, and his son, a schoolteacher, received his arrear pay. Two fellow villagers, who learned that there was now about Rs.600 in the house, crossed over to a nearby village in Comilla (Pakistan) where they met with friends. That night they raided and looted Nowab Ali's house. But things went wrong for them: Nowab's wife resisted and seriously wounded one robber with a spear, and villagers caught another man just before he could cross back into Pakistan and they beat him to death. When the injured robber, also from Pakistan, recognized one of the local initiators of the robbery among the bystanders and pointed him out, that man clubbed him to death.[55]

This example illustrates the local nature of robbery, both in terms of participants and of spatial range. It also shows how villagers usually meted out retaliatory justice with very simple means and without involving the state judiciary.

This pattern was to change in various ways. An important factor was the increasing availability of more sophisticated weaponry in the borderland. After 1947, armed border guards appeared on the scene and in several parts insurgent groups acquired firearms of their own. It was in the borderland that robbers first graduated from bamboo clubs, large knives and iron bars to rifles, revolvers and bombs. Now robbery required networking that involved people with access to this new technology: insurgents, border guards, policemen and smugglers. Most ordinary borderlanders remained unarmed except for traditional bamboo clubs, spears, machetes and so on, and therefore they were easy victims for robbers with firearms.[56] As a result, violent crime became an increasingly attractive option for those who needed quick money to support a lifestyle, rebellion or election campaign.

The spread of arms was very uneven. There were sections of the borderland where firearms were available from right after Partition (for example, the Burma/East Pakistan border), there were periods when they were more plentiful (for example in the early 1970s, after the huge influx of weaponry during the Bangladesh Liberation War), and there were certain times and places in which criminal networks were more effective than in others. By the 1990s, borderland robberies looked different.

In mid-1999 the Bangladesh government declared an amnesty for 'criminal gangs' who were active in the southwestern borderland, where they had established 'shadow regimes of private adjudication, penal action and toll collection.' Some of these had developed out of insurgent revolutionary groups that had been active in the area in the 1970s and were then known as *rat bahini* ('night troops', i.e. those who rule at night). Later most of them became brigands, terrorizing the countryside. They were known by the name of their leader, or continued to think of themselves as political insurgents. They survived by means of extortion and robbery and their arsenal now included sub-machine guns, self-loading rifles, Sten-guns, revolvers and bombs. The amnesty was followed by an 'anti-terrorist drive' that led some to surrender, others to cross the border into West Bengal, and yet others to ensconce themselves in the coastal Sundarban forest.[57]

The more sophisticated weaponry changed the character of violent crime in the borderland, tilting the balance of power towards robbers and their suppliers.[58] Another factor was the scope of their organizations. The village-based gang became less important as borderland bandits linked up with new underground political movements, smuggling operations and poaching networks, as well as with legal political and commercial activities. Borderlanders found it more difficult to resist violent crime but continued to do so, sometimes by becoming better organized themselves.[59] In some cases cross-border robbers were better armed than border guards and the latter therefore preferred to look the other way rather than challenge them. For example, when a group of 25 heavily armed men in military fatigue crossed the border from Bangladesh to Assam (India) in September 2003, they did so only a few metres from the Indian border outpost of Balia, which was manned by five guards with inferior arms. The guards did nothing as the group looted houses, abducted a contractor and a teacher across the border and demanded a Rs.3 million ransom for each man. According to Indian police sources, the group consisted of 'National Liberation Front of Tripura (NLFT) rebels and Bangladeshi miscreants who ... act in collusion with local collaborators.'[60]

In other cases police and border guards did not look the other way, but actually were among the robbers or provided them with support.[61] Some cross-border raids were carried out in close cooperation with border guards who rented out their arms for an agreed amount for a certain duration. For example, one member of a group of 13 robbers (10 Bangladeshis and 3 Indians) who attacked an Indian border village from Bangladeshi soil in 2003 later alleged that they had hired an AK-series weapon from the 33rd battalion of Bangladesh border guards in Ramgarh for Tk.1,000 per night, and that they had returned it after the robbery.[62] Bangladeshi villagers reported in 2001 that an Indian gang known as the Ghose Bahini, armed with cut rifles and pistols and 'backed by the [Indian border guards], frequently intrude into Bangladesh territory, harass the residents and forcibly take away cattle and crops from the field.'[63] And a spectacular robbery at a borderland Catholic church in India during Christmas 2002 turned out to be linked directly to a recent disruption of the illegal border trade that was an important source of wealth for smugglers and border guards alike. India had suddenly clamped down on a stretch of the border because of fears of 'terrorist' intrusions. Quickly regrouping, an alliance of local Bangladeshi and Indian smugglers turned themselves into a band of armed robbers. They swooped down on the church during midnight mass, injured priests and members of the 1,200-strong congregation, made off with jewellery and about Rs.200,000 in cash, and disappeared across the border, unmolested by border guards.[64]

One region where the newer forms of violent crime blossomed was the Sundarbans, a vast coastal mangrove forest straddling the border between Khulna (East Pakistan/Bangladesh) and 24-Parganas (India). Here people lived by fishing and collecting forest produce. State surveillance was mainly through the Forestry Department, whose officials were known to exploit their positions for private gain: they played a pivotal role in the poaching of timber, deer meat and tiger skins.[65] The Sundarbans also provided shelter for those who lived off river robbery and who exploited the existence of the border to develop two new specializations: kidnapping and piracy.[66]

Kidnapping for ransom was neither new nor restricted to this region.[67] But in the Sundarbans kidnappers chose new targets. Here their victims were not primarily rich landholders, tea-garden managers or entrepreneurs, but fishermen and collectors of shrimp fry. Kidnapped people were taken out to sea or hidden across the border by Indo-Bangladeshi gangs, and routinely killed if ransom was not forthcoming.[68] When border guards caught kidnappers, networks of illegal transborder cooperation could briefly come into view. For example, Bangladeshis charged with kidnapping, illegal fishing and smuggling in West Bengal were released because Indian politicians exerted pressure to that effect.[69]

The Sundarbans also provided an excellent base from which to launch attacks at sea. Pirates had not been much in evidence in the early years after Partition but by the 1980s and 1990s they had become very active. The sea borders of Bangladesh, India and Burma were alive with smugglers, ships (visiting the ports of Calcutta, Chalna, Chittagong and Akyab/ Sittwe) and mechanized fishing craft. As there was no coastal guard to speak of, pirates had a free hand.[70] Using trawlers, they occupied offshore islands where they kept hostages and from where they attacked fishermen and ships.[71] Some regulated their income from fishermen by creating private systems of taxation.[72] It was commonplace for them to challenge the power of the state. When marine border patrols came too close, pirates would attack and fight pitched battles with them. Because the firing power of pirates was frequently superior to that of the border police, it was often more sensible for border guards to seek accommodation and alliances rather than confrontation with pirates.[73]

Challenging the state's power

The borderland proved an excellent site for both rebels and bandits to defy the state and as a result none of the three states – Burma, India and Pakistan/ Bangladesh – have enjoyed a truly 'pacified' borderland. On the contrary, as they overcame early challenges involving tenant cultivators and communists, they were confronted with a growing array of militant regionalisms that expressed themselves increasingly in the idiom of nationalist separatism.[74] In some cases, they were able to come to an agreement with insurgents (e.g. the Indian state and the Mizo National Front in 1986), after which a section of the borderland quietened down.[75] But in the vast majority of cases, they saw no other option than threats and repression.

State officials' inability to engage effectively with regional autonomy movements often found expression in a standardized language shot through with a lofty paternalism, a refusal to take regional demands seriously or treat them as legitimate, and threats of retribution. The following quotation contains a number of typical catchwords ('mainstream', 'extremists', 'terror', 'misguided youths'). Here the Chief Minister of West Bengal, Buddhadeb Bhattacharjee, addresses a relatively small rebel group in the North Bengal borderland in 2001:

The KLO [Kamtapur Liberation Organization] has ignored the government's overtures to join the mainstream. It is our last message to them: either surrender before it's too late or face the music. The government is in no mood to compromise with extremists and those who perpetrate terror. It is time these misguided youths saw sense and gave up arms.[76]

Not surprisingly, words of this kind did little to persuade rebels to give up their struggle, and the state elite usually tried to crush them militarily.[77] Where police and border guards proved unable to cope with the challenge, the army, meant for defence against external enemies, was turned upon the state's own citizens. Whole stretches of the borderland were put under military command and special commando units (in India named 'Black Panthers', 'Black Cats', etc.) were deployed for years on end. In these areas, civil administration was relegated to an inferior position and army personnel were put in charge.[78] It was no coincidence that India located its counter-insurgency training school in the Mizoram borderland soon after Mizoram declared its independence from India in 1966 and became embroiled in secessionist war for 20 years.

The Indian Army's Counter-Insurgency and Jungle Warfare School was established at Vairengte in Mizoram in 1970. It provides training for personnel from the Indian Army as well as the Navy, Air Force, Rashtriya Rifles, paramilitary forces and police. It has also given counter-insurgency training to officers and soldiers from Bangladesh, Nepal, Bhutan, Sri Lanka, Singapore, Kenya, Ghana, Mauritius, Botswana, Iraq and the United States. Training includes quick-response shooting, ambush, jungle lane shooting, chance encounter, mobile firing, hostage rescue operation, urban shooting and pursuit, and airborne drop. In addition, the school provides language familiarization courses in Nagamese, Tangkhul, Assamese, Manipuri and Bodo.[79]

· India, Bangladesh and Burma all used punitive actions, 'combing operations', the herding of borderlanders into 'grouped villages' and other counter-insurgency techniques to control unruly border regions.[80] The results of these policy decisions were predictably bloody, and human rights organizations, both domestic and international, protested strongly.[81] In sections that descended into protracted regional war (e.g. Tripura, the Chittagong Hill Tracts and northern Arakan), borderlanders were caught in the middle for years as neither the state nor its challengers were able to establish dominance.[82] The vicinity of the border provided rebels with a resource that helped them evade the full force of state retaliation and allowed them an independent supply of arms. For the states that deployed armed forces against their own citizens, on the other hand, the border was a useful symbolic resource: they routinely legitimized their actions by invoking the language of national security and threats to territorial integrity.

The other challenge to the states' monopoly of power in the borderland came from bandits or brigands. These had access to increasingly sophisticated weaponry bought, often with proceeds from smuggling and extortion, from arms dealers on both sides of the border. In certain parts of the borderland, they successfully challenged the state and established their own rule.[83] By expanding into piracy, they demonstrated that even the maritime border, which India, Bangladesh and Burma had long treated as an unchallenged territorial marker, was now out of control.

The states sharing the borderland claimed to control their territory and defend its integrity. Such claims should be weighed against the sustained challenges to that control and integrity that rebels and bandits posed in many parts of the borderland. These challenges came from insurgents and violent entrepreneurs outside the state structure but also from within. We have seen that there could be close links between members of law-enforcing agencies and rebels and bandits. It was of course a major weakness of the state that it was not able to control its own personnel. But its weakness was more fundamental: it was a question not just of unwitting cooperation but of conscious coopting. Insurgents who surrendered were often inducted into the state structure and even entrusted with law enforcement.[84] For example, when the Bangladesh government offered an amnesty to 'outlaws' in the southwestern borderland, many of those who surrendered were immediately recruited into the paramilitary Ansar force, even though they did not meet its educational and fitness requirements. This allowed them to continue their activities by other means and with even better protection. It was alleged that in this area,

> where the presence of the ruling party is thin ... outlaws who indicated willingness to join and work for the party [Awami League] were allowed to surrender ... The government ... may be working on the strategy for next elections, where these terrorists will have a role to play.' Evidently, however, state protection was not all that important for these 'rehabilitated' recruits: some of them soon deserted because they disliked 'the disciplined life in the barracks.'[85]

These state tactics were not exceptional. States with weak territorial control have often used one group of predators to catch others.[86] In the Bengal borderland the distinction between border rebel, outlaw and state agent could be almost imperceptible.[87]

Conclusion: unruly borders and the 'border effect'

After Partition, a multitude of relatively well armed and well organized groups sprang up to challenge state strategies of territoriality in the borderland. With the exception of the movement for Bangladesh, these rebellions did not grow into major threats to state survival, but neither were these states able, in the long run, to eliminate armed challenges to their sovereignty in the borderland. Rebellion could be episodic, forms of organization could vary, and protagonists and ideologies could change with amazing rapidity, but nevertheless some long-term trends were noticeable.

Violent territoriality. The state elites of India, Pakistan, Burma and Bangladesh frequently saw no other way of controlling their border regions than by sending in their armed forces. Before Partition, the population of these areas had had very little experience of military presence.[88] Since 1947, however, every part of the borderland (and not just the boundary line itself) has been under military control at one time or another. For some sections of the border this was merely a brief interlude, with militarization primarily focusing at securing the border, after which civil administration regained the upper hand.[89] But several parts of the borderland experienced long periods during which the state's armed forces were deployed to discipline the borderland population. It is important to realize that Burma, Pakistan and Bangladesh all experienced long spells of military rule, which naturally included a strong military presence in the border areas, and that the northeastern states of India have seen equally long periods in which military force has been used as a parallel system of governance and a routine tool of statecraft.[90] But even during periods of parliamentary democracy, sections of the borderland remained under military control and their inhabitants were excluded from democratic procedures and rights.[91] Borderlanders sometimes found themselves living as guinea pigs in what the armed forces considered as laboratories for counter-insurgency training and for testing techniques ranging from 'winning hearts and souls' to styles of patrolling, forced resettlement, and the effective use of crowd control, torture and the latest weaponry.[92]

It was in these sections of the borderland that the inability of post-Partition states to exert territorial control without resorting to systematic violence could best be observed. Over time, militarization became an indispensable instrument of rule, used against enemies within, but also holding much larger groups of borderlanders hostage (Plates 10.10 and 10.11).

As we have seen, the exact locations of borderland militarization shifted over time but it was the practice itself, and particularly the suspension of the human and civil rights of borderlanders that it entailed, which drew wider attention to military violence as a state routine. Not only did this practice of violent territoriality receive more attention nationally and internationally over time, but its effect on these states themselves became more visible, in terms of the emergence of regional parties, terrorist attacks beyond the borderland, the spawning of new insurgencies, and increased military spending.[93]

Global links. The scale of many armed challenges to state sovereignty was quite large, both in terms of the numbers of people involved and the border areas affected. But these challenges posed no immediate threat to the survival of the state and for this reason many politicians and analysts of state and nation in India, Bangladesh and Burma have simply ignored them, or marginalized

Plate10.10: The borderland under military rule. An army camp on a denuded hill top overlooks Lake Kaptai and all traffic moving on it. Near Betchhari, Chittagong Hill Tracts, Bangladesh, 2001.

Plate 10.11: Bangladesh Rifles patrolling Lake Kaptai by speedboat, 2001.

them as purely 'local' problems – little sores festering quietly in remote parts of the nation's body. It has not been easy for them to stick to this position, however, when thousands of refugees fled the national territory, or when airplanes were hijacked, trains blown up, foreign aid workers kidnapped, or ambassadors to the United Nations embarrassed by noisy demonstrators.

As we have seen, borderland rebels' international connections varied over time and between rebellions but the long-term trend has been for them to grow. As a result, India, Bangladesh and Burma have found it increasingly difficult to treat borderland rebellions as local and domestic affairs. They have had to acknowledge that other states lent military, financial and political support to these rebellions, and that international organizations became more intent on calling each of these three states to account for their human rights violations in border areas.

For example, until the late 1980s the Bangladesh state had been successful in projecting itself in the international arena as a victim of a horrendous war of independence, natural disasters and world-economic inequities. It was widely seen as an innocent state struggling heroically against huge odds. But this image underwent drastic readjustment when news about the borderland rebellion of Jummas in the Chittagong Hill Tracts began to circulate worldwide. International human rights groups, organizations of indigenous peoples and United Nations bodies were instrumental in exposing a string of massacres and other human rights abuses perpetrated by the Bangladesh armed forces.[94] Through their publications, and by creating an international platform for the voices of borderland rebels, they put unprecedented pressure on the Bangladesh state elite, and on the states that funded it so lavishly with development aid. In international forums, representatives of the Bangladesh state suddenly found themselves accused of genocide and the country's international image was tarnished considerably.[95]

Borderland rebels supported their movements financially not only by means of donations, toll collections, ransoms or robberies. They also tapped into international trade flows to support themselves, taxing producers and traders operating in their section of the borderland, or becoming (illegal) traders themselves. Their dependence on international trade networks was considerable: tea, timber, opium and arms were among the most important commodities of international trade that sustained borderland revolts in one way or another. By the beginning of the 21st century, opium appeared to be emerging as a dominant source of income, not only as an item of borderland trade, but increasingly as a cash crop grown in the borderland itself, and under the protection of rebels.[96]

The ability of borderland rebels to link up with international networks of information, lobbying, funds and trade allowed them, more than ever before, to 'jump scale,' to break out of the iron grip of the nation state and to mobilize support and resources from abroad.[97] Their international networking made them review their own strategies and aims. Increasingly they saw their struggles in the borderland not so much as local, domestic affairs, more or less contained by state counter-insurgency, but as local manifestations of revolts against state power going on all over the world. The struggles continued to be local but the views informing them grew more global. Most borderland rebellions came to depend increasingly on funds from diasporic borderlanders – in, for example, Canada, Australia or Saudi Arabia – who could be described as long-distance nationalists.[98] For the state elites of India, Bangladesh and Burma, this implied that the strategy of violent territoriality now came at a higher price. They found it more difficult to apply the old tactics of containment, isolation, repression and expulsion because they were pitted against borderland adversaries who were not only better armed and less easily intimidated but whose crucial advantage lay in being much better connected than before.[99] To the extent that they could mobilize external support, borderland rebels became players in international arenas as well as in local and national ones.[100]

The border effect.   By defying state power, rebels and bandits contributed to a continual reproduction of the border. The states reacted to the challenge by opting for violent forms of territoriality in the borderland, but also by emphasizing their control of the border itself. Military, administrative and symbolic control of the boundary was of the essence wherever state sovereignty was put into question. Anti-personnel mines, fences, outposts, border roads and armed patrols served as emphatic expressions of state sovereignty in parts of the borderland where that sovereignty was being challenged. Events in the borderland became an important factor in shaping these states.

In a general discussion of the role of bandits, rebels and other military entrepreneurs in the history of state formation, Thomas Gallant speaks of the 'border effect'.[101] Very often, border banditry and rebellion pose real challenges to a state's monopoly of violence. In order to eradicate these challenges, the army is sent to the border regions, followed by bureaucrats. The state's attempt to abolish borderland unruliness and to establish its law and order has a dual effect. On the one hand, it introduces the mechanisms of centralized state control, incorporating border regions more firmly into the national polity and leading to a more precise demarcation of the state's territorial sovereignty. On the other hand, however, it facilitates and shapes the internal consolidation of the state. The need to eradicate border unruliness acts as a tool to create both a stronger, more centralized state apparatus and a new balance of power within the state, between the military, the bureaucracy and politicians. The relative success, or failure, of military and political campaigns in the borderland is an important determinant of this balance of power. It also impinges on the state's wider policy options, especially in terms of whether it opts for accommodation with, or repression of, other forms of opposition.

The border effect was of particular significance in the formation of the fledgling post-Partition states. Preoccupied, from the moment of their creation, with eradicating borderland unruliness, they sought to establish law and order. At the same time, however, they were shaped by their border policies. There can be no doubt that the activities of rebels and bandits in the Bengal borderland contributed in a major way to the emergence of the armed forces as rulers and administrators in East Pakistan, Bangladesh, Burma and Northeast India. The consolidation of these states in the second half of the twentieth century owed a great deal more to borderland unruliness, and the border effect, than is commonly realized.

But it was not just that rebels made states reinforce their grip on the border and thereby contributed to a consolidation of these states. Rebels themselves reproduced the border by restricting their territorial imagination to one side of it. All borderland revolts challenging the post-Partition states pitted themselves against only one of these states, and hence their territorial claims were restricted to parts of that state's territory. True, nation-based revolts often referred vaguely to broad swathes of territory that had historically been inhabited by ancestors and to which they might one day lay claim. Rebel visionaries could dream of a future 'Greater Mizoram' or a (partly overlapping) 'Jummaland', both covering parts of Burma, India and Bangladesh. But the actual strategies of rebel politicians were securely nested in post-Partition geography. They strove to carve an independent country out of a single post-Partition state. Failing that, they wished for a zone of relative autonomy within one of these states. The political activities of borderland rebels underlined the defining power of Radcliffe's cartography.

The defining power of Radcliffe's cartography plays a crucial role in the next chapter as well. It documents a very specific kind of violent territoriality: the Radcliffe line itself has become a zone of everyday killing and maiming; it has become a 'killer border'. Although rebels and bandits play a role in this violence, there are many other protagonists. In the following pages I plot these practices of everyday violence and identify their victims.

Notes

1 Thomas Gallant, who suggests this term especially to categorize 'armed predators ... who operate in the interstice between legality and illegality', describes military entrepreneurs as 'men who take up arms and who wield violence or the threat of violence as their stock in trade ... They are entrepreneurs in the sense that they are purveyors of a commodity – violence.' Military entrepreneurs may pit themselves against a state (which then brands them as bandits, rebels, brigands, pirates, warlords, etc.) or they may put themselves at the service of a state (which then incorporates them as border patrols, freedom fighters, coastguards, or tax collectors). Thomas W Gallant,

'Brigandage, Piracy, Capitalism, and State-Formation: Transnational Crime from a Historical World-Systems Perspective', in: Josiah McC Heyman (ed.), *States and Illegal Practices* (Oxford and New York: Berg, 1999), 27.

2 Among the more prominent rebellions were, starting from the southeast, various independence movements in Arakan (Burma; 1948–present); the revolt in the Chittagong Hill Tracts (Bangladesh; 1972–97); the Mizoram uprising (India; 1947–86); the civil war in Tripura (India; 1980s–present); the Nankar revolt in Sylhet (East Pakistan; 1940s); the Assam movement (India; 1979–85); and the Naxalbari/ Atrai rebellion (India–Bangladesh; 1967–1970s).

3 The two identities could also be seen to alternate in the long term. The late 1940s and early 1950s were a period in which class-based border rebellions were more noticeable than nation-based ones, and the Naxalbari uprising in 1967 set the tone for a new series of class-based insurgencies that remained active throughout the 1970s. Nation-based border rebellions were relatively weak in the immediate post-Partition period but picked up in the 1950s and have been very noticeable ever since. As a result of these two trends, the late 1960s and the 1970s presented the most complex configuration of borderland rebellions to date, and the period since then has been dominated by borderland challenges to state control that based themselves more on national identities than on class ones.

4 E.g. when the Assam government had to transfer communist prisoners in Silchar jail (Cachar) to Guwahati in 1948, they worried that transport by rail would cause popular disturbances. To avoid these, they approached the East Pakistan government to transport the prisoners in well-guarded trucks from Silchar through Sylhet (East Pakistan) to Guwahati (Pol. EBP7P-3/48 (8-48)).

5 Pol. 13-1/48 (10-48). West Bengal and Assam were, however, equally worried about communist influence. The West Bengal government declared the Communist Party of India illegal (CR 5R-1/50 (1-53b)) and the Deputy Commissioner of Sylhet (East Pakistan) observed: 'It also appears that the Assam Govt. externed a large number of veteran and dangerous communists and they all came to Sylhet district and pushed their programmes here' (Pol. P3I-33/49 (12-49)).

6 Circular from the Chief Secretary, Government of East Bengal, to all Departments, Directorates, Commissioners, District and Subdivisional Officers (Government of East Bengal, Home Department, General Administration and Appointment Branch, IE-29/49 (B. Proceedings of 1949); hereafter G&A IE-29/49).

7 This high official, the Commissioner of the Rajshahi Division, had originally launched this plan in December 1947 but had found the results disappointing (Pol. P10A-20/49 (4-49)).

8 The role of communists in these rebellions was related to a period of heightened activism between 1948 and 1950. Communists used the border in other ways as well. In February 1949, the Revolutionary Communist Party of India (RCPI) attacked Calcutta airport, an ammunitions factory and Basirhat police station. After a battle between police and about 40 armed men, the 'gang tried to escape across the border to East Pakistan but two were apprehended after a chase with the help of local people.' Saroj Chakrabarty, *With Dr. B.C. Roy and Other Chief Ministers (a Record Upto 1962)* (Calcutta: Benson's, 1974), 115–16.

9 Cf. Taj ul-Islam Hashmi, *Pakistan as a Peasant Utopia: The Communalization of Class Politics in East Bengal, 1920–1947* (Boulder, Col.: Westview Press, 1992), 231–7.

10 CR 6M3-8/54 (1-55).

11 Pol. P5R-28/49 (8-49); Pol. P3P-125/49 (11-49); Pol. P5R-61/49 (12-49); Pol. P3I-4/50 (3-51); CR 6M1-1/51 (7-53). Cf. Promotho Gupto, *Muktijuddhe Adibashi (Moymonsingh)* (Calcutta: National Book Agency, 1964). These attacks by hundreds of Hajongs on police stations and patrols led to frequent casualties. See e.g. 'Punoray pulish o Hajonge shonghorsho: Momenshahi shimante ekjon nihoto o 6-jon ahoto', *Azad* (15 February 1949); 'Pulish – Hajong shonghorsher protibad: Momenshahi Communistder hortal prochesta byortho', *Azad* (27 February 1949); 'Momemshahi zelay Hajong upodrob: pulisher shonge shonghorsher phole koekjon hotahoto', *Azad* (26 July 1949).

12 Under the Police Act of 1861, after declaring the area 'disturbed'. *The Dacca Gazette Extraordinary* (26 September 1949).

13 CR 4M-1/50 (3-53). After 1950 the movement subsided.

14 Pol. EBP10C-18/47 (4-48). The Additional District Magistrate of Sylhet concurred: 'Nankar dispute in this district cannot be put down unless drastic actions against the Communists are taken' (Pol. P10C-17/48 (9-48)).

15 'It appears that nearly in all the areas of Sylhet there is a deep laid and well spread communist organisation ... Inciting leaflets and pamphlets defying the law and order and instigating people against the Pakistan State and exciting the mazdoors [labourers] were being widely distributed by the communists ... Processions were paraded shouting slogans like "Pakistan Dhangsha Hok [Down with Pakistan], Inquilab Zindabad [Victory to the Revolution], etc. etc." ...They became bold after the repeated successes of communists in China and started their anti-State activities openly and fearlessly. They chose inaccessible and Hindu areas for their head quarters and centres of activities though some Muslim students and youths were trapped by them ... To confine my report to the Beanibazar and Borlekha area ... towards the end of 1947 the brainy and clever communists started instigating the Nankars (holders of chakran lands) of these areas to create troubles against the landlords and the Govt. ... They went so far as to attack the Bahadurpur Police camp in November 1947 ...attacked [the police chief of Beanibazar] in March 1948 ... In May 1948 ... they observed Nankar Day in Beanibazar and Borlekha ... In June 1949 the communists again raised their heads [and] Independent Communist and Mazdoor Raj was proclaimed in June 1949' (Pol. P3I-33/49 (12-49); cf. Pol. P10C-17/48 (4-49)). Cf. Ajay Bhattacharya, *Nankar Bidroho* (Dhaka: Punthipotro, 1973-1976; 2 vols.).

16 CR 3R-1/54 (3-55). Cf. Mesbah Kamal and Ishani Chokroborti, *Nacholer Krishok Bidroho Shomokalin Rajniti O Ila Mitro* (Dhaka: Muktijuddho Bongobondhu O Bangladesh Gobeshona Institute, 2001). Other communist-supported movements in the borderland that survived Partition were among (largely non-Muslim) tobacco and betel nut growers in northern Rangpur (Pol. P15P-47/48 (4-49)), and the agitation in Khulna that was influenced by the movement in 24-Parganas, across the border in West Bengal. Adrienne Cooper, *Sharecropping and Sharecroppers' Struggles in Bengal, 1930–1950* (Calcutta: KP Bagchi, 1988), 225.

17 Their most active post-Partition period was between 1948 and 1950. See Cooper, *Sharecropping*, 211–42; Krishnakanta Sarkar, 'Kakdwip Peasant Insurrection,' in: AR Desai (ed.), *Agrarian Struggles in India After Independence* (Delhi: Oxford University Press, 1986), 618–59.

18 Naxalbari is a *thana* (police station) in the southern tip of Darjeeling district (West Bengal, India).

19 For introductions, see Asish Kumar Roy, *The Spring Thunder and After: A Survey of the Maoist and Ultra-Leftist Movements in India, 1962–75* (Calcutta: Minerva, 1975);

Sumanta Banerjee, *In the Wake of Naxalbari: A History of the Naxalite Movement in India* (Calcutta: Subarnarekha, 1980); Edward AJ Duyker, *Tribal Guerrillas: West Bengal's Santals and the Naxalite Movement* (Delhi: Oxford University Press, 1987); Marius Damas, *Approaching Naxalbari* (Calcutta: Radical Impression, 1991).

20 In March 1967 the pro-Moscow CPI (Communist Party of India), the pro-Beijing CPI(M), and other parties formed the United Front government in West Bengal. A few weeks later, a peasant conference was held under the auspices of the CPI(M) leadership of Siliguri, the subdivision of the district of Darjeeling bordering both East Pakistan and Nepal. The conference led to peasant committees being organized and armed all over the region, and to land occupations and finally confrontations with the police. Important leaders of the insurgence – e.g. Jangal Santhal, Kanu Sanyal, and Charu Mazumdar – were all from the area.

21 Banerjee, *In the Wake*, 111; Roy, *Spring Thunder*, 51–2, 68.

22 Photographer unknown. From the Mazumdar family collection.

23 On jumping scale, see chapter 1.

24 'Spring Thunder over India', *People's Daily* (5 July 1967), quoted in Roy, *Spring Thunder*, 105 and Damas, *Approaching Naxalbari*, 82; cf. Amiya K Samanta, *Left Extremist Movement in West Bengal: An Experiment in Armed Agrarian Struggle* (Calcutta: Firma KLM Private Ltd., 1984), 111.

25 Samanta, *Left Extremist Movement*, 111–12. Members of the Communist Party of India (Marxist-Leninist) in West Bengal, interviewed by Shahriar Kabir in December 1996. Recordings deposited in the International Institute of Social History, Amsterdam, The Netherlands.

26 For this reason, Indian support for the Hajongs remained restricted to providing a safe haven for refugees and petitioning the Pakistani state to return confiscated property.

27 S Mahmud Ali, *The Fearful State: Power, People and Internal War in South Asia* (London: Zed Books, 1993), 181.

28 Several of these groups also sought, and gained, support from China, which turned into an implacable enemy of India, especially after the India-China War of 1962, and which, together with the USA, acted as a political patron to Pakistan.

29 Ali, *The Fearful State*, 15.

30 According to Chatterjee, there were Naga training camps in Rangamati, Ruma, Bandarban, the Rainkhiang Reserved Forest and Alikadam. Between 1959 and 1965, four batches of Naga guerrillas were sent there for training, returning home with arms and ammunition given by the Pakistan government. In 1965, the Indian press reported that 1,500 Naga 'hostiles' had re-entered Indian territory after receiving arms and training in East Pakistan. In 1969, Chatterjee writes, the Chinese opened a training centre for guerrilla warfare and a 'small air-strip was built in a place 15 kms South-east of Rangamati in the Chittagong Hill Tracts to train insurgents [from India] in air operation.' Naga training in East Pakistan came to an abrupt end in 1971 (but rebels from Nagaland returned in 1991). According to Ali, citing the Indian Home Minister, Mizo training camps were located in Ruma, Bolipara, Mowdok, Thanchi, Alikadam and Dighinala. Nibedon (1980) gives a detailed account of the escape of the Mizo rebels from Bangladesh in December 1971; they returned in 1979. See RK Chatterjee, *India's Land Borders: Problems and Challenges* (Delhi: Sterling Publishers, 1978), 207–8; 'Minorities in East Pakistan: Government watching situation – Naga hostiles', *The Statesman* (14 September 1965); Ali, *The Fearful State*, 39, 182; Sen Gupta, *Eclipse of East Pakistan*, 392–5; Nirmal Nibedon, *Nagaland: The Night of the Guerrillas* (Delhi:

Lancers Publishers, 1978), 83; Nirmal Nibedon, *Mizoram: The Dagger Brigade* (Delhi: Lancers Publishers, 1980), esp. 150–78; Phanjoubam Tarapot, *Insurgency Movement in North-Eastern India* (Delhi: Vikas, 1996), 130, 201; Sanjoy Hazarika, *Strangers of the Mist: Tales of War & Peace from India's Northeast* (Delhi: Viking, 1994), 117, 171; Dinesh Chandra Jha, *Indo-Pakistan Relations (1960–1965)* (Patna: Bharati Bhawan, 1972), 295–8; 'Mizoram double mission to Dhaka', *The Telegraph* (11 December 2002); 'Mizo "hand" in Bangla creation: MNF leaders had thought of executing Zia-ur Rahman', *The Telegraph* (3 June 2003).

31 Near Mohajontora, in the Chittagong Hill Tracts. They formed close links with the Mizo fighters there, and took training in their camps in 1978, according to Tarapot, *Insurgency Movement*, 177, 179. After 1975, they returned here. According to the Chief Minister of Tripura, in 1999 there were 'at least 25 camps of the different insurgent groups in Bangladesh', which the Bangladesh government denied. In 2000, Indian newspapers reported a Bangladesh army crackdown on insurgents from Tripura in the Sajek range of the Chittagong Hill Tracts. In 2001, an Indian newspaper published what it claimed to be 'the complete list of training camps [of] insurgent outfits [from India] deep within Bangladesh territory'; this list contained 24 locations. In 2002, other press reports put the number of camps of 'Tripura militants' alone in Bangladesh at 39, and the total number of camps (run by 10 different 'Northeast ultra' groups) in Bangladesh at 99. By 2003, the Indian government claimed that there were 155 terrorist training camps in Bangladesh, run by at least ten different insurgent groups from India's northeastern states. Bangladesh consistently denied the existence of these camps. This same pattern of accusation-and-denial could also be observed at a lower administrative level, between states in India: Tripura accused Mizoram of harbouring 7 camps of National Liberation Front of Tripura (NLFT) rebels, a charge refuted by the Home Minister of Mizoram who accused Tripura of letting leaders of the Bru National Liberation Front (BNLF – a group of exiles from Mizoram) use 6 camps in Tripura. Brahmanand Mishra, 'India: Tackling hostility on two fronts,' *Far Eastern Economic Review*, 84:18 (6 May 1974), 14; '"No camps of insurgents in Bangladesh"', *The Daily Star* (1 February 1999); cf. Man Mohan, 'Tripura wants Centre to get ultra camps in Bangladesh closed', *The Times of India* (9 September 1998); *XII Lok Sabha Debates, Session III* (23 December 1998); '42 guerrillas arrested from Indo-Bangla border', *Rediff on the Net* (11 March 1999); Subir Bhaumik, 'Dateline Lalu Kalu: Here NE rebels train side by side', *The Northeast Daily* (21 May 2000); 'Bangla army kills 11 Tripura militants', *The Times of India* (19 June 2000); 'Bangla Army commandos kill 11 NLFT militants', *The Assam Tribune* (20 June 2000); Chandan Nandy, 'Revealed: Bangla Covert Camps', *The Telegraph* (14 June 2001); 'NSCN (I-M), PLA, ULFA, Tripura ultras sharing camps', *The Assam Tribune* (20 March 2002); 'NLFT, ATTF battle it out in Bangladesh', *The Assam Tribune* (22 June 2002); 'India identifies 99 NE ultra camps in Bangla', *The Assam Tribune* (4 November 2002); 'India seeks closure of 155 ultra camps in Bangladesh', *The Assam Tribune* (12 May 2003); 'Tripura CM furnishes list of 7 camps', *The Assam Tribune* (3 July 2003).

32 When the Bangladesh Liberation War broke out in 1971, these trainees fought on the side of the Pakistan army, ambushing Indian border security personnel in Cachar, Karimganj and Dharmanagar. They left what had become Bangladesh in December 1971 but were said to have re-established camps at Chhotodamai (Sylhet) in 1987. In 1999 some were arrested in Sylhet, together with a local helper, for illegal border crossing and possession of illegal Chinese arms. In 2002, Meithei rebels belonging to various

insurgent groups were reported to be training in nine bases in the Bangladesh districts of Sylhet, Moulvi Bazar and Srimongol; they were said to be 'shopping for cellular phone interceptors, night vision binoculars and spy listening devices, besides sophisticated arms and ammunition.' Tarapot, *Insurgency Movement*, 41–6, 139, 172; BG Verghese, *India's Northeast Resurgent: Ethnicity, Insurgency, Governance, Development* (Delhi: Konark, 1996), 118, 120, 180; '4 alleged ULFA men acquitted of charge of keeping illegal arms', *The Daily Star* (25 July 1999); 'Meitei ultras go high tech in Bangladesh', *The Sentinel* (17 March 2002).

33 'Purbo Pak hoite Barmay hana,' *Azad* (2 January 1949); Ali, *The Fearful State*, 187.

34 Nibedon, *Mizoram*, inserted after 16; Nirmal Nibedon, *North East India: The Ethnic Explosion* (New Delhi: Lancers Publishers, 1981), inserted after table of contents (photographers unacknowledged). The guerrillas retreated to India as their Pakistani protectors were losing the war against the Bangladesh freedom fighters and the Indian army. The Mizo leader Laldenga appears in the top photograph (standing in the middle).

35 Notably the United Liberation Front of Asom (ULFA) whose 'anti-Bangladeshi-infiltrators' stand contrasted with its links with Bangladesh. An improvement in relations between Bangladesh and India, after the Awami League came to power in Bangladesh in 1996, led to army raids on training camps of Assamese and Naga insurgents in Bangladesh. ULFA then transferred its major command bases to Bhutan. Hazarika, *Strangers of the Mist*, 170–5; Tarapot, *Insurgency Movement*, 170, 172; Verghese, *India's Northeast Resurgent*, 60; SK Ghosh, *Unquiet Border* (New Delhi: Ashish Publishing House, 1993), 82-84; 'Bangla begins crackdown on NE ultras,' *The Sentinel* (2 February 1997); 'Ultras trying to enter India via Indo-Bangla border', *The Sentinel* (8 July 1999); see also evidence given by ULFA men in the documentary 'India: Assam Tea Wars' (Reporter: Mark Corcoran; Australian Broadcasting Corporation, 23 May 2001).

36 Tarapot, *Insurgency Movement*, after 134. Photographer unacknowledged. It is not completely clear whether the photograph was taken at Chhotodamai or at another camp in Bangladesh.

37 See for example Hasan Zaheer, *The Separation of East Pakistan: The Rise and Realization of Bengali Muslim Nationalism* (Karachi: Oxford University Press, 1995).

38 Mohammed Ayoob and K Subrahmanyam, *The Liberation War* (Delhi: S Chand and Co., 1972), 155; DK Palit, *The Lightning Campaign: The Indo-Pakistan War 1971* (Salisbury: Compton Press, 1972), 63–4; Ghosh, *Unquiet Border*, 90–1. Pakistani sources have insisted that these links predated the war and that the Indian Border Security Force became involved in 'subverting' East Pakistan from as early as 1966. See AMK Maswani, *Subversion in East Pakistan* (Lahore: Amir Publications, 1979), 177–87; cf. Jha, *Indo-Pakistan Relations*, 298–9.

39 Palit, *The Lightning Campaign*, 59, 61; and e.g. 'Pakistani army violating border regulations,' *The Statesman* (15 April 1971); 'Exchange of fire on border: 30 Indian villagers reported killed', *The Statesman* (28 April 1971).

40 The identity of the cartoonist is unclear. Reaz Ahmed, from whose compilation this cartoon derives, writes in his introduction: 'I could not gather any information on him [Ahmed] and the sources of where and when these cartoons were published. We can presume that probably they were published around October 1971.' Reaz Ahmed (comp. and ed.), *Gonomadhyome Bangladesher Muktijuddho, Kartun, Prothom Khondo / Media and Liberation War of Bangladesh, Cartoons, Volume 1* (Dhaka: Centre for Bangladesh Studies, 2002), 17, 22, 42.

41 *Bangla Name Desh* (Calcutta: Anondo Publishers, 1972), 86. Photographer

unacknowledged.

42 Lachhman Singh, *Indian Sword Strikes in East Pakistan* (Sahibabad: Vikas Publishing House, 1979), facing 114. Photographer unacknowledged.

43 On this episode, see Hazarika, *Strangers of the Mist*, 278–90. On the background of the Chittagong Hill Tracts war, see for example Siddhartho Chakma, *Proshongo: Parbotyo Chottogram* (Calcutta: Nath Brothers, 1392 BE [1985–6]); Ali, *The Fearful State*, 162–203; Willem van Schendel, Wolfgang Mey and Aditya Kumar Dewan, *The Chittagong Hill Tracts: Living in a Borderland* (Bangkok: White Lotus, 2000). On the term Jumma, see Willem van Schendel, 'The Invention of the "Jummas": State Formation and Ethnicity in Southeastern Bangladesh', *Modern Asian Studies*, 26:1 (1992), 95–128. On militarization and human rights abuses, see Chittagong Hill Tracts Commission, *Life is Not Ours: Land and Human Rights in the Chittagong Hill Tracts, Bangladesh* (Copenhagen/Amsterdam: International Work Group on Indigenous Affairs (IWGIA)/ Organising Committee Chittagong Hill Tracts Campaign, 1991). *Update 1* (1992); *Update 2* (1994); *Update 3* (1997); *Update 4* (2000); Bhaumik, Subir, Meghna Guhathakurta and Sabyasachi Basu Ray Chaudhury (eds.), *Living on the Edge: Essays on the Chittagong Hill Tracts* (Calcutta: South Asia Forum for Human Rights/ Calcutta Research Group, 1997). Although a peace accord was signed in 1997, many of its crucial elements were never implemented and violent clashes continued to occur. For a recent confrontation, see Pinaki Roy, 'Ethnic villagers live under spectre of fear: Over 1,500 live in the open, burn-out houses dot ravaged Mahalchhari villages', *The Daily Star* (4 September 2003).

44 The Kader Bahini were a guerrilla group headed by Kader Siddiqui. See Lawrence Lifschultz, *Bangladesh: The Unfinished Revolution* (London: Zed Press, 1979), 64; Ellen Bal, 'They Ask If We Eat Frogs': Social Boundaries, Ethnic Categorisation, and the Garo People of Bangladesh* (Delft: Eburon, 2000). For official reports and Bangladeshi demands that India should dismantle the 'miscreants'' training camps in Meghalaya and return the inmates to Bangladesh, see Avtar Singh Bhasin (ed.), *India-Bangladesh Relations: Documents – 1971–2002* (New Delhi: Geetika Publishers, 2003), IV, 1911–16.

45 From the collection of the Organising Committee Chittagong Hill Tracts Campaign. Photographer unacknowledged.

46 From the collection of the Organising Committee Chittagong Hill Tracts Campaign. Photographer unacknowledged.

47 Obviously, arms smuggling was one form of illicit trading, as discussed briefly in chapter 7. Money for arms came largely from toll collection, ransoms, bank robberies, donations by foreign governments, donations by locals living abroad, and involvement in various other forms of smuggling. Arms were often hidden close to the border. When Bangladesh armed forces discovered two hideouts in 'deep forest' near Dochhari on the Bangladesh-Burma border, they found '130 kilograms of powerful plastic explosives, 26 containers of other explosives, 226 grenades, 61 M-16 rifle bullets, 18 containers full of chemicals, 50 time-regulating watch[es] used in explosive devices, a shotgun, 12 detonator boosters, 40 battery connectors, and a range of other accessories'. They were not sure who these belonged to, although they observed that 'militant operatives from Myanmar' frequented the area. Cf. V Chitra, 'The great triple-border arms bazaar', *Tehelka* (24 October 2000); 'Arms cache seized from deep CHT forests: Army suspects subversive activities', *The Daily Star* (20 September 2003).

48 See Nibedon, *Mizoram*, 240–60.

49 The Advisory Group on Northeastern States, consisting largely of officials of the Indian

Ministry of Home Affairs, concluded: 'even Chief Ministers kept MLAs [Members of Legislative Assemblies] on their side on a consideration which sometimes went as high as Rs.11 lakh [US$23,000] per month per MLA.' The money came from 'State funds, extortion at check-gates and commissions on supplies and recruitment ... money is also required to pay off the insurgent groups or to allow them to raise taxes ... insurgency helped in getting money from the Centre.' 'Illegal Money Collection NE's Canker: Advisory Group', *The Shillong Times* (7 May 2003).

50 For a comparative perspective, see Gallant, 'Brigandage, Piracy'.

51 For an introduction, see Ranjit Sen, *Social Banditry in Bengal: A Study in Primary Resistance, 1757–1793* (Calcutta: Ratna Prakashan, 1988).

52 CR 1B3-16/53 (11-54).

53 For a description of a cross-border gang of Chakmas from Assam (India) and East Pakistan, see CR 1B4-12/52 (6-54).

54 Dacoities often went (and continue to go) unreported. According to figures on 'serious crime' compiled by the government of East Bengal between 1947 and 1950, however, there were on average 4,283 cases of dacoity and robbery, and 3,533 cases of rioting, each year (Pol. P3R-7/48 (8-49); Pol. P3R-68 (1)/48 (3-49); Pol. P3R-5/50 (3-51); Pol. P3R-68/48(2-x) (4-49); Pol. P3R-17/49 (10-49)).

55 It was then that the villagers called in the police, leading to the events being recorded in CR 3I-63/55 (10-55).

56 'Border crime incidents in Tripura continue unchecked', *The Sentinel* (29 April 2003).

57 A notorious group in Kushtia was known as 'Ruhul's Fighters', and various competing groups in Khulna and Jessore called themselves factions of the Revolutionary Communist Party, the East Bengal Communist Party, the People's Fighters, etc. See e.g. 'Chalan Beel now a den of extremists', *The Independent* (7 August 1999); Zahid Hossain Biplob, 'It was a sweet revenge to Ruhul Bahini but an endless nightmare to villagers', *The New Nation* (10 August 1999); '464 former outlaws to be recruited to Ansar forces today – 250 more extremists to surrender at Kushtia July 23', *The Independent* (18 July 1999); 'Protecting fishermen', *The Independent* (22 August 1999); 'Atrai, a centre of Biplab Bahini's terrorism', *The Daily Star* (4 September 1999); '23 gangs of robbers control Sundarban,' *The Independent* (16 September 2002). For a replay of this operation, and 'underground activists and criminals' once again crossing the border to India, see 'Anticrime crackdown in southwestern dists begins', *The Daily Star* (19 July 2003); '10,000 outlaws rule 10 districts in SW region', *The Daily Star* (19 July 2003); '11,000-strong joint force swings into action in southwestern region', *The Daily Star* (20 July 2003).

58 Better arms also allowed smugglers to return to the more confrontational tactics that they had employed in the early years after Partition. When members of the Bangladesh Rifles tried to confiscate a truck laden with sugar near the border in a village in Comilla district in 1999, 'the people of the locality, led by the "smugglers" blocked the road at Padua Bazar and locked in a clash with the BDR members by exploding bombs and damaging [fifty] vehicles on the highway ... the crowd went violent creating a panic in the area. The mob also kept seven members of the BDR hostage for hours.' The fight, which left one person dead and 30 injured, blocked all traffic on the crucial Dhaka-Chittagong highway for six hours ('One killed as BDR men, alleged smugglers clash in Comilla', *The Independent* (29 June 1999)). For a similar case in Dinajpur, and further examples of smugglers attacking border guards who blocked their way in Mymensingh and Rajshahi, see 'One killed as smugglers clash with BDR', *The Daily Star* (10 June

1999); 'Two Indian intruders killed in Mymensingh', *The Independent* (9 August 1999); 'Smugglers attack BDR men, snatch contraband items', *The Independent* (21 August 1999)

59 E.g. in a 'People's Platform against Terrorism' (Santrashbad Birodhi Gana Mancha) in Lower Assam. 'Nalbari people unite against militant outfits', *The Assam Tribune* (29 July 1999); cf. 'Villagers beat 3 outlaws to death in Kushtia', *The Daily Star* (13 February 1999).

60 'BSF failure in Barak border', *The Sentinel* (14 September 2003).

61 As admitted by the Inspector-General of Police in Bangladesh. A survey by the Bangladesh Society for Enforcement of Human Rights revealed that police officers 'earned 600 to 1,000 times more than their salaries, mainly through bribes and extortion.' Robberies by members of the Nasaka (Burmese border guards) in southern Bangladesh also occurred occasionally. See '1600 outlaws surrender; amnesty deadline expires', *The New Nation* (31 July 1999); 'BSEHR survey: Police officers earn 1000 times more than their salaries', *The Daily Star* (17 April 1999); 'Bangladesh arrests Myanmar men with live grenades', *ShweInc News* (16 March 1999).

62 "'BDR provided arms to Bangladesh dacoits'", *The Assam Tribune* (10 June 2003). For two other groups of cross-border robbers, see 'Calcutta-Khulna crime corps – Bangladeshi rob-and-run mastermind held at Sealdah station', *The Telegraph* (16 July 2003); 'Bangla band of robbers held', *The Telegraph* (23 July 2003).

63 In one of these raids, on 3 July 2001 on the Bholahat/ Malda border, they critically injured two Bangladeshi villagers and took away 200 heads of cattle. This group was still active in 2003, and was reported to have killed 22 people from Bangladesh territory and abducted some 200. 'Over 100 Indians trespass into Bangladesh', *The New Nation* (5 July 2001); cf. 'Forays of Indian bandits make C'Nawabganj villagers panicky', *The Independent* (24 November 2001); 'Seven Bangladeshis killed by BSF in C'Nawabganj in ten years', *The Independent* (6 May 2002); '109 killed in 13 months in Indo-Bangla border: BSF atrocities on rise', *The New Nation* (16 May 2003).

64 The church at Maliapota (Nadia district, West Bengal) served as an informal bank to many locals who thought their money was safer there. Pranab Mondal and Rabi Banerjee, 'Marauders at midnight mass: Band of 40 terrorises Christmas gathering', *The Telegraph* (26 December 2002); Rabi Banerjee, 'Smuggle block sends plunderers to church', *The Telegraph* (28 December 2002).

65 These operations sometimes led to confrontations, as when, in 1950, foresters from the Pakistan side raided Indian Forest Department officials in 24-Parganas because 'you make delay in giving allotment to men from Pakistan' (CR 1B2-1/51 (2-54)). In the 1990s, the trade in the skin of Royal Bengal tigers, a severely endangered species, was extremely lucrative as the Bangladeshi and Indian elites were prepared to pay large sums of money for this exclusive item of interior decoration. Unlike tiger skins, timber could be extracted legally. Here Forest officials earned by applying the tax (in Bangladesh: Tk.500 per 3,600 kg) and adding a personal fee (Tk.2,000) to it. 'Involvement of forest officials alleged: Smugglers plundering timbers, animals in Sundarbans', *The New Nation* (24 April 1999). On poaching in other borderland forests, see for example Shehab Ahmed, 'Elephant poachers still active', *The Daily Star* (18 April 1998); 'Gangsters in Forests', *The Independent* (17 April 1999).

66 '23 gangs of robbers control Sundarban', *The Independent* (16 September 2002).

67 It also became a favourite means of acquiring money for insurgents in different parts of the borderland where steady toll collection was not sufficient for their needs. In 2000–

1, insurgents in Tripura kidnapped about 600 people for ransom, killing 40 of them in captivity. The kidnapping of tea garden managers was particularly lucrative. It was very common in Cachar (Assam) in the 1990s, as was the abduction of Bengali woodcutters by Jumma insurgents in the Chittagong Hill Tracts (Bangladesh), and the kidnapping of businessmen and state officials in Tripura (India). According to press reports, at least 13 planters were killed and more than 30 tea executives kidnapped for ransom from Tripura's 58 big tea plantations between 1994 and 2001, and the tea industry paid at least Rs.30 million in ransom. In Cachar, where tens of millions of rupees also changed hands in this way, the tea industry responded by paying insurgents protection money on a regular basis and, when state interference made this more difficult, by setting up their own Tea Garden Security Force. This force could also be used to discipline the plantation labourers, as was the case when three labourers, demonstrating for better pay, were shot dead by the Tea Garden Security Force. 'Dogra, Singh's grilling over: 2 tea executives arrested', *The Sentinel* (24 October 1997); 'Cachar planters may deploy Tea Security Force', *The Telegraph* (9 August 1999); 'NDBF collected over 40 million as Boroland tax', *The Assam Times* (8 July 1997); 'Ultras push tea in Tripura to the brink,' *The Sentinel* (6 August 2001); 'Tension grips Barak tea gardens after Jalenga firing', *The Sentinel* (21 October 2001); 'NLFT militants kill vendor from Bengal', *The Telegraph* (30 May 2003).

68 At least 100,000 shrimp fry collectors, many of whom were females, lived off catching shrimp fry from the rivers and canals that crosscut the Sundarbans. '100 kidnapped from Sundarbans in a month', *The Independent* (17 April 1999).

69 '24 Bangla pirates arrested after mid-sea encounter', *The Telegraph* (20 December 1991). Many gangs operating in the Sundarbans consisted of both Indian and Bangladeshi citizens. E.g. 'Four dacoits arrested in Satkhira', *The New Nation* (24 August 1999).

70 Bangladesh had no coast guard till 1995, when a 200-man force was created, apparently chiefly to fight illegal fishing by Thai, Burmese and Indian trawlers who were thought to have looted marine fish worth Tk.23 billion over the last 20 years. But a plan to create 37 coast guard stations was not implemented, and in 1999 'the coast guard units, formed some years back to protect some 710 kilometres of coastal areas, have so far been, to say the least, not up to the task.' In 2001 the coast guard was described as 'virtually idle' for lack of vessels to patrol with; its single ocean-going vessel, purchased for over Tk.300 million in 1999, could not take to sea for technical reasons. In 2002 the Bangladesh coast guard was reported to have 'only two patrol boats at its disposal since its inception.' In 2003 it received four 30-year-old vessels from the Bangladesh Navy. Aroop Talukdar, 'Pirates unleash reign of terror in South', *The Daily Star* (26 February 1999); 'Lack of logistic support, manpower: Coast guards turn ineffective in coastal belt', *The New Nation* (26 April 1999); 'Coast guard remains idle', *The New Nation* (22 June 2001); 'Coast Guard vessel remains idle', *The New Nation* (25 November 2001); Nurul Amin, 'Ctg outer anchorage safe haven for pirates', *The Independent* (7 September 2002); '4 Navy ships handed over to Coast Guard', *The Daily Star* (6 March 2003).

71 'Police-pirates gunfight: 7 dacoits with arms held at N Talpatti', *The Daily Star* (7 October 1997); 'Five Myanmar pirates held', *The Independent* (16 March 1999); '7 abducted by Bangla pirates', *The Statesman* (11 July 1999); 'Police hardly raid hideouts of pirates: Defence cargo ship had no security escort', *The Daily Star* (18 July 1999); Suhrid Shankar Chattopadhyay, 'Terror in the Sunderbans', *Frontline*, 18:15 (21 July–3 August 2001).

72 For example, after five groups of pirates had been robbing fishing gear and trawlers

from fishermen in the Meghna estuary and the adjoining area of the Bay of Bengal for some years, they graduated to a joint system of more stable taxation. They divided the waters into five zones and charged each trawler Tk.20,000–Tk.50,000 for a 'pre-paid security card' and an 'identification flag' that provided protection from all pirate attacks. Protection by government officials was essential in maintaining such systems. Akter Faruk Shahin, 'Pirates issue "security cards" for fishermen!' *The Daily Star* (12 July 2003); 'Pirates rule Meghna: 20 trawlers looted, 20 fishermen abducted for not having "pre-paid security card"', *The Daily Star* (12 August 2003); 'Fishermen protest attack by pirates,' *The Independent* (23 August 2003).

73 For example, when pirates attacked a police party that came too close to North Talpatti island, a gun battle ensued. 'During this fight for about two hours the miscreants opened 100 rounds of gunfire. Police in self-defence shot 41 rounds of fire.' 'Police-pirates gunfight: 7 dacoits with arms held at N Talpatti', *The Daily Star* (7 October 1997); cf. 'Police hardly raid hideouts of pirates: Defence cargo ship had no security escort', *The Daily Star* (18 July 1999); Krishnendu Bandyopadhyay, 'Pirates active in the Sunderbans', *The Times of India* (8 September 2003).

74 Willem van Schendel, 'Bengalis, Bangladeshis and Others: Chakma Visions of a Pluralist Bangladesh', in Rounaq Jahan (ed.), *Three Decades of Bangladesh: Promise and Performance* (Dhaka: University Press Limited Press, 2000), 65–105; 'The Arakanese communities in neighbouring countries mark the 218th anniversary of the loss of their national sovereignty', *Narinjara News* (1 January 2003).

75 Although the dream of an independent state of Mizoram never died; it was even expressed by the Chief Minister of Mizoram, Zoramthanga, in an interview in 2003. 'Mizoram CM still for independent State', *The Assam Tribune* (30 July 2003).

76 In the same speech he dismissed the Kamtapur People's Party's charge of human rights violations by government agents. 'CM warns separatists, watches infiltrators', *The Telegraph* (5 November 2001).

77 Such words rarely impressed other borderlanders either. In the aftermath of rebels killing 14 villagers in Kamalnagar (Tripura), the Chief Minister, Manik Sarkar, 'sounded a dire warning against banned military outfits [and] declared that "extremely tough measures would soon be initiated to curb the mindless violence in the name of insurgency in Tripura with an iron hand"'. Residents of Kamalnagar were not in the least reassured by these verbal pyrotechnics. When the Chief Minister, 'who always shies away from visiting trouble spots', deputed five of his cabinet colleagues to visit the area, inhabitants set up a road block and 'the ministerial team was hit with brickbats and abused after their arrival. It left within minutes, having failed to persuade the people to listen.' '5 Ministers heckled at carnage site', *The Telegraph* (19 August 2003); 'Police rescue family of ex-rebel in Tripura', *The Telegraph* (19 August 2003).

78 For overviews, see *India – Para-Military Forces* (New Delhi: Institute of Peace and Conflict Studies, 1998) and Sanjib Baruah, 'Generals as Governors: The Parallel Political Systems of Northeast India', *Himal South Asian*, 14:6 (June 2001).

79 'Elite forces trained to counter terrorism', *The Assam Tribune* (4 June 2002); 'Indo-US wargames in Mizoram', *The Statesman* (18 November 2002); 'Joint Indo-US military exercise in Mizoram', *The Assam Tribune* (3 May 2003); 'Indo-US exercise ends in Mizoram', *The Sentinel* (3 May 2003); 'Indo-US drill at Vairengte', *The Telegraph* (3 May 2003). In 2001 another Counterinsurgency School was established in Kalucherra, Dhalai district, Tripura. 'Rebels kill TSR jawan', *The Telegraph* (30 August 2003).

80 On the Indian Army's 'village grouping' in Mizoram, see Rajesh Rajagopalan, '"Restoring

Normalcy": The Evolution of the Indian Army's Counterinsurgency Doctrine', *Small Wars and Insurgencies*, 11:1 (2000), 44–68. For a more recent example, see 'Killing blow to Tripura cluster village plan', *The Telegraph* (18 July 2003). On cluster villages in Bangladesh, see Chittagong Hill Tracts Commission, *Life Is Not Ours: Land and Human Rights in the Chittagong Hill Tracts, Bangladesh*, Report (1991).

81 On Arakan, see e.g. 'Bangladesh: A new blight on the border', *Far Eastern Economic Review*, 100:23 (9 June 1978), 35; The *Return of the Rohingya Refugees to Burma: Voluntary Repatriation or Refoulement?* (Washington, DC: US Committee for Refugees, 1995); Human Rights Watch, *Burma: The Rohingya Muslims – Ending a Cycle of Exodus?* (New York: Human Rights Watch/ Asia, 1996); Human Rights Watch, *Malaysia/Burma: Living in Limbo – Burmese Rohingyas in Malaysia* (New York, etc.: Human Rights Watch, 2000). On the Chittagong Hill Tracts, see note 43; on Northeast India, see note 30.

82 For example, in 1997 a mission consisting of lawyers, journalists and various women's groups from India's northeastern states published a report that established that the Armed Forces (Special Powers) Act operating there had disrupted life, legitimized arbitrary killings by security forces and led to illegal detention and custodial violence. It accused the security forces of treating everyone as militants and secessionists to be suppressed. On the other hand, according to the Indian government, in the year 1997 no less than 739 'extremist and terrorist attacks' took place in Assam, Meghalaya, Tripura and Mizoram, and 2,102 people (including 470 members of security forces) were killed. Insurgents sometimes killed borderlanders to protect cross-border escape routes, as in a night-time attack on Simna Colony (Tripura), a border village astride the route to the All Tripura Tiger Force's training camp at Satchhari, just inside Bangladesh. 22 villagers were killed. One borderlander in Assam who lost three members of his family to rebel attacks and was then subjected to several violent raids by the Indian army said: '[We] are caught between militants and the army'. 'Centre failed in NE: Report', *United News of India* (3 April 1997); *XII Lok Sabha Debates, Session II (Monsoon)*, 29 July 1998 (Available from: http://alfa.nic.in/lsdeb/ls12/ses2/2429079801.htm); Satyabrata Chakraborti, 'Border route used regularly by ultras', *The Statesman* (9 May 2003); 'Assault slur on army in Dhubri', *The Telegraph* (6 August 2003).

83 One example was Joynal Abedin Hazari, a successful 'military entrepreneur' in the Feni region of the borderland of southeast Bangladesh. Hazari, whose control of local society was based on a strictly organized armed force (the Hazari Bahini or Steering Committee), amassed wealth and influence by means of extortion, the collection of tolls, occupation of government land, false tenders, etc. He became a member of parliament for the Awami League but ran into trouble when 14 criminal cases, including murder, were started against him. He was powerful enough, however, to fight off the Awami League government till it resigned in August 2001. Then Hazari fled just across the border to Tripura (India), waiting for better times and still being informed by followers crossing the border illegally on a daily basis. See e.g. 'Hazari Bahini may stage a comeback as "godfather" is still absconding', *The Daily Star* (25 August 2001); 'Hazari's cadre caught while crossing border', *The Daily Star* (20 November 2001).

84 The offer of state employment as part of the 'rehabilitation' of guerrillas was regulated in peace agreements between the states and insurgents as well, for example the Indian government and the Mizo insurgents in 1986, and the Bangladesh government and the Jumma insurgents in 1997. In another case, surrendered rebels accused the Tripura government of reneging on its pledge. After four years they went on hunger strike to

make the government stop its 'dilly-dallying tactics' and give them a proper job in the paramilitary. In Assam, too, the state wanted to induct surrendered rebels into Reserve Police Battalions. 'Ex-separatists to fight for India now', *The Assam Tribune* (9 August 2001); 'Tripura govt. in a piquant situation: Surrendered ultras turning down job offers,' *The Assam Tribune* (26 September 2001); '"Create battalions with surrendered ultras"', *The Assam Tribune* (4 March 2003); '282 MNF returnees given employment', *The Telegraph* (22 July 2003).

85 '464 former outlaws to be recruited to Ansar forces today: 250 more extremists to surrender at Kushtia July 23,' *The Independent* (18 July 1999); '"Terrorists" now have legal weapons and legal protection', *The New Nation* (19 July 1999); 'Absorption of outlaws in Ansar resented', *The New Nation* (19 July 1999); '223 ex-outlaws recruited as Ansar so far', *The Independent* (26 July 1999); 'Ansar deserters', *The Independent* (10 September 1999); 'Ansars sold bullets looted from jute mills in Daulatpur', *The Daily Star* (31 May 2003).

86 Gallant, 'Brigandage, Piracy'. For reverse cases – a member of the Special Police force in Tripura deserting with a service rifle, joining a local rebel group, and fleeing to safety in Bangladesh; and a Bangladeshi Ansar man looting 20 rifles and 600 bullets and joining a banned communist group in the Khulna borderland – see 'Jawan joins Tiger Force', *The Telegraph* (15 July 2003); 'Joint forces comb Sundarbans', *The Daily Star* (23 July 2003).

87 For example, a group of car lifters, extortionists and highway robbers who 'would at times disguise themselves as "militants"' and who were apprehended by villagers in Meghalaya turned out to be a sub-inspector and a former assistant sub-inspector of the Meghalaya Police, a head constable of the Assam Rifles, and six civilians. 'Police take to crime in Meghalaya', *The Telegraph* (9 August 2003).

88 In some parts, however, colonial annexation had involved episodes of militarization (e.g. the various 'punitive' expeditions that the British sent into what is now Mizoram) and World War II militarization touched the southernmost section of the borderland where Arakan and Bengal meet.

89 The East Pakistan border came under military control during Operation Closed Door in 1957, and so did the Indian border during the war of 1971.

90 Military juntas have been ruling Burma from 1962 to the present, and Pakistan/ Bangladesh from 1958 to 1971 and from 1975 to 1990. For Northeast India, see Baruah, 'Generals as Governors'.

91 A good example is the Chittagong Hill Tracts, which remained highly militarized after the rest of Bangladesh reverted to parliamentary democracy in 1990, and even after the government concluded a peace accord with the regional autonomy movement in 1997.

92 Cf. Rajagopalan, '"Restoring Normalcy"'; Ali, *The Fearful State*; Martin Smith, *Burma: Insurgency and the Politics of Ethnicity* (London: Zed Press, 1994).

93 The emergence of countless regional political parties in the borderland, and their electoral successes, caused considerable complications for the state elites and the national parties; borderland militarization could lead to counter violence not only in the borderland itself, but also elsewhere in the state territory or its representations abroad; the proliferation of insurgent organizations in the borderland over time was partly in reaction to the activities of the armed forces; and a reputation of genocide could interfere with the state's income from development aid or investment. For the example of Bangladesh, see Chittagong Hill Tracts Commission, *Life Is Not Ours*; Van

Schendel, 'Bengalis, Bangladeshis and Others'.

94 Among the active international organizations were Anti-Slavery Society, Survival International, International Work Group on Indigenous Affairs (IWGIA), Amnesty International, Unrepresented Nations and Peoples Organisation (UNPO), South Asian Human Rights Documentation Centre (SAHRDC), Asia Watch, etc. Among the United Nations bodies were the UN Subcommittee on Indigenous Populations and the International Labour Organization (ILO). The European Parliament also exerted pressure. An international Chittagong Hill Tracts Commission was formed with support of several of these organisations, and this commission monitored developments in this part of the borderland and reported widely on them.

95 See also Van Schendel, 'Bengalis, Bangladeshis and Others'.

96 Opium was not a new crop in the region and it had long been grown in small quantities for local use. State authorities in India, Bangladesh and Burma occasionally destroyed poppy fields (e.g. in Arunachal Pradesh, the Chittagong Hill Tracts and Arakan) but with little impact on production. The growing user markets for heroin in these countries, as well as the beckoning international markets, made poppy cultivation an increasingly attractive way of financing border rebellions.

97 By the early 21st century, insurgent organizations were also using the Internet to get their message out. See for example the home pages of the Arakan Rohingya National Organisation (www.webtecharabia.com/1final3/arno.htm) and the United Liberation Front of Assam (www.geocities.com/CapitolHill/Congress/7434/ulfa.htm).

98 Cf. Benedict R O'G Anderson, *Long-Distance Nationalism: World Capitalism and the Rise of Identity Politics* (Amsterdam: Centre for Asian Studies Amsterdam, 1992).

99 Rebels also became transnational investors. When Indian police arrested an activist of a relatively small group, the Hynniewtrep National Liberation Council, and seized his computer, they found out that the organization had been collecting Rs.250,000 monthly from Shillong alone, and that this money was invested in land and property in Bangladesh. 'Bangla link', *The Telegraph* (15 May 2003).

100 The Rohingyas of the Burma (Arakan) borderland are a case in point. In the 1980s and 1990s they built up an international network of support based on their Muslim identity. Tapping into flows of funds from the Gulf states and from groups in South Asia, diasporic Rohingyas emerged as competent lobbyists for their cause.

101 Gallant, 'Brigandage, Piracy', 46–50.

11

'RIFLE RAJ' AND THE KILLER BORDER

'The incident is not serious ... There is nothing at army-to-army level.' This is what a government spokesman in New Delhi told the press after Indian border guards gunned down two Bangladeshi men working their fields near the border.[1] The Bengal border is usually portrayed as a distant and peaceful meeting point of friendly states, quite unlike the violent borderland between India and Pakistan. Of course, even here 'minor incidents' may occur, as they do at any border, but these unfortunate moments are best soon forgotten in the name of restoring peaceful relations and good will.

This chapter qualifies that portrayal. It looks at the Bengal border as a landscape of fear, originating in Partition, where both civilians and state personnel fall victim to violence almost on a daily basis.[2] The modern state has been described as a form of 'violence directed towards a space', and nowhere is this perspective more helpful than at state borders.[3] It forces us to abandon the idea that borders are remote peripheries and that what happens there is of little wider concern – as remote from important issues of state as the border itself is from the state capital.

Borders embody the formation of states, always a violent process, and they often have violent origins themselves. Policing them is a crucial manifestation of state territoriality, requiring the threat of force and sometimes its application. Overt violence can be an initial feature of border making that disappears when states settle into a more regulated existence and manage their borders by negotiation. But there is little reason to assume that this is the dominant pattern in the world: most international borders are zones where armed men gather and where they use those arms. State surveillance and interdiction lead to border violence. The level of this violence fluctuates with the nature of the states involved and their relationship with each other, with the capacity for violence displayed by non-state actors in the borderland, and with moments of political or economic stress.

The Bengal borderland is a good example. It may be marginal to the concerns of the elites ruling the region, but it is here that the antagonism of post-Partition state building is most intensely felt. It is here that the states' inability to pursue territoriality without victimizing citizens – their own as well as their neighbours'

– is clearly visible. And it is here that citizens can be seen to resort to violence in order to strike back at the state and its strategy of territoriality. In other words, it is here that the violence of 'normal' relations between friendly states is demonstrated on a daily basis.

Friendly states with violent borders

In view of the seismic way in which the Bengal borderland was formed and the many unresolved issues surrounding it, it is no surprise that high levels of border violence are an everyday fact of life. The origins of the Bengal borderland were certainly violent. When Burma seceded from the rest of British India to become a separate colony in 1937, the break-up had been relatively amicable. But when the rest of British India split apart in 1947, it was a bitter divorce that left deep wounds of anger and recrimination. The power elites of the new states, themselves scarred by the experiences of 1947, were unable to jettison the antagonistic politics that had led to state fragmentation in the first place. They were unable to normalize interstate relations. Three of their territorial strategies in particular were liable to result in armed confrontation at the border: using the border as a diplomatic resource; using it as a choke point of international trade; and using it as a site to suppress rebellion.

The border had important diplomatic and strategic uses. Even though heads of government, in public statements, could grow lyrical about the warm relations and eternal friendship between their country and its neighbours, realities at the border told a very different story. The borderland fluctuated between tension and outright confrontation, and interstate relations at the border have always been marked by strain, suspicion and suspense.[4] As we have seen, even at the best of times almost the entire border was officially closed and guarded (Plate 11.1). There were designated border crossings but these were few and far

Plate 11.1: Patrolling a closed border: Indian border guards on the Brahmaputra river.[5]

between – to be exact, there were only 13 of them in 2003, or one for every 300 km of border. Here people and goods were allowed to pass from one territory to the other but always under strict state surveillance.

Moreover, it was not unusual for these border crossings to be closed without prior notice whenever tension between the states increased. Such closures were often for brief periods, political signals of displeasure that were not allowed to interfere too much with economic exchange. At times of more intense conflict between the states, however, sabre-rattling would drown out all other sounds (Plates 11.2 and 11.3).

Plate 11.2: An armed Bangladeshi guarding the closed border after lethal clashes between Indian and Bangladeshi border guards. Tamabil checkpoint, Meghalaya (India) / Sylhet (Bangladesh) border, 2001.[6]

Plate 11.3: Indian truck drivers having lunch at the border. Held up for days at a closed checkpoint, these men from far-off Uttar Pradesh are forced to camp out in their trucks. Mahadipur check post (Malda, West Bengal, India), 2001.

There were also certain parts of the borderland that were especially prone to violence. Where stretches of the border were disputed and undemarcated, gunfights between border guards of the two states could be so frequent that people who happened to live there had little option but to flee their houses repeatedly. In these areas, the recurring threat of state violence permeated all aspects of life.[7]

But the border was more than an arena where the political and military elites of neighbouring states could posture, slap each other in the face, and test their weaponry. It was an equally important site of economic policy. Over the years the governments of India, East Pakistan/ Bangladesh and Burma devised and implemented various economic plans. These economic policies were in no way coordinated with each other and differed markedly in character. The one thing that they did have in common, however, was each state's ambition to put strict controls on external trade. Realities at the border showed this ambition to be untenable. Not only did disparate economic systems meet at the border, but here they became undone, shaded into each other and merged. Outlawed cross-border trade was common and state attempts at interdiction could lead to border violence. Smugglers were shot at and border villages were raided and burned by border guards. But sometimes smugglers had the upper hand, intimidating the border population and attacking border patrols.

Struggles over sovereignty between states and non-state military entrepreneurs constituted a third source of border violence. Many open or hidden border wars over people and resources led people to cross the border. Insurgents seeking to establish a base across the border, refugees being compelled to flee to the safety of the neighbouring state, and migrants seeking cross-border employment – all had to navigate the tense border zone. They could fall victim to the border guards of either state but they could also contribute to border violence themselves. Often, armed insurgents being given shelter by the neighbouring state unleashed terror on the local population. They could also come to blows with other insurgent groups in the area, or ambush border patrols. Cross-border bands of robbers, cattle rustlers and pirates added to the general sense of insecurity.

The interplay of these factors varied over time and between sectors of the border. Some sectors never experienced high levels of border violence. Others became very disturbed during a particular period, only to revert to low levels of tension afterward. Sometimes violence was much more intense on one side of the border than on the other.[8] And, as we have seen, there were some periods of general border violence (e.g. 1957, 1965, 1971), as well as some parts of the borderland that were particularly violent throughout.[9]

Measuring border violence

The incidence of border violence since 1947 has never been analysed, and it would be difficult to provide a full picture of it. The problem lies in the fragmented and contradictory nature of the source material as well as in its poor accessibility, coverage and reliability. State records deal with border violence only to the extent that officials at the border considered it relevant to inform their superiors in the state bureaucracy. Moreover, as many 'joint enquiry' reports by border officials from India and East Pakistan/ Bangladesh attest, it was sometimes difficult for them to agree on what had actually happened. It is not possible to say how many cases of border violence were never recorded, and state records are not (yet) available for the early 1960s onward. Nevertheless, the rich collection in the Bangladesh National Archives makes it abundantly clear that in its early years the Partition border was a true killer.[10]

But what about more recent times? One way of getting a sense of border violence since the 1960s is to use reports in newspapers, especially local ones. This is a daunting task, not only because it requires searching dozens of newspapers from three countries and in several languages, but also because old issues of many (local) newspapers were never systematically preserved and are now almost impossible to find.

I have not been able to collect detailed information about violence along the entire border for the entire period. What I have been able to do, however, is a much more restricted survey, covering only the most recent years and based on information culled from the Internet editions of a number of newspapers in English and Bengali, mainly from India and Bangladesh.[11] In some cases, I was able to crosscheck this information in interviews with borderlanders.[12] Despite the historical and methodological limitations of such a survey, it does provide us with a tool for measuring and comparing violence.[13]

The period covered by this survey starts from 1998. This was one of the most relaxed periods in the relationship between India and Bangladesh. In 1996, elections in Bangladesh had returned a government that was more favourably inclined toward India than any in the previous 21 years. This government managed quickly to settle two major issues between the two countries. In December 1996 India and Bangladesh signed the Farakka Water Treaty that regulated how they would share the water of the Ganges.[14] In December 1997 the Bangladesh government signed a peace accord with insurgents in the Chittagong Hill Tracts, thereby making it possible for tens of thousands of refugees to return from India. By early 1998 other plans were on the drawing board: cross-border railway connections and bus services; an exchange of enclaves; and the sharing of the waters of the Tista river. Relations of official friendship and good neighbourliness prevailed and border tension was at its lowest level. The official relationship between Bangladesh and Burma (in this period officially known as Myanmar) was also good. In other words, in view of the much tenser circumstances that historically have characterized relations at this border, the border violence reported in this chapter should be seen as unusually low.[15]

In this period of official harmony, the power elites of India, Bangladesh and Burma tended to disregard the violence that befell their fellow citizens at the border. Such matters should not stand in the way of political deals that were now within reach. State officials and the media of the three countries typically met border violence with indifference, only stirring occasionally if border guards were shot down in a direct showdown with their counterparts from across the border. Such 'incidents' were sometimes exploited by opposition politicians, who would portray the incumbent government as weak on national honour, or by border guards who would capitalize on the event by demanding an expansion of their numbers in the cause of national security.[16] Meanwhile, the victims of border violence remained largely nameless and faceless.

Although it was not always possible to ignore border violence, state authorities treated it as a minor irritant. For example, in July 2000, India and Bangladesh were busy arranging mutually profitable agreements involving the border. Early in the month, they decided to resume the movement of goods trains across their border at Benapol-Petrapol – a service that had been suspended during war some 35 years previously. Towards the end of the month, they also agreed on a cross-border bus service between Dhaka and Agartala (Tripura).[17] At the same time, Bangladesh and Burma arranged for the repatriation of some Rohingya refugees to Burma. Clearly, the governments sharing the border were getting on well.

But this did not mean that the border was quiet. On the contrary, in that same month press reports mentioned serious incidents in nine border locations. In these unrelated confrontations, 12 civilians and 16 members of the armed forces were killed, mostly by gunfire, and 18 civilians and 11 members of the armed forces were seriously injured. Among the casualties of these nine incidents were 3 Burmese nationals, 19 Bangladeshis and 35 Indians.

All three states played down the significance of these deaths.[18] To them, the deaths were clearly a routine matter with no political repercussions. This debonair assessment is a telling comment on their attitudes towards their own citizens and those across the border: in pursuing territoriality, you cannot make an omelette without breaking eggs.

But how many eggs were broken? How many people got killed, wounded or abducted at the border between India, Bangladesh and Burma in recent years? And who were they? The survey covers five years, from January 1998 to December 2002. It includes only incidents that occurred on the boundary line itself, or very near it. It excludes the frequently reported incidence of violence away from the border, in the wider borderland, and also the many acts of border violence that did not result in the killing, maiming, or kidnapping of people.[19] Table 11.1 provides a summary of the findings.

Table 11.1: Persons killed, wounded and abducted on the India-Bangladesh and Bangladesh-Burma borders, 1998–2002 (Sources: Internet editions of various newspapers[20])

	Persons killed	Persons wounded	Persons abducted	Total
1998 (8 incidents)	17	68	16	101
1999 (50 incidents)	76	363	158	594
2000 (70 incidents)	115	290	237	645
2001 (86 incidents)	107	341	47	495
2002 (149 incidents)	218	142	233	593
Total	533	1,204	691	2,428

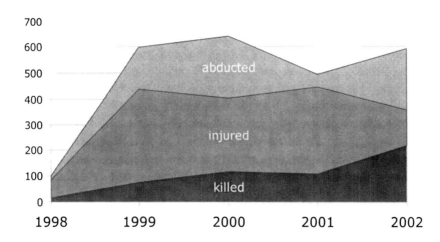

Table 11.1 shows that violence on the border was an everyday affair and that it came in small packages. There were numerous incidents, each typically claiming one or a few victims. Over the five-year period, the number of incidents rose steadily while the number of victims per incident decreased.[21] In the early years injuries were more common than killings and abductions, but in 2002 killings outstripped injuries by a considerable margin. Table 11.1 does not show the spatial spread of the border incidents but the underlying news reports testify to the fact that they occurred all along the border.[22]

Who killed whom?

What underlay this killing and wounding at the border? Who were the perpetrators and who were the victims? If we want to write a social history of border violence, we need to find the people behind the faceless figures quoted above. The pattern that emerges is complex and surprising.

Fire across the border.   In the majority of reported incidents, border guards (and other state agents) harmed nationals of the other state (Plate 11.4). Death or injury was usually caused by bullets but border guards also used firearm butts to bludgeon people to death. Some victims were tortured till they died, others drowned in border rivers trying to escape attacking border guards. Between 1998 and 2002 border guards killed 230 'neighbouring' civilians, and injured or abducted another 636.[23]

Plate 11.4: **The wife of Mohammad Yusuf wails over her husband's body. He was shot dead by border guards near Benapol checkpoint in 2002.**[24]

Who were the victims? First of all, people who happened to live near the border. Sometimes border villagers were shot in their homes when border guards fired across the border. For example, five Bangladeshi villagers were hit in their sleep in December 2000 when Indian border guards opened fire on Bangladeshi colleagues after a salt smuggling deal had gone wrong.[26] At other times, border guards would cross the border to intimidate villagers who had incurred their displeasure. Villagers were also shot or arrested when they came too close to the border or when they worked their fields very near it.[27]

Everyday tales of border violence

Plate 11.5: Stone collector and his workplace, the Mohanondo river, separating Bangladesh from India (background).

A few weeks ago three brothers from our village were collecting stones from the river right here and loading them on to their raft. Suddenly, the BSF [Indian border guards] called out to them and told them that they had crossed the mid-river borderline into India. Then the brothers said: "OK, so take our raft," but the BSF started beating them, and then shot them at close range! Two of them dived under water and so escaped, but the third was killed immediately and his corpse floated down the river. The BSF collected it an hour or so later, brought it to the police station [on the Indian bank of the river], and laid it out at the market place there. We couldn't go and see it ... Two days later, after a flag meeting, they returned the body to us. It was hideously swollen.

... And this hut here on the riverbank belongs to Mokshed. Robbers came from across the river a couple of days ago. Just killed him and went back to India! We have no idea why. He was a good, friendly man, just a small trader in jute and paddy. Probably mistook him for someone else... We could not do anything against them because they had rifles and hand bombs. They actually left a bomb behind; it is still here. Some of us living on the edge of the river got very scared and moved inland, and now we patrol at night.

From an interview on the Bangladeshi bank of the Mohanondo river (separating Panchagarh district, Bangladesh from Darjeeling district, India), March 2000. Interviewers: Md. Mahbubar Rahman and Willem van Schendel.[25]

Children cutting grass for their cattle near the (often unmarked) boundary line were not safe, nor were women and men collecting firewood, or the many fishermen, boulder collectors and shell collectors earning a living on the border rivers (see Box: 'Everyday tales of border violence').[28] It was also not uncommon for drunken border guards to cross the border in search of young women to rape. Male villagers who put up resistance to such forays risked being bayoneted or shot dead.[29] Then there were the victims of anti-personnel mines: the borderlanders who trod on Burmese anti-personnel mines in the no man's land of the undemarcated Burma-Bangladesh border.[30] Merely living and working near the border was hazardous.

A second group of victims were those who were caught while crossing the border on purpose, usually because they were involved in unauthorized trade, emigration or robbery. These people played lethal cat-and-mouse games with the border guards.[31] Countless smugglers were killed as they crossed the border, usually shot by border guards, but many also drowned when their boats capsized as they were making their escape.[32] Indian border guards in Assam regularly killed Bangladeshis who cut holes in the border fence.[33] In a few cases, nationals of other countries (e.g. Sri Lanka, Thailand, the Philippines and Taiwan) were killed or injured as they fished off the coast in the Bay of Bengal.[34]

Border crossers falling victim to violence were not always in pursuit of economic gain. Some were celebrating their religious unity across the border. This was the case with a crowd of Muslims attending Id prayers at a mosque in Cooch Behar (India), yards from the border, in December 2000. Among the thousands were Bangladeshis who had crossed the border to attend. As they were returning home, Indian border guards challenged them. Both Bangladeshis and Indians protested. Suddenly one of the guards opened fire, killing four Indians and one Bangladeshi, and injuring six.[35] In another case, Indian border guards shot dead two Bangladeshis returning from a pilgrimage to Ajmer (Rajasthan, India).[36]

There was, of course, nothing legal about border guards gunning down unarmed civilians. According to the laws of these countries, border crossers should be apprehended and charged with unauthorized entry under the passport and visa regulations.[37] Although this did happen occasionally, the border guards' standard response to unauthorized entry was to open fire, and shoot to kill. For countries that were ostensibly on the best of terms with each other, this was remarkably bellicose behaviour. And yet, in the five years covered by the survey, there was not a single mention of border guards being disciplined by their superiors for violence towards border crossers.[38] On the contrary, both politicians and reporters usually glorified border shootings as being necessary for the protection of national interest. According to them, border guards were dealing with a security problem: foreigners who were excluded from the nation should be stopped from entering its territory. Not surprisingly, border guards of all three countries frequently used this argument.[39] For example, after Indian border guards had opened fire on ten Bangladeshis who were collecting boulders and sand from the Pyain, a border river, killing five of them, officials of the Indian Border Security Force argued that these boulder collectors had been well inside Indian territory – a charge denied by the Bangladeshi authorities – and that the killing was completely justified because the 'intruders' were in Indian territory (Plate 11.6).[40] In another case a high-ranking BSF officer proudly claimed: 'Our *jawans* [men] have shot dead many timber smugglers along the border.'[41]

Plate 11.6: Bangladeshis collecting boulders and sand from a border river, viewed from the hills of neighbouring Meghalaya (India) near Dawki, 2000.

In most cases, the matter would end here. The local border guards would conclude the incident with a ritual flag meeting at which the parties sat down on the boundary line, each on their own side.[42] The main point of these meetings was to 'restore confidence', to reduce tension in the borderland and to induce local inhabitants, who usually fled during shootings, to return to their homes. Victims' dead bodies, which were often carried away by the border guards who had killed them, were released to their families, proclamations of goodwill were made, and the participants parted after declaring their determination to keep the peace.[43]

But the case of the murdered boulder collectors did not end here. In a new development, three human rights organizations in Bangladesh took issue with the standard argument condoning state-sponsored border killings. They petitioned their government, stating that

> the international code of conduct of border patrol provides that even if a person is found to have crossed an international border, he/she should be detained or returned to the proper authorities of his/her home country, and in no way be violently dealt with.[44]

A few days later the Bangladesh government took the unusual step of lodging an official protest with the Indian government.

Road rage and Rifle Raj.   Border guards did not only use violence against foreigners. They also turned violent against their own nationals. As one old Indian living near the border expressed it: 'Our own border guards are worse than those British ever were! They push us beyond all limits of endurance ... They should protect us, not kill us.'

Between 1998 and 2002 border guards killed 59 co-nationals and injured no less than 464 others.[45] Quite a number of these casualties occurred in pitched battles between border guards and borderlanders. Border villages, markets and roads formed the stage for these battles, for which there were generally two main scenarios. In the first, border guards tried to apprehend smugglers whom they suspected of hiding in a border market. They would attack the market, ransack houses and indiscriminately beat up village men, women and children. Villagers would retaliate by bringing out protest processions, damaging vehicles belonging to the border guards and demanding a judicial inquiry into the atrocity.[46] If the battle took place at a border check post, local people and transport workers would barricade the border crossing in protest.[47]

The second scenario revealed an even deeper rift between the nation's sentinels and the borderlanders whom they were supposed to serve and protect.[48] The border guards' readiness to use violence against co-nationals is demonstrated by the rapidity with which small quarrels could escalate. In a Bangladeshi border town, border guard Alauddin quarrelled with a shopkeeper over the sale of a soft drink and hit him. Bystanders intervened and settled the matter. Then, however, Alauddin 'went back to his camp and returned in the area along with 25 to 30 BDR men equipped with sticks. They beat up the people standing on the road and damaged some houses, leaving 15 people injured.'[49]

In a case in Cooch Behar (West Bengal, India), a truckload of border guards encountered a rickshaw and quarrelled over who had the right of way. The guards gave the rickshaw-puller a beating and then opened fire, killing five bystanders and wounding two. Enraged by what they described as sheer brutality, all local political parties declared a general strike in the area. They demanded that the responsible border guards be punished after a judicial inquiry and that compensation be paid to the victims' families. In addition, they demanded an immediate end to the frequent harassment of villagers by border guards. BSF headquarters responded merely by withdrawing the company currently posted in the area and promising an internal inquiry into the incident.[50] In the Indian parliament in Delhi, MPs from West Bengal accused border guards of often overstepping their jurisdiction, of humiliating and assaulting the border population, and of creating havoc in the border areas, leading to frequent skirmishes between guards and local people.[51] When these MPs demanded exemplary punishment of the perpetrators of the 'road rage' killings in Cooch

Behar and financial assistance to the victims' families, they were frequently interrupted and most of their testimony was expunged from the record. The Deputy Speaker concluded the fierce parliamentary debate with the words:

> We are proud of our BSF and other Forces. The Members cannot irresponsibly utter anything and everything on the Forces ... I will not allow you to say anything more ... Nothing will go on record.[52]

Such metropolitan disdain for borderland grievances translated into powerful protection – indeed impunity – for border guards and posed serious practical problems for borderlanders.[53] Border guards who acted as 'thugs in fatigues' – who terrorized and victimized their 'own' borderlanders – appeared to be above the law.[54] They enjoyed the protection of their superiors and were not deemed accountable to the local civil administration, let alone their victims' surviving relatives.[55]

But local administrators did not always take this lying down. In 2003 tensions boiled over in West Bengal. Officials in Malda district accused the Border Security Force of unlawful raids on villages along the border with Bangladesh, forcing their way into houses, seizing livestock at gunpoint, gunning down villagers without any provocation, and sexually harassing local women. It was no surprise, they said, that the Indian border population regarded the Indian border guards as their enemies. The superintendent of police denounced the border guards for unleashing 'a reign of terror ... [if they] are not taught to behave themselves, things might go out of hand any moment.' And the district magistrate threatened: 'We are fed up with [the BSF] ... If they do not stop harassing the villagers, we will lodge a complaint against the battalion with the Union Home Ministry.' In response to this campaign, Home Ministry officials intervened and the director-general of the Border Security Force announced that his men 'would attempt to arrest transborder criminals before opening fire. Even when shooting, they would target at their legs. "Shooting to kill will be the last resort," he said.'[56] Critics mocked such assurances, and a local politician scoffed:

> The BSF killed a middle-aged woman in cold blood a few months back when she went to give food and water to her son working in the field beyond the border fencing. Do they consider her a smuggler or an ISI operative?[57] (cf. Plate 11.7)

In view of such violent realities, it was no wonder that the inhabitants of the borderland lived in fear of the border guards, speaking of *Rifle Raj* – Border Guard Rule[59], and that local politicians dreamed of freeing the borderland from it.[60]

Plate 11.7: Village woman and patrolling Indian border guard near Dhubri, Assam.[58]

Killing colleagues. In the preceding sections we have come across border guards in the role of killers; however, they themselves also fell victim to violence at the border. Half of those who died or were injured were attacked by colleagues from across the border, and the other half by violent civilians. Between 1998 and 2002, no less than 42 border guards of these friendly nations were killed by their cross-border colleagues, and 32 more were injured or abducted – most of them Indians.[61] Border guards fell victim to violence in one of three situations: trespassing, cross-border shooting and invasion.

It was not uncommon for border guards to trespass into the neighbouring territory. They could do so by accident, in hot pursuit of smugglers, on an espionage mission, or intent on committing rape. For most of them, such an adventure ended in being arrested and handed back to their own authorities but sometimes they had to pay more heavily for their transgression.[62] Two Bangladeshi border guards were shot dead by Indian colleagues on the Ganges river as they were chasing smugglers trying to return to India.[63] One Indian border guard was killed by Bangladeshi fire as he tried to rescue colleagues who had entered Bangladesh in an attempt to kidnap two women collecting stones near the border.[64] And another Indian border guard lost his life when a Bangladesh border patrol found that he and a colleague were visiting in a Bangladeshi border village with 'an ill motive'.[65]

Trespassing took on a special character in disputed areas along the border. When Indian cultivators, backed up by border guards, began ploughing fields in a tiny disputed area on the Sylhet border, Bangladeshi guards rushed to the spot and tried to stop them 'trespassing'. Four Bangladeshi guards were disarmed by their Indian colleagues and taken to Indian territory. A fierce gunfight broke out, followed by a flag meeting and the return of the Bangladeshis and their guns.[66] Sometimes such shootings in disputed areas resulted in border guards getting killed or injured.[67]

Cross-border shootings were frequent, and some localities were particularly prone to them. One was Hili, the town in Dinajpur that was divided between India and Bangladesh. Here the border closely followed the (Bangladeshi) railway line and both Bangladesh and India had erected walls that violated the agreement stipulating that no constructions are allowed within 150 yards from the boundary line.[68] Since Partition, gunfights have been commonplace here. In one twenty-hour exchange of fire during the period under review in this chapter, a Bangladeshi border guard was killed and another injured, together with several civilians, including a little girl.[69]

But cross-border shootings could occur anywhere, and they often developed from small incidents. In the early stages, civilians would become victims; in the later stages border guards could also be killed. Such an escalation of violence can be seen quite well in a lethal clash on the Kushtia/Nadia (Bangladesh/West Bengal) border in April 1999. The immediate cause was the death of Babu. According to villagers, Indian border guards tried to abduct Babu, a Bangladeshi who was working his field near the border, and killed him when he resisted. According to Indian border guards, however, they tried to stop robbers coming across the border from Bangladesh. Everybody agreed, however, that, next, a large group of Bangladeshi villagers assembled at the spot to claim Babu's body. The Indian border guards fired guns and mortars at them, leaving one person dead and about forty wounded. Finally, Bangladeshi border guards arrived on the scene and soon they were locked in a gun battle with their Indian colleagues that lasted throughout the day. When the shooting stopped, a total of nine people were dead and about 60 injured. Among the dead were two Bangladeshi and two Indian border guards.[70]

This incident showed a very rapid escalation of violence but sometimes it took much longer to reach the final stage of border guards killing each other. In a conflict at the Bangladesh-Assam border, the violence stretched over more than three weeks. In the final stage, four (according to other reports, eleven) Indian border guards were shot dead by their Bangladeshi colleagues.[71] Other border guards lost their lives in similar clashes along the border.[72]

Full-scale invasion of the neighbouring territory occurred only once during the five-year period from 1998 to 2002. In a highly publicized confrontation between Indian and Bangladeshi border guards, 19 men met a violent end. The confrontation involved two disputed border areas. The first, Padua or Pyrdiwah, was a small strip of land claimed by Bangladesh but occupied by India; in the case of the second, Boroibari, the situation was the reverse.[73] Partly in response to Indian road-building activities nearby, Bangladeshi border guards suddenly occupied Padua in April 2001 and encircled its small Indian border outpost. The action did not result in casualties but it enraged the Indian authorities. A few days later Indian border guards invaded Boroibari, about 100 km to the west. What was intended as a retaliatory move turned into a strategic and publicity disaster. Sixteen Indian border guards died and two were injured in the attack, which also left three Bangladeshi border guards dead and five injured. About 10,000 civilians fled the area after several were wounded in the shooting (see Plates 11.8–11.10).[74]

Hitting the rulers. Border guards could also die at the hands of civilians. Between 1999 and 2002, 46 border guards and other state employees were killed in this way and 46 others were wounded.[78] Most of these casualties fell in encounters between border guards and armed insurgents.

Plate 11.8: A Bangladeshi border guard with two blindfolded Indian guards, who were wounded while attacking Boroibari, in a helicopter taking them to a Dhaka hospital, 2001.[75]

Plate 11.9: Indian border guards, helped by villagers, are loading a coffin containing the corpse of a colleague onto a truck after the Boroibari attack, 2001.[76]

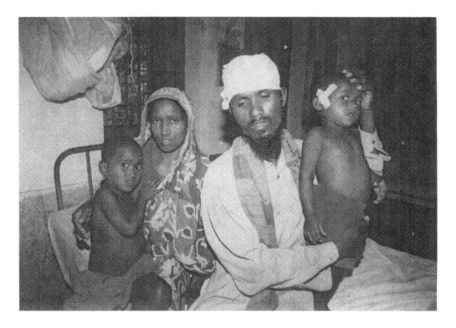

Plate 11.10: Bangladeshi borderlanders wounded during the invasion of Boroibari, 2001.[77]

For example, the Burma-Bangladesh border was the scene of several battles between Burmese border guards and the separatist Rohingya Solidarity Organisation (RSO). On one occasion, RSO rebels killed 11 guards who were laying anti-personnel mines along the border with Bangladesh. Another encounter left one border guard and two RSO fighters dead, and 32 others from both sides wounded.[79] Insurgents frequently ambushed Indian border patrols and sometimes raided their camps. The most risky area for Indian border guards was the Tripura sector, but spectacular attacks by insurgent groups also took place in Mizoram and Meghalaya during these years.[80] Some rebel groups also considered labourers, whom the state employed to repair border roads, as agents of the state and these could also fall victim to insurgent fire.[81]

Sometimes state agents encountered smugglers or robbers who wounded or killed them.[82] In one instance, a group of 50 to 60 smugglers overpowered a patrol team of four Bangladeshi border guards, took them hostage, beat them up, and later handed them over to Indian border guards. The hapless Bangladeshis were returned after a flag meeting; a month later they were still recovering in hospital.[83] Occasionally villagers roughed up border guards who had strayed across the border.[84] Border guards could also get caught in the crossfire when rival gangs of smugglers had a dispute over control of a strategic border crossing.[85]

Robbers, rivals, ransom. Finally, the border was also a site where many civilians killed and wounded each other in a wide variety of altercations. In the five-year period under review, 108 people died in this way and 723 others were injured or abducted.[86] Much of this violence had to do with struggles over who controlled border resources. Quarrels over borderland commons – grazing land, firewood, and fish in border rivers – could escalate and lead to killings.[87] Insurgent groups also killed border villagers to secure escape routes across the border.[88] Control of borderland trade was another source of violence. When smugglers fell out, their disputes could often be settled only by the use of force. Fights over the control of illegal border crossings, where powerful men would tax trade flows, produced many victims.[89] But cross-border traders could also rob their partners, and kill them in the process. This occurred frequently on the Naf river. Robbers originating from Maungdaw in Burma (but now settled on the Bangladesh side) would rob Burmese smugglers and kill them by hand or drown them in the border river.[90]

Cross-border robbery took many other forms as well. Looting borderlanders' property was a popular activity and when intended victims tried to defend themselves, casualties could easily occur. For example, the inhabitants of a Mru village on the Bangladesh-Burma border put up strong resistance when 30

Burmese robbers attacked them. They killed three and wounded thirteen attackers, while only two of them were wounded.[91] Another common form of cross-border robbery was kidnapping for ransom. In the district of Meherpur (Kushtia) in western Bangladesh, police said that 'at least 50 Bangladesh nationals were kidnapped [and taken to India] from frontier villages of the district in last one and half years and they were later released on payment of ransoms.' Some rebel groups used cross-border kidnapping as a technique to finance their struggle. In this way, Arakan Democratic Party activists abducted two Marma men from Bangladesh to Burma for ransom, and the Bru National Liberation Front kidnapped three Mizos from an Indian border village, abducting them to Bangladesh.[92] When kidnappings went wrong, the victims were often killed.

Civilians could also kill each other for different reasons. In one case, a cross-border brawl appears to have originated in a denial of borderland inclusiveness. On a day in March 2001, a section of the border was alive with religious sociability. On the Bangladeshi side the Muslim feast (urs) of Hazrat Arfin was being celebrated, and on the Indian side hundreds of Hindu devotees had gathered to attend the Baruni Fair (mela). When young men from Bangladesh crossed over to the Indian side, they were attacked and, according to press reports, 150 were injured. That evening, angry Bangladeshis attacked villages across the border, injuring about 50 Indians.[93]

Conclusion: panic and bodies

These examples show that a border between 'friendly states' can be a site of quite considerable violence. The dominant image of the Bengal border ignores this violence. Even though both borderlanders and border guards regularly fall victim to violence, their deaths and injuries are treated as insignificant, as minor occurrences, typically reported in small newspaper entries under the heading of 'district news'. In the press, deaths at the border are presented as unfortunate minor 'incidents' whose importance – if any – lies in the possible injury they do to the nation's pride. Reporters rarely consider border 'incidents' worthy of further investigation. State officials, on their part, are also keen to project an image of a peaceful, friendly border where killings are isolated aberrations – moments of inexplicable loss of control – that punctuate the normality of neighbourly goodwill.[94]

Needless to say, these perspectives are not shared by borderlanders who know the border to be a zone of concentrated violence and a landscape of fear. To them, the border is the embodiment of a state system of spatial control that could not exist without routines of intimidation and killing. At the border, the state is largely 'Rifle Raj' (Border Guard Rule), and inhabitants of the borderland experience border guards both as an occupying force and as protectors of the national territory, directing state-sponsored violence towards both sides of the dotted line. As one borderlander expressed it: 'They are the tigers in our garden.'[95] And yet, these tigers are not all-powerful, because there are definite limits to how far they can use coercion to make border populations comply. Borderlanders may strike back, and in the long run border guards may find a strategy of accommodation and working with the grain of borderland society more effective than the application of excessive violence.[96]

For inhabitants of the borderland, the border is never 'normal' or placed beyond question. They never belittle the violence of the Partition border because every day many of them put their lives on the line in lethal border games that have their origins in Partition. It is along the border that the antagonism of state building in South Asia continues to be most intensely felt. Here borderlanders confront the fact that their lives are 'abstracted, and in some cases even dehumanized, by concepts of citizenship, sovereignty, and territoriality'[97] – and that they may die because of this.

Border panic.   To make matters worse, politicians in India and Bangladesh are increasingly focusing on the border as a zone of national vulnerability. This new interest is linked to the emergence of hypernationalism (including forms of Hindutva and Islamism), an ideology that emphasizes the supremacy of the nation and demands safe territorial borders in order to construct a nation with clear-cut social boundaries. For hypernationalist politicians, unauthorized cross-border trade and population movements are an affront to the nation and a threat to its very survival as a territorial identity: they cannot be seen to be 'soft' on such issues. To them, pushing for an open border does not make political sense, and the lifting of border controls in the name of globalization is out of the question. Quite the opposite: they turn the border into a sacred symbol of the nation, thereby employing it as a useful resource in creating moral panic around border-related issues such as illegal immigration, infiltration, international terrorism, human trafficking and smuggling.[98]

Fear of the border has nothing to do with trying to understand borderland societies better or making the victims of border violence less faceless and nameless. Nor does border panic change the view that borderlands are peripheral and distant. Rather, these fears are the currency of a national politics that exploits and deepens popular stereotypes of the border. Such fears allow nationalist politicians and state officials to forge new strategic alliances aimed at recrafting the image of the border and symbolically reaffirming the state's territorial authority.[99] A border panic is a godsend for those in charge of border control, because they can use it both to underline just how indispensable they

are and to demand more state resources to allow them to be more efficient.[100]
If such appeals are supported by politicians, as they increasingly are, they lead
to more attempts at state surveillance and interdiction at the border, a further
militarization of border society, and a sharper divide between borderlanders
and their minders. The outcome will inevitably be higher levels of border
violence.

Borders and bodies.   Borders embody the modern state as a form of violence
directed towards a space. Inevitably, border politics are violent and violence at
borders is political – but not only on the scale outlined above. Borders do not
only violate geographical space; they can also invade human space – the human
body. This points to what Hastings Donnan and Thomas Wilson have described
as the 'body politics' of borders.[101] The relationship between state borders and
the human body is often thought of in terms of a biological metaphor: the
border embodies a state system of spatial control, or acts as an outer skin
protecting a national social order. However, the physical destruction of human
bodies at the Bengal border demonstrates that the relationship between state
borders and the body can be much starker. Here, power relations have an
immediate impact on the individual body by training, clothing and arming it
(border guards or guerrillas), by observing, categorizing, searching and approving
it (authorized border crossers), or by violently opposing its movement across
space (smugglers, labour migrants or terrorists).

For this reason, border violence can be understood as an instrument to classify
bodies. Perpetrators of border violence can distance themselves from their
victims by classifying these as bodies belonging to a particular category that the
border excludes. Whether this is done in the service of the state, transnational
trade or insurrection is perhaps immaterial. A state border facilitates the
dehumanizing of 'infiltrators', 'smugglers', 'enemy agents', 'border guards', and
so on, and provides instant ideological support for physical abuse: 'dehumanising
violence perpetrated on a body is a major element of identity formation in
contexts where drawing the border round the nation is in dispute.'[102]

Thus armed rebels or smugglers who set out to attack men whose bodies are
clad in state uniforms have first identified these men as specimens of a category
of obstructors who need to be eliminated. Similarly, Indian border guards'
frequent complaint that they cannot tell Indian and Bangladeshi citizens apart
translates easily into their categorizing the entire borderland population as
suspect, unworthy of civil rights, and outside the nation.[103] From this it is but a
small step to treating all borderlanders as subhumans and disciplining them by
physical means. For this reason, Indian border guards take out their frustration
on the bodies of Indian inhabitants of the borderland by beating, shooting,

raping and killing them without compunction.[104] In the process of perpetrating violence, they exclude their victims from the nation and reaffirm their own identity as the definers of the nation's political borders who have a right – indeed a duty – to destroy foreign bodies. Even though borderland politicians may object to both this arrogation of power by border sentinels and the exclusion and physical destruction of borderlanders' bodies that result from it, it is routinely condoned by national politicians.

The conviction that people ought to be only in a certain place, a homeland, and nowhere else – unless authorized by higher powers – leads to the violent categorization of bodies at borders.[105] Territoriality not only produces borders; by the same token it also destroys bodies. This destruction is made palatable, even laudable, by dehumanizing certain bodies as belonging to excluded and devalued categories – infiltrators, foreigners, ultras, terrorists, smugglers, anti-social elements, or borderlanders. In this way, dead bodies at the border come to stand for a greater good: they symbolize security. Far from being an aberration, Rifle Raj exemplifies the post-Partition social order. At South Asia's borders, the violence of Partition is not over: it is still happening, and we had better take notice.

In this chapter I have focused on physical violence at the Partition border in the most recent period. The next chapter deals with the Bengal borderland as a battlefield of a rather different kind. It considers how Partition gave rise to new forms of self-identification and in particular how the new nations sought to leave their imprint on the borderland. Tensions between the exclusivity of the new territorial nationalisms and the realities of cross-border connections and flows turned the borderland into a crucial site of symbolic interaction, an enduring battleground of identity politics.

Notes

1 'India, Bangladesh agree to talks after border firing', *Sawaal News* (15 July 2000). In similar vein, the chief of the Bangladesh Rifles (BDR), visiting New Delhi, played down the killing of 19 border guards during border skirmishes at Pyrdiwah/ Padua and Boroibari in April 2001 as 'a localised problem – as long as we see them locally and we do not allow them to spark, I think we would have done a good job.' 'BSF concern over Bangla influx', *The Assam Tribune* (30 October 2002).

2 Yi-Fu Tuan, *Landscapes of Fear* (Oxford: Blackwell/ New York: Pantheon Books, 1979).

3 Henri Lefebvre, *The Production of Space* (Oxford: Blackwell, 1991), 280.

4 The only exception was a brief period of relaxation during a few months in late 1971 and early 1972, when the border between India and Bangladesh appeared to have vanished in the wake of the Bangladesh Liberation War.

5 Photograph by Shib Shankar Chatterjee (AC Dasgupta Road, Ward Number - II, Dhubri, Assam-783 301, India).

6 *Bangladesh Observer* (23 April 2001).

7 Cf. the case of the Muhuri river and other examples in chapter 4.

8 For example, the border between Mizoram (India) and the Chittagong Hill Tracts (Bangladesh), where violence was high on the Indian side from 1966 (when Mizoram made a bid for independence from India) to 1986 (when a peace treaty was signed), and violence was high on the Bangladeshi side from the mid-1970s (when the Chittagong Hill Tracts made a bid for regional autonomy) till 1997 (when a peace treaty as signed).

9 For example the Kushtia/ Nadia border, Hili, the Tin Bigha corridor, Muhuri/ Belonia. On Tin Bigha, see Willem van Schendel, 'Stateless in South Asia: The Making of the India-Bangladesh Enclaves', *The Journal of Asian Studies*, 61:1 (February 2002), 115–47.

10 The Ground Rules of 1959 suggested the following reasons for frequent cross-border firing, all of which continue to be operative today:

   a) Often, border security forces on both sides do not know where the International Boundary lies on the ground. Therefore, when nationals of the other country cross into what they think is their territory, fire is opened to prevent the ingress.

   b) Where the boundary in the riverine area is criss-cross and portions of land on the home side of the river are owned by the other country, fire is opened when these lands are cultivated or attempts are made to dispossess their rightful owners.

   c) When a char land is formed after the floods, whether in the bed of the river or as an accretion of the mainland, attempt is made by nationals of both countries to seize the newly formed char lands. This leads to claims and counter-claims as to which side owns the char lands. Firing is resorted to support claims of the respective sides.

   d) When the river falls on the international boundary, fishing and navigational disputes occur and fire is opened to stop cattle lifting or other raids by local inhabitants on both sides..

   e) Occasionally fire is opened because of suspected movement in the vicinity of border security posts – this happens usually at night.

   f) Sometimes a build-up of border security forces leads to a race between the two countries and tempers are frayed. A "trigger happy" person lets off a round and this develops into a shooting match.

   Ground Rules Formulated by the Military Sub-Committee of the Indian and Pakistan Delegations (20 October 1959), reprinted in Avtar Singh Bhasin (ed.), *India-Bangladesh Relations: Documents – 19712002* (New Delhi: Geetika Publishers, 2003), V, 2737.

11 There are clear limitations to this information. First, these newspapers are in English and Bengali, not in other borderland languages (e.g. Khasi, Garo, Kokborok, Mizo) in which newspapers are available in print but not yet on the Internet. Second, these newspapers are national or regional ones, published from Calcutta, Dhaka, Shillong and Guwahati; local newspapers published from provincial towns have not yet spawned Internet editions. Third, Internet editions often excerpt printed editions that may be richer in information on border violence than the editions I have used. Fourth, before 1998 most of the newspapers I used were still experimenting with Internet and their coverage was not complete; therefore, my survey starts from 1998. And finally, there are obvious limitations to what editors found newsworthy enough to include in their newspapers. For example, if we compare the Indian and Bangladeshi newspapers, it is

immediately clear that some border incidents are seen as highly significant on one side of the border but do not get any coverage on the other. Clearly, we have no way of accessing border violence which reporters and editors of all these newspapers considered insignificant. However, a number of interviewees at the border reported shootings and other violent incidents that I also found reported in one or more newspapers. In addition to newspapers from India and Bangladesh, I have used a variety of press reports on violence on the Burma-Bangladesh border. A list of newspaper sources can be found in the References at the end of this book.

12 See for example the Box 'Everyday tales of border violence' below.

13 The definition of violence used in this chapter excludes a number of harmful relations in which the cause of the harm and its effects are less easily established than in a shooting or a fist fight, and where the effects may be distributed in an area well beyond the boundary line. Thus I do not deal here with 'environmental violence', such as the pollution of the border river Churni by a liquor factory in Bangladesh that killed fish and possibly humans in the borderland at the Nadia/ Kushtia border during six months each year. Aditya Ghosh, 'Bangla liquor blackens river', *The Times of India* (30 August 2001).

14 See Bhasin (ed.), *India-Bangladesh Relations*, II, 1099–1103.

15 In October 2001, a new government was voted into power in Bangladesh. Dominated by the Bangladesh Nationalist Party (BNP), the cabinet also included Islamist ministers for the first time. Although relations with India deteriorated, no perceptible heightening of border violence resulted from this change.

16 See the BDR plan to construct border roads, double the strength of the BDR and add an air wing. Indian border guards often complained that they were overstretched and that the 'psychological and the physical strain was bound to affect the operational efficiency of the force.' Such strains came to the surface in regular reports of Indian border guards settling a quarrel with their colleagues by shooting them, or committing suicide by shooting themselves. 'BDR chief suggests ring roads along borders', *The Daily Star* (16 July 2000); Aloke Tikku, 'The price of "guarding" the nation', *The Statesman* (1 June 2003); Avijit Sinha, 'Morning mayhem at BSF camp', *The Telegraph* (20 August 2003).

17 Three years later, however, this plan was still on the drawing board, and Bangladesh had not yet constructed the 13-km road that was needed to link the Tripura border to the Bangladesh highway system. 'Push for Indo-Bangla bus service', *The Telegraph* (25 April 2003).

18 In one of the incidents, Indian border guards shot dead two brothers working their fields near the border in northern Bangladesh. A spokesman of the Indian Ministry of Defence in Delhi, pressed by journalists, dismissed the incident as insignificant, framing it in terms of infiltration and playing down the states' involvement: 'The incident is not serious. People are infiltrating from Bangladesh and so security has just been tightened. There is nothing at army-to-army level.' 'India, Bangladesh agree to talks after border firing', *Sawaal News* (15 July 2000).

19 The incidents reported here occurred on the borderline, or at most at a little distance from that line. Depending on the type of attack, this could be the cross-border reach of a shotgun, an arrow, or a short dash across the border. The press also carried numerous reports on cross-border shootings and border scuffles without people getting injured, and on cross-border robbery, looting and piracy that led to material loss but no bodily harm. There were also many reports on failed attempts at cross-border abduction or

rape. I excluded all these cases from the survey.

20 Assessing the quality of the coverage of these reports is difficult for the following reasons:

    a) The coverage itself was extensive. Six Indian newspapers, five Bangladeshi newspapers and one Burmese newsgroup were searched daily (in addition to many more newspapers and weeklies that were searched for details on particular incidents). Usually, incidents were reported in more than one source. It may well be that the coverage is biased toward 'high-tech' encounters involving fire-arms, towards larger-scale events, toward encounters in which adult men rather than women or children were involved, and toward incidents in which state personnel was involved, but there is no way of assessing these biases.

    b) Reporting on Burmese victims is probably poorer than on Bangladesh victims because of the severe muzzling of the press in Burma (Myanmar).

    c) Much information on border incidents comes from official sources rather than from eyewitness accounts gathered by journalists. Apart from the biases inherent in official reporting, figures from official sources sometimes contradict each other.

    d) The lower numbers for 1998 may reflect a relatively more peaceful atmosphere at the border during that year, or poorer coverage of border incidents in a year in which newspapers were still professionalizing their Internet editions.

For other attempts to measure border violence perpetrated on Bangladeshis in recent years, see the reports of the human rights organization Odhikar (http://www.odhikar.org); cf. 'Odhikar report: 202 killed by BSF, Indian criminals in last 2 years', *The Daily Star* (2 December 2002).

21 From 12.6 victims per incident in 1998 to 4.0 in 2002. It is likely that this was a 'real' decline and not attributable primarily to better reporting of minor incidents in more recent years.

22 Some stretches were, however, less prominent than others. Looked at from the Indian side, the Mizoram border was clearly the least violent section of the Partition border. It stood in sharp contrast to the exceptionally violent Tripura border to the north and the fairly violent Burma-Bangladesh border to the south.

23 In this five-year period, Bangladesh Rifles (BDR) killed 6 Indians and injured or abducted 66 Indians; Indian Border Security Force (BSF) killed 193 Bangladeshis and injured or abducted 325 Bangladeshis; and Burmese Nasaka killed 31 Bangladeshis and injured or abducted 244 Bangladeshis. In other words, foreign border guards killed 124 Bangladeshis, 6 Indians, and no Burmese nationals. In a few cases, the killers were other state personnel: police, forest guards, coast guards, or paramilitary personnel.

24 *The Daily Star* photograph. Mohammad Yusuf (40) was a cultivator of Shakharipota village in Bangladesh. On 24 July 2002, he was killed instantly when Indian border guards (BSF) opened fire at the busy border crossing of Benapol, apparently to scare away a group of 20 Bangladeshi nationals trying to cross into India. According to the Additional Inspector-General of the BSF, Ramseh Singh, 'some bullets ... hit a person, killing him instantly, and injured another.' Bangladesh border guards said, however, that Mohammad Yusuf was killed four to six yards inside Bangladesh territory, and that there 'was no question of any trespassing into the Indian territory.' The killing sparked off shooting between border guards of the two countries, followed by an expression of regret by the local BSF commander and an official condemnation by the Bangladesh government. 'Skirmish at Benapole: BDR, BSF exchange fire over farmer's killing', *The Daily Star* (25 July 2002); cf. 'Bangladesh Rifles fire on BSF at Bongaon', *The Times of India* (25 July 2002).

25 For Indian villagers just across the river border also carrying out night patrols, in connection with a conflict over constructing additions to a riverside Shiva temple, see Probir Pramanik, 'Temple village on vigil after border standoff', *The Telegraph* (6 February 2003). The use of bombs in cross-border attacks was also reported for Bangladeshi cattle robbers attacking villagers in Malda. 'Twelve wounded in rustler attack', *The Telegraph* (30 May 2003).

26 Indian smugglers had taken 50 sacks of salt through a border fence gate to the Bangladeshi village of Radhanagar (northwestern Bangladesh) late at night, where Bangladeshi border guards arrested them. The Indian border guards then opened the gate and demanded the salt back. When the Bangladeshi guards refused, the Indians opened fire, injuring the sleeping villagers. 'BSF opens fire on sleeping people in Naogaon: 5 hurt', *The Independent* (25 December 2000). In another case, about 12 Indian border guards crossed into a Bangladesh border village and 'started charging baton on the villagers indiscriminately', probably in connection with cross-border cattle theft. When village men tried to stop the border guards taking cattle to India, the guards opened fire, killing three and wounding fifteen. '3 killed by BSF firing in Kaliganj', *The New Nation* (10 March 2000).

27 'Dinajpur-Fakirganj border tense: 2 Bangladeshis shot dead by BSF', *The Independent* (18 September 1999); 'Bangladesh lodges protest over alleged killings by BSF', *India Today* (20 September 1999).

28 For example, 'BSF won't free 2 Bangladeshi boys', *The New Nation* (1 June 2001); '4 Bangladeshi boys abducted by BSF', *The New Nation* (16 July 2003); 'Bangladeshi fisherman shot dead by Nasaka', *The Independent* (9 September 1999); 'Nasaka abducts 32 Bangladeshis: Three others shot, 5 missing', *The Independent* (5 November 1999); 'Border tense: BSF hands over body of abducted Bangladeshi', *The New Nation* (12 April 2000); 'Bangladeshi killed in BSF firing', *The New Nation* (21 August 2000); '2 shot dead by BSF in Sherpur, Mymensingh', *The Daily Star* (21 June 2001).

29 'Villager shot dead: BDR-BSF gunfight at Haluaghat', *The Daily Star* (29 June 1999); 'Two BSF men caught in Netrakona', *The New Nation* (15 November 1999); 'BDR, BSF flag meet flops: Villagers flee homes as tension mounts', *The New Nation* (29 August 2000); cf. 'Intoxicated BSF man intrudes into Bangladesh', *The Independent* (24 June 2002).

30 According to the Landmine Monitor Report 2000, 'at least' 53 people were killed and 125 injured by land mines along the Bangladesh-Burma border since 1993. This estimate seems too low, although the much higher figures (500 Bangladeshi nationals killed between 1995 and 1999, and 120 Bangladeshis who became disabled by mines in 1998– 9) published by Mizzima News cannot be verified. The Burma security forces, who had abandoned the planting of mines in 1998, resumed the practice in 2000. 'Land mines exploded in Bangladesh-Burma border', *Mizzima News Group* (22 October 2000); 'Two killed in landmine blast on border with Myanmar', *The Independent* (11 November 2000); *Landmine Monitor Report 2000: Toward a Mine-Free World* (New York: Human Rights Watch, 2000). See also chapter 4.

31 Often border guards did not know the national identity of smugglers till after they had killed them. Indian border guards gunned down a man who was smuggling 15 heads of cattle across the Padma river at night. Then they found out that he was Ranjit Mondol from Raninagar in Murshidabad (India). His father later explained: 'We are very poor and my son worked for a big fish. He used to be paid Rs.300 for every pair of cattle that he managed to take to Bangladesh. He had to risk his life, brave the Padma and the

BSF. I had told him several times to stay away from the smuggler, but he never listened.' 'BSF guns down cattle smuggler', *The Telegraph* (5 August 2003). Cf. 'Villagers cry foul after shootout on Padma', *The Telegraph* (19 August 2003).

32 For example, on a winter's day in 2000, Indian smugglers crossed the border river Kalindi (between southern West Bengal and Bangladesh) and safely reached the Bangladeshi bank. They loaded their boat with goods from Bangladesh and were on their way back home when Bangladeshi border guards spotted them and began to chase them. Then Indian border guards joined the hot chase, and in the mêlée the smugglers' boat capsized. All seven men on board drowned; later villagers downstream saw only two bodies floating in the river. 'Bodies of two Indians found in Satkhira', *The New Nation* (21 January 2000). For a similar case, see 'Two Indians drown in Padma', *The Daily Star* (5 July 2001).

33 For example, 'Bangladeshis cut open border fence to sneak into Assam', *The Sentinel* (21 May 2000); 'Bangladeshi killed', *The Assam Tribune* (16 July 2001).

34 '20 Lankan fishermen held near St. Martins', *The New Nation* (29 April 2000); '59 foreign fishermen held, three trawlers seized', *The Daily Star* (25 September 2000).

35 Probir Pramanik, 'Tragedy on border over prayer', *The Telegraph* (29 December 2000); 'BSF firing kills three near Indo-Bangladesh border', *The Hindustan Times* (29 December 2000). In another incident, a group of Bangladeshis went to a border village in India to enjoy an open-air opera (*jatragan*), only to be arrested by Indian border guards. After a meeting with Bangladeshi border guards, most of them were released. 'BSF free 13 Bangladeshis', *The Daily Star* (13 December 2000).

36 'BSF killed two Bangladeshis,' *The Daily Star* (6 August 2003).

37 *Ground Rules Formulated by the Military Sub-Committee of the Indian and Pakistan Delegations* (20 October 1959), reprinted in Bhasin (ed.), *India-Bangladesh Relations*, V, 2735–42. These rules were confirmed in the *Joint India-Bangladesh Agreement for Border Authorities of the Two Countries, 1975* (reprinted in Bhasin (ed.), *India-Bangladesh Relations*, IV, 1902–7), and in a 1991 agreement between India and Bangladesh: 'According to this mechanism, any person caught crossing the border illegally is to be handed over by the side apprehending him to the other side.' Pranay Sharma, 'Twin talks with Bangla', *The Telegraph* (27 April 2003).

38 In general, public pronouncements regarding professional discipline and punishment were rare, and usually very vague. There were no press reports pertaining to the punishment of border guards regarding particular killings. Responding to the allegation that Bangladeshi border guards were inefficient, a Commanding Officer of the Bangladesh Rifles, Lt. Col. ASM Shamser Ali, told a journalist in general terms: 'there are good officers and bad officers in every force but you will be surprised how many staff are sacked for professional delinquency. Some of the *jawans* (men) are given jail sentences for minor offences.' M. Asiuzzaman, 'Smugglers take BDR men hostage', *The New Nation* (19 March 2002). Indian border guard (BSF) sources, quoted in a newspaper report about BSF involvement in smuggling across the border with Bangladesh, explained that 'if caught ... the punishments were stringent. Courts of inquiry were held, similar to a court martial. If connivance was proved, the BSF personnel lost his job as well as pension. Even if guilt could not be proved, the authorities often took the precaution of posting the person back to disturbed Kashmir. "Six constables and two officers were recently sent home".' Nirmalya Banerjee, 'Fencing problem plagues border', *The Times of India* (16 April 2002).

39 They also were prone to argue that they had shot dead border crossers in self-defence, because these had 'challenged them', or 'threatened them with sharp instruments.'

40 The killing occurred on the Pyain river. The Inspector-General of the Indian Border Security Force (BSF) told Indian journalists that the killing of five Bangladeshis was perfectly justified as 'the intruders were more than 200 yards inside Indian territory despite the warning. Further, a BSF inspector was lynched by intruders last year.' VS Sirohi (IGP (BSF) Shillong frontier), quoted in 'BSF firing: Toll goes up to 5', The Assam Tribune (14 July 2000). For a case involving Bangladesh border guards who killed two Indian teenagers suspected of attempted cattle theft, see 'Two Indian intruders killed in Mymensingh', The Independent (9 August 1999).

41 Anirban Roy, 'BSF jawan abets smugglers', The Telegraph (10 March 2000). In July 2000, a BSF patrol unit shot dead a suspected smuggler after 'lay[ing] in waiting for an hour' on the bank of the border river. They then seized a few sacks of sugar that had been in his possession. 'Cachar smuggler shot', The Telegraph (2 July 2000).

42 This could be an occasion to assert the rightfulness of killing border crossers point blank. At a flag meeting in mid-2001, BSF officers were reported to have clearly announced to their Bangladeshi counterparts: 'Any person infiltrating into India will be shot at.' They argued that 'the BSF was compelled to shoot' Namar Ali, a Bangladeshi citizen catching fish near the border at Jakiganj, on the ground that he came to the Indian side of the border and 'challenged the BSF'. His body was later returned to Bangladesh. 'BSF reborn with vigour', The Sentinel (2 August 2001).

43 No mention was made in these press reports of any reparations having been made to relatives of people killed by border guards.

44 The three human rights organizations were Odhikar, Ain-O-Shalish Kendra and the Bangladesh Legal Aid and Services Trust (BLAST). 'BSF firing: Toll goes up to 5', The Assam Times (14 July 2000); 'HR groups concerned at border violence by BSF', Holiday (21 July 2000); 'Killings by BSF: Dhaka lodges protest with Delhi', Daily Star (25 July 2000).

45 In this five-year period, Bangladesh Rifles (BDR) killed 5 Bangladeshis and injured 398 other Bangladeshis at or very near the border; Indian Border Security Force (BSF) and Assam Rifles killed 48 Indians and injured 43 other Indians; and Burmese Nasaka killed 6 Burmese and injured 23 other Burmese. These figures exclude dozens of Burmese nationals being killed by anti-personnel mines laid by the Burmese army and Nasaka in the no-man's land at the Burma-Bangladesh border.

46 After one of these attacks in a Bangladesh border market, a national daily wrote in an editorial about 'a remorseless show of strength' and 'excesses committed on innocent civilians.' It demanded that the BDR should make a formal apology to the villagers. 'We condemn the BDR action ... People already have a somewhat negative perception of their failure to have the desired impact on smuggling, drug and arms racketeering and trafficking of women and children across the border. Such an incident of highhandedness is bound to put further dent on their credibility ... the BDR high command should immediately initiate an investigation into the matter and take stringent disciplinary measures against the responsible jawaans [men].' 'Villagers, BDR clash in Chuadanga: 100 hurt', The New Nation (13 March 2000); 'Editorial: BDR men going haywire', The New Nation (14 March 2000). For a similar case involving Indian border guards and villagers, see 'Atrocities by BSF alleged', The Assam Tribune (1 May 2000). For Murshidabad, see 'Token end to border row', The Telegraph (9 April 2002). Sometimes border guards clashed with people living further from the border, e.g. Indian border guards getting involved in a pitched battle with inhabitants of Gughupara, a village 5 km from the border in Murshidabad where 30 buffaloes 'were huddled together ... for smuggling.' The guards gunned down three villagers, killing one and seriously

injuring two others, and the villagers injured three guards with 'sharp weapons' and bricks. Such confrontations in the borderland, but far from the boundary line, have not been included in the figures given in this chapter. 'BSF battles rustlers', *The Telegraph* (6 February 2002).

47 For protests at the border crossings ('land ports') of Sona Masjid, Benapol and Hili, see 'Deadlock at Sonamasjid Land Customs station continues for 10 days', *The Independent* (16 April 2000); 'Export-import thru' Benapole suspended', *The Daily Star* (25 November 2000); 'Trucks to Bangla held up on border', *The Telegraph* (5 January 2001).

48 Such antagonism is common at borders. Speaking of the border between the Gold Coast and French Togoland in the 1920s and 1930s, Paul Nugent describes how 'the local communities and those in uniform regarded each other as aliens.' Paul Nugent, 'Power Versus Knowledge: Smugglers and the State Along Ghana's Eastern Frontier, 1920–1992', in Michael Rösler and Tobias Wendl (eds.), *Frontiers and Borderlands: Anthropological Perspectives* (Frankfurt am Main, etc.: Peter Lang, 1999), 86.

49 'BDR men clash with people in Joypurhat: 15 injured', *The New Nation* (25 March 2000). For a similar case in Meghalaya (India), see 'One hurt as BSF opens fire on mob – Police to probe incident', *The Telegraph* (6 November 2002). Cf. 'BSF jawans kill 2 near Bangladesh border', *The Times of India* (20 January 2003).

50 A very similar case of 'unprovoked firing' involved trucks inadvertently blocking a BSF vehicle on a road in Murshidabad; this enraged the BSF constables so much that they shot to death one of the truck drivers and injured a bystander, after which they fled the wrath of the locals by hiding in a police station. 'BSF road-rage shooting kills 5 in Cooch Behar', *The Statesman* (4 December 1999); 'BSF probe into Cooch Behar violence', *The Telegraph* (5 December 1999); Sudip Sinha, 'Bengal: Cooch Behar villagers cry for justice', *The Statesman* (5 December 1999); 'Border guards gun down truck driver', *The Telegraph* (3 December 2001). Cf. Main Uddin Chisti, 'Fence bruises border villages', *The Telegraph* (3 June 2003).

51 Another West Bengal politician who was vocal on this issue was Kamal Guha, the state Agriculture Minister, who made BSF misbehaviour an issue in local elections. He spoke of the 'atrocities' being committed by the Border Security Force that had 'unleashed a reign of terror in the name of containing infiltration along the entire stretch of the India-Bangladesh border.' And yet, he alleged, senior ministers, although aware of the plight of citizens in the borderland, were 'totally indifferent to their problems.' An MP from South Dinajpur also accused the BSF of committing atrocities and added that the border guards forced local farmers to run errands for them without any remuneration. 'If the people refuse, the jawans often beat them up', he said. 'Farmers in border areas being ignored', *The Times of India* (11 April 2002); Abhijit Chakraborty, 'Land-locked in BSF territory', *The Telegraph* (28 August 2002); cf. 'Tiller row sparks BSF fury', *The Telegraph* (29 January 2003); 'BSF accused of excesses', *The New Nation* (8 August 2002); 'BSF jawan shoots at student', *The Statesman* (20 January 2003); 'Kamal trains guns at BSF "excesses"', *The Telegraph* (1 March 2003).

52 *XIII Lok Sabha Debates, Session II (Winter Session), Monday, November 29, 1999/ Agrahayana 2, 1921 (Saka)* (available from: http://alfa.nic.in/lsdeb/ls13/ses2/ 17291199.htm); *XIII Lok Sabha Debates, Session II (Winter Session), Thursday, December 9, 1999/Agrahayana 18, 1921 (Saka)* (available from: http://alfa.nic.in/lsdeb/ls13/ses2/ 31091299.htm).

53 Similarly, Bangladeshi borderlanders greeted with mixed feelings their Prime Minister's declaration that 'BDR members have been playing a commendable role in discharging

their major responsibility with utmost honesty, sincerity and performance.' 'BDR members playing commendable role: Khaleda', *The New Nation* (9 March 2002). On BDR men harassing borderlanders, see Francis Rolt, *On the Brink of Bengal* (London: John Murray, 1991), 141–2.

54 The term 'thugs in fatigues' is taken from Debarati Agarwala, 'BSF jawans snare cattle booty', *The Telegraph* (7 January 2003).

55 Two weeks after these raids on border villages, BSF men in Malda created a new furore when – chased by border villagers who tried to recoup a confiscated power tiller – they opened fire and shot a youth. Debarati Agarwala, 'Malda calls meet on BSF "excesses"', *The Telegraph* (14 January 2003); Debarati Agarwala, 'Govt draws the line for border guards', *The Telegraph* (15 January, 2003); 'Tiller row sparks BSF fury', *The Telegraph* (29 January 2003). Cf. Rousik Sen, 'BSF martial law robs villages of marital joy', *The Telegraph* (30 January 2003); Debarati Agarwala, '"Assault" sparks BSF boycott: Jawans beat up Congress leader, brother', *The Telegraph* (10 February 2003). Similarly, general strikes were called against rising BSF atrocities after BSF personnel shot at a group of schoolchildren in Murshidabad and manhandled a businessman in South Dinajpur. 'BSF fires on students in slap case', *The Telegraph* (19 January 2003); 'BSF jawan shoots at student', *The Statesman* (20 January 2003); Abhijit Chakraborty, 'Bandh to protest BSF "excesses"', *The Telegraph* (18 January 2003). Cf. Alamgir Hossain, 'Traders' ire on violent jawans', *The Telegraph* (7 November 2002); 'Cattle battle with BSF', *The Telegraph* (28 July 2003). For complaints about hostile BSF from villagers in Meghalaya, see Rajeev Bhattacharyya, 'Border village in dire straits', *The Telegraph* (26 February 2003). For a borderlander in Dhubri (Assam) staging a legal battle against the BSF who confiscated his timber, see 'Person turned barren land into forest, only to be deprived of its fruits', *The Sentinel* (13 August 2003). For BSF attempts to convince borderlanders that 'manning the international borders is not all about grim-faced jawans with fingers on the trigger, ready to shoot at the slightest provocation', see Bidhayak Das, 'Charity begins at the border: BSF tries to improve quality of life in interiors of Meghalaya', *The Telegraph* (18 July 2003).

56 The director-general also suggested that the conflicts were caused by the border villagers' ignorance of what the BSF's statutory duties were. He suggested that this problem could be overcome easily: lists of these duties 'would now be displayed in Bengali in villages and copies would also be handed over to village panchayat pradhans [council heads].' 'BSF steps to better relations with villagers', *The Times of India* (15 March 2003); 'Bengali barrier in border rows', *The Telegraph* (16 March 2003); 'BSF pledge caution on border fire', *The Times of India* (17 March 2003); cf. Sakyasen Mitra, 'BSF plans to deploy Bangla-speaking men along border to reduce tension', *The Daily Star* (15 June 2003).

57 Gobinda Roy, Forward Bloc MLA from North Bengal, quoted in 'BSF "firing" goes up at border area', *The Times of India* (19 February 2003). ISI = Inter-Services Intelligence, Pakistan's foreign intelligence agency. In Cooch Behar another MLA, Nripen Roy, was equally indignant: 'The BSF reign supreme … we have been flooded with complaints.' Main Uddin Chisti, 'Fence bruises border villages', *The Telegraph* (3 June 2003).

58 Photograph by Shib Shankar Chatterjee (AC Dasgupta Road, Ward Number - II, Dhubri, Assam-783 301, India).

59 Rifle Raj could go further than mere harassment. The All-Assam Students' Union not only gave a list of BSF extortions and 'atrocious activities' in the Dhubri area that had pushed 'the people of the border district … to the last limit of tolerance' but also

alleged that 'some BSF personnel are leasing out some of the Brahmaputra chars to some dreaded criminals of Bangladesh.' See '"BSF harassing border villagers"', *The Assam Tribune* (18 August 2001).

60 For example, the Chief Minister of Meghalaya who 'mooted the setting up of a northeastern paramilitary type force, comprising recruits from the seven northeastern states. He feels that such a force will lead to less friction and help the state governments monitor human rights abuses and avoid excesses.' 'Lapang to focus on border plan – Roads on priority list', *The Telegraph* (25 April 2003).

61 In this five-year period, Bangladesh Rifles (BDR) killed 33 BSF men and injured or abducted 23 others; and Indian Border Security Force (BSF) killed 9 BDR and injured or abducted 9 others. No press reports made mention of Nasaka harming BDR or vice versa, despite frequent border shootings in this section. Shootings without casualties have been excluded from the figures in this chapter.

62 For example, BSF constable Ram Kishore Rathore was found 450 meters inside Comilla district (Bangladesh). He was arrested, and the next day he was deported to India. A similar treatment befell Sree Beenny Singh in Kushtia district. In a bizarre incident in northern Sylhet, two Indian border guards 'entered into Bangladesh territory through Takerhat border, hired a rickshaw and started proceeding towards Lakmachora area in the thana'; they were arrested and handed over. And two police constables from Meghalaya (India) named Ling Pai and B Hasa entered Bangladesh to 'get released a truck seized with smuggled coal from India'; they triggered an exchange of fire between the border guards of the two countries but remained unharmed themselves. They were arrested and later sent back to India. 'BSF personnel returned', *The New Nation* (20 December 2000); 'BSF man held inside Bangladesh territory, released', *The Independent* (12 May 2001); 'Situation tense in Tahirpur bordering area', *The Independent* (6 February 1999); 'Arrested Indian policemen freed', *The Daily Star* (4 November 1999); 'BSF member caught inside Bangladesh', *The New Nation* (20 March 2003); 'Five intruding BSF men caught by villagers, freed after flag meeting', *The Independent* (5 April 2003).

63 'Two Bangladeshi guards killed in clash', *The Times of India* (23 September 1999).

64 This occurred on the Dinajpur/West Dinajpur border. Some reports spoke of attempts to dishonour or rape them. 'BSF man killed in encounter with BDR', *The Independent* (28 March 2000); 'Villagers flee homes as BSF, BDR dig in along Magurbari border', *The Independent* (29 March 2000); 'Unwanted border clashes', *The New Nation* (31 March 2000). .

65 'BSF man killed in gunfight with BDR in Sherpur', *The Daily Star* (14 September 1998).

66 An area of 60 ha on the Saropar-Naogram border (Sylhet) has been in dispute since 1958. 'Abducted BDR men freed', *The Daily Star* (21 August 1999).

67 E.g. two Indian border guards were injured in August 1999 when clashes broke out in Muhurir Char, a 30 ha disputed area on the Tripura (India)-Feni (Bangladesh) border. See chapter 4 for some background. 'Tripura rebels set terms for hostage release', *The Telegraph* (11 September 1999).

68 *Ground Rules Formulated by the Military Sub-Committee of the Indian and Pakistan Delegations* (20 October 1959), reprinted in Bhasin (ed.), *India-Bangladesh Relations*, V, 2738. The Ground Rules were confirmed in the *Joint India-Bangladesh Agreement for Border Authorities of the Two Countries, 1975*, reprinted in Bhasin (ed.), *India-Bangladesh Relations*, IV, 1902–7.

69 During this battle, an Indian and a Bangladeshi girl were also killed, and three Bangladeshi and two Indian civilians were reported to be injured. 'Dhaka seeks

compensation', *The Hindu* (31 August 1998); 'BSF firing: Dhaka demands compensation for the victims', *The Daily Star* (31 August 1998).

70 The Indian and Bangladeshi versions of the origins of the clash differed considerably. See e.g. 'Unprovoked BSF firing in Kushtia border: BDR Naik, 5 others killed, 40 injured', *The New Nation* (20 April 1999); 'Nine killed in Indo-Bangla border firing', *The Times of India* (21 April 1999); '"Clashes on Kushtia border ensued from firing by Bangladeshi intruders," claim BSF', *News from Bangladesh* (22 April 1999).

71 This clash, which became known as the Pakhi Urar Char incident, began on 13 September 1999 when the Indian Border Security Force (BSF) killed a Bangladeshi. On 1 October they killed another Bangladeshi. On 6 October, BSF men abducted a Bangladeshi from the border, and the Bangladesh Rifles (BDR) abducted an Indian in return. Troops were massed on both sides, and they resorted to intensive cross-border shooting. This left eleven Indian border guards dead (or, according to other reports, four dead and seven seriously injured) while border villagers fled in terror. 'BDR-BSF skirmish on Kurigram border', *The Independent* (7 October 1999); Mamun Islam, 'India masses troops on Kurigram border: BDR sends reinforcements to 32 posts: Panicky villagers fleeing homes', *The Independent* (8 October 1999); 'Kurigram border still tense', *The Independent* (10 October 1999); Mamun Islam, 'BSF creating panic along Kurigram border', *News from Bangladesh* (18 October 1999); Mamun Islam, 'Three tension-filled weeks in a border village', *The Independent* (29 October 1999).

72 For example, six Indian border guards were killed and 13 others injured under Bangladeshi fire at the Cooch Behar (India)-Kurigram (Bangladesh) border in July 2000. At least three Indian civilians were killed and 8 injured, and about 18,000 people fled their homes. 'BDR-BSF meet held: Borders quiet', *The Independent* (14 July 2000); 'Kurigram returning to normalcy', *The Daily Star* (16 July 2000).

73 Padua/Pyrdiwah is on the border of the East Khasi Hills (Meghalaya, India) and Sylhet (Bangladesh). Boroibari is on the border of Mankachar (Assam, India) and Roumari (Kurigram, Bangladesh). Padua is held 'in adverse possession' by India, as is Boroibari by Bangladesh. See also chapter 4.

74 All national newspapers in India and Bangladesh covered the confrontations for several weeks following 18 April 2001. The incidents were also featured widely in the international media.

75 *The Independent* (19 April 2001).

76 Photograph by Shib Shankar Chatterjee (AC Dasgupta Road, Ward Number - II, Dhubri, Assam-783 301, India).

77 Photograph by Zia Islam, April 2001.

78 In 1998, there were no press reports on civilians harming state agents. According to press reports, 14 Burmese state agents were killed, 23 Indian state agents were killed (and 26 injured), and 9 Bangladeshi state agents were killed (and 20 injured) in border encounters with civilians between 1999 and 2001. Most of these state agents were border guards, but some were border police or customs men.

79 Nurul Alam, 'BDR lodges protest with NASAKA: Planting of mines along border', *The Daily Star* (14 November 2000); 'Myanmar deploys troops along Bangladesh border', *The Times of India* (16 November 2000); 'Tension along Bangladesh-Myanmar border', *The Times of India* (18 November 2000); '3 reported dead as guards fight rebels', *The Mekong Digest* (28 January 1998).

80 For border patrols being ambushed and killed by the National Liberation Front of Tripura (NLFT) in Tripura, see e.g. 'BSF Jawan killed in Tripura mine blast', *The Telegraph* (29

July 1999); 'Separatists' attack: 8 BSF men killed in Tripura', *The New Nation* (27 September 1999). In Mizoram, seven members of the elite anti-terrorist Hunter Force of the Mizoram police were killed, and four injured, in an ambush by the Bru National Liberation Front along Indo-Bangladesh border ('Bodies of cops brought to Aizawl', *The Assam Tribune* (2 July 2000)). And two Indian border guards were killed by fighters of the United Liberation Front of Asom (ULFA) and the A'chik National Volunteer Corps (ANVC) during a raid on the Dumkasol observation post on the Meghalaya-Bangladesh border, during which the insurgents captured the border guards' arms ('2 BSF jawans killed in ULFA, ANVC attack', *The Assam Tribune* (24 February 2001)).

81 Seven labourers were killed and eight injured by rebels who intercepted their Border Roads truck, lined them up and sprayed them with bullets, on the Tripura border. Man Mohan, 'Tripura wants Centre to get ultra camps in Bangladesh closed', *The Times of India* (9 September 1998). In another case, the army escort of border road workers was attacked, leaving nine soldiers dead and three injured. 'Massive hunt launched to nab NLFT ultras in Tripura, Bangla border sealed', *The Sentinel* (11 October 2002). In Tripura, insurgents also resented the construction of a railway along the border with Bangladesh because it would connect Agartala with the rest of India by rail for the first time since 1947, making the transport of troops into Tripura easier. Hence they attacked labourers working on the construction of this line. '6 railway labourers abducted in Tripura', *The Sentinel* (30 December 2002).

82 On battles between smugglers (of heroin, phensidyl, sugar, buffaloes, rice, salt and timber) and Bangladeshi border guards, policemen and forest rangers, see e.g. 'Smugglers beat cops, snatch seized heroin', *The Independent* (22 July 2000); 'Timber smugglers open fire on forest officials at Ukhia: 10 including Forest Range Officer hurt', *The Daily Star* (25 December 2000); '2 BDR men hurt as smugglers open fire', *The New Nation* (16 February 2001); 'Buffalo smugglers clash with police', *The Independent* (19 October 2001); 'Smugglers attack BDR patrol in Hilli, jeep damaged', *The Independent* (30 January 2003); 'Smugglers attack BDR patrol in Natore: 15 hurt', *The Independent* (1 February 2003). On smugglers giving battle for two hours to a force consisting of Indian revenue intelligence men, railway police and local police, intent on searching a local train known as the 'Contraband Express', see Probir Pramanik, 'Cops, smugglers clash at Bagdogra station', *The Telegraph* (5 August 2001).

83 This incident occurred near Charghat, on the Rajshahi/Murshidabad border, in February 2002. Asiuzzaman, 'Smugglers take BDR men hostage'.

84 On Bangladeshi villagers carrying out 'citizens' arrests' of Indian border guards for rape or stealing cows, see 'Two BSF men caught in Netrakona', *The New Nation* (15 November 1999); 'Arrested BSF men handed over', *The Daily Star* (4 December 2000). On a case of Indian villagers injuring and capturing a trespassing Bangladeshi border guard, see 'BDR jawans clash with farmers', *The Telegraph* (13 February 2002). On shoot-outs between border guards and cross-border kidnappers, see 'Cop injured in clash with armed terrorists in Meherpur', *The Independent* (2 March 2000). On a border vigilante group asking state permission for arms to protect the border against the neighbouring state's border guards in the face of the uselessness of the Indian Border Security Force, see 'Khasi chiefs meet in Shillong, ask Delhi for people's army', *The Sentinel* (17 October 2001); 'Shankadeep Choudhury, 'Villagers' army to take on Bangla raiders', *The Times of India* (10 November 2001).

85 For example, 'BDR man, 2 others killed by Indians', *The New Nation* (26 October 2000).

86 In this type of encounter 65 Bangladeshis were killed (and 528 others injured or abducted), 38 Indians killed (and 161 injured or abducted), and 5 Burmese killed (and 34 injured or abducted) between 1998 and 2001. These figures exclude one Korean national who was injured during a pirate attack on his ship.

87 Lethal fights over border fishing rights are reported in 'Three killed in shootout', *The Telegraph* (29 January 2000); and 'Border tense: BSF hands over body of abducted Bangladeshi', *The New Nation* (12 April 2000); the death of three Indians and a Bangladeshi in a quarrel over grazing rights in '4 villagers killed in clash at India, Bangla border', *The Times of India* (21 July 2001); and the killing of a Bangladeshi firewood collector by Indian civilians in '2 Bangladeshis killed by Indians', *The New Nation* (22 August 2000). Thirteen Bangladeshi construction workers, building a sluice gate in the disputed Muhuri river (Tripura/ Feni border) were attacked and wounded by a large crowd of Indians ('Sluice gate over Muhuri: 13 Bangladeshis hurt in Indian attack', *The New Nation* (25 April 1999)).

88 As happened in Simna Colony, a village in Tripura on the border with Bangladesh and within view of Satchhari, a training camp of the All Tripura Tiger Force (ATTF) inside Bangladesh. Twenty-two inhabitants of Simna were killed in a night attack, and survivors said: 'The mass killing was done to force us to leave our villages for good. But we are poor, we have no means to go anywhere else for safety … They want an unhindered movement in the area by scaring away villagers.' Satyabrata Chakraborti, 'Border route used regularly by ultras', *The Statesman* (9 May 2003).

89 For example, one Bangladeshi died and 25 others were injured when a mediation meeting over the sharing of money between two rival smuggling organizations failed on the Nadia/ Kushtia border ('One killed as smugglers trade fire in Kushtia', *The Daily Star* (23 July 2001)). In a similar incident on the Rajshahi/ Murshidabad border, a fight with bombs and guns broke out between groups over an important river crossing on the Ganges, where goods and cattle from India crossed over to Bangladesh, killing one and injuring 30. Among the methods of eliminating rivals was the cutting of leg tendons, a punishment meted out to five people on this occasion. 'Control over river ghat: One killed, 30 hurt in gunbattle in Rajshahi', *The Independent* (2 November 2000). Cf. Willem van Schendel, 'Easy Come, Easy Go: Smugglers on the Ganges', *Journal of Contemporary Asia*, 23:2 (1993), 189–213.

90 'Smugglers robbed at Bangladesh-Burma water', *Mizzima News Group* (13 July 2000). Similarly, in an attempt to corner the profits of the illegal cattle trade, a group of Indians stormed a border farmhouse in Chapai Nawabganj (Rajshahi, Bangladesh) and took away 294 cows, killing one person and injuring four. '7 Bangladeshis killed by BSF in 18 months', *The New Nation* (25 June 2001).

91 'Myanmar gunmen killed in Bangladesh border battle', *ShweInc News* (24 October 1998).

92 'Bangladeshi abducted by Indian in Meherpur', *The Daily Star* (8 July 2000). For other reports of cross-border kidnapping, see e.g. 'Boy kidnapped by Indians yet to be rescued,' *The New Nation* (15 January 2000); 'Bangladeshis kidnapped 2 Tripura teachers', *The Times of India* (19 July 2001); 'Two abducted men released in Bandarban', *The New Nation* (23 June 1999); 'Mizoram refuses to pay ransom to rebels', *The Telegraph* (28 April 2000).

93 '200 hurt as Bangladeshis, Indians clash in Sunamganj border area', *The Independent* (26 March 2001).

94 Social scientists have followed suit; in their accounts everyday border violence is simply

overlooked. As Vazira Zamindar argues with respect to the India-(West) Pakistan border: 'the graphic violence of 1947 was only a part of the violence of Partition, while the bureaucratic and institutional forms of everyday violence that went into the making of the Indo-Pak border, and [sustain] it to this day, have instead been naturalized, or in other words, nationalized. One could argue that if the genocidal violence has been treated historiographically as a civilizational aberration, then this institutional violence has been civilized as part of a two-state national order.' Vazira Zamindar, 'Divided Families and the Making of Nationhood in India and Pakistan 1947–65' (Ph.D. thesis, Columbia University, 2002), 14.

95 Interview, Bagha, 1988.

96 See the protests by Malda district authorities, mentioned above, and Paul Nugent, *Smugglers, Secessionists & Loyal Citizens on the Ghana-Togo Frontier: The Lie of the Borderlands Since 1914* (Oxford: James Curry/ Athens: Ohio University Press/ Legon: Sub-Saharan Publishers, 2002), 274.

97 As Chaturvedi argues for communities in the Pakistan-India borderland. Sanjay Chaturvedi, 'Common Pasts and Dividing Futures: A Critical Geopolitics of Indo-Pak Border(s)', in Paul Ganster (ed.), *Cooperation, Environment and Sustainability in Border Regions* (San Diego: San Diego State University Press/ Institute for Regional Studies of the Californias, 2001), 414.

98 For example, after 15 years 'on the fringes of national politics', Swami Chinmayanand, a Hindutva activist turned politician, became the Indian junior minister in charge of border management in 2003. Immediately he let it be known that he hoped 'to yank the eastern borders into the mainstream of security cover while still at the Centre.' The Indian government had realized that the country's 'eastern flank', especially the border with Bangladesh, needed special attention because 'militants were assembling a network in the east to subvert the country's heartland.' His two main techniques to counter this threat were border fencing and winning the hearts and minds of borderlanders. Seema Guha, 'Swami turns security spotlight towards east', *The Telegraph* (20 August 2003).

99 Cf. Andreas, *Border Games*, x.

100 For example, in the wake of 'border incidents' in 2000, the chief of the Bangladesh border guards (BDR) launched a plan to construct border roads to 'beef up national security, increase vigilance and curb smuggling drastically.' This implied, he said, that the strength of the BDR should be doubled from 37,000 to 70,000 men (and its Army officers from 300 to 600), and that an air wing comprising of helicopters should be added. 'BDR chief suggests ring roads along borders', *The Daily Star* (16 July 2000). In 2002, in the wake of growing concern in Indian political circles about Islamic militants and Indian rebel groups in Bangladesh, the Indian Border Security Force (BSF) unveiled a plan to raise 78 new battalions and strengthen the command structure. 'BSF "eastern theatre" to counter Bangla threat,' *The Telegraph* (30 November 2002).

101 Hastings Donnan and Thomas M Wilson, *Borders: Frontiers of Identity, Nation and State* (Oxford and New York: Berg, 1999), 129–50.

102 Donnan and Wilson, *Borders*, 141.

103 'The common man living close to the border is not treated like an Indian citizen.' Kamal Guha, the West Bengal Minister of Agriculture, quoted in 'Kamal trains guns at BSF "excesses"', *The Telegraph* (1 March 2003).

104 A similar process of dehumanizing borderlanders' bodies could be observed on the Bangladeshi side of the border. Here Bangladesh border guards (BDR) could turn violent

against Bangladeshi citizens. One form of violence was rape. Zuan Rahman, a border guard of Sonatia border outpost in Panchagarh, abducted a local woman and raped her. When her co-villagers heard about this, they chased and caught him, and kept him confined in the village. Colleagues of the BDR man then rushed to the site and attacked the villagers. After wounding five people, including the woman who had been raped, they 'snatched the rapist from the villagers.' 'Five injured as BDR men, villagers clash,' *The Independent* (31 May 2003).

105 It is an example of territoriality at the scale of the human body. On the human body as a geographical scale, see Sally A Marston, 'The Social Construction of Scale', *Progress in Human Geography* 24:2 (2000), 219–42.

12

NATION AND BORDERLAND

Borders are not always easy to discern. As one traveller observed, looking down from his airplane in 1954:

> Somewhere in that misty, watery greenness below was the frontier between West and East Bengal, between India and Pakistan; a frontier which few Bengalis really wanted; a barrier to trade and the free movement of men; an incentive to smugglers of goods and currencies; a breeding place for corrupt officials. I couldn't see it. All I could see was the unity of a province which the follies of men had denied.[1]

This lack of obviousness is precisely the reason why borders become zones of national concern. They demarcate a nation's imagined homeland and a state's territorial jurisdiction, and this should be visible to all. They must be symbolically marked with the nation's imprint. This imprint evokes the nation, locates the border in the mind, physically separates the included from the excluded, and stakes out the arena where neighbouring nations confront each other. It is for this reason that borderlands are essential sites for the study of nations, and the study of borderlands must address the ways in which competing nations continually mark their side of the border.[2]

The Bengal borderland inevitably became an important battlefield of identities, a place where worldviews met and where new forms of self-identification were shaped. The sudden creation of the border forced a frantic reworking of categories of inclusion and exclusion in terms of citizenship, ethnicity, gender, generation, religion, lifestyle and phenotype. It created new majorities and minorities and new ways of signalling who belonged, who was expelled and who opted out.

Arguably the most powerful new symbols were those associated with the emergence of new *national* identities. Among these symbols, the border itself was of paramount importance because of the territorial way in which modern nations are conceived. The post-Partition states were the principal architects of nation-building, strengthening their nations by constantly reproducing the territorial borders and giving these the appearance of being sacred, not in need of explanation, beyond question and natural. Bordering the nation meant taking symbolic control of the nearest half of the borderland that was claimed by the nation as 'inside', and disowning the other half that was excluded as 'outside'. It was imperative to mark and separate the two halves as clearly as possible, and – in order to project an image of autonomy, impermeability and sovereign power – to exclude the 'outside.' In this way, the construction of pure, unadulterated, clearly bounded and self-enclosed nations of Indians, Pakistanis/ Bangladeshis and Burmese only served 'to mask the reality of a boundary that is *necessarily* porous to economic flows ... Indeed, the stability of the "inside" depends upon such flows from the "outside".'[3] The tensions between the territorial exclusivity of the new state-sponsored nationalisms and the reality of cross-border identities and flows turned the borderland into a crucial arena of symbolic interaction, an enduring battleground of identity politics.

Sites of memory

How are historians to study these tensions? It may be useful to consider the work of Pierre Nora and others.[4] They argue that historians of the nation should give priority to the study of 'sites of memory' – monuments, museums, archives, events, texts, ideas, and so on – that support the notion of the nation. These memory sites, they suggest, are not *what* people remember about the nation but *where* and *when* they remember it. They are reminders of the nation. Studying them, according to Nora and his collaborators, may help us in understanding the relationship between individual memories and public memory, and between both of these and power.

Studying sites of memory is of particular importance at a time when many people feel ambivalent about nations, on the one hand recognizing that they are participants in a national history but on the other hand feeling a critical distance from what is presented as 'national tradition'.[5] If memory sites are reminders, then their existence points to the fact that remembering does not come spontaneously: 'If we still inhabited our memory, we would have no need to consecrate sites to it.'[6] In other words, the appearance of memory sites may indicate an anxiety over a possible loss of public memory. Creating memory sites is therefore always a political act, an attempt to retain a memory that is fading away, reviving one that has disappeared altogether or creating a new one. Neglecting or destroying sites can be read as an attempt at effacing memory, or obstructing its resurrection or construction.

This approach allows us to map the cultural landscape of a borderland. Sites of national memory, or symbols of the nation, can tell us about the success of nation-building projects and the 'territorialization of memory' that they entail.[7] And memory sites celebrating cross-border unity can show us how borderlanders challenge the imprint of the nation. This is a complex theme requiring extensive consideration; in this chapter I cannot do more than hint at the possibilities of this approach. I look briefly at five types of memory sites: territorial symbols, monuments, events, language and body codes. In a final section, I also consider the reverse: the borderland's role as a memory site in the construction of the nation-state.

Symbols of territorial sovereignty.   Because borders mark the end of a nation's territory, they are spaces of intense national anxiety. Here the nation's spatial dimensions are demarcated visibly and in opposition to a neighbouring nation. Not only are borders spaces where nations burst into view as nowhere else (except perhaps in the centres of capital cities), but borders are also locations where nations must engage in a direct symbolic confrontation with each other. Depending on the political relationship, this confrontation may take the form of a friendly conversation, a spirited dialogue, or a bitter altercation. Symbols of territoriality are one idiom in which nations express themselves here, and nations need symbols that are readily understood. At the border between India, Bangladesh and Burma, most of the symbols have been derived from the international repertoire of territoriality.

We have seen how much effort it had taken these states to establish the exact location of the border between their territories, and how often the symbolic confrontation between them had taken the form of a quarrel. By the 21st century, the demarcation of the border was still incomplete and more than a few inhabitants of the borderland still had no idea in which country they were living.[8] In most sections of the border, however, the nations had imprinted their territories by means of markings that were unequivocal and easy to recognize.

First, there were joint territorial symbols. These were the boundary pillars and buoys that showed the exact location of the borderline (Plates 12.1 and 12.2). True landmarks, the neighbouring states could create them only by mutual consent, and they wore the names of the states on opposite sides. The boundary 'pillars' of the Bengal borderland were in fact pyramids of drab white or gray concrete.[9] Over time, bureaucrats of India and Pakistan/Bangladesh produced a long, irritable correspondence about the proper location and maintenance of these pillars. Today it is still possible to find some boundary pillars marked 'Pakistan' instead of 'Bangladesh,' a sure sign of territorial dispute.[10] Borderlanders did not take particular care of these pillars. On the contrary, in official correspondence, they were sometimes accused of damaging or removing them.[11] Although many of the boundary pillars looked forlorn, they were crucial in stabilising territorial claims and in indicating to all concerned where one state's territory ended and that of the other began. By the same token, these memory sites marked the metaphysical line separating Indians from Bangladeshis.

Plate 12.1: Pillar marking the border between Bangladesh and India, with the Indian border fence in the background, 2000.[12]

Plate 12.2: This buoy in the mouth of the river Naf forms the southernmost joint marker of the Burma-Bangladesh boundary. The mountains of Arakan can be seen in the distance, 2001.

Another joint territorial symbol, or rather a joint territorial ritual, was the flag meeting between border officials. A flag meeting was usually held on the boundary line itself, with the two groups of officials facing each other across a table that actually straddled the border. Flag meetings were important practices in the performance of the nation and the maintenance and reproduction of the border (Plate 12.3). Although perhaps too transient to be called sites of memory, they were certainly institutions shaping public memory and they did tend to recur intermittently at specific points along the border.

Plate 12.3: A flag meeting of Indian (right) and Bangladeshi border guards, Hili border, 2001.[13]

A second type of territorial symbol was the mirrored territorial symbol. By means of these, both nations signalled their freedom to do as they pleased in their own territory, but in remarkably parallel ways. Good examples are the border outposts and customs houses, established independently by each state but amazingly similar in form and function.[14] In the 1950s, a European traveller described his experience as follows:

Then we turn a bend and find ourselves at Tamabil, the Customs-post at the [East] Pakistan border. I get my rucksack down and stagger with it to the office of the little inquisitors. The passport and customs officers were housed in a shining prefabricated building made of corrugated aluminium … The inquisition was soon over. A hundred yards or so farther up the road, just beyond the Indian Custom-post, I waited to board the Indian bus.[15]

Other mirrored territorial symbols were the uniforms and insignia displaying the nation on the bodies of the border guards (Plate 12.4) – or the red, blue or yellow flags hoisted by border guards on one side to signal anger, a willingness to talk, or an invitation to come to the borderline to their counterparts on the other side.[16] The nations also mirrored their claims on the border territory by assigning nationalist names to places.[17]

Plate 12.4: **A member of the Bangladesh Rifles (BDR) in front of his border outpost overlooking the Ganges at the Rajshahi-Murshidabad border, 1988.**

These symbols differed markedly from the third type of territorial symbol, which was one-sided. Neither the Indian barbed-wire fences and watchtowers, nor the Burmese anti-personnel mines had their counterparts on the Bangladesh side of the border. Plate 12.5 shows a rather different one-sided symbol of territorial sovereignty. A Pakistani tank, conquered by Indians during the war of 1971, is displayed prominently in an Indian border town as a symbol of national pride.

Plate 12.5: Pakistani tank in the border town of Cooch Behar (India).

Monuments.   Another important way of claiming the borderland for the nation was by erecting monuments near the border. After Partition, public monuments of the colonial state were torn down everywhere (although an occasional statue of Queen Victoria can still be seen, e.g. in the Indian border town of Dhubri). Such colonial monuments were replaced by symbols of the new nation. At first, these symbols were of the more portable kind: flags, new national colours (green-white for Pakistan, saffron-white-green for India, blue-red-white for Burma) daubed on walls and trees, new national currencies and stamps, signboards, licence plates and nationalist graffiti. Later, statues of anti-colonial leaders appeared on the streets and squares of borderland towns. On the Indian side, Mahatma Mohandas Gandhi, Netaji Subhas Chandra Bose, Pandit Jawaharlal Nehru and Khudiram Bose were favourites (Plate 12.6).

Plate 12.6: Statue of anticolonial hero Khudiram Bose (1889–1908), erected by the 'Committee to Preserve the Memory of Khudiram', Cooch Behar, India.

On the other side of the border, statues of humans were less in evidence – possibly because of the impact of religious indictions against depicting the human form – but non-figurative statues became particularly frequent after the birth of Bangladesh in 1971. The three stooped pillars of the Monument to the Martyrs (*Shohid Minar*), commemorating all those who had fallen during the Language Movement and the Bangladesh Liberation War, appeared in many border towns and villages (Plates 12.7 and 12.8).[18]

Plate 12.7: The Central Monument to the Martyrs in Patgram, a border town in northern Bangladesh.

Plate 12.8: 'Place of Pilgrimage for Independence' (*Shadhinotar Tirthokkhetro*) on the banks of the border river Mahananda in Tetulia (Bangladesh). Across the river, Indian territory can be seen. The monument is decorated with the *shapla* (water lily, the national flower of Bangladesh), and the poem '*Shadhinota Tumi*' ('You, Independence').[19]

By contrast, symbols and monuments of the territorial unity of the borderland were much less prominently visible. They were not rare but they were usually so unobtrusive that outsiders were often unaware of them. They consisted of smugglers' paths, holes cut into border fences, or houses built defiantly across the border by people whose villages had been cut in two.[20] If these symbols became more than light traces on the landscape, they were likely to be annihilated. Plate 12.9 shows the remains of a small market that inhabitants of a border *chor* (island) in the Ganges had initiated in order to save themselves the considerable inconvenience of having to travel to the far side of the huge river to do their shopping or sell their produce. According to local people, the market attracted villagers from neighbouring *chor* areas in both India and Bangladesh and 'was really what all of us needed. It was a great help, and fun too.' The Bangladesh authorities closed it down because it was thought to be facilitating smuggling. The locals resented the move as yet another sign of the thwarting of borderland life, and they retained the skeletons of the market stalls as a subdued monument to cross-border solidarity.[21]

Plate 12.9: Quashed borderland market, Mazhardiar Chor, Bangladesh.

In some cases, however, borderland monuments were used very publicly, as a gauntlet flung down in front of the nation. For example, Indian police killed two activists of the movement for Kamtapur – an independent state for the Rajbongshi and Koch minorities living on both sides of the India-Bangladesh border in North Bengal – in 2000. Two years later, a public ceremony was organized to unveil life-size busts of these two martyrs and a leader said:

the entire exercise of unveiling the busts of our *shahids* [martyrs] is an open challenge to the state government ... The death of our two comrades inspired us to continue the struggle.[22]

Such confrontational tactics created a dilemma for state authorities: allowing sites of counter-memory and borderland defiance to stand could be as risky as destroying them.

Events.   Territorial symbols and monuments were not the only ways in which the tension between national and borderland culture surfaced. Immediately after Partition both India and Pakistan tried to nationalize cross-border events. Both attempted to destroy older forms of regional (now 'cross-border') sociability, whether religious events, markets or annual fairs.[23] Instead, new events celebrating the nation were introduced.[24] Some of these were annual commemorations in which officials as well as locals participated (Plates 12.10 and 12.11). Such celebrations were held all over the territory where they had .the effect of legitimizing, naturalizing and sacralizing the nation, but in the borderland they served another purpose as well: to make 'our' borderlanders turn their backs on 'their' borderlanders.

Plate 12.10: A national event in the borderland: Pakistan's Liberation Day (15 August) being celebrated in the Chittagong Hill Tracts, around 1959.[25]

Plate 12.11: Borderlanders dressed up as Bangladesh freedom fighters during a national holiday (Rajshahi district, Bangladesh, 1988). India is in the background, a few hundred metres away.

Other events were less frequent but no less effective in differentiating the two sides of the borderland. Elections were particularly important because politicians often worried about (or hoped for) illegal voters from across the border, or feared sabotage by borderland insurgents. Therefore, border crossings were sometimes restricted or forbidden during elections, and security measures were strengthened.[26] As we have seen, however, borderlanders were known to cast their votes in elections across the border anyway.[27]

The nation manifested itself not only in the sacralization of certain moments in time, but also in the measurement of time itself. In Bengal, several calendrical systems coexist. Important among them is the Bengali calendar, which uses a solar year that starts in April. In the mid-1990s, the government of Bangladesh introduced a specifically Bangladeshi Bengali calendar that differed from the Bengali calendar used in neighbouring West Bengal and Tripura (India) by one day. As a result, New Year's celebrations in the borderland now take place on 14 April on the Bangladeshi side and on 15 April on the Indian side.[28]

There is no doubt that the rhythms of the nations installed themselves firmly in the borderland and differentiated the populations on either side of the dividing line. But how hegemonic did these rhythms become? Borderlanders certainly joined in national celebrations. But did this make them relinquish their involvement in borderland events? Usually such events were more difficult to discern, as they were less formal and large-scale than those sponsored by the state and often escaped the notice of outsiders. This was partly on purpose because demonstrations of cross-border solidarity were sure to draw censure from agents of the nation and often involved infringements of state law. But the low-key nature of events expressing borderland unity was also linked to their naturalness; unlike the new 'events of the nation,' they were embedded in well-established cultural patterns and often did not require new forms of organization.

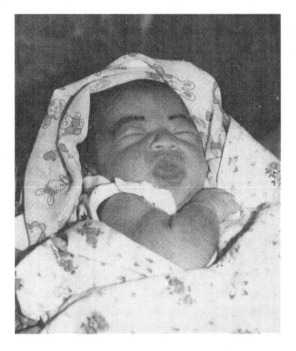

Plate 12.12: A cross-border birth. This three-day-old baby, born in her mother's parental house in Bangladesh, will grow up in her father's village across the border in India, and so become an Indian citizen (Rangamati, Bangladesh, 2001).

So what were these 'borderland events'? In addition to various forms of ignoring and defying the border, a multitude of small events and acts symbolized cross-border solidarities and a shared borderland culture. Cross-border kinship continued to be cemented by borderland marriages, as a result of which citizens of one country were often born in the other (Plate 12.12).[29] A shared borderland culture also expressed itself in patterns of reproductive behaviour that disregarded the border.[30] Similarly, religious ceremonies continued to sustain religious communities across the border.[31] Borderlanders ignored passport and visa rules *en masse* to see a doctor, meet friends and relatives, or go to work, a market, or a cinema across the border.[32] In the words of one borderlander:

> Most of them don't have passports. If someone crosses the border, he'll say: "Oh, I don't need a passport, I have friends on the other side!"'[33]

Cross-border traders also created 'borderland events' when they resisted state forces that thwarted them. Occasionally they would attack border guards, take them hostage, or barricade roads to get their way.[34] And various cultural flows, or forms of 'border art', across the borderland made it easy for people to remain emotionally linked.[35] Consider the multiple border crossings involved in the performance of folk singer Mujib Pardeshi (Mujib the Foreigner), whose forefathers moved from Assam to what is now Bangladesh:

> Transcending all geographical, political and cultural boundaries between the two neighbouring countries – India and Bangladesh – renowned Bangladeshi folk singer Mujib Pardeshi enthralled a unique audience here [on a huge *chor* in the Brahmaputra river in India] … singing about the struggling life of the people living along the banks of Bangladesh's Padma [Ganges] river. Mujib came across the Bangladesh border to sing at "Pardeshi Cultural nite" organised for raising fund[s] for a local youth association … The entire char came alive to the tune of Pardeshi's ballads on the downtrodden.[36]

Similar cross-border cultural links came into view every time people from both sides of the border came together to enjoy an open-air opera or a party, or to pray together at a festive day, e.g. the end of the month of Ramadan or Kali Puja.[37] Such links were not only based on traditional contacts but were also created by new events. For example, in 2002 a Calcutta-based theatre group staged a play entitled *Osama bin Laden: Terror of the World* in two villages in West Bengal very near the Bangladesh border. Local officials became jittery because they expected 'a large number of Bangladesh nationals to cross the border and make up the audiences on the two days', and they felt powerless to stop these border crossers.[38]

Abdul Alim from the border town of Rajshahi (Bangladesh) expressed the strength of cross-border identities as follows:

> There are differences in lifestyle between the border region and the interior.

In terms of occupation, because most people in the border region are linked with all that trade ... smuggling. There are also people like that in the interior, but not as many. And you know what is so funny? It is difficult to tell people on either side of the borderline apart. They are very close in their culture. For example there are some traditional practices that the people on that side and this side follow. The border has no authority over them at all. Because the border came into existence in a peculiar way and often cuts right through houses. So how can you tell things apart? Neighbours have lived with each other for many years, and now suddenly my house is in Pakistan and yours in India...?![39]

In many cases 'borderland events' coexisted with 'events of the nation'. Inhabitants of border regions thought of themselves as members of the nation when they took part in events celebrating the nation – and as borderlanders when they joined in borderland events. But the two types of event could also clash. Spokesmen for the nation could exclude borderlanders, or accept them only on conditions that they would never be able to meet. A good example is a speech by Sheikh Mujibur Rahman, Bangladesh's first Prime Minister, at a public meeting in the Chittagong Hill Tracts in 1975. In this speech, which turned into a critical event, he addressed the non-Bengali inhabitants of this part of the borderland as 'brethren and told them to become Bengalis, to forget the colonial past and join the mainstream of Bengali culture.'[40] His government's rejection of the languages, religions and cultural identities of the region fuelled a borderland revolt that successive governments of Bangladesh tried in vain to quell by sending in armed forces and hundreds of thousands of Bengali settlers. These borderland 'events' set the scene for the physical expulsion of tens of thousands of borderlanders who spent over 20 years in refugee camps just across the border in Tripura (India) (Plate 12.13).

Similar forms of exclusion in India and Burma led groups to choose to break away from the nation and reject its events. For example, various rebel groups in Northeast India declared Indian Independence Day a 'black day' and obstructed its celebration, arguing that 'the northeast was never a part of India and so the question of celebrating Independence Day does not arise.'[42] And in 2000 a Rohingya organization in Arakan (Burma) argued that:

the "Union of Burma" is still an un-liquidated and undecolonised colonial empire with Burman replacing Britishers as colonial masters.' Therefore, 4 January 1948, Burma's Independence Day, 'was marked in the history of Arakan as the calamitous day that [served] to fabricate the artificial and false nationhood of "Burma".'[43]

Plate 12.13: Borderlanders expelled from the nation. Refugees from the Chittagong Hill Tracts (CHT, Bangladesh) during a visit by a human rights commission. Pancharampara refugee camp, in Tripura (India), near the Bangladesh border, 1990.[41]

Borderlanders could also reject the nation on purely economic grounds. Some Indian border villages in Tripura were completely neglected by the authorities and lacked even a road to the nearest Indian town. As a result, their inhabitants had to depend on illegal trips across the border into Bangladesh for shopping, health care and drinking water. In protest, they raised the flag of Bangladesh and *ghera*oed (besieged) the Chief Minister of Tripura when he dared show his face in the area.[44]

Generally speaking, borderlanders maintained and created identities that were not nested in the national identity but cut across the boundaries constructed for the nation.[45] These identities vied with national identities in a continual round of symbolic events, and the relative popularity of these events over time could be seen as an indicator of the variable success of nationalist projects in the borderland.

Language. The nation left its imprint on the culture of the borderland in many other, less tangible, ways. Indian border guards often complained that they could not distinguish illegal Bangladeshi immigrants from local Indian citizens because these spoke the same language, dressed similarly and shared the same culture. But Indian border guards were not usually Bengalis; they came from faraway parts of India.[46] For borderlanders themselves, however, there were many telltale signs by which to distinguish people from either side of the border. Language was one.

In the borderland, the nation as a cultural notion emanated primarily from the village school and the mass media. But literacy was low and mass media not very widespread. There were primary and secondary schools in many larger villages, catering to a small but growing proportion of the children. Newspapers had a relatively small readership but their contents spread more widely by word of mouth. Radio sets were prized status symbols (often lovingly protected by a custom-made cloth cover) but until the 1970s their density was quite low. Television did not reach the border areas till the 1980s.[47] Other forms of national integration and indoctrination, e.g. a conscript army bringing recruits together from all over the country, were completely absent.

The contents of the mass media were rarely attuned to the needs of borderlanders. A group of Indian ministers, charged with reviewing national security, was acutely aware of this. They wrote:

[Lest] the battle for the mind of our people is lost, ... an imaginative media policy and information sharing approach need to be evolved to orient the border population towards national development goals, security concerns and national integration ... National electronic media have to address the needs and concerns of [the] border population as they see it and not as we see it ... local culture and traditions need to be highlighted in programmes of AIR [All-India Radio] and Doordarshan [Indian state television].[48]

Even though instruments of national cultural integration were weakly developed or ineffective in the Bengal borderland, the nation entered the local language in many ways. Vocabularies began to diverge and borderlanders could increasingly use these clues to work out whether a person was from India, East Pakistan/ Bangladesh, or Burma.[49] There were three main sources of differentiation. First, there was a conscious effort in Pakistan to 'Islamize' the Bengali language, which the state elite considered to be too 'Hinduized.' It chose words of Persian or Arabic origin, many of which were already in use among some Muslim Bengalis, over words derived from Sanskrit. Some of these words became much more widespread in Bangladesh than in West Bengal and now act as markers of Bangladeshiness.[50] Second, many objects and institutions that gained currency after 1947 were given different names in India and Bangladesh.[51] And third, half a century of living under different states threw up specific vocabularies relating to administration and politics that differed on either side of the border.[52] At the border, two nations used the same tongue but rather diversified idioms.

The language of the border was not just a story of divergence, however. Borderlanders also developed a common cross-border vocabulary to deal with their new reality of separation-and-connection. For example, smuggling was commonly known as 'trade number 2' (*dui nombor bebsha*) or 'crossing the river' (*epar-opar*). Many other new terms, especially those referring to border management and cross-border trade, gained currency among people on both sides of the border but remained largely unknown beyond the borderland.[53]

Body codes of the nation. Another sign by which borderlanders were able to distinguish people from either side of the border was dress. The ways in which borderlanders-to-be had clothed their bodies before 1947 had provided them with innumerable clues regarding gender, religious community, region, wealth and educational status. After 1947, however, many also adopted new 'national' styles of dress. These styles were elaborations of those of the religious communities in Bengal, to which were added new elements. For example, the checkered or coloured *lungi*, an ankle-long sarong worn by Bengali Muslim males, became a symbol of East Pakistan; by contrast, the white *dhoti* (an elaborate loincloth) that had become associated with upper-caste Hindu dominance, was marginalized. 'Before Partition, Bengali Muslims were proud to wear the *dhoti*', an elderly borderlander reminisced,[54] but that practice died out soon after Partition and gradually even Hindus in East Pakistan adopted the *lungi*. Increasingly, *dhoti* signified India, *lungi* Bangladesh. Other body codes of the nation were the Nehru cap and *khadi* cloth (in India), and the *kamiz-salwar*, Mujib costume and *jamdani* sari (in Bangladesh). Since various post-Partition political struggles expressed themselves symbolically in fashion styles that differed between the nations, very complex and shifting patterns of meaning came to be attached to these codes. In the India-Bangladesh borderland, where people had access to clothes produced in both countries and were exposed to different 'national' fashions, the elaboration of distinct body codes could signal various shades of national identity.

These body codes of the nation can be observed in Plate 12.14. It shows a cartoon from India depicting an Indian national – a light-skinned, snub-nosed Khasi man from Meghalaya dressed in his 'national' costume – facing a Bangladeshi national, a darker skinned, aquiline-nosed Bengali man with the Muslim symbols of beard, cap and *lungi*. The two appear to be in good cheer as they exchange trade goods across a border fence that is represented as low, innocuous and shared.

Plate 12.14: Body codes of the nation: A cartoon showing two ethnic stereotypes, Bengali and Khasi, meeting at the Partition border.[55]

The borderland as imagined by the nation

The symbols and events of the post-Partition nations found a place in borderland society, continually reminding borderlanders of the nation to which they had been assigned. But the borderland also played an important role in the self-image of the post-Partition nations. The borderland itself became a national memory site. The most obvious symbol was the map, often reduced to an outline, the boundary line itself. The power of this spatial representation was particularly clear in Bangladesh. When Bangladeshi independence was declared in 1971, the new nation's flag showed a bottle green background with a red circle in the middle. In the circle was the yellow outline of the new country. Radcliffe's handiwork was now complete: the border that he had designed had become accepted as an intensely emotive symbol of a new nation (Plates 12.15 and 12.16).[56]

Plate 12.15: The flag of independent Bangladesh being raised for the first time during a mass meeting at Dhaka University on 2 March 1971, just before the beginning of the Bangladesh Liberation War. The map of the new country is seen in reverse.[57]

Plate 12.16: **The flag of independent Bangladesh covers the corpse of a victim of the Liberation War, 1971.**[58]

This remarkable emergence of the Radcliffe line as a core symbol of the nation is also visible in every Bangladesh passport, which shows the border on every page as well as on the front cover (Plate 12.17). After Bangladesh came into existence, the nation was often described in territorial terms. For example, it was common to refer to Bangladeshis as a national community living 'between Tetulia and Teknaf', the two extremes of the national territory in the north and south (Plate 12.18).

Plate 12.17: **Outline of the national territory on a visa page of a Bangladesh passport.**

Plate 12.18: Signpost at Banglabandha (Tetulia), the northernmost point of Bangladesh, proudly showing its distance (1021 km) to Teknaf, the country's southernmost border. Only locals read this signpost because no traffic passes this road: the border crossing to India (and nearby Nepal) is closed.[59]

These positive images of the border as a symbol of the inviolability of Bangladesh's national territory received a jolt in 2001 when armed clashes between Indian and Bangladeshi border guards left 19 men dead.[60] The fear that the borderland was vulnerable to foreign invasion was also exemplified by a computer game that became available on the Internet in early 2003. Its creator described himself as an 'independent nationalist animation developer'. The game ('Bangladesh BDR'[61]) was set in the borderland near Rangamati in the Chittagong Hill Tracts. It showed a border marked with a barbed-wire fence running through hilly terrain. The player was instructed that he/she was a patriotic Bangladeshi border guard whose sacred duty it was to provide a 'teeth-shattering rebuff' to invading Indian border guards by killing them with grenades whenever they popped up from behind the pretty green bushes. The game was remarkable for its aggressiveness (the enemy border guards were described as 'Indian dogs') as well as for the fact that the defence of the nation was entrusted to border guards rather than to the regular army.

In the construction of Indian nationalism, on the other hand, the border with Bangladesh was much less important. Of course, as long as the territory had been East Pakistan, its borders had been a major concern: India felt that the main threat to its territorial integrity came from Pakistan (and later, after 1962, also from China). But after India's invasion of East Pakistan and the subsequent dissolution of Pakistan, the new nation of Bangladesh was seen as both too friendly and too weak to pose any military threat. In India it is not at all uncommon to come across maps of the national territory that simply ignore the existence of the border with Bangladesh. Plate 12.19 shows an example from one of India's most respected national newspapers.

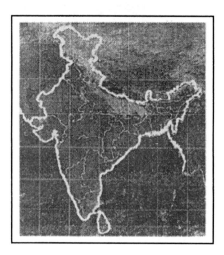

Plate 12.19: 'Today's National Weather': Bangladesh overlooked in the daily weather map of Indian newspaper *The Hindu*.[62]

In India the border with Bangladesh was, however, important in another way. It figured prominently in the construction of a demographic threat. As we have seen in chapter 8, it came to stand for demographic invasion, a deliberate, large-scale and sustained infiltration by Bangladeshis. Some saw a sinister design to dismember the Indian nation, a plan to create a Greater Bangladesh and to provide Lebensraum for Bangladeshis by destabilizing northeastern India, Islamizing it, and ultimately severing it from the rest of the country.

It has been argued that the successor states to British India display a remarkable and persistent 'cartographic anxiety', largely the result of the traumatic carving up of the territory at the time of Partition.[63] Soon after the transfer of power, the new leader of Pakistan described his territory as 'moth-eaten' and the new leader of India felt that 'the body of India' was 'broken'. These images of infirmity revealed how vulnerable these leaders considered their nations to be to threats from outside as well as from within. Their resolve to nurse their nations back to robust health implied a strong emphasis on national unity and border maintenance. According to Sankaran Krishna, their policies were indicative of 'a larger postcolonial anxiety – of [societies] suspended forever in the space between the ex-colony and not-yet nation.'[64] This made it extremely difficult to sort out the territorial loose ends resulting from Partition because every concession was felt as a weakening of the nation. Maps were used as weapons in border disputes, with the disputed area shown as belonging to the nation's territory, even if it was in fact well out of reach.[65]

The legend of Mujibnagar. The most dramatic way in which the borderland insinuated itself into the core of national consciousness was through the image of 'Mujibnagar' in Bangladesh:

> On 17 April 2000, Bangladesh observed 'historic Mujibnagar Day.' The President announced that this was 'a red letter day in our national history' and called upon all to 'maintain national solidarity, practise democracy and work together for the nation's progress.' Meanwhile, the Minister of Foreign Affairs placed a wreath at the Mujibnagar Mausoleum, and the Prime Minister declared: 'On this sacred day, I pay my deep respect to the memory of the Father of the Nation.'[66]

What was this all about? The story goes like this. The Bangladesh Liberation War broke out in East Pakistan in March 1971 and most leaders of the movement for Bangladesh escaped to India. A few weeks later they returned to a border village just inside East Pakistan/ Bangladesh. Here a local 'Border Action Committee' had been formed to support the Bangladesh cause, and this committee helped in the preparation of a ceremony on 17 April 1971. Gathered in the village mango grove and protected by Indian border guards, the insurgent

Plate 12.20: Installing the Provisional Government of Bangladesh, April 1971.[69]

leaders established the Provisional Government of Bangladesh. The village was renamed Mujibnagar (Mujib Town) after Sheikh Mujibur Rahman, later honoured with the title Father of the Nation, who could not attend because he was in Pakistani captivity.[67] Mujibnagar is therefore the place where the Bangladesh nation began its formal independence (Plate 12.20).[68]

Ever since, narrations of the nation have stressed Mujibnagar's role as midwife to the nation's independence. In the 1980s, an impressive mausoleum was built in the mango grove; its 23 pillars symbolize the 23 years of Pakistani (mis)rule (Plates 12.21 and 12.22). Few outsiders came to see it, however, because it was unsafe to visit this section of the borderland; most of the time, it was under the control of groups of armed bandits. As a result the state neglected the area but locals tried to cash in on their village's special status by demanding an immigration check post at Mujibnagar, urging the government 'to consider their demand keeping in mind the historic importance of Mujibnagar.'[70]

Plates 12.21 and 12.22: The mausoleum at Mujibnagar.[71]

The legend of Mujibnagar placed the borderland squarely within the national imagination. Its symbolic role was reinforced when the party that had spearheaded the Bangladesh independence movement, the Awami League, returned to power in 1996 after an absence of 21 years. It created Mujibnagar Day, a new national celebration.[72] All this is particularly poignant in view of reports that the original Mujibnagar gathering actually may never have taken place at all.[73]

Conclusion: the nation and its borderland

In this chapter I have suggested that borderlands are important localities for studying nations, because here nations spread their tails and parade for each other. We can read borderland symbols of the nation as sites that reflect complex struggles over public memory. These struggles can be highly intricate, as the example of the Mujibnagar Mausoleum reveals. At first glance, it seems to be a reminder of the first government of Bangladesh. Or is it a reminder of Pakistani misrule, as its 23 pillars imply? The timing of the construction of the Mausoleum and its location at the very edge of Bangladeshi territory also allow us to see it as an expression of national sovereignty vis-à-vis India.[74] Or is it – together with the recently created national Mujibnagar Day – best understood as an attempt to silence voices that claim that Mujibnagar never happened and that the first provisional government of Bangladesh was installed on Indian soil?

Similarly, what can we learn about struggles over memory from the fact that the statue of Khudiram (Plate 12.6) is in mint condition whereas the Monument to the Martyrs (Plate 12.7) is in a dilapidated state? By raising questions like these, borderland memory sites can open up productive new ways of analysing the nation.

If memory sites point to anxiety over possible memory loss, the proliferation of national symbols in the borderland is of particular significance. The flurry of symbols surrounding two nations meeting at a border is a display directed not only at the homeland and the other, but also at a borderland population that may otherwise not be duly impressed by the glory of the nation. In the borderland, the 'lest we forget' attitude inherent in sites of memory anywhere is imbued with a more liberal dose of 'lest they, our borderlanders, forget.' Or perhaps 'lest their counter-memory elbows out our national memory.' And conversely, the infrequency of memory sites dedicated to borderland identity may point not just to repression but also to the fact that borderland memories are alive and kicking, and that therefore there is as yet no need to support them with elaborate sites.[75] If so, we can take any future establishment of memory sites celebrating the borderland as a sign that the memory of borderland unity is fading.

Notes

1 Bernard Llewellyn, *From the Back Streets of Bengal* (London: George Allen & Unwin, 1955), 24. For another description of the elusiveness of the West Bengal-Bangladesh border, see Ranabir Samaddar, *The Marginal Nation: Transborder Migration from Bangladesh to West Bengal* (New Delhi, etc.: Sage Publications, 1999), 52–5.

2 Paul Nugent observes that it 'is arguably at the margins of national territory that one can most fruitfully study the shaping of state institutions and the development of elements of a national culture', while Hastings Donnan and Thomas Wilson add that 'perhaps foremost among all the anthropological tasks at borders ... is the investigation and interpretation of the symbolic aspects of the state.' Paul Nugent, 'Power Versus Knowledge: Smugglers and the State Along Ghana's Eastern Frontier, 1920–1992', in Michael Rösler and Tobias Wendl (eds.), *Frontiers and Borderlands: Anthropological Perspectives* (Frankfurt am Main, etc.: Peter Lang, 1999), 77; Hastings Donnan and Thomas M Wilson, *Borders: Frontiers of Identity, Nation and State* (Oxford and New York: Berg, 1999), 13.

3 Joseph Nevins, *Operation Gatekeeper: The Rise of the 'Illegal Alien' and the Making of the U.S.–Mexico Boundary* (New York and London: Routledge, 2002), 161, 176–7.

4 Pierre Nora (ed.), *Les lieux de mémoire* (Paris : Gallimard, 1997), 3 vols.

5 This sentiment is also expressed by Krishna when he states: 'The vocation of the postcolonial intellectual: to decouple our histories from the narrative of the nation, to miscegenate the stories of our pasts, and, perhaps most importantly, to decolonize our vision of the future by liberating that space from the modulations of ersatz pasts.' Sankaran Krishna, *Postcolonial Insecurities: India, Sri Lanka and the Question of Nationhood* (Minneapolis: University of Minnesota Press, 1999), 245.

6 Pierre Nora, 'Entre mémoire et histoire: la problématique des lieux,' in : Nora (ed.), *Les lieux*, I, 24.

7 Anthony D Smith, 'Culture, Community and Territory: The Politics of Ethnicity and Nationalism', *International Affairs*, 72:3 (1996), 445–58.

8 Zarir Hussain, 'A small "country" called Sheet Bangla that India & B'desh forgot', *The Northeast Daily* (22 May 2000); R Dutta Choudhury, 'Tale of a village trapped in no-man's land', *The Assam Tribune* (16 April 2000); R Dutta Choudhury, 'Dhubri border farmers live in India, till in Bangla', *The Assam Tribune* (17 April 2000); Faruque Ahmed, 'They are Indian but earn their livelihood in Bangladesh: With no health care centre, no post office, no grocery shop, 900 Bhogdanga villagers deprived of basic necessities', *The Northeast Daily* (14 November 1999).

9 'Down the broad river valley [at the Tamabil/ Dawki border], dotted through the fields, were concrete border markers, painted white, like large mushrooms.' Francis Rolt, *On the Brink of Bengal* (London: John Murray, 1991), 133.

10 See chapter 4. No such correspondence exists between Burma and Pakistan/ Bangladesh because the demarcation of their border has not been completed. The pillars marking the India-Bangladesh enclaves are of a different shape; see Willem van Schendel, 'Stateless in South Asia: The Making of the India-Bangladesh Enclaves', *The Journal of Asian Studies*, 61:1 (February 2002), 115–47.

11 For example, after the Indian authorities found that two boundary pillars on the Jalpaiguri-Dinajpur border were damaged in 1952, the Deputy Secretary of West Bengal impressed on his counterpart in East Pakistan the symbolic nature of the crime and his nationalist reading of it: 'Only those sides of the pillars which have the words "India" engraved,

have been damaged.' A local Pakistani official, sent to the spot, reported that 'only a portion of the pillar is broken but the name plate "India" is still there. Our people say that they did not damage it. It may be that cowboys of India might have done it. We have warned our people not to play with boundary pillars' (CR 1B1-2/52 (7-54); cf. CR 1B3-2/49 (11-50); CR 1B2-18/52 (2-54)).

12 In the region where this photograph was taken, no less than 62 per cent of the border pillars were damaged beyond repair, 25 per cent had disappeared, and only 13 per cent were intact. 'Bangladesh regains 150 acres of land from India', *The Independent* (19 July 2003).

13 *Doinik Ittefak* (1 May 2001).

14 Although national autonomy could be expressed in many rituals. For example, customs offices on the Indian and Bangladeshi sides of the border kept different working hours and closed on different days of the week. The need to coordinate timings, at least for one of the border crossings (Petrapol/ Benapol), was not tabled till 55 years after Partition. 'Agreed Minutes of the First Meeting of the India-Bangladesh Joint Group of Customs Officials, Dhaka, November 3, 2002', in Avtar Singh Bhasin (ed.), *India-Bangladesh Relations: Documents – 1971–2002* (New Delhi: Geetika Publishers, 2003), III, 1868.

15 Llewellyn, *From the Back Streets*, 95–6.

16 E.g. Niraj Lama, 'Tension persists on Bangla border', *The Statesman* (8 March 2002); 'Dhaka rules out joint verification,' *The Statesman* (6 February 2003). The use of flags (and light signals at night) was initiated in 1959. See *Ground Rules Formulated by the Military Sub-Committee of the Indian and Pakistan Delegations* (20 October 1959), reprinted in Bhasin (ed.), *India-Bangladesh Relations*, V, 2741.

17 For example, border markets in Pakistan/ Bangladesh were renamed *Pakistanhat* (Pakistan Market), *Jinnahrhat* (Jinnah's Market), or (later) *Joybanglahat* (Victory-to-Bangladesh Market), and refugee camps in the West Bengal borderland were given names such as *Jayhindpolli* (Victory-to-India Village), *Muktinogor* (Freedom Town), *Congresspolli* (Congress Village) or *Indira Gandhi Colony*. Chakrabarti, *The Marginal Men*, 483, 488.

18 For a pictorial exploration of nationalist monuments in Bangladesh, see Aftab Ahmod, *Amra Tomader Bhulbo Na* (Dhaka: Borna-Shagor Prokashoni, 1994).

19 On this poem and its relationship to the national anthem of Bangladesh, 'Amar Shonar Bangla' (My Golden Bengal), see Dina M Siddiqi, 'In Search of Shonar Bangla', *Himal* (21 July 2003).

20 See photograph in Van Schendel, 'Stateless in South Asia', 135.

21 For Indian border guards similarly 'eradicating a market that thrived on barter of goods from across the border' in Meghalaya, see Rajeev Bhattacharyya, 'Border village in dire straits', *The Telegraph* (26 February 2003).

22 Anupam Dasgupta, 'Kamtapuris salute Tarbandha "*shahids*"', *The Telegraph* (29 November 2002).

23 See e.g. chapter 6 on the breaking up of the Phuldol festival by Pakistani authorities in 1948 and on the prohibition against visiting cross-border markets.

24 For example, on the Indian side of the border: Republic Day (26 January), Independence Day (15 August) and Netaji's Birthday (23 January); on the Pakistan/ Bangladesh side: Liberation Day (15 August), and later Ekushe (21 February) and Victory Day (16 December).

25 Photographer unknown. Hans Meier collection.

26 E.g. 'Border in Tripura to be sealed before LS polls', *The Assam* Tribune (9 September 1999); R Dutta Choudhury, 'To prevent insurgents during LS polls: Army to launch

special operations', *The Assam* Tribune (7 September 1999). 'Pre-poll vigil on Bangla border', *The Statesman* (19 September 1999). LS stands for Lok Sabha, the Lower House of the Indian Parliament.

27 Chapter 9. See e.g. Aloke Banerjee, 'Where Two Nations Slip into Each Other', *The Statesman* (29 May 1993).

28 Willem van Schendel, 'Modern Times in Bangladesh', in Willem van Schendel and Henk Schulte Nordholt (eds.), *Time Matters: Global and Local Time in Asian Societies* (Amsterdam: VU University Press, 2001), 37–55.

29 Customarily, pregnant women returned to their parents' house to give birth. Birth registration being lax, these cross-border babies either remained unregistered (and of uncertain nationality) till they entered primary school, or were registered in their country of residence when they returned there with their mother several weeks or months after their birth.

30 Amin et al. advance this argument in their study of reproductive behaviour in contiguous border districts of West Bengal and Bangladesh. Sajeda Amin, Alaka Malwade Basu and Rob Stephenson, *Spatial Variation in Contraceptive Use in Bangladesh: Looking Beyond the Borders; Working Paper 138* (New York: The Population Council, 2000).

31 For example, the Hujur Shaheber Mela, an annual fair at the mausoleum (*mazar*) of Pir Hujur Shaheb in the border town of Haldibari (Cooch Behar, India). This two-day celebration, held during February, draws hundreds of thousands of visitors from West Bengal, Bangladesh, Sikkim, Bhutan and Assam. Main Uddin Chisti, 'Haldibari decks up for amity carnival', *The Telegraph* (3 January 2003).

32 For example, in January 1999, two Buddhist monks from Cox's Bazar in southern Bangladesh were arrested on their way back from Burma. They were carrying bronze Buddha statues and Burmese money that their disciples in Burma had donated to them. The local magistrate sent the two to jail. 'Two Buddhist monks nabbed', *The New Nation* (27 January 1999). See also Maseeh Rahman, 'Separated at Birth,' *Time* (11 August 1997); 'Indo-Bangla border in Karimganj only in name', *The Assam Tribune* (31 August 1999); '8 Indian nationals arrested in Rajshahi', *The Daily Star* (7 July 1999); 'Malaria patients taking treatment in Bangladesh', *The Assam Tribune* (19 June 1999).

33 Abdul Alim (born c. 1935), interviewed by Md. Mahbubar Rahman, Rajshahi, January 1999.

34 For example: 'One killed as smugglers clash with BDR', *The Daily Star* (10 June 1999); 'One killed as BDR, smugglers clash in Jaipurhat,' *The Independent* (10 June 1999); 'One killed as BDR men, alleged smugglers clash in Comilla', *The Independent* (29 June 1999).

35 The idea of 'border art' is examined in Gloria Anzaldúa, 'Chicana Artists: Exploring *Nepantla, el Lugar de la Frontera*', in: Antonia Darder and Rodolfo D Torres (eds.), *The Latino Studies Reader: Culture, Economy, and Society* (Malden and Oxford: Blackwell Publishers, 1998), 163–9.

36 Mani Mahanta, 'A "pardeshi" enthralls river people with night-long ballads: Brahmaputra char people swing to the tune of Mujib's folk tales of the people along the Padma', *The Northeast Daily* (10 December 1999). For a song about another Bangladeshi river, the Dharla, being sung on an Assam *chor*, see Hazarika, *Rites of Passage*, 128–9.

37 Border guards sometimes disastrously disturbed such joint activities. For example, when a group of 13 Bangladeshi Hindus crossed the border to join the Durga Puja festival in the Indian border town of Chandgaon in West Bengal, Indian border guards opened fire on them. Two of them were killed, and two others injured. '2 Bangladeshis killed in BSF firing in Dinajpur', *The Independent* (14 October 2002). Cf. 'BSF free 13 Bangladeshis',

The Daily Star (13 December 2000); Probir Pramanik, 'Tragedy on border over prayer', *The Telegraph* (29 December 2000). On cross-border sociability, see Rolt, *On the Brink*, 136–40. On cross-border religious community networks, see Debarati Agarwala, 'Border hop to pray for peace', *The Telegraph* (16 November 2001); 'Bangladeshi nationals sneak into NE as pilgrims, says Centre', *The Assam Tribune* (25 April 2002); 'Border immersion on DD festive fare', *The Times of India*, 19 September 2003).

38 Among these authorities (in Murshidabad district) there was no feeling that they could actually stop these visitors from attending. Even the Indian border guards were asked merely to 'intensify vigil on the border to ward off trouble'. The theatre company, Jugantar Opera, did not consider a mixed borderland audience a problem at all: 'Our aim is to entertain the rural people and nothing else. So, if this creates a law-and-order problem, we have nothing to do with it.' 'Border *jatra* on Laden puts police on toes', *The Telegraph* (21 October 2002).

39 Abdul Alim (born c. 1935), interviewed by Md. Mahbubar Rahman, Rajshahi, January 1999.

40 'At this', Chakma adds, 'the tribal people left the meeting.' AB Chakma, 'Look Back From Exile: A Chakma Experience', in Wolfgang Mey (ed.), *They Are Now Burning Village After Village: Genocide in the Chittagong Hill Tracts, Bangladesh* (Copenhagen: IWGIA, 1984), 58.

41 Photograph by Wolfgang Mey. For a report, see Chittagong Hill Tracts Commission, *Life Is Not Ours: Land and Human Rights in the Chittagong Hill Tracts, Bangladesh* (Copenhagen/ Amsterdam: International Work Group on Indigenous Affairs (IWGIA) / Organising Committee Chittagong Hill Tracts Campaign, 1991).

42 For example, the Hynniewtrep National Liberation Council (HNLC) called a 36-hour general strike in Shillong (Meghalaya) from 14 August 1999 'to prevent the celebration of Independence Day'. In the same vein the National Liberation Front of Tripura (NLFT) imposed a ban on the celebration of India's Republic Day (26 January) in 2000 and 'made it mandatory for the people to raise a black flag to protest Tripura's merger with the Indian Union on October 15, 1949.' A man who hoisted the Indian tricolour in defiance of the ban had his finger chopped off in retaliation. In 2001 at least a dozen rebel groups in a joint statement protested against New Delhi's 'colonial and repressive' rule and called for a boycott of Independence Day. 'Cachar alert to thwart attacks on I-Day eve', *The Telegraph* (13 August 1999); 'Teacher's finger lopped off', *The Telegraph* (29 January 2000); cf. 'Need to enthuse respect for national flag', *The Assam Tribune* (1 February 2000); 'Rebel groups call for Independence Day boycott', *The Times of India* (31 July 2001); 'NE ultra outfits call for R-Day boycott', *The Assam Tribune* (24 January 2003).

43 Aman Ullah, 'Arakan: An un-decolonised colonial territory', *The Newsletter Monthly: News and Analysis of the Arakan Rohingya National Organisation*, Arakan (Burma), 2:4 (April 2000; see www.anfal.co.uk/ 2000April.htm).

44 'Four youths abducted to Bangladesh', *The Telegraph* (14 May 2003).

45 For examples, see e.g. Van Schendel, 'Stateless in South Asia'.

46 In recent years apparently mostly from Kashmir. Kazim Reza, 'BDR plea to stop cross-border shootings: India should deploy forces having Bengali origin', *The New Nation* (21 May 2000).

47 By the early 21st century, many border villages were still without access to television, and many Indian border villages that did have access to it could not get Indian channels. This prompted a campaign by Indian state television, Doordarshan, to 'reach out to

parts of Assam, Meghalaya and Tripura that have access to only Bangladesh channels ... the idea was to negate the possible influence of "anti-India propaganda" on residents of the border areas.' 'Doordarshan in border war with Bangla television', *The Telegraph* (18 November 2002).

48 Government of India, *Reforming the National Security System - Recommendations of the Group of Ministers* (New Delhi: Ministry of Defence, 2001), 94–5.

49 I restrict myself here to examples from the Bengali language, but other partitioned languages (Garo, Chakma, Khasi, Arakanese, etc.) also began to diverge in terms of vocabulary.

50 For example, *mehman/ othiti* (guest), *gost/ mangsho* (meat), *pani/ jol* (water), *goshol/ snan* (bath), different greetings and goodbyes (*khoda hafez, nomoshkar*), and the use of the respectful *'ji'* for yes in Bangladesh. Moreover, from 1947 to 1971 Eastern Bengali came under the influence of the would-be national language of Pakistan, Urdu, and increasingly became focused on the Bengali dialect of Dhaka. Western Bengali was similarly influenced by Hindi, and remained more oriented towards the Bengali dialect of Calcutta, the old cultural capital of all Bengal. Public writing also differed in the borderland: on the Indian side, Hindi script was much in evidence on posters, signboards and public buildings, but was completely absent on the Bangladesh side. In the early years of Pakistan and India, slogans in Arabic and Hindi were often used as symbolic weapons in cross-border animosities, people from the Pakistani side of the border shouting *'Allah-o-Akbar!'* (Arabic: God is Great!), to which the reply from the Indian side would be *'Jay Hind!'* (Hindi: Victory to India!). See CR 1B3-2/50 (7-52).

51 For example, *baby-taxi/ auto-rickshaw*, or *minibus/ Maruti van*. The *mishuk* (a lighter version of the *baby-taxi*) and the *Ambassador* (a car) provide examples of terms that exist only on one side of the border, since *mishuks* do not exist in India and *Ambassadors* are not used in Bangladesh.

52 For example, the terms for various units of administration (e.g. *thana/ taluk, block*) and officials, the *ponchayot* (panchayat, institution of local government in India but not in Bangladesh), and political events (for example, a general strike is known as *hortal* in Bangladesh and as *bondh* in India). A separate history of several decades also has thrown up different ways of dividing time; for example, in Bangladesh it is common to speak of *Ayuber amole* (= 1958–68) or *Shadhinotar pore* (= after 1971), expressions that have no equivalents in India.

53 For *dui nombor bebsha, epar-opar* (both: smuggling), *direct party* (smugglers who do not hide their business at all), *ranar* ('runner', or paid smuggler), and other local terms relating to smuggling, see Van Schendel, 'Easy Come, Easy Go'. Words relating to border management and smuggling included *sappilar* (sub-pillar), *jiro* (the borderline, from 'zero point'), *lukano* (here: hoodwinking border guards on patrol), *heli* (for helicopter, here: bicycle or flat cart used to transport bulky smuggled items), *baggage party* (smuggling on motorcycles), *linemen* (supervisors), *dhur* (hired smuggler), and many others. It is likely that terminologies varied in different sections of the borderland.

54 Md. Sofi in an interview with Md. Mahbubar Rahman, Rajshahi, 1999.

55 Souvik Chowdhury, 'Meghalaya-Bangladesh border: The dangers of mixed loyalties', *Tehelka* (26 February 2001).

56 The map was omitted when Bangladesh, as an independent state, chose its official flag. For Indian representations, see e.g. Sankaran Krishna, 'Cartographic Anxiety: Mapping the Body Politic in India', in Michael J Shapiro and Hayward R Alker (eds.), *Challenging Boundaries: Global Flows, Territorial Identities* (Minneapolis: University of Minnesota Press,

1996), 193–214.

57 Aftab Ahmod, *Shadhinota Shongrame Bangali* (Dhaka: Borna-Shagor Prokashoni, 1998 (3rd ed.), 61. Photographer unacknowledged.

58 Ahmod, *Shadhinota Shongrame*, 142. Photographer unacknowledged.

59 The person depicted in this photograph is Dr. Md. Mahbubar Rahman whose interviews were a crucial source of information for this study. Cf. 'Landlocked Nepal to use Mongla port: Govt to offer 50pc discount on service charges', *The Daily Star* (13 October 2002).

60 See chapter 11.

61 See http://www.uradhura.com/bdnationalists/bdrbsf.html. Mostofa Zaki developed the game.

62 *The Hindu*, 12 December 2001. This map also allots southeastern Bangladesh to Burma, and (more conventionally) all of the disputed state of Jammu and Kashmir to India.

63 Krishna, 'Cartographic Anxiety'.

64 Postcolonial anxiety, Krishna argues for India and Sri Lanka, is the fear of national disunity and fragmentation that produces actions and policies that hasten precisely that very outcome. If the cartographic anxieties of Pakistan and Bangladesh are brought into play as well, it becomes even clearer how absolutely crucial the Partition borderlands are as fracture zones of the imagined bodies of these three nations. Krishna, 'Cartographic Anxiety'; Krishna, *Postcolonial Insecurities*, 240–1.

65 This becomes clear when we look at how Kashmir is depicted as fully Indian in Plate 12.19, whereas in reality half of it is occupied by Pakistan. An example from the Bengal borderlands is provided by comparing Indian and Bangladeshi maps of the Berubari region. This region on the border of Jalpaiguri and Dinajpur districts has been disputed from 1947, owing to a discrepancy between the text and the map of the Bengal Boundary Commission. See chapter 4, and Van Schendel, 'Stateless in South Asia'.

66 'Mujibnagar Day today', *The Daily Star* (17 April 2000); Shahidul Islam, 'Thousands join Mujibnagar Day celebrations in Meherpur', *The Independent* (18 April 2000).

67 The border village was known as Boiddonathtola (near Bhaborpara, Meherpur, Kushtia district). 'Those turbulent days of 1971: Mujibnagar: Where the path to freedom was designed', *The Daily Star* (15 December 1999).

68 For glowing accounts of these events, see *Bangla Name Desh* (Calcutta: Anondo Publishers, 1972), 82; MA Bari, *Muktijuddher Roktim Smriti/ Memoirs of a Blood Birth: an account of the Liberation War and the role played by Mujibnagar in the struggle for freedom...* (Dhaka: Banimahal Prokashani, n.d. [c. 1996]).

69 *Bangla Name Desh*, 82. Photographer unacknowledged.

70 'Masterplan for uplift of Mujibnagar', *The Daily Star* (30 April 2000).

71 Ahmod, *Amra Tomader*, 80. Photographs by Aftab Ahmad.

72 The Mujibnagar legend continues to be elaborated and embellished with miraculous elements. A good example is the story that appeared in a national newspaper in 2001. It tells of the village boy who was selected to recite the Quran at the 1971 ceremony but later was caught by Pakistan soldiers who tortured him, covered his body with ants and left him for dead. The boy survived, however, and miraculously his body showed not one bite mark. 'Allah's ants did not sting the sacred body of the elocutionist of the Holy Quran.' Musa Sadik, 'Fate of the elocutionist of the Quran at Mujibnagar', *The Daily Star* (26 March 2001).

73 'The Indian government invented a place called Mujibnagar within Bangladesh from which the provisional government supposedly operated. In fact, Mujibnagar was simply a part of Calcutta where the Bangla leaders were housed. The Indian press dutifully

swallowed this myth. All very patriotic, you understand.' Swaminathan S Anklesaria Aiyar, 'The dark side of patriotism', *The Times of India* (22 August 1999); cf. Kuldip Nayar, 'Between the lines: Military's cooked-up brew', *The Kathmandu Post* (30 June 1997). A US reporter visiting Mujibnagar on 18 April reported: 'Only yards from the Indian border, Bangla Desh held a ceremony in a mango grove at a village called Mujibnagar last Saturday ... But glory fades quickly for Bangla Desh. The day after the ceremony, the village is deserted except for a few dozen residents. The reviewing stand still sits under a spreading mango tree, but only several ducks and a goose strut around it. The memory of glory lives on, however. Back on the Indian side of the border, a Bangla Desh official is still dreaming about the previous day. "It was a wonderful day", he declares, "Seven ministers and 27 eminences. Very good speeches. A fine ceremony"'. Peter R Kann, 'A flickering cause: East Pakistanis pledge to fight to the death but mostly they don't – They lack leadership to prolong their revolt: No aid by other nations. Too many Patrick Henrys?', *The Wall Street Journal* (21 April 1971).

74 It was built during the regime of General Ershad whose politics were not pro-India.

75 It would be unthinkable, for example, to have a Monument to the Heroic Smuggler in this borderland – but in borderlands where smuggling has become a thing of the past, such monuments may actually come up with official approval. For a case on the Belgian-Dutch border, where a customs official and two ex-smugglers jointly unveiled a smugglers' monument to commemorate 'an important aspect of local history', see Ed Ragas, *Baarle op de grens van twee eeuwen: Enclavedorpen in beeld* (Baarle-Nassau: Bruna), 1999.

13

CONCLUSION: BEYOND STATE AND NATION

Borderlanders hardly think of themselves as living in the margin. The borderland is the centre of their world. In my exploration of the Bengal borderland I have adopted this perspective: the borderland is the stage and borderlanders are the protagonists. The aim has been to bring to life a regional history that is little known and to rethink three fields of enquiry: the history of the Partition of British India, borderland studies and sociospatial theory. In these concluding pages, I briefly revisit these fields and suggest ways of incorporating borderlanders' everyday transnationality into social theorizing.

Writing the history of Partition

A borderland perspective highlights the need to rethink our understanding of Partition, the demise of British India and the creation of the states of Pakistan and India. Despite the fact that the borderland is where Partition actually happened – and, as many borderlanders would assert, continues to happen[1] – historians of that Partition have largely ignored it.

The forging of international borders between the two new countries has been a core theme in Partition studies but, remarkably, the borders themselves remain largely invisible in these accounts. We learn a great deal about the politics leading up to the territorial division, and histories of Partition are peppered with the names of certain middle-aged men: Louis Mountbatten, Jawaharlal Nehru, Mohammad Ali Jinnah and Cyril Radcliffe. We also learn much about national interests – British, Indian, Pakistani – and how these were served or betrayed by the territorial decisions of the final days of colonial rule. A crucial practice in most of these accounts is a periodization of Partition that stops in 1947, at the very moment when the new borders came into existence, as if the process of Partition came to an end at that point. Writings on Partition can be said to be abundantly political but still quite weak on the spatial restructuring, or reterritorialization, that was such an essential element of Partition. As a result, the border remains a symbol of partition, reconfiguration, independence, nationhood, and uprootedness – it has not yet become a subject of serious enquiry.[2]

For those who experienced the forging of the Bengal borderland, however, it was a life-changing and often devastating upheaval. Even today, very few people beyond the reaches of this elongated region are aware of the many forms of conflict, inequity, injustice and violence that have confronted its inhabitants ever since. Politicians and scholars alike have shown little inclination to listen to voices from the borderland, or to explore how millions of people managed to recover from the disaster and incorporate the border into their everyday lives. As a result, the study of this borderland has remained a curiously neglected no man's land.

This book is an invitation to imagine the Bengal borderland as a useful unit of social research and as a crucial but neglected site for the study of Partition. It suggests that much of what currently passes as received wisdom about it is less fact than fiction. It is important to uncover what Paul Nugent, in a deliberately ambiguous phrase, has referred to as 'the lie of the borderlands', in order to counter discursive oblivion and distortion and to inscribe the borderlands' permutations into the larger historiography of post-1947 South Asia.[3] Without direct reference to the borderlands as a historical reality it is not possible to understand how post-colonial societies in South Asia developed, the extent to which South Asian economies actually became bounded by borders, or the ways in which national identities became internalized. How did the 'Radcliffe line', made public in Delhi on 17 August 1947, turn into a material reality and a social fact with a huge impact on the lives of millions of people today? How was it established, maintained, challenged and subverted? How could certain people turn it to their economic, political or social advantage? How did it affect social transformations on either side?

With respect to such questions, this study has tried to break some ground. It focused on selected aspects of the evolving borderland with a view to demonstrating that new perspectives on the aftermath of Partition are possible – perspectives that go beyond the usual View-from-the-Citadel and the dichotomous categories of We and They that plague it. Taking a borderland perspective helps to break down the one-dimensional world in which heroic nationalist politicians shoot from the hip at menacing cardboard Others-across-the-Border. In the complex border world, categories and identities are inescapably blurred, and Othering is a subtle and partial matter. If there is a principal lesson to be learned from the view from the Bengal borderland, it is that the main oppositional categories of post-1947 South Asian history-writing – nation, religious identity, state – are of very limited use if treated as containers of exclusivity. We need to go back to the drawing board to come up with more carefully calibrated tools. Some pointers to what these tools might be emerge from the fields of borderland studies and sociospatial theory.

Borderland studies

The view from the Bengal borderland may enrich the field of borderland studies. In recent years, theorizing about borders and borderlands has become quite sophisticated but the empirical evidence on which border theorists base themselves remains geographically very uneven. It is derived mostly from Europe, the US-Mexico border and Africa. The world's largest and most populous continent, Asia, is poorly represented in borderland studies and, within it, South Asia is an almost complete blank. And yet the study of South Asia's borderlands appears indispensable because here a major and intensely contested experiment in twentieth-century border making took place, providing us with a laboratory-like situation. Here we have the well-documented imposition of a modern international border, a brusquely partitioned society and myriad individual and group strategies producing a contemporary borderland. The novel geographies thrown up by the political earthquake of Partition, further reconfigured by over half a century of social negotiations and struggles, have exerted an immense influence on the course of human events in South Asia. Antagonistic state politics – now nuclear-missile fuelled – continue to be fed by numerous unresolved interstate conflicts in the border regions, most notoriously the Kashmir issue, but also along the Bengal border, a far more dynamic and contested region than many imagine it to be. This antagonism not only makes itself felt well beyond South Asia, but it has also forced South Asians to live in the shadow of a regional Cold War long after the Cold War of the superpowers had come to an end. If proof were needed that events in borderlands influence processes of state and nation formation, or indeed the world interstate system, a glance at South Asia should suffice.

Another reason for borderland theorists to consider South Asia more closely is the need to compare the dynamics of borderlands resulting from partitions, or state divorce. Partitions continue to be carried out today as solutions to ethnic conflict (e.g. the former Yugoslavia), but comparisons with older partitions are still in their infancy.[4] How are the conflicts that result from a partition managed in the new borderland? To what extent do partition borderlands share certain characteristics, and follow similar trajectories?[5] Do partition borderlands differ from other borderlands and, if so, why? Some of the answers to these questions may be found in the extensive borderlands of South Asia.

But it is not only the case that South Asian experiences can enrich the field of borderland studies more generally; approaches in borderland studies can also help to refocus the way in which we look at South Asian societies and thereby help to develop a more comparative understanding of Partition. The concept of 'borderland' itself provides a useful starting point. We may describe a borderland as a zone (region, landscape[6]) within which lies an international border, and a borderland society as a social and cultural system straddling that border. Therefore a borderland is much more than the peripheral meeting point of two states and their institutions. Rather than considering a borderland as a transition zone, or even a crush zone between centres of sovereign territorial power, we should consider it in its own right.

Students of borderlands emphasize that borders not only join what is different but also divide what is similar.[7] This is an essential point in South Asia, where post-1947 history writing has been prone to assume division – in terms of nation, economy, sovereignty and religion – rather than connectedness. The aftermath of Partition has produced intense security concerns and these influence strongly how states and many citizens see borderlands: as the vulnerable outer rim of the national territory, which extends to the borderline, where the known world ends.[8] These concerns are echoed in many scholarly debates in South Asia. Sanjib Baruah speaks of 'the din of national security talk among the pan-Indian intelligentsia', and Itty Abraham and MSS Pandian similarly remark that 'What is most troubling is the all-too-easy recourse to invoking the sacred cow of national security when in trouble and the even greater ease with which so many intellectuals and commentators swallow this line.'[9] Writings on South Asia's borderlands are replete with national security jargon. It is common to read in the press, as well as in academic studies, about 'hardcore militants' who are 'holed up' in border 'strongholds', or about 'security' that is 'beefed up' in order to 'seal the border', while patrols are deployed for 'search and combing operations', poised for a 'massive crackdown' that will 'flush out' the 'ultras' from their borderland 'hideouts'. Such verbal machismo serves to make the borderland legible for the state, but cannot hide the state's basic dyslexia.[10] As long as it sees cross-border links as a violation of the natural order, as forms of trespassing or treason, it will not be able to grasp the realities of borderland society.[11]

We need urgently to humanize the borderlands of South Asia. The security discourse – which sees border regions as landscapes of defence, securityscapes, or zones of subversion, interdiction and exclusion[12] – seriously hampers an understanding of their human dynamics.[13] It also legitimizes the often horrific consequences of conflicts over spatial control. Borderland studies that are not afraid to abandon the cantonment perspective and cross the border – and thereby risk the wrath of hypernationalists – can act as a powerful corrective. In academic terms, they serve a double purpose. South Asian borderland studies need to make up for lost time and start contributing to the worldwide field of borderland theory. In addition, the study of South Asia's borderlands requires a joint effort and can therefore make a significant contribution to reassembling South Asia's partitioned academy.

Politically speaking, South Asian borderland studies are highly relevant in a period in which hypernationalist ('majoritarian') historical discourses are resurgent and the demonizing of cross-border Others is commonplace. In India, Bangladesh and Burma alike, homogenizing Grand National Narratives present the past as a triumph of Good over Evil, and the future as a Common Destiny that has little time for 'marginals' such as borderlanders.[14] But writing histories of borderlands is *not* writing about margins. It is looking anew at the big stories that create fictive bonds of community by constructing a national past that is territorial, authentic, moral, unitary, linear, orderly, approved by the powers-that-be, and often self-congratulatory.[15] Such hypernationalist histories speak to a 'postcolonial anxiety', or an intense fear of national disunity and fragmentation.[16] Borderland histories, like many other forms of alternative history built around what Shahid Amin describes as 'not foundational but recalcitrant events', offer the possibility of modifying established narratives and of escaping from the 'production of ghettoised mainstream histories.'[17] The particular recalcitrance of border histories lies in their questioning of historical narratives predicated upon strategies of state territoriality. They explore how the resultant 'geographies of knowing' simultaneously create 'geographies of ignorance'.[18] For this reason alone the unfamiliar stories from borderlands are important to the practice of history writing: they are an antidote to the partitioning of memories, the politics of forgetting and the naturalization of exclusion that lie at the root of borderlands' political, discursive and academic oblivion.

Sociospatial theory

Sociospatial theory is the third field of enquiry that this book addresses. There are promising connections to be made between developments in sociospatial theory and the study of social practices at the margins of geographical units. In recent years, human geographers have pointed to the necessity of historicizing the way we think about geographical scale. Traditional notions of geographical scale as a fixed, bounded, self-enclosed container of social practices are being superseded by an emphasis on process, flow, transformation and social contestation. Scales, or levels of spatial representation, are never static.[19] Hierarchies of scale may appear to be fixed but they are better understood as temporary outcomes of ongoing processes of 'scalar structuration', powered by everyday social practices and struggles.[20]

Anthropologists have approached the same theme from a slightly different angle. Theorizing about the cultural disjunctures that characterize modernity and post-modernity, they have developed notions of space and culture that are no longer organically connected to the bounded entities of nation or state. Such notions appear to be especially applicable to people who live transnational lives and who have crossed geopolitical and metaphorical borders. But these people may themselves still believe in a natural correspondence between nation, state and identity – all seen as bounded units – and their actions may be rooted in a sense of bounded culture that clashes with the culturally interstitial places where they live.[21]

The imagery of borders has become a popular metaphor in the study of culture but it rarely connects with the idea of scalar structuring that is being developed in human geography. The study of borderlands may be of particular importance in bringing together these trends in sociospatial theorizing. Borderland studies challenge the tendency in the social sciences to study the world as a given patchwork of state-defined societies, economies and cultures (a territorialist epistemology) as well as their tendency to analyse spatial forms as self-enclosed geographical units (methodological territorialism). Hastings Donnan and Dieter Haller suggest that 'a focus on these liminal border zones may compel us to reconceptualise many of our most cherished assumptions about the nature of the relationships between people, place, identity and culture.'[22] Where cultures and identities overlap, mingle, or melt into each other, we need more than a territorial epistemology. At the same time, the study of borderlands must qualify the main discursive contender to the territorialist epistemology: the sweeping imagery of 'globalization' with its predictions of the 'end of geography' and a borderless, homogeneous world. We have to find 'more modest and more discerning ways of analyzing processes that cross borders but are not universal, that constitute long-distance networks and social fields but not on a planetary scale.'[23]

Here, sociospatial theory's increasing emphasis on the historicity of social space dovetails with the study of borderland societies. Borders are not just lines in the landscape, inert elements shaping the societies and cultures that they enclose, the pre-given ground on which events take place.[24] They are better understood as a spatial dimension of social relations that are continually being reconfigured, and in this process the meaning of borders is produced, reconstructed, strengthened or weakened. Historians argue that current accounts of global restructuring could do with a good dose of comparative history. The movement of people, capital and commodities has always revealed the unevenness of internationalization, the 'lumpiness of cross-border connections, not a pattern of steadily increasing integration.' The current wave of heightened transnational activity in the world (generally termed 'globalization') may well be overtaken by a triumph of nationalism and protectionism, as happened to its precursors.[25] Rather than dusting off 'a tattered modernization theory' and repackaging it as globalization, we need to compare 'past eras of transportation and communication revolution and market expansion with the current period, indicating similarities and differences.'[26]

In their efforts to rethink social space, however, both historians of transnational connections and theorists of sociospatiality tend to invoke borders discursively rather than study them empirically.[27] And yet, borderlands are useful for studying how global reterritorialisation takes place because here geographical scales of various levels always meet. At borders the national scale provides a bounded landscape, an already partitioned geography that encounters the geographical imaginations of borderlanders. The content of these imaginations is not predetermined. Empirical investigation is required to understand how borderlanders analyse the various webs of relations in which they are involved, or from which they are excluded. Knowing how borderlanders 'scale the world' is essential if we are to make sense of their social activities, struggles, and strategies – their politics of scale. The ways in which borderlanders invent and contest divergent geographical scales may provide illuminating examples of how struggles between the powers of territorial control and those that challenge them unfold. Studies of scalar structuration have so far neglected such practices of 'scaling at the margins'. Borderlands make particularly good research sites because they tend to exist for relatively long periods of time and are continually reconstituted and rescaled.

Rescaling in the Bengal borderland

The borderland that resulted from the carving up of British India in 1947 marked the abrupt imposition of a new scale – the nation-state – on an unprepared society, leading to novel politics of scale.[28] In the preceding chapters we have considered several dimensions of this process. The need for border making and border maintenance impelled the new states rapidly to develop their bureaucratic powers of territorial control (e.g. border survey parties, joint enquiry committees, customs departments, intelligence services, passport systems, national currencies, mechanisms of cross-border land exchange) as well as their military and logistic capability (for example paramilitary border personnel, border road and fence construction, counterinsurgency) and identity regimes (schools, mass media, sites of memory). These agencies and tools of territoriality were always pitted against practices that opposed the hegemony of the national scale, and sought to impose other geographies of power. Networks of smuggling, regional autonomy movements and unauthorized cross-border labour migration were among the cases that we looked at in some detail. Several of these attempts at scalar structuration were pitched at a regional or local scale, others at transnational scales whose horizons went far beyond the state.

Before we look further into the dynamics of these struggles, let us first consider the wider context of scalar structuring. The Partition of British India occurred at a time when the world scalar fix was under severe strain. During the previous century and a half, a bundling of territoriality to state sovereignty had turned the world into a giant jigsaw puzzle of national pieces that was now beginning to fall apart. After the Second World War, processes of production, marketing and consumption had become so transnational that the national scale of economic organization was losing its former effectiveness. Postwar states were able to stave off their weakening for another generation, however, by means of trade and immigration restrictions, currency controls, militaristic display, and inter-state institution-building (e.g. the United Nations and the Bretton Woods institutions). This 'Ramboesque reaffirmation of national boundaries' did not last very long. It began unravelling in the 1970s, and the late twentieth century saw the growth of a new dispensation in which territoriality and sovereignty were being parcelled out differently and new relations came up between economies, polities and identities. The world appeared to be entering a new phase of scalar structuring.[29]

The dynamics of the Bengal borderland showed a remarkable but partly accidental parallel to this global process. In the 1940s and 1950s, the newly created states of India, Pakistan and Burma were busy affirming the bundling of territoriality to state sovereignty because they saw it as an essential element in establishing themselves as sovereign modern states, and their efforts were not without success. The creation and control of national borders was an important indicator of this success. As we have seen, establishing and demarcating the border was a long drawn-out process that was completed in most parts but remains crucially unfinished in others today. Similarly, these states' control over their borders in terms of the movement of people and goods remained very haphazard. They also engaged in extraterritorial games intended to destabilize the territorial ambitions of the neighbouring state. Hence, incapable of imposing clear-cut territorial sovereignty – i.e. controlling resources and people by controlling area – these states faced serious problems in normalizing and routinizing relations between themselves. In a period in which states worldwide were much concerned with territoriality, the post-Partition states of this region retained frayed edges that prevented them from becoming truly undisputed sovereign territorial units.

In the 1970s, the dynamics of the borderland changed. As Pakistan disintegrated and the state of Bangladesh emerged, a new element was introduced into South Asian politics and the equation of borderland power was altered. Gone was the intense antagonism of the pre-1971 period, when Pakistan and India had eyed each other belligerently across the Bengal border. There was now room for more state cooperation and less suspicion. But peaceful borders remained well out of reach: most outstanding border disputes remained unresolved, border violence and unauthorized border crossing continued to be everyday affairs, and the states were soon back to their cross-border destabilizing designs.[30]

But by now the world had entered a new phase of scalar structuring, and the national scale was losing some of its centrality. All over the world, forces opposed to state territoriality were having an easier time, and intensified struggles over scale could be observed in the Bengal borderland. In this period, the states presiding over the Bengal borderland largely lost their ability to exert territorial control over trade. Their earlier efforts to enclose the cross-border regional economy had weakened, and illicit trade increasingly began to rescale these states themselves. Similarly, territorial control over people lessened, and unauthorized (and undocumented) migration across the border boomed. Regional autonomy groups multiplied, acquiring better arms and plunging sections of the borderland into intense territorial wrangles with state forces. In other words, borderland struggles and negotiations over power, livelihood and identity moved with the winds of global rescaling. But they did not all move in the same direction.

How borderlands diversify

Since its birth, the Bengal borderland has been shaped and reconfigured by a multitude of human activities. How can we characterize this reconfiguration, and how does it relate to current theoretical fashions that suggest a worldwide withering of borders? In general terms, the assertion of an impending borderless world has been sharply criticized. For example, Gearóid Ó Tuathail argues that while transformations in markets and telecommunications

> are creating a global village, this village is characterized by a functional global apartheid that separates and segregates certain affluent neighborhoods from other deprived and disconnected zones and neighborhoods. The development of borderless worlds does not contradict but actually hastens the simultaneous development of ever more bordered worlds characterized by stark inequalities and digital divides.[31]

This image of global apartheid and the interplay of borderless and ever more bordered worlds may be applicable to borderlands, although the spatial metaphor of zones and neighbourhoods is perhaps less helpful here. Evidence from the Bengal borderland suggests that struggles over bordering are not clearly segregated in spatial terms. Rather, they occur simultaneously, in different mixes of competing social practice, or 'entanglements of power', all along the borderland.[32] It is not so much that certain spaces are more global than others but rather that 'borderless world' discourses 'need to be problematized by old

political economy questions: Who benefits? What class promotes the discourse
of "borderless worlds"? For whom is the world borderless?'[33]

Understanding the permutations of borderlands should start from the
recognition that struggles over bordering always lead to diversification – between
borderlands, between segments of borderlands, between groups of actors in
borderlands, and over time. The late twentieth century saw such diversification
on a world scale. Certain borderlands (e.g. those between member states of the
European Union) became much more interdependent and integrated but others
(for example, those joining Israel and Palestine, or Pakistan and India) hardened
and became increasingly alienated.[34]

The hardness, or impermeability, of a border can also differ along its length.
This can be the result of physical features (when a section of the border runs
through water, a desert, a mountainous area or a city), of more or less intensive
policing of a particular section of the border (as in Operation Gatekeeper on
the California-Mexico border[35]), of local cross-border agreements (e.g. between
border districts or semi-autonomous border regions in neighbouring countries),
of varying degrees of physical or linguistic difference between borderlanders on
either side, or a combination of these.

Third, borders appear as more, or less, of an obstacle to different groups of
people. Citizens from one side may find it easier to cross the border than their
counterparts from the other side. People with particular cultural, economic,
political or physical characteristics may experience the border as a more
formidable barrier than others. Age and gender also play a role. Consider, for
example, the different treatment meted out to two Pakistani citizens when
they crossed the tense border with India on consecutive days. A young Muslim
girl who strayed across as she was grazing her calf was given shelter in an Indian
border village and returned to the Pakistan authorities the next day. A Hindu
man who crossed the border unarmed, without any possessions and claiming to
be fleeing an oppressive family situation, was taken into custody as the Indian
border guards suspected him of being 'on a reconnaissance mission.'[36]

Finally, the hardness of borders changes over time. The power of neighbouring
states waxes and wanes and the relationship between them is always in flux. At
the border, changing interstate relations combine with the varying demands of
cross-border labour and commodity markets, as well as with trade and migration
policies, to produce complex patterns of hardening and weakening. In analysing
such patterns in borderlands, it is useful to distinguish three levels of temporality.
'The impact of a particular world historical transformation (world time) on
social change in borderlands must be related to the developmental phases of
the states concerned (state time), as well as the stages of the life cycle in which
particular borderlands find themselves (borderland time).'[37]

In other words, borderlands are processes of continual reconfiguration, invention and diversification. We need new conceptual tools to grasp these processes. In the following three sections, we look at some concepts that are helpful: life-cycle stages, patterns of control and constellations of scale.

Borderlands and time: a life-cycle approach

It has been suggested that a life-cycle approach may be useful for comparative research into borderlands and time. A model outlined by Michiel Baud and myself proposes six possible stages in a borderland's existence: embryonic, infant, adolescent, adult, declining and defunct.[38] Today, the entire Bengal borderland has moved beyond the first two stages of such a borderland life cycle – the embryonic borderland[39] and the infant borderland[40] – and most parts appear to be in the next stage – the adolescent borderland. In this stage the border is 'an undeniable reality, but its genesis is still recent, and many people remember the period before it existed.' Economic and social relations are beginning to be confined by the existence of the new border, but old cross-border networks have not yet disintegrated and still form powerful links across the border.[41] This is an accurate description of most of the Bengal borderland but particularly of those parts that are less heavily policed (Mizoram/ Chittagong Hill Tracts, or the Sundarban region[42]) and where old cross-border networks of kinship and trade appear to be relatively vigorous.

In certain sections, however, the borderland can be said to have moved into a fourth stage: it has become an adult borderland. Here the border has become a firm social reality. Social networks now implicitly accept and follow the contours of the border and cross-border social and kin networks have become scarcer and are increasingly viewed as problematic. New cross-border networks, such as those supporting smuggling, are based on an acceptance of the border as a fixed reality.[43] This description fits sections of the Bengal borderland that have been fenced and are carefully patrolled on the Indian side, e.g. the Dhubri/ Rangpur section.[44] It also applies to well-guarded sections of the borderland that mark a clear ethnic divide, for example the two banks of the Naf river near Teknaf.[45]

The life-cycle approach suggests that borderlanders can also come to regard their borderland as part of a natural order handed down by earlier generations and almost impossible to question. No part of the Bengal borderland has reached that stage. Although most inhabitants now are too young to have personal recollections of the period before the border existed, they perceive the border as very much a social rather than a natural fact.[46]

Looking at the Bengal borderland in this way is not without its problems because of the evolutionary and deterministic connotations that a life-cycle model can have. Still, the concept of stages is useful in mapping a borderland's diversification over time. The Bengal borderland shows how quickly and unevenly such diversification may occur in a relatively young borderland.

Borderlands and power: patterns of control

A second way of looking at how borderlands diversify is to compare power balances in a borderland. A simple way of doing this is by distinguishing three patterns of control. A borderland can be quiet, it can be unruly, or it can be rebellious.[47] In a quiet borderland, territorial control by the two states does not lead to major confrontations with borderland groups.[48] We have seen that there are few sections of the Bengal borderland that were ever completely quiet on both sides of the border at the same time.[49] By contrast, the second variant, the unruly borderland, has been very common. In an unruly borderland, local society openly resists the border and the rules that come with it. States usually react by stationing troops in the borderland or arming the borderland elite in an attempt to enforce state rule. If this attempt is successful, the states create a militarized quiet borderland; if it is not, the borderland remains disorderly and turbulent. The latter outcome has been quite common in the Bengal borderland, and where it has persisted for many years, it has contributed to a lengthening of the adolescent stage. A good example of a section of the borderland that has been unruly over long periods of time is the Sundarban region. Even more common than the unruly borderland has been the 'half-unruly' borderland, characterized by turbulence on one side of the border combined with quietness on the other. An example is the section where, in the 1980s and 1990s, a very disorderly and highly militarized Tripura (India) faced the quiet districts of Comilla and Sylhet in Bangladesh (see Appendix, Figure 1).

A rebellious borderland is one in which the regional elite sides with the borderland population and takes up arms against a state that seeks in vain to impose its authority. We have seen that the Mizoram/ Chittagong Hill Tracts borderland was rebellious in the 1970s and 1980s, when guerrillas fought the armies of India and Bangladesh in separate wars for autonomy along hundreds of kilometres of borderland. Rebellion on one side of the border but not the other was, however, much more common.[50]

The patterns of control presented in this section can be combined with the life-cycle stages of the previous section. In the Bengal borderland such combinations were complex, with a predominance of sections that were both adolescent and unruly.

Borderlands and rescaling: constellations of scale

A third way of looking systematically at borderland diversification is to compare different constellations of scale.[51] The Bengal borderland can be described as a site of frantic rescaling from its inception. The new state elites of India, Pakistan and Burma were major rescalers. Their conceptions of spatial reality were remarkably similar: they each strove to establish territorially defined state structures and national identities. Although they might fall out over the exact location of each other's territorial limits, they did agree strongly on the principle of territoriality and their projects of national scalar structuring complemented and strengthened each other.[52] The material consequences made themselves felt in the borderland through a host of bureaucratic, military, logistic and symbolic practices. These established the border as an undeniable physical and political reality.

The hegemony of the national scale was never complete, however, because the new states failed as 'gatekeeper states' and never could eliminate the cross-border practices that they forbade.[53] There were continual challenges to their territorial ambitions as a vibrant borderland society sprang up astride the border and produced quite different projects of scalar structuring. We have described the Bengal borderland as largely adolescent and unruly: the border was an undeniable reality but social and economic networks formed powerful links across the border and there was considerable local resistance to the border and the rules that came with it. Three types of scale appear to be especially relevant for people in such borderlands. The first type is formed by *scales-we-almost-lost*, pre-border webs of relations that have weakened but have not quite vanished. The second is the *state scale*, the web of relations that came with the border and is linked to the national territory. And the third is made up of *border-induced scales*, cross-border webs of relations that sprang up because of the border's existence. These three types of scale originate at different times and can therefore be distinguished as pre- and post-border phenomena. Although borderlanders can readily make such distinctions, they are rarely interested in the historicity of these scales. Rather, they juggle constellations of scales that are interlinked and change over time. How borderland time, power and rescaling pan out in certain localities and at certain times determines the changing geographies and diverging social practices of the Bengal borderland.[54] Such geographies and practices can be visualized by imagining constellations of scales. One way of developing this approach further is to consider how borderlanders represent their spatial environment and their own place in it.

Cognitive maps of the borderland

In many ways, the Bengal borderland was a creation of the imagination of its inhabitants. It was their sense of the world that informed their everyday behaviour which in turn considerably shaped the borderland environment. Cognitive maps (organized representations of people's spatial environment and their own place in it) can be stored externally in the form of physical maps, but usually they are not. Studying the changing geographies of a borderland therefore requires us to access 'maps in minds', internally stored cognitive maps.[55] The sources of information on which this book is based do not allow us systematic access to borderlanders' mapping practices but they do provide important leads. There is considerable scope here for further research on cognitive mapping to elucidate borderlanders' conceptions of space and forms of spatial knowledge.[56]

Just as the term *nepantla* (a state of being in-between[57]) is now being used to understand how Mexican-US borderlanders map their world, so the terms that Bengal borderlanders use to refer to their social and physical environment (e.g. *asha-jaoa, epar-opar*[58]) point us towards specific borderland styles of scaling the world. The available evidence also underlines the multiplicity of cognitive maps in borderlanders' minds. For example, when a smuggler uses the pronoun 'we' to refer not only to a group of citizens (Indians), but also to a cross-border trade organization (arms smugglers) and a regional religious category (Bengali-speaking Muslims in India and Bangladesh), he demonstrates a capacity to position himself simultaneously in a variety of scales, only one of which is national. When a dozen rebel groups in a joint statement call for a boycott of India's Independence Day, arguing that 'the northeast was never a part of India and so the question of celebrating Independence Day does not arise', they reject the national scale altogether.[59] When people from both sides of the border come together to enjoy an open-air opera, to pray together or to sell their produce in a border market, they defy the restrictions imposed by the national scale and insist on a cognitive map that includes the world beyond the state border.[60] When an old borderland revolutionary reminisces about how Chinese Minister of Foreign Affairs Zhou Enlai fêted him in Beijing in 1970, he invokes a transnational brotherhood of revolutionary socialists.[61] And when an Indian man takes three months' leave from his government job to accompany his pregnant wife to her parents' house in Bangladesh for the birth of their first child, they may flout the citizenship laws and visa regulations of both states, but they affirm the scale of borderland kinship that links individuals and family groups across the border.

In the partitioned geography of a borderland, cognitive maps will never overlap completely because individuals must frame their conceptions of spatial reality in non-consonant ways, some accepting the border, others not.[62] The concepts of 'cognitive map' and 'scale' have moved much closer together since theorists of scale have begun to criticize an overemphasis on thinking about scale as size (as in map scale) and scale as level (as in a pyramid or hierarchy of scales). Instead, they suggest, we should think of scale primarily as a web of relations.[63] This allows us to picture individuals as being involved in several such webs at the same time and as harbouring several corresponding representations of their spatial environment. Significantly, some people have access to webs at different levels or webs with a wider geographical span, whereas others do not. In a borderland, it may not be simply that 'the rich and powerful revel in their freedom and ability to overcome space by commanding scale [but] the poor and powerless are trapped in place.'[64] For example, in cross-border trade or migration, the social 'invisibility' of poor borderlanders may actually allow them to participate in webs of relations that are as spatially dispersed as, or even more dispersed than, those of their better-off neighbours.[65]

The state as a *local* scale

If we think of scale as a socially constructed mental representation of webs of relations, a cognitive map, a number of questions present themselves. How do people who scale their world imagine such webs to be bordered? What are the spatial limits of scales? How do they come about, how do they evolve and disappear?[66] In the preceding chapters, we have encountered many examples of the politics of scale that focused on the issue of bordering. Often, state practices were ignored by borderlanders who continued to scale their world in ways that did not coincide with state borders. These scales spilled over the spatial limits set by the state's territory even at periods of extreme tension or war between these states.

Today, there is no indication that the state scale has won the cognitive war. True, it has established itself as a very important web of relations among borderlanders, and many inhabitants of borderlands live in 'communities that face both ways, but which lean more towards their national centres.'[67] But this does not mean that the state scale has attained hegemony. Overt defiance is visible in pitched battles between smugglers and border guards, in numerous armed insurrections, and in joint mass prayers (and illegal border crossings) during annual religious festivals.[68] And covert defiance is visible in holes cut into border fences, assistance given to illegal immigrants, and unauthorized transborder production and marketing systems.[69] Borderlanders certainly use the state scale – when they hide behind the border, make citizenship claims, celebrate national holidays, or pull border guards into local conflicts and so elevate these to the status of international border incidents – but the confines of this scale are frequently dissonant with borderlanders' other, and often more powerful, conceptions of spatial reality.[70]

What makes borderlanders most noteworthy in terms of their scaling practices is that for them the state scale is not overarching and does not encompass the more 'local' scales of community, family, the household, or the body. Unlike 'heartlanders' (and most theorists on scale), borderlanders usually do not think of the state as an intermediate layer between the local and the global (or

transnational). To them it is, in many ways, the state that represents the local
and confining, seeking to restrict the spatiality of their everyday relations. Scales
that most heartlanders experience as neatly nested within the state scale –
community, family and face-to-face relations of production – are experienced
very differently by borderlanders. In their case, these scales are often less 'local'
than the state; they breach the confines of that scale, spill over its limits, escape
its mediating pretensions, and thereby set the scene for a specific borderland
politics of scale.[71]

It was the persistence of highly meaningful pre-border scales that provided
inhabitants of the Bengal borderland with a sense of stability in times of dramatic
change. After 1947 many of them spent much energy on maintaining cross-
border family networks, religious communities, marketing regions, property
relations, trade routes, political connections and webs of sociability. Not only
were these persistent scales not obliterated by the state, but they actually formed
the foundations on which new border-induced scales emerged. These new scales
were not simply continuations of pre-1947 webs of relations, however. They
tended to be much more expansive (e.g. smuggling and illegal migration
networks that developed links across South Asia and far beyond) and less stable.
Many borderlanders became directly involved in them, as smugglers, illegal
migrants, traffickers of humans (or trafficked humans), or receivers of migrants'
remittances. Others, not directly involved, were well aware of how these
activities rescaled the borderland, and their cognitive maps also came to include
the new transnational topographies.[72]

In other words, diversification in terms of spatial representations (or scale)
occurred in any locality in the Bengal borderland, between different groups of
people. Here the politics of scale – continual struggles over ways to organize
daily life – involved redefinitions and scale 'jumping' that altered the geometry
of social power by strengthening some people while disempowering others.[73]
These struggles were most visible where states attempted to rein in expansive
scales. Much of the defiance described in chapter 6, and much of the border
violence described in chapter 11, can be read as clashes between state agents'
localizing politics of scale and borderlanders' attempts to organize their lives
according to less territorially confining scales. The outcome of these clashes
was uncertain because state practices of territoriality differed. In the borderland,
even the outlines of the state were often vague: state agents were drawn into
cross-border politics of scale, and borderlanders' politics of scale could entail
infiltrating a porous state structure.[74] For this reason, a heavily guarded segment
of the border could easily be a segment where border guards were heavily
involved in private gain from cross-border trade.[75] Their uniforms and other
visible trappings of territorial discipline did not necessarily match the spatiality
of their everyday relations, or how they scaled their environment and their

place in it. If the evidence is to be believed, the very sentinels of the state were often 'domesticated' by borderlanders and became highly susceptible to the lure of the borderland. Thus they could become active agents in forms of scalar structuring that actually weakened state territoriality.[76]

Rethinking state-centrism

Borderlanders may have kept the state scale at arm's length; social scientists by and large have not. The state scale dominates our thoughts, a situation that has become rather an embarrassment to many now that the world political map is fraying and becoming undone.[77] The inherited model of state-defined societies, economies, histories and cultures looks increasingly contrived and ahistorical. As John Torpey shows in his study of the invention of the passport, the state's concern with authorizing, or interdicting, the movement of human beings and goods across sharply-defined lines in the landscape is a rather recent development in human history.[78] Yet these lines of control have come to exert extraordinary power over how we view the world and how we divide human beings into distinct groups.

Today, the social sciences are struggling to free themselves from the iron grip of the nation-state. As 'postmodern cracks in the Great Westphalian Dam' have opened up, we are increasingly aware of the limitations of the 'territorialist epistemology' that has so long held sway in the social sciences.[79] In order to prepare ourselves for a new world of post-Westphalian territorialities, we need to question our broad acceptance of the often violent border practices of states, and the attendant definitions of what (and who) is legal or illegal, included or excluded.

Now that the social sciences are beginning to move beyond a paradigm based on how state elites define the world order, the question is what to put in its place. The deterritorialization thesis (which prophesies a borderless world of flows, and an end to geography, territory and distance) is hardly convincing. It takes insufficient account of the fact that global flows must be premised upon various forms of spatial fixity and localization.[80] It also pays too little heed to the political backlash of scalar structuring and the cognitive dissonance it produces. Those who feel that disorder and insecurity are growing around them demand that their state grow stronger to protect them from threatening transnational flows by creating a safe territory behind impermeable borders. At this juncture, the 'everyday transnationality' of borderlanders may point the way.

Everyday transnationality

In their endeavours to rethink state-centrism, social scientists could do worse than take a leaf out of the borderlanders' book. Around the globe, inhabitants of 'borderscapes' have devised practices and worldviews that take account of the state but never as an overarching entity that encompasses the local scales of community, production unit, family or body. Of necessity, borderlanders see the state as both plural and confining. Inhabitants of borderlands are faced with (at least) two state entities bent on restricting the spatiality of their everyday lives in the name of law and order, national security or territorial sovereignty. Inevitably, borderlanders' everyday practices are suspended between toeing the borderline and transgressing it, continually exploring and challenging the territorial pretensions of two states. The result, a variety of forms of everyday transnationality, can be understood only if we transcend the territorial epistemology inherent in state-centrism. These transnational practices point to two alternative approaches: transborder arrangements and transborder flows.

Transborder arrangements

Many borderland practices are not spatially confined to the territory of one state. They are embedded in social arrangements and regulatory systems that cross the border, forming the backbone of borderland society, a social and cultural system straddling that border. Although states are based on territoriality, they can sanction, or accept, certain transborder arrangements, usually in conjunction with their neighbours. Thus, in the Bengal borderland, there were numerous state-initiated 'binational' institutions that crossed the borderline (survey parties, joint enquiry committees, flag meetings, trade agreements, land exchange deals and many more[81]). In addition, these states covertly interfered in the 'domestic' affairs of the other when they supported regional autonomy groups across the border or made secret incursions into the neighbouring territory.[82] But it was not only the states that breached the spatial confines of their territories in the pursuit of territoriality.[83] There were numerous non-state initiatives that were accepted by both states, for example contacts between Chambers of Commerce in Northeast India and adjoining areas of Bangladesh, or socio-religious links between Buddhists in Arakan (Burma) and southeastern Bangladesh.

In addition to these arrangements that were acceptable to the states administering the borderland, millions of borderlanders were also involved in transborder arrangements of which the states did not approve. These included transborder networks of kinship, landholding and population movement; and transborder systems of production, marketing and consumption. The states could either tolerate these or actively oppose them. Sometimes, intervention was beyond the technical and administrative capacities of the state. For example, when borderlanders in India began using cell phones tuned to the frequencies of neighbouring Bangladesh, Indian officials were appalled:

No government agency in India has any control over this system and, therefore, cannot monitor the conversation. The consequences can be disastrous ... No one knows anything about what is going on and, in these troubled times, these tools could be the terror-exporter's dream come true.[84]

Transborder arrangements, and the everyday transnationality they embodied, were not unique to the Bengal borderland. On the contrary, social scientists have identified similar transborder connections wherever state territories meet. Because these occur in geographical spaces of close-knit human interaction, they differ from the virtual worlds of financial markets, the Internet and the media that tend to dominate discussions on transnational linkages and global restructuring. Borderlands form arenas of practice that illuminate, in their own way, the changing configuration of state and non-state entities in the modern world. They should be more central in an anthropology of the transnational because they provide grounding and substance to notions such as reterritorialization, and because they highlight how state practices of territoriality have always been contested by trans-state entities, regulatory systems and alliances. Looking at competing forms of territoriality in borderlands and their shifting configurations has already provoked lively debates on territorial and social boundaries,[85] border landscapes,[86] comparative models of borderlands,[87] partitioned culture areas and transborder communities,[88] borders as a resource for local communities,[89] and border livelihoods and subversive economies.[90] These debates on competing territorialities in borderlands may help contextualize the often freewheeling and highly abstract discussions on transnationality.

On the other hand, the conceptual creativity of discussions of the transnational-on-a-world-scale may also enrich the study of borderland transnationality. Concepts developed to analyse 'glocal' diasporas and cultures – 'hybridity', 'creolization', 'bricolage', 'ideoscape', 'interstitiality', and so on[91] – may be of use in understanding the intensely rooted, local forms of transnationality and modernity occurring in borderlands. But this can be effective only if we make a clear distinction between the borders and borderlands that are the topic of this book, and the metaphor of borders and borderlands that is frequently invoked in diaspora studies.[92] The borderlands in this book are marked by a physical borderline, a spatial boundary, a divided geography, an inescapable structural bipolarity. When we talk about the transnational in this context, we refer to the crossing of territorial boundaries and to the linking of localities that are spatially separated by a state-enforced line.

The use of the term 'borderland' in the study of global diasporas and postcolonial identities is altogether different. It is figurative and much less precise because it is neither spatially grounded nor does it involve a clearly recognizable boundary. Rather, it is a theoretical construct used to explore the cultural complexity and fluidity of cosmopolitan (and mostly urban) environments, and it is applied especially to narratives of identity and difference – of 'roots' and 'routes' – among diasporic communities from the South established in North America.[93] In other words, spatial borderlands are quite distinct from discursive borderlands but both embody forms of transnationality.[94] Studying them challenges, in different ways, the tradition of representing nations and cultures as geographically discrete. In this sense, they are part of the same project.[95] Just as the study of diasporic communities is indispensable in advancing our knowledge of transnationality, so is the study of 'communities which live across borders, survive despite them, routinely cross them and constantly network around them.'[96]

Transborder flows

Another practice of everyday transnationality, the movement of people and goods across international borders, may also help us transcend the territorial epistemology inherent in state-centrism. How do various forms of trade and migration negotiate space? How do they relate to competing forms of territoriality in borderlands? How do they beat, circumvent and shape regulatory systems, entities and alliances? Extraterritorial flows of goods and people do not stand in simple opposition to territorial organizations but in a relationship of mutual constitution. For example, states that challenge flows create more barricaded and violent borders as well as more sophisticated, albeit outlawed, organizations to keep flows going. In this way, policies of state interdiction and surveillance produce new transborder arrangements that may turn out to be a bigger challenge to state territoriality.[97] The image of states as simply reactive, responding to the growth of clandestine transnational flows, is misleading because it understates the degree to which states actually structure, condition and even enable clandestine border crossings.[98]

State-centric discourses on unauthorized transborder flows are usually one-sided in the following ways. First, they focus attention on what enters the state territory but not on what leaves it. We have seen how the Bangladesh discourse on international migration exemplifies this. It is vocal about unauthorized entry (e.g. Rohingya refugees from Burma) but silent about the much larger flow of Bangladeshi migrants to India whose departure from the territory of Bangladesh is unauthorized and about whom complaints from India are very audible indeed. Similarly, US discourses on unauthorized flows of goods highlight flows into US territory (mainly of drugs and migrants) but ignore the fact that the USA is probably the world's single largest exporter of smuggled goods as well.[99]

Second, these discourses tend to ignore the fact that it is consumer demand within the state territory that fuels unauthorized transborder flows. Thus goods and services that the local economy cannot provide, and that the state deems undesirable (or admissible only if suitably taxed), become contraband as a result of state action. There is often a striking gap between state pronouncements about the need to stamp out unauthorized transborder flows and state policies to stop them. For example, in both India and the USA, dominant discourses on unauthorized immigration project images of borders as being subverted by infiltrating and unwanted aliens, and inspire state policies of border interdiction and deportation. In neither country, however, do these discourses lead the state to penalize domestic employers of 'illegal aliens'. As a result of state inactivity in this respect, demand for cheap immigrant labour, and hence strong incentives for further unauthorized immigration, continue to exist.[100]

Third, state-centric discourses on unauthorized transborder flows are one-sided because they refuse to take into account counter-discourses of legitimacy that underlie these flows.[101] For example, many unauthorized labour migrants maintain that their actions are justified – because of an inalienable right to migrate, a disadvantaged position in the world economy, the predatory nature of their state, or other moral or economic reasoning. Arguments to the effect that migration is a basic human right that transcends the principle of national sovereignty turn illegal migration into a morally justified act that, moreover, helps family members back home, provides labour to the destination society and contributes hard currency to the home economy. In other words, state-centric discourses disregard the moral justifications that may underpin these flows in the eyes of both participants and some ethicists.[102]

Fourth, state-centric discourses on unauthorized transborder flows are usually one-sided in that they ignore how states facilitate these flows and benefit from them. To stick to the example of labour emigration, states may come to rely on it as an export-led strategy, a safety valve for problems of unemployment and blocked social mobility. Emigration allows them to implement economic policies that aim at growth rather than at creating jobs, and so encourage workers to look for employment abroad.[103] Such states take no steps to curb unauthorized emigration but they are keen to tax the remittances that migrants send back home. To this end they try to make sure that these remittances flow through official banking channels. Bangladesh is a good example of a labour-exporting country that is continually struggling to stamp out privatized forms of remitting money (here known as *hundi* or *hawala*).

States benefit from unauthorized transborder flows in other ways as well. For example, if national industries can get their products to foreign consumers cheaply by evading import duties in the countries of destination, the home state may assist them because it benefits from these exports, for example by taxing the industries. Many Indian companies access the Bangladesh market in this way,[104] and this is also how products from countless industrialized countries around the world clandestinely find their way to millions of consumers in India, via Bangladesh.[105] The link between the state and unauthorized transborder flows is even closer when the state is involved in the production and trade of goods (e.g. drugs, arms) that are banned in the markets of destination. Power holders in Burma, Afghanistan and Colombia have been accused of running 'narco-states' – states that are dependent on income from the trade in outlawed drugs – but many governments that denounce this practice are themselves involved in large 'grey market' transfers of arms.[106]

Conclusion: a worldwide web

In analysing unauthorized transborder flows of goods and people it makes little sense to construct a sharp opposition between these flows and territorial organizations such as states. States actually structure and enable clandestine border crossings, and unauthorized flows can entrench borders and rescale states.[107] The challenge is, rather, to look at territorial states, transborder arrangements and transnational flows as complementary elements in processes of reterritorialization. The current drift of these processes appears to be towards making institutions at the state level less central because stronger direct links are developing between localized arenas (e.g. borderlands) and transnational ones.

In this three-cornered struggle over reterritorialization, state elites hold some very important cards: access to state institutions with their rich pickings from tax; their legitimizing authority; their access to other states and supranational organizations; and their superior military clout. 'Unauthorized' entrepreneurs, on the other hand, hold important cards as well: the power to operate profitably while remaining largely illegible to states; a high degree of organizational and regulatory flexibility; the capacity to be spatially mobile; and the skill to redirect state institutions, undermine state territoriality, and rescale states. Transnational entrepreneurs and state elites can form alliances that simultaneously prop up state structures and allow these to serve the interests of 'unauthorized' transnational flows. In this process, sometimes described as the criminalization of the state,[108] those who routinely undermine the state's territoriality emerge as its kingmakers and office bearers.

There is, however, a third group holding important cards: borderlanders. Their power is based on a detailed knowledge of topography, social fields and constellations of overlapping scales that allows objects and persons to navigate border regions safely. Borderlanders incorporate such flows into transborder projects of scalar structuring that are not easily manipulated by either states or transnational entrepreneurs. The three-cornered ambivalence is expressed in a mixture of trust, rewards, threats, violence, avoidance and subterfuge. When states attempt to interdict clandestine border crossings and unauthorized access to markets beyond the border, they usually highlight the fact that they are waging war against transnational crime lords: these are campaigns against people traffickers, battles with international organized crime, wars on drugs cartels. But what is often forgotten is that states attempting to interdict clandestine border crossings are also joining battle with borderland societies and their projects of scalar structuring.

In other words, global reterritorialization is best approached by looking simultaneously at states, transborder arrangements and transnational flows because these are complementary arenas of power, profit and imagination. They are far more difficult to separate than theorists often assume. It is frequently only states, or states and flows, which figure in analyses of reterritorialization, while transborder arrangements are overlooked – usually considered to be derivative, marginal, or insignificant. I suggest that this is a serious misjudgement. Borderlanders are active partners in reterritorialization. They are anything but passive, supine marginals on whom states and markets impose their will.[109] On the contrary, many states stand or fall by how their borderlands handle them. The economic and political activities of border power-holders, traders and rebels often induce state elites to find ways of co-opting or crushing them. These policies may build up state capabilities and increase the state's clout throughout its territory (the 'border effect'[110]) but may also lead to the state's collapse amidst borderland rebellions and desertions. What happens at borders exerts a powerful, but too rarely recognized, influence on processes of state and nation formation. For example, the new pressures that states are experiencing today – and that many perceive as a 'crisis of the nation-state' – often make themselves felt first in their borderlands.[111]

In this book we have witnessed the birth of the Bengal borderland and the invention of a borderland society, an endeavour in which millions participated. This is a big story, and yet it is just one example out of many. A web of international borders covers the world, and many of the Bengal borderland's features are repeated around the globe. Far too often scholars of transnational linkages, reterritorialization and globalization have remained oblivious to the significance of border regions and, as a result, borderland societies form a missing link in their theoretical reflections. The Bengal borderland – like its counterparts from Tierra del Fuego to Jerusalem, from Dover to the Mekong river, from Lake Victoria to Tijuana – acts as a pivot between territorial states and transnational flows. Arrangements quietly worked out in the world's myriad borderlands have a direct impact on the shape, legitimacy and effectiveness of both states and flows – and thus on the future of the world.

Notes

1 Obviously, this sense of Partition as a lived experience is not restricted to borderlanders, although the borderland environment may be more densely packed with reminders than other environments, and borderlanders' memories may have particular characteristics. The rapidly growing literature on Partition and memory focuses on how strongly Partition lives on in South Asia. In the words of Butalia, Partition's 'deep, personal meanings, its profound sense of rupture, the differences it engendered or strengthened, still lived on in so many people's lives. I began to realize that Partition was surely more than just a political divide, or a division of properties, of assets and liabilities. It was also, to use a phrase that survivors use repeatedly, a "division of hearts".' Urvashi Butalia, *The Other Side of Violence: Voices from the Partition of India* (New Delhi: Penguin Books, 1998), 8. Cf. Gyanendra Pandey, *Remembering Partition: Violence, Nationalism and History in India* (Cambridge: Cambridge University Press, 2001); Niaz Zaman, *A Divided Legacy: The Partition in Selected Novels of India, Pakistan, and Bangladesh* (Dhaka: University Press Limited, 1999).

2 Only a few authors – notably Joya Chatterji, Ranabir Samaddar and Sanjoy Hazarika – have recently taken up the challenge of borderland studies in Bengal and Assam. Joya Chatterji, 'The Fashioning of a Frontier: The Radcliffe Line and Bengal's Border Landscape, 1947–52', *Modern Asian Studies*, 33:1 (1999), 185–242; Ranabir Samaddar, *The Marginal Nation: Transborder Migration from Bangladesh to West Bengal* (New Delhi, etc.: Sage Publications, 1999); Sanjoy Hazarika, *Rites of Passage: Border Crossings, Imagined Homelands, India's East and Bangladesh* (New Delhi: Penguin Books, 2000).

3 Paul Nugent, *Smugglers, Secessionists & Loyal Citizens on the Ghana-Togo Frontier: The Lie of the Borderlands Since 1914* (Oxford: James Curry/ Athens: Ohio University Press/ Legon: Sub-Saharan Publishers, 2002).

4 In a recent article, Radha Kumar looks at partitions in Ireland, India-Pakistan, Israel-Palestine, Cyprus and Yugoslavia, but not at borderlands in particular. Radha Kumar, 'Settling Partition Hostilities: Lessons Learnt, the Options Ahead', *Transeuropéennes*, 19/20 (2000–1), 9–28. Cf. Gilles Bertrand (ed.), 'La partition en question: Bosnie-Herzégovine, Caucase, Chypre', *Cahiers d'études sur la Méditerranée Orientale et le Monde Turco-Iranien*, 34 (2002), 137–233.

5 For example, according to Paul Nugent, the Togo-Ghana borderland was 'never arbitrary in any simple sense [because this partition border was] superimposed upon a long-standing pre-colonial frontier zone.' This was not the case for parts of the Bengal borderland (the West Bengal/ Bangladesh stretch and the Mizoram/ Chittagong Hill Tracts stretch) but other parts (e.g. the Meghalaya/ Bangladesh and Tripura/ Bangladesh stretches) could be described as long-standing frontier zones. The significance of such differences could be explored in a comparative study of 'foreshadowed' and 'novel' partition borderlands. Nugent, *Smugglers, Secessionists*, 273.

6 Donnan and Wilson draw attention to a tendency among geographers to speak of 'border landscapes' whereas political scientists tend to refer to these as 'border regions' and historians as 'borderlands.' Hastings Donnan and Thomas M. Wilson, *Borders: Frontiers of Identity, Nation and State* (Oxford and New York: Berg, 1999), 44–60.

7 Tobias Wendl and Michael Rösler, 'Introduction: Frontiers and Borderlands: The Rise and Relevance of an Anthropological Research Genre', in Michael Rösler and Tobias Wendl (eds.), *Frontiers and Borderlands: Anthropological Perspectives* (Frankfurt am Main, etc.: Peter Lang, 1999), 2.

8 For the image of the world ending, see Berdahl, *Where the World Ended*.

9 Sanjib Baruah, *India against Itself: Assam and the Politics of Nationality* (Philadelphia: University of California Press, 1999), xv; Itty Abraham and MSS Pandian, 'Autonomy of Scholarship and the State', *The Hindu* (15 August 2001).

10 On state projects of legibility and simplification, see James C Scott, *Seeing Like A State: How Certain Schemes to Improve the Human Condition Have Failed* (New Haven and London: Yale University Press, 1998). For examples of the confusion felt by Indian border guards and other state officials trying to 'read' the borderland between West Bengal and Bangladesh, see Samaddar, *The Marginal Nation*, 52–63.

11 Cf. Robert R Alvarez Jr., 'Toward an Anthropology of Borderlands: The Mexican-U.S. border and the Crossing of the 21st Century', in Rösler and Wendl (eds.), *Frontiers and Borderlands*, 229. Obviously, such conflicts are not restricted to borderlands but they are particularly widespread there. For a study of how affective family ties between Delhi (India) and Karachi (Pakistan) similarly challenged the 'two-state order, engaging an array of disputes over belonging and citizenship', see Vazira Zamindar, 'Divided Families and the Making of Nationhood in India and Pakistan 1947–65' (Ph.D. thesis, Columbia University, 2002).

12 Cf. Maoz Azaryahu, 'Israeli Securityscapes', in John R Gold and George Revill (eds.), *Landscapes of Defence* (Harlow: Pearson Education Limited, 2000), 102–13.

13 The plea for a 'critical geopolitical perspective' with regard to South Asia's borders is most eloquently made in Sanjay Chaturvedi, 'Common Pasts and Dividing Futures: A Critical Geopolitics of Indo-Pak Border(s)', in Paul Ganster (ed.), *Cooperation, Environment and Sustainability in Border Regions* (San Diego: San Diego State University Press/ Institute for Regional Studies of the Californias, 2001), 405–22.

14 Cf. Shahid Amin, *Alternative Histories: A View from India* (Calcutta: Centre for Studies in Social Sciences/South-South Exchange Programme for Research on the History of Development (SEPHIS), 2002). Chaturvedi speaks of 'the discourse and practices of reflexive otherness'. Sanjay Chaturvedi, 'Process of Othering in the Case of India and Pakistan', *Journal of Economic and Social Geography*, 93:2 (2002), 149–59.

15 Amin, *Alternative Histories*.

16 It can be seen as a narrative form of the over-centralization and concentration of power by state elites on behalf of majorities they supposedly represent. Krishna links these strategies to postcolonial anxiety. Sankaran Krishna, *Postcolonial Insecurities: India, Sri Lanka and the Question of Nationhood* (Minneapolis: University of Minnesota Press, 1999), 240–1.

17 Amin, *Alternative Histories*.

18 On 'geographies of knowing,' see Derek Gregory, *Geographical Imaginations* (Cambridge, Ma./ Oxford: Blackwell, 1994); cf. Willem van Schendel, 'Geographies of Knowing, Geographies of Ignorance: Jumping Scale in Southeast Asia', *Environment and Planning D: Society and Space*, 20 (2002), 647–68.

19 Scales are ways in which we frame conceptions of spatial reality, and the outcomes of these framings have material consequences. See e.g. Neil Smith, 'Contours of a Spatialized Politics: Homeless Vehicles and the Production of Geographical Scale', *Social Text*, 33 (1992), 66; Katherine T Jones, 'Scale as Epistemology', *Political Geography*, 17:1 (1998), 27; Sallie A Marston, 'The Social Construction of Scale,' *Progress in Human Geography*, 24:2 (2000), 221.

20 Cf. Neil Brenner, 'The limits to scale ? Methodological reflections on scalar structuration,' *Progress in Human Geography*, 25:4 (2001), 592.

21 Donnan and Wilson, *Borders*, 9–10. See also Ricky Lee Allen 'The Socio-Spatial Making and Marking of "Us": Toward a Critical Postmodern Spatial Theory of Difference and Community', *Social Identities*, 5:3 (1999), 249–77.

22 Hastings Donnan and Dieter Haller, 'Liminal No More: The Relevance of Borderland Studies', *Ethnologia Europaea: The Journal of European Ethnology*, 30:2 (2000), 8.

23 Frederick Cooper, 'What Is the Concept of Globalization Good For? An African Historian's Perspective', *African Affairs*, 100:399 (2001), 189.

24 Cf. Donnan and Haller, 'Liminal No More', 10.

25 Cooper, 'What is the Concept', 190. For example, Hanagan suggests that if we are interested in understanding the effect of rapidly improving communications and transportation on the movement of labour, and on labour movements, it would be useful to compare the current period since 1945 with the period of the Second Industrial Revolution, from 1870 to 1913. Michael P Hanagan, 'An Agenda for Transnational Labor History' (unpublished paper, 2002). Cf. Jim Glassman, 'State Power Beyond the "Territorial Trap": The Internationalization of the State', *Political Geography*, 18:6 (1999), 669–96.

26 Hanagan, 'An Agenda'.

27 But see contributions to Thomas M Wilson and Hastings Donnan (eds.), *Border Identities: Nation and State at International Frontiers* (Cambridge: Cambridge University Press, 1998), as well as Donnan and Wilson, *Borders*, and the special issues on borders and borderlands in *Regional Studies* (33:7, 1999) and *Ethnologia Europaea* (30:2, 2000), for some studies that demonstrate that 'studying communities which live across borders, survive despite them, routinely cross them and constantly network around them has become an indispensable aspect of the discourse of transnationalism.' Dan Rabinowitz, 'National Identity on the Frontier: Palestinians in the Israeli Education System', in Wilson and Donnan (eds.), *Border Identities*, 142.

28 Or, to use alternative terms suggested by Brenner, politics of scaling or politics of scalar structuration (Brenner, 'The Limits', 604).

29 Neil Smith and Ward Dennis, 'The Restructuring of Geographical Scale: Coalescence and Fragmentation of the Northern Core Region', *Economic Geography*, 63 (1987), 160–82.

30 Unauthorized border crossings could also involve state personnel. An example of not respecting a friendly neighbouring state's territorial integrity was an Indian incursion into Bangladesh, reported without apology in the Indian press: a 'team of four Border Intelligence Corps (BIC) officials sneaked into the country recently to probe the ground reality ... "We knew that sneaking into Bangladesh w[ould] be a risky decision. But we were determined to know what is going on there."' 'Border-cross for influx insight', *The Telegraph* (3 November 2001).

31 Gearóid Ó Tuathail, 'Borderless Worlds? Problematising Discourses of Deterritorialisation', in Nurit Kliot and David Newman (eds.), *Geopolitics at the End of the Twentieth Century: The Changing Political Map* (London: Frank Cass, 2000), 139–54; cf. Nevins, *Operation Gatekeeper: The Rise of the 'Illegal Alien' and the Making of the U.S.–Mexico Boundary* (New York and London: Routledge, 2002), xi, 185–6.

32 Sharp et al. use the image of 'entanglements of power' in their discussion of geographies of domination and resistance: 'societies are much less neat than orthodox accounts have presumed, and ... relationships in the power webs of everyday mundane political and social practices are much more entangled – with many more spaces for resistance – than most versions of liberal and Marxist thought ever imagined ... despite the

apparent ubiquity of modern state power as woven into the everyday routines of its subjects, domination is in no way complete or secure. Individual citizens or groups may reject the state ... In addition, resistance is woven into the heart of the state apparatus itself ... Power is thereby entangled within the state, and resistances are insinuated through its varied apparatuses ... This power is also entangled spatially, since state power emerges in part from its territoriality, but this territory is never a homogeneous place.' Joanne P Sharp, Paul Routledge, Chris Philo and Ronan Paddison, 'Entanglements of Power: Geographies of Domination/Resistance', in: Joanne P Sharp, Paul Routledge, Chris Philo and Ronan Paddison (eds.), *Entanglements of Power: Geographies of Domination/Resistance* (London and New York: Routledge, 2000), 7. For a further elaboration of the association of power with space, see John Allen, *Lost Geographies of Power* (Malden, etc.: Blackwell Publishers, 2003).

33 Ó Tuathail, 'Borderless Worlds?'.

34 For these terms to describe and compare borderlands, see Oscar Martínez, *Border People: Life and Society in the U.S.–Mexico Borderlands* (Tucson: University of Arizona Press, 1994), 5–10. Cf. Wendl and Rösler, 'Introduction,' 9–10.

35 Nevins, *Operation Gatekeeper*.

36 '8-yr-old girl strays across border, handed to Pak', *Times of India* (16 February 2002). The most bizarre entanglement of gender and age could be seen in the case of Shahnaz Pravin Akhtar Kausar, a Pakistani woman who in 1995 washed up on the Indian bank of the Jhelum river after a quarrel with her husband. She was arrested for illegal entry and thrown into an Indian jail. There she was raped by a policeman, resulting in the birth of a daughter in 1997. The Indian authorities tried to deport mother and daughter to Pakistan, but Pakistan refused to accept the daughter who was an Indian citizen. Released from jail in 2002, the two were living in government quarters in the city of Jammu. The mother appeared to be officially tolerated as long as her daughter was a minor. In this way, Shahnaz became the only case in India's official records of a Pakistani national overstaying. Binoo Joshi, 'Flushout fix: mother Pakistani, child Indian', *The Telegraph* (16 January 2003). On gender and borders, see also AP Cheater, 'Transcending the State? Gender and Borderline Constructions of Citizenship in Zimbabwe', in Wilson and Donnan (eds.), *Border Identities*, 191–214.

37 Michiel Baud and Willem van Schendel, 'Toward a Comparative History of Borderlands', *Journal of World History*, 8:2 (1997), 236.

38 Baud and Van Schendel, 'Toward a Comparative History,' 223–5.

39 The *embryonic borderland* is the stage in which clear borderlines are not yet distinguishable but where two or more frontiers (zones of political, cultural, economic and demographic expansion) close into, and sometimes clash with, each other (Baud and Van Schendel, 'Toward a Comparative History', 223). Few parts of the Bengal borderland could be described as such. Although frontiers of Bengali expansion clearly existed in the pre-1947 period, they rarely coincided with the border that was imposed in 1947. Among the sections that could arguably be described as embryonic were the borderland now separating Meghalaya (India) from Mymensingh/ Sylhet (Bangladesh) and the Burma/ Bangladesh borderland. In many parts of the borderland, however, there was absolutely *no* embryonic stage preceding the imposition of the border; the entire West Bengal (India)/ Bangladesh borderland is a case in point.

40 The 'infant borderland' is the stage that exists just after the borderline has been drawn. National identities are still vague, cross-border social and economic networks strong, and the possible disappearance of the border seems to be a serious option to many

borderlanders (Baud and Van Schendel, 'Toward a Comparative History', 224). The entire Bengal border went through this stage but moved beyond it in a number of steps, of which the riots of 1950, the imposition of a passport and visa system in 1952, and the abolition of legal cross-border land exchange in 1965 were the most decisive. See also Md. Mahbubar Rahman and Willem van Schendel, '"I Am *Not* a Refugee": Rethinking Partition Migration', *Modern Asian Studies*, 37:3 (2003), 551–84.

41 Baud and Van Schendel, 'Toward a Comparative History', 224.

42 See Appendix Figure 1. The Sundarban region straddles the southern reaches of the districts of 24-Parganas (India) and Khulna (Bangladesh).

43 Baud and Van Schendel, 'Toward a Comparative History', 224.

44 See Appendix Figure 1. The impermeability of even this section should not be overrated: more than half of it remains unfenced and man-made holes can be seen in the fences that have come up. 'Border fencing in Dhubri incomplete', *The Assam Tribune* (2 February 2002),

45 On this stretch of the border between the districts of Maungdaw (Burma) and Chittagong (later: Cox's Bazar) in Bangladesh, it is not only physical characteristics (a mighty border river) and ethnic differences, but also an active policy of population expulsion (of Bengali-speaking Rohingyas) from the Burmese side that has contributed to the weakening of old-cross-border kin networks.

46 The life-cycle model suggests two more stages: the 'declining borderland' (when a border is losing its political importance and new cross-border links emerge that are no longer seen as a threat to the state), and the 'defunct borderland' (when the border is abandoned, physical barriers are removed and border-induced networks fall apart). Baud and Van Schendel, 'Toward a Comparative History', 224.

47 For details, see Baud and Van Schendel, 'Toward a Comparative History', 226–9.

48 This can be either because there is a general acceptance of, or support for, the existence of the border (the 'harmonious' variant of the quiet borderland), or because state power is so overwhelming that challenges against the existence of the border are not articulated in open confrontations (the *enforced* variant of the quiet borderland). See Baud and Van Schendel, 'Toward a Comparative History', 227.

49 There were areas that came relatively close to this state, e.g. the Dinajpur (Bangladesh)/ West Dinajpur (India) borderland in the 1980s.

50 For example, during the Naxalbari uprising in Darjeeling district (India) in 1967, the adjoining border regions of Dinajpur (East Pakistan) remained quiet; the Bangladesh war of 1971 reversed the pattern.

51 Scales are spatial representations, ways in which we frame conceptions of spatial reality, and the outcomes of these framings have material consequences.

52 The states clearly reinforced each other in the borderland. Not only did they share an interest in dominating the border population, controlling the cross-border movement of goods and people, and making borderlanders committed to the nation, but in the case of India and Pakistan (and later Bangladesh) their very antagonism made the job easier. Every attempt at state surveillance and control on one side of the border could be used to tie inhabitants on the other side more closely to their own state. Every attempt at official nation building implied a slur on the nation in the neighbouring state, thereby strengthening its appeal across the border (see chapter 5).

53 Here I use the term 'gatekeeper state' in the sense of a state that can open or close the border at will. This is a more restrictive use than the one proposed by Nevins, from whom I derive the term. According to Nevins, the gatekeeper state is a state 'the task

of which is to provide extraterritorial opportunities for national territory-based capital (thus intensifying the process of globalization) while, somewhat paradoxically, providing security against the perceived social costs unleashed by globalization – especially immigration'. Nevins, *Operation Gatekeeper*, 178. For an example of a state (the German Democratic Republic) that came close to the image of a 'gatekeeper state', see 'Die Todesgrenze der Deutschen', *Der Spiegel* (24 June 1991, 58–83; 1 July 1991, 52–71; and 8 July 1992, 102–16); Berdahl, *Where the World Ended*.

54 Cf. Ansi Paassi, 'Boundaries as Social Process and Discourse: The Finnish-Russian Border', *Regional Studies*, 33:7 (1999), 669–80.

55 See Roger M Downs and David Stea, *Maps in Minds: Reflections on Cognitive Mapping* (New York, etc.: Harper & Row, 1977), 6. On scale and cognitive maps, see also Peter Orleans, 'Differential Cognition of Urban Residents: Effects of Social Scale on Mapping', in Roger M Downs and David Stea (eds.), *Image and Environment: Cognitive Mapping and Spatial Behavior* (Chicago: Aldine Publishing Company, 1973), 115–30. People can explain their internal representations of space in words, gestures or drawings. For the interactive nature of these representations, and their content, selectivity and organisation, see Downs and Stea, *Maps in Minds*, esp. 99–145.

56 Which could contribute to problematizing how 'the construction and implementation of certain powerful groups' spatial knowledge form hegemonies that denigrate and silence the spatial language of people constituted as the "Other," while normalising and regulating their own partially-constituted spatial mis/understandings.' Allen, 'The Socio-Spatial Making', 253.

57 '*Nepantla* is the Nahuatl word for an in-between state, an uncertain terrain one crosses when moving from one class, race, or gender position to another, when travelling from the present identity into a new identity. The Mexican immigrant at the moment of crossing the barbed-wire fence into the hostile "paradise" of *el norte*, the United States, is caught in a state of *nepantla*.' Gloria Anzaldúa, 'Chicana Artists: Exploring *Nepantla*, *el Lugar de la Frontera*', in Antonia Darder and Rodolfo D Torres (eds.), *The Latino Studies Reader: Culture, Economy, and Society* (Malden and Oxford: Blackwell Publishers, 1998), 165.

58 The Bengali expressions *asha-jaoa* and *epar-opar* commonly translate as 'coming and going' and 'this side and that' but they have many connotations. *Epar-opar* can also be translated more literally as 'both banks of the river' and as a verb (*epar-opar kora*) it means 'crossing and recrossing' or 'to ferry over'.

59 'Rebel groups call for Independence Day boycott', *The Times of India* (31 July 2001). The same rejection of the national scale occurred when such groups described other Indian citizens entering their area as 'illegal foreigners' and 'infiltrators'. For an example from Meghalaya, see '"Foreigner" tag on Hindu migrants', *The Telegraph* (3 February 2003).

60 'BSF free 13 Bangladeshis', *The Daily Star* (13 December 2000); Probir Pramanik, 'Tragedy on border over prayer', *The Telegraph* (29 December 2000).

61 Sourin Bose was a leader of the Maoist uprising in Naxalbari in 1967 and an emissary of the Communist Party of India (Marxist-Leninist) – also known as the Naxalites – to China in 1970. Cited from the video interview with Sourin Bose recorded by Shahriar Kabir and Willem van Schendel in Siliguri, West Bengal (India), 1996, now in the collections of the International Institute of Social History.

62 This does not necessarily lead to what social psychologists, following Leon Festinger, refer to as 'cognitive dissonance.' Leon Festinger, *A Theory of Cognitive Dissonance* (Evanston, Ill, etc.: Row, Peterson, 1957).

63 Richard Howitt, 'Scale as Relation: Musical Metaphors of Geographical Space', *Area*, 30:1 (1998), 49–58.

64 Erik Swyngedouw, 'Excluding the Other: The Production of Scale and Scaled Politics', in Roger Lee and Jane Wills (eds.), *Geographies of Economies* (London: Arnold, 1997), 175.

65 Donna Flyn suggests that invisibility is also in the eye of the beholder. In her study of a West African borderland, where locals turned the border into something benefiting them (by means of smuggling and taxing other cross-border traders), she concluded that 'borderlanders can be empowered by their positioning on boundaries and crossroads. Far from being invisible, they claim to embody the border.' Donna K Flyn, '"We Are the Border": Identity, Exchange and the State along the Bénin-Nigeria Border', *American Ethnologist*, 24:2 (1997), 311–30.

66 For empirical explorations in other contexts, see John Agnew, 'The Dramaturgy of Horizons: Geographical Scale in the "Reconstruction of Italy" by the New Italian Political Parties, 1992–95', *Political Geography*, 16:2 (1997), 99–122; and Philip F Kelly, 'Globalization, Power and the Politics of Scale in the Philippines', *Geoforum*, 28:2 (1997), 151–71.

67 Paul Nugent, *Smugglers, Secessionists*, 9.

68 Smugglers not only resisted state interdiction of unauthorized cross-border trade, but also rejected its authority to interdict. '"For the poverty-stricken village[s] along the 96-km long border area, smuggling has become one of the main occupations," says a senior BSF official, on condition of anonymity. Nobody treats it as illegal. 10-year old Rafiq Mian Kurbah [of Dawki village] proudly proclaims his ambition to be a smuggler when he grows up, and 70-year old Wanli Khatun says all her four sons are employed in the trade. She reveals that one of her sons – a graduate from Shillong College – had been a smuggler for seven years before he got a job as a school teacher in Nongstoin.' Souvik Chowdhury, 'Meghalaya-Bangladesh border: The dangers of mixed loyalties', *Tehelka* (26 February 2001).

69 For example, illegal cross-border manufacturing systems brought Indian capital and Bangladeshi labour together on Bangladeshi soil (see the case study of the assembly plant in Nabharon (Jessore, Bangladesh) in chapter 7), and cheap Bangladeshi labour travelled to Indian production units across the border (chapter 8). Smuggling involved the borderland in trade networks that could be anything from regional (e.g. Assamese oranges, Bangladeshi rice) to transcontinental (e.g. Swiss watches, American M-16 assault rifles, Korean electronics, Burmese heroin). And a multitude of autonomy movements in the borderland fought for various forms of territorial rescaling. An excellent study of how war can lead to even sharper spatial diversification between rebel-held and government-held sectors than in the Bengal borderland is JoAnn McGregor, 'Violence and Social Change in a Border Economy: War in the Maputo Hinterland, 1984–1992', *Journal of Southern African Studies*, 24:1 (1998), 37–60

70 There were, however, also groups of borderlanders for whom claims on citizenship were highly problematic. The Rohingyas of Arakan (Burma) were denied citizenship rights by their state. The Burmese authorities considered Rohingyas not to be one of the country's 'national races' and denied them Burmese nationality under the 1982 Burma Citizenship Law. To the Burmese government, Rohingyas are mere 'resident foreigners', not citizens. Human Rights Watch, *Burma/Bangladesh – Burmese Refugees in Bangladesh: Still No Durable Solution* (New York, etc.: Human Rights Watch/ Asia, 2000).

71 For examples of the complexities involved, see Willem van Schendel, 'Stateless in South Asia: The Making of the India-Bangladesh Enclaves', *The Journal of Asian Studies*, 61:1 (February 2002), 115–47.

72 Willem van Schendel, 'Easy Come, Easy Go: Smugglers on the Ganges', *Journal of Contemporary Asia*, 23:2 (1993), 189–213.

73 Swyngedouw, 'Excluding the Other', 169. Cox has nuanced Smith's original formulation of the concept of jumping scale (to organize the production and reproduction of daily life and to resist oppression and exploitation at a higher scale) by showing that such resistance can also be expressed at a more local scale. As we have seen, however, in a borderland situation the architectural imagery of higher and lower scales (or more local and more global ones) breaks down, and the direction of scale jumping is in the eye of the beholder. Smith, 'Contours', 60; Cox, Kevin, 'Spaces of Dependence, Spaces of Engagement and the Politics of Scale, Or: Looking for Local Politics', *Political Geography*, 17:1 (1998), 1–23.

74 Van Schendel, 'Easy Come, Easy Go', 204–5.

75 There is ample evidence for this in various surveys. For example, Ghafur et al. reported that 'an overwhelming proportion of illegal trade is conducted within a system of connivance and co-operation of the law-enforcement agencies with the operators in exchange of financial payments.' They also found a 'widespread and increasing practice of rent-seeking among the rank and file of these agencies' and abysmally low figures for arrests and convictions of suspected smugglers (Abdul Ghafur, Muinul Islam and Naushad Faiz, *Illegal International Trade in Bangladesh: Impact on the Domestic Economy* (Dhaka: Bangladesh Institute of Development Studies, 1990), Phase I, 50; 47–8, 100). Cf. 'Border crime on the rise in West Bengal', *The Statesman* (15 April 1992); SK Ghosh, *Unquiet Border* (New Delhi: Ashish Publishing House, 1993), 64–8. For a discussion of a similar 'disjuncture between official threats and the reality in which state officials were actually aiding and abetting smuggling' on the Ghana-Togo border, see Paul Nugent, 'Power Versus Knowledge: Smugglers and the State Along Ghana's Eastern Frontier, 1920–1992', in Rösler and Wendl (eds.), *Frontiers and Borderlands*, 94.

76 This was easier on the Bangladesh side, where border guards and local population usually shared a language and a regional culture, than on the Indian side, where communication was often much more difficult.

77 Timothy W Luke and Gearoíd Ó Tuathail, 'The Fraying Modern Map: Failed States and Contraband Capitalism', *Geopolitics*, 3:3 (1998), 14–33.

78 See e.g. John Torpey, *The Invention of the Passport: Surveillance, Citizenship and the State* (Cambridge: Cambridge University Press, 2000).

79 Scott Relyea, 'Trans-State Entities: Postmodern Cracks in the Great Westphalian Dam,' *Geopolitics*, 3:2 (1998), 30–61. On the Treaty of Westphalia, see chapter 1.

80 Brenner, 'Beyond State-Centrism?', 62.

81 Border survey parties, joint enquiry committees and flag meetings are discussed in chapters 4, 5 and 11; the arrangements for transit and sanctioned trade are discussed in chapter 7; and the mechanisms for land exchange are discussed in Rahman and Van Schendel. In addition there were many others: the Inter-Dominion Information Consultative Committee, Provincial and District Minority Boards, Evacuee Property Management Boards, monthly Inter-Dominion meetings, Joint Riot Enquiry Commissions, the Joint Rivers Commission, the Joint Border Working Groups, and so on. See A Appadorai, *Select Documents on India's Foreign Policy and Relations, 1947–1972* (Delhi: Oxford University Press, 1982), 80–93; Rahman and Van Schendel, '"I

Am *Not* A Refugee"'; and Avtar Singh Bhasin (ed.), *India-Bangladesh Relations: Documents – 1971–2002* (New Delhi: Geetika Publishers, 2003), 5 Volumes.

82 See chapter 10. On a covert Indian incursion into Bangladesh, see 'Border-cross for influx insight', *The Telegraph* (3 November 2001).

83 In chapter 5 we have seen that state actors also employed different strategies according to where they were situated. Thus, in their pursuit of border stability, officials in the border districts often quietly employed practices of cross-border cooperation and conflict management that flew in the face of the confrontational policies of territoriality employed by their superiors in the capital.

84 Sunando Sarkar and Alamgir Hossain, 'Border mobiles fox security eavesdroppers', *The Telegraph* (4 March 2002); 'Mobile phones in Tripura? Yes, courtesy B'desh's Grameen Phone!' *The Sentinel* (28 December 2002). In another cross-border telephone deal, booth owners in the southwestern Bangladesh borderland had an understanding with colleagues in India. They charged their customers phoning people across the border international rates but secretly linked up to Indian numbers at local-call rates: 'Booth-owners on both sides are filling coffers giving damn to security concerns.' Sunando Sarkar and Pronab Mondal, 'Phone ring blurs border divide', *The Telegraph* (29 July 2003). Cf. Subrata Nagchoudhury, 'No hanging up on cross-border telephonism', *The Sunday Express* (10 August 2003).

85 Donnan and Wilson, *Borders*, 19–41; Wilson and Donnan (eds.), *Border Identities*.

86 Donnan and Wilson, *Borders*, 44–9.

87 Donnan and Wilson, *Borders*, 49–53.

88 AI Asiwaju (ed.), *Partitioned Africans: Ethnic Relations across Africa's International Boundaries, 1884–1984* (London and Lagos: C Hurst & Company / University of Lagos Press, 1985); Demetrios G Papademetriou and Deborah Waller Meyers (eds.), *Caught in the Middle: Border Communities in an Era of Globalization* (Washington, DC: Carnegie Endowment for International Peace, 2001).

89 Nugent, *Smugglers, Secessionists*, 93–112; cf. Willem van Schendel, 'Working through Partition: Making a Living in the Bengal Borderlands', *International Review of Social History*, 46 (December 2001), 393–421.

90 Donnan and Wilson, *Borders*, 87–106.

91 For a brief overview, see Wendl and Rösler, 'Introduction,' 11–12; cf. Donnan and Wilson, *Borders*, 9–10.

92 'The construct of the "border," a trendy term within literary and cultural studies, has been used to refer to any number of boundaries within disparate semantic fields. Some critics tend to exalt and fetishize the border or "the borderlands" ... [The border is] a historical construct, a product of social and political relations used to demarcate hegemonic power.' Rosaura Sánchez, 'Mapping the Spanish Language along a Multiethnic and Multilingual Border', in Antonia Darder and Rodolfo D Torres (eds.), *The Latino Studies Reader: Culture, Economy, and Society* (Malden and Oxford: Blackwell Publishers, 1998), 106.

93 For example Gloria Anzaldúa, *Borderlands/La Frontera: The New Mestiza* (San Francisco: Spinsters/ Aunt Lute, 1987); Carl Gutierrez-Jones, *Rethinking the Borderlands: Between Chicano Culture and Legal Discourse* (Berkeley: University of California Press, 1995); Scott Michaelson and David E Johnson (eds), *Border Theory: The Limits of Cultural Politics* (Minneapolis and London: University of Minnesota Press, 1997). For an application of this concept to Asian studies, see Shirley Hune, 'Asian-American Studies and Asian Studies: Boundaries and Borderlands of Ethnic Studies and Area Studies',

in: Johnella E Butler (ed.), *Color-Line to Borderlands: The Matrix of American Ethnic Studies* (Seattle/ London: University of Washington Press, 2001), 227–37.

94 Vazira Zamindar's study of the making of nationhood in India and Pakistan between 1947 and 1965 presents an intermediate case. She analyses how these new nations became bounded by a number of institutional practices (rehabilitation of refugees, dealing with evacuee property, systems to regulate cross-border movement) that excluded North Indian Muslims from both Pakistan and India. These 'border-making practices' were not necessarily located in the *spatial* (territorial) borderland but they were crucially important in defining the *discursive* borderland between the nations of India and Pakistan. According to this analysis, North Indian Muslims ended up in a discursive no man's land between these two nations. This case differs from the Chicano case in that the spatial border between the states of India and Pakistan was an absolutely inescapable image in the construction of Indian and Pakistani identities, whereas the spatial reality of, for example, the US–Mexican border was a more optional element in the construction of Chicano identities in the United States. Zamindar, 'Divided Families'. Cf. Sankaran Krishna, 'Cartographic Anxiety: Mapping the Body Politic in India', in Michael J Shapiro and Hayward R Alker (eds.), *Challenging Boundaries: Global Flows, Territorial Identities* (Minneapolis: University of Minnesota Press, 1996), 193–214.

95 For an attempt, employing Soja's concept of 'Thirdspace', to frame and link these different forms of spatiality theoretically, see Allen, 'The Socio-Spatial Making'. Cf. Edward W Soja, *Thirdspace: Expanding the Geographical Imagination* (Cambridge, Ma.: Blackwell Publishing, 1996).

96 Rabinowitz, 'National identity', 142; cf. Anderson and O'Dowd, 'Borders, Border Regions', 602–3.

97 Andreas describes how an escalation of US border policing in the US–Mexico borderland led to a sharp shift from self-smuggling by individual migrants to highly-organized smuggling operations by transnational criminal networks. Peter Andreas, *Border Games: Policing the U.S.–Mexico Divide* (Ithaca and London: Cornell University Press), 2000.

98 Andreas, *Border Games*, 7. On the Bangladesh-India border at Benapol, the pattern of legal/ illegal crossing changed perceptibly after the Bangladesh government doubled the travel tax and also applied it to Indian nationals. The Indian authorities followed suit, slapping a travel tax of their own on travellers. Many could not afford the double burden and paid brokers to help them cross more cheaply and illegally. Syed Mehdi Momin, 'Illegal border crossing – Benapole style', *The Independent* (7 September 2003); 'Spurt in influx of illegal migrants', *The Assam Tribune* (9 September 2003).

99 'The United States is by far the world's number one smuggling target, with illegal drugs and migrants leading the list of imports. The United States is also probably the single largest exporter of smuggled goods if one considers, for example, the mass quantities of American cigarettes, pornographic material, money, weapons, and stolen cars that are smuggled out of the country every year. Most of the attention, not surprisingly, is on what is coming into the country rather than on what is going out. For example, complaints by Mexico that large quantities of illegal weapons from the United States end up south of the border in violation of Mexican gun control laws generate relatively little U.S. media coverage or concern among Washington policy makers (particularly in comparison with the concern over the influx of drugs and immigrants). Similarly, while Mexico is chastised for being a key transshipment point for Colombian cocaine bound for the U.S. market, largely ignored is the fact that the United States is a major transshipment point for cocaine exported to Canada.' Andreas, *Border Games*, 16–17.

100 In India, employer sanctions were absent; in the US they have been described as largely symbolic and as forming the basis of an 'enormous underground business in fraudulent documents'. On India, see chapter 9; on the United States, see Andreas, *Border Games*, 32–9.

101 A female Dutch cocaine smuggler put it like this: 'It is ridiculous that states prohibit cocaine. In my view everybody has his own responsibility for using it or not. Nobody forces them to take it, do they? I have never dealt in anything but pure cocaine, and that is really not harmful at all.' Frank Bovenkerk, *La Bella Bettien* (Amsterdam: Meulenhoff, 1995), 73. Cf. Nancy Ries, '"Honest Bandits" and "Warped People": Russian Narratives about Money, Corruption, and Moral Decay', in Carol J Greenhouse, Elizabeth Mertz and Kay B Warren (eds.), *Ethnography in Unstable Places: Everyday Lives in Contexts of Dramatic Political Change* (Durham and London: Duke University Press, 2002), 276–315.

102 For example, in 2002 the United States Conference of Catholic Bishops stated: 'Every person has an equal right to receive from the earth what is necessary for life—food, clothing, shelter ... The native does not have superior rights over the immigrant. Before God all are equal; the earth was given by God to all. When a person cannot achieve a meaningful life in his or her own land, that person has the right to move' (http:// www.nccbuscc.org/mrs/cst.htm). Cf. Brian Barry and Robert E Goodin (eds.), *Free Movement: Ethical Issues in the Transnational Migration of People and of Money* (New York, etc.: Harvester Wheatsheaf, 1992).

103 On Bangladesh, see chapter 9; on Mexico, Andreas, *Border Games*, 37–8.

104 For example, Indian companies producing phensidyl, a cough syrup that is very popular in Bangladesh, although it is banned there because of its addictive properties owing to its high codeine content. Other Indian products are woollen shawls from Kashmir, silk *saris* from South India, table fans, cosmetics, razor blades, medicines, and components of trucks and buses.

105 In chapter 7 we have seen that a bewildering variety of commodities entered Bangladesh largely to be traded illegally across the border to India, e.g. Japanese, Korean and Taiwanese electronics; Danish, Dutch and Australian milk powder; Russian, Chinese and Israeli assault rifles; American cigarettes and cosmetics; French perfumes; Thai concrete and fertilizers; and Swiss watches.

106 'Grey market transfers are usually covert, conducted by governments, government-sponsored brokers, or other entities, that exploit loopholes or intentionally circumvent national and/or international law or policies. Grey market transfers include sales to recipient countries that have no identifiable legal government or authority (e.g. Somalia) and transfers by governments to non-state actors (i.e. rebel and insurgent groups). In addition, there are cases where governments illegally hire brokers to transfer weapons (e.g. the 'Iran-Contra Affair').' *Small Arms Survey 2001: Profiling the Problem* (Geneva/ Oxford: Graduate Institute of International Studies / Oxford University Press, 2001), 166.

107 Paul Nugent argues that smuggling at the border between Togo and Ghana had the effect of entrenching rather than undermining the border. Nugent, *Smugglers, Secessionists*, 231–71.

108 This process has been most thoroughly analysed for Africa. See Jean-François Bayart, Stephen Ellis and Béatrice Hibou, *The Criminalization of the State in Africa* (Oxford/ Bloomington: Currey/ Indiana University Press, 1999), and Patrick Chabal and Jean-Pascal Daloz, *Africa Works: Disorder as a Political Instrument* (Oxford/ Bloomington:

James Currey/ Indiana University Press, 1999). For an interpretation of the resulting 'sovereigntyscapes,' see JD Sidaway, 'Sovereign Excesses? Portraying Postcolonial Sovereigntyscapes', *Political Geography*, 22:2 (February 2003), 157–78.

109 Peter Sahlins, *Boundaries: The Making of France and Spain in the Pyrenees* (Berkeley: University of California Press, 1989), 8.

110 Cf. Thomas W Gallant, 'Brigandage, Piracy, Capitalism, and State-Formation: Transnational Crime from a Historical World-Systems Perspective', in Josiah McC Heyman (ed.), *States and Illegal Practices* (Oxford and New York: Berg, 1999), 25–61. McCoy provides a detailed example of the 'border effect' in his discussion of Khun Sa and the Burmese state. Alfred W McCoy, 'Requiem for a Drug Lord: State and Commodity in the Career of Khun Sa', in Heyman (ed.), *States and Illegal Practices*, 129–67.

111 Donnan and Wilson, *Borders*, 158..

APPENDIX

Appendix Figure 1: The Partition border and adjacent districts

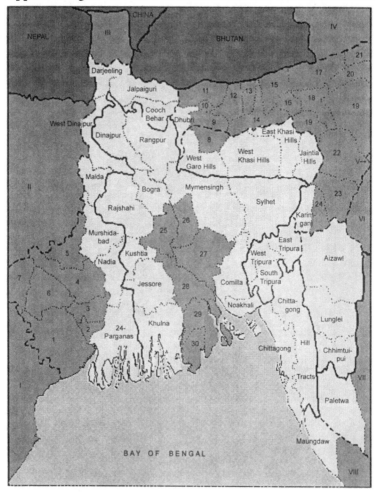

Since 1947, in an ongoing process, many districts have been subdivided, reorganized or otherwise changed. For clarity's sake, I present what by now are known as 'greater districts.'

DISTRICTS

STATES

In West Bengal (India):
1 Medinipur
2 Haora
3 Hughli
4 Barddhaman
5 Birbhum
6 Bankura
7 Puruliya

In Meghalaya (India):
8 East Garo Hills

In Assam (India):
9 Goalpara
10 Bongaigaon
11 Kokrajhar
12 Barpeta
13 Nalbari
14 Kamrup
15 Darrang
16 Marigaon
17 Sonitpur
18 Nagaon
19 Karbi Anglong (2 pts)
20 Golaghat

21 Lakhimpur
22 North Cachar Hills
23 Cachar
24 Haliakandi

In Bangladesh:
25 Pabna
26 Tangail
27 Dhaka
28 Faridpur
29 Barisal
30 Patuakhali

In India:
I Orissa
II Bihar
III Sikkim
IV Arunachal Pradesh
V Nagaland
VI Manipur

In Burma (Myanmar):
VII Chin State
VIII Arakan (Rakhine) State

Appendix Figure 2: New administrative units in the borderland, 1947–2003

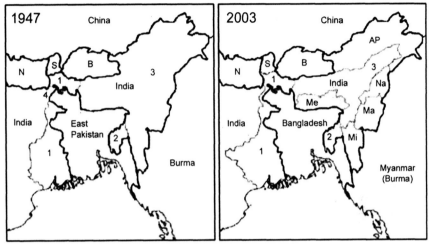

1 = West Bengal   AP = Arunachal Pradesh   N = Nepal
2 = Tripura   Ma = Manipur   S = Sikkim
3 = Assam   Me = Meghalaya   B = Bhutan
4 = Bihar   Mi = Mizoram
   Na = Nagaland

REFERENCES

Unpublished records

National Archives of Bangladesh, Dhaka

Government of East Bengal (East Pakistan)

Home (Political) Department, Branch C.R. [Confidential Records],
B. Proceedings   (CR)
Home (Political) Department, Branch Records, B. Proceedings
Home (Political) Department, Branch Political, B. Proceedings   (Plt.)
Home (Police) Department, Branch Police, B. Proceedings   (Pol.)
Home Department, General Administration and Appointment Branch,
B. Proceedings   (G&A)
Agriculture, Co-operatives and Relief Department, Branch Relief, B. Proceedings;
Agriculture, Co-operatives and Relief Department, Branch Forests, B. Proceedings;
Agriculture Department, Branch Development, B. Proceedings;
Land Revenue Department, Branch Excluded Areas, B. Proceedings;
Public Relations Department, Branch P & D, B. Proceedings;

Newspapers (titles and authors of newspaper articles are mentioned only in footnotes)

India: Current Internet address

Amrita Bazar Patrika (Calcutta)
Ananda Bazar Patrika (Calcutta)   http://www.anandabazar.com/
The Assam Tribune (Guwahati)   http://www.assamtribune.com/
Deccan Herald (Bangalore)   http://www.deccanherald.com/
The Financial Express (Bombay)   http://www.financialexpres.com/
The Hindu (Chennai)   http://www.hinduonnet.com/
Hindusthan (Calcutta)
The Hindustan Times (Delhi)   http://www.hindustantimes.com/
Hindusthan Standard (Calcutta)
Indian Express (Mumbai)   http://www.expressindia.com/
Ittehad (Calcutta)
Navhind Times (Goa)   http://www.navhindtimes.com/
The Northeast Daily (Guwahati)   http://assam.org/
                                            (currently discontinued)
The North East Times (Guwahati)   http://www.glpublication.com/net/
The North East Tribune (Guwahati)   http://www.northeasttribune.com/
The Oriental Times (Guwahati)   http://www.nenanews.com/

Outlook	http://www.outlookindia.com/
Rediff on the Net	http://www.rediff.com/
Rozana Hind (Calcutta)	
Sawaal News	http://news.sawaal.com/
Tehelka	http://www.tehelka.com/
The Sentinel (Guwahati)	http://www.sentinelassam.com/
The Shillong Times (Shillong)	http://www.theshillongtimes.com/
The Statesman (Calcutta)	http://www.thestatesman.net/
The Sunday Express (Bombay)	http://www.indianexpress.com/
The Telegraph (Calcutta)	http://www.telegraphindia.com/
The Times of India (Delhi)	http://www.timesofindia.com/
The Tribune (Chandigarh)	http://www.tribuneindia.com/
The Week (Kottayam)	http://www.the-week.com/

East Pakistan/ Bangladesh:

Azad (Dhaka)	
Azan (Chittagong)	
Bangladesh Observer (Dhaka)	http://www.bangladesh.net/observer/
Daily News (Dhaka)	
The Daily Star (Dhaka)	http://dailystarnews.com/
Doinik Ittefak (Dhaka)	http://www.ittefaq.com/
Holiday (Dhaka)	http://www.bangla.net/holiday/
The Independent (Dhaka)	http://www.independent.com.bd/
Muktakantha (Dhaka)	http://www.muktakantha.com/
News from Bangladesh (Dhaka)	http://bangladesh-web.com/news/
The New Nation (Dhaka)	http://www.nation-online.com/
Pakistan Observer (Dhaka)	
Prothom Alo (Dhaka)	http://www.prothom-alo.com/
Sangbad (Dhaka)	
Zindegi (Dhaka)	

Burma/ Myanmar and exile groups

Kaladan News	
Mizzima News Group	http://www.mizzima.com/
Narinjara News	
New Light of Myanmar (Rangoon)	http://www.myanmar.com/nlm/
ShweInc News	http://www.shweinc.com/news

Other:

Arab News (Jeddah/ Riyadh/ Dhahran)	http://www.arabnews.com/
Dawn (Karachi)	http://www.dawn.com/
The Kathmandu Post	http://www.nepalnews.com.np/
Mekong Digest (Washington, DC)	http://www.mekongdigest.com/
The Morning News (Karachi)	

The New York Times   http://www.nytimes.com/
The News International (Karachi)   http://www.jang.com.pk/thenews/
One World   http://www.oneworld.net/
People's Daily (Beijing)   http://english.peopledaily.com.cn/
Pakistan Times (Karachi)
South China Morning Post (Hong Kong)   http://www.scmp.com/
The Wall Street Journal (New York)   http://www.wsj.com/

Unpublished PhD theses

Chester, Lucy Payne, 'Drawing the Indo-Pakistani Boundary During the 1947 Partition of South Asia' (PhD thesis, Yale University, 2002).

Zamindar, Vazira, 'Divided Families and the Making of Nationhood in India and Pakistan 1947–65' (PhD thesis, Columbia University, 2002).

Books and articles

Abraham, Itty, and MSS Pandian, 'Autonomy of Scholarship and the State', *The Hindu* (15 August 2001).

Abraham, Itty, and Willem van Schendel, 'Introduction: The Making of Illicitness', in Van Schendel and Abraham (eds.), *Illicit Flows: How States, Borders and Language Produce Criminality* (Bloomington: University of Indiana Press, forthcoming).

Acharya, Jagat Mani, Manjita Gurung and Ranabir Samaddar, *Chronicles of a No-Where People on the Indo-Bangladesh Border* (Kathmandu: South Asia Forum of Human Rights, 2003).

Agnew, John, 'The Territorial Trap: The Geographical Assumptions of International Relations Theory', *Review of International Political Economy*, 1:1 (1994), 53–80.

———, 'The Dramaturgy of Horizons: Geographical Scale in the "Reconstruction of Italy" by the New Italian Political Parties, 1992–95', *Political Geography*, 16:2 (1997), 99–122.

———, *Making Political Geography* (London: Arnold, 2002).

Agnew, John, and Stuart Corbridge, *Mastering Space: Hegemony, Territory and International Political Economy* (London and New York: Routledge, 1995).

Agreement on Demarcation of Bangladesh-India Land Boundary 1974 (Act No.LXXIV of 1974) (Dacca, 1974)

Ahmad, Nafis, 'The Indo-Pakistan Boundary Disputes Tribunal, 1949–1950', *The Geographical Review* (New York), 43:3 (1953), 329–37.

Ahmed, Haroon, 'Bangladeshi Immigrants in Sindh', in Tapan K Bose and Rita Manchanda (eds.), *States, Citizens and Outsiders: The Uprooted Peoples of South Asia* (Kathmandu: South Asia Forum for Human Rights, 1997), 345–52.

Ahmed, Imtiaz (ed.), *Memories of a Genocidal Partition: The Haunting Tales of Victims, Witnesses and Perpetrators* (Colombo: Regional Centre for Strategic Studies, 2002).

Ahmed, Reaz (comp. and ed.), *Gonomadhyome Bangladesher Muktijuddho, Kartun, Prothom Khondo / Media and Liberation War of Bangladesh, Cartoons, Volume 1* (Dhaka: Centre for Bangladesh Studies, 2002).

Ahmod, Aftab, *Amra Tomader Bhulbo Na* (Dhaka: Borna-Shagor Prokashoni, 1994).

———, *Shadhinota Shongrame Bangali* (Dhaka: Borna-Shagor Prokashoni, 1998; 3rd ed.).

Akanda, SA, 'Referendum in Sylhet and the Radcliffe Award, 1947', *Journal of the Institute of Bangladesh Studies*, 14 (1991), 21–47.

Ali, Chaudhri Muhammad, *The Emergence of Pakistan* (New York and London: Columbia University Press, 1967).

Ali, Salamat, 'Trouble Flares up on Bangladesh Border', *Far Eastern Economic Review*, 124:18 (3 May 1984), 12.

Ali, S Mahmud, *The Fearful State: Power, People and Internal War in South Asia* (London & New Jersey: Zed Books, 1993).

Allen, John, *Lost Geographies of Power* (Malden, etc.: Blackwell Publishers, 2003).

Allen, Ricky Lee, 'The Socio-Spatial Making and Marking of "Us": Toward a Critical Postmodern Spatial Theory of Difference and Community,' *Social Identities*, 5:3 (1999), 249–77.

Alvarez Jr., Robert R, 'Toward an Anthropology of Borderlands: The Mexican–U.S. Border and the Crossing of the 21st Century', in Michael Rösler and Tobias Wendl (eds.), *Frontiers and Borderlands: Anthropological Perspectives* (Frankfurt am Main, etc.: Peter Lang, 1999), 225–34.

Amin, Shahid, *Alternative Histories: A View from India* (Calcutta: Centre for Studies in Social Sciences/South-South Exchange Programme for Research on the History of Development (SEPHIS), 2002).

Amin, Sajeda, Alaka Malwade Basu, and Rob Stephenson, *Spatial Variation in Contraceptive Use in Bangladesh: Looking Beyond the Borders, Working Paper 138* (New York: The Population Council, 2000).

Anderson, Benedict R O'G, *Long-Distance Nationalism: World Capitalism and the Rise of Identity Politics* (Amsterdam: Centre for Asian Studies Amsterdam, 1992).

Anderson, James, and Liam O'Dowd, 'Borders, Border Regions and Territoriality: Contradictory Meanings, Changing Significance', *Regional Studies*, 33:7 (1999), 593–604.

Andreas, Peter, *Border Games: Policing the U.S.–Mexico Divide* (Ithaca and London: Cornell University Press, 2000).

Ansari, Sarah, 'The Movement of Indian Muslims to West Pakistan after 1947: Partition-Related Migration and Its Consequences for the Pakistani Province of Sind', in Judith M Brown and Rosemary Foot (eds.), *Migration: The Asian Experience* (Oxford: St. Martin's Press, 1994), 149–68.

Anzaldúa, Gloria, *Borderlands/La Frontera: The New Mestiza* (San Francisco: Spinsters/ Aunt Lute), 1987.

———, 'Chicana Artists: Exploring *Nepantla, el Lugar de la Frontera*', in Antonia Darder and Rodolfo D Torres (eds.), *The Latino Studies Reader: Culture, Economy, and Society* (Malden and Oxford: Blackwell Publishers, 1998), 163–9.

Appadorai, A, *Select Documents on India's Foreign Policy and Relations, 1947–1972* (Delhi: Oxford University Press, 1982).

Ashikho-Daili-Mao, *Nagas: Problems and Politics* (New Delhi: Ashish Publishing House, 1992).

Asiwaju, AI (ed.), *Partitioned Africans: Ethnic Relations across Africa's International Boundaries, 1884–1984* (London and Lagos: C Hurst & Company/ University of Lagos Press, 1985).

———, 'Partitioned Culture Areas: A Checklist,' in: AI Asiwaju (ed.), *Partitioned Africans* (1985), 252–9.

Auden, WH, *City without Walls and Other Poems* (London: Faber and Faber, 1969).

Ayoob, Mohammed, and K Subrahmanyam, *The Liberation War* (New Delhi: S Chand & Co., 1972).

Azaryahu, Maoz, 'Israeli Securityscapes', in John R Gold and George Revill (eds.), *Landscapes of Defence* (Harlow: Pearson Education Limited, 2000), 102–13.

Bal, Ellen, *'They Ask If We Eat Frogs': Social Boundaries, Ethnic Categorisation, and the Garo People of Bangladesh* (Delft: Eburon, 2000).

Banerjee, Sumanta, *In the Wake of Naxalbari: A History of the Naxalite Movement in India* (Calcutta: Subarnarekha, 1980).

Bangla Name Desh (Calcutta: Anondo Publishers, 1972).

'Bangladesh – Facts on Trafficking and Prostitution', *Coalition Against Trafficking in Women* (1998).

'Bangladesh: A New Blight on the Border', *Far Eastern Economic Review*, 100:23 (9 June 1978), 35.

Bangladesh Human Rights Practices, 1995 (Washington, DC: United States Department of State, 1996).

'Bangladesh Lodges Protest over Alleged Killings by BSF', *India Today* (20 September 1999).

Bari, MA, *Muktijuddher Roktim Smriti / Memoirs of a Blood Birth: An Account of the Liberation War and the Role Played by Mujibnagar in the Struggle for Freedom....* (Dhaka: Banimahal Prokashani, c. 1996).

Barry, Brian, and Robert E Goodin (eds.), *Free Movement: Ethical Issues in the Transnational Migration of People and of Money* (New York, etc.: Harvester Wheatsheaf, 1992).

Baruah, Sanjib, *India against Itself: Assam and the Politics of Nationality* (Philadelphia: University of California Press, 1999).

———, 'Generals as Governors: The Parallel Political Systems of Northeast India', *Himal South Asian*, 14:6 (June 2001).

Baruah, Srinath, 'Certain Observations on Informal Trade with Neighbouring Countries and Economic Prospects of the North Eastern Region', in Gurudas Das and RK Purkayastha (eds.), *Border Trade: Northeast India and Neighbouring Countries* (New Delhi: Akansha Publishing House, 2000), 53–86.

Baud, Michiel, and Willem van Schendel, 'Toward a Comparative History of Borderlands', *Journal of World History*, 8:2 (1997), 211–42.

Baxter, Craig, *Jana Sangh: A Biography of an Indian Political Party* (Philadelphia: University of Pennsylvania Press, 1969).

Bayart, Jean-François, Stephen Ellis, and Béatrice Hibou, *The Criminalization of the State in Africa* (Oxford / Bloomington: Currey/ Indiana University Press, 1999).

Berdahl, Daphne, *Where the World Ended: Re-Unification and Identity in the German Borderland* (Berkeley, etc.: University of California Press, 1999).

Bertrand, Gilles (ed.), 'La partition en question: Bosnie-Herzégovine, Caucase, Chypre', *Cahiers d'études sur la Méditerranée Orientale et le Monde Turco-Iranien*, 34 (2002), 137–233.

Bhasin, Avtar Singh (ed.), *India-Bangladesh Relations: Documents – 1971–2002* (New Delhi: Geetika Publishers, 2003), 5 Volumes.

Bhattacharjee, SR, *Tribal Insurgency in Tripura: A Study in Exploration of Causes* (New Delhi: Inter-India Publications, 1989).

Bhattacharya, Ajay, *Nankar Bidroho* (Dhaka: Punthipotro, 1973–6; 2 vols.).

Bhattacharya, Birendra Kumar, *Murshidabad: West Bengal District Gazetteers* (Alipore: West Bengal Government Press, 1979).

Bhattacharyya, Bhubaneswar, *The Troubled Border: Some Facts About Boundary Disputes Between Assam-Nagaland, Assam-Arunachal Pradesh, Assam-Meghalaya and Assam-Mizoram* (Guwahati: Lawyer's Book Stall, 1995).

Bhattacharyya, Gayatri, *Refugee Rehabilitation and Its Impact on Tripura's Economy* (New Delhi/ Guwahati: Omsons Publications, 1988).

Bhattacharyya, Harihar, 'The Emergence of Tripuri Nationalism, 1948–1950', *South Asia Research*, 9:1 (1989), 54–71.

Bhaumik, Subir, Meghna Guhathakurta, and Sabyasachi Basu Ray Chaudhury (eds.), *Living on the Edge: Essays on the Chittagong Hill Tracts* (Calcutta: South Asia Forum for Human Rights/ Calcutta Research Group, 1997).

Bikram-Kisor, Sahadev, and Jagadis Gan-Chaudhuri (comp.), *Tripura: Historical Documents* (Calcutta: Firma KLM Private Limited, 1994).

Bose, Ajoy, 'Nation in Migration', *Time* (11 August 1997).

Bose, Sugata, *Agrarian Bengal: Economy, Social Structure and Politics, 1919–1947* (Cambridge: Cambridge University Press, 1986).

Bose, Tapan K, and Rita Manchanda (eds.), *States, Citizens and Outsiders: The Uprooted Peoples of South Asia* (Kathmandu: South Asia Forum for Human Rights, 1997).

Bovenkerk, Frank, *La Bella Bettien* (Amsterdam: Meulenhoff, 1995).

Boyce, James K, *Agrarian Impasse in Bengal: Institutional Constraints to Technological Change* (Oxford: Oxford University Press, 1987).

Brenner, Neil, 'Between Fixity and Motion: Accumulation, Territorial Organization and the Historical Geography of Spatial Scales', *Environment and Planning D: Society and Space*, 16 (1998), 459–81.

———, 'Beyond State-Centrism? Space, Territoriality, and Geographical Scale in Globalization Studies', *Theory and Society*, 28 (1999), 39–78.

———, 'The Limits to Scale? Methodological Reflections on Scalar Structuration', *Progress in Human Geography*, 25:4 (2001), 591–614.

Brown, J Coggin, and AK Dey, *India's Mineral Wealth: A Guide to the Occurrences and Economics of the Useful Minerals of India, Pakistan and Burma* (London: Oxford University Press, 1955).

Butalia, Urvashi, *The Other Side of Violence: Voices from the Partition of India* (New Delhi: Penguin Books, 1998).

———, 'An Archive with a Difference: Partition Letters', in Suvir Kaul (ed.), *The Partitions of Memory: The Afterlife of the Division of India* (Delhi: Permanent Black, 2001), 208–41.

Chabal, Patrick, and Jean-Pascal Daloz, *Africa Works: Disorder as a Political Instrument* (Oxford/ Bloomington: James Currey/ Indiana University Press, 1999).

Chakma, AB, 'Look Back From Exile: A Chakma Experience', in Wolfgang Mey (ed.), *They Are Now Burning Village After Village: Genocide in the Chittagong Hill Tracts, Bangladesh* (Copenhagen: IWGIA, 1984), 35–62.

Chakma, Siddhartho, *Proshongo: Parbotyo Chottogram* (Calcutta: Nath Brothers, 1985–6 [1392 BE]).

Chakrabarti, Prafulla K, *The Marginal Men: The Refugees and the Left Political Syndrome in West Bengal* (Calcutta: Naya Udyog, 1999; 2nd ed.).

Chakrabarty, Saroj, *With Dr. B.C. Roy and Other Chief Ministers (a Record Upto 1962)* (Calcutta: Benson's, 1974).

Chatterjee, RK, *India's Land Borders: Problems and Challenges* (Delhi: Sterling Publishers, 1978).

Chatterji, Joya, *Bengal Divided: Hindu Communalism and Partition, 1932–1947* (Cambridge: Cambridge University Press, 1995).

———, 'The Fashioning of a Frontier: The Radcliffe Line and Bengal's Border Landscape, 1947–52', *Modern Asian Studies*, 33:1 (1999), 185–242.

————, 'Right or Charity? The Debate over Relief and Rehabilitation in West Bengal, 1947–50', in Suvir Kaul (ed.), *The Partitions of Memory: The Afterlife of the Division of India* (Delhi: Permanent Black, 2001), 74–110.

Chattopadhyay, Dilip Kumar, *History of the Assamese Movement since 1947* (Calcutta: Minerva, 1990).

Chattopadhyay, Suhrid Shankar, 'Terror in the Sunderbans', *Frontline*, 18:15 (21 July–3 August 2001).

Chaturvedi, Sanjay, 'Common Pasts and Dividing Futures: A Critical Geopolitics of Indo-Pak Border(s)', in Paul Ganster (ed.), *Cooperation, Environment and Sustainability in Border Regions* (San Diego: San Diego State University Press/ Institute for Regional Studies of the Californias, 2001), 405–22.

————, 'Process of Othering in the Case of India and Pakistan', *Journal of Economic and Social Geography*, 93:2 (2002), 149–59.

————, 'The Excess of Geopolitics: Partition of "British India"', in Stefano Bianchini, Rada Iveković, Ranabir Samaddar and Sanjay Chaturvedi, *Partitions: Reshaping States and Minds* (forthcoming), 119–53.

Chaudhuri, Binay Bhushan, 'Commercialisation of Agriculture', in Sirajul Islam (ed.), *History of Bangladesh, 1704–1971* (Dhaka: Asiatic Society of Bangladesh, 1992), vol. 2, 371–427.

Chaudhuri, Kalyan, 'Protest in West Bengal', *Frontline* (15–28 August 1998).

Cheater, AP, 'Transcending the State? Gender and Borderline Constructions of Citizenship in Zimbabwe', in Thomas M Wilson and Hastings Donnan (eds.), *Border Identities: Nation and State at International Frontiers* (Cambridge: Cambridge University Press, 1998), 191–214.

Chittagong Hill Tracts Commission, *Life Is Not Ours: Land and Human Rights in the Chittagong Hill Tracts, Bangladesh*, Report (1991); *Update 1* (1992); *Update 2* (1994); *Update 3* (1997); *Update 4* (2000) (Copenhagen/ Amsterdam: International Work Group on Indigenous Affairs (IWGIA)/ Organising Committee Chittagong Hill Tracts Campaign, 1991–2000).

Chopra, PN, *The Sardar of India: Biography of Vallabhbhai Patel* (New Delhi: Allied Publishers, 1995).

The Code of Criminal Procedure, 1898 (Act V of 1898) [as Modified up to the 31st December 1980] (Dacca: Bangladesh Forms and Publications Office, 1981).

Cole, John W, and Eric R Wolf, *The Hidden Frontier: Ecology and Ethnicity in an Alpine Valley* (New York: Academic Press, 1974).

Cooper, Adrienne, *Sharecropping and Sharecroppers' Struggles in Bengal, 1930–1950* (Calcutta: KP Bagchi, 1988).

Cooper, Frederick, 'What Is the Concept of Globalization Good For? An African Historian's Perspective', *African Affairs*, 100:399 (2001), 189–213.

Copland, Ian, 'The Further Shores of Partition: Ethnic Cleansing in Rajasthan, 1947', *Past and Present*, 160 (1998), 203–39.

Cox, Kevin, 'Spaces of Dependence, Spaces of Engagement and the Politics of Scale, Or: Looking for Local Politics', *Political Geography*, 17:1 (1998), 1–23.

Crow, Ben, with Alan Lindquist, and David Wilson, *Sharing the Ganges: The Politics and Technology of River Development* (Delhi: Sage Publications, 1995).

Cumming, JG, *Survey and Settlement of the Chakla Roshnabad Estate in the Districts of Tippera and Noakhali, 1892–99* (Calcutta: Bengal Secretariat Press, 1899).

Damas, Marius, *Approaching Naxalbari* (Calcutta: Radical Impression, 1991).

Das, Amiya Kumar, *Assam's Agony: A Socio-Economic and Political Analysis* (New Delhi:

Lancers Publishers, 1982).

Das, Veena, *Critical Events: An Anthropological Perspective on Contemporary India* (Delhi: Oxford University Press, 1995).

Das Gupta, Jyoti Bhusan, *Indo-Pakistan Relations (1947–1955)* (Amsterdam: De Brug-Djambatan, 1958).

Das Gupta, Malabika, 'Greater Mizoram Issue and Tripura', *Economic and Political Weekly*, 21 (13 September 1986): 1629–30.

———, 'Nationalities, Ethnicity and Cultural Identity: A Case Study of the Mizos of Tripura', in B Pakem (ed.), *Nationality, Ethnicity and Cultural Identity in North-East India* (New Delhi: Omsons, 1990), 369–74.

Das Gupta, Ranajit, *Economy, Society and Politics in Bengal: Jalpaiguri 1869–1947* (Delhi: Oxford University Press, 1992).

Dasgupta, Abhijit, *Growth with Equity: The New Technology and Agrarian Change in Bengal* (Delhi: Manohar, 1998).

Dasgupta, Anindita, 'Denial and Resistance: Sylheti Partition "Refugees" in Assam', *Contemporary South Asia*, 10:3 (2001), 343–60.

Dasgupta, Subodh, 'Gouribari: What Next?' *Economic and Political Weekly* (29 September 1984): 1696.

De, Amalendu, *Swadhin Bangabhumi Gathaner Parikalpana* (Calcutta: Ratna Prakashan, 1975).

'Die Todesgrenze der Deutschen', *Der Spiegel* (24 June 1991, 58–83; 1 July 1991, 52–71; and 8 July 1992, 102–16).

Disturbances in the Punjab, 1947 (Islamabad: National Documentation Centre, 1995).

Donnan, Hastings, and Dieter Haller, 'Liminal No More: The Relevance of Borderland Studies', *Ethnologia Europaea: The Journal of European Ethnology*, 30:2 (2000), 7–22.

Donnan, Hastings, and Thomas M Wilson, *Borders: Frontiers of Identity, Nation and State* (Oxford and New York: Berg, 1999).

Downs, Roger M, and David Stea, *Maps in Minds: Reflections on Cognitive Mapping* (New York, etc.: Harper & Row, 1977).

Dutta, Rajesh, 'Coal Export from Meghalaya to Bangladesh: A Case Study of the Barsora Trade Route', in Gurudas Das and RK Purkayastha (eds.), *Border Trade: Northeast India and Neighbouring Countries* (New Delhi: Akansha Publishing House, 2000), 200–8.

Duyker, Edward AJ, *Tribal Guerrillas: West Bengal's Santals and the Naxalite Movement* (Delhi: Oxford University Press, 1987).

East Bengal, Government of, Home Department (Political), *Note on the Genesis of Communal Disturbances in West Bengal* (Dacca: East Bengal Government Press, 1950).

East Pakistan District Gazetteers: Dacca (Dacca: East Pakistan Government Press, 1969).

East Pakistan District Gazetteers: Sylhet (Dacca: Government Press, 1970).

Eaton, Richard M, *The Rise of Islam and the Bengal Frontier, 1204–1760* (Berkeley: University of California Press, 1993).

Festinger, Leon, *A Theory of Cognitive Dissonance* (Evanston, Ill. etc: Row, Peterson, 1957).

Finkenauer, James O, 'Russian Transnational Organized Crime and Human Trafficking', in David Kyle and Rey Koslowski (eds.), *Global Human Smuggling: Comparative Perspectives* (Baltimore and London: The Johns Hopkins University Press, 2001), 166–86.

First Annual Report on the Ansars (Dacca, 1949).

Five Years of Pakistan (August 1947–August 1952) (Karachi: Pakistan Publications, 1952).

Fleischmann, Klaus, *Arakan: Konfliktregion zwischen Birma und Bangladesh* (Hamburg: Institut für Asienkunde, 1981).

Flyn, Donna K, "'We Are the Border": Identity, Exchange and the State along the Bénin-Nigeria Border', *American Ethnologist*, 24:2 (1997), 311–30.

Foucher, Michel, *Fronts et frontières: Un tour du monde géopolitique* (Paris: Fayard, 1991).

Fraser, TG, *Partition in Ireland, India and Palestine: Theory and Practice* (London and Basingstoke: The Macmillan Press, 1984).

Frederick, John, 'The Black Route', in John Frederick and Thomas L Kelly (eds.), *Fallen Angels: The Sex Workers of South Asia* (New Delhi: Lustre Press/ Roli Books, 2000), 68–9.

Frederick, John, and Thomas L. Kelly (eds.), *Fallen Angels: The Sex Workers of South Asia* (New Delhi: Lustre Press / Roli Books, 2000).

Gallant, Thomas W, 'Brigandage, Piracy, Capitalism, and State-Formation: Transnational Crime from a Historical World-Systems Perspective', in Josiah McC Heyman (ed.), *States and Illegal Practices* (Oxford and New York: Berg, 1999), 25–61.

Ganster, Paul (ed.), *Cooperation, Environment and Sustainability in Border Regions* (San Diego: San Diego State University Press/ Institute for Regional Studies of the Californias, 2001).

Gardner, Katy, *Global Migrants, Local Lives: Travel and Transformation in Rural Bangladesh* (Oxford: Clarendon Press, 1995).

Ghafur, Abdul, Muinul Islam, and Naushad Faiz, *Illegal International Trade in Bangladesh: Impact on the Domestic Economy* (Dhaka: Bangladesh Institute of Development Studies, Phase I 1990; Phase II 1991).

Ghosh, Gautam, "'God is a Refugee": Nationality, Morality and History in the 1947 Partition of India', *Social Analysis*, 42:1 (1998), 33–62.

Ghosh, Papiya, 'Partition's Biharis', *Comparative Studies of South Asia, Africa and the Middle East*, 17:2 (1997), 21–34.

Ghosh, Partha S, *Cooperation and Conflict in South Asia* (Delhi: Manohar, 1995).

Ghosh, SK, *Unquiet Border* (New Delhi: Ashish Publishing House, 1993).

Glassman, Jim, 'State Power Beyond the "Territorial Trap": The Internationalization of the State', *Political Geography*, 18:6 (1999), 669–96.

Goswami, Dhirananda, *Nodiyar Songkot*, vol. 1 (Santipur: Nodiyar Progotisil Kormider pokkhe, 1951).

Gravers, Mikael, 'The Karen Making of a Nation', in Stein Tønnesson and Hans Antlöv (eds.), *Asian Forms of the Nation* (London: Curzon Press, 1996), 237–69.

Gregory, Derek, *Geographical Imaginations* (Cambridge, Mass./ Oxford: Blackwell, 1994).

Gupta, Ravi, and Sanjay Kumar, 'Rules on Mapping Technologies in India Heading Nowhere!', *GISDevelopment* (November–December 1998).

Gupto, Promotho, *Muktijuddhe Adibashi (Moymonsingh)* (Calcutta: National Book Agency, 1964).

Gutierrez-Jones, Carl, *Rethinking the Borderlands: Between Chicano Culture and Legal Discourse* (Berkeley: University of California Press, 1995).

Hanagan, Michael P, 'An Agenda for Transnational Labor History' (unpublished paper, 2002).

Haque, Azizul, 'Bangladesh 1979: Cry for a Sovereign Parliament', *Asian Survey*, 20:2 (1980), 217–30.

Hashmi, Taj ul-Islam, *Pakistan as a Peasant Utopia: The Communalization of Class Politics in East Bengal, 1920–1947* (Boulder, Col.: Westview Press, 1992).

Hazarika, Sanjoy, *Strangers of the Mist: Tales of War & Peace from India's Northeast* (Delhi: Viking, 1994).

———, *Rites of Passage: Border Crossings, Imagined Homelands, India's East and Bangladesh* (New Delhi: Penguin Books, 2000).

Heyman, Josiah McC, 'The Mexico-United States Border in Anthropology: A Critique and Reformulation', *Journal of Political Ecology*, 1(1994), 43–65.

Heyman, Josiah McC (ed.), *States and Illegal Practices* (Oxford/ New York: Berg, 1999).

Hodson, HV, *The Great Divide: Britain - India – Pakistan* (New York: Atheneum, 1971).

Hossain, Golam, *General Zia and the BNP: Political Transformation of a Military Regime* (Dhaka: University Press Limited, 1988).

Hossain, Mobarak, *Chorer Manush Chorer Jibon* (Dhaka: Mass Line Media Centre, 1999).

Hossain, Monirul, 'Terrorism in Post-Colonial Assam', *The Eastern Anthropologist*, 52:1 (1999), 13–30.

Howitt, Richard, 'Scale as Relation: Musical Metaphors of Geographical Space,' *Area*, 30:1 (1998), 49–58.

Human Rights Watch, *Landmine Monitor Report 2000: Toward a Mine-Free World* (New York, etc.: Human Rights Watch, 2000).

———, *Malaysia/Burma – Living in Limbo: Burmese Rohingyas in Malaysia* (New York, etc.: Human Rights Watch/ Asia, 2000).

———, *Burma/Bangladesh – Burmese Refugees in Bangladesh: Still No Durable Solution* (New York, etc.: Human Rights Watch/ Asia, 2000).

Hune, Shirley, 'Asian-American Studies and Asian Studies: Boundaries and Borderlands of Ethnic Studies and Area Studies', in Johnella E Butler (ed.), *Color-Line to Borderlands: The Matrix of American Ethnic Studies* (Seattle/ London: University of Washington Press, 2001), 227–37.

Hussain, Monirul, *The Assam Movement: Class, Ideology and Identity* (Delhi: Manak Publications, 1993).

India, Government of, *Reforming the National Security System – Recommendations of the Group of Ministers* (New Delhi: Ministry of Defence, 2001).

'India-Bangladesh Border: Dangerous Situation', *Economic and Political Weekly* (30 March 1991).

India/Bangladesh: "Push In – Push Out" Practices at the Border Not Acceptable (London: Amnesty International, 2003).

India – Para-Military Forces (New Delhi: Institute of Peace and Conflict Studies, 1998).

Influx – Infiltratie uit Oost-Pakistan ('s-Gravenhage: Information Service of India, Ambassade van India, 1964).

Inter-Dominion Conference at New Delhi (December 6–14, 1948), Appendix V: Boundary Disputes (New Delhi, 1948).

Islam, Sirajul, *Rural History of Bangladesh: A Source Study* (Dacca: Tito Islam, 1977).

Iveković, Rada, 'From the Nation to Partition, through Partition to the Nation: Readings', *Transeuropéennes*, 19/20 (2000–1), 201–25.

Jahan, Rounaq (ed.), *Three Decades of Bangladesh: Promise and Performance* (Dhaka: University Press Limited, 2000).

Jalal, Ayesha, *The Sole Spokesman: Jinnah, the Muslim League and the Demand for Pakistan* (Cambridge: Cambridge University Press, 1985).

Jasimuddin, *Nokshi Kāthar Math* (Calcutta: Pabalisarsa, 1975; 4th ed. [1928]).

Jha, Dinesh Chandra, *Indo-Pakistan Relations (1960–65)* (Patna: Bharati Bhawan, 1972).

Jones, Katherine T, 'Scale as Epistemology', *Political Geography*, 17:1 (1998), 25–8.

Kamal, Mesbah, and Ishani Chokroborti, *Nacholer Krishok Bidroho Shomokalin Rajniti O Ila Mitro* (Dhaka: Muktijuddho Bongobondhu O Bangladesh Gobeshona Institute, 2001).

Kamaluddin, S, 'Slap in the Middle of a Row: Negotiations over the Ownership of a Tiny Island Strain Relations between New Delhi and Dacca', *Far Eastern Economic Review*,

108:19 (2–8 May 1980), 38.

———, 'Bangladesh: The Country Has Become a Smuggler's Paradise: Trade without Tariff', *Far Eastern Economic Review*, 153:32 (8 August 1991), 16.

Kar, M, *Muslims in Assam Politics* (New Delhi: Vikas Publishing House, 1997).

Kaul, Suvir (ed.), *The Partitions of Memory: The Afterlife of the Division of India* (Delhi: Permanent Black, 2001).

Kearney, Michael, 'Transnationalism in California and Mexico at the End of Empire', in Thomas M. Wilson and Hastings Donnan (eds.), *Border Identities: Nation and State at International Frontiers* (Cambridge: Cambridge University Press, 1998), 117–41.

Keck, Margaret E, and Kathryn Sikkink, *Activists Beyond Borders: Advocacy Networks in International Politics* (Ithaca, NY Cornell University Press, 1998).

Kelly, Philip F, 'Globalization, Power and the Politics of Scale in the Philippines', *Geoforum*, 28:2 (1997), 151–71.

Kemp, A, and U Ben-Eliezer, 'Dramatizing Sovereignty: The Construction of Territorial Dispute in the Israeli-Egyptian Border at Taba', *Political Geography*, 19 (2000), 315–44.

Khan, Mohammed Ayub, *Friends Not Masters* (London: Oxford University Press, 1967).

Khan, Sadeq, 'Indian BSF Go Berserk', *Holiday* (27 August 1999).

Kirkwood, Neville A, *Independent India's Troubled Northeast, 1952–69: An Australian Missionary's Story*. (n.p.: Griffith University, Centre for the Study of Australia-Asia Relations, 1996).

Klieman, Aaron S, 'The Resolution of Conflicts through Territorial Partition: The Palestine Experience', *Comparative Studies in Society and History*, 22:2 (1980), 281–300.

Krishna, Sankaran, 'Cartographic Anxiety: Mapping the Body Politic in India', in Michael J Shapiro and Hayward R Alker (eds.), *Challenging Boundaries: Global Flows, Territorial Identities* (Minneapolis: University of Minnesota Press, 1996), 193–214.

———, *Postcolonial Insecurities: India, Sri Lanka and the Question of Nationhood* (Minneapolis: University of Minnesota Press, 1999).

Kumar, Arun, *The Black Economy in India* (New Delhi, etc.: Penguin Books India, 1999).

Kumar, Radha, 'The Troubled History of Partition', *Foreign Affairs*, 76:1 (1997), 22–34.

———, 'Settling Partition Hostilities: Lessons Learnt, the Options Ahead', *Transeuropéennes*, 19/20 (2000–1), 9–28.

Kyle, David, and John Dale, 'Smuggling the State Back In: Agents of Human Smuggling Reconsidered', in David Kyle and Rey Koslowski (eds.), *Global Human Smuggling: Comparative Perspectives* (Baltimore and London: The Johns Hopkins University Press, 2001), 29–57.

Kyle, David, and Rey Koslowski (eds.), *Global Human Smuggling: Comparative Perspectives* (Baltimore and London: The Johns Hopkins University Press, 2001).

The Labour to Be Led in Fighting against Disturbances; Anti-Riot Leaflet No. 3 (Calcutta: Communist Party, 1950).

Lefebvre, Henri, *De l'État* (Paris: Union Générale d'Éditions, 1976–8, 4 vols.).

———, *The Production of Space* (Oxford: Blackwell, 1991).

Lifschultz, Lawrence, *Bangladesh: The Unfinished Revolution* (London: Zed Press, 1979).

Lin, Sharat G, and Madan C Paul, 'Bangladeshi Migrants in Delhi: Social Insecurity, State Power, and Captive Vote Banks', *Bulletin of Concerned Asian Scholars*, 27:1 (1995), 3–27.

Lintner, Bertil, 'Distant Exile: Rohingyas Seek New Life in Middle East', *Far Eastern Economic Review*, 156:4 (28 January 1993), 23.

———, *Burma in Revolt: Opium and Insurgency since 1948* (Chiangmai: Silkworm Books, 1999).

Llewellyn, Bernard, *From the Back Streets of Bengal* (London: George Allen & Unwin, 1955).

Ludden, David, *India and South Asia: A Short History* (Oxford: Oneworld Publications, 2002).

———, 'The First Boundary of Bangladesh on Sylhet's Northern Frontiers', *Journal of the Asiatic Society of Bangladesh* (forthcoming).

Luke, Timothy W, and Gearóid Ó Tuathail, 'The Fraying Modern Map: Failed States and Contraband Capitalism', *Geopolitics*, 3:3 (1998), 14–33.

McCoy, Alfred W, 'Requiem for a Drug Lord: State and Commodity in the Career of Khun Sa', in Josiah McC Heyman (ed.), *States and Illegal Practices* (Oxford and New York: Berg, 1999), 129–67.

McGregor, JoAnn, 'Violence and Social Change in a Border Economy: War in the Maputo Hinterland, 1984–1992', *Journal of Southern African Studies*, 24:1 (1998), 37–60.

Mahanta, Prafulla Kumar, *The Tussle between the Citizens and Foreigners in Assam* (Delhi: Vikas, 1986).

Mahatdhanobol, Vorasakdi (and edited by Pornpimon Trichot), *Chinese Women in the Thai Sex Trade* (Bangkok: Institute of Asian Studies, Chulalongkorn University, 1998).

Mansergh, Nicholas (editor-in-chief), *The Transfer of Power, 1942–7: Constitutional Relations between Britain and India* (London: Her Majesty's Stationery Office, 1970–83, 12 vols.).

Marston, Sallie A, 'The Social Construction of Scale,' *Progress in Human Geography*, 24:2 (2000), 219–42.

Martínez, Oscar, *Border People: Life and Society in the U.S.–Mexico Borderlands* (Tucson: University of Arizona Press, 1994).

———, 'The Dynamics of Border Interaction,' in: Clive H Schofield (ed.), *Global Boundaries: World Boundaries, Volume I* (London: Routledge, 1994), 8–14.

Maswani, AMK, *Subversion in East Pakistan* (Lahore: Amir Publications, 1979).

Mathur, SM, 'Restrictions on Survey of India Maps: Logic and Rationale,' *GISDevelopment* (July–August 1999).

Menon, Ritu, and Kamla Bhasin, *Borders & Boundaries: Women in India's Partition* (Delhi: Kali for Women, 1998).

Michaelson, Scott, and David E Johnson (eds), *Border Theory: The Limits of Cultural Politics* (Minneapolis and London: University of Minnesota Press, 1997).

Mishra, Brahmanand, 'India: Tackling Hostility on Two Fronts', *Far Eastern Economic Review*, 84:18 (6 May 1974), 14.

Misra, Udayon, *The Periphery Strikes Back: Challenges to the Nation-State in Assam and Nagaland* (Shimla: Indian Institute of Advanced Studies, 2000).

Mohsin, Amena, *The Politics of Nationalism: The Case of the Chittagong Hill Tracts, Bangladesh* (Dhaka: University Press Limited, 1997).

———, 'Partitioned Lives Partitioned Lands', in Imtiaz Ahmed (ed.), *Memories of a Genocidal Partition: The Haunting Tales of Victims, Witnesses and Perpetrators* (Colombo: Regional Centre for Strategic Studies, 2002), 19–42.

Monmonier, Mark, *Spying with Maps: Surveillance Technologies and the Future of Privacy* (Chicago: University of Chicago Press, 2002).

Morgenstern, Oskar, *On the Accuracy of Economic Observations* (Princeton, NJ: Princeton University Press, 1963; 2nd ed.).

Mosley, Leonard, *The Last Days of the British Raj* (London: Weidenfeld and Nicolson, 1961).

Muhith, AMA, *The Deputy Commissioner in East Pakistan* (Dacca: National Institute of Public Administration, 1968).

Mukherjea, SN, *A Brief Agricultural Geography of West Bengal* (Calcutta: Directorate of Agriculture, Government of West Bengal, 1956).

Nag, Sajal, *Roots of Ethnic Conflict: Nationality Question in North-East India* (Delhi: Manohar, 1990).

Nayar, Kuldip, *Distant Neighbours: A Tale of the Subcontinent* (New Delhi: Vikas, 1972).

Nazem, Nurul Islam, 'The Impact of River Control on an International Boundary: The Case of the Bangladesh-India Border', in Carl Grundy-Warr (ed.), *Eurasia: World Boundaries* (London and New York: Routledge, 1994), 101–10.

Nevins, Joseph, *Operation Gatekeeper: The Rise of the 'Illegal Alien' and the Making of the U.S.–Mexico Boundary* (New York and London: Routledge, 2002).

Nibedon, Nirmal, *Nagaland: The Night of the Guerrillas* (Delhi: Lancers Publishers, 1978).

———, *Mizoram: The Dagger Brigade* (Delhi: Lancers Publishers, 1980).

Nora, Pierre (ed.), *Les lieux de mémoire* (Paris: Éditions Gallimard, 1997), 3 vols.

Nugent, Paul, 'Power Versus Knowledge: Smugglers and the State Along Ghana's Eastern Frontier, 1920–1992', in Michael Rösler and Tobias Wendl (eds.), *Frontiers and Borderlands: Anthropological Perspectives* (Frankfurt am Main, etc.: Peter Lang, 1999), 77–99.

———, *Smugglers, Secessionists & Loyal Citizens on the Ghana-Togo Frontier: The Lie of the Borderlands Since 1914* (Oxford: James Curry/ Athens: Ohio University Press/ Legon: Sub-Saharan Publishers, 2002).

Ó Tuathail, Gearóid, 'Borderless Worlds? Problematising Discourses of Deterritorialisation', in Nurit Kliot and David Newman (eds.), *Geopolitics at the End of the Twentieth Century: The Changing Political Map* (London: Frank Cass, 2000), 139–54.

One Year of Popular Government in East Pakistan (Dacca: Government of East Pakistan, 1957).

Orleans, Peter, 'Differential Cognition of Urban Residents: Effects of Social Scale on Mapping', in Roger M Downs and David Stea (eds.), *Image and Environment: Cognitive Mapping and Spatial Behavior* (Chicago: Aldine Publishing Company, 1973), 115–30.

Paasi, Anssi, *Territories, Boundaries and Consciousness: The Changing Geographies of the Finnish-Russian Border* (Chichester, etc.: John Wiley & Sons, 1996).

———, 'Boundaries as Social Process and Discourse: The Finnish-Russian Border,' *Regional Studies*, 33:7 (1999), 669–80.

Padmanabhan, R, 'The Deportation Drive', *Frontline* (15–28 August 1998).

Painter, Joe, *Politics, Geography and 'Political Geography': A Critical Perspective* (London, etc.: Arnold, 1995).

Pakistan, Government of, *Pakistan O Bharoter Moddhe Jatayater Jonne Passport O Visa Niyomaboli / Passport System to Regulate the Entry of Indian Nationals into Pakistan* (Dacca: Ministry of Foreign Affairs and Commonwealth Relations, 1952). See also: *Passport System*, 1952.

Pakistan 1957–1958 (Karachi: Pakistan Publications, 1958).

Pakrasi, Kanti B, *The Uprooted: A Sociological Study of the Refugees of West Bengal, India* (Calcutta: Editions Indian, 1971).

Palit, DK, *The Lightning Campaign: The Indo-Pakistan War 1971* (Salisbury: Compton Press, 1972).

Pandey, Gyanendra, 'Voices from the Edge: The Struggle to Write Subaltern Histories', in Vinayak Chaturvedi (ed.), *Mapping Subaltern Studies and the Postcolonial* (London and New York: Verso, 2000), 281–99.

———, *Remembering Partition: Violence, Nationalism and History in India* (Cambridge: Cambridge University Press, 2001).

Papademetriou, Demetrios G, and Deborah Waller Meyers (eds.), *Caught in the Middle: Border Communities in an Era of Globalization* (Washington, DC: Carnegie Endowment for International Peace, 2001).

Partition Proceedings, Volume VI: Reports of the Members and Awards of the Chairman of the Boundary Commissions (New Delhi: Government of India, Partition Secretariat, 1950).

Passport System to Regulate the Entry of Indian Nationals into Pakistan (Dacca: East Bengal Government Press, 1952). See also: Pakistan, 1952.

'Porous Borders, Divided Selves: A Symposium on Partitions in the East', *Seminar*, no. 510 (February 2002).

Prabhakar, MS, 'Ferment in Manipur', *Frontline* 6:1 (1989), 32–9.

Prescott, JRV, *Political Frontiers and Boundaries* (London: Unwin Hyman, 1987).

Rabinowitz, Dan, 'National Identity on the Frontier: Palestinians in the Israeli Education System', in Thomas M Wilson and Hastings Donnan (eds.), *Border Identities: Nation and State at International Frontiers* (Cambridge: Cambridge University Press, 1998), 142–61.

Radcliffe, Cyril, *Report of the Bengal Boundary Commission* (New Delhi, 12 August 1947).

————, *Report of the Bengal Boundary Commission (Sylhet District)* (New Delhi, 13 August 1947).

Rae, Heather, *State Identities and the Homogenisation of Peoples* (Cambridge: Cambridge University Press, 2002).

Rahman, Atiur, and Abdur Razzaque, 'Informal Border Trade between Bangladesh and India: An Empirical Study in Selected Areas', in Forrest E Cookson and AKM Shamsul Alam (eds.), *Towards Greater Sub-regional Economic Cooperation: Limitation, Obstacles, and Benefits* (Dhaka: University Press Limited, 2002), 129–213.

Rahman, Maseeh, 'Separated at Birth', *Time* (11 August 1997).

Rahman, Md. Mahbubar, and Willem van Schendel, '"I Am Not a Refugee": Rethinking Partition Migration', *Modern Asian Studies*, 37:3 (2003), 551–84.

Rajagopalan, Rajesh, '"Restoring Normalcy": The Evolution of the Indian Army's Counterinsurgency Doctrine', *Small Wars and Insurgencies*, 11:1 (2000), 44–68.

Ram, Mohan, 'Eyeball to Eyeball: The Issues That Triggered the Massacres in Assam State in February Remain Unresolved, and Both Sides Are Standing Firm', *Far Eastern Economic Review*, 120:20 (19 May 1983), 29.

Ramachandran, Sujata, 'Of Boundaries and Border Crossings: Undocumented Bangladeshi "Infiltrators" and the Hegemony of Hindu Nationalism in India', *Interventions*, 1:2 (1999), 235–53.

Rao, Nivedita, et al., see: Internet sources.

Ray, Jayanta Kumar, *Democracy and Nationalism on Trial: A Study of East Pakistan* (Simla: Indian Institute of Advanced Study, 1968).

Ray, Manas, 'Growing Up Refugee: On Memory and Locality', *History Workshop Journal*, no. 53 (2002), 149–79.

Razac, Olivier, *Barbed Wire: A Political History* (New York: The New Press, 2002).

Razzaq, Abdur, and Mahfuzul Haque, *A Tale of Refugees: Rohingyas in Bangladesh* (Dhaka: The Centre for Human Rights, 1995).

Red Light Traffic: The Trade in Nepali Girls (Kathmandu: ABC/ Nepal, 1996).

Relyea, Scott, 'Trans-State Entities: Postmodern Cracks in the Great Westphalian Dam', *Geopolitics*, 3:2 (1998), 30–61.

Report of the Committee of Review on Educational Facilities for New Migrants from East Pakistan to West Bengal (Calcutta: West Bengal Ministry of Labour, Employment and Rehabilitation, 1968).

Report to the Government of Pakistan on a Survey of Labour Problems in Inland Water Transport in East Pakistan (Geneva: International Labour Office, 1961).

The Return of the Rohingya Refugees to Burma: Voluntary Repatriation or Refoulement? (Washington, DC: US Committee for Refugees, 1995).

Ries, Nancy, '"Honest Bandits" and "Warped People": Russian Narratives about Money, Corruption, and Moral Decay', in: Carol J Greenhouse, Elizabeth Mertz and Kay B Warren (eds.), *Ethnography in Unstable Places: Everyday Lives in Contexts of Dramatic Political Change* (Durham and London: Duke University Press, 2002), 276–315.

Rohingya Reader (Amsterdam: Burma Centrum Nederland, 1995; 2 vols.).

Roitman, Janet, 'The Garrison-Entrepôt', *Cahiers d'Études Africaines*, 38:2–4 (1998), 297–329.

Rolt, Francis, *On the Brink of Bengal* (London: John Murray, 1991).

Rösler, Michael, and Tobias Wendl (eds.), *Frontiers and Borderlands: Anthropological Perspectives* (Frankfurt am Main, etc.: Peter Lang, 1999).

Roy, Asish Kumar, *The Spring Thunder and After: A Survey of the Maoist and Ultra-Leftist Movements in India, 1962–75* (Calcutta: Minerva, 1975).

Roy-Chaudhury, Rahul, *Trends in the Delimitation of India's Maritime Boundaries* (Delhi: Institute of Defense Studies and Analysis, 1998).

Rumley, D, and JV Minghi (eds.), *The Geography of Border Landscapes* (London: Routledge, 1991).

Sack, Robert David, *Human Territoriality: Its Theory and History* (Cambridge: Cambridge University Press, 1986).

Sahlins, Peter, *Boundaries: The Making of France and Spain in the Pyrenees* (Berkeley: University of California Press, 1989).

Samaddar, Ranabir, *The Marginal Nation: Transborder Migration from Bangladesh to West Bengal* (New Delhi, etc.: Sage Publications, 1999).

———— (ed.), *Reflections on Partition in the East* (Delhi: Vikas Publishing House, 1997).

Samanta, Amiya K, *Left Extremist Movement in West Bengal: An Experiment in Armed Agrarian Struggle.* (Calcutta: Firma KLM Private Ltd., 1984).

Sambanis, Nicholas, *Ethnic Partition as a Solution to Ethnic War: An Empirical Critique of the Theoretical Literature* (Washington, DC: The World Bank, 1999).

Sánchez, Rosaura, 'Mapping the Spanish Language along a Multiethnic and Multilingual Border', in Antonia Darder and Rodolfo D Torres (eds.), *The Latino Studies Reader: Culture, Economy, and Society* (Malden and Oxford: Blackwell Publishers, 1998), 101–25.

Sarkar, Krishnakanta, 'Kakdwip Peasant Insurrection', in AR Desai (ed.), *Agrarian Struggles in India after Independence* (Delhi: Oxford University Press, 1986), 618–59.

Schaeffer, Robert K, *Severed States: Dilemmas of Democracy in a Divided World* (Lanham, MD: Rowman and Littlefield, 1999).

Scott, James C, *Seeing Like a State: How Certain Schemes to Improve the Human Condition Have Failed* (New Haven and London: Yale University Press, 1998).

Selected Indo-Pakistan Agreements (New Delhi: Ministry of External Affairs, 1970).

Sen Gupta, Jyoti, *Eclipse of East Pakistan: Chronicles of Events since Birth of East Pakistan Till October 1963* (Calcutta: Renco, 1963).

Sen, Ranjit, *Social Banditry in Bengal: A Study in Primary Resistance, 1757–1793* (Calcutta: Ratna Prakashan, 1988).

Sharma, Chavi, 'A Division of India/A Partition of the Self', in Imtiaz Ahmed (ed.), *Memories of a Genocidal Partition: The Haunting Tales of Victims, Witnesses and Perpetrators* (Colombo: Regional Centre for Strategic Studies, 2002), 1–17.

Sharma, Surya P, *India's Boundary and Territorial Disputes* (Delhi: Vikas Publications, 1971).

Sharp, Joanne P, Paul Routledge, Chris Philo and Ronan Paddison, 'Entanglements of Power: Geographies of Domination/Resistance', in Joanne P Sharp, Paul Routledge, Chris Philo and Ronan Paddison (eds.), *Entanglements of Power: Geographies of Domination/Resistance* (London and New York: Routledge, 2000), 1–42.

Shrikantia, SV, 'Restriction on Maps in India: An Anachronism That Needs Removal, *GISDevelopment* (March-April 1999).

Sidaway, JD, 'Sovereign Excesses? Portraying Postcolonial Sovereigntyscapes,' *Political Geography*, 22:2 (February 2003), 157–78.

Siddiqi, Dina M, 'In Search of Shonar Bangla', *Himal* (21 July 2003).

Siddiqui, Kamal, et al, *Land Reforms and Land Management in Bangladesh and West Bengal: A Comparative Study* (Dhaka: University Press Limited, 1988).

Singh, Amrik (ed.), *The Partition in Retrospect* (Delhi: Anamika Publishers, 2000).

Singh, Gurharpal, 'The Partition of India in a Comparative Perspective: A Long-Term View', in Ian Talbot and Gurharpal Singh (eds.), *Region and Partition: Bengal, Punjab and the Partition of the Subcontinent* (Karachi: Oxford University Press, 1999), 95–115.

Singh, Lachhman, *Indian Sword Strikes East Pakistan* (Sahibabad: Vikas Publishing House, 1979).

———, *Victory in Bangladesh* (Dehra Dun: Natraj Publishers, 1981).

'Situation of Rohingya Refugees in Bangladesh,' *The Newsletter Monthly – News and Analysis of the Arakan Rohingya National Organisation, Arakan (Burma)*, 2:2 (February 2000).

Sleightholme, Carolyn, and Indrani Sinha, *Guilty without Trial: Women in the Sex Trade in Calcutta* (Calcutta/ New Brunswick, NJ: Stree/ Rutgers University Press, 1996–7).

Small Arms Survey 2001: Profiling the Problem (Geneva/ Oxford: Graduate Institute of International Studies/ Oxford University Press, 2001).

Smith, Anthony D, 'Culture, Community and Territory: The Politics of Ethnicity and Nationalism', *International Affairs*, 72:3 (1996), 445–58.

Smith, Martin, 'Sold Down the River: Burma's Muslim Borderland', *Inside Asia* (July–August, 1986), 5–7.

———, *Burma: Insurgency and the Politics of Ethnicity* (London: Zed Press, 1994).

———, *Ethnic Groups in Burma: Development, Democracy and Human Rights* (London: Anti-Slavery Society, 1994).

Smith, Neil, 'Contours of a Spatialized Politics: Homeless Vehicles and the Production of Geographical Scale', *Social Text*, 33 (1992), 55–81.

———, 'Remaking Scale: Competition and Cooperation in Prenational and Postnational Europe', in Heikki Eskelinen and Folke Snickars (eds.), *Competitive European Peripheries* (Berlin: Springer, 1995), 59–74.

Smith, Neil, and Ward Dennis, 'The Restructuring of Geographical Scale: Coalescence and Fragmentation of the Northern Core Region', *Economic Geography*, 63 (1987), 160–82.

Soja, Edward W, *Thirdspace: Expanding the Geographical Imagination* (Cambridge, Mass.: Blackwell Publishing, 1996).

Spate, OHK, 'The Partition of the Punjab and of Bengal,' *The Geographical Journal*, 110 (1948), 201–22.

Spruyt, Hendrik, *The Sovereign State and Its Competitors: An Analysis of Systems Change* (Princeton, NJ: Princeton University Press, 1994).

Sreedhar, and John Kaniyalil, *Indo-Pak Relations: A Documentary Study* (New Delhi: ABC Publishing House, 1993).

The State of the World's Refugees: A Humanitarian Agenda (Oxford: UNHCR/ Oxford University Press, 1997).

Stoddard, ER, 'Illegal Mexican Labor in the Borderlands: Institutionalized Support of an Unlawful Practice', *Pacific Sociological Review*, 19:2 (1976), 175–210.

Swain, Ashok, *The Environmental Trap: The Ganges River Diversion, Bangladeshi Migration and Conflicts in India* (Uppsala: Uppsala University, Department of Peace and Conflict Research, 1996).

Swyngedouw, Erik, 'Excluding the Other: The Production of Scale and Scaled Politics', in Roger Lee and Jane Wills (eds.), *Geographies of Economies* (London: Arnold, 1997), 167–76.

Tan, Tai Yong, and Gyanesh Kudaisya, *The Aftermath of Partition in South Asia* (London and New York: Routledge, 2000).

Tarapot, Panjoubam, *Insurgency Movement in North-Eastern India* (Delhi: Vikas, 1996).

Taylor, Peter, 'Embedded Statism and the Social Sciences: Opening up to New Spaces', *Environment and Planning A*, 28:11 (1996), 1917–28.

Tayyeb, A., *Pakistan: A Political Geography* (London: Oxford University Press, 1966).

Ten Years of Pakistan, 1947–1957 (Karachi: Pakistan Publications, 1957).

Torpey, John, *The Invention of the Passport: Surveillance, Citizenship and the State* (Cambridge: Cambridge University Press, 2000).

Tripura, Government of, *The Tripura Land Revenue and Land Reforms Act, 1960* (Agartala: Law Department, 1960).

Tripura District Gazetteers: Tripura (Agartala: Government of Tripura, 1975).

Tuan, Yi-Fu, *Landscapes of Fear* (Oxford: Blackwell/ New York: Pantheon Books, 1979).

Union Home Secretary Chairs a High Level Empowered Committee (Washington, DC: Embassy of India, 10 December 2000).

Vakil, CN, *Economic Consequences of Divided India: A Study of the Economy of India and Pakistan* (Bombay: Vora & Co., 1950).

Van Schendel, Willem, *Peasant Mobility: The Odds of Life in Rural Bangladesh* (Assen/ New Delhi: Van Gorcum/ Manohar, 1981–2).

———, 'Self-Rescue and Survival: The Rural Poor in Bangladesh', *South Asia*, 9:1 (1986), 41–59.

———, *Three Deltas: Accumulation and Poverty in Rural Burma, Bengal and South India* (Delhi, etc.: Sage Publications, 1991).

———, 'The Invention of the "Jummas": State Formation and Ethnicity in Southeastern Bangladesh', *Modern Asian Studies*, 26:1 (1992), 95–128.

———, 'Easy Come, Easy Go: Smugglers on the Ganges', *Journal of Contemporary Asia*, 23:2 (1993), 189–213.

———, *Reviving a Rural Industry: Silk Producers and Officials in India and Bangladesh, 1880s to 1980s* (Dhaka/ Delhi: University Press Ltd./ Manohar Publications, 1995).

———, 'Bengalis, Bangladeshis and Others: Chakma Visions of a Pluralist Bangladesh', in Rounaq Jahan (ed.), *Bangladesh: Promise and Performance* (Dhaka: University Press Limited, 2000), 65–105.

———, 'Modern Times in Bangladesh', in Willem Van Schendel and Henk Schulte Nordholt (eds.), *Time Matters: Global and Local Time in Asian Societies* (Amsterdam: VU University Press, 2001), 37–55.

———, 'Working through Partition: Making a Living in the Bengal Borderlands', *International Review of Social History*, 46 (December 2001), 393–421.

———, 'Stateless in South Asia: The Making of the India-Bangladesh Enclaves', *The Journal of Asian Studies*, 61:1 (February 2002), 115–47.

———, 'Geographies of Knowing, Geographies of Ignorance: Jumping Scale in Southeast

Asia', *Environment and Planning D: Society and Space*, 20 (2002), 647–68.

———, 'Spaces of Engagement: How Borderlands, Illicit Flows and Territorial States Interlock' in Van Schendel and Abraham (eds.), *The Criminal Life of Things: How States, Borders and Language Produce Illicitness* (Bloomington: University of Indiana Press, forthcoming).

Van Schendel, Willem, and Itty Abraham (eds.), *Illicit Flows: How States, Borders and Language Produce Criminality* (Bloomington: University of Indiana Press, forthcoming).

Van Schendel, Willem, and Ellen Bal (eds.), *Banglar Bohujati: Bangalir Chhara Banglar Ononyo Jatir Prosongo* (Calcutta: International Centre for Bengal Studies, 1998).

Van Schendel, Willem, and Aminul Haque Faraizi, *Rural Labourers in Bengal, 1880 to 1980* (Rotterdam: Comparative Asian Studies Programme, Erasmus University Rotterdam, 1984).

Van Schendel, Willem, Wolfgang Mey, and Aditya Kumar Dewan, *The Chittagong Hill Tracts: Living in a Borderland* (Bangkok: White Lotus, 2000).

Verghese, BG, *India's Northeast Resurgent: Ethnicity, Insurgency, Governance, Development* (Delhi: Konark, 1996).

Victims of Trafficking and Violence Protection Act 2000: Trafficking in Persons Report (Washington, DC: United States of America, Department of State, 2002).

Vumson, *Zo History, with an Introduction to Zo Culture, Economy, Religion and Their Status as an Ethnic Minority in India, Burma, and Bangladesh* (Aizawl: the author, c.1992).

Walker, Andrew, *The Legend of the Golden Boat: Regulation, Trade and Traders in the Borderlands of Laos, Thailand, China and Burma* (Honolulu: University of Hawai'i Press, 1999).

Waterman, Stanley, 'Partitioned States', *Political Geography Quarterly*, 6:2 (1987), 151–70.

Wendl, Tobias, and Michael Rösler, 'Introduction: Frontiers and Borderlands: The Rise and Relevance of an Anthropological Research Genre', in Michael Rösler and Tobias Wendl (eds.), *Frontiers and Borderlands: Anthropological Perspectives* (Frankfurt am Main, etc.: Peter Lang, 1999), 1–27.

West Bengal District Gazetteers: Koch Bihar (Calcutta: West Bengal District Gazetteers, 1977).

Whyte, Brendan R, *Waiting for the Esquimo: An Historical and Documentary Study of the Cooch Behar Enclaves of India and Bangladesh* (Melbourne: Research Paper 8, School of Anthropology, Geography and Environmental Studies, University of Melbourne, 2002).

Wilson, Thomas M, and Hastings Donnan (eds.), *Border Identities: Nation and State at International Frontiers* (Cambridge: Cambridge University Press, 1998).

Wolf, Eric R, *Europe and the People without History* (Berkeley, etc.: University of California Press, 1982).

Yunus, Mohammad, *A Memorandum on the Genocide of the Rohingya Muslims of Arakan in Burma* (Arakan: Rohingya Solidarity Organization, 1995).

Zaheer, Hasan, *The Separation of East Pakistan: The Rise and Realization of Bengali Muslim Nationalism* (Karachi: Oxford University Press, 1995).

Zaman, Niaz, *A Divided Legacy: The Partition in Selected Novels of India, Pakistan, and Bangladesh* (Dhaka: University Press Limited, 1999).

Film

'India: Assam Tea Wars'; documentary in the series *Foreign Correspondent*, Australian Broadcasting Corporation (reporter: Mark Corcoran), 23 May 2001.

Internet sources

http://alfa.nic.in/lsdeb/ls11/ses2/14180796.htm. *XI Lok Sabha Debates, Session II, (Budget Session) 18 July 1996/ Asadha 27, 1918 (Saka)*

http://alfa.nic.in/lsdeb/ls12/ses2/2429079801.htm *XII Lok Sabha Debates, Session II (Monsoon Session), 29 July 1998.*

http://alfa.nic.in/lsdeb/ls13/ses2/17291199.htm. *XIII Lok Sabha Debates, Session II (Winter Session), Monday, November 29, 1999/ Agrahayana 2, 1921 (Saka).*

http://alfa.nic.in/lsdeb/ls13/ses2/31091299.htm. *XIII Lok Sabha Debates, Session II (Winter Session), Thursday, December 9, 1999/ Agrahayana 18, 1921 (Saka).*

http://www.anfal.co.uk/2000April.htm. Aman Ullah, 'Arakan: An un-decolonised colonial territory', *The Newsletter Monthly: News and Analysis of the Arakan Rohingya National Organisation, Arakan (Burma)*, 2:4 (April 2000).

http://www.webtecharabia.com/1final3/arno.htm. Arakan Rohingya National Organisation.

http://www.cia.gov/cia/publications/factbook/. Central Intelligence Agency, *The World Handbook 2000.*

http://www.ciionline.org/news/pressrel/2000/Nov/28nov2.htm. Confederation of Indian Industry. *Press Release* November 2000.

http://www.indianembassy.org/. India, Embassy of, 'Union Home Secretary Chairs a High Level Empowered Committee', Washington, DC, 1998.

http://alfa.nic.in/rs/rsdebate/synopsis/189/su17052000.htm. *Rajya Sabha: Supplement-I to the Synopsis of Debates; Wednesday, May 17, 2000/ Vaisakha 27, 1922 (Saka).*

http://www.mnet.fr/aiindex/i_csss/deport.html. Rao, Nivedita, *Deportations of Bengali-Speaking Muslims from Mumbai: A Fact-Finding Report Produced by a Joint Team from CPDR, EKTA and WRAG.* Mumbai, 1998.

http://www.trade-india.com/dyn/gdh/shipping_corner/bangladesh.htm.Trade-India.com, Trades and Routes.

http://www.geocities.com/CapitolHill/Congress/7434/ulfa.htm.United Liberation Front of Assam.

http://www.nccbusc.org/mrs/cst.htm. United States Conference of Catholic Bishops, Migration and Refugee Services.

http://shakti.hypermart.net/petroleum.html

http://www.gasmin.com/energy/ex.html

http://www.stopgatekeeper.org/

INDEX

Breinigsville, PA USA
29 April 2010
237093BV00003B/1/P